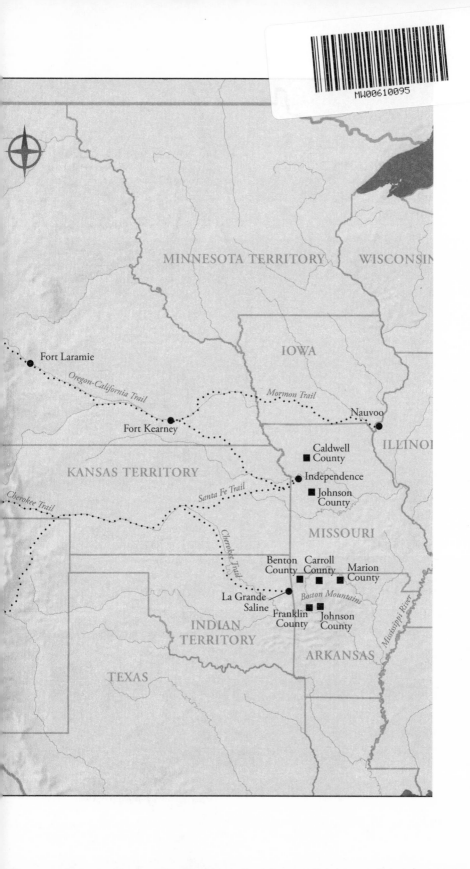

Vengeance Is Mine

Vengeance Is Mine

*The Mountain Meadows Massacre
and Its Aftermath*

RICHARD E. TURLEY JR.

AND

BARBARA JONES BROWN

OXFORD
UNIVERSITY PRESS

Oxford University Press is a department of the University of Oxford. It furthers
the University's objective of excellence in research, scholarship, and education
by publishing worldwide. Oxford is a registered trade mark of Oxford University
Press in the UK and certain other countries.

Published in the United States of America by Oxford University Press
198 Madison Avenue, New York, NY 10016, United States of America.

Library of Congress Cataloging-in-Publication Data
Names: Turley, Richard E., Jr., author, Jones, Barbara Brown
Title: Vengeance is mine : the Mountain Meadows Massacre and its
aftermath / Richard E. Turley Jr., Barbara Jones Brown
Other titles: Mountain Meadows Massacre and its aftermath
Description: New York, NY : Oxford University Press, [2023] |
Includes bibliographical references and index. |
Identifiers: LCCN 2023004613 (print) | LCCN 2023004614 (ebook) |
ISBN 9780195397857 (hardback) | ISBN 9780197675694 (epub) | ISBN 9780197675731
Subjects: LCSH: Mountain Meadows Massacre, Utah, 1857. | Massacres—Utah. |
Murder—Investigation—Utah. | Mormons—Utah—History—19th century. |
Lee, John D. (John Doyle), 1812–1877—Trials, litigation, etc.
Classification: LCC F826.T87 2023 (print) | LCC F826 (ebook) |
DDC 979.2/02—dc23/eng/20230131
LC record available at https://lccn.loc.gov/2023004613
LC ebook record available at https://lccn.loc.gov/2023004614

DOI: 10.1093/oso/9780195397857.001.0001

Printed by Sheridan Books, Inc., United States of America

To Juanita Brooks

Vengeance is mine; I will repay, saith the Lord.
Be not overcome of evil, but overcome evil with good.
Romans 12:19, 21

Contents

PART 6 PROSECUTION

PART 7 PUNISHMENT

Illustrations

Preface

On September 11, 1857, a group of Mormon settlers in southwestern Utah used false promises of protection to coax a party of California-bound emigrants from their encircled wagons and massacre them. The slaughter left the corpses of more than one hundred men, women, and children strewn across a highland valley called the Mountain Meadows.

"Since the Mountain Meadows Massacre occurred," wrote southern Utah historian Juanita Brooks decades later, "we have tried to blot out the affair from our history." Brooks believed she was doing her church a service by publishing her landmark book, *The Mountain Meadows Massacre,* in 1950, maintaining "that nothing but the truth can be good enough for the church to which I belong." Though no official condemnation of her work came from authorities of the Church of Jesus Christ of Latter-day Saints, neither did any recognition.[1]

Just over fifty years later, historian Will Bagley introduced his own book on the subject, *Blood of the Prophets: Brigham Young and the Massacre at Mountain Meadows*, with the criticism that "the modern LDS church wishes the world to simply forget the most disturbing episode in its history."[2]

In 2008, agreeing with Brooks's conclusion that the atrocity "can never be finally settled until it is accepted as any other historical incident, with a view only to finding the facts," and acknowledging that "only complete and honest evaluation" of the crime can bring true catharsis, we (along with coauthors Ronald W. Walker and Glen M. Leonard) published *Massacre at Mountain Meadows.*[3] The book was a turning point, marking the first time that the Church of Jesus Christ of Latter-day Saints encouraged its historians to publicly lay bare this shameful episode in its history. The church's support of that effort included unfettered access to its previously restricted massacre-related sources and funding for researchers to scour archives and other sources across the United States.

The scope and findings of that research led to reckoning and change. *Massacre at Mountain Meadows* made its way into the hands of tens of thousands of readers and led church leaders, members, and others to understand and accept "more than we ever have known about this unspeakable episode," said Latter-day Saint apostle Henry B. Eyring. Speaking to massacre victims' descendants gathered at a September 11, 2007, sesquicentennial commemoration at the Mountain Meadows, Eyring shared an official apology on behalf of the church.[4]

Continued reconciliation efforts between the church and organizations of the victims' relatives resulted in these disparate entities coming together to petition for and receive, in 2011, National Historic Landmark status for the Mountain Meadows, where monuments today memorialize the victims' final resting place in the valley. "The designation means the United States has recognized that this site is among the most important in U.S. history," National Park Service historian Lisa Wegman-French declared in a ceremony at the Mountain Meadows.[5]

All of the sources gathered and used in writing *Massacre at Mountain Meadows* were made available to the public in Salt Lake City's Church History Library. Some of the most revealing sources were also published in two documentary histories: *Mountain Meadows Massacre: The Andrew Jenson and David H. Morris Collections* (2009) and *Mountain Meadows Massacre: Collected Legal Papers* (2017).

Yet the efforts that produced *Massacre at Mountain Meadows* were not complete. As the book's preface explained, after considering the overwhelming amount of source material gathered, "we concluded, reluctantly, that too much information existed for a single book. Besides, two narrative themes emerged. One dealt with the story of the massacre and the other with its aftermath—one with crime and the other with punishment. This first volume tells only the first half of the story, leaving the second half to another day." With the publication of *Vengeance Is Mine: The Mountain Meadows Massacre and Its Aftermath*, that day has come.

As one of the authors and the content editor of *Massacre at Mountain Meadows*, we combined our efforts to coauthor *Vengeance Is Mine*. We have concluded that the decision to tell the massacre story in two volumes was the right one, as it allowed us to explore the aftermath of the atrocity in greater detail than any previous work. The depth of that exploration has led us to new conclusions that change how the story has been told for generations.

Multiple raids on emigrant wagon trains in Utah Territory, both before and weeks after September 11, 1857, demonstrate that the train massacred at Mountain Meadows was not the only one attacked. These assaults were motivated by political wrangling over federal and local rule and tensions between church and state that reached a deadly peak in 1857 but roiled Utah for decades. Modern readers may recognize similar tensions today, not only in Utah but throughout the United States. This jostling for power between Latter-day Saints and federal authority continued long after the massacre. Attempts to wield the case as a political weapon resulted in justice delayed—and justice denied—for the innocent victims of the massacre and their families.

For generations, the telling of the massacre and its aftermath has been shaped by an 1877 book titled *Mormonism Unveiled; or the Life and Confessions of the Late Mormon Bishop, John D. Lee; (Written by Himself)*. Attorney William W. Bishop published the volume a few months after the execution of his client, John D. Lee—the only man convicted for his role in the mass murder. *Mormonism Unveiled* went through nineteen printings within fifteen years of its publication and several more modern reprints, demonstrating just how influential this book has been for more than a century.[6]

Other books and portrayals of the massacre have liberally cited and quoted the words that Bishop claimed to be Lee's. Based on our research, we conclude that Bishop altered and expanded Lee's original and significantly shorter "confession" to publish *Mormonism Unveiled*. We have therefore not relied on the account that Bishop attributed to Lee in *Mormonism Unveiled*, but on primary research, including new transcriptions of the original short-hand records of Lee's two trials and other documents.

With the rare ability to read and transcribe nineteenth-century Pitman shorthand, our colleague LaJean Purcell Carruth created new transcripts of the original shorthand records of John D. Lee's trials, along with never-before-transcribed passages from other legal proceedings and additional types of records. We cite Carruth's transcriptions throughout our book. Readers can view the side-by-side comparison of her trial transcriptions and the transcriptions made by nineteenth-century shorthand reporters at www. MountainMeadowsMassacre.org, under the "Trial Transcript Archive" tab.

Partly because of their reliance on *Mormonism Unveiled*, prior massacre historians have concluded that Lee's trials and conviction were a mere ap-peasement to justice that closed the massacre case and vindicated church leaders. Our book shows that the pursuit of further convictions continued after Lee's execution.

From the beginning of this project, our goal has been to make our work approachable for nonacademic readers, not just professional scholars. We believe our decision to tell the story in a narrative style is another reason

Massacre at Mountain Meadows reached so many readers. We chose to continue that narrative format in this volume, though with interpretive signposts along the way to share our conclusions based on our decades of researching and writing about the massacre. While *Vengeance Is Mine* essentially picks up where *Massacre at Mountain Meadows* left off, the use of flashback and summary—often with new insights—will bring readers up to speed even if they have not read the first volume.

The primary sources we rely on for our book's narrative reflect some of the erroneous beliefs of their time. While we feel it is important for modern readers to see how these prejudices of the past shaped the Mountain Meadows Massacre and its aftermath, we do not subscribe to them.

Nineteenth-century Euro-Americans did not typically distinguish between the vastly diverse original peoples and nations of the Americas, instead monolithically referring to all simply as *Indians*. In general, we have used tribal or band names—such as *Paiute, Pahvant, Ute,* and *Shoshone*—to identify these groups when we can, using *Indian, Native,* and *Indigenous* as synonyms occasionally for variety. Similarly, both Mormon and non-Mormon sources of the era refer to non–Latter-day Saints as *gentiles*. We find this term objectionable today but use it in the text to reflect nineteenth-century parlance, in part because the alternative *non-Mormon*, which we also use for variety, has its downside.

Though this volume, like the first, benefited from extensive research funded by the Church of Jesus Christ of Latter-day Saints History Department, for the past several years we have written *Vengeance Is Mine* independent of church funding. From start to finish, we have had sole editorial control over our manuscript, and we alone are responsible for its contents.

Richard E. Turley Jr.
Barbara Jones Brown

PART 1
CRIME

1

The Angel of Peace Should Extend His Wings

Salt Lake City and Mountain Meadows, September 11, 1857

On September 11, 1857, a tall, slender girl approached a pair of offices nestled between two mansions. The elegant structures must have intimidated the sixteen-year-old, who lived her life in rough-hewn houses and stone forts. Gathering her skirts and her nerve, she stepped through the door marked "President's Office."

As her eyes adjusted to the coolness of the brick-and-plaster interior, she made out several clerk desks. In a ledger labeled "Sealings Record," a clerk recorded her name, birthdate, and birthplace: "Sarah Priscilla Leavitt; 8 May 1841; Nauvoo, Illinois." On the line above, the clerk took down the same information for the man who came in with her: "Jacob Hamblin; 2 April 1819; Ashtabula County, Ohio."[1]

Priscilla and Jacob creaked up a staircase to the second story, where they met with the man who was both Utah's governor and president of the Church of Jesus Christ of Latter-day Saints, fifty-six-year-old Brigham Young.[2]

Priscilla and Jacob clasped hands as Young pronounced the words of their marriage ceremony, which the Latter-day Saints called a "sealing." When Priscilla accepted Jacob's proposal weeks before, he gave her the options of marrying in southern Utah, where they lived, or waiting until he could bring her here, to Salt Lake City. She chose this place. Priscilla Leavitt's marriage was unusual by American standards, but not because of her youth. Rural girls of the day often wed by sixteen, sometimes marrying established men who were much older. Priscilla's marriage was peculiar because Jacob already had a wife.[3]

At that moment, thirty-five-year-old Rachel Hamblin—whom Jacob called his "kind[,] effctionate companion"—was three hundred miles south in a highland basin called the Mountain Meadows. The year before, Rachel

Figure 1.1 Left to right: Brigham Young's Lion House, church president's office, governor's office, and Beehive House. Courtesy Church History Library.

Figure 1.2 Brigham Young, 1855. Courtesy Church History Library.

and Jacob had moved their family to the north end of the pristine valley to start a summer ranch.[4]

The Hamblin and Leavitt families had long been intertwined. Two of Priscilla's older sisters both married Jacob's brother William, and Rachel employed Priscilla around the house. In early August 1857, when Brigham Young called Jacob to head his church's Southern Indian Mission, Jacob chose Priscilla's brother Dudley as one of his two mission counselors. Rachel chose Priscilla to be not only a "plural wife" for Jacob but also a helpmeet and companion for herself.

"I told them both," Priscilla said, "that I loved this family well enough to help them, and to give them my love and care. Since Brother Jacob had to be away from home so much on church business and missionary work with the Indians, I felt very humble in accepting this great responsibility." In polygamous Latter-day Saint culture, a plural wife did not just marry a husband; she married his family.[5]

As Priscilla and Jacob took their marriage vows at 11:55 a.m., dozens of Mormon militiamen readied themselves for action at the Mountain Meadows, four miles south of the Hamblin ranch. They lined the wagon trail that ran through the valley's luxuriant grass. The ragtag men faced a circle of besieged wagons some distance from where they stood. Above the encircled wagons, they could make out a white flag, hung from a pole in desperation.[6]

The militiamen watched as a leader from their ranks, Major John D. Lee, hoisted his own white swag on a stick and walked toward the wagon fort. After a brief negotiation, iron jangled as the emigrants inside removed chains connecting their wagons at the wheels. After their barricade opened, Lee disappeared into the circle with two other men, both driving wagons. One was Samuel Knight, Jacob Hamblin's other counselor in the Indian mission. The remaining militiamen outside waited for an hour or more, clutching their guns, sweating in the midday sun, thinking about what they were soon to do.[7]

That evening in Salt Lake, a newly arrived visitor joined his Latter-day Saint hosts for supper. Captain Stewart Van Vliet was a quartermaster for hundreds of U.S. troops headed for Utah. The army had sent Van Vliet ahead with the "ostensible errend . . . to Learn wheather certain Supplies could be procured for the troops 'enroute' for this place," Young concluded, "but it is generally thought that he has been Sent here as a feeler to know & find out the mind of the people." Young gave Van Vliet his answer: the soldiers must not come into Utah's settlements. If the troops continued their advance, his people would resist.[8]

This was not Van Vliet's first meeting with the Mormons. A decade earlier, he gained their trust when he visited their refugee camps along the Missouri River after mobs drove them from their homes in Illinois. Now, at the September 11 dinner, Van Vliet arose and asked the privilege to speak. "He warmly expressed gratitude for his former and present acquaintance and associations" with the Saints. "His prayer should ever be," he said, "that the Angel of Peace should extend his wings over Utah."[9]

About the same time, near sundown at the Mountain Meadows, Lee, Knight, and several other militiamen arrived at the Hamblin shanty in time for their supper, drawing two wagons to Rachel Hamblin's door. Though she had heard gunshots throughout the week and "a firing greater than before" earlier that day, Rachel must have been shocked at what she saw in the wagon beds—seventeen blood-stained children, most of them crying. Their hair was tangled and their clothes filthy from what they had endured over the past five days. Seven were infants not yet two years old. The other ten ranged from ages two to six.[10]

Blood oozed from one toddler's ear. A one-year-old girl's left arm dangled by the flesh just below the elbow. The ghastly wound made one militiaman think she would die. Yet these children were lucky to make it this far. Behind them on the killing fields lay the butchered bodies of their parents, siblings, grandparents, aunts, uncles, and cousins. The children in the wagons were all who remained of what had been a bustling train of more than a hundred California-bound emigrants.[11]

The tear-stained girls and boys, along with two quilts, were pulled from the wagons and passed to Rachel, who was already caring for several children of her own. Some were her stepchildren, some adopted, and three she'd had with Jacob. She could not shield her youngsters from the trauma of seeing the bloodied and wailing little ones. Instead, the older Hamblin children must have helped their mother care for the survivors, who cried in vain for their own mothers. Rachel left no account of how she and some two dozen children at the ranch got through that horrific night. Her adopted Shoshone son, a teenager named Albert, recounted that "the children cried all night." He never got over the horror of that September 11.[12]

Outside, in the Mountain Meadows, the militiamen made their own beds under the blackening heavens. John D. Lee unrolled his blanket, laid his head back, and fell into an oblivious sleep.[13]

2

Sermons Like Pitch Forks

New York to Utah, 1830–57

In the summer of 1857, Elizabeth Knight Johnson bent over her handiwork, her aging fingers pulling needle and thread through scraps of fabric. She and her Salt Lake City neighbors were making quilt squares they hoped to bind together in time for October's territorial fair. Beginning in late July, they had another reason to hurry. They worried they might soon be abandoning their homes. Their fears were born from experience, and, perhaps more than any of them, Elizabeth knew the trauma of fleeing.[1]

At age thirteen in 1830, she joined a church just established not far from her home in Colesville, New York. Elizabeth and her extended Knight family formed most of one of its first congregations. Believing God had chosen the faith's prophet-leader, Joseph Smith, to restore Jesus Christ's primitive church in modern times, or "the latter days," the Knights supported Smith during his translation of the Book of Mormon. A man in his early twenties, Smith taught that early inhabitants of the Americas—descendants of the biblical Israel—recorded the book of scripture on gold plates he found buried near his home in Palmyra, New York.[2]

Smith eventually called the new faith the Church of Jesus Christ of Latter-day Saints. Its divine mission was to usher in Christ's millennial return by building a new Zion on the American continent. To follow their prophet and escape persecution, Elizabeth Knight's family left Colesville, gathering to Ohio with a growing body of "Latter-day Saints" or "Saints," as they came to call themselves. A few months later they were on the move again.[3]

As the Saints proliferated, so did the controversy surrounding them and their prophet. Through the 1830s and 1840s, they tried to establish their permanent home and Zion, sojourning in Ohio, Missouri, and Illinois. Some of their beliefs and practices—including communitarianism, theocracy, bloc voting, and the emerging practice of polygamy—ran against American mainstream values of capitalism, individualism, democracy, and monogamy.

Reacting to these practices, vigilante mobs used violence, including mass murder, to drive "Mormons," as they called them, from their communities. At times the Saints fought back, only to be overwhelmed by more violence and then fleeing to a new place. With their religious minority status, the Saints' petitions to federal and local governments failed to bring redress or lasting protection.[4]

The Latter-day Saints, including Elizabeth Knight and her kin, paid a heavy toll for their beliefs. The greatest blow came in 1844, five years after they established a city called Nauvoo on the Illinois side of the Mississippi. A mob disguised with painted faces assassinated Joseph Smith and his brother Hyrum in the nearby Carthage Jail. The two were awaiting a hearing on a treason charge for declaring martial law and calling out their state militia unit to protect Nauvoo from anticipated attack. The Smiths' murder struck close to home for Elizabeth. Not only had her family known Joseph since she was a child, Hyrum had baptized her in 1830 and performed her marriage to Joseph Johnson in 1842.[5]

After the Carthage murders, Latter-day Saint apostle Brigham Young became the leader of the main body of Smith's followers, continuing his legacy. Illinois governor Thomas Ford later observed that the Smiths' murders, instead of ending their religion, "as many believed it would," only "gave them new confidence in their faith."[6]

At Nauvoo, they finished building the temple Smith began. Before his murder, the prophet-leader introduced a ceremony called the endowment through which initiates made covenants to prepare Zion for Christ's Second Coming and their souls to return to God in the afterlife.[7] The temple was a holy place where Latter-day Saints received their endowment and "sealed" their marriages for eternity. Elizabeth Knight Johnson and her husband were among several thousand Saints who were endowed and sealed in the Nauvoo temple after Smith's death.[8]

The endowment was a strictly oral ceremony, believed too sacred to write down.[9] Speaking in 1845 of one promise or "covenant" of the rite, a church leader shared his interpretation that "I have covenanted, and never will rest nor my posterity after me until those men who killed Joseph and Hyrum have been wiped out of the earth."[10] Abraham Cannon, son of apostle George Q. Cannon and an apostle himself, said his father told him "that he understood when he had his endowments in Nauvoo that he took an oath against the murderers of the Prophet Joseph as well as other prophets, and if he had ever met any of those who had taken a hand in that massacre he would undoubtedly have attempted to avenge the blood of the martyrs."[11]

The concept of avenging the blood of martyred prophets appeared in the Book of Mormon, in which the blood of slain prophets cried unto "God for vengeance upon those who were their murderers."[12] But it was not unique to Latter-day Saint thought. The Old Testament records that God commanded an Israelite king to "avenge the blood of my servants the prophets."[13] In the New Testament, Jesus taught that "the blood of all the prophets, which was shed from the foundation of the world, may be required of this generation," and the apostle John shared a related vision of the world's end days. "I saw . . . the souls of them that were slain for the word of God," John wrote. "They cried with a loud voice, saying, How long, O Lord, holy and true, dost thou not judge and avenge our blood?"[14]

Latter-day Saints had varying interpretations of what avenging the blood of the prophets meant. The people of Nauvoo did not use violence to avenge the Smiths' deaths. Instead, apostle Willard Richards, who witnessed the brutal murders, urged his people to remain still. After hearing Richards's impassioned speech, "a vast assemblage" in Nauvoo, "with one united voice," wrote a Mormon reporter, "resolved to trust to the law for a remedy of such a high handed assassination," and "to call upon God to avenge us of our wrongs!"[15]

Brigham Young believed that God would command his people to avenge the blood of prophets before the world's end, though he did not know exactly how or when. He told apostle Wilford Woodruff in 1856 that "were we now Commanded to go & avenge the Blood of the prophets," the Saints would not "know what to do." Fortunately, Young confided to Woodruff, "there is one thing that is a consolation to me[.] And that is I am satisfied that the Lord will not require it of this people untill they become sanctifyed & are led by the spirit of God so as not to shed inocent Blood."[16]

In late 1845, Latter-day Saint leaders in Nauvoo planned yet another mass exodus. "To hasten their removal," Illinois governor Thomas Ford admitted, the twelve apostles "were made to believe that the [U.S.] President would order the regular army to Nauvoo" to arrest them as soon as the frozen Mississippi thawed and troops could travel upstream by riverboat.[17] Speaking to a congregation, apostle Heber C. Kimball expressed his belief that "the Twelve [apostles] would have to leave shortly, for a charge of treason would be brought against them" for swearing their people "to avenge the blood of the anointed ones."[18]

Young and other apostles began leading the Saints' westward flight across the icy Mississippi in early 1846. Knowing that the Mormons had no choice but to sell out, "people from all parts of the country flocked to Nauvoo to purchase houses and farms," Ford said, "which were sold extremely low, lower than the prices at a sheriff's sale."[19] Isaac Haight, later a church leader in southern Utah, was one of those forced to sell, trusting "in the Lord," he said, "that he will open the way for us to get away from this wicked nation, stained with the blood of the Prophets."[20]

Carrying provisions in their wagons and bitterness in their souls, the Saints put behind them not only the state of Illinois but the borders of the nation. "We owe the United States nothing," railed British-Canadian apostle John Taylor. "We go out by force as exiles from freedom. The Government and people owe us millions for the destruction of life and property in Missouri and in Illinois. The blood of our best men stains the land, and the ashes of our property will preserve it till God comes out of his hiding place, and gives this nation a hotter portion than he did Sodom and Gomorrah."[21]

Elizabeth Knight Johnson and her husband left Nauvoo and the graves of their first two children. They and the other refugees spent months in makeshift camps across Iowa and along the Missouri River. Hundreds of graves peppered their path from Nauvoo to their winter quarters as hunger, malaria, tuberculosis, and scurvy took their toll.[22]

In these conditions, Elizabeth gave birth to another child and buried her father and an older brother. Her now-orphaned nephew, fourteen-year-old Samuel Knight, had already suffered the death of his mother in Missouri.[23] Working as a wagon driver, Samuel set out with an advance train of Saints in the summer of 1847, traveling more than a thousand miles west. Believing the West would free his people from their trials, Brigham Young envisioned the isolated Great Basin as the place they would permanently call Zion.[24]

The Saints were not the only Americans looking west. Their migration unfolded in an era of expansionism, when Anglo-Americans claimed a divine mandate, a "Manifest Destiny," to spread "white civilization" throughout the Western Hemisphere. Government leaders encouraged emigration as a means of colonizing new territory, empowering the nation through occupying the land and exploiting its resources.[25]

In 1845, the United States annexed the independent Republic of Texas, which had been part of Mexico, and provoked the U.S.-Mexican War.[26] West Point graduate Stewart Van Vliet fought in the conflict, helping win the war.[27] The resulting 1848 Treaty of Guadalupe Hidalgo forced Mexico to sell much of its northern territory in what became all or large parts of California, Nevada, Arizona, New Mexico, Colorado, Wyoming, and Utah.[28]

After his Mexican tour, Van Vliet transferred to Fort Kearny, in what would become Nebraska. Van Vliet visited the Mormon refugee camps in the area and over the years gave some Saints much-needed work.[29]

Joseph and Elizabeth Knight Johnson trekked to the Salt Lake Valley in 1848 when Elizabeth was pregnant with twins. Her babies died on the plains the day they were born.[30] After settling in Salt Lake, the couple took in Elizabeth's orphaned nephew, Samuel. Joseph taught him his trade of making adobe bricks for building.[31]

The 1848 treaty with Mexico brought the Latter-day Saints, barely forging a new life in the Salt Lake Valley, back under the U.S. rule they had traveled more than a thousand miles to escape. They first drafted a petition for territorial status, then sought statehood instead after learning it would give them far more autonomy, including the right to elect all their own leaders. But Congress made Utah a territory instead. The vast territory essentially extended from upper California's eastern border to the continental divide, encompassing all or parts of what later became Utah, Nevada, Wyoming, and Colorado.[32]

President Millard Fillmore granted the Saints some self-rule when he appointed Mormons to half the territorial positions in 1851, including Young as governor and superintendent of Indian affairs. The other appointees were non-Mormons, or "gentiles," as early Mormons called them.[33]

Though the Saints were unpopular, at first their westward migration fulfilled the U.S. government's desire for white Americans to colonize the newly acquired territory. Believing in their own manifest destiny, the Saints began expanding their "kingdom of God" on earth as soon as they arrived in the Salt Lake Valley. Their version of expansionism included polygamy, a marital system they believed extended into the afterlife.[34]

By the mid-1850s, Mormon settlement expanded as far north as Oregon Territory's Salmon River, as far west as Carson Valley near northern California's border, and southwest to San Bernardino, California. Mormons built settlements along the "northern route," which led from Salt Lake City to Oregon Territory or northern California, and along the "southern route," which passed from Salt Lake through the deserts of southwest Utah to southern California. Watering places along the trails brought settlers and travelers into contact with Indigenous people, who relied on the same water sources. When Mormons arrived in the Great Basin, several Native groups inhabited the area—the Bannock, Shoshone, Ute, Goshute, Paiute, and Navajo.[35]

Latter-day Saints believed American Indians descended from the prophet Israel of the Old Testament. According to the Book of Mormon, a group of Israelites—two of them named "Laman" and "Lemuel"—left Jerusalem and migrated to the Western Hemisphere. Descendants of these migrants, said the book, became "Lamanites"—an Indigenous people of the Americas. The Saints believed that when Christ's Second Coming was imminent, the Lamanites would gather with them and accept the latter-day gospel.[36] "If the Gentiles do not repent," the Mormon scripture warned, the Lamanites would rise against and "cut off" their enemies.[37]

The Saints began proselytizing Natives soon after arriving in the Salt Lake Valley. In 1853, Young created an Indian mission in southern Utah and called Samuel Knight as one of its missionaries. Knight and fellow missionaries Oscar and Jacob Hamblin, Dudley Leavitt, Ira Hatch, and others began building a fort settlement on the banks of the Santa Clara River, along which lived large numbers of Paiutes. The fort was some thirty-five miles south of the Mountain Meadows, a popular camp spot on the southern route to California.[38]

With the Latter-day Saint belief that both they and the Lamanites were of the house of Israel, the missionaries told the Natives they were brothers—that Mormons were different from Americans who might mistreat them. "I well remember," missionary Jacob Hamblin wrote of his initial visits to the Santa Clara Paiutes, "seeing thare women cetch up thare Childrin and run and hide for feer we had come to steel thare childrin but the news soon spred among them that we ware mormans thare white Brothers." Ute warriors had long used their advantages of horses and guns to kidnap Paiute women and children, selling them in a slave network extending from Santa Fe to Los Angeles. The Mormons tried to stop the Utes' raiding and soon earned many Paiutes' trust. Grateful, some "incisted on baptisiam," Hamblin said.[39]

At the end of 1854, with Young's four-year term as governor soon to expire, word spread that President Franklin Pierce wanted to replace him. A Paiute told the missionaries "he had herd [t]he Americans did not want Brigham to be Capt. any longer [and] they was a going to Send an American Capt here," Hamblin wrote in his diary. "He Said if the Americons ever came here to fight the Mormans the Piedes [Paiutes] would all help the Mormans."[40]

President Pierce named Lieutenant Colonel Edward J. Steptoe, who was wintering with his troops in Utah, to replace Young. But Steptoe declined

Figure 2.1 Latter-day Saints baptizing Paiutes in southern Utah, 1875. Courtesy Church History Library.

Pierce's appointment and continued on to the Pacific in the spring. Though Young was pleased to retain an interim governorship, he felt furious about some soldiers' unruly behavior towards Mormon women and that some women left with Steptoe's command. "We ought to have slain" the soldiers, Young preached, "and hung up their bodies or thrown them to the wolves."[41]

His concerns were compounded by the view—expressed in at least two prominent newspapers—that non-Mormons had set their sights on the Latter-day Saint Zion, as they had before in Missouri and Illinois. "The Salt Lake Valley is a point of paramount importance to the emigration and commerce across the continent," opined one writer. "Americans will avail themselves of the great facilities and advantages it affords." Within ten years, "hostile collisions" would erupt between gentiles and Mormons, "the result of which will be that the Mormons will be forced from the Valley."[42]

Young warned that the Saints would never again give up their home. "It has been leaked out, to a few individuals, that the government of the United States is going to send troops here to drive out the 'Mormons,'"

Young announced in March 1856. "I say to such threateners, cease your folly." If troops came again, his people would flee to the mountains and, if forced, fight. "If any more mobs come," Young preached, "cut their damd throats."[43]

Raised in Vermont and New York in the early nineteenth century, Young came of age in a culture steeped in violent rhetoric, an era that glorified Revolutionary War heroes and their language.[44] As one study of American political rhetoric noted, "the use of violent language should not always be read literally" as intending to incite violence but rather "as one of the few strategies available to those who regard themselves as politically powerless to capture public attention, dramatize an issue, and build a new political movement."[45]

Young acknowledged he often used violent rhetoric for effect. "I frequently say 'cut his infernal throat,' " he said in 1848. "I don't mean any such thing." He used such language when he felt "strenuous" about a topic, Young explained, speaking just how he pleased because that was how he knew to express himself. "How I have had the headache, when I had ideas to lay before the people, and not words to express them," he said, apparently hindered by his lack of formal education. "But I was so gritty that I always tried my best."[46]

By 1856, Young increasingly felt that all was not well in Utah's Zion. Crop failure and famine burdened the territory. The number of gentiles and dissenting Mormons in Utah was growing. He believed the Saints' religious fervor was fading, that their righteousness, obedience, and unity were decreasing. "He considered the people were not ownly asleep but working wickedness," recorded apostle Wilford Woodruff. Young and other church leaders called on people to renew their dedication in what became known as the "Mormon Reformation."

Young dispatched apostles to preach repentance, resolving that church leaders must "preach sermons like pitch forks tines downwards that the people might wake up." Jedediah M. Grant, one of Young's two counselors in the church's ruling First Presidency, "rained down pitch forks & forked lightni[n]g" also "upon the Gentiles who were working wickedness upon this people & defiling the females."[47]

Young urged Latter-day Saints to show their dedication by taking on the commitment of marriage—including "plural marriage," which required church authorization. The prophet's exhortations were effective. One clerk felt "astonished at the number of applications for permission to take wives."[48]

Twenty-three-year-old bachelor Samuel Knight heeded the call. In the summer of 1856, he visited Salt Lake, where he married Caroline Beck before bringing her back to his home at the Santa Clara fort.[49]

Besides preaching marriage, Young taught the doctrine of "blood atonement." According to the Old Testament, atonement for sin required a blood sacrifice, made by cutting the throat of an animal, then burning part of the carcass as an offering to God. Traditional Christian theology held that Jesus's sacrifice of his own blood atoned for the world's sins, replacing the need for animal sacrifice. But while "it is true that the blood of the Son of God was shed for sins," Young taught in September 1856, "yet men can commit sins which it can never remit. . . . They must be atoned for by the blood of the man."[50]

Some might consider "cutting people off from the earth" to be "strong doctrine," Young acknowledged, "but it is to save them, not to destroy them." If serious transgressors understood "the only condition upon which they can obtain forgiveness" and be saved in the next life, they "would beg of their brethren to shed their blood, that the smoke thereof might ascend to God as an offering to appease [His] wrath."[51] Such speeches of Young and his counselors "sent arrows into the harts of men," Woodruff wrote, making "the Harts of many tremble."[52]

Young and other leaders expounded the doctrine over the next several months. Though he did not clarify which sins warranted blood atonement, they seemed to include murder and repeated adultery.[53] When confronting those whose sins could not "be atoned for without the shedding of the blood," Young asked an audience in February 1857, "will you love that man or woman well enough to shed their blood?" Spilling their blood so they might obtain salvation, he said, "is loving our neighbour as ourselves."[54]

Young meant the reform movement to shake his followers from spiritual slumber. "The work of reformation is working mightely among the people and the Spirit is searching deeply their hearts and causing them to confess their sins with weeping and sorrow," Isaac Haight wrote Young in October 1856. Since leaving Nauvoo, Haight had become the president (or ecclesiastical leader) of southwestern Utah's Cedar City "stake." Latter-day Saint stakes encompassed smaller church units, called wards and branches. Haight also served as Cedar City's mayor and an Iron County militia major—a reflection of Utah's limited separation of powers.

In his letter, Haight told Young that a man in nearby Fort Harmony confessed to having "connexion" with a woman before he married her. "He had had his [temple] Endowments," Haight said, and "wishes to know what he shall do. I think he has deeply repented of the sin and Says that if the Law of God requires his Blood to be spilled he will most willingly comply with Any thing required that he may be saved." Despite Young's preachings on blood atonement, he counseled Haight to tell the man to "goe and sin noe more repent of all his sins and be Baptized for the same." He counseled Haight again later, "in the name of the Lord, remission and pardon, even of adultery, are promised to all that truly repent."[55]

Young's letter reflected a sympathetic side that surfaced more in his private interactions than his public speaking. This softer trait developed through his own sufferings and caring for others in theirs. Due to his family's poverty, his principal education as a youth was manual labor. With a mother who slowly died of tuberculosis and an oft-absent father, the teenaged Young became a surrogate parent to his younger brother. Later, when his first wife languished from the same disease as his mother, he cared for her and their young children until she too succumbed. The soft spot beneath Young's sharp-tongued, acerbic exterior prompted one man to compare him to a sweet-and-sour apple.[56]

Even if Young merely meant the Reformation's preaching to prod people to change, acts of violence by some of his followers showed how dangerous such strong rhetoric could be. According to the Cedar City Stake minutes, a man named Rasmus Anderson was brought before his "congregation for an attempt to commit adultery on the Person of His stepdaughter," only eleven years old at the time. Anderson confessed and promised to "do better." Speaking to the congregation, Cedar City bishop Philip Klingensmith "showed to what it would lead if not checked." Both Anderson and the girl were rebaptized as a symbol of repentance.[57]

But now, stake president Haight reported in a June 1857 letter to Young, the two had been caught together again after the girl married someone else. When they were called before Bishop Klingensmith, Anderson "confessed that he had been in the constant habit of having Conexion with her[.] When they were catachised they both lied and had partook of the Sacrament living in Adultery," Haight wrote. "I felt that he was not worthy to live upon the Ea[r]th any longer So I Sent some of the police they Start him for Calafornia." Nineteenth-century southern Utahns used expressions like "starting someone for California" or "getting to California" as euphemisms for killing.[58] Responding to Haight's letter, Young wrote advice about the girl but nothing of Anderson.[59]

Years later, a trial attorney accused Klingensmith of being in a party that took Anderson from his house "in the darkness of the night" and executed him. "His grave was dug and [his] throat cut upon the bank and the body thrown in," the attorney charged. Though Klingensmith testified that he knew Anderson personally and believed his killing was a penalty for committing adultery, he denied participating in the execution.[60]

Despite violent excesses, Young saw the Mormon Reformation as a "refiner's fire" that, on balance, bettered his people's lives and increased their religious commitment.[61] But the fire burned some out. Many disaffected Mormons fled Utah, along with some gentiles and federal appointees. Young saw that too as a blessing. "The Territory," he wrote, "has taken an emetic," regurgitating "Lawyers, Loafers, Special pleaders, Apostates, Officials, and filth."[62] Before long, the "runaway" appointees reported their experiences to officials in Washington, bringing results Young hardly saw as a blessing.

The Latter-day Saints only briefly found the isolation and peace they had sought in the uncolonized West. As their fears of again losing their homes and their autonomy increased in the 1850s, so did their violent rhetoric against dissenters, outsiders, and U.S. federal control. Combined with church leaders' teaching of violent doctrines like vengeance, blood atonement, and prophecies that "Lamanites" would join with them to "cut off" their enemies, by 1857 Utah was headed for an inferno.

3

Imposed Upon No More

Arkansas to Utah, January–September 1857

In January 1857, during the heat of the Mormon Reformation, Utah's territorial legislature convened. Fed up with the colonial-like rule under which Utah (like other U.S. territories) existed, Governor Brigham Young and the legislature sent two resolutions or "memorials" to Washington, demanding "the right to have a voice in the selection of our rulers." While federal appointees from the East complained that Mormon society took its cues from church leaders rather than federal authority, Utah's leaders contended that "we will not tamely submit to being abused by the Government Officials, here in this Territory."[1]

If appointees to Utah continue "to corrupt our community, set at defiance our laws, trample upon the rights of the people, . . . and endeavor to influence the General Government against us," one of the memorials warned, "we will send them away."[2] It was "almost another declaration of independence," a legislative clerk wrote.[3] Though the memorial did not match the firebrand language of Southern "states' righters" of the era, its timing proved explosive.[4]

James Buchanan had recently won the U.S. presidency. Shortly after Buchanan took office, Utah territorial delegate John M. Bernhisel presented Utah's memorials to Secretary of Interior Jacob Thompson. Within forty-eight hours, another member of Buchanan's cabinet received two letters condemning Latter-day Saint leaders.

One was from Utah's chief justice, John Kinney, charging that Mormons obeyed Young over federal law and that missionaries were forging Indian alliances "in case of any difficulty with the U.S.," poisoning "their minds against the government and Americans." He also charged that polygamy was taught as a religious duty and that gentiles and religious dissenters were not safe in the territory. Kinney recommended replacing Young as governor. The second letter, from Utah's surveyor general, David Burr, contained its own allegations, including that Young's successor would be in danger of assassination. Both letters recommended that a small military presence be established in Utah to enforce federal authority.[5]

Arriving in Washington at the same time as the two letters, the Utah legislature's memorials proved incendiary. Secretary Thompson called one of them "a declaration of war" and asked delegate Bernhisel if Utah intended to set up its own "independent Government." Thompson also brought up polygamy. Feelings against it were growing stronger, not only in Washington, but throughout the country. "It would be slandering God to say that he approved of polygamy," Thompson told Bernhisel, and "the Government intended to put it down."[6]

With their polygamous and theocratic practices, the Mormons' ten-year colonization of former Mexican territory was becoming a threat to U.S. aspirations of a coast-to-coast expansion of a unified democracy. Within a few weeks, President Buchanan decided to replace Governor Young and was determining how many troops to send to Utah to ensure Mormon compliance with federal authority.[7] Ignoring Latter-day Saint leaders' call for Washington to investigate the charges against them, Buchanan's administration issued military orders on May 28, declaring Utah "in a state of substantial rebellion."[8]

Hearing that General William S. Harney and 2,500 troops were destined for Utah, and receiving no explanation from Buchanan, the Saints feared the army was coming to drive or destroy them—or at best threaten the independence they sought in Utah. The distress of Missouri and Illinois was still raw in their minds, as were the more recent rumors that federal troops would someday come to drive the Saints from the now-developed Salt Lake Valley. Holding the same church position Joseph Smith had when assassinated, Young also feared for his life. While Utah would accept his replacement and the other new appointees if they "would behave themselves," Young said, he and his advisors devised strategies to keep the troops out and persuade Buchanan to pull them back.[9]

First, Mormon militiamen would slow the army's approach by intercepting their supply trains and burning the prairie grass their animals needed to survive. If they could keep the troops from entering Utah's settlements before snows stalled them on the plains, Young reasoned, he and his people could buy time until the American public and Congress might turn against Buchanan's decision to send the army. Second, if the troops did make it through, the Saints would lay their settlements in ashes and flee to the mountains or some other remote region.[10]

In early August, Young and one of his counselors, Daniel H. Wells, sent two circular letters throughout Utah explaining this strategy. Wells—who was also lieutenant general of the territorial militia, the Nauvoo Legion—wrote to militia leaders. He wanted every military district prepared "to march any-where in the territory with arms, ammunition, transportation, and clothing for a winter campaign."[11]

As church president, Young addressed ecclesiastical leaders—often the same men as the militia heads—instructing the Saints to prepare "for sur-vival if they came under siege." Guns must be in working order, ammunition saved, grain cached. This vital food source must not be trampled by livestock or sold to gentile merchants and passing emigrants.[12]

Couriers carried the two letters throughout the territory. Departing at daybreak on August 3, George A. Smith delivered them in settlements south of Salt Lake all the way through southwestern Utah, preaching their contents and reviewing militia drills as he went. It was not just his 250-pound bulk on a five-foot, ten-inch frame that made Smith a heavyweight. He was a church apostle, Joseph Smith's first cousin, and had led initial efforts to settle southern Utah in the early 1850s. He still had a plural wife and child living in the southern town of Parowan.[13]

As church leaders prepared the territory for a standoff with the U.S. mil-itary, hundreds of non-Mormon emigrants were crossing Utah, following their own dreams west. Many traveled as neighbors and extended families from Missouri, Arkansas, or Texas, driving cattle west and then north along the Cherokee Trail before converging with the Oregon-California Trail. California-bound emigrants who passed through Salt Lake City could take either the northern route to the Sacramento gold fields or the southern route to San Bernardino, Los Angeles, or San Diego. Some emigrants who owned cattle hoped to sell the beef there at a premium before returning home. Others, whether they brought cattle or not, hoped to start a fresh life in the nation's newest state of California.[14]

Word of Latter-day Saints' plans to resist the approaching army reached emigrants passing through Utah. Stephen B. Honea, headed for California from northwest Arkansas's Franklin County, reported what they were hearing. Before reaching Salt Lake in mid-August, Honea met mounted companies of well-armed Utah militiamen near Fort Bridger in what later be-came Wyoming. Over a shared campfire, one English-born militiaman "re-ferred in bitter terms to the treatment the Mormons had received in Illinois and Missouri, reflected on the unjustness and tyranny of the people of the

United States, and said that the time was come to get even." The militiamen were going "to meet Gen. Harney," the soldier said. "If he was coming peaceably, we will let him come, but if not, we will drive him back."

A Mormon who lived on the trail outside of Salt Lake "spoke bitterly against the United States," Honea said, denouncing federal appointees and rejoicing "that the time had come when the saints would be avenged on their enemies—that men were found who could face the enemy, and that Harney, with his 2,500 men, never would enter Salt Lake." The man told Honea's train that "Young had ordered the people to prepare for war," instructing them not to sell food to emigrants and to stockpile provisions, guns, and ammunition.[15]

Soon, a third element of Young's resistance strategy developed, this one involving Native people. Previous wars on American soil taught feuding European powers that Indian alliances helped assure military victory. Latter-day Saint leaders believed they needed Utah's Indigenous people to fight with them—or at least not against them—to withstand the approaching troops.

On August 4, Young sent a letter to Jacob Hamblin, calling him to be the new president of the Southern Indian Mission. Hamblin chose fellow missionaries Dudley Leavitt and Samuel Knight as his two counselors in the mission presidency. Samuel and Caroline Knight were then living in a wagon box next to the Hamblins' board shanty at the north end of the Mountain Meadows. Samuel was working for Hamblin, building him a more substantial home of adobe brick.[16]

"Continue the conciliatory policy toward the Indians, which I have ever recommended," Young instructed Hamblin. "Seek by works of righteousness to obtain their love and confidence, for they must learn; that they have either got to help us, or the United States will kill us both."[17]

As Utah's governor and superintendent of Indian Affairs, Young had worked for years to maintain peace as settlers and emigrants encroached on Indigenous people's homelands. Following federal policy, Indian agents sought to convert Native peoples to the white man's way of life and farming, dispensing "presents" like plows, livestock, blankets, and clothing. Such efforts were made to discourage Indian raiding of cattle for food. When conflicts broke out, interpreters worked to negotiate peace by distributing food and gifts to Indians.[18]

In early August, Young received word that emigrants and Indians were skirmishing on the northern route. Emigrants had killed two Native men after Indians took some of their livestock. "Much excitement prevailed," apostle Lorenzo Snow wrote on August 7 from Brigham City, sixty miles north of Salt Lake. "We had much difficulty in protecting [an]other company of emigrants from being massacred" by Indians in retaliation for the two killings.[19] A company of California-bound emigrants involved in the difficulty changed their route, turning around to take the southern route to California instead.[20]

That company was likely Missourian Nicholas Turner's wagon train. Eight years earlier, Turner led a train west along the northern route. After a return trip to Missouri, he was now headed back a second time to his new home in northern California. Earlier in life, Turner fought against the Saints. During 1838 conflicts with Mormons in Caldwell County, Missouri, he commanded the nearby Johnson County militia.[21]

Peyton Welch, a herdsman in both of Turner's California treks, spoke of the August 1857 troubles on the northern route. After Turner's company found that route too dangerous because "Indians had stopped it up," the train's members chose a different course. Hearing two other trains had taken the southern route from Salt Lake City and were but a few days ahead, Welch said, Turner's company decided to follow them. The two trains ahead, led by Jack Baker and Alexander Fancher, came mostly from northwest Arkansas.[22]

Responding to the troubles on the northern route, Young sent his brother-in-law, interpreter Dimick Huntington, with gifts to prevent more difficulties. Huntington first visited "Little Soldier," leader of a Shoshone band living north of the Great Salt Lake.

While there, Huntington said, "I asked him if he knew that the US troops were a coming."

"Yes," Little Soldier answered, but he did not want to join the Saints' fight. He told Huntington he feared the troops and would "go a way off into the mountains . . . & wait & see how the Mormons come out."

Huntington told Little Soldier the troops would kill Indians just as readily as they killed Mormons. He advised the Shoshone to cache all the berries and wheat they could in case of a siege, "for B[righam] said so."

That, Little Soldier said, "was good & he would do it."[23]

Near Brigham City the next day, Huntington gave a peace offering of six cattle and wagonloads of vegetables and bread to four hundred Shoshone in the area. He also gave them Young's instructions to cache food.

When Huntington told a Shoshone leader there that he heard some of the tribe recently stole emigrant stock, "the chief looked much down," the interpreter recorded. The Shoshone man admitted he knew something of the theft and asked if Huntington was mad. "I told him no he then asked if Brigham was mad I told him no." Hearing this, the Shoshone told Huntington all about the raid and showed him where the horses were hidden in the mountains. Huntington left the Shoshone "feeling quite well."[24]

The incident marked a striking change in Superintendent Young's Indian policy. By the time he received Lorenzo Snow's August 7 letter about the emigrant-Indian skirmishes north of Salt Lake, Young and his agents had previously mediated disputes between Indians and emigrant parties that season. But now determining that the Saints needed the Native groups on their side as the troops approached, Young decided he would no longer hold Indians back when emigrants shot at them.[25]

Young recorded his policy change in an August 11 diary entry shortly after Huntington left for northern Utah. Young determined that "unless the Government assumes a more pacific attitude," he would "declare emigration by the overland route Stopt. And make every preparation to give the U. S. a Sound drubbing[.] I do not feel to be imposed upon any more."[26]

Young and his advisors believed the Saints' strategic position astride America's transcontinental emigration routes gave them their best leverage in negotiating with the government. Major trails leading to the resource-rich Pacific passed through Utah Territory. Euro-Americans knew that keeping those trails open for emigration and trade was crucial to national expansion. They also believed that keeping the trails safe meant controlling the West's Indians. If the Mormons could persuade Washington that their presence in Utah was crucial to doing that, perhaps Buchanan might reverse his decision. But if the troops continued towards Utah, Young threatened he would no longer mediate between emigrants and Indians, forcing overland emigration to stop.[27]

On August 13, Wells sent another letter to militia leaders throughout Utah, this one regarding Young's Indian strategies. "Instruct the Indians that our enemies are also their enemies" and "are continually fighting against them somewhere," he wrote. Federal aggression would eventually come upon the Sioux, Cheyenne, and Utah's Indians, Wells predicted. The tribes of Utah "must be our friends and stick to us, for if our enemies kill us off, they will surely be cut off by the same parties."[28] In a public prayer that day, Young evoked Book of Mormon prophecies when he petitioned God that "the Lamanites . . . may do thy will & be as a wall of defense around about us."[29]

Young wanted his new policies broadly known. "[If] I have to fight I wish to give my enemies fair warning," he explained in his diary, "and then if the[y] will not take it they must! abide the consequences. I wish to meet *all men* at the judgment Bar of God without any to fear me or accuse me of a wrong action." Young publicly laid out his policies on Sunday, August 16.[30]

Thousands of Saints and a few gentiles packed Salt Lake's bowery to hear Young's Sabbath address. He reminded them of the Saints' suffering in the church's early days. He blamed their trials on "the Government under which we live," which had "been the means of the death of thousands and thousands of men women and children," he asserted, including "Joseph and Hiram [Smith] in prison, while they were under the pledge of the Government of the State of Illinoi[s]." He even charged the government with responsibility for the recent murder of apostle Parley P. Pratt in Arkansas. (In reality, Pratt was killed by an abusive husband from San Francisco whose wife left him and became Pratt's polygamous wife.)[31]

Young accused Washington of ignoring defiance of federal authority in southern parts of the country while "underhandedly, sneekingly" sending troops west to Utah "in the form of a mobb" to "destroy and kill" the Saints who had "always lived most strictly according to the Constitution and laws of the United States." While he did not object to the government's "sending Governors and judges here," he said, "I do object to their injuring this people." He speculated the army had secret orders to kill Mormon leaders, scatter the people, "and break up this kingdom called Latter Day Saints."

In the face of all this, "I have come to this decision," Young announced, "that the last mobb has come to afflict this people that ever has come." From now on, if the government or "any people whatever rise up against this people," then "in the name of Israel's God I say, lift the sword and slay them."

"Amen!" roared the crowd.

"The Lord Almighty and the Elders of Israel being our helpers," the troops "shall not come to this Territory," Young said. "I will fight them and I will fight all hell." But if the army did manage to reach Utah's settlements, how many in the community will "do as I do and take the road I shall travel?" Young asked.

Cries of "We are ready!" rang throughout the congregation.

If necessary, Young said, the Saints would follow a scorched-earth policy, leaving nothing behind for the army. "I shall lay this building in ashes," he said, "I shall lay my dwelling house in ashes, I shall lay my mills in ashes, I shall cut every shrub and tree in the Valley, every pole, every inch of board, and put it all into ashes." After all was laid waste, Young asked, "Dare you all go into the Mountains?"

"Yes!" the congregants cried out.

To anyone not willing to follow this course, Young said, "I want you to pick up and leave now while you can in peace, for if a man refuses to come to the scratch if the time ever should come that we lay waste everything, we will hue him down."

"Can you flee to the mountains, men, women and children," Young asked, "and lay wast[e] and desolate every thing before [you]? If you can, show your hands."

Thousands of hands shot into the air, then broke into thunderous applause. "The feeling that prevailed in the meeting," recorded a clerk, "cannot be discribed."

Young wanted his strategies widely circulated. "Report it, ye gentiles, you hickory [lapsed] Mormons," he urged. "Publish it abroad."

Laying out the next part of his policy, Young spoke of how he had endeavored to keep the trails through Utah safe for emigration, declaring that Latter-day Saint influence kept Indians from robbing or killing emigrants. But "if the United States send their army here and war commences," cross-continental travel must cease, he vowed.

"Write to your friends, if the United States armies come," Young told his audience, "then say to your friends don't pretend to cross this continent. . . . I will not hold the Indians still while you shoot them, as you have hitherto, but I will say to them, go and do as you please."

All Young asked of the government was "to let us alone," he said, "and we will live our religion, serve our God, preach the gospel, gather the Saints, build up Zion, and fill the earth with the peace of God."[32]

The speech was "the Greatest D[is]course . . . I ever he[a]rd by Man," recorded one Latter-day Saint.[33]

"I have never Seen the time," Young recorded in his diary that night, "when the people Seemed more united than they are at present to resist the powers of darkness, and defend and maintain the rights of Isreal."[34]

The day after Young's speech, Honea's wagon train reached Salt Lake City but hurried south after just a few hours. A local merchant told the company that Young had declared Utah an independent territory that "owed no obedience or allegiance to any form or laws, but those of their own enactment, and called upon the people to stand together, and support him in maintaining the cause of God and the church."[35]

Though publicly Young simply said he would no longer "hold the Indians" back, privately, interpreter Dimick Huntington encouraged Indians to raid emigrants' livestock. On August 30, after learning many Shoshone were gathering north of Salt Lake City, Young sent Huntington north once again. The interpreter brought them cattle and wagonloads of produce. Like Young, he referenced Book of Mormon prophecies about Lamanites, telling the Indians "the Lord had come out of his Hiding place & they had to commence their work."

Huntington recorded that he "gave them all the Beef cattle & horses that was on the Road to Cal Afornia the North Rout," encouraging the Shoshone to raid emigrant livestock and drive the animals into the mountains. Surprised at the Saints' about-face teaching, the Indians replied that this "was some thing new," and "they wanted to Council & think of it." One Indian told Huntington he didn't think the time had come to "rise up & fight" but asked Huntington to "tell Brother Brigham that we are his friends & if he says the soldiers must not come, it is anough[,] the[y] wont come in. . . . Tell B that he can Depend upon us."[36]

Not many days later, as the moon rose above a camp spot called Warm Springs, "we was suddenly aroused by the Fireing of Guns and the Yelling of the Invaders," an emigrant on the northern route recorded on September 9. The raiders ran between the camp and herd of the McKuen, Dunn, and Lincoln company in the darkness, "fireing about 15 or 16 Gunshots—and Yelling at a considerable rate," J. W. Dunn wrote. "The intention of them was without doubt to stampede our Stock . . . not to kill any cattle or any person but simply to Steal as many as they could." In the morning, when the emigrants saw tracks of shod horses and one or two pairs of boots, they concluded at least some of the raiders were white men. The train's herd was soon raided again a short distance away at City of Rocks.[37] On September 12-13, apostle George A. Smith wrote Parowan stake president William H. Dame that Shoshone had stolen "a host of cattle" from passing emigrants.[38]

Smith had returned to Salt Lake from his southern tour on August 31.[39] Among those who fell in with him along his way north were Jacob Hamblin; his fiancée, Priscilla Leavitt; and a dozen Native leaders from southern Utah. The group included Paiutes Tutsegavits of Santa Clara and Youngwuds of the Ash Creek band near Harmony, Kanosh of central Utah's Pahvant Utes, a Beaver Creek Ute called Ammon, and Ammon's wife.[40]

En route to Salt Lake, the travelers spent the night of August 25 at Corn Creek, a campsite some 150 miles south of Salt Lake and 12 miles south of Fillmore. Corn Creek's cool springs and abundant grass made it a popular stop for travelers and local Pahvants. When Smith's and Hamblin's groups arrived, a large, southbound party of emigrants was already camped there. Their hundreds of cattle grazed under guard nearby.[41]

Three of the emigrant men, one a train captain, walked to Smith's and Hamblin's camp to ask about traveling conditions—the roads, good places to water and graze their livestock, and southern Utah's Indians. Hamblin described all the camping spots from Corn Creek to the Muddy River near Las Vegas. The grassy Mountain Meadows, he informed them, was the place to recruit their stock before entering the long desert. When the emigrants said they had forty or fifty males in their group able to bear arms, Hamblin replied they could protect their livestock from possible Indian raids with only "half that number."[42]

The emigrants "seemed to be ordinary frontier 'home-spun' people," Hamblin remembered, most traveling as families.[43] The three emigrants Hamblin met called their captain "Mr. Fancher." A cattle rancher with land in northwest Arkansas's Benton County, Alexander Fancher had driven cattle to California in 1850, bringing his wife Eliza Ingram and their children with him. The Fancher family was making the journey again, this time with their nine children, ages two to nineteen.

Saladia Ann Brown Huff, whose husband, Peter, died on the plains weeks before, also hailed from Benton County. She continued on for California with their six children, aging from early childhood to fourteen.[44]

The large group of emigrants encamped at Corn Creek was not a single unit but a combination of smaller trains that had left Arkansas for California in the spring of 1857. The biggest contingent came from north of the Boston Mountains in northwest Arkansas. This group was led by the family of fifty-two-year-old John Twitty Baker, a wealthy land and livestock owner in Carroll County. Jack Baker and his older son in the train, George W., left Arkansas with nearly three hundred cattle. Jack's other son in the company, Able, was nineteen and single. Jack's wife, Mary, stayed home, but George traveled with his wife, Manerva Beller Baker, and their four children, ages nine months to seven years. Jack's daughter, Sarah Baker Mitchell; her husband, Charles; their infant son; and Charles's brother, Joel, rounded out the extended Baker family. The Mitchell brothers brought sixty-two head of cattle.[45]

The Baker company included the Marion County families of Jesse Dunlap Jr. and Lorenzo Dow (L. D.) Dunlap. The Dunlap brothers married sisters Mary and Nancy Wharton. Jesse and Mary had ten children, ages one to eighteen. L. D. and Nancy traveled with their eight children, ages eighteen months to eighteen years.[46]

From Johnson County, Arkansas, south of the Boston Mountains, came the wagons of widowed Cyntha Tackitt and her eight children, ages twelve to twenty-six. Cyntha's oldest daughter traveled with her husband, John Milum Jones; at least one child; and John's brother, Newton. Cyntha's oldest son, Pleasant, and his wife, Armilda Miller, had two children, ages nineteen months and four years.[47]

Emigrants William and Martha Cameron and their seven children, ages eight to twenty-four, also hailed from Johnson County. The Camerons' older daughter, Matilda, and her husband, Josiah Miller, traveled with their four children, one an infant and the oldest age nine.[48]

After sharing a camp near this combined company at Corn Creek, Hamblin's and Smith's groups continued north for Salt Lake. Soon after arriving on September 1, the southern Utah Indians of Hamblin's party spent about an hour with Young and Huntington in Young's office. In that meeting, Huntington said, "I gave them all the cattle that had gone to Cal[ifornia] the south rout."

The Indians opened their eyes wide in surprise, responding, "You have told us not to steal."[49]

"So I have," Huntington answered, "but now they have come to fight us & you for when they kill us then they will kill you."

The Native leaders replied they were "afraid to fight the Americans & so would raise grain" and let the Mormons fight it out with the army.[50]

This was a typical—and wise—response from Utah's Indigenous leaders. In mid-August, Goshutes had told Huntington "they was afraid of the troops & would go home & wait and see" how the battle turned out. The Mormon rebuttal was always the same. "If the troops Killed us they would then Kill them," Huntington repeated. "I told them all that they & the mormans was one but the Lord had thro[w]ed the Gentiles a way."[51]

Though the Native leaders expressed reluctance to fight, Young recorded in his September 1 diary, "A Spirit Seems to be takeing posses[s]ion of the Indians to assist Isreal. I can hardly restrain them from exterminating the 'Americans.'"[52]

The Saints kept up their efforts to strengthen relationships with Utah's Indigenous people. While in Salt Lake, Hamblin showed his Native guests around the city, where they were "treted with mutch res[p]ect," he wrote.[53] Huntington lodged "Ammon and wife" and "Kanosh and fourteen of the band" for four days beginning September 1.[54]

Indian agents presented the visitors with gifts. Ammon received a wagon, blankets, tobacco, powder, and lead. On September 11, Paiute headman and Mormon convert Tutsegavits received a few butcher knives, powder, and pistol caps. Young ordained Tutsegavits to the Latter-day Saint priesthood on Sunday evening, September 13, instructing him "to go & preach the Gospel & Baptise among the House of Isreal."[55]

Even before this meeting, marauders began attacking emigrant trains in central and southern Utah. By early September, emigrant Nicholas Turner's wagon company reached Corn Creek near Fillmore, where they concluded Indians were as hostile towards emigrants on the southern route as they had been on the northern one. "We found the Indians very ill disposed toward us, and were informed that the Indians and Mormons together had stopped the trains ahead of us and killed a number of persons belonging to them," Peyton Welch said. Turner's group likely learned this information after an express rider passed through the area, carrying an urgent message to Brigham Young about an emigrant company under siege at the Mountain Meadows.[56]

The merged trains of Wilson Collins and William Dukes, whose members (including Stephen Honea) hailed from Arkansas and Missouri, followed closely behind Turner's company. When the Collins and Dukes group reached Corn Creek, an Indian agent there "told us that a train had passed a short time before us," Honea said, "who had poisoned an ox, and that they had been attacked by the Indians. He spoke in abusive terms of the men of that train, for having acted in an improper manner."[57]

Another emigrant heard similar rumors while at Beaver, thirty-five miles further south. Dubious, the emigrant asked an Indian if there was any truth in the poisoning story. The Native man confirmed that a few Indians had died and several more were sick, he believed from watermelons poisoned by Mormons.[58]

Tensions came to a head when Pahvants attacked the Turner company near nightfall on September 8. Hearing of the assault, Beaver's Latter-day Saint bishop, Philo T. Farnsworth, approached the Dukes and Collins companies, camped just outside Beaver. Farnsworth persuaded some of those emigrants to help Mormon militiamen escort the beleaguered Turner group to the Dukes and Collins larger camp near Beaver.[59]

When the rescue party of emigrants and militiamen reached Turner's train, Indians were firing at the company's wagons, and a Native man had been wounded. As the guides led Turner's group towards the camp of the

Dukes and Collins companies, Indians kept firing at the train, "wounding some of the cattle, but doing no other injury," emigrant Honea said. The interpreters prevented the emigrants from firing back, telling them "that if they injured an Indian, [they] would all be killed."[60]

After Turner's wagons joined the Dukes and Collins camp, the merged company's three leaders—Turner, Dukes, and Collins—went into Beaver to talk with Bishop Farnsworth. There, Indians attacked again, wounding all three emigrant leaders. The injured men hobbled back to their campsite where, in a scene eerily similar to the one simultaneously taking place further south at Mountain Meadows, the combined companies quickly "corralled their wagons" and dug pits inside for self-defense.[61]

"We then made preparations for a fight," said Honea, "but no fight took place." The influential Native leader Ammon, just returned from his trip to Salt Lake City, came to the camp with Bishop Farnsworth to end the stand-off. "All was peace," Ammon said—then demanded livestock. After turning over six head of cattle and a horse, the combined Dukes train was able to continue its journey.[62]

A different story was unfolding at the Mountain Meadows. Just hours after the siege set in, militiamen William Stewart and Joel White encountered two emigrants—oblivious to the attack on their company—rounding up stray cattle outside the Meadows. The two emigrants were stopped at Leach's Spring, on the stretch of trail between Cedar City and Pinto called Leach's Cutoff. Thinking they needed to contain the situation, Stewart and White fired on the two emigrants, killing William Aden but only wounding the other. Aden's companion "put spurs to his horse and fled" towards his company at the Meadows, where he made it into their wagon corral. Now, everyone inside the corral would know that white men were involved in their attack. Already anxious about the approaching U.S. Army, Cedar City's leaders worried about the consequences if they let the emigrants go on to California with that knowledge.[63]

The assaults on the emigrant companies near Beaver and at Mountain Meadows erupted as Captain Stewart Van Vliet, now serving as quartermaster for the approaching U.S. troops, arrived in Salt Lake, again riding into the Saints' midst in a time of crisis. "He has invariably treated [us] kindly, as he would a Baptist, a Methodist, or any other person," Young said after Van Vliet's arrival.[64]

As quartermaster, Van Vliet wanted to buy supplies and arrange winter quarters for the approaching troops.[65] He calmed the Saints when he told them the troops en route to Utah now numbered fewer than a thousand and that they and their worn-out stock could not reach the settlements by winter without Mormon assistance.

Young's response alarmed Van Vliet: He would "not let the troops come in." Surprised, Van Vliet asked if Mormon leaders had "counted the cost?"

"We ha[ve]," Young replied, then asked if Uncle Sam had counted his.[66]

Though Young insisted that soldiers not enter Utah's settlements, he made diplomatic overtures toward Van Vliet. On the morning of September 10, "I Showed the Captain my whole family and establishment," Young said, "wherewith he expressed himself highly pleased." Van Vliet was amazed at how far the Saints had come since he last saw them in desperate circumstances ten years before.[67]

After Van Vliet's visit—at "about 12," recorded an office clerk—"an Express arrived from Iron Co[unty]."[68] The rider, thirty-one-year-old James Haslam of Cedar City, was admitted into Young's office, where the church president looked up from a meeting with Daniel Wells, apostle John Taylor, and several others. Young asked who the express was from.

Isaac Haight, answered Haslam.[69]

Young took the note and gazed at it in silence. The express, according to a contemporary account, was sent "to President Young with the intelligence that some California emigrants had been attacked by the Indians, and were entrenched behind their wagons, and to get his instructions what to do with the *Americans*."[70]

"Go and lie down and take a little sleep," Young told Haslam, instructing him to come back at one o'clock.[71]

Wells drafted a response to Cedar City stake president Haight, probably as dictated by Young. As was custom with Young's outgoing correspondence, a clerk neatly recopied the draft, Young signed it, and an ink copy of the letter was made by pressing it, in sequential order, in a bound, letterpress copybook.[72]

"Your note of the 7th inst [September 7] is to hand. Capt Van Vliet acting Commissary is here," began the letter to Haight. "We do not expect that any part of the army will be able to reach here this fall." From this beginning to its concluding exhortation of patience, the letter seemed designed to calm concerns shared in Haight's express. Young did not seem to realize the emigrants were in mortal danger. The response was ready for Haslam when he returned to the office.[73]

Young asked if he could "stand the trip back."

"Yes," the expressman replied, though he had spent most of the last sixty hours in the saddle, carrying the express some 250 miles from Cedar City.[74]

Taking the letter, Haslam mounted his horse and "shot off like an arrow" for the south.[75]

4

Too Late

Mountain Meadows to Cedar City, September 12-13, 1857

Hooves pounded the ground at Hamblin's ranch as several riders approached in the predawn darkness of September 12. The wailing of the surviving children answered the question the men carried in their minds all night from Cedar City. The deed had been done.[1]

Leading the group were Cedar City mayor, stake president, and militia major Isaac Haight and district militia commander and Parowan stake president William Dame—the only man in southern Utah who outranked Haight militarily.[2]

The men dismounted and walked to the wagon-box shelter of Caroline and Samuel Knight, looking for something to eat. As the consequences of their decisions dawned on them, Dame and Haight quarreled. Awakened, militiamen at the ranch listened in. John D. Lee heard Dame tell Haight "he would have to report the destruction of the emigrant camp."

"How?" Haight asked. "As an Indian massacre?"

Dame said he was not sure he would lay the responsibility on Indians.

"How the h—l can you report it any other way without implicating yourself?" Haight retorted.[3]

One of the militiamen, Bishop Philip Klingensmith, recalled Haight telling "Colonel Dame, that, if he was going to report of the killing of [the] emigrants, he should not have ordered it done."[4] Overhearing the dispute, Samuel Knight ascertained that no leader in Salt Lake had sanctioned "the dastardly deed."[5] Though cattle raiding by Indians and—secretly—their Mormon interpreters was part of Brigham Young's strategy for convincing Washington to pull back its troops, the murder of emigrants was not part of that plan. Had Young wanted his men to commit a massacre, Dame and Haight would not have argued over which of them would take responsibility for the atrocity, or whether to even report white perpetrators' involvement.

Noticing the eavesdroppers, Dame and Haight lowered their voices to a whisper before falling silent. They finished their breakfast and climbed back on their animals, ready to inspect what lay south. Lee and other militiamen who had slept at Hamblin's ranch went with them "to bury the dead." As the group rode a few miles deeper into the Mountain Meadows, the sun dawned, slowly drawing a blanket of darkness from the forms on the ground.[6]

Strewn among the sagebrush were dozens of blood-spattered corpses, most of them children between the ages of seven and sixteen. Here and there among them lay the twisted forms of their mothers and a few infants. The women and children's bodies were "in almost every condition," Klingensmith said, "some throats cut, some heads smashed, some shot." They were scattered along the ground for quite a distance, as if they had been running for their lives when hewn down.[7]

Dame seemed terror-stricken, said Lee, who followed the two armchair leaders closely to watch their reaction. Haight also grew distraught, making "quite a lamentation" according to one witness. Yet ultimately the two leaders seemed more concerned with assigning blame than with mourning the dead at their feet. Dame again told Haight he would have to report the massacre.

"You know that you counselled it," Haight snapped back, "and ordered me to have them used up."

Dame reminded Haight of the intelligence, now so obviously false, that Haight gave him privately a few days before—that Indians had already slain most of the emigrants at their wagon corral. "I did not think there were so many women and children," Dame pleaded. "I thought they were nearly all killed by the Indians."

"It is too late in the day for you to back water," Haight said. "You know you ordered and counselled it, and now you want to back out."

"Have you the papers for that?" Dame demanded, hardening. "Show the papers for that."

"You throw the blame of this thing on me and I will be revenged on you if I have to meet you in hell to get it," Haight shouted as Dame turned his back on him and walked off. Enraged, the leaders pulled themselves back onto their saddles and continued south.[8]

Soon they heard the rhythmic sound of iron striking grit. In a ravine fifty yards from the road, Cedar City militiamen were tossing up dirt with picks and shovels. Along this stretch of trail the day before, about forty emigrant men and older teenaged boys had collapsed to the dust in a ragged line, shot in the head at close range. A few men's bodies, their throats slashed, lay further off from the rest. By the time Dame and Haight's group rode up, the line of corpses was disappearing as militiamen, talking and laughing as if to shake off the horror, dragged the bodies to a mass grave in the ravine.[9]

It could hardly be called a burial. The militiamen had brought instruments for killing, not digging. A dozen or so men from the southern settlements of Santa Clara and Washington, eager to quit the morbid scene, did not bother to help and instead set off for their homes. Contending with limited tools, the hard ground, and the harder reality of what they had done, the remaining men dug superficial graves.[10] The effort was not so much an attempt at proper burial as it was a cover-up of how the emigrant men died. The execution-like shooting of lined-up victims along the road was a dead giveaway of white participation.

The militiamen heaped the bodies, already "stinking in the boiling sun," into the ravine, throwing dirt over them as quickly as they could to cover the ghastly sight and smell. "It was a horrid awful Job," Lee said. "The whole air was filled with an awful stench."[11] Amos Thornton from nearby Pinto helped bury the dead but "wished he had not," recounted his stepson, "as the memory of that terrible sight he could not forget."[12]

Riding south another mile, the leaders reached the encircled wagons, now strangely silent except for the occasional bellowing of scattered cattle. Like the bodies of their owners, the wagons were pocked with bullet holes, and their covers had been stripped from their frames. Feathers, freed from beds slashed open in search of plunder, floated around the corral. Some drifted into a pit inside the wagon fort's perimeter. The emigrants had used picks and shovels to dig the pit for protection. Militiamen now used those same picks and shovels, looted from the corral, to dig the emigrants' graves.[13]

Somewhere in the eerie scene, the leaders found twenty-three-year-old Nephi Johnson. Two days earlier, Haight had summoned him from his home six miles north of Cedar City and ordered him to the Meadows. A missionary to the Indians, Johnson spoke the Paiutes' language and had their trust. Memories of his role in the killing fields would haunt him to his deathbed.[14]

Johnson had spent the night of September 11 at the corral site, where Lee sent him after the massacre "to keep the Indians from taking things out [of] the wagons." When Johnson reached the site and found Paiutes ransacking the wagons, he told them to stop. "Some of them would and some of them would not," he said. Still, plenty of truck was left by the time the leaders showed up, most of it white men's tools and utensils.[15]

The militiamen unchained the wagons from each other, breaking apart the corral, then rounded up the emigrants' oxen to draw the wagons away. Charging Johnson to keep the matter secret, Klingensmith and Cedar City militia major John M. Higbee had him lead the wagons north out of the Meadows to Iron Springs—a temporary hiding place for the loot. The militiamen left the remaining cattle in the valley for the time being.[16]

Finally, there was the matter of what to do with the surviving children, still in Rachel Hamblin's care at the north end of the Meadows. After returning to Hamblin's ranch, "John D. Lee seemed to have the distribution of the children," Rachel said. As a federal "farmer to the Indians" with some knowledge of the Paiute language, Lee claimed to act as agent for the Indians, trading goods for each of the children as if the Indians owned them. "I told the Indians," Lee explained, "that we would buy the children of them."[17]

Rachel Hamblin saw Lee's purchasing of the children for what it was— "a mere sham." She wanted to keep badly injured Sarah Dunlap. With both bones of Sarah's forearm severed by a bullet, the one-year-old could hardly endure the bone-shaking ride back to the settlements. When six-year-old Rebecca and four-year-old Louisa begged not to be separated from their baby sister, Hamblin's "mother-heart was touched." Perhaps she saw in the sisters the faces of her three biological children, who were the same ages as the three Dunlap girls.[18]

Normally timid, Hamblin found the courage to stand up to Lee—the only Mormon to do so at the Mountain Meadows. "I persuaded Lee not to separate them, but to let me have all three," she said. "This he finally agreed to. The children stayed with me, and I nursed the wounded child, though it has lost forever the use of its arm."[19] Because of Hamblin, the Dunlap sisters were the only survivors permitted to stay together for their entire time in Utah. The sisters helped each other remember who they were. The fourteen other children—already suffering the loss of parents and older brothers and sisters—were soon torn from surviving siblings, cousins, and playmates; placed in separate homes; and encouraged to forget.[20]

After Lee's "purchase" of the children, Klingensmith took charge of them. As Cedar City's bishop, his duty was to look after the welfare of his flock. With many local settlers already struggling to provide for their families, "I made it my business to get these children places where there was not many children," Klingensmith said, failing to see the irony in providing for children whose parents he had helped murder. He and others lifted the remaining survivors into the wagons of Cedar City militiamen John Willis and Sam McMurdie.[21]

The children had been in McMurdie's wagon before. A few hours before the massacre, the emigrants had allowed him and Samuel Knight to drive their wagons inside the besieged corral under Lee's false promises of protection. Following Lee's instructions, the emigrants had loaded the two wagon beds with their guns, baggage, wounded, and young, "as if they were going on a journey," McMurdie said. McMurdie's and Knight's wagons had led the emigrants' procession out of the corral, with Lee walking between the two single-file wagons. Older children and women, some carrying infants, followed on foot, trailed by the men and oldest teenaged boys.[22]

On that September 11 afternoon, the militia leaders had hurried the wagons and women and children past the militiamen lining the road nearby, not wanting their ranks to think too much about what lay in store for those passing before them. But the leaders halted the emigrant men when they reached the militia line. Some of the emigrants raised a cheer, believing the militiamen were their saviors, their armed escorts out of the valley. Major Higbee ordered his men to line up, single file, four or five feet to the right of each emigrant. High on the back of his horse, Higbee then led the two columns of men forward, following some distance behind the women and children.

About a mile into the trek, McMurdie's lead wagon had come to a bend in the road, skirting a low-lying ridge that extended from the east side of the valley towards the west. Here the scrub oak and sage grew thick and close across both sides of the trail. Higbee knew what he was supposed to do there, but hesitated. Perhaps it was the sight of dozens of children and women ahead that kept him silent for another quarter mile as his horse plodded on. Finally, he turned his horse across the road and looked back at the men. Only then did he shout *"Halt!"*—the signal for the killing to begin.[23]

The horrific slaughter took less than six minutes.[24]

After fulfilling his role in the militia line, Klingensmith had moved up the road to perform his next grisly task. Little Rebecca Dunlap emerged from a clump of sagebrush and begged for help when she saw a white man approach. Two of her older sisters lay dead beside her. She had pulled baby Sarah from their motionless mother's arms and hidden with her in the brush. The bullet that created the growing blood stain on their mother Mary's dress may have been the one that nearly severed Sarah's arm. Rebecca was one of only two six-year-olds to be spared. The other fifteen survivors were all younger.

Though some of the surviving children had been in McMurdie's and Knight's wagons, Klingensmith found others shrieking on the ground near their slain mothers or stumbling about in shock. He gathered the smallest together and turned the older ones over to be killed. Nancy Saphrona Huff, four years old at the time, remembered seeing "one girl, some ten or twelve years old they said was to[o] big and could tell so they killed her. . . . I saw them shoot the girl after we were gathered up." Five-year-old Martha Elizabeth Baker recalled watching two men lead her seven-year-old sister, Mary Lovina, over a ridge. She never saw her again. Klingensmith loaded the last survivors into the two wagons and brought them to Rachel Hamblin's door.[25]

Eliminating witnesses old enough to "tell tales" was the motive perpetrators later gave for wiping out all of the wagon company besides the littlest children. Referring to the killing of William Aden and his companion's escape into the emigrants' corral, Major Higbee had explained to the militiamen gathered to the Meadows, "white men ha[d] interposed" in the earlier attacks "and the emigrants know it, and there lies the danger in letting them go." Someone added, "If we let them go, . . . they will raise hell in California, and the result will be that our wives and children will have to be butchered and ourselves too."[26]

Now, the day after the massacre, Klingensmith lifted the surviving children again into McMurdie's wagon, as well as Willis's, and climbed in. Traveling northeast from the Meadows back towards Cedar City, McMurdie and Willis drove the children away from the last vestiges of their families. Huff remembered that Willis "carried me off from the spot." As the two wagons made the journey back, the children—most of them babies or toddlers— were likely held in the arms of militiamen who massacred their families.[27]

The two wagons stopped first at Pinto, where Klingensmith found a home for Martha Elizabeth Baker with newlyweds Amos Thornton and Mary Whittaker. Mary's father, James, was one of Klingensmith's counselors in Cedar City's bishopric. Klingensmith may have also left Betsy's younger sister, Sarah Frances, still suffering with a wounded ear. He remembered leaving one or two children at Pinto, including "one that was wounded." If two-year-old Frances was initially at Pinto, it was not for long. Over the ensuing months, some of the children were shuffled from home to home in southern Utah.[28]

Two smaller groups of militiamen took the same trail, traveling ahead of Klingensmith and the children. At mid-afternoon on that Saturday, September 12, the first group of four militiamen ran into a California-bound mule train of a dozen Mormon freighters and their non-Mormon passengers, Philetus (P. M.) Warn and George Powers. Warn, a New Yorker, had booked passage with the freight train in Salt Lake City. Seeking safety in numbers, Powers, of Little Rock, Arkansas, joined his own three-wagon train to the Mormon freighters at Parowan when the rumor hit that a company was under Indian attack at the Mountain Meadows. When the militiamen returning from the Meadows ran into the mule train, freight captains Sidney Tanner and Billy Mathews pulled them aside to talk privately.

After the militiamen moved on, Mathews related their report that "the entire train [ahead] had been cut off." The freighters had planned to camp at Leach's Springs, but "as it was still dangerous to travel the road," George Powers was told, they "concluded it was better for us to pass the spot in the night." More likely, the leaders wanted to pass through the Meadows at night to keep their gentile passengers in the dark. Sobered, the Tanner-Mathews train drove on towards the scene of death "without much conversation."[29]

Near dusk, a mile east of Leach's Springs, the mule train ran into more militiamen headed back for the settlements—Dame, Haight, and two others, "in company with a band of some twenty Indian warriors," Powers said. "These Indians had a two-horse wagon, driven by a white man, and beside him, there were two or three Indians in it!" Powers was stunned to see the white men and Indians on friendly terms. "They were all in high spirits, as if they were mutually pleased with the accomplishment of some desired object," Powers said.

As the returning militiamen and Indians thronged around the Mormon freighters "with noisy cordiality," Powers took a closer look. Many of the Indians were wearing shawls, he said, "and bundles of women's clothes were tied to their saddles. They were also all supplied with guns or pistols, besides bows and arrows. The hindmost Indians were driving several head of the emigrants cattle." Their wagon, he noticed, was "filled with something I could not see, as blankets were carefully spread over the top." Powers felt his blood boil but dared not speak.[30]

Dame returned two mules he had borrowed from Tanner to ride from Cedar City to the Meadows the previous day.[31] He and Haight told Tanner and Mathews "that they found *Ninety-five dead bodies upon the ground,* and left a part of the [militia] company to inter them as decently as possible."[32] After the freight company passed on, Powers asked the question on everyone's minds. "Why had it been done?"

"[You] must not grieve or take on, for the women were all prostitutes," Mathews answered, according to Powers. "Their bodies had been examined by President Dame, and this ought to console." This statement was one of many lies that would be repeated by some perpetrators in an attempt to justify the emigrants' murder. Other Mormons, including church leaders, would believe and circulate such lies. Some Mormons would continue to blame the victims for generations.

George Powers observed that "Matthews rejoiced greatly at the massacre, and considered it the beginning of long delayed vengeance," while "Tanner regretted it, and seemed to be deeply grieved."[33] The two men's views would represent both ends of the spectrum of Latter-day Saint feeling about the atrocity.

Somewhere along the trail that evening, the Tanner-Mathews train unknowingly passed McMurdie's and Willis's wagonloads of militiamen and the surviving children returning to Cedar City. Klingensmith ordered the two wagons off the road, where he quieted the children with food and water and silently watched the freight train go by at a distance.[34] When the freighters reached Pinto, a settler told them to watch for an emigrant said to have escaped the massacre. A rescued girl of about six "said that she saw her mother killed by an arrow," but "her father had escaped to California."

The girl was likely the child Klingensmith placed at Pinto earlier that day, Martha Elizabeth Baker. For years, local settlers and others would refer to the escaped emigrant simply as "young Baker." Freight train passenger P. M. Warn said that "the matter of the escape was talked over by the Mormon captains, and Mathews made the remark, 'If the man comes into our train, he shall not be received!'"[35]

The Tanner-Mathews company descended into the Mountain Meadows before dawn. Powers and Warn laid low in the back of the wagons, covered with blankets, a condition they accepted so they could journey forward with the train. Distinguishing Mormons from Americans, Dame had told them in Parowan that, "as the Indians were deadly hostile to all Americans," Powers and Warn must not be identified as non-Mormons or "it would endanger the safety of the whole train." Dame was also motivated to hide what was unfolding at the Meadows. Powers and Warn fell asleep as they lay under blankets in the wagons, later saying they thought the train "drove all night in silence."[36]

The passengers' slumber shielded them from the reality. Billy Mathews's teenaged son, E. C., "didn't see a soul in Mountain Meadows," or at least, "not a living soul." E. C. was driving the third or fourth wagon in the train when the teams ahead turned "a little out to the left." When he came to the spot, he saw why. In the greyness just giving way to light, he made out several bodies "lying on the ground without clothes on them, naked bare," he said.[37]

As the freighters took in the shocking sight, the emigrants' abandoned cattle "came rushing around our wagons, making the night hideous with their bawling," said seventeen-year-old teamster Francis Marion Lyman, son of Latter-day Saint apostle Amasa Lyman. That sound, "mingling with the unearthly stench from the decaying bodies of the human beings," Francis said, made it the most terrifying night of his life. "I felt great relief as we put distance between us and the fatal spot."[38]

Powers and Warn awoke when the wagons stopped at daylight on Sunday, September 13, three miles beyond the scene of slaughter. The men of the train napped for just a few hours before pushing on again. Eager to put distance between themselves and the Meadows, they drove twenty more miles before camping near a Paiute village on the Santa Clara River, finally unharnessing their mules more than twenty-four hours after leaving Cedar City.[39]

Early that same day, Isaac Haight arrived home in Cedar and got a little rest. He missed the first part of Sunday morning's services to look for James Haslam, the express rider he sent to Young six days before. Haight heard that Haslam had just returned, and he felt anxious to see him. With the violent rhetoric and teachings of the Reformation, as well as the hysteria over the approaching troops, Haight seemed to hope there was a chance Young's response might validate the decision he had made.

Haight found Haslam in the street, headed toward Haight's house with Young's letter. Haight took it from his outstretched hand and read:

G.S.L. City Sept. 10th 1857

Elder Isaac C. Haight
Dear Brother,

Your note of the 7th inst is to hand. Capt. Van Vliet acting commissary is here having come in advance of the army to procure necessities for them. We do not expect that any part of the army will be able to reach here this fall. There is only about 850 now coming, they are now at or near Laramie. A few of the freight trains are this side of that place, the advance of which are now on Green River. They will not be able to come much if any farther on account of their poor stock. They cannot get here this season without we help them, so you see that the Lord has answered our prayers and again averted the blow designed for our heads.

In regard to emigration trains passing through our settlements we must not interfere with them until they are first notified to keep away. You must not meddle with them. The Indians we expect will do as they please but you should try and preserve good feelings with them. There are no other trains going south that I know of if those who are there will leave let them go in peace. While we should be alert, on hand and always ready we should also possess ourselves in patience, preserving ourselves and property, ever remembering that God rules. He has overruled for our deliverance this once again and he will always do so if we live our religion, be united in our faith and good works. All is well with us. May the Lord bless you and all saints forever.

I remain as ever your Brother in the Gospel of Christ.

Brigham Young[40]

Haslam watched as Haight, the most powerful man in Cedar City, broke down and "cried like a child." All he could manage to say was "too late, too late."[41]

After half an hour, Haight pulled himself together and walked into the church service, where Elisha Groves, visiting from Fort Harmony, spoke of the "Lamanites" being "the battle axe of the Lord." At the meeting's close, Haight took the stand, lowered his head, and offered the benediction.[42]

PART 2
COVER-UP

5

Forget Everything

Southern Utah, Mid-September 1857

On the morning that Isaac Haight read Brigham Young's letter in Cedar City, John Hamilton Sr. noticed unfamiliar people and cattle in the fields of his settlement of Sidon (Hamilton Fort) seven miles south. When he and his son went to investigate, they spied thirty or forty Indians encamped, stoking a fire. Two appeared wounded. These were not the Indians Hamilton knew who lived near the fort and worked his fields for food. Some had "a little black on their faces" as if they had been painted, testified Hamilton and his son, John Jr. The younger Hamilton was not sure where these Indians came from, though he had seen some of them before at Cedar. The Hamiltons' description of this group of Indians matched the one George Powers gave of the group he saw leaving the Meadows the day before.[1]

Guns and white men's clothing littered the ground around their camp. Some Indians were apparently washing the clothes, working from a three-foot-high pile of bloody raiment. Male and female garments of all kinds were "thrown out to dry, some on the ground, some on the bushes," said John Jr. As the Hamiltons stared, the Indians shot down two head of cattle to eat. "You may guess," John Sr. said, "I was afraid to speak to them."[2]

The Indians later sold some of the garments to the settlers. Mary White of Hamilton's settlement admitted buying from an Indian the dress of a little emigrant girl. Many southern settlers were living in poverty, "destitute of clothing," and White had three young daughters to clothe.[3]

Meanwhile, on that morning of September 13, word reached Fort Harmony that John D. Lee and his party were about to return from an "expedition South west." The fort's residents climbed the stairs to the second-story meeting room, where they watched for the expedition's return. Soon they saw "a greate number of Indians," Harmony's church minutes recorded, "with Bro J. D. Lee."[4]

"I looked out and saw John D. Lee at the head of the Indians," remembered Annie Elizabeth Hoag. "With very much the air of a hero," another witness testified, Lee led the group single file around the fort. Harmony's inhabitants had watched a similar scene the Sunday before when Lee and his party prepared to leave on their expedition.[5]

That previous Sunday, September 6, happened to be Lee's forty-fifth birthday. He dressed himself up that day "as much like a military officer as he could with the clothes he had," tying "a red sash around his waist," one witness said. Taking the speaker's stand, Lee told "of an emigrant company of gentiles that was going through," recalled Hoag.[6]

Lee told the congregation he had not seen the emigrants himself but learned of them from Haight, who summoned him after the train passed through Cedar City. Haight called on Lee—a government subagent teaching farming to Indians—to gather Paiutes and lead them to the emigrants' camp at the Mountain Meadows.[7]

Hoag remembered Lee seeking the congregation's approval so they would share responsibility for going after the emigrants. Maintaining that stake presidents Isaac Haight and William Dame endorsed the measure, Lee asked the congregants to raise their right hands in support.[8]

"The Saints of course lifted their hands up for they knew that his word was the law," Hoag said. When Lee asked if any stood contrary, only two or three hands went up. Hoag lifted hers briefly but then felt guilty when she did not have the courage to keep it raised. Her fear was not irrational. Another Harmony resident said that when he tried to speak against the plan, Lee threatened that "if he did not carry himself straight, he would get his tail cut off just below the ears."[9]

After the affirmative vote, Lee tromped down the stairs. About noon he "mustered in" several dozen Paiutes who lived nearby. Brandishing "a sword in his right hand," he marched them "military style" around the fort while residents looked on. "All that wish success to Israel," he shouted, "say 'Amen.'" When only a few answered, he "called for a better response, which he got, but in very faint voices."[10]

Now a week later, on Sunday, September 13, Lee marched the group of Paiutes around Fort Harmony again. Only this time they were returning instead of leaving, and "laden with booty," witnesses said, "loaded with plunder such as beds and tinwair," blankets, shoes, hats, and guns. Lee waved his sword above his head and shouted, "Thanks to the Lord God of Isriel that has delevered our enemies into our hands."[11]

The Indians gathered round Lee as he handed out melons, squash, and pumpkin pies from the fort. After all were treated, he climbed the stairs to the meeting room where the settlers sat to hear him. "Thank God [I] ha[ve] come back all right," Lee declared as he took the stand. Looking over his audience, he claimed to have seen a vision months before. In it he saw ninety-six sheep lying in a pile—bucks, ewes, and lambs. He proclaimed "he had just seen the vision fulfilled."[12]

Lee later took aside Hoag's then-husband, Peter Shirts, and told him "the whole storry, relating it as an actual occurrence and not as a vision." At the Meadows, Lee had wanted the gathered Indians "to attack the emigrant party before daylight when they would be in the most profound slumber, and to massacre them before they could awake and arm themselves," Shirts remembered. Not wanting to appear at the main assault, Lee crept up on a herdsman sleeping on a knoll above the cattle. When he pulled the trigger of his caplock pistol to kill the man, it failed to fire. Startled, the herdsman leaped up and raced down the rocky knoll for the camp, with Lee in close pursuit. As the man stooped to dive into a tent, Lee shot him dead.[13]

The shot and barking dogs woke the emigrants, who fired on their attackers. Gunshots thundered through the valley for half an hour as the raiders fired and the camp's defenders shot back. Some emigrants' bullets hit their mark, splintering the femurs of two Indians and driving all the attackers back.[14]

As Lee recounted the story to his congregation on September 13, he showed them bullet holes in his clothing. Though he had painted his face dark in disguise, riflemen spotted him on the knoll and fired, he explained. Bullets whizzed through his sleeve and hat, but they "didn't even as much as graze" him—evidence, Lee claimed, that "the Lord had blessed him."[15]

The emigrants had known what to do when attacked. Some used rifles to keep the marauders at bay while others circled the wagons. Lee watched with consternation as they quickly shoveled away dirt from beneath the wheels, lowering the wagon beds to the ground and chaining the wheels together, creating a makeshift fort. Inside the enclosure, men, women, and children huddled in a dugout pit for protection.[16]

The emigrants entrenched themselves so well that the attackers "could not get to them," Lee said. Exasperated and suffering casualties, the Paiutes complained that Lee had gathered them for the attack. "They was not going to do the dirty work alone," they insisted, gesturing towards the Mormon settlements.[17]

According to Shirts's account, Lee sent messengers south to Santa Clara to bring more Paiutes to the Meadows. By Friday, September 11, there were also "a good many whites come along." That morning, the militiamen gathered near the besieged wagons and raised a white "flag"—a handkerchief on a stick—signaling they were there to help.[18]

The emigrants allowed Lee into their corral for negotiation. Hoag remembered how Lee relayed the story to the Harmony congregation.

The emigrants' spokesman asked Lee if "he meant what he showed by the flag."

"Yes," Lee answered, he "meant peace."

"Do you give us peace?" Lee asked in return.

"Yes," the negotiator replied, but another emigrant protested, "No!"

"All I wish," Lee insisted, is for you "to surrender your arms and we will see that you go unhurt."

"If you give up your arms you are a fool," the protesting emigrant urged their spokesman.

"I don't know," the negotiator hesitated. "He promises peace."

"Don't you be such [a] god damned fool as that," a third man jumped in. "If you do you are dead men."

"No, I will promise you peace," Lee assured. "All I want is your arms."[19]

After a tense parley, the emigrants finally surrendered their guns on Lee's promise to protect them back to Cedar City. Separating the women and children from the men, Lee instructed them all to walk out in a line. Outside the corral, militiamen and Indians waited, also separated into two groups. After the militiamen marched the company for a distance, the emigrant men were "all shot dead at the first fire," Lee said, with the exception of a few. He did not say how the women and children were killed, and so Shirts later asked Indians. "The women and children were knocked down with stones, clubs and gun barrels," they told him.[20]

According to Hoag's recollection, Lee told his congregation about encountering an emigrant man holding his baby.

"Give up that child," Lee demanded.

The emigrant seemed to know Lee and his beliefs. "No, Lee," he replied. "I recognize you," and "you know the penalty of shedding innocent blood." If Lee was going to shoot, the man said, Lee would have to kill the child too, and bear the consequences.

The Bible condemned those who shed innocent blood, meaning those who were blameless, and Latter-day Saints taught that shedders of innocent blood forfeited their chance to enter the highest heaven.[21]

Lee gave the emigrant another chance to hand over the baby, but he refused.

"Then," Lee told his congregation, "it was [my] turn to shoot." He killed the baby and the man with the same bullet. Defending his actions to the stunned Harmony residents, Lee explained that he did not "consider himself under the penalty of shedding innocent blood." The killing of the baby, he said, could not be helped.[22]

As the congregation listened to Lee's chilling account, a messenger interrupted, entering the room and walking up to hand Lee a note. Reading it, Lee went silent about the massacre.[23]

The message was likely from Haight, informing Lee of Young's letter. The account Lee just gave placed responsibility for the massacre on himself, other white men, and Paiutes. But after receiving the messenger's note, he began covering up white involvement and laying blame solely on Indians. Not long after, Shirts said, "the citizens of Harmony were called together and told that if they ever mentioned a word of . . . Lee's speech of Sunday their throats would be cut."[24]

As the congregation came downstairs from Lee's Sunday speech, Hoag spotted children she had not seen before. One of them, a boy called Calvin, was weeping. Though he was only six, his height made him look seven or eight.

Pointing to a man called "Indian Joe," the boy cried "that was the Indian" who killed his Pa, "for he had his best coat and pants on."[25]

Hoag did not see the child again. "They said they had to keep the child secreted," she said. Another child taken in by Lee's family was a five-year-old boy Lee called Charles. "Lee said we was not to ask 'em any questions whatever," Hoag said. Nothing was to be said to the surviving children that might "cause them to remember. . . . They wanted them to forget everything that had transpired from this affair."[26]

Scenarios like the one in Harmony played out through southern Utah as massacre perpetrators returned home and word of Young's letter spread. "After Haslem had returned," said Cedar City resident Mary Campbell, "he told in public what Prest Young had told him[,] to spare no horesflesh . . . but hurry on and tell Haight to let the emigrants pass and not molest them."[27]

Authorized by Dame, Haight had started the cover-up of Mormons' involvement in emigrant cattle raiding and Aden's murder by ordering militiamen to massacre witnesses at the Meadows. He hoped to make the atrocity appear to outsiders as if it was solely committed by Indians. After receiving Young's letter instructing him to "let [the emigrants] go in peace," he started covering up the crime not only to outsiders, but to other Mormons.

He quickly sent notice of Young's letter to leaders of other settlements where massacre perpetrators came from and, at Cedar's afternoon service that Sunday, he spoke on "the spirit of the times," accusing "cousin Lemuel"—Mormon slang for Indians at the time—of being "fired up with the spirit of their fathers."[28]

Messengers "were sent around enjoining upon the people to keep their mouths closed," Mary Campbell said. They said, for example, that even if you were to "see a dead m[a]n laying on your wood pile, you must not tell but go about your business." Mary White likewise remembered that "everybody was silenced not to speak about it." Haight knew he had to enforce silence. "The people of Cedar was aware of the white's being guilty," she said.[29]

Before news of Young's letter and Haight's order of silence traveled fifty miles south of Cedar to Washington, Utah, "there was a great deal of excitement," said John Hawley, "and those that was at the scene of death was the most excited." Just returned from the Meadows, a few of the men spoke with great zeal in a church meeting. They "declared to us that the dividing line was then drawn between Jew and Gentile, and all must die that passed through the Territory who were not of our faith," Hawley recalled. "The work of death they applauded very much." Massacre participant Harrison Pearce seemed the most extreme. According to Hawley, Pearce proclaimed "he could see all the Gentiles stripped naked and lashed on there back and hav[ing] the sun scorch them to death by inches." Two others offered similar rants.[30]

Hawley seethed at what he was hearing. In July, while visiting Salt Lake City to receive his endowment rites, he had spoken with apostle Wilford Woodruff about the "the excitable times" unfolding in 1857 Utah. "I told him I took no stock in a good many revengeful speeches that had been indulged in by some of my brethren," Hawley said. Woodruff said "he was satisfied that some of our brethren had gone farther with this reformation and vengeance than they ought."[31]

Oblivious to what was surging through Hawley's mind, Washington's leaders invited him to share news from his recent trip to church headquarters. Hawley stood and railed with "as much zeal against the work of death" as the previous speakers had for it. "I should have to know it would be a saving of my own life before I would take the life of my fellowman," he chided.[32]

"And as far as the a[v]enging the blood of the prophets that some had been said today, who of you know that this company had any hand in killing the prophets?" None of them had any such knowledge, he insisted. "You only suppose and that will not do." Ironically, Hawley's brother William was one of the militiamen who went to the Mountain Meadows.[33]

John Hawley's defiance riled the Washington settlement's leaders, who took his "case under advisement." In a council meeting, Harrison Pearce and others reportedly discussed putting him out of the way. Fortunately for Hawley, "Uncle Billy Young"—the oldest militiaman at the massacre—pled his case. Fifty-two-year-old Young carried the day, but the council told him to issue a warning.

"I am sent to tell you," he told Hawley, "to be more on guard and not oppose the authority."

Steeled, Hawley responded, "You may tell the council I still stand on the same ground I took yesterday."[34]

Word of Brigham Young's letter to Haight finally reached Washington on Monday, September 14. "This day brought Brother Brigham's message and it was read in our branch," Hawley said. "When this was done there was a different tune played and these men that thought I ought to die thought different." From then on "they was my friends and I was more bold in proclaiming against such acts than before." Though Hawley eventually left the faith, into his old age he attributed the massacre to the "excitment inherited by the reformation" and those who "sent an express to Brigham Young to know what to do with this company, but did not wait till they got returns from Brigham before they massacred the company."[35]

William Dame returned home to Parowan by September 13. Over the prior few days, he had ridden nearly seventy miles to the Meadows, seen the horrific carnage, then made the journey back. But there would be little rest for him.[36]

About the time Dame returned, another California-bound train of some 125 men, women, and children, driving twenty-three wagons and some 450 loose cattle, rolled into Parowan. The company was the combined "Dukes train" of emigrants from Missouri, Texas, and Arkansas—the merged trains of Nicholas Turner, William Dukes, and Wilson Collins—recently besieged near Beaver. "The emigrants were very much frightened for fear of the indians," the Parowan Stake Historical Record noted.[37]

Word had reached the Dukes train that the company ahead was no longer under siege, but "murdered," reported Stephen Honea of the train, "and that it would not be safe for us to proceed any further." The shocking news struck close to home for Honea, who knew people in the slaughtered company. The massacred train "was under the charge of Captain Baker, familiarly known as 'Uncle Jack,' from Carroll county, Arkansas," Honea's account said. He also said a son of Baker was in the train.

Mormon settler Elisha Hoopes felt no remorse at the news. Honea heard him say that "he was glad the train had been killed, for they carried poison with them, and had only got their just reward."[38]

Reaching Parowan, the emigrants of the Dukes train "placed themselves almost entirely under the counsel and direction of Pres. Dame," the Parowan Stake Historical Record stated, "asking his counsel in every thing." Shocked by what he had seen at the Meadows, Dame did what he could to prevent another attack. He encouraged the emigrants to stay in Parowan to replenish supplies and gave the company written orders to show militia leaders when they ventured further south.[39]

Addressed to "Majors, Commandants of Posts and Captains of Companies," the order advised leaders "to allay all excitement with the indians which they may have towards the emigrant and traveler, and assist in passing through the trains now upon the road, affording them what assistance may be necessary to secure a safe journey." Though Dame knew militiamen had instigated the attack at the Meadows, his veiled language directed that they "send forward the best interpreters and clear the way by sending the indians off from the road, and guarding them through the different tribes now showing signs of hostility."[40]

Meanwhile, the Tanner-Mathews freight train continued its journey south along the Santa Clara River. There a group of local Paiutes approached, led by a headman called Jackson. Within minutes, Jackson identified passengers George Powers and P. M. Warn as gentiles, circling around Powers and drawing back his bowstring in threat.

"At the very moment that we were wishing for him most," said Powers, interpreter Ira Hatch rode up. Hatch was a missionary from nearby Fort Clara, "and of great influence among" the Indians, freight captain William Mathews assured Powers.[41]

After being convinced that Powers and Warn were not the Americans they were hunting, Jackson sent several of his men forward on the trail to California, while Hatch traveled on with the freighters. Reaching the sands of Beaver Dam Wash some fifty miles southwest of the Meadows, Hatch identified footprints made by white men's boots. Then he too left the freight train, hurrying ahead on the trail.[42]

The freighters were winding up another day's drive when Hatch returned, riding with two other Mormons. Powers later accused the two brothers, Henry and McCan Young, of being horse thieves escaping to Utah from San Bernardino, California. Hatch told the freighters he had encountered the Youngs on the Muddy River, "in company with an emigrant, who escaped the massacre." Hatch would later tell the approaching Dukes company that the emigrant's name was "Baker."

Hatch told the freighters that when he came upon these three, "there was not an Indian in sight, and that he had to give the whoop to call them from concealment." Powers began doubting Hatch when the interpreter contradicted himself, claiming "that on his arrival he found the Indians hotly pursuing the three men; and that they jumped upon the emigrant, and killed [Baker] before his eyes, before he could interfere to prevent it." Hatch said he was only able to save the two Mormons.[43]

By then, Young's policy of encouraging Indians to join the Saints' efforts resisting federal troops had extended even to these far reaches of the territory. When the Tanner-Mathews train reached Las Vegas, Powers said, a headman of the band there "asked our interpreter whether our captain had brought him no word from Brigham Young, whether he was nearly ready to fight the Americans yet; adding, that he was ready, had got his arrows poisoned, &c." At Cottonwood Springs, fifteen miles past Las Vegas, Powers said "the chief" of another band, who called himself "Brigham Young, said he was afraid of the emigrant train behind"—the approaching Dukes company—"and wished to know if they would shoot."[44]

6

The Sound of War

Salt Lake City to Beyond the Muddy River,
September–October 1857

As the Tanner-Mathews freighters and the Dukes company made their way through the havoc in the south, Brigham Young continued efforts to keep the army at bay in the north. Though Captain Van Vliet had informed the Saints that the troops could not reach them by winter, an express arrived on September 12 that made them wonder. Seven hundred soldiers had left Fort Laramie, pushing towards Salt Lake City about five hundred miles to the west. Hoping to avert a conflict, Van Vliet and Utah territorial delegate John Bernhisel prepared to head towards the approaching troops and then to Washington, DC. Young sent letters east with them.[1]

"I think we may count upon [Van Vliet's] assistance in staving off a collision with the United States this year," said Young's letter to apostle Orson Pratt, "and he thinks the Union(!) within that time will have ceased to be." With civil war looming in the East, Young wondered if the time had come for his people to declare their own independence. "We shall not permit troops to enter our Settlements," he wrote. "We are now free, and we have determined to remain so."[2]

Young reiterated his strategy to defeat the troops if they continued towards Utah's settlements. The people would set fire to their own homes and wage a guerilla war from hiding places in the mountains, he told Pratt. "Besides all this, cousin Lemuel by thousands only wait the word to use their best endeavors to fulfil the prophecies," Young claimed of the Indians. "Just let Uncle Sam make one movement proclaiming actual hostilities, and the war cry will resound."[3] In a similar letter to a church leader in Philadelphia, Young added that "for years I have been holding the Indians, [but] the check rein has broken, and cousin Lemuel is at length at large; in fact he has been already collecting some of his annuities. Day after day I am visited by their Chiefs to know if they may strike while 'the iron is hot.'" Young did not mention that he and Indian interpreters were encouraging Indians to join their fight.

"My answer depends on M^r. Buchanan's policy," Young continued. If the president did not respect the Saints' rights, "travel will be stopped across the continent—the deserts of Utah become a battle ground for freedom. It's peace and our rights—or the knife and tomahawk—let uncle Sam choose."[4]

Hoping to persuade Washington to pull back the troops, Young again warned of Indian aggression toward emigrants and the army in a letter to the U.S. commissioner of Indian Affairs. "The sound of war quickens the blood and nerves of an Indian," Young alleged, playing on nineteenth-century stereotypes. "The report that troops were wending their way to this Territory has also had its influence upon them. In one or two instances this was the reason assigned why they made the attacks which they did upon some herds of Cattle[.] they seemed to think if it was to be war they might as well commence and begin to lay in a supply of food," he wrote. If Washington would only heed his advice, Young urged, travelers could pass through Utah and "no Indian would disturb or molest them."[5]

Finally, Young wrote an old friend in Philadelphia, Thomas L. Kane. In 1846, after the Saints fled Illinois, Kane used his political ties to win national sympathy for the exiles' plight and support for their relocation to the American West. Kane's humanitarian efforts made him a beloved figure among the Mormons. Young wrote him of their new predicament, hoping the Saints might again "rely upon your aid and influence in averting the fearful storm."[6]

In a sermon the next day, Young "rather warmly" preached the same messages he wrote in his letters, directing his words to the federal government as much as to the crowd before him. "President Young," recorded one listener, "arose & said he was angry & Ritously angry & he would not have any of their Soldiers here but would treet all as a mob[,] for [the] government now wishes to Send Soldiers here to hold the mormans till the mob could come and rob & plunder us & kill inocent men women & children."[7]

Young again warned all who would listen that "the Indians Now are coming hundreds of miles to me to know if the[y] may kill the Emegrants that are passing through[.] I tell them not to do it[,] to cees their contentions & sheding of blood. But I can hold them noe longer." The express letter Young received from Haight three days earlier must have been on his mind. To anyone with "friends in the Stat[e]s," Young warned, "let them send them word to not cross over land for the[y] are noe more safe."[8]

Though Young's tough talk was meant to stop the army's approach, he also counseled his people against hoping for a collision. Some, he cautioned, are wishing the troops to come "that the[y] might fight."

"This," he warned, "is a [w]rong Spirit."[9]

After Van Vliet and Bernhisel headed east with Young's letters the next morning, Young called a meeting with top territorial, militia, and church leaders, including his counselor and Nauvoo Legion commander Daniel H. Wells. The group discussed a proclamation he had asked Wells to prepare on August 29, to be made public only if "the troops proceed to enter the Territory."[10]

After that weekend's news of troops proceeding past Fort Laramie, the leaders decided to issue the proclamation. Though addressed to the "Citizens of Utah," its words were also clearly meant for the eyes of the nation.

"We are invaded by a hostile force who are evidently assailing us to accomplish our overthrow and destruction," the proclamation began. Detailing persecutions in Missouri and Illinois, the document stated that the Saints had been forced to seek, among "hostile savages" in the "barren wilderness," protection and shelter they could not find "in the boasted abodes of Christianity and civilization."

The Saints had been given no opportunity to defend themselves from the charges recently leveled against them by "corrupt officials," "anonymous letter writers," "hireling priests and howling editors," the proclamation declared. They now claimed freedom of conscience and their right to defend themselves from the approaching army, calling it an "armed, mercenary mob."

The proclamation ended with a declaration of martial law. Governor Young forbade "armed forces, of every description, from coming into this Territory," commanded Utah's militiamen to prepare to march against any invasion, and prohibited anyone from entering, traveling through, or leaving the territory without a permit from a militia officer.[11]

The Saints' fears about the approaching troops were not unfounded. Though some soldiers had no desire to forge a bloody path into the Salt Lake Valley, others, like Captain Jesse A. Gove, hoped the Mormons would dare give battle. "If the Mormons will only fight," he wrote, "their days are numbered. We shall sweep them from the face of the earth and Mormonism in Utah will cease."[12]

Copies of Young's proclamation were posted throughout Salt Lake City's streets as couriers carried copies to other parts of the territory. Jacob Hamblin, still visiting the city with southern Utah Indians after his marriage to Priscilla Leavitt, picked up copies and accompanying letters of instruction to deliver to southern settlements.[13] The letters, signed by Young and Wells, reiterated the same strategies: if the army reached the settlements before winter, the people were to burn their communities, take to the hills, destroy the troops' supplies, and starve them out. In the meantime, the Saints must cache supplies and make "fast friends" of the Indians.[14]

"Keep things perfectly quiet and let all things be done peacefully but with firmness and let there be no excitement," the letters said, adding, "Keep alive the spirit of the Reformation." The documents contained mixed messages, with Young talking tough publicly while privately promoting calm. "Save life always when it is possible," Young and Wells concluded. "We do not wish to shed a drop of blood if it can be avoided. This course will give us great influence abroad."[15]

But blood already soaked the ground at Mountain Meadows.

With these letters and the martial law declaration in hand, Jacob Hamblin and his wagon party left for home. Hearing that the "Army was marching toward Salt Lake City," Priscilla felt "relieved to be coming back to southern Utah" and her future home at the Mountain Meadows. She did not know what lay ahead.[16]

As the Hamblins traveled south, John D. Lee saddled his horse in Harmony. Now a week after his return from the massacre, he left home again. This time he rode with William R. Davies, who was both his bishop and his militia adjutant, to attend their church's semiannual general conference in Salt Lake City in early October.[17]

Lee had another reason for going. After Young's September 10 letter arrived telling Haight to let the besieged emigrants go in peace, Haight had a talk with Lee. Haight and William Dame had argued at the Meadows over how to report the massacre. Now Haight insisted that Lee be the one to report it to Young, and in person.

Lee hesitated, asking why Haight didn't "send a written report" instead?

Lee "could tell him more satisfactorily than [I] could write," Haight replied, encouraging Lee to "stand up and shoulder as much of the responsibility as [he] could conveniently."[18]

Though Haight and Dame knew that they too were going to Salt Lake for general conference, they wanted to hide behind Lee, and he played right into their hands.[19]

As Lee headed north and Hamblin's party traveled south, rumors of the massacre spread. "I hear that a company of Emigrants en route for Callifornia were all killed by the Indians near Iron Co," Homer Brown recorded in Nephi on September 20, "all killed excep 15 small children, part of them sucking babes." Hearing the atrocity was committed solely by Indians, Brown and others associated the massacre with the recent, inexplicable deaths among Pahvants at Corn Creek.

"The Emigrants killed a beef and poisoned the meat and then gave it to the Indians, which caused some of them to die, and the[y] soon had their revenge," Brown surmised in his journal.[20] Central Utahns did not yet realize the massacre took place at Mountain Meadows, located in Paiute country more than 150 miles south of the Pahvant territory around Corn Creek.

On September 21, the day after Brown recorded this theory, a Fillmore boy died from the same mysterious malady affecting the Pahvants. Cattle, though "fat & sleek," collapsed on the Mormon range around Corn Creek in the days after the emigrants allegedly poisoned an ox carcass. Fourteen-year-old Proctor Robison was harvesting the cattle's hides when "he scratched a pimple on his face & soon his head swelled," one local said. Robison died the next day.[21]

The local people expanded their theory to explain the deaths of Robison and the cattle. Not only had emigrants killed and poisoned an ox for the Pahvants at Corn Creek, locals reasoned, they must have also poisoned the spring, killing the cattle that drank from it and the boy who skinned their carcasses.

Hamblin heard this explanation when his party passed through on the day of Robison's burial. "There was some considerable excitement about it among the citizens of Fillmore," Hamblin said, "and among the [P]ah-Vent Indians who live within eight miles of that place. I was told that eighteen head of cattle had died from drinking the water; that six of the [P]ah-Vents had been poisoned from eating the flesh of the cattle that died; and that one or two of these Indians had also died." Robison's bereaved father told Hamblin "the boy had been poisoned in 'trying out' the tallow of the dead cattle." Hamblin felt satisfied the father genuinely believed what he said. Hamblin also "thought, *at the time*, that the spring had been poisoned."[22]

Less than two years later, Hamblin told army investigator James H. Carleton that he camped that night "with a company from Iron county." In 1857, Iron County's two major towns were Parowan and Cedar City. Further south in Washington County were Fort Harmony, Santa Clara, and Washington. The company from Iron County informed him the accused emigrants "had all been killed off at Mountain Meadows, except seventeen children."[23]

As the Hamblins continued south, "Jacob seemed to be worried and depressed about something," Priscilla noted. He learned more about the massacre when they ran into Dame, on his way to catch up with a group of about twenty Parowan Saints headed to Salt Lake for general conference—probably the group Hamblin's party had camped with.[24] Hamblin said Dame "confirmed what these people from Iron county had said."[25]

Dame also told Hamblin about the second company of emigrants traveling not far behind the one massacred, likely relaying what he had done to protect the Dukes company from yet another attack, including his written orders to militia leaders.[26]

"Send forward the best interpreters" to "clear the way" for the passing company, Dame's orders had said, keeping Indians away from the road and guarding the emigrants "through the different tribes now showing signs of hostility."[27]

Having just left Salt Lake, Hamblin knew Dame's instructions to prevent a cattle raid countermanded Young's strategy to encourage such attacks as motivation for Washington to pull the troops back. Before their conversation ended, Dame gave Hamblin "an order to press into service any animals" he needed to catch up to the Dukes train. Hamblin later told Carleton he rushed forward to stop Indians that Dame told him were gathering at the Muddy River to "wipe out" this second company. But Hamblin did not explain why Dame, who had already sent orders to prevent a second attack on the Dukes company, would need to rush another messenger south with those same instructions.[28]

Hamblin's group reached Beaver by 8:00 p.m. There he swung himself onto a borrowed horse and hurried into the night, leaving Priscilla and their wagon party to come home at a slower pace. Stopping in Parowan and then Cedar for just ten minutes, Hamblin pursued the Dukes train.[29]

In Leach's Cutoff, Hamblin saw two or three hundred head of Texas cattle plodding towards him. He had seen this drove before at Corn Creek on his way to Salt Lake, only then it had seemed twice its current size. The company of emigrants who drove the longhorns were now nowhere to be seen. Hamblin paused to talk with two Cedar City men driving the cattle, who said they were taking them to Iron Springs, a grazing spot seven miles from Cedar. He later saw the herd on the Harmony range.[30]

Hamblin soon reached Pinto, northeast of the Meadows. Among the missionary families living there, he found Dudley Leavitt, his counselor in the Southern Indian Mission and, since September 11, his brother-in-law.

Hamblin relayed what he heard from Dame. Leavitt confirmed that the emigrants ahead had several interpreters from Santa Clara to see them through to California, following Dame's orders.[31] Those interpreters included Ira Hatch, two of Jacob Hamblin's younger brothers, and a couple of unnamed men.[32]

Hamblin told Leavitt to hurry to his ranch at the Meadows, "get the best animal he could," and chase after the company ahead. Hamblin told Carleton he sent his counselor "to stop further mischief from being done." But more "mischief" would soon occur.[33]

When Jacob rode the last leg to the Meadows the next morning, he found his home "anything but cheerful." Rachel Hamblin carried heavy burdens. Besides caring for seventeen children through the traumatic night of September 11, she was still nurturing the three suffering Dunlap sisters, as well as her own brood. She would feel relief when Jacob's new wife arrived a few days later. "Dear Rachel welcomed me with open arms," Priscilla said. "Yet I had not expected to find this terrible situation." Priscilla remembered sad, gloomy days after the "terrible massacre," days "so full of work . . . and trying to comfort those who had been through such tragedy—the heart grew faint and sick at times."[34]

One-year-old Sarah suffered in body as well as mind. Jacob observed she "had been shot through one of her arms, below the elbow, by a large ball, breaking both bones, and cutting the arm half off."[35] Jacob's family told him what they knew of the carnage that erupted south of their ranch. "The account of the massacre my family gave me," Jacob said, "made my heart ache."[36]

Knowing Jacob had just returned from meeting with Salt Lake leaders, Rachel asked if he "thought such work was right, and was counciled by the Authorities," Jacob said. "I told her no."

Not wanting his family to have any part in the crime, Jacob asked Rachel "if she had any of the spoil of the Company, about the House." She showed him the "two nice quilts" brought to the ranch after the massacre. He told her it was all right to keep them for the three little Dunlap girls in her care.[37]

Jacob had his adopted Shoshone son Albert lead him to the massacre site. Three miles south of the ranch and about a mile north of the emigrants' siege site, they approached a place on the trail near a sloping ridge. There, "a few acres of oak brush and sage" grew tall and close to both sides of the road, "the only thing of the kind I saw in the valley," a federal investigator would soon observe.[38]

As Albert led Jacob through the area "where those unfortunate people were slain," Jacob recoiled. "Oh! horrible, indeed was the sight," he said. "Language fails to picture the scene of blood and carnage."[39]

At three places, hungry scavengers had "strewn in every direction" the remains of what Jacob believed were "over one hundred men, women and children," he said, "stripping the bones of their flesh." The bodies were "in a state of putrification." At one site, he counted nineteen wolves disinterring bodies "and eating the flesh. My feelings, upon this occasion," he said, "I will not attempt to describe—The gloom that seemed to diffuse itself through the air and cast a shade over the hills and vales, was dismal in the extreme."[40]

Albert also showed Jacob two girls, their bodies left lying where they "had run some ways off before they were killed." The girls looked about fourteen or fifteen, "lying there with their throats cut," Jacob said.[41]

The remains of fifty-two-year-old Jack Baker lay somewhere along the ground. Before leaving Arkansas he had prepared his will, "knowing the uncertainty of life and the certainty of death and not knowing the time of my dissolution." He had expressed his desire that upon his death, his body would receive "a decent burial in the bosom of it[s] mother Earth."[42]

Hamblin did not attempt to bury the bodies that fall. Instead, he would wait until "the following summer, when the bones had lost all their flesh."[43]

As horrific as the scene was for Jacob, it was worse for Albert, who witnessed the slaughter. Though many perpetrators and witnesses of the atrocity, including the surviving children, left the massacre site never to return, Albert lived in it. As a key witness and a herdsman at the Meadows, the teenager had to repeatedly visit the scene of the massacre, both literally and figuratively.

"He had a hard time adjusting to life again," Priscilla Hamblin said of Albert, who was close to her age. "The Indians and the white men both claimed 'the devil or evil spirits' were after Albert."[44]

As Albert and Jacob took in the carnage at the Meadows, the Dukes company wended its way along the Santa Clara River to the south, several days behind the Tanner-Mathews freighters. To keep them from seeing the grisly scene at the Mountain Meadows, Dame had instructed their Mormon guides to take the company south on a much rougher road that skirted Harmony and Washington before reaching the Santa Clara. With news of the massacre and the memory of their own siege at Beaver fresh in their minds, the emigrants felt spooked by the presence of hundreds of local Paiutes who frequently surrounded their train.[45] When the train reached the southwesterly flowing Virgin River, "we had to give more beeves to the Indians," emigrant

Stephen Honea said. The company became increasingly suspicious of their hired interpreters, who got along well with the Indians.[46]

Somewhere on the difficult fifty-mile stretch along the Virgin, Dudley Leavitt caught up to the train. The emigrants wondered why he suddenly showed up in the middle of the desert, not knowing that Jacob Hamblin had sent him here. "A man named Lovett, joined us," said Honea, "who had no ostensible reason for coming to us."[47]

The trail left the Virgin River to cut west through the desert, eventually intersecting the Muddy River, where some nine hundred Paiutes lived on their farm of melons, corn, and vegetables. When the train reached the farm, about three hundred Indians surrounded their wagons. "The interpreters told us the Indians wanted ten beeves," said Honea. "We gave them six, and thought they were well satisfied." The company formed a temporary encampment as they watered their animals and waited out the worst heat of the day.[48]

The nervous emigrants kept up their guard. From Hatch they knew that "here was where they had killed the last of the train that was ahead of us"— the emigrant that Hatch called Baker. In the late afternoon, the travelers pushed onto the dreaded sixty-mile stretch of desert between them and the next water at Las Vegas. The emigrant herdsmen led out, driving some 450 cattle a half-mile ahead of the long line of twenty-three wagons. Three of the Mormon interpreters brought up the rear.[49]

The trail soon brought the company into Big Wash, a dry stream bed so long and deep that the emigrants called it a canyon or "holler." As night came on, they trudged several miles through the ravine's gravel and sand, choking on dust kicked up by their animals. As they moved toward the end of the wash, Honea saw one of Jacob Hamblin's brothers speaking with a young Indian who had traveled with the company since the Muddy. The Indian pointed towards the hill just ahead of the train.[50]

The herdsmen stopped the drove and waited as Hamblin's brother rode along the hilltop, as if looking for something. By the time the interpreter rode back down, the wagons had caught up to the herd, and the whole train lumbered on.[51]

Suddenly, the young Indian broke into a run towards the front of the herd, giving "a whoop." In response, a chorus of yelling and whooping rent the night air. The startled emigrants looked up towards the source of the din. In the moonlight just beginning to shine over the top of the ravine, hundreds of Indians rushed down the hill.[52]

7

An Awful Tale of Blood

Northern Utah and Southern California, September–October 1857

John D. Lee and his Harmony bishop, William Davies, made good time as they headed north for general conference in Salt Lake. They passed through Fillmore about the same time as Jacob Hamblin's southbound party. Like Hamblin, Lee heard of the supposed poisoning deaths of the teenaged Proctor Robison and several Indians in the area.[1]

After reaching Provo a few days later, Lee ambled into a church service on Sunday morning, September 27, where local stake president James C. Snow offered him the pulpit. Though Lee was "a stranger to most of you," Snow said, he thought the congregation might "like too hear from" him.[2]

A clerk scrawled ink across paper, recording the meeting's minutes. Lee took the stand to talk about the massacre, as he had in Harmony two Sundays before. Only this time he omitted mention of white participation and added details of the "poisoning" story he had just heard in Fillmore.

"There was some Emigrants passd through," Lee began, who "boasted verry much & they killd an ox & poisened it for the Indians[.] four or five of them Died[.] one Mormon boy died." In Cedar City, the marshal (John M. Higbee) arrested one of the emigrants and "they said where is your god Damd Bishop & such like conduct" before leaving town. Local Indians then told the Mormons "that they was friends too the cause of Isreal" and "enemies too the Gentiles." The Indians "killd all but three [emigrants] that got away in the night," Lee said. "One was overtaken the next day & they was on the track of the other two. . . . Seventeen Children was saved & brought intoo the settlements." Lee concluded that "this was the condition of the Lamonites out where he was living." To him, the massacre demonstrated that Indians were fulfilling their scriptural destiny, fighting on the Saints' side in the face of impending war.

Having told of the mass murder, Lee said "he was trying too live near untoo the Lord" and hoped "we all might have an interest in the Kingdom[,] that we might be permitted too return too our [heavenly] father & mother in peace."

As Lee spoke, Snow grew irritated, not because of Lee's callous talk but because he sensed sympathy among his flock for the slain emigrants. Such "sympathy will be the means of Destroying many," he chided. "I have no sympathy for such people." If the emigrants threatened and poisoned people as Lee claimed, Snow seemed to reason, they deserved no pity. "Saints should know when too sympathize," he preached.

Snow said he felt the spirit of the Reformation "tight" within himself. "The day is fast approaching when we must be prepared too stand." He railed against "Old Buck" Buchanan and the approaching army. Word had just reached Provo of the troops' latest "forced march" towards Salt Lake City.[3]

Though reaction to the massacre varied, Latter-day Saint settlers in northern and central Utah believed the white perpetrators' story that Indians were solely responsible. Around the time of Lee's speech, a Provo farmer noted in his diary, "a com[pany] of 100 emigrants killed South of Iron County By the indians." A Nephi resident recorded that a Cedar City visitor told him "it was True about the Indains Killing the emegrant[s]— he also said th[at] 2 Thousand Indains could be raised shortly if needed."[4] The day after Lee's speech in Provo, a Church Historian's Office clerk in Salt Lake wrote, "Reports reached town that the companies of Cala[fornia] Emigrants going south were all used up by the Indians—100 men. & 1000 head of cattle,—at Mountain Meadows."[5] In none of these contemporary Utah accounts—including John D. Lee's—did the writers or speakers say that the slain emigrants were from Arkansas, only that they were bound for California.

On September 29, two days after his speech in Provo, Lee walked into Brigham Young's Salt Lake City office. He looked "travel-worn" in the morning light, an office worker noted, "as if he had come in haste from a long journey."[6]

Lee's arrival was a distraction from other alarming events. Young and Wells had received a series of distressing expresses from Mormon scouts who were watching the movements of the U.S. Army's Utah Expedition. In spite of Governor Young's demands that they stop, the troops had continued to advance.[7]

When the eastbound party of Captain Van Vliet and Utah territorial delegate John Bernhisel encountered the advance troops, Van Vliet gave them the warning he received from Young. If the troops tried to enter Utah's settlements, Van Vliet told them, "they would find a diferent warfare from any thing they had met with." As quartermaster, he advised the infantry to winter on the waters of Hams Fork, a short distance ahead but still east of Fort Bridger—the Mormons' line in the sand. The troops may simply have been following Van Vliet's advice when they pushed towards Hams Fork at the end of September, but the Saints saw the move as aggressive.[8]

Responding to news of this latest advance, Young wrote the commanding officer of "the forces now invading Utah" to either turn the troops around or deposit their arms with Utah militia leaders. He enclosed in his letter a copy of his martial law proclamation.[9]

These worries occupied Young's mind when John D. Lee appeared at his door. Though Lee requested a private interview, Young had fifty-year-old Wilford Woodruff join them in Young's inner office. With piercing blue eyes and a short, greying beard, Woodruff was familiar to Lee. Like Lee, he had joined the Saints in the 1830s and served missionary tours in Kentucky and Tennessee. Unlike Lee, Woodruff also served missions in Arkansas and England, and became a church apostle in 1839. An inveterate diarist, Woodruff had been assistant church historian since 1856.[10]

Strain, already heavy in Young's office, intensified as Lee walked in. Nearly three weeks had passed since Young received Haight's express about troubles with an emigrant company. Within the last two weeks, a Ute named Arapene told interpreter Dimick Huntington "that the Piedes had killd the whole of a Emigrant company & took all of their stock & it was right," which Huntington likely reported to Young.[11] Just the day before, rumors of an Indian massacre at Mountain Meadows reached Salt Lake. Now Lee, a federal agent to Paiutes near the Meadows, came before the church president. Though the massacre took place eighteen days earlier, Lee feigned that he came as an express rider, implying the atrocity occurred more recently. Telling the real date of the crime would have cast suspicion on southern Utah leaders for taking so long to report it. This deception caused confusion for decades over when the massacre occurred.[12]

Lee brought "an awful tale of blood," Woodruff recorded. A company of California-bound emigrants, totaling about 150 men, women, and children, came through the territory with numerous cattle and horses, Lee began. He asserted they "belonged to the mob in Missouri & Illinois." As they traveled south, "they went damning Brigham Young [and Young's counselor] Heber C Kimball & the Heads of the Church saying that Joseph Smith ought to have been shot a long time before he was." Lee knew mention of Smith's murder rankled Latter-day Saint nerves, especially Young's.[13]

Next, Lee launched into the poisoning story. The emigrants "wanted to do all the evil they Could," he claimed, "so they poisond Beef & gave it to the Indians & some of them died." Lee also said "several of the saints died" from springs the emigrants poisoned.[14]

After dishing up plenty of both Indian and white motive, Lee said only that "the Indians became inraged" at the emigrants' conduct, surrounding them on a "prairie." To defend themselves, "the Emigrants formed a Bulwark of ther wagons." But "the Indians fought them five days" until "they killed all their men about 60 in number." Omitting mention of his and other white men's roles in decoying the emigrants from their wagon fort, Lee lied that Indians "rushed into their Carrall & Cut the throats of their women & Children except some 8 or 10 Childrn which they brought & sold to the whites." Finally, he said, the Indians "strip[p]ed the men & women Naked & left them stinking in the boiling sun."[15]

At some point, Young interrupted the chilling account. Despite Lee's accusations against the emigrants, Young said the story of their slaughter "was heart rending," and "that Emigration must stop as he had before said." The church president's reaction gave Lee pause. Young did not express satisfaction with the emigrants' deaths, as Provo stake president Snow had, but rather showed the sympathy for which Snow had chided his congregation. Young's response made an impression on Lee. Years later he wrote in his journal, "Brigham Young knew nothing of the Mountain Massacre until it was all over; & verry Much regretted it when he heard of it."[16]

After seeing Young's reaction, Lee began to express some empathy for the emigrants in his massacre accounts. At the same time, as if to salve his and others' feelings, he intensified his efforts to demonize them.

Lee told Young and Woodruff that when he heard about the massacre, "he took some men & went & buried their bodies," which "was a horrid awful Job." He then continued his victim blaming. "Many of the men & women was rotten with the pox [venereal disease] before they were hurt by the Indians," he claimed, reflecting what freighter Billy Mathews said William Dame told him the day after the massacre. He "did not think their was a drop of innocent Blood in their Camp." He had taken in two of the surviving children and "could not get but one to kneel down in prayer time & the othe[r] would laugh at her for doing it." And, he added, the children "sw[o]re like pirats."[17]

Lee asserted that after the massacre, he sent interpreters to assist the passing Dukes train. "Their was another large Company of Emigrants," Woodruff recorded Lee saying, "who was also damning both Indians & Mormons[.] they were afraid of shareing the same fate[.] Brother Lee had to send interpeters with them to the Indians to try to save their lives while at the same time they are trying to kill us."

Though Lee and other militiamen took control of much of the slain emigrants' property, he again lied to Young and Woodruff that "Indians obtain[ed] all ther Cattle Horses & property guns &c."[18]

By the time Lee finished his story, Young had to escape the four walls of his office. His efforts to stop the army's approach, so pressing over the previous days, came to an abrupt halt. "President Young left the Office 11 a.m. in his carriage for his upper mill, his health being feeble," recorded a clerk. Young could have retreated to either of his mansions that flanked his offices but instead sought the solitude of the mill.[19] Though he had hoped to avoid "shedding a drop of blood" in the present crisis, civilians had been slaughtered on Utah soil. He must have wondered whether his strategy to encourage Indian cattle raiding was to blame.

From that point on, Young's efforts to engage Indians in raiding emigrant cattle and fighting U.S. troops ceased. He did not mention the strategy again. Instead, he told Indian leaders, "I do not want you to fight the Americans nor to fight us for them, for we can take care of ourselves."[20] Lee's telling Young of the supposedly all-Indian massacre changed Young's stance just as Young's reaction against the atrocity changed Lee's.

Young's solitude at the mill did not last long. He returned to the office that evening to handle another disturbing express. A militiaman brought word from the east that part of the army had again advanced. Nauvoo Legion general Daniel Wells, who left the city for the front two days before, sent the messenger to urge militia companies "to rush forward" to him at Echo Canyon. Some fifty miles northeast of Salt Lake City, the long and often-narrow canyon of towering red cliffs was a natural gateway into Utah's northern settlements. The Nauvoo Legion would make a stand there if the U.S. troops came that far.[21]

Woodruff spent that evening at home. His Salt Lake congregation, the Fourteenth Ward, was to send fifty men to Echo Canyon in the morning, and he needed to prepare his seventeen-year-old son to go.[22]

In 1833, Joseph Smith prophesied that "not many years shall pass away before the United States shall present such a scene of *bloodshed* as has not parallel in the hystory of our nation." Woodruff recalled the prophecy as he recorded Lee's news of the massacre and the imminent threat of war. "The scene of Blood has Commenced," he told his diary. "Joseph said we should see so much of it that it would make our hearts sick."[23]

The beating of drums woke the city early the next morning. Four hundred militiamen paraded in the streets, ready to join at a moment's notice the eight hundred already stationed in Echo Canyon and further east. The people watched with "solemnity" and "a good deal of anxiety" for the raising of a signal flag, which would mean a call from Wells for reinforcements. "It is a solum time the Armies of the Gentiles are making war upon us because of our religion & we have to defend ourselves against a Nation of 25,000[,]000 of people," said Woodruff. "We have to trust in God."[24]

The fear of war loomed large in the minds of the Saints that fall of 1857. They could not fathom then that the Mountain Meadows Massacre would cast a shadow far darker and longer than the specter of war itself.

The war preparations cast a gloom on Utah's territorial fair taking place in the city. Woodruff's wife Phoebe, along with Elizabeth Knight Johnson and the other Fourteenth Ward quilters, pieced together their album quilt in time for the fair and won a first-place prize. But "their were so many of the Brethren gone to the Mountains to meet the Enemy," Wilford wrote, "that but little is doing in the fair."[25]

As the Salt Lake militiamen mustered, the Tanner-Mathews freighters wound their way through California's Cajon Pass, where they encountered a San Bernardino–bound mail carrier. Someone in the train spoke about the massacre to the carrier, who "brought news of the terrible calamity that befel an emigrant company coming on their way to Cal[ifornia]," wrote San Bernardino resident Louisa Barnes Pratt, a Latter-day Saint. "A band of Indians had pursued after them, massacred the whole company! The news caused a terrible excitement!"[26]

By the time the freighters reached San Bernardino on October 1, a local man was already on his way to Los Angeles, where he shared the news with the *Los Angeles Star*. "Rumored Massacre on the Plains," announced the headline of the *Star*'s October 3 lead article.

Because the story had come to the newspaper as a rumor, "we confess our unwillingness to credit such a wholesale massacre," its editors wrote, publishing only what they heard without assigning blame. "Ninety-five persons" traveling from Salt Lake "had been cruelly massacred" somewhere between the last settlements of Utah and California's border, the article reported. The company's property "had been carried off" and surviving children "picked up on the ground." Beyond that, "no further particulars are known."[27]

Though the *Star* editors initially refrained from assigning responsibility for the massacre, others had their own ideas. California's faithful Saints, like their counterparts in northern Utah, believed claims that Indians were solely responsible, while "unbelievers began at once to blase about, that the indians had 'Mormon allies,' " wrote Pratt. "A few began to be vindictive towards [us] in that Country: as though [we] could be confederate when hundreds of miles from the scene!"[28]

The Saints could not believe anyone of their faith was connected with such an atrocity. Teenaged Francis Marion Lyman of the Tanner-Mathews company wrote his father, apostle Amasa Lyman, that gentiles and apostates blaming the Saints was "nothing more than could be expected." Like Pratt, the younger Lyman reported "considerable talk" about the massacre. "Some say that if they had . . . any friends in the company they would kill the first damed Mormon that they met."[29]

Freighter Billy Mathews sensed dangerous repercussions for local Saints. He told his non-Mormon passenger George Powers "not to associate with the damned apostates"—many of whom had left Utah for San Bernardino—because "they were cut throats of the worst character." The Saints would give Powers a steady job at their mill, Mathews offered, while warning Powers to "be careful not to talk too much of what [he] had seen."

Attending the southern California Saints' conference on October 6, Powers heard a speaker say from the pulpit "that the hand of the Lord was" in the massacre, and "whether it was done by white or red skins, it was right! The prophesies concerning Missouri were being fulfilled, and they would all be accomplished." Billy Mathews added that "the work had just begun, and it should be carried on until Uncle Sam and all his boys that were left, should come to Zion and beg for bread."[30]

Louisa Pratt wrote that Mathews "gave us a full account of the horrible deed; perpetrated by the Indians, according to the best of his knowledge. If he believed they had 'white allies,' he was careful to conceal it. Had he intimated suspicion of that nature, our indignation would have known no bounds!" While Pratt said she and those around her felt "horror and astonishment" at the crime, Powers said he "heard many persons express gratification."[31] Like their Utah counterparts, California Mormons' reactions to the massacre varied.

Within days of his arrival in the mostly Mormon community, Powers passed up Mathews's job offer and left town. So did P. M. Warn, the other non-Mormon who traveled with the Tanner-Mathews freighters to California. "I did not stay in San Bernardino, because it did not appear to be a free country," Powers said, "for I am an American, and like freedom of thought and speech."[32]

Powers exercised his right to speak as soon as he reached Los Angeles, where his report created a stir. "Placards . . . posted throughout the city brought out a very large number" of citizens—some of them disaffected Mormons—to an October 12 public meeting. There they listened to the statements of Powers and Warn, detailing their journey from Salt Lake. Though both stated they traveled just a week to ten days behind the massacred company, like the early accounts of Utah settlers, they did not mention knowing the names of the emigrants or where they were from.[33]

Warn reported that as he journeyed behind emigrant groups passing through Utah's settlements, "he every where heard the same threats of vengeance against them, for their boisterousness and abuse of Mormons and Mormonism, as was reported." Powers spoke of specific troubles at only two settlements. At Buttermilk Fort, north of Corn Creek, he "found the inhabitants greatly enraged at the train which had just passed, declaring that they had abused the Mormon women, calling them w—s, &c., and letting on about the men." Because of the Latter-day Saint practice of polygamy, outsiders sometimes called Utah women "whores." Powers said these townspeople "appeared to be bitterly hostile, and would hardly speak to us. We were unable to get anything we stood in need of."

Further south at Beaver, Powers heard "an ox died." By then, Beaver resident Elisha Hoopes had spread the rumor that he saw an emigrant poison a dead ox before offering it to Pahvants. "The people at Beaver," Powers said, "seemed also to be incensed against the train."

"We hope for the sake of our common humanity," the Los Angeles Star editors added to their publication of the Powers and Warn reports, "that the character of this people may be redeemed from the black catalogue of crime here preferred, and that it will yet appear that they are not the fiends incarnate they are represented."[34]

Southern Utah leaders had tried to cover up Aden's murder, Mormon involvement in cattle raiding, and the attack at Mountain Meadows by silencing all witnesses of these acts. They refused to let the emigrants go for fear they would "raise hell in California." But that happened anyway.

As reports spread, northern California newspapers laid responsibility for the massacre with the Mormons and called for retribution. "The blood of American citizens cries for vengeance from the barren sands of the Great Basin," the *San Francisco Daily Evening Bulletin* declared. "Virtue, christianity and decency, require that the vile brood of incestuous miscreants who have perpetrated this atrocity shall be broken up and dispersed."[35]

The "Mormon massacre," along with Utah Territory's declarations of independence, the article predicted, would surely bring the Saints "in speedy conflict with the United States—and this insures their final extermination." Once the hatred "pervading the whole country against the Mormons is given legal countenance and direction, a crusade will start against Utah which will crush out this beastly heresy forever. From this State alone thousands of volunteers could be drawn, who would ask no better employment than the extermination of the Mormons."[36]

8

Hostile to All Strangers

Eastern Utah to Eastern California, September–October 1857

The day after John D. Lee gave his report to Brigham Young, an Indian agent in Provo, George Armstrong, did likewise. Young had been serving as superintendent of Indian Affairs. Armstrong's letter, written three days after Lee spoke in Provo, aligned with what Lee told Young—that Natives alone committed the atrocity.[1]

Armstrong wrote of the rumored poisoning of Pahvants "by a Company of emigrants from the States to California, While the company were camped a short distance from Fillmore." When the Pahvants asked the encamped company for food, Armstrong reported, the train's captain replied "they would give them a beef the next day." When the Pahvants returned, "the beef was killed and poisoned and given to the Indians." Four of them died, and more became dangerously ill. "When the cause of this unhappy circumstance was discovered by the Indians," Armstrong asserted, "they held a council and determined to be revenged."

Armstrong repeated the false rumor that Pahvants followed the train to the "Mountain Meadows where they attacked the camp and after a desperate fight they killed fifty seven men and nine women." Armstrong intimated that the emigrants, through the alleged poisoning, had brought on their own destruction.[2]

Between Armstrong's and Lee's reports, Young heard a long list of accusations against the slain emigrants: that they were part of Missouri and Illinois mobs, that they boasted Joseph Smith should have been killed sooner than he was, that they cursed Young and other church leaders as they passed through Utah, and that they killed Indians and settlers near Fillmore by poisoning them. Though the two accounts were filled with hearsay, supposition, and—in Lee's case—deliberate lies, they seemed to support each other.

The following Sunday, October 4, Young spoke to thousands of Utahns gathered for the church's general conference. He preached that his people would be sustained "against all that can come to annoy, destroy, desolate, and drive the Saints of God" because "God will fight our battles."[3] Young expressed similar sentiments in a letter that day to Daniel Wells and other militia leaders stationed at Fort Bridger east of Echo Canyon. "The spirit of our God guides and blesses you in your views and plans," he told them.[4]

On October 2, U.S. Army colonel Edmund Alexander had received Young's martial law proclamation and September 29 letter telling the soldiers to either turn around or winter where they were after surrendering their arms. Hearing Young's letter read to them, the soldiers scoffed that they would turn over their six-shooters after they turned "the wheel 6 times." Unshaken by Young's warning, Tenth Infantry Captain Jesse Gove exclaimed, "We will show him on which side of his bread the butter should be spread."[5]

Later that day, apparently in response to the troops' reaction, Wells made his next move, calling together a company of mounted militia with young Lot Smith as its captain. Their instructions were to head east to the Fifth U.S. Infantry's camp and "cripple them" by stampeding their cattle and burning their supply trains. But "if the soldiers fired on us," said one man in the company, "we were not to return the fire." This directive lined up with the September 14 letter from Young and Wells instructing Utah's leaders to "save life always" when possible and not "shed a drop of blood if it can be avoided."[6]

The militiamen soon spied the heavily laden wagons traveling a day behind the troops. At midnight Smith's men crept up on the fifty-one corralled wagons and their sleeping teamsters. Smith told the surprised wagon master "to get all of his men and their private property as quick as possible out of the wagons, for I meant to put a little fire into them."

The slumbering teamsters woke to the shock of armed raiders ordering them to get up and grab their things. "I (never) saw a scareder lot in my life," said a militiaman, "until they found that they was not going to be hurt." Fifty-one burning wagons "made a grand light," he said. "The country was lit up for miles around." The next day, militiamen captured twenty-six more wagons.[7]

An express carried word of the attacks to an army encampment on the Sweetwater River, several days' travel to the east. The camp included the Utah Expedition's new commander, Colonel Albert Sidney Johnston of Texas, and Utah's newly appointed chief justice, Delana R. Eckels. Both Johnston and Eckels shared the explosive news of the attacks in letters to their superiors in the East.[8]

About the time Lot Smith and his men burned the supply wagons, the California-bound Dukes company faced yet another attack in the desert east of Las Vegas. The emigrants paused on the trail in the sandy bottom of Big Wash, stopped by a terrifying chorus of yelling and whooping that rippled along the hills above them "where previously we could not perceive a single Indian," emigrant Stephen Honea said. Riding out front with the herd, the company's startled drovers heard one of the Hamblin brothers holler to them "to fall back and leave the cattle." The guide urged that "if they thought anything of the women and children," they must race "back to the wagons and protect them."[9]

In the confusion, the herdsmen obeyed. Some men of the train had families with them, like twenty-three-year-old William Wilson of Jackson County, Missouri, whose wife and baby rode in one of the roughly two-dozen wagons. The forty-four emigrants who bore arms had to defend the seven dozen who did not.[10]

On the crest of the hill ahead, Indians seemed to appear out of nowhere. "As the moon shone brightly on the desert they were easily seen," herdsman Peyton Welch said. Some emigrants thought they saw about two hundred. To others it seemed more like four or five hundred. Welch thought he recognized them as Indians from the Muddy. The emigrants watched in horror as the raiders descended the hills toward them. They were under attack for the second time in less than a month, with recent news of the massacre at Mountain Meadows fresh in their minds.[11]

The cattle lurched into a stampede as the raiders reached them. Some emigrants drew their guns to fire at the Indians, but an interpreter stopped them, warning them not to shoot or the entire train would be massacred. Dust and terror filled the air as hundreds of cattle thundered through the ravine.[12]

Agonizing moments passed for the emigrants. The Indians drove the cattle out of the wash and onto the desert flats. When the tumult and dust settled, the emigrants realized their lives had been spared. But the Indians were slipping away, and with them the herd and the emigrants' dreams of a bright future in California.[13]

Welch "called for men" to pursue the cattle. Seven volunteers, he said, "were all I could get."[14] Most of the men stayed near the wagons with their families. "The men that had no families wanted to go," Wilson's wife said, "but we were afraid of the Indians, that they would come in and kill the women and children while they were gone."[15]

Welch and his volunteers charged after the herd until an interpreter intervened. He told them they might be able to get their cattle back if they didn't go after the Indians but let him intercede. The emigrants gave the interpreter a chance, watching hopefully as he rode after the cattle. Soon he returned. The Indians "sent word," he said, that "if we wanted to fight to come on."[16]

Welch's posse of emigrants asked the interpreter to lead them to the Indians. The guide agreed, and the posse started out, a bright moon lighting their way. The other Mormon guides had already left, ostensibly to recover loose stock.

The Indians herded the cattle along the plateau above Big Wash, back towards the Indian farm at the Muddy. Soon the emigrant posse and their interpreter came up on the Indians, paused in a hollow. The posse members stopped, thinking it unsafe to go closer.

Again the emigrants implored their interpreter to negotiate. The guide agreed but said he needed to exchange his old gun for a pistol first. Someone handed him "a valuable navy revolver," and the interpreter explained his plan. "If danger threatened," he said, "he would fire the pistol, which would be the signal for them to return to the wagons."[17]

The horsemen waited as their guide rode down toward the Indians. Soon two pistol shots rang out, sending the riders racing back to their wagons, where they waited for their interpreters' return. As the minutes ticked by, with no sign of their guides, the emigrants realized they had been fooled. "We was on the edge of the de[s]ert and had to go on," Welch lamented. "We couldn't go back." Roughly forty miles lay between them and the next water at Las Vegas. The waterless stretch had to be traversed in the coolness of night for livestock to survive.[18]

The company had hired the interpreters to safely guide them from Cedar City to Cottonwood Springs, a little west of Las Vegas. But the men into whose hands the emigrants placed their money and their trust had deserted them.[19]

The Mormon guides later shared their own version of the raid, saying they had prevented another massacre.[20] According to Dudley Leavitt's granddaughter Juanita Brooks, Leavitt claimed being a guide on that expedition "was like taking our lives in our hands." Leavitt said he found the Indians "gathered and dressed in their war paint," but "he talked with them and persuaded them to take the cattle and let the company go in peace." Then "tying a red bandana around his head and giving a mighty whoop," wrote Brooks, "he led the stampede himself."[21]

Not long after the raid, a California-bound emigrant traveling with a different party saw what he thought were the tracks of some three hundred cattle, heading from the Muddy toward the Mormons' Santa Clara fort. Among the cattle tracks were those of "several shod horses and mules," the emigrant, John Aiken, said. The "drove of Cattle" that ended up at the fort, wrote a Santa Clara resident, "was called the publick herd."[22]

Shortly after the Indian interpreters' return to Santa Clara, Jacob Hamblin wrote to Brigham Young. "The Indians here are very hostile to all Strangers[,] allmost ungovernable," Hamblin said in his letter. "I dare not go to far with them or to much against the Spirit of them for fear of loosing influance and govermant over them[.] the last company of emigrants went without any loss of life but they took all of their loos cattle but 100 head of lame ones." Hamblin told Young the Indians divided the cattle among the various bands and brought a hundred cows to the Santa Clara missionaries for breeding.

Hamblin also wrote of his efforts in building up the fort and the Southern Indian Mission. "If any movements we have taken does not meet your approbacion," Hamblin concluded his letter, "please let us know[.] a word from you is incouraging to the Boys especially these times."[23] No record of a reply from Young exists.

Meanwhile, the Dukes company limped along the trail to California, abandoning wagons as their oxen collapsed in the heat. One of them later "swore he would kill the first man who said he was a Mormon."[24]

This third attack on the combined Dukes company was yet another of the multiple raids on emigrant trains that took place that fall of 1857, all aligned with Young's strategy to stop emigration until Washington pulled its troops back from Utah. Had the attack on the company at Mountain Meadows not gone murderously awry, Young's cattle-raiding strategy might have been largely forgotten. Instead, the massacre of emigrants at Mountain Meadows would haunt Young, his legacy, and his people.

9

The Spirit of the Times

Southern Utah to Southern California, October–November 1857

Sunday morning, October 18, 1857, saw John D. Lee preaching again at Harmony's pulpit. Feverish with the flu and the war hysteria he carried home from Salt Lake's general conference, he spent the entire meeting "giving the spirit of the times north," a clerk recorded. "Said that thare [were] 1,500 troops on the way to the [Salt Lake] Valley. Said we had to prepare for a big fight next year."[1]

After Lee and other southern Utah leaders returned from the conference, they decided what to do with the massacred emigrants' property and the surviving children. On September 29, Lee had lied to Brigham Young that "Indians obtain[ed] all ther Cattle Horses & property guns &c." But Lee and Cedar City bishop Philip Klingensmith claimed Young told Lee to "take charge" of the slain emigrants' cattle and property.[2]

According to Bishop Klingensmith's clerk, George Bowering, Klingensmith had a history of lying about property he pilfered. On October 12, Bowering wrote the church's presiding bishop at church headquarters that Klingensmith had just released him as clerk because "he sees I understand the way he does business." Bowering accused Klingensmith of using donations "paid into the office for his own use and no charge made in the books, as for instance 9/10 of tithing paid in clothing &c he takes to his own house for safe keeping and that is the last of it."[3]

The emigrants' cattle rounded up at the Mountain Meadows were driven to Fort Harmony's range.[4] Lee's sudden increase in wealth was conspicuous.[5] He said his ownership of the cattle was a trust "for the benefit of the Indians" and that he gave them "considerable of the beef."[6]

In late October and early November, the surviving children were given new names in a Latter-day Saint ritual similar to christening. In these ceremonies, a local church leader typically held a new baby before a congregation, blessing the infant and publicly pronouncing the child's name. Older, adopted children received the same rite, only the leader placed his hands on the child's head for the ceremony. A young child's blessing was not baptism into church membership. That rite was only administered to persons aged eight or older.

Following a blessing, a clerk might enter the child's name, birthdate, birthplace, and parents' names in the congregational record, along with the name of the person who pronounced the blessing. On Sunday, October 24, eleven children in all were blessed in Cedar City. Unlike the others, four of these children's entries listed no birthplace or parentage. Only their new names and estimated birth years were recorded: Albert Morris, 1856; Betsy Whittaker, 1855; Maria Smith, 1855; and Eliza K. Smith, 1857.[7]

In Harmony's November 1 services, a few more children of unnamed parentage were blessed, though the minute book did not list estimates of those children's ages. Lee blessed a boy, Charles, with his surname. He later said the boy, whom he called Charlie, was the son of the massacred company's captain.[8]

Harmony bishop William Davies blessed another boy as John Groves—the six-year-old survivor mentioned by Annie Elizabeth Hoag who identified himself as Calvin and was taken in by Harmony resident Elisha Groves. The bishop blessed another boy as Louis Gordon Ingram. Alexander and Agnes Ingram, a childless couple in their mid-thirties, adopted this infant massacre survivor.[9] Agnes was "happy to death to get this child," remembered a Harmony resident. The Ingrams had gone "a good ways" to pick up the baby—probably from Cedar City.[10]

Some of the surviving children remained with the same families throughout their time in Utah. The Dunlap sisters stayed with the Hamblins. Martha Elizabeth Baker continued to live with the Thorntons at Pinto. The boy John D. Lee named Charles remained with the Lees, John Calvin remained with the Groves, and the baby called Louis stayed with the Ingrams.[11]

Other children were shuffled from home to home. Klingensmith temporarily took in "a nice little baby girl," he said, "a babe at the breast" he gave to one of his wives, who was nursing her own baby. This was the baby he blessed as Eliza K. Smith on October 24. After "Eliza" was weaned, "that child was given to Birkbeck [at] Cedar City because they had no child. Told my wife let 'em have it," Klingensmith said.[12]

Two girls of unknown parentage and birthplace, with estimated birthdates of 1854 and 1856, were not blessed in Cedar City until February 1858, suggesting that they too were shifted from somewhere else.[13]

Cedar City resident Mary Campbell recalled that an emigrant girl recognized a massacre perpetrator, exclaiming, "There is the man who killed my father." The girl, Campbell remembered, "afterwards disappeared." An entry appears in Cedar City's blessing record for April 24, 1858, when a girl of unknown birthdate, birthplace, and parentage was blessed as Angeline Jewkes. She was "about 6 years" old and born in the "U States." The lateness of her blessing date, compared with other surviving children's, suggests that she too was moved from another home.[14]

On November 2, 1857, the day after Agnes and Alexander Ingram's adopted baby boy was blessed along with the other children in Harmony, Alexander and another man drove away from the fort with a wagon and draft animals provided by Lee. As planned, they met at Pinto that night with other men and wagons from Cedar City, including massacre participants Klingensmith, William Bateman, and one of the two men who had driven a wagon at the massacre, Samuel McMurdie.

Eight men of this combined company were headed for the mountains near Las Vegas to mine lead for ammunition to use in the anticipated war. The other two men were Cedar City missionaries, Jehiel McConnell and Commodore Perry Liston, called to serve among Paiutes on the Muddy River. McMurdie, who kept a journal of the trip, mentioned nothing of the grisly scene they passed through at the Mountain Meadows en route to Las Vegas, probably because he was one of the massacre's perpetrators.[15]

After Klingensmith's group left, Isaac Haight put on an auction of the emigrants' property at Cedar City's tithing house, where much of the loot had been stored in the cellar. In pioneer Utah, Latter-day Saint tithing houses functioned not only as revenue collection points for the church but also as general stores and welfare agencies, disbursing goods to the needy. Though Klingensmith, as bishop, was primarily in charge of the tithing house, stake president Haight chose to disperse the emigrant property while Klingensmith was away.[16]

The local people packed into the tithing house for the auction, eager to purchase badly needed items. Most of the community was in desperate straits. The iron industry they had moved to southern Utah to establish had not gone well. As one Iron County man put it, "they had been living upon little else than bread."[17]

The people had painstakingly but fruitlessly pursued making iron "till every person engaged in the enterprise was reduced to poverty," observed Louisa Barnes Pratt, who had learned of the massacre from the Tanner-Mathews freighters while living in San Bernardino. She had recently relocated to southern Utah, along with many other California Saints after Young called them back under the threat of war. "Great was the poverty of the people in Cedar City," she wrote. "Every day my house was thronged with women, wanting to buy groceries, cloth, and every thing I had."[18]

In a November 12 meeting of Cedar City's Female Relief Society, one of Isaac Haight's wives, "Sister A Haight," had "made some remarks on the poor, their want of clothing &c." When Relief Society leaders reported to Bishop Klingensmith that some of the women of the town "were destitute of clothing," he answered "that it was quite right, and that it was good for us."[19]

In this environment of severe want, the slain emigrants' property was pulled from the cellar and held out to the people. Thomas Willis, a Cedar City teenager at the time, remembered being in the tithing house when the "traps that would naturally be along with a train of that kind" were auctioned— kitchen utensils like skillets, bake ovens, milk pans, pails, and churns, along with tools like saws, axes, log-chains, augurs, plains, and chisels. Larger items like wagons, oxbows, wagon covers, and bedding were also sold. Willis said auctioneers spent "pretty much all afternoon crying it off."

The cash-poor settlers bid in grain futures. Bidding grew so brisk that Haight cautioned the people "not to bid up so high on the goods; that when they went to their grain bins they would find that they were lower than they expected."[20]

Still, "the bidding ran high," each article bringing "nearly or quite its value." The final prices were recorded in an account book for later collection, but in the end, few bidders ever paid for what they got. The incriminating evidence in the account book was reportedly later burned, and no leader ever demanded "payment for the goods of the murdered emigrants."[21]

Massacre survivor Nancy Saphrona Huff, who lived with the Willis family until she was about six, recalled recognizing the emigrants' belongings in the possession of local people. "The Mormons got all the plunder. I saw many of the things afterward. John Willis had, in his family, bed clothes, clothing, and many other things," she said. "When I claimed the things, they told me I was a liar, and tried to make me believe it was the Indians that killed and plundered our people, but I knew better."[22]

In mid-October, not long before the auction, a California-bound traveler at Pinto saw Mormons drawing what he thought were some of the stolen wagons towards Cedar City. "They did not explain to me anything of their business, or of their possession of the wagons," said John Aiken. They "seemed very distant and indifferent in their communications." Concerned for his safety, Aiken did not ask too many questions. "I wished to avoid suspicion," he said.

Aiken soon encountered interpreter Ira Hatch, who told him the Dukes train, raided about two weeks earlier, "had lost over 200 head of cattle by the Indians." Hatch's telling a California-bound traveler that Indians were raiding emigrant cattle was consistent with Young's strategy to create fears about emigrating through Utah. Aiken, his suspicions roused, listened in on a conversation between Hatch and a "Mr. Hamblin." Hamblin "told Hatch to go and brand *his own* cattle, before he turned them out with his," Aiken said. Aiken also said Hamblin "sold a steer" to one Mormon, saying the steer was in poor condition because it "had bee[n] driven to the Muddy and back."

After staying several days at Pinto, Aiken joined the San Bernardino–bound mail company of John Hunt, a Latter-day Saint. Hunt agreed to let Aiken ride with his company to California but guaranteed him no protection in the event of Indian conflict. Hunt told Aiken he would have "to fight [his] own battles, as they were friendly with the Indians" and wished to remain so.

When the company reached what Aiken called "the field of blood" at the Mountain Meadows, like Jacob Hamlin before him, he saw some twenty wolves "feasting upon the carcasses of the murdered," the nude bodies in "a state of putrefaction." He noted "that the women and children were more generally eaten by the wild beasts than the men." Hunt drew his gun and fired at the wolves. The scavengers ran only a short distance before halting, ready to return to the carnage.

"Although this terrible massacre occurred within six miles of P[into] Creek settlement, and thirty from Cedar City," Aiken surmised, it appeared to him "the Mormons are determined to suffer their carcasses to remain uncovered, for their bones to bleach upon the plains."[23] Aiken was right. Jacob Hamblin had already decided it was pointless to attempt to bury the bodies that fall. He would wait until "the bones had lost all their flesh."[24]

As Hunt's mail company passed through the Meadows, "Mr. Hunt and his companions often laughed," Aiken said, "and made remarks derogatory to decency, and contrary to humanity, upon the persons of those who were there rotting, or had become the food to wild beasts."[25]

Though Aiken was an acquaintance of "Cap. Baker" and others whose remains now lay scattered around him, he "dared not express [his] sentiments" in front of Hunt's company, feeling "I was traveling with enemies to my country and countrymen," he said.

Several miles south of the Meadows, Aiken and the mail company came upon the tracks of a herd that appeared to include at least three hundred head. The tracks veered east off the California trail at the fork leading to the Santa Clara Fort. For the next one hundred miles between that fork and the Muddy, the southbound mail company passed over the northbound cattle tracks, supposing them "to be the stolen cattle that were run off from the trains of Captains Dukes and Turner," Aiken said.

The fast-paced mail company soon passed the combined Dukes and Turner companies, still limping their way through the desert. Since the raid in early October, the company had made its way to Las Vegas "without molestation," said emigrant Stephen Honea. "The Indians were peaceable, and the [Mormon] interpreters not being with us," he noted, "we had to give them only one animal."

Cottonwood Springs was the next oasis on the desert trail. Here too, "there being no Mormons," Honea said, "the Indians [were] peaceable and friendly." With their remaining animals worn out, the emigrants decided to stay put until their stock gained enough strength to survive the trek ahead through the punishing Mojave Desert. But their provisions were running low. Finally, Honea and eight others determined to walk the remaining 275 miles to San Bernardino for help.

Before departing, "we were told by the Captains and the company that on arriving in San Bernardino, we must say nothing against the Mormons, as that city was composed of Mormons," Webb said. They "must not excite" the Latter-day Saints for fear they would not "forward supplies to keep the company alive" or, worse yet, "cut them all off." It was no longer Indians but Mormon aggression the emigrants feared.

Over the next several days, the nine men walked across the desert, "enduring almost incredible sufferings from the want of food and water," Honea said. They "reached San Bernardino" on October 17, "almost exhausted."

The emigrants' fears about violence from the California Saints proved unfounded. After Honea and his party arrived, Mormons and non-Mormons of San Bernardino sent wagons of supplies to the stranded emigrants. The Dukes company finally made it into the town on October 31, and the Turner company arrived several days later, at last marking the end of their harrowing journey.

The emigrants soon went public with their Utah experiences, talking to newspaper editors and drawing up affidavits. "I have no hesitation in saying," one emigrant told a notary public, "that from my knowledge and belief, the late horrible massacre and robberies, perpetrated upon the emigrant trains in Utah Territory, were committed by the Mormons and Indians under Mormon influence." This assessment was universal among the many Turner and Dukes company emigrants who signed affidavits.

Newspaper accounts of the massacre and its surrounding events exploded, spreading to the East Coast via the Panama Canal mail route and then across the nation by telegraph. While the *Los Angeles Star* editors had been cautious in the first published story of the massacre on October 3, after hearing the accounts of the recently arrived emigrants, they held nothing back.

"From the statements made regarding the preaching of the Mormon Prophet, and the sentiments of the people, there can be no doubt but a deep rooted animosity exists amongst them against the people and Government of the United States," the newspaper now proclaimed. Referring to the U.S. troops of the Utah Expedition, the *Star*'s editors predicted that the first shot the Mormons "fired against that band of 'Uncle Sam's boys' will be the signal for lighting the torch of a long and sanguinary war, which will not be quenched till Mormonism is exterminated from the soil of the United States."[26]

Southern Utah's massacre leaders had deemed it "necessary to kill all [the Arkansas emigrants] to silence" those who knew white Mormons were involved in their attack. "It had to be done," they had reasoned, for if word of their involvement "should come to the ears of President Bucanann, it would endanger the lives of the Bretheren." And yet endangering their people was precisely the result of their murderous decision, one that most would regret the rest of their lives. "There is where we did wrong," Isaac Haight later admitted to a friend, "and I would give a world if I had it" to take it back.[27]

PART 3
NEGOTIATION

10

A Lion in the Path

Utah; Washington, DC; Arkansas; and Pennsylvania,
November 1857–January 1858

Within days of the Turner and Dukes companies' arrival in San Bernardino, a
non-Mormon merchant walked into Brigham Young's office, following up on
a deal. William Bell found that in Utah, prejudice "against Gentiles in general
is very certain, but it has no practical results, if they mind their own business." Bell and his business partners had minded theirs, to the tune of half-a-
million dollars' profit over the previous eight years. But now, with the threat
of war closing in, Bell wanted out.[1]

He had recently married British immigrant Marian Benbow, whose family
wished to leave Utah.[2] Young and the church owed much to the Benbows.
Marian's parents, William and Ann, had befriended Young and Wilford
Woodruff when they went as missionary apostles to England in 1840. William
introduced the two young men around his home county of Herefordshire,
where they baptized Benbow family members and nearly two thousand of
their neighbors. William's brother John paid to publish England's first five
thousand copies of the Book of Mormon and, when the Benbow families and
their neighbors immigrated to their American Zion, donated to help other
British Saints make the journey.[3]

But Utah and their new religion did not work out for the William Benbow
family, prompting William Bell to seek a new home in the Midwest for his
wife, their young child, and his in-laws. The merchant had what the Mormons
needed—supplies for a possible war—and a Utah Saint owned something
Bell wanted—land on the Iowa side of the Mississippi. Young helped arrange
the swap, and Bell came to his office to say goodbye. The merchant planned
to take his five-wagon train to southern California, sail to New York, then go
by rail to Iowa.[4]

Anticipating that California and New York newspapers would ask Bell for
insider information on the Utah conflict, Young spelled out the message he

hoped Bell would share. "I say that the troops shall never enter this valley!" he declared, emphasizing each word.

Again Young laid out the strategies he hoped would keep the troops out of Utah's settlements until "Congress will have time to consider the matter thoroughly" and "withdraw the troops." But if the troops continued forward, "we are determined to resist," he told Bell. "The Lord will protect his own. If the troops attempt to enter, we will destroy them." Though Young was "emphatic in his denunciations of the government," Bell thought he had "a wholesome dislike of gunpowder himself." Newspapers on both coasts would publish Bell's comments over the coming winter, which may have influenced Congress's view of the conflict.[5]

Young soon wrote southern Utah leaders Isaac Haight and John D. Lee about the Bell company. Just over a month had passed since Young heard Lee's account of the massacre, and Young's letter made clear he did not want the Bell train raided. William Bell, the letter began, "a person with whom you are both well acquainted," would soon be passing through southern Utah to California. "As the Indians beyond you are reported to be somewhat troublesome and hostile to travelers," Young wrote in a veiled reference, "I wish you to procure for M^r. Bell and all in the company . . . the services of an interpreter and a good Indian." He suggested Jacob Hamblin and Tutsegavits, the Paiute leader he recently met and ordained in Salt Lake.

Contradicting his late August directive to save every kernel of grain, Young wrote that the Bell company would "probably want to buy some oats in our southern settlements, which I trust the brethren will be able to sell them." In case he had not made it clear enough, in closing Young wrote, "I wish Mr. Bell and company to pass safely to San Bernardino with all their effects." In keeping with Utah's September 14 martial law proclamation, Young provided passports for each man in the company to show militia leaders and Indians alike.[6]

Bell's company of sixteen men and four women—which included his family and his store clerks—left Salt Lake on November 8, certain that Utah militiamen and federal troops were about to clash. "Mounted couriers were constantly passing between Echo Cañon and the city, conveying news"— covering the 113-mile distance in just ten hours, Bell said.[7]

In spite of their passports from Young and the letter Young wrote to Haight and Lee about seeing Bell and his party safely through, the company experienced a harrowing journey south. "It was necessary, at each settlement," Bell reported, "to call on the Bishop, hire an interpreter, and send them ahead of the company to treat with the Indians for their safe passage." Near Cedar City, Isaac Haight, as Young's letter directed, employed guides for the company "to see them safe thro to California," though Haight disparagingly described the company's members as "gentile merchants and apostates."[8] As Young had requested, Jacob Hamblin and Tutsegavits were those guides, along with Nephi Johnson and a few others.[9]

When the Bell company neared the Muddy River, Hamblin rode out ahead. At the Muddy, he met two Indian missionaries stationed there, Jehiel McConnell and Commodore Perry Liston, who had hitched a ride there with Klingensmith's party that went to Las Vegas to mine lead. Hamblin had trouble convincing McConnell and Liston that the approaching Bell company should not be attacked.

"A plan had been laid and matured in their minds to kill off this company and take the spoil," Hamblin said. "I told them the instructions I had from Gov. Young; but they held out the idea to me that there was secret instructions that I knew nothing of." Hamblin insisted, "I had written instruction from Brigham Young to take this company through safe, and that I would stand by them to the last."[10]

This contemplated attack on the wagon company was narrowly avoided. After the Bell company safely reached Los Angeles, Hamblin wrote a report to Young. "The company which I was called to go through with, they & their effects passed through in safty, thoug attended with some difficulty in consequence of certain personsons having been sent to the Muddy" from Cedar City, "and there giving the Indian[s] such instructions as we know nothing about." Interpreter Ira Hatch, Hamblin wrote, "is now on his way there to correct those errors, & set things to wright as soon as possible."[11]

Meanwhile, across the country in Washington, DC, a Philadelphia lawyer strode into the White House on November 10, eager to talk to President James Buchanan. The young man was Lieutenant Colonel Thomas L. Kane, the non-Mormon friend of the Saints whom Young had recently petitioned for help.

Two letters Kane received in October, along with news reports of events in Utah, had left him "inexpressively shocked." The first letter was from Samuel Richards, an England-bound missionary Young had asked to inquire of Kane what he knew about the government's "designs against us." Finding Kane away from his Philadelphia home, Richards left him a note. Buchanan's sending troops, combined with "the universal cry" against polygamy,

Richards wrote, "indicate to us that the present intention[s] of Gov. towards us are extremely hostile."

The Saints believed the government was trying to "break us up," Richards said. "From the knowledge you have of us, Dear Col., and the character of Prest. Young, you must well know that we could never submit to be interfered with in our religious views and practices, after what we have already passed through."[12]

The second letter Kane received was Young's of September 12, one that Utah territorial delegate John Bernhisel carried as he and Captain Stewart Van Vliet journeyed from Salt Lake to Washington. "In turning my thoughts upon you," Young wrote, "reminiscences of the past crowd thickly upon me." Though forever grateful to Kane for helping the Saints through their struggles of 1846, Young's memories of the calamities that elicited Kane's assistance filled him with foreboding. Buchanan's unexplained deployment of troops, Young said, made the Saints suspicious about the government's intentions. Though they had enjoyed peace from "our enemies" for ten years, Young concluded "the Crusade was again commenced against us."

The Saints hoped they could rely on Kane's "influence in averting the fearful storm, but if it breaks upon us," Young predicted, "it will also break upon the whole Country. . . . Discord shall rend the nation asunder." The day before Young wrote these words, Van Vliet had told him he thought the United States were headed for civil war. Young believed a clash in Utah would set off a national conflict.[13]

After reading the letters from Richards and Young, Kane shared his alarm with George Plitt, a family acquaintance who was a friend of Buchanan. Plitt urged Kane to visit the president, hoping Buchanan might send him to Utah as a peace commissioner.

But when Kane met with the president on November 10, Buchanan showed no interest. "The advance of the troops would be slow," he assured Kane, and their orders and his instructions to the new governor traveling with them were designed to prevent conflict. Buchanan's response reflected the government's general lack of concern. "The public feeling at present in relation to Utah is pretty tranquil," Bernhisel wrote Young from Washington on November 13. "It is not generally believed that there will be any difficulty between the people of our Territory and the Government of the United States."[14]

After the meeting with Buchanan, Kane admitted, "I thought myself fortunate in evading a proposal" from the president to go to Utah. Due to family hardships and the difficulty of reaching the Rocky Mountains in winter, the trip would have been daunting.[15]

But the tranquility in Washington soon ended. On the day Bernhisel wrote Young, Judge Delana Eckels's October 13 letter from the plains reached Washington, confirming Kane's warning that Buchanan brushed off. Eckels's letter reported that Mormon militiamen had burned dozens of the Utah Expedition's supply trains. Young's martial law declaration reached Washington a few days after Eckels's letter.[16]

A week later, the *New York Times* reported that Mormon missionaries in England had sought "from the British Government permission to settle in the British possessions" in North America.[17] The report was one of many speculations that Latter-day Saints were planning yet another exodus from U.S. territory as the federal troops advanced. The reports said the Saints were looking north to Russian America (later Alaska) or Canada, or south to northern Mexico or Central America—areas coveted by American imperialists.[18] As rumors of the militia raids and Mormon exodus spread, Buchanan made political hay of "the Mormon question" to achieve his expansionist goals.

In mid-November, Buchanan spoke with Russian minister Edward A. de Stoeckl in Washington. Stoeckl had heard "that the Mormons, although animated with the most warlike resolution, foresee the eventuality of a new emigration." Buchanan "smilingly alluded" to Stoeckl that they might even head to Russian America.

Would the Mormons "resort to us as conquerors or as peaceful colonists?" Stoeckl asked.

"It is for you," Buchanan replied, "to settle that question; as for us, we shall be very happy to be rid of them."

Stoeckl reported the conversation to Russia's foreign minister, Aleksandr Gorchakov. If rumors were true that Mormons might head to Russian America as conquerors, Stoeckl warned, Russia must either provide armed resistance or give up that part of its territory. Gorchakov shared Stoeckl's news with Russian tsar Alexander II.

"This supports the idea of settling henceforth the question of our American possessions," the tsar reacted. Gorchakov instructed Stoeckl to discuss the "sale of its North American possessions." The transaction took place a decade later, with the Civil War causing a delay. Though Buchanan's 1857 intimation of Mormon encroachment was not the sole reason for Russia's sale of Alaska, it was a factor.[19]

Buchanan began lobbying for a larger force to send to Utah in his annual message to Congress on December 8. Because Congress adjourned before he ordered troops to Utah earlier that year, it was his first public explanation of his decision. "This is the first rebellion which has existed in our Territories; and humanity itself requires that we should put it down in such a manner that it shall be the last," he insisted. "We ought to go with such an imposing force as to convince these deluded people that resistance would be vain, and thus spare the effusion of blood."

Buchanan argued this strategy would convince the Mormons "that we are their friends, not their enemies." He asked Congress "to raise four additional regiments," increasing the nation's standing army by more than a third at a cost of seven million dollars. "At the present moment of depression in the revenues of the country I am sorry to be obliged to recommend such a measure," he said, referring to a recent financial panic, "but I feel confident of the support of Congress, cost what it may, in suppressing the insurrection."[20]

Secretary of War John Floyd's report to Congress backed Buchanan. As American expansion spread to the Pacific, Floyd knew as well as Young that Utah occupied a key position at the crossroads of the westbound trails. But Young's strategy to convince the government that it needed his help there backfired. Floyd argued that the Mormons' strategic position was the very reason that they must be removed.[21]

"They stand a lion in the path," defying the government's authority, Floyd argued. They had encouraged "nomad savages . . . to the pillage and massacre of peaceful and helpless emigrant families." The settlement of Pacific territory, the rights of emigrants, and communication between the nation's populations on its two coasts "all depend upon the prompt, absolute, and thorough removal of a hostile power besetting this path." Floyd recommended raising the new regiments for a "thorough repression." Paradoxically, many of the events Floyd and Buchanan cited to justify deploying troops to Utah occurred only after they had sent the troops.[22]

The day after Congress received Buchanan's and Floyd's messages, Buchanan's political advisor, U.S. Attorney James Van Dyke, urged the president to reconsider Kane's peaceful alternative. A Philadelphia acquaintance of Kane, Van Dyke wrote Buchanan that after hearing of the Mormon raids and consulting with Utah delegate Bernhisel, Kane was determined to go to Utah to broker peace, with or without Buchanan's endorsement. But the president's approbation, Van Dyke wrote, might ensure Kane's success.[23]

The president received Van Dyke when he appeared at the White House in late December. Buchanan asked if Kane still intended to follow through with his plan, saying it was "fraught with dangers" and "doubting whether any good would result."

Van Dyke responded he had no doubt of Kane's power to influence the Mormons.

Buchanan asked Van Dyke if he had confirmed that belief with Bernhisel, prompting Van Dyke to quickly meet with the Utah delegate.

Bernhisel reiterated Young's contention that Latter-day Saint influence on Utah's Indians was essential for the safety of emigration to the Pacific coast. He charged that the government's removal of Young as superintendent of Indian Affairs had resulted in "depredations . . . by the Indians." But Bernhisel also expressed "a lively interest in anything" that might avert hostilities between Utah and Washington.

Though Bernhisel lamented Kane had not intervened earlier to persuade the Saints "to return their allegiance to the U.S.," the territorial delegate assured Van Dyke "there was no person here nor there who could exercise such a wholesome influence" on the situation as Kane.

Bernhisel wanted Kane to understand what he was getting into. While he "would be perfectly safe" in Salt Lake because of "the kind feelings of Gov. Young and the better class of the people towards" him, "hostility to the United States," especially in southern Utah through which Kane would pass, had reached such a pitch that "they would sacrifice" him if they discovered his plans.

Convinced Kane could influence Mormon leaders if he could only reach Salt Lake, Van Dyke related to Buchanan all Bernhisel said. "It seemed to make a favorable impression upon him," Van Dyke said, and Buchanan agreed to see Kane again.

Back in the White House, Kane tried convincing Buchanan "that a large portion of the Mormons labor under a mistake as to the intentions of the Federal Government." Buchanan refused to believe it. Even if it were so, he insisted, his recent message to Congress would "disabuse their minds."

The two men discussed a possible solution to the Mormon question—the "peaceful" eviction of the Latter-day Saints from the nation. If Kane could talk Mormon leaders into another mass exodus, it would solve Buchanan's dilemma—he could cleanse America of the Mormons and polygamy while still preserving his support of popular sovereignty and slavery. The president did not mention to Kane that the Russian government was considering a sale of Russian Alaska under threat of Mormon encroachment.

Buchanan promised to send Kane letters of introduction to show U.S. officers and Mormon leaders in Utah. Kane returned home to Philadelphia, purchased a ticket to sail from New York to California, and gave up his clerkship.

"God's will be done!" recorded his wife, Elizabeth, who wondered how she and her family, already in dire straits, would survive without him.[24]

As Kane prepared to leave, another man sat hundreds of miles away in the northwest Arkansas town of Dubuque, sharing his own urgent message with Washington. "Sir," he wrote Arkansas senator and U.S. Indian Affairs chairman William K. Sebastian. "Two of my sons were in the train that was massacred on their way to California . . . by the Indians and Mormons." The grieving father, fifty-year-old William C. Mitchell, was a businessman and former state senator.[25]

Anguish had filled Mitchell's home since news of the massacre hit Arkansas. He and his wife, Nancy Dunlap Mitchell, lost not only their sons, Joel and Charles—both in their twenties—and Charles's wife, Sarah Baker Mitchell, but also Nancy's kin on the Dunlap side. Nancy's two younger brothers, Lorenzo and Jesse Dunlap, their wives Nancy and Mary, and their combined total of eighteen children were "unmercifully butchered," Mitchell believed. What was more, the Mitchells' daughter-in-law Sarah was one of nine Baker family members in the massacred train.[26]

As Mitchell wrote Senator Sebastian, he referred to a report he read in a California newspaper. "The bodies of 118 persons, men, women and children were lying upon the ground, a prey to the buzzards," the article said. Mitchell felt incensed. "From all accounts the President has not made a call sufficient to subdue" those responsible, he wrote Sebastian. "Four regiments together with what regulars can be spared is too small a force to whip the Mormons and Indians, for rest assured that all the wild tribes will fight for Brigham Young. I am anxious to be in the crowd—I feel that I must have satisfaction for the inhuman manner in which they have slain my children, together with two brothers-in-law" and their families.

Though the newspaper report grieved Mitchell, it also provided a glimmer of hope. "Fifteen infants" had been saved, it claimed. The Mitchells' son and daughter-in-law, Charles and Sarah, had a baby boy. The Mitchells hoped their grandbaby was among the survivors. "I could designate my grandson if I could see him," William wrote. He asked Sebastian and the Arkansas delegation to press the government to retrieve the children. Over the next eighteen months, Mitchell led the bereaved families' efforts to recover their little ones.[27]

Two days after Mitchell wrote Washington, Buchanan's letters of introduction for Kane reached Philadelphia. They were hardly the endorsements Kane wanted. Though Van Dyke had asked Buchanan to declare that Kane's "personal word would have great weight" with the president, Buchanan did not give Kane any authority to speak on his behalf.

"Whilst reposing entire confidence in the purity of patriotism of your motives," the president wrote in Kane's letter to show Mormon leaders, "I would not at the present moment in view of the hostile attitude they have assumed against the United States send any agent to visit them on behalf of the Government." In his letter for Kane to show federal officers, Buchanan wrote, "as you have been impelled by your own sense of duty to visit Utah & having informed me that nothing can divert you from this purpose, it affords me pleasure to commend you to the favorable regard of all officers of the United States whom you may meet."

After seeing the letters, Plitt and others thought Buchanan had "behaved badly," Elizabeth Kane said. "His exceedingly non-committal letters are, they say, 'Buck all over, so that if Mr. K[ane] succeeds, he may approve him, if he fails disavow him.'"[28]

But Buchanan's letters were the best support Kane had as he boarded his California-bound ship in New York. Elizabeth saw him off, trying to keep a cheerful face as her husband "looked the last look as his vessel bore him off." To protect himself from anti-Mormons as he traveled to Utah and from vigilante Mormons once he reached Utah, Kane traveled incognito as "Dr. Osborne," a fictive Philadelphia botanist.[29]

Unpacking his trunk, Tom found a letter Elizabeth slipped inside from his father, U.S. district judge John K. Kane. "I have been so strenuous an opponent of your whole project," the letter said, "that I think it right to say to you once and for all, at the moment of our parting, that you carry with you all the blessing that a father's prayers can involk."

And yet, the father told his son, "I do not think you are to succeed; and I want you to be prepared for the worst. The Mormons can hardly have misconceived the honest and kindly aims and purposes of the President." He did not believe Tom could change the Saints' course, in spite of "how anxious Mr. Buchanan is to prove himself their friend." Because of the "blindness" of Tom's Mormon friends, "I have very faint hopes connected with your mission," Judge Kane wrote. "You are going, I apprehend, to fail."

These were the last words Thomas Kane ever had from his father.[30]

11

The Mormon Game

Northern and Eastern Utah, November 1857–January 1858

As Thomas L. Kane sailed from New York, the troops of the Utah Expedition suffered through a miserable winter in the wilderness.[1] After watching Mormon militiamen hamper the army's progress through the fall—driving off animals, burning grass, and destroying river fords—the Tenth U.S. Infantry's Jesse Gove realized that the militiamen's "only intention" was to "cripple our movements in that way." He correctly deduced that "the Mormon game" was to keep the troops from entering Utah's settlements before winter snows forced them to stop.[2]

When Colonel Albert Sidney Johnston finally reached his troops in early November, he ordered a march to Fort Bridger for shelter, though the Mormons had recently abandoned and burned the settlement. Severe snowstorms hampered the short march of the army's miles-long caravan to Bridger, killing hundreds of livestock.[3]

Brigham Young again offered supplies to the army, this time sending "mules laden with 800 lbs of salt, as a present to the commanding officer here," wrote Elizabeth Cumming, wife of Utah's newly appointed governor, Alfred Cumming of Georgia. "They were, of course sent back instantly—notwithstanding the longing for it."[4] Rejecting the offer from the enemy, Colonel Johnston instead sent a force south to New Mexico to procure supplies, horses, and mules to replace those lost.[5] Meanwhile, Young's emissaries dumped the rejected salt, it being common in the Salt Lake Valley, and Indians later found and sold it at a high cost to the troops who could have had it for free.[6]

Johnston established winter quarters for the army near the ashes of Fort Bridger, where a tent garrison called Camp Scott sprang up.[7] The Cummings, along with most of the other federal appointees who had hoped to reach Utah that season, camped near the army in a civilian enclave named Eckelsville, after recently appointed territorial chief justice Delana Eckels.[8]

Garland Hurt, an Indian agent who fled the Indian farm at Spanish Fork, Utah, when hostilities erupted earlier that fall, found his way to the troops and wintered with them in Camp Scott.[9] Governor Cumming forwarded to Washington a report he received from Hurt "on the subject of outrages said to have been committed in Great Salt Lake City."[10] Hurt's account of the massacre was the first to reach Washington from a federal appointee.

Bivouacked in the mountains with the army, Cumming pronounced Camp Scott, located in Utah's Green River County, the seat of territorial government. He issued a proclamation and letter of transmittal to "Brigham Young, Ex Governor of Utah Territory," proclaiming that the president had appointed him Utah's governor on July 11, 1857. The "many acts of violence...committed on the highways, in the destruction, and robbery of property belonging to the United States," Cumming told Young, "indicate that the territory is in a state of rebellion, [and] are ascribed, how truly I do not know, to yourself." Cumming had read orders taken from a captured Mormon militiaman that commanded "violent and treasonable acts . . . which subject their actors to the penalties awarded to traitors." He gave Young a chance to "promptly disavow them" and enclosed a copy of his own proclamation to Utahns.[11]

Cumming's proclamation announced his arrival in Utah Territory as governor, his weather-induced delay in reaching Salt Lake City, and his intention to establish a "temporary organization of the territorial government" where he was. It also condemned the "many treasonable acts of violence . . . supposed to have been commanded by the late executive," Brigham Young, and declared that offenders would soon be prosecuted in Judge Eckels's new court at Camp Scott.

"It is my duty," Cumming wrote, "to enforce unconditional obedience to the Constitution, to the organic law of this territory, and to all other laws of Congress." If Utahns refused to comply, the military would force them to, but Cumming promised to restrain the army if the citizens cooperated. "I will, in the event of resistance, rely, first, upon a posse comitatus of the well disposed portion of the inhabitants of this Territory, and will only resort to a military posse in case of necessity," he wrote.

"I come among you with no prejudices or enmities," Cumming insisted, "and by the exercise of a just and firm administration, I hope to command your confidence." In a veiled reference to polygamy, he professed that "freedom of conscience, and the use of your own peculiar mode of serving God, are sacred rights, the exercise, guaranteed by the Constitution, with which it is not the province of the government or the disposition of its representatives in this territory to interfere." Finally, by virtue of his "authority as Commander-in-Chief of the Militia of this Territory," he ordered the Utah militia forces "to disband and return to their respective homes," those refusing being subject "to the punishment due to traitors."[12]

Eight days later, Cumming's letter to Young and his proclamation reached Salt Lake, where they were promptly dismissed. "Says he has been appointed by the 'President', Governor of Utah Territory—the Territory is in a state of rebellion &c &c," a clerk who summarized the letter's contents wrote dryly.[13] Mormon lawyer Hosea Stout recorded that the letter from Cumming "the Pretender" was read in a public meeting in the Salt Lake Tabernacle. Stout called the proclamation an "informal[,] injust and illegal document sought to be palmed on us."[14]

While the troops' and appointees' failure to reach Salt Lake before winter meant misery for them, Young and his people viewed the army's halt as a God-given respite from invading forces.[15] But the federally appointed officials' spending a bitter winter encamped next to the army also had profound negative consequences, causing schisms among the executive, military, and judiciary that would stymie the investigation and prosecution of the Mountain Meadows Massacre.[16]

While the State Department's instructions led Governor Cumming to expect the army would support him as Utah's chief executive, Colonel Johnston believed his orders from the War Department gave him authority to make decisions independently. The two men vied for ascendency during their months at Camp Scott. Johnston kept a tight rein on military intelligence, leading Cumming to report to Secretary of State Lewis Cass that key correspondence between army officers and Mormon leaders was kept from him.[17]

Cumming asked Cass to get an order requiring "that all information touching civil affairs of the Territory, which may come to the knowledge or into the possession of the military be communicated without delay" to him.[18]

While Cumming's proclamation to Utahns seemed harsh to Latter-day Saints, it seemed too compromising to some at Camp Scott, who believed only force would cow the Mormons into submission. The hardliners coalesced around Judge Eckels, who, like soldiers he marched with, had come to deeply resent the Mormons. Their shared experiences and views created a tacit alliance between the judge and the military, while Governor Cumming and Young's replacement as superintendent of Indian Affairs, Jacob Forney, followed a more pacifist approach.[19]

The new, federally appointed officers underestimated the depth of local resistance to them as outsiders. Though President Buchanan could appoint new territorial officers, he could not easily displace Utah's territorial legislature. The legislature soon exerted itself against the new appointees in a struggle for political control. Though Cumming asserted himself as governor and Eckels endeavored to try Mormons in his court, unless the people recognized them as leaders and funded their offices, the new officials could have little power in Utah despite their titles.[20]

Although Cumming's proclamation threatened legal action, he harbored private doubts about the legality of such prosecution. The organic act under which Congress formed Utah Territory gave the territorial legislature authority to decide when and where courts would be held. In late November, Cumming wrote Lewis Cass asking to vest decisions about the courts in the governor and judges on the grounds that the people were in rebellion.[21]

Judge Eckels worried about the lack of funding to carry on judicial business. Despite instructions from Cumming and the federal government not to interfere with the Mormons' religious practice of polygamy, Eckels did just that. Unable to find authority for his actions in either Utah territorial or federal law, he formulated a legal theory under which polygamy was illegal because Utah had once been under Mexican control, and Mexican law forbade it. Eckels's persistent anti-polygamy bias created a rift between him and Utah's new governor. Cumming's wife, Elizabeth, wrote from Camp Scott that "Alfred over & over t[old] the Judge, 'Sir, the government does not meddle with their 'peculiar institutions'—Congress *cannot* do it—*I* have, *you* have no business with it. To enforce the U. S. laws is all we have to do.'"[22]

In his December 1857 Green River County court, Eckels seated a grand jury from civilian camp followers living in Camp Scott. Guided by Eckels, the jury indicted Brigham Young, Daniel H. Wells, Lot Smith, and dozens of other Saints for treason, charging that they were responsible for attacking government supply trains and other acts. In response, the territorial legislature redrew county lines, merging Green River County into Salt Lake County "for election, revenue and judicial purposes," effectively annulling Eckels's court.

The legislature took other measures to thwart the federal appointees—cutting off local funding for them and moving the seat of government from Salt Lake City to Iron County hundreds of miles south. The legislature also sent another memorial to Washington, reminding officials there of the one sent the previous January and asking why it had not been answered, unless the new appointees, "backed by an army to enforce them upon us . . . is to be deemed an answer." The legislators asked why their petitions were "treated with silent contempt, and a hostile course pursued," based solely on the accusations of critics who, "if justice had its due, . . . would either be pulling hemp by the neck, or learning a trade in the confines of a prison."

The new memorial challenged the notion that the army was just "a harmless demonstration intended for our good," alleging the soldiers had boasted "from the time they left the Missouri River, and even before, that they were coming to destroy the leaders of our people" and "to take our lives and to sport at pleasure with our wives and daughters." The memorial implored, "Are the horrid scenes of Missouri and Illinois to be re-enacted by the General Government? Are we to be robbed and plundered—our best men slain—and the residue again driven from their homes by merciless and infuriate soldiery under authority usurped by the General Government[?]"

If the government wished to be fair, it should "restore unto us our rights in Missouri and other States . . . ; bring to justice the murderers of Joseph and Hyrum Smith, who were massacred while in the custody of the law . . . , punish the assassins of [Latter-day Saint apostle] Parley P. Pratt, who slew their unresisting victim beneath the portals of the court, which had pronounced him guiltless," and "restore unto us our political, religious and inalienable rights, that we may have reason to believe that you are our friends, and not our enemies."

The signers vowed, "We shall not again hold still, while fetters are being forged to bind us." Utahns wanted to be part of the American system. "Withdraw your troops," they demanded, and "give us our Constitutional rights."[23]

As for Washington, sentiments swung from excitement against Utah to moderation. Despite initial efforts to bar Utah delegate John Bernhisel from his seat in the House of Representatives, Congress eventually allowed him to retain it.[24] In late January, Senator Henry Wilson introduced a nonbinding joint resolution to have the president appoint a peace commission to visit Utah and investigate the difficulties there "with a view to their settlement"—just as Latter-day Saint leaders and Thomas L. Kane had earlier suggested.[25]

Meanwhile, Kane reached Panama, crossed the isthmus by railroad, and boarded another ship for San Francisco. From there, he sailed down the coast of California to the port of San Pedro. Stopping briefly in San Bernardino, he made his way toward Salt Lake City, traveling north along the same route taken south by the Arkansas emigrants a few months earlier. Still traveling under the alias of "Dr. Osborne," Kane did not know that some of the Mormons who assisted him on his way were participants in the Mountain Meadows Massacre.[26]

12

Fearful Calamities

Arkansas, Oregon, Utah, and Washington, DC, January–February 1858

As Arkansas resident William C. Mitchell wrote to his U.S. senator about the slaughter of his family members, word spread through the state about the massacre. On January 5, 1858, a Carroll County citizen wrote a letter later published in a Little Rock newspaper. "We have rather melancholy news from the Plains," the unidentified writer lamented. "Some of our best citizens murdered."

According to the letter, the news had reached Carroll County via a California newspaper—clearly the *Los Angeles Star*'s account from Stephen Honea of the combined Dukes train—which said the leader of a massacred train was "familiarly known as 'Uncle Jack of Crooked Creek, Carroll co., Ark.'"

"If this be true," the Arkansas letter writer surmised, "we have lost some of our best citizens, as Mr. Baker was one of that class," a prominent landowner. "Mr. Jno. T. Baker" was the kind of man you wanted on your side, "a warm friend and a bitter enemy." He departed Carroll County with a drove of cattle and some of his family—a "son and daughter"; son-in-law Charles R. Mitchell and Charles's brother, Joel; and "several others," the writer said. Baker left his wife and other children at home, planning to return and move more of his family to California if he liked what he saw.

"What will the Government do with these Mormons and Indians?" the letter writer asked. "Will it not send out enough men to hang all the scoundrels and thieves at once, and give them the same play they give our women and children?"[1]

Alarm grew as word of the massacre spread through northwest Arkansas. On February 1, Carroll County residents deliberated on the "painful intelligence" in a meeting at the county seat of Carrollton, a thriving town with a public square bordered by a courthouse and businesses.[2]

The citizens mourned the news that "an emigrant train with 130 persons from Arkansas was attacked by the Mormons and Santa Clara tribe of Indians" in southern Utah. The meeting's attendees constructed a partial list of those known to be in the massacred train:

"John T. Baker and sons, George and Able"

"George Baker's wife and four children"

"Allen Deshazo" [John T. Baker's son-in-law]

"Charles and Joel Mitchell, sons of Col. Wm. C. Mitchell, of Marion county"

"Charles Mitchell's wife and child"

"Milam Jones and his brother"

"[Milam's] mother-in-law and family"

"Pleasant Tacket and family"

"Alexander Fancher and family"

"Wm. Cameron and family"

"Widow Huff (whose husband, Peter Huff, died after they had started on the route)"

"Some others."[3]

These were "our most estimable citizens, countrymen and friends," people at the meeting declared in a resulting resolution. Those "who constituted the company that left Carroll county in April last," they said, "was known as Baker's company."

Aggrieved at the loss of so many of their neighbors and the "outrages committed upon the persons and property of our citizens by the Mormons and Indians acting under their instigation," the citizens petitioned the federal government to investigate the massacre "and deal out retributive justice to the parties guilty of the monstrous deed."

They also believed "the government should immediately adopt decisive measures" to subdue the insubordination and rebellion they perceived among the Mormons. They offered to send at least four volunteer companies from Carroll County to Utah. Ironically, in a few years the same federal government would send its armies to Arkansas and other southern states to put down a secessionist rebellion. Most of Carrollton would burn to ashes during the Civil War.[4]

Not knowing war would soon bring calamity to their own families, people at the 1858 meeting expressed sympathy for the "distressed parents and immediate relations" of the departed emigrants. Worried for the welfare of the reported "fifteen infant children" said to have been turned over to Cedar City

Mormons, they called on the government to recover the children and return them to relatives in Arkansas. They also petitioned their congressional delegation to seek an appropriation to defray the costs.[5]

Six weeks later, citizens of Newton County, Arkansas, held a similar meeting in the town of Jasper. They adopted the same resolutions as the people at Carrollton, with one addition. Though they did not mention any additional names, they said the massacred emigrants came not only from Carroll and Marion Counties to the north of the Ozarks' Boston Mountains, but also Newton and Johnson Counties. Johnson lay south of the Boston range, while Newton straddled the mountains.

The Arkansans' statements that the murdered emigrants came from several counties supported Jacob Hamblin's memory of his August 1857 conversation with them at Corn Creek. There they told him their combined company was "made up near Salt Lake City of several trains that had crossed the plains separately." It also helps explain why the people of Carroll County, when they identified their missing neighbors, only named a fraction of the total number of emigrants slain.[6]

Like their Carroll County neighbors to the north, the people of Newton County stated their readiness to raise army volunteers should the government need assistance in subduing Utahns.[7] But events of February 25, 1858, changed the course of the march towards war. In just a twelve-hour period—at the Saints' Fort Limhi mission in Oregon Territory, in their capital of Salt Lake City, and in the nation's capital—dramatic incidents transformed the policies on both sides of the conflict.

At midmorning, a Fort Limhi settler was working at the mill on the Salmon River when he spotted a group of Bannock and Shoshone Indians riding toward the settlement's large herd of cattle and horses. The man sprinted from the mill to the fort to signal an alarm. The settlers grabbed their guns and ran for the livestock, but by then Indians had already surrounded the herd. One herdsman managed to race away unscathed, but two others were shot down and their heads bludgeoned until they lay still. Incredibly, they survived.[8]

The attackers also turned on the settlers who rushed towards the herd. "They kept fireing at us and riding . . . close to us," fatally shooting one man and wounding a few more, wrote a settler.[9] One horseman, George McBride, waved his hat, then charged down a hill in an attempt to round up stray cattle. Indians shot him off his horse before taking his revolver, his shirt, his hat, and finally, his scalp. The other bloodied settlers retreated towards the fort. The assailants pursued them, one riding McBride's horse and another holding his scalp in the air. "Sino mich Mormon Narient," the Indian on McBride's horse yelled, meaning, "One Mormon is brave."[10]

Seventy-one men, women, and children of the fort prepared for a siege while debating what to do. They were "over 300 miles from friends," with few horses or teams left to attempt an evacuation. Finally, they decided to send two young men to Salt Lake for help on the only two horses that were fit for the ride. Fort Limhi's leader, with one arm shot just below the elbow, dictated a letter for Brigham Young. A woman sewed the letter inside one of the messengers' coats before the two riders slipped out of the fort. As the two men left, the settlers sent up prayers, straining their ears for the sound of gunshots, believing their messengers' death would mean their own.[11]

Unaware of the attack on their northern counterparts at Fort Limhi, Latter-day Saints in Utah's settlements went about business as usual. But Salt Lake City was about to experience its own dramatic episode. Wilford Woodruff was working in the Church Historian's Office when Young called for him and other top church leaders to meet. Apostle Amasa Lyman had just arrived in Salt Lake with "a messenger dire[c]t from Washington," and Young wanted his closest advisers to meet the visitor.

By the appointed hour of 7 p.m., Woodruff was waiting in the warmth of Young's Beehive House mansion. The church president and his two counselors, Heber Kimball and Daniel Wells, were there too, along with apostles Orson Hyde, John Taylor, Charles C. Rich, and Lyman.

At 8 p.m., the mysterious messenger arrived. Young's twenty-three-year-old son, Joseph, introduced him "as Dr. Osborne," Woodruff wrote, "which was *Col T. L. Kane*." The men must have been astonished to see Kane, not only because he had risen to legendary status in Mormon memory, but also because he had grown so thin, weighing only 104 pounds on a five-foot, four-inch frame. "He was vary pale and worn down having travelled night and day," Woodruff said. The men quickly seated him "in an easy chair."[12]

Young relished the moment that Kane walked in. Earlier that day, when Kane and Lyman had not quite reached Salt Lake, Kane sent an express rider ahead with a note for Young. "Your friend of old times is now within an hour's march of your dwelling," he wrote, asking "for the interview which he has travelled so far to seek; and, so near you, having no more occasion for the name of . . . *Osborne*, signs himself, Yours truly Thomas L. Kane."[13]

Elated, Young dashed off a response. "My Dear friend," he scrawled, "I will not multiply words upon paper but I will be happy to wait upon you at my Beehive House at Eight o'clock this evening." He would send his carriage to

Kane's lodgings. "I cannot express my joy and surprise at your arrival," Young wrote. "God bless you."[14]

At Young's house, Kane "found the Governor surrounded by a large circle of friends and advisers," he wrote. These men "cordially received [me] according to the character of my acquaintance with them."[15] Whether from emotion, exhaustion, or both, Kane "had great difficulty in speaking" as he made his "very formal" introductory remarks, Woodruff recorded.

"Governor Young and Gentlemen, I Come as an ambassador from the Cheif Executive of our Nation," he exaggerated, "duly authorized to lay before you . . . the feelings and views of the Citizens of our Common Country and . . . the executive towards you." Kane next explained his second purpose, "to enlist your sympathies in behalf of the poor soldiers who are now suffering in the cold & snows of the mountains and request you to render them aid and Comfort and to assist them to Come here and to bid them a Hearty welcome into your hospitable valley."[16]

Kane then requested a private interview with Young. The church president showed Kane into another room, where they met "in secret session."[17] Kane presented to Young the letter he asked delegate John Bernhisel to write for him before he left for Utah.

Kane has "asked me," Bernhisel said, to write a letter arguing that the people of Utah make the troops "as comfortable as possible at Rush Valley [a federal military reservation fifty miles southwest of Salt Lake] by building them quarters with dispatch, entertaining the sick and officers at the City, etc. I have offered to write what he desires," Bernhisel explained, though he doubted Kane would convince Young to follow this course. That said, Bernhisel made a hopeful allusion to Kane's propositions for the Saints' future. "I am most fully convinced of the wisdom of Colonel Kane's far-seeing views as to our present and future interests, and believe that he is divinely guided," he said. "But he can present them to you better than any one else."[18]

Kane may have broached the possibility of another Mormon exodus from U.S. territory. Though Young had been sending men into Utah's western deserts to search out a possible new home for the Saints, after Kane's arrival he wrote Bernhisel and a leader in the church's British Mission that "we have our eyes upon the Russian possessions." It is not clear whether Young was seriously considering a move to what later became Alaska—or whether he simply hoped to keep outsiders guessing. He concluded his letter, "P.S. Postmasters, clerks, and others: when you have read this letter, please close it again and forward it to its destination."[19]

When Young and Kane returned from their confidential meeting, the group of old acquaintances settled into a long conversation, and Kane finally relaxed.

"I wish you knew how much I feel at home," he said.

"I want to take good care of you," Young replied, later adding, "I think a great deal of a friend[,] a true friend."[20]

Haunted by the depression that had plagued him since the 1856 death of his brother, renowned explorer Elisha Kane, and the recent national financial crisis that left his family in dire straits, Tom revealed his feelings "that my life dont pay and I feel like going away as soon as it is the will of God [to] take me."

Young tried to encourage his friend. "Life is worth preserving and blessings will follow our living in this life if we do right," he said, adding later, "Brother Thomas the Lord sent you here and he will not let you die. No you Cannot die till your work is done. I want to have your name live with the Saints to all Eternity. You have done a great work and you will do a greater work still."

Kane attempted to satisfy the leaders' hunger for news from the States, answering their many questions. The previous fall's economic panic was caused by the failure of financial institutions in the East, he told them. Captain Stewart Van Vliet had represented the Saints' case well in Washington. Bernhisel had been permitted to take his seat in Congress, though "he was opposed by the Arkansaw members & a few others."

Young wanted to know how President Buchanan's December 8 message to Congress was received in Washington. "I suppose they are united in putting down Utah," he said.

"I think not," Kane replied.[21]

Though none of the men in the Beehive House knew it, Congress had just spent the previous hours debating what to do about Utah.

Earlier that day, Senator Robert Johnson of Arkansas had grown weary of the endless private bills, reports, petitions, and memorials brought up on the Senate floor. Finally, he stood to interrupt. If the Senate had "leisure to take up" private bills, he said, then certainly it had time to take up the president's and secretary of war's proposed bill to increase the size of the standing U.S. military. "For a month we have been considering the Army bill," Johnson said, but "it has been laid over and deferred, until now we have the most serious question of the session pressing right upon us."

At Johnson's urging, the debate finally turned to the bill and its substitute offered by Senator Andrew Johnson of Tennessee. Six years later, Andrew

Johnson would become Abraham Lincoln's vice president and, after Lincoln's assassination, president of the United States. His substitute bill proposed to authorize Buchanan to raise temporary, volunteer troops for the Utah crisis rather than a permanent increase of four regiments in the regular army.

Senator Albert Brown of Mississippi opposed Andrew Johnson's proposal to raise volunteers instead of regular troops. "Brigham Young would not fight unless he was forced to," he insisted. But "if you send volunteers from Missouri and Illinois, from which two States they are more likely to come, . . . they will go to wreak vengeance on the Mormons, and they will bring on a war."

Brown abhorred the thought of the government making war on its own citizens. "There never has been an American musket fired against the bosom of an American citizen by order of the Government," he claimed. "I shall deplore the hour when the first blood is shed in a fratricidal war." Though Brown spoke of Utah, he was also likely alluding to the South.

John Bell of Tennessee rose to speak. Though he initially supported the increase of the regular army, he had changed his mind. Bell made it clear he was no Mormon sympathizer. "I regarded these people as fanatics, standing in pretty much the same character in which I regard the Abolitionists of the North," he said. The Saints should never have been granted self-rule. Allowing them to appoint their own leaders as territorial officers had given them "the ambition of building up a great community," he said. "I have seen it unequivocally and boldly announced, even in the Charleston Mercury, that, under the principles recognized by the Congress of the United States, the Mormons had as much right to form a constitution, and demand admission into the Union, as the people of any other Territory," Bell said, aghast.

Yet Bell criticized Buchanan's handling of Utah. "I think the idea of a Mormon war is monstrous," he said. "To make war upon the Mormons, and denominate it a Mormon war, I say, is horrible to my feelings." The administration should have employed "negotiations to see whether these people could not be brought to their senses" and convinced "not to engage in a resistance to the power of this Government," Bell said. "It would have been sufficient to send Governor Cumming alone with a small escort," which would have cost less than one hundred thousand dollars. Instead, the president had made "a very erroneous" move in sending the army to Utah, "costing millions of money to the Government" at a time when the nation's finances were in an "embarrassed condition."

As for rumors "that the Mormons have instigated the Indians on their frontiers to mischief upon emigrants and other American citizens passing through that country," Bell said, "I doubt that very much. I do not give full confidence to the reports we receive on that subject."[22] Such rumors had circulated in newspapers and dime novels for nearly a decade.[23]

Robert Johnson of Arkansas, the senator who brought up the army bill that day, knew that at least one of the recent rumors was true. In recent weeks, William Mitchell had written Arkansas's delegation about the Mountain Meadows Massacre and worried that the four regiments headed to Utah were "too small a force to whip the Mormons." Senator Johnson now insisted that the regular army must be increased to secure peace. "The declarations of the Administration" show "their earnest conviction that we shall have serious difficulties in Utah" and "a war there. . . . It is their duty to use all the powers they may have at their command to achieve the object they have in view in Utah," he said. "I do not believe that peace will be secured without a battle and bloodshed."[24]

Senator Graham Fitch of Indiana then arose, making the final argument favoring the regular army's increase. "Mormon emissaries," he argued, had "been seeking to 'smoke'" western and northwestern Indians "into an alliance with them" against the army and the American people.

There was another reason to increase the army, Fitch suggested, a reason not yet laid before Congress. "If there is any one tradition of our people more cherished than another," Fitch said, it is that the entire continent would be controlled "by our enterprise and our institutions; that it is to be united to us by a community of interest and feeling, and a common opposition to European interference." Such policy was "not a mere selfish desire to enlarge our boundaries," he claimed, in order "to add to our individual and national wealth," but "a wise policy of self-preservation." Mexico was about to "crumble to pieces." A large part of it could "fall into" U.S. possession, "if we are prepared to avail ourselves of the opportunity to receive it."

Fitch made his final pitch. "We have these difficulties presented to us— Utah, the Indians, and the probable difficulties—or . . . if not difficulties, a probable opportunity to benefit ourselves—on our southwestern frontier," he said. "It will be extremely unwise not to prepare."

It was now four o'clock in the chamber. In spite of the lateness of the hour, a senior senator arose and, in his bass voice, asked permission to speak. Though the sixty-four-year-old's whiskers and thinning hair had turned white, his chiseled face, barrel chest, and six-foot-three-inch height still made him an imposing figure.[25]

"As for the [issues] in the northern portion of Mexico, I think I understand them perhaps as well as most persons, that being rather in the neighborhood of my home," said Senator Sam Houston of Texas, who had received a letter from Seth Blair, his friend in Utah. "I apprehend no danger resulting from our vicinity to Mexico, that would require the increase of our regular Army." Rather, "it is the indoctrination of this Union with false sentiments that I fear," boomed Houston. "That is what I am warring against."

The Constitution's authors "declared their open detestation of anything like the employment of a Federal force to control citizens, and reduce them to subordination to the laws," he said. Though he was not opposed to allowing temporary volunteers, "I am opposed to the increase of the regular Army; and if it is intended for the Mormons," he said, "[i]f they have to be subdued . . . and the valley of Salt Lake is to be ensanguined with the blood of American citizens"—including that of Saints and soldiers—"I think it will be one of the most fearful calamities that has befallen this country."

Houston censured the president, saying he was satisfied Buchanan had not sought "the information he ought to have" before sending troops to Utah. "His wisdom and patriotism should have dictated the propriety of ascertaining, in the first place, whether the people of Utah were willing to submit to the authority of the United States," he said. "If this course had been taken by the Executive, I am sure he would never have recommended war."

"In my opinion," he offered, "whether we are to have a war with the Mormons or not, will depend on the fact whether our troops advance or not." If, instead, "negotiations be opened; if we understand what the Mormons are really willing to do; that they are ready to acquiesce in the mandates of the Government, and render obedience to the Constitution; if you will take time to ascertain that," Houston urged, "we may have peace." But if the troops advanced on Utah, "you will only add to the catastrophe, not diminish human suffering. These people expect nothing but extermination, or abuse more intolerable than even extermination would be, from your troops, and they will oppose them."

Two members of the military affairs committee that introduced the original army bill stood to say that although they had earlier supported it, they had changed their minds. Senator Cameron of Pennsylvania, later Lincoln's first secretary of war, now felt convinced "there can be no such emergency as we were some time ago told existed. . . . There seems to be a determination to force upon the country an increase of the regular standing Army, to which I can never consent."[26]

Two days before the congressional debate on the bill, the *New York Herald* had published its interview with William Bell, the Salt Lake merchant who met with Brigham Young the previous October before journeying to the East. "Brigham thinks that through the winter the government and Congress will have time to consider the matter [of the Utah Expedition] thoroughly, and, if they wish, withdraw the troops and send in special commissioners," Bell told the *Herald*.[27]

Instead of an increase to the standing army, Congress decided to grant the president just two regiments of volunteers. As Latter-day Saint leaders hoped would happen, cooler heads prevailed in Washington that winter. With the exception of Senator Johnson of Arkansas, the senators who argued in favor of the army bill on February 25 were from the northern states, while those who argued against it were from the South. Southern statesmen wanted Buchanan to make peace with the Saints, rather than increase the standing army to fight them. This was because "they thought that they might be placed in the same position as the Mormons, at some future time," surmised a Latter-day Saint leader in the East. Even Arkansas senator William K. Sebastian, to whom William Mitchell had written that "four regiments" was "too small a force to whip the Mormons," helped defeat the bill to increase the army's size.[28]

Buchanan gave up and searched for peace commissioners to send to Utah. His decision had little if anything to do with Kane's arrival in Salt Lake City on February 25. Kane's first communication from the territory, dated March 5, did not reach Washington until about April 15—after Buchanan had already appointed a peace commission.[29]

In his presidential address later that year, Buchanan asserted that "it was my anxious desire that the Mormons should yield obedience to the Constitution and the laws, without rendering it necessary to resort to military force." Claiming the desires dictated to him by Congress as his own ideas, Buchanan dispatched peace commissioners bearing "a proclamation addressed by myself to the inhabitants of Utah," he said, "warning them of their true condition, and how hopeless it was on their part to persist in rebellion."[30]

But as the U.S. troops lived out their bitter winter on the plains, neither they nor the Mormons who waited for them knew of the change of winds in Washington.

13

Peacefully Submitting

Salt Lake, Camp Scott, and Spanish Fork, March–May 1858

On March 8, 1858, the two messengers who had fled Fort Limhi raced up to Brigham Young's Salt Lake City office. The young men had ridden more than three hundred miles in eight days to bring Young "the disastrous intelligence" of the Bannock and Shoshone attack on their fort. Not knowing that the settlers and their attackers had managed to make peace in the previous few days, Young hastily sent a rescue party of a hundred men to escort the fort's inhabitants back to Utah.

Though these Latter-day Saint settlers would later return safely after an arduous journey, news of the Indian attack must have struck a blow to Young's hopes that all Natives would side with his people in the face of an invasion by U.S. troops. The news may have also contributed to Young's more conciliatory approach towards the army.[1]

Thomas Kane left Salt Lake for the army's winter quarters on the day the Fort Limhi messengers arrived: March 8, 1858. Through deep snows he carried Brigham Young's invitation for Governor Alfred Cumming to come to Salt Lake, along with Young's offer to supply the troops with cattle and flour so long as they stayed where they were. Kane rode into Camp Scott alone, leaving his Latter-day Saint escort behind as he approached the tent city.[2]

Kane's arrival only widened the breach between Governor Cumming and Chief Justice Delana Eckels over how to resolve the war. Cumming, open to reconciliation and slow to condemn Utah's entire populace, found himself outnumbered by many denizens of Camp Scott who sided with Eckels's aim to crush rebellion in the territory. Kane provided Cumming an ally.[3]

Kane's ties to government leaders in the East, confirmed by the letters he carried from President Buchanan, bolstered Cumming's belief that Washington would accept a peaceful resolution.[4] And the message Kane brought from Mormon leaders gave Cumming confidence that Utah's citizens would accept him as governor if he could protect them from military occupation.[5]

Cumming agreed to go with Kane to Salt Lake without a military guard, even though recently breveted General Albert Sidney Johnston warned against it.[6] Elizabeth Cumming wrote that her husband's plan was to reissue his proclamation while in Salt Lake, "take possession of the seals of office, & order the [Mormon militia] troops to disband. If any or all of these things are refused, he will have recourse to the aid of the military—but he will give them the chance of peacefully submitting." The governor also planned to attend to "other matters" she was not "at liberty to mention." One matter he would attend to during his visit was launching an investigation of the Mountain Meadows Massacre.[7]

Young prepared his people for the possibility of an exodus south, keeping up efforts to scout for places to relocate.[8] In church meetings he continued to present the policy he planned to pursue, "to remove the grain, and the women and the children from the city, and then, if needs be burn [the city] and lay it in waste."[9] Young acknowledged that although the Saints had "been preparing to use up our enemies by fighting them, . . . if we take that course and shed the blood of our enemies, we will see the time, . . . when we will have to flee from our homes and leave the spoil to them."[10] By March 30, Young was preparing to move his large family south to Provo, along with the other settlers of northern Utah.[11]

After Cumming left for Salt Lake with Kane, Eckels capitalized on the new governor's absence, fueling speculation about his motives. Only newly appointed Indian Affairs superintendent Jacob Forney and a few others defended the territorial executive. "There are some persons here," Elizabeth Cumming wrote, "who pretend to the Governor's face that they are his well-wishers" but talk "the fastest against him & the loudest, when they are not in his presence." Forney considered heading for Salt Lake himself to warn the governor of the growing movement against him at Camp Scott.[12]

"God grant you health & wisdom to steer your course aright among these quicksands," Elizabeth wrote her husband, "& enable you especially to keep clear of false friends—*Mormons* & Gentiles."[13] She had hoped the intensifying rumors "were only the result of a disappointment on the part of certain persons, who had hoped . . . for a chance of promotion if a war were to take place." But she concluded there was "a settled purpose to misrepresent you at Washington."[14] Forney decided to write U.S. Attorney General

Jeremiah Black about Eckels's behavior. "Why Judge Eckels is thus striving to bring war upon us, after what the Gove[r]nor has accomplished is certainly strange," he wrote.[15]

Meanwhile Cumming and Kane passed quietly through the militia defenses on their way to Salt Lake. Everywhere he went, the new governor received an outwardly dignified reception from a respectful, if dubious, citizenry. Hearing of Cumming's pending arrival, Young discussed with other leaders how to receive him. Though Young's colleagues resented his being displaced as governor, Young told them "he did not care anything about it; the Lord would overrule it for good." Young considered giving Cumming a chilly reception, but Kane advised him to see Cumming's presence as an opportunity. Young "had caught the fish," Kane told the outgoing governor, "now you can cook it as you have a mind to."[16]

Initial meetings between the two leaders were strained. When Cumming demanded the use of Young's governor office, Kane told the new governor twice "that Gov. Youngs office was a part of his private residence." And while Young believed it necessary to move the people south to protect them from the approaching troops, "Gov. Cumming came pretty near commanding him . . . to forbid the people leaving their homes; as there would be nobody left here but renegades who followed the army for Juries."

In another meeting with Cumming, Young blamed recent tensions with Indians—especially the recent attack on Latter-day Saints at Fort Limhi—on Garland Hurt.[17] "The Indians say that Dr. Hurt is laying in Uinta valley with a body of Indians who are stealing horses and cattle[,] coming in to plunder the settlements," Young told Cumming, "and they send messengers to the Indians in the settlements to incite them." Cumming said this was not possible, but Young implied it would be difficult to convince his people otherwise. To placate Young, Cumming showed him instructions from Secretary of State Lewis Cass, which contained the caution not to interfere with the Latter-day Saints' religious institutions, "however deplorable in themselves or revolting to the public sentiment of the Country."

The night of his meeting with Cumming, Young had supper with local leaders, including Daniel H. Wells and George A. Smith. Young said that at Cumming's request, he would briefly postpone his plans to relocate to Provo. But he added he was "fully satisfied" Cumming "desired the destruction of the Saints" since he seemed willing to expose them to the army. Young reiterated "he would rather burn everything he had than submit to them 5 minutes."[18]

For his part, Cumming wrote General Johnston that he had been "everywhere recognized as governor of Utah" and "universally greeted" with respect. "Ex-Governor Brigham Young" had paid him "a call of ceremony" and "evinced a willingness to afford me every facility which I may require for the efficient performance of my administrative duties." Cumming repeated the Mormon charges against Hurt for "having incited to acts of hostility the Indians in Uinta valley" and expressed hope that Hurt could "vindicate himself from the charges," which called for "a thorough investigation."[19]

Caught between a people who grudgingly accepted his leadership and critics back at Camp Scott, Alfred Cumming knew he walked a fine line. To Elizabeth, he confided, "My *troubles* are now only beginning."[20]

On April 16, Young wrote "His Excellency Governor Cumming" and again offered to send provisions to the army.[21] Young still distrusted the troops and wanted his people out of the army's path when it entered the Salt Lake Valley. "The northern settlements are now principally vacated," Young soon wrote to territorial delegate John Bernhisel in Washington, "and this city will be in a few more days; so if the Officers do come in they will have to chase up the people to get any subjects; and if the army comes they will find blackened desolation."[22]

While Young prepared to implement his scorched-earth policy, Cumming began carrying out business as governor. On April 24, Daniel H. Wells reported to Young that Cumming planned to head south in two days, "intending to investigate the Mountain Meadows affair and will I expect go as far as Harmony"—John D. Lee's home. Cumming requested a guard of Latter-day Saints for his expedition. "The boys dont any of them feel much like going," Wells wrote Young, "but he must be cared for while he remains in our midst for it would be entirely to[o] responsible a concern to go down on our hands, and I feel as though it is rather risky to let him stay so long, and hope that his life is insured long enough to last him back to camp."[23]

Despite Cumming's intentions to go south, he soon learned "that a number of persons who were desirous of leaving the Territory were unable to do so, and considered themselves to be unlawfully restrained of their liberty." Cumming seemed irked that this news forced a postponement of his "journey of importance" south, but dutifully sent out notices expressing his "readiness to relieve" all aggrieved persons.

Cumming spoke the next day to a congregation of three thousand on "an occasion of intense interest" in the Salt Lake Tabernacle. "The most profound quiet was observed when I appeared," he said of the meeting, with Young introducing him "by name as the governor of Utah."

Cumming told his audience "that I had come among them to vindicate the national sovereignty; that it was my duty to secure the supremacy of the Constitution and the laws; that I had taken my oath of office to exact an unconditional submission on their part to the dictates of the law." He also emphasized "that they were entitled to a trial by their peers; that I had no intention of stationing the army in immediate contact with their settlements, and that the military posse would not be resorted to until other means of arrest had been tried and failed."[24]

Cumming was impressed that the audience "listened respectfully to all that I had to say—approvingly even, I fancied." But they showed "no consciousness of having done wrong, but rather, as it were, indicat[ed] a conviction that they had done their duty to their religion and to their country." He observed the Saints' reverence for the Constitution. "The Mormons profess to view the Constitution as the work of inspired men, and respond with readiness to appeals for its support."

Concluding his speech, Cumming invited response from the congregation. "Several powerful speakers" arose in turn, he wrote. "They harangued on the subject of the assassination of Joseph Smith, junior[,] and his friends; the services rendered by the Mormon battalion to an ungrateful country [during the Mexican War]; their sufferings on 'the plains' during their dreary pilgrimage to their mountain home, &c." The speakers excited the crowd to "the wildest uproar."[25]

One speaker challenged Cumming's assertion that the approaching army was coming to protect the citizens from Indians.[26] Cumming dropped any pretense that the federal officials were united in their views, acknowledging that he was "not for the bayonets that come to inforce your respect."[27]

Apostle John Taylor, who survived gunshot wounds suffered during the mob assassination of Joseph Smith, gave an impassioned speech against the new, federally appointed governor and the government's treatment of the Saints. The audience became so aroused that Young had to tell Taylor to stop. Taylor complied, "reluctantly, saying that Gov. Young is the most merciful man in the World, and had it not been for him, the Army at Bridger, would not have been in existence now, as the people of the Territory would have annihilated them."[28]

Young then stood, explaining that "the sercumstances that bro Taylor was inclined to bring before the people I do not wish to hear them myself,

and I know there are a great many he[re] that do not, for we have already
seen to[o] much of such scenes." Though Young had riled the crowd in the
Tabernacle the previous August, this time, with Utah's new governor present,
he said he "felt a little mortified to see manifested so much enthusiasm,"
adding that he "would like to see men and women cool, and not become excited upon any subject."[29] Cumming seemed relieved that Young succeeded
in "calming the tumult."[30]

During his speech, Cumming alluded to his forthcoming investigation
of the Mountain Meadows Massacre. "I have it in contemplation to visit the
southern parts of the territory, and to present myself to the people."[31] He also
promised asylum to anyone who wanted protection in leaving the territory,
inviting them to contact him privately.[32] He stayed in Salt Lake for a few days
after his speech, keeping his "office open at all hours of the day and night" for
any who sought his aid. He "registered no less than 56 men, 33 women, and
71 children, as desirous of my protection and assistance in proceeding to the
States."[33]

Finally, on May 2, Cumming wrote Secretary of State Cass that he was
heading for southern Utah the next day. "After I have finished my business
there," he wrote, "I shall return as soon as possible to the army, to complete
the arrangements which will enable me, before long, I trust, to announce that
the road between California and the Missouri may be travelled with perfect
security by teams and emigrants of every description."[34]

Cumming told Young of his plans to eventually return to Camp Scott
and there "require the army to remain where they were until he got returns
from the dispatches he had just sent" to his superiors in the East. If General
Johnston's troops "refused to obey his orders he should call on the militia of
the Territory."[35]

Soon Cumming, Kane, and their escort reached the Indian farm at Spanish
Fork. There, they questioned Indian agent George W. Armstrong, a Latter-
day Saint, and perhaps others on a range of matters, including the Mountain
Meadows Massacre. A record of the interview in Kane's diary reflects a more
detailed version of the report that Armstrong sent to Young the previous
September.[36]

According to Kane's notes on Armstrong's comments, when the emigrants
camped at Corn Creek, the Pahvants visited them to trade and seek compensation for grass eaten by the cattle. When the emigrants resisted, the Indians
backed off. Once the emigrants left, the Pahvants returned and "noticed in
places a white like flour upon the grass." Mormon and Indian cattle were

grazing in the area, and the Indians "notic[e]d one critter went off a little and died right off." The Indians skinned it, and "one took it on his shoulder . . . up to camp and it nearly killed him." One Indian who drank from the spring died, "and a number more came very near dying." Against Kanosh's wishes, friends of the dead man followed a group of emigrants that night, "shot into their camp[,] wounded one man & stole four head of cattle."

Armstrong's account claimed the Pahvants "passed this word on" to the Paiutes near Mountain Meadows, where a similar poisoning unfolded. "Then," Kane's journal records, "they got so mad! they passed the word round & gathered all together and used them up." The Paiutes who participated in the massacre, according to the account, were "Quanra's band[,] Younggwitch's[, and] Tutsegabbot's," as well those from the "Moahpah."[37]

Cumming, already familiar with Hurt's report of the massacre, now had another account, and the inconsistencies were obvious. Hurt's account included a report from Paiutes who acknowledged participating in the massacre but said white men had orchestrated it. The version Cumming and Kane got at the Spanish Fork Indian farm was the developing Mormon settlers' story that the massacre was carried out by Indians in revenge for poisoning.

Later that evening, Joseph Young and a companion caught up with Cumming and Kane. Young "came riding up to meet me," Kane wrote, bringing confirmation that Kane's father had died of pneumonia. Cumming and Kane abandoned their investigation of the massacre, returning the next day to a largely abandoned Salt Lake City.[38]

14

The Moment Is Critical

Salt Lake, Camp Scott, and Provo, May–June 1858

"Every preparation is making for the conflagration," Brigham Young wrote Utah territorial delegate John Bernhisel as his people abandoned their northern settlements in early May 1858. They were prepared to sacrifice their comfortable homes rather than "submit to a military despotism." Young sent his letter east with Thomas L. Kane.[1]

Kane and Governor Alfred Cumming left Salt Lake for Camp Scott on May 13.[2] Before leaving, Cumming again tried to convince Young there was no need to fear the army, promising he would "restrain the troops at Bridger from a further advance" until he received a response to the letters he sent to Washington. But Young remained unpersuaded.[3]

When Cumming reached Camp Scott, he learned the full details of Justice Delana Eckels's attempts to undermine him. "How angry he was, when he found all out," Elizabeth Cumming wrote. The governor moved to regain control, firing two officers who had betrayed him. "Then," Elizabeth wrote, he "resigned himself to wait" for his dispatches to reach Washington, confident the Buchanan administration would support him.[4]

Even before Cumming's or Kane's letters and their news of conciliation reached the nation's capital, President Buchanan had acquiesced to Congress and appointed peace commissioners—Lazarus W. Powell, a U.S. senator-elect and former governor from Kentucky, and Ben McCulloch, a distinguished veteran of the Texas Revolution and the Mexican War and then the U.S. marshal for the eastern district of Texas—a Sam Houston protege.[5] They carried to Utah "a proclamation addressed by myself to the inhabitants of Utah," Buchanan wrote, "warning them of their true condition, and how hopeless it was on their part to persist in rebellion." Dated April 6, 1858, the president's proclamation "offered all those who should submit to the laws a full pardon for their past seditions and treasons."[6]

Secretary of War John Floyd instructed the two commissioners to "bring these misguided people to their senses, to convert them into good citizens and to spare the effusion of human blood." The commissioners were to repeat the administration's assurances "that the movement of the army to Utah has no reference whatever to their religious tenets or faith." Once the appointed federal officers were received and Utahns "yielded to the laws and to their official acts," the need for troops in the territory would disappear, Floyd said, "except what may be required to keep the Indians in check and to secure the passage of emigrants to California."[7]

As Powell and McCulloch journeyed west, some soldiers at Camp Scott, unaware of the administration's softened stance, worried that Cumming had forfeited a chance at war in favor of diplomacy.[8] Captain Jesse Gove wrote that "the moment is critical in the extreme between the military and civil powers."

Gove wrote his wife, "We have been cursing old Cumming." He "makes an ass of himself," Gove fumed. "He seems to have the idea that he is the commander-in-chief. He will learn too late, perhaps, that he has but a small control on the army." Gove hoped "the government will have sense enough to declare the Territory in rebellion. If they do that we will settle their coffee very soon."[9]

Despite Gove's hopes, at Camp Scott Cumming and General Johnston temporarily settled their differences, documented by an exchange of letters. Cumming's letter to Johnston announced that all Mormon militia forces had disbanded except "a small party subject to my orders in and near Echo Cañon." Johnston's reply acknowledged Cumming's letter and stated that federal troops would "oppose no further obstruction to the carrying of the mails, or the commercial pursuits, or to a free intercourse of the inhabitants of [Utah] Territory."[10]

Cumming enclosed a copy of his communications with Johnston in a proclamation he asked a Latter-day Saint leader to publicize. "There will certainly not be any movement of troops for more than 30 days," the new governor affirmed. "Before moveing, the General in command will publish a proclamation notifying the community that he does not advance with any hostile views, nor will he encamp near any dense settlement."[11]

Peace commissioners Powell and McCulloch reached Camp Scott in late May, carrying with them Buchanan's presidential proclamation. Though pleased with the progress towards peace, Elizabeth Cumming seemed disappointed that the late-coming commissioners were "sent out to Utah to do what Alfred had *already* done."[12] At approximately the same time, in Philadelphia, Elizabeth Kane worried that Buchanan's dispatch of the peace commissioners to Utah would rob her husband of the credit he deserved for moving the peace process forward.

Buchanan's proclamation also disappointed Captain Gove. It fell "upon us like a thunderbolt," he wrote. He hoped Young would not heed it so he and other soldiers might still get a chance at military action and career advancement. "The pardon only extends to rebellion and treason," Gove reasoned. Other crimes, "such as murder, robbery, and theft," were "subject to trial and conviction," and for that reason, he believed the Saints "will never submit."[13] Unstated was the issue of whether culpability for the Mountain Meadows Massacre—a murderous but not treasonous act—was covered by Buchanan's blanket pardon for Utah's entire population.

The first reports of the commissioners' arrival at Camp Scott reached Latter-day Saint leaders at the same time as newspaper accounts about the reinforcement of federal soldiers in the region.[14] Unsettled by the conflicting reports, the Saints' leaders continued the move south and defensive preparations for the army's approach.[15]

On June 5, Mormon militia leader James Ferguson carried a copy of Buchanan's proclamation to Young in Provo.[16] That same day, a dispatch arrived from the south reporting that an expedition Young sent to find a new place of refuge for the Saints had "explored the whole desert to near Carson Valley all around to the rim of the bason." Although they found places for a small number of people to hide, in general the region was "rather open to the north."[17] Other reports received about the same time were likewise discouraging.[18] Increasingly, it looked as though accepting the government's proffered olive branch was the best option.

A militia leader in Salt Lake wrote Young on June 6 that Governor Cumming and the federal appointees would soon arrive in the city. We will "do all we can to hustle everything moveable out of here in the morning," wrote the leader.[19] Ferguson wrote with the same news that night, adding the intelligence that reinforcements were approaching Camp Scott, where the soldiers were busy preparing for a move on the Salt Lake Valley.[20]

"How shall we receive the Commissioners?" Ferguson asked, saying the presidential proclamation offended him and his men. "I have done nothing to be pardoned for," he protested.[21] Young directed Ferguson and other militia leaders in Salt Lake to visit Cumming and insist that until a peace conference was completed, the "troops ordered to Utah must in strict good faith entirely refrain from advancing any nearer to the settlements."[22]

While Young wrote from Provo, the peace commissioners' party—including Utah's new Indian Affairs superintendent, Jacob Forney—reached the near-empty city of Salt Lake.[23] Alfred and Elizabeth Cumming knew "the city was to be abandoned by its inhabitants, until after the army had passed through," but Elizabeth "was *not* prepared for the death like stillness which existed." She admired the "large, beautiful city, the houses all separate—each with its garden—wide streets, with a pebbly stream running on each side—city capable of containing twenty thousand inhabitants—as level as Augusta Georgia—houses mostly about two stories high, built of adobes, which are like bricks in shape & size." She marveled that the gardens were "full of flowers & vegetables & promise of fruit—but the doors of all houses closed—not a window to be seen—only boards instead—not a carriage or wagon or mule or horse or man to be seen." The surreal setting moved her: a lovely city backed by snow-capped peaks, yet empty of people, with "the rushing of the water on each side the only sound."

The Cummings' carriage ride brought them to their temporary quarters at the William Staines home. On the frontier it was a mansion, and Elizabeth thought it "very pretty." She hoped Staines would "rent us his house . . . if he does not burn it—but if there is any trouble when the army enters, the whole city is to be burned."[24]

On the afternoon of the Cummings' arrival, several Latter-day Saint militia officers called on the Cummings as Young requested. Elizabeth seemed surprised to find "their manners . . . polished" and their conversation "very varied & interesting." The Cummings learned that Young and his counselors would come for a visit the next day. "B. Y. says that he & Govr Cumming have settled matters, & seems to think it superfluous to see the Commissioners—but the gentlemen Commrs bring a proclamation & pardon from the President, & it is thought better there should be a conference with them—also, the time & manner of the entrance of the army is to be settled."[25]

Before leaving Provo for Salt Lake, Young wrote William Dame, who was among those scouting out new settlement sites. Young explained he was "going to G. S. L. City tomorrow, where we shall, probably, soon be able to learn a few items which may have a bearing on our next movement."[26]

Two days later, Young and other Latter-day Saint leaders met with peace commissioners Powell and McCulloch, who stated they were there to persuade the Mormons to submit to the authority and laws of the United States. The president had the right to send the U.S. Army anywhere at any time, if it benefited the American public, they said. The secretary of war could establish military posts as he thought "necessary to protect the emigration to and from the Pacific, prevent Indian depredations, and to act as a *posse comitatus* to enforce the execution of civil process should it be necessary." They affirmed that the army would not jeopardize the Saints' religious rights.[27]

Powell and McCulloch accused the Mormons "of treason & some 50 other Crimes," for which President Buchanan had offered a pardon if they would subject themselves to federal authority and allow the military into the valley.[28] The church leaders denied all the charges, except burning supply trains and driving off the army's cattle, "and for that they accepted the President's pardon." The Saints expressed gratitude that Buchanan had sent commissioners as a sign of diplomacy but complained of former territorial appointees and reviewed the persecutions through which their people had passed.[29]

The commissioners gave the church leaders a letter from Captain Stewart Van Vliet, expressing hope that "moderation will prevail in your counsels," and encouraging Young to "submit freely & willingly to the authority of the U.S." as a "duty so long as you remain within the limits of this country," a "duty to God as well as to man."

Van Vliet repeated what he told Young in Utah the previous year: the Mormons might keep out the troops for the winter, but spring would bring "an overwhelming force" of five thousand more, leaving the Latter-day Saints no prospect "but war & bloodshed" unless they submitted. "You may annoy our troops for some time," Van Vliet warned, "but in the end you must be overcome."

Van Vliet confirmed that the government had "no intention of troubling" the Saints' religion. "Mr Buchanan told me," Van Vliet wrote, "that his instructions to Gov Cumming were not to interfere or meddle with the Mormon religion in any way—If your religion cannot withstand the contact of the world, it cannot be true—If the presence of a thousand U.S. troops . . . can shake the faith of your people, that faith can be of little value."[30]

In the evening of the first day of the peace conference, the two commissioners met privately with the First Presidency. Young finally accepted the entrance of General Johnston and the army into the valley—but only if they followed Governor Cumming's orders and did not remain near any settlements. Allowing the army into the territory would justify "the Mormon's peaceful intentions," Young said, "and their willingness to comply with federal law."[31]

A large audience gathered when the peace conference resumed the next morning. Powell and McCulloch spoke, expressing gratitude at the peaceful settlement and assuring the citizens that the federal government would protect them if they remained law-abiding. They reassured the crowd that as the army passed through the Salt Lake Valley it "would not molest or injure any peaceable citizen" or their property, and asked the people to return to their homes in Salt Lake and other northern settlements. That night, the commissioners sent a messenger to General Johnston, announcing the apparent agreement "and suggesting that he issue a proclamation to the people of Utah, and march to the valley at his earliest convenience."[32]

Young remained cautious. When he returned to Provo on June 13, he announced to the Saints there the peaceful resolution but did not encourage them to return north yet. Still, he saw divine intervention in this diplomatic conclusion, saying, "the hand of God . . . has brought us to our present position of peace and has hedged up the way of our Enemies."[33]

Apostle Wilford Woodruff recorded his view that "Buchanan had made war upon us & wished to destroy us because of our religion thinking that it would be popular but He found that Congress would not Sustain him in it. He had got into a bad scrape and wished to get out of it the best he Could. Now he wants peace because he is in the wrong & has met with a strong resistance by a strong high minded people."[34]

If Cumming, the peace commissioners, and Latter-day Saint leaders saw the official end to the conflict as salutary, many in the army considered the expedition "a farce from beginning to end."[35] The New York Daily Tribune reported, "We have heard a great deal heretofore about the danger of personal violence a[n]d loss of property to which the Gentiles in the Territory of Utah have been exposed on the part of the Mormons. At present, the danger seems to be entirely the other way. Nothing can exceed the rancorous and even ferocious feelings against the Mormons with which the army at Camp Scott appears to be penetrated. They regard themselves as engaged not so much in a public service as in the prosecution of a private quarrel."[36]

"The Mormons have accepted the pardon," Captain Gove surmised, "but it is no more in earnest than the wind." He thought the Saints as "impudent and villainous as ever" and believed they had "accepted only to gain time." Gove hoped "to give them a sound whipping, hang about 100 of them, and then the rest will submit." As for Buchanan's pardon, he thought "the President has damned himself and the country."[37]

PART 4

INVESTIGATION

15

Make All Inquiry

Provo and Salt Lake, June 1858

On June 19, 1858, as the Utah Expedition stood poised to enter Salt Lake City, Jacob Hamblin ducked out of the rain and into the Provo office of church historian George A. Smith. Just arrived from southern Utah, Hamblin "called and had conversation with G.A.S. in regard to the Santa Clara Indians" and "gave a[n] account of the Massacre at Mountain meadows," a clerk recorded. The clerk noted no further details of their conversation. Nor did anyone record an interaction between Hamblin and Brigham Young at that time.[1]

The church president was in his own temporary office in Provo that morning, completing a long letter to Governor Alfred Cumming. He protested the troops' recent advance on Salt Lake in spite of General Johnston's promise to stay put until Cumming gave him the go-ahead. Cumming and the peace commissioners could not expect the people to return to their homes, Young insisted, if "large bodies of troops are Camped in their immediate suburbs."[2]

That afternoon, Smith and assistant church historian Wilford Woodruff went to see Young, his counselor Daniel H. Wells, and his secretary Albert Carrington. Though Johnston had issued a "proclamation to the Inhabitants of Utah upon receiving the news of peace," his advance left Young feeling skeptical. "The arrival of the Peace Commissioners in no wise ha[s] benefitted us," he complained.[3]

On June 21, two days after stopping in Provo, Hamblin rode through the abandoned streets of Salt Lake City, arriving at the Staines mansion, where the Cummings were staying. A quarter century later, Hamblin's autobiography claimed that George A. Smith went with him, introducing him to Cumming and urging the new governor to use Hamblin's southern Utah intelligence to investigate the massacre. Contemporary sources do not comport with this reminiscent account. The Historian's Office journal shows that Smith remained in Provo, dictating letters and meeting with Young and fellow apostle Amasa Lyman until ten that night.[4]

After meeting Hamblin and receiving Young's letter, Cumming sent Indian missionary Hamblin to Jacob Forney, Utah's superintendent of Indian Affairs, who had been making inquiries about massacre survivors.[5] Forney had just read William C. Mitchell's December 31 letter asking for federal assistance in retrieving the surviving children. Mitchell's forwarded letter was enclosed in another from acting U.S. commissioner of Indian Affairs Charles E. Mix. Mix, based in Washington, wanted Indian agents in California and Utah "to make all inquiry" to find the survivors, "who may be in the possession and keeping of some of the Indians, and, if they can be discovered, to use every effort to get possession of them." If Forney heard anything about the children, Mix wrote, he was to report it at once. If he discovered the children alive, Forney was to arrange for their care until they could be "turned over to their friends."[6]

Forney was likely astonished when Hamblin appeared at his door. This stranger from southern Utah had not only heard of the surviving children—he knew where some of them were. One of them, he stated, even lived under his roof. Others, Hamblin told Forney, were near his home, "in the care of whites." Forney accepted Hamblin's claim that "these unfortunate children were for some days among Indians," and that "with considerable effort, they were all recovered bought & otherwise from Indians."[7]

The normally quiet frontiersman revealed more than just the whereabouts of the children. He told the Indian Affairs superintendent about the crime that made them orphans. Forney pulled out pen and paper to take down Hamblin's statement:

> Mr Hamblin, who lives two miles from where the massacre was committed, was not at home at the time. Mr H, made strict enquiry among the Indians, of the causes which lead to the unfortunate difficulties between the Indians and Arkansas emigrants, who were murdered last September, and believes the emigrants, through ignorant indiscretion, incited the Indians to the perpetration of the Massacre.
>
> *First*—The Indians believed, that, at or near Fillmore, the said Emigrant Party poisoned a spring, from the effect of which 3 Indians died, and 3 more were sick for some time The Chief of these, has influence among the Tribes between Fillmore and Santa Clara. The Emigrants placed a guard to guard the cattle, [N]o—an Indian returning from a hunt with considerable venison[,] was shot by said Guard. Mr H says the Indians told him and other

whites, that if they interfered in behalf of the Emigrant Party, all would be considered their enemies and dealt with accordingly.

The people at Cedar City told the Emigrants that they might expect an attack from Indians to kill them or drive off their stock. The Emigrants replied that they were not affraid—that they could whip all the Ute Indians.

They (the Emigrants) remained 3 days in Camp at Mountain Medows.

A Message was sent to their camp from Cedar City, that they might expect an attack that night. Next morning between day-light and sun-rise the Emigrants were fired on and fifteen killed and wounded.

Hamblin's statement contained both fact and fiction. It was true he was not in southern Utah at the time of the massacre, that Indians near Fillmore believed poisoning had sickened and killed some of their band, and that the emigrants were first attacked on the third day of their encampment at the Mountain Meadows. But his account omitted anything that could be interpreted as white motive in the massacre. It was the emigrants' "ignorant indiscretion," Hamblin said, that "incited the Indians to the perpetration of the Massacre." Hamblin even recited one of the oft-repeated claims of southern Utah's cover-up—that if the local settlers had intervened on behalf of the emigrants, the Indians would have considered the settlers their enemies and dealt with them accordingly.[8]

Because Hamblin was not an eyewitness to the crime, it is not clear how much of this account he actually believed. Massacre ringleaders had tried to cover up the whites' role in the crime from the beginning, laying the blame entirely on Indians. Yet Hamblin likely knew more than what he told Forney. At the beginning of his statement, he said he "made strict enquiry among the Indians, of the causes which lead to the unfortunate difficulties between the Indians and Arkansas emigrants."

Indian agent Garland Hurt did the same. Ten days before Hamblin made his statement to Forney, a correspondent at Camp Scott reported what Hurt and others there had learned from Indian sources. "This massacre was perpetrated by the Piedes, or Santa Claras, under Mormon leaders," the correspondent wrote on June 12. "One hundred and fourteen men, women, and children, were butchered almost before they had time to see their assailants."[9] The report recounted:

A trusty Indian spy, who was sent down among the Piedes to ascertain the facts, reported that they expressed deep regret for this act, and said they never would have perpetrated the outrage, except for the counsel and exhortations of JOHN D. LEE, President of the Mormon Stake at Cedar City, Iron County. [The correspondent conflated the titles of Lee and Cedar City stake president Isaac Haight.] LEE came to them, they said, told them that the Americans "always killed Indians whenever they saw them, and advised them, therefore, to go and kill them." He stated, also, that the Americans killed Mormons, (this was not long after PARLEY P. PRATT was killed,) and therefore that they didn't like them either. The Indians expressed the fear that they were not strong enough to attack the large emigrant party with safety. LEE replied, that if they would undertake it, the Mormons would help them—a promise which they fulfilled by furnishing a party of Danites to lead the fray and make it horribly successful. LEE also told the Indians that they should have all the plunder, including the blankets and cattle, except the wagons, which the Mormons wanted for themselves. After the massacre, the Mormons cheated their savage allies, and appropriated the cattle also, which came near creating a row between them at the time, and left the Indians in no amiable mood toward their saintly employers, who left them with all the responsibility and scarcely any of the spoil. It was this bit of bad faith, probably, which made the Indians so ready to expose their prompters in the evil deed.[10]

If Hamblin had made the same "strict enquiry among the Indians" as he stated to Forney, he too would have learned of the local settlers' role. In short, even if the settlers had tried to deceive Hamblin, his Indian contacts would have told him of white men's involvement.

Forney's actions showed he believed Hamblin and his version of events. Forney hired the Indian missionary as his subagent and sent him back to southern Utah with "a general letter to the chiefs & a few presents." He told Hamblin to locate the massacre survivors, and that he would come himself to southern Utah in late July. If he did not arrive in southern Utah by that time, Forney instructed, Hamblin was to return to him in Salt Lake.[11]

After his meeting with Hamblin, Forney felt pleased with himself. Pulling out a fresh sheet of paper, he wrote back to Mix. "It affords me great pleasure to inform you and the friends of the children in question . . . that I learned to day where the children are."[12]

As Forney wrote to Mix, Young wrote a letter about Forney to "Arrowpeen, Chief of the Utahs." President Buchanan had "sent on a new Agent of Indian Affairs by the name of Forney who will probably try and see you after a while,"

Young told the Ute leader. "I trust that all things will go right, and that we shall be able to preserve peace, which you know I have always most earnestly taught and desired." Though Young had sought to preserve peace with Utah's Indians since the Saints' arrival in 1847, his letter to Arrowpeen brushed over the fact that, less than a year before, he had encouraged Indians to raid emigrant cattle and to ally with the Saints in withstanding the approaching troops.[13]

Hamblin was soon back in Provo, reporting to Brigham Young. William Dame and his Indian interpreter Nephi Johnson were there too.[14] Young had summoned Dame and, apparently, Hamblin to give an account of their recent explorations.[15] Since April, Dame and Johnson had followed Young's call to explore the White Mountains in the deserts west of Parowan. They led a group of sixty southern Utah men in finding a refuge for the Saints, a place to hide from the approaching troops. Dame reported to the First Presidency that his men had created a camp in that area, where they cleared forty acres and put in crops. "Received their approbation," Dame said of the First Presidency's assessment of his report.[16]

Hamblin reported on his explorations in what became Arizona, where he met local Indians and investigated rumors that "Gentiles" were steaming up the Lower Colorado River "to find whare they can get suplys to an army." Hamblin learned that the rumors were true—U.S. Army lieutenant and topographical engineer Joseph C. Ives was exploring the limits of navigation up the river. After the Mormons began "open hostilities" on the Utah Expedition, Ives learned that Secretary of War John B. Floyd's "War Dept. may wish to send a strong force to Great Salt Lake by the Colorado river & Virgin river."[17]

Hamblin and Dame apparently gave their accounts in the same meeting. "Hamblin made a report of the progress of the [mission to the] Indians to the President," Young's clerk recorded on June 24. "The President talked to Bro Dame of Parowan about the making of Gunpowder, who informed him that they were manufacturing good gunpowder. Bro Jacob Hamblin also stated that Capt Ives and command coming up the Colorado from California, had some conversation with some Indians who told him to be careful of the Mormons, as they would fight."[18] In the Historian's Office that same afternoon, Woodruff, Smith, and Amasa Lyman "had much Conversation upon the subject of being betrayed by the Government & their officers," Woodruff wrote.[19] The discussions in both the President's Office and the Historian's Office showed how dubious church leaders were about the recent peace accord.

Eighteen years later, Hamblin testified that he told Smith and Young "everything I could" about the Mountain Meadows massacre "pretty soon after it happened." He said Young responded that "as soon as we can get a court of justice we will ferret this thing out, but till then don't say anything about it."[20] No contemporaneous or later source documents such a conversation with Young and Smith, and Hamblin said quite a bit about the massacre to Forney on June 22 and again to another federal investigator less than a year later.[21]

On June 26, General Johnston finally arrived in Salt Lake City, leading his command through the abandoned streets. The procession of officers, dragoons, artillery, infantry, animals, and supply wagons stretched for more than eight miles and took nearly eleven hours to pass through the city. Man and beast sweated in the intensity of labor and heat. Dense clouds of wagon-stirred dust enveloped them, coating their wet skin until they looked as dark as the earth on which they strode.[22]

After months of drilling, marching, camping, and preparing for a fight, the grand entrance felt anti-climactic to the troops, although they marveled at the beauty of the city, the first one they had seen since leaving the Missouri River in July 1857. "We marched through the city with colors flying and bands playing," Captain Randolph Barnes Marcy said, "but, to our astonishment, we only saw here and there a very few persons," who "never even condescended to look toward our sacrilegious cavalcade."[23]

Marcy did not seem to notice some four hundred pairs of eyes secretly observing the procession from between the slats of the city's boarded-up windows.[24] Assistant Adjutant General Fitz-John Porter did. "Almost every house contained 2 men, while many of them contained 40 to 50—all peeping through the windows ashamed or afraid to show their faces," Porter guessed. "I fancy most of them were counting our conveyances & strength. If so they must have become crazy before the end of the day."[25]

Brigham Young's twenty-one-year-old nephew, John R. Young, remembered spying with other guards from an upstairs room of Brigham's Lion House. The church president had instructed them to torch the buildings if the troops broke their pledge not to occupy the city. The guards felt strained to their limits as they watched the army "march through the deserted streets of the dead city," John R. recalled. "To us western mountain boys, the solemnity of the march was oppressive."[26]

They felt great relief when the army kept its promise to pass through the city peacefully, making its temporary camp at a designated spot on the far side of the Jordan River. "Not a man nor a mule stepped out of place," said

Elizabeth Cumming. "Not a stick nor stone belonging to Zion was touched," a soldier added. "The army passed through it as hastily as possible, and then shook the dust from off their feet by leaping into the Jordan for a bath."[27]

Nauvoo Legion adjutant general James Ferguson wrote Young that when the Tenth Infantry marched through, "Col. Alexander[,] (mounted) at the head of his Column[,] doffed his Cap as he passed the very small crowd that stood at the Corner watching his march." Yet even with the troops' orderly passage through the city and a peace settlement in place, "Govr. C. advises the postponement of any return of families to the City at present," Ferguson wrote to Young.[28]

"The feeling of the army is anything but friendly to the Mormons," wrote Elizabeth Cumming, "& these last reciprocate the feeling."[29]

Assistant Adjutant General Porter echoed Cumming. "We have at last reached the land of the 'honey Bee,'" he wrote, "& peaceably so far as any open opposition by the Mormons but hostile in all that concern intercourse between them & us." The Saints and soldiers lived "in a state of Quarantine," with the army relegated to the west side of the Jordan River, and the Mormons to the east. "As for the war it is now at an end," Porter wrote, though he believed that "this people are not conquered & never will submit to the authority of the U.S. Government so long as the present rulers are left among them."[30]

16

Join the Know Nothings

Northern and Southern Utah, June–July 1858

Camped in the open pasture between the Jordan River's west banks and the Great Salt Lake into which the Jordan flowed, the U.S. troops awoke in alkali and dust. In the light of the rising sun, the city of Salt Lake appeared like a panorama, backed by snow-capped peaks reaching into the clouds.[1] Riding into town with dozens of other army officers, a stunned Second Lieutenant John Van Deusen Du Bois thought it the loveliest place he had ever seen. "The city is beyond my power of description," he wrote. "It is beautiful—even magnificent."[2]

That day, the officers called on Governor and Mrs. Cumming at the Staines mansion. In the lavishly decorated parlor, General Johnston and his staff made peace with Cumming, smoking pipes and agreeing on terms. Johnston would keep most of his troops on the west side of the Jordan as they moved to a permanent camp farther from Salt Lake City. Cumming would advise Young and the other refugees in Provo to return to their homes in northern Utah, traveling up the road on the east side of the river. "It is well to have some distance put between the fire & the gunpowder," Elizabeth Cumming remarked.[3]

The officers spent a few days rambling through the abandoned city, "everywhere finding something to admire," Lieutenant Du Bois said. Salt Lake was "laid out with perfect regularity," its wide streets "bordered by large trees beneath which & on either side run murmuring brooks with pebbly bottoms." Adobe houses neatly washed with brown earth dotted the streets, bordered by gardens "green with summer foliage." Stone walls surrounded "large & handsomely ornamented" public buildings, including Brigham Young's "magnificently finished" Beehive House. Between the gates of the high walls that surrounded Young's two homes and offices, the curious officers spied gardens filled with grapevines and fruit-laden trees. A handful of sober-faced men hung around, tending the city's gardens.

"Can it be true," Du Bois asked himself, "this story of their crime?" Some had painted Salt Lake as "a den of thieves & murderers," but to the soldier's eyes it seemed "an abode of purity and happiness, a going back to the Golden Age." Despite the evidence he had heard of Mormon crimes, the lieutenant felt unsettled as he walked the lovely streets, witnessing the evidence of their humanity. "I know it is true," he thought, "but feel that it cannot be." Du Bois finally reconciled himself by concluding that Salt Lake was "a whitened sepulchre," a city whose beauty was "not unlike the foliage of plants nourished by corruption."

Du Bois thought just as little of those who made overtures towards the Saints. "Governor Alfred Cumming is becoming a Mormon rapidly," catering to Young, he said. Mrs. Cumming even "receives & returns the calls of [Young's] Chief Concubine or first wife," which Du Bois found "a disgrace to the American ladies." In pardoning the Mormons, President Buchanan had failed, Du Bois believed, leaving the army disgusted and degraded. "Brigham's power is stronger than ever," he concluded. "We certainly have the most cowardly government on the globe. Any strength can bully it & only to the weak tribes of Indians dares it ever to show its power." The federal government had "made a great mistake in allowing Territories to make their own laws."[4]

The day after meeting with General Johnston, Cumming headed to Provo to meet with church leaders.[5] He also issued a proclamation that the army had passed through peacefully and that residents of northern Utah could return home safely. Soon a procession of some five hundred Latter-day Saint wagons choked the road on their way back to the northern settlements. "They left their homes at the call of the Prophet & now at the same call they are on their return," one Saint wrote admiringly of the sight. "If this doesn't show that this people are more united than any other that have ever been upon the earth than I have read history wrong. Israel in her palmiest days was never so obediant to Moses as we are to Brigham." On the other side of the Jordan, the army's procession wended its way south to make a permanent camp in the uninhabited Cedar Valley west of Lehi and Utah Lake.[6]

The troops and the migrants came into close contact at "the point of the mountain" north of Lehi, where only one road passed through. There "a Latter-day Saint tipped over his wagon," the Historian's Office journal noted, "in sight of the passing army. A soldier remarked he was glad to see it, whereupon his officer ordered him to go with him and made him help the Mormon to right up his wagon."[7]

On returning to Salt Lake, Young's counselor Heber C. Kimball felt dreary. Taking in the boarded-up windows and the untended orchards suffering from drought, all seemed sad to him. Even "the trees wept," he said. Kimball shared his gloom as he visited the Historian's Office, its desks, walls, and unpacked boxes still covered with dust. He predicted "many would apostatize" because of "the army locating here."[8] Fearing for his safety, Young discontinued public meetings and stayed within the walls of his complex, where an armed guard stood watch.[9]

As the refugees returned to the other northern settlements, William Dame and Nephi Johnson left Provo for southern Utah. In spite of the reported truce, Colonel Dame remained on guard, sending out orders for an Iron County Militia drill. Along with the orders, Dame sent word to Major John D. Lee that he wished to see him in Parowan.[10]

For days Lee had been a whirlwind of activity, preparing Harmony to receive hundreds of local settlers for a Fourth of July celebration. As the "chairman & also Ma[r]shal of the day," he engaged twelve hands in painting and wallpapering his "mansion" and ornamenting the meetinghouse with pine. Rich in cattle, Lee traded two cows and calves for cash and provisions. The Lee family butchered an 800-pound beef, a "fine ox," and two goats, "in all about 2000 lbs" of meat, and brewed three hundred gallons of malted beer to wash it all down.[11]

During the festivities, Lee married his adopted Paiute son, "Lemuel Lee," to a Paiute woman the whites called "Mohale Laman."[12] Having received word that Dame wished to see him "on Some Special & private business," Lee headed to Parowan after the three-day party ended.

Dame put up Lee in his home that night. He reviewed "the Proclamation of President Jas. Buckhannon & Govenor Alfred Cumming to the Territory of Utah & the inhabitants thereoff," said Lee, "offering a free Pardon for all their Sedition, Treasons & Rebellion against the goverment of the U.S. & all other acts growing out or arrising therefrom." Dame told Lee of the peace conference and the refugees' return home. "We acknowledge the hand of the Lord in all these Moves," Lee told his diary. "He is overruling all things for our good; even Governor Comings is held by the hand of the Lord & Swears that the (U.S.) Statues & the Territoritorial enactments shall be faithfully executed."

This would hardly seem to warrant Dame's summoning Lee forty miles to Parowan for a private talk. Lee already knew of Buchanan's pardon, and Dame could have shared the more recent news through the same courier who delivered his orders for the military drill. The closing of Lee's long and rambling account of the meeting, however, suggests something more was on Dame's mind. Some of the U.S. troops, Dame told Lee, would be passing through to California. "Reports also says that some 1000 Troops are expected to establish a Post at the Mountain Meadows," Lee recorded.[13] Dame may have also shared Hamblin's news that Indian Affairs superintendent Jacob Forney was investigating the massacre and planned to come south to retrieve the surviving children.

Dame likely had a similar conversation with Haight the next day during the countywide militia musters. Colonel Dame left his adjutant in charge of the muster at Parowan so he could speak to the Cedar City militiamen. "The Col who had just returned from the north addressed us upon the spirit of the times," recorded a regiment clerk. That evening, Major Haight "told us all to join the [k]no[w] nothings, to mind our own business & hold our tongues &c."[14]

In a Cedar City church meeting the following day, one man "spoke on Keeping A Close mouth & minding the Mormon Creed" of minding your own business. Another leader also "spoke on the mormon Creed & Kn[owing] nothing that will injure our brethern in righteousness." It was the same message that had reverberated through southern Utah in recent weeks—local priesthood leaders preaching of "bridling the tongue," of "the evil in speaking against our neighbours," and of "watch[ing] ourselves in the place of watching our neighbours, and of being united."[15]

Cedar City's Relief Society members, including "Sister A. Haight," "Sister Smith," and "Sister Hopkins"—wives of massacre leaders—advised the women "to guard agains tattling &c," "to be watchful of their words & not to misrepresent anything," and to mind "our own business, that we were not called to watch the whole city, but to watch ourselves."[16]

During Harmony's services, Lee reminded the congregation of "the reformation." Then, at the bishop's request, he went "from house to House [to] stir up the Saints" and pin down their loyalties. "Commenced with my family first," he said. "All felt humble & desired to do right, with the exception of Mary Ann who was then under a heavy trial."[17]

Lee had married Mary Ann the year before when she was twelve years old. A few weeks before the massacre at Mountain Meadows, Lee and Mary Ann's stepfather had whisked the girl away to Parowan over her mother's objections. There, after Lee lied to apostle George A. Smith, claiming that Mary Ann was over the age of fourteen and that her mother approved of the marriage, Smith sealed the girl to Lee. "Since she has been sealed to him she has been d[i]ssatisfyed & says that she is in a perfect hell," Mary Ann's mother wrote Young, requesting a divorce for her now thirteen-year-old daughter. She "says that she would rather die than to Live with him." Young granted the divorce.[18]

As the people of southern Utah held their meetings, top church leaders in northern Utah had meetings of their own amidst the unpacking of homes and offices in Salt Lake City. Young held a council with presiding bishop Edward Hunter, apostles George A. Smith and Amasa Lyman, and a few others. With the refugees' weeks-long abandonment of their farms and their wheat crop blighted by disease, the leaders worried "whether there was bread stuff on hand throughout the Territory to last another year." They directed Bishop Hunter to write a letter advising the people to buy only what they needed and to save grain against the projected scarcity. Missionaries were appointed to deliver the letter throughout the territory and preach its message, with Smith and Lyman assigned to preach in southern Utah.

On July 12, at Young's suggestion, Smith visited Governor Cumming. The record of their meeting reflects only their discussion of the appointment of a new Indian agent, but there may have been more to their talk. On July 14, Smith and Lyman held a final meeting with Young, then embarked for southern Utah the next morning. The two apostles were in for far more than they expected.[19]

17

A Line of Policy

Southern Utah, Arkansas, and Washington, DC, July–December 1858

Traveling south in July 1858, George A. Smith and Amasa Lyman passed multitudes of Saints headed in the other direction, back to their northern Utah homes. On a mission to preach self-reliance, Smith and Lyman urged listeners from Provo to Parowan to preserve their grain and livestock. The goal was to survive the winter despite a disease infestation of crops.[1]

Smith and Lyman stayed with their respective polygamous families in Parowan before embarking on the rest of their tour, taking a circuitous route through Cedar City, Pinto, the Mountain Meadows, Santa Clara, Washington, Toquerville, Harmony, and Sidon, then back again to Parowan. Smith and Lyman reached their first stop of Cedar City on a Sunday morning, where they found local leaders conducting church services in the shade of a new bowery.[2]

The pulpit was turned over to Smith, who spoke "on the necessity of Zion's children subsisting on the products of their own labour" and "preserving their grain and cattle."[3] Lyman preached the same message in the afternoon service. Gentile "merchants offering coveted trade goods," Lyman said, was even "a greater enemy than the previous year's danger from military invasion." This was "another kind of war," in which the people must "keep 'at least two years of provisions on hand' so that they would not need to trade for food with non-Mormons."[4]

That night, "I was kindly received and entertained by bro I. C. Haight," Smith recorded. Smith praised Haight's large and "excellent two story house" made of "burned brick laid in flemish bond style and the corners of hewed stone."

Haight and his counselor John Higbee escorted Smith and Lyman around Cedar, showing them the coal beds of Coal Creek Canyon, the community "Iron works," and Haight's woolen factory. Smith felt pleased with everything he saw, until he asked about Cedar's food supply. The infestation meant that only a medium crop was expected, and the community's surplus wheat was gone, sold to the hungry San Bernardino Saints who migrated to the area earlier that year. It was one of many soon-to-emerge signs that all was not well in southern Utah's Zion.

Smith and Lyman left the next morning, planning to follow the trail as it led through Leach's Cutoff, the Mountain Meadows, and the Santa Clara canyon, before heading east towards Fort Clara and Washington. Haight did not go with them for this part of their tour. Instead, he took the rougher road that led past Harmony and the new community of Toquerville before meeting up with Smith's party again in Washington. He left it to Nephi Johnson to guide the apostles until then. James McKnight, a *Deseret News* foreman, traveled with the party as Smith's clerk.

In Pinto, Smith and Lyman again preached self-reliance, urging "a line of policy calculated to make us free from gentile bondage." The next day, the group made its way through the Mountain Meadows, where Smith and McKnight first laid eyes on the carnage. "It is truly a melancholy spectacle to behold skulls and every kind of human bones bleaching upon the plain in such profusion," McKnight wrote. While the sight of the killing field evoked emotional accounts from others who beheld it, Smith's description was more matter-of-fact and even judgmental of the male victims.

"We visited the ground where the emigrants & Indians had their battle last year," he said. "The wolves had, apparently, torn out nearly all the bodies from the graves. Their bones, lying scattered all around, were undergoing a process of rapid decomposition, an item that seemed singular, having so recently enjoyed life. The hair of the women indicated where most of them were buried and, from appearance, the men had run away and left the women." The men "were killed beyond them and buried about where they were shot." Smith's account made no mention of the many child victims of the massacre. His version of events that day was highly flawed, despite his being surrounded by southern Utah men who knew the truth.

Smith wrote about "a splendid flock of sheep" at Hamblin's ranch; the crops of corn, wheat, cotton, grapevines, and peach trees he saw growing along the Santa Clara; and the watermelon and succotash he feasted on at Fort Clara. Heading east from the fort, Smith's party passed through eighteen miles of "naked hills of red and greyish sandstone" littered with "immense piles of volcano rock." Covered in dust, Smith's group rolled into Washington near sundown on July 31. Like the scattered mesquite shrubs and cacti around them, the people of the fledgling settlement struggled for existence in the "drought and desolation," with families living in makeshift camps along "a cluster of springs."

The following day, Smith and Lyman preached in Sunday services under the shade of the local bowery, again encouraging "Zion's independence" through home trade and manufacture. Haight met back up with Smith's party at Washington, where he promptly sent Nephi Johnson on another errand.

Monday morning saw the men of Washington back under the bowery for Utah Territory's general elections. Gunfire rocked the little community around 9 a.m., when local resident Rufus Adair was shot in the head. Just fourteen years old, Adair was "one of the most active and exemplary young men" in Washington, Smith wrote, and a "superior shot with a bow." Rufus took his last breath at 5 p.m. A coroner's inquest concluded "that the deceased came to his death by the accidental discharge of a revolver in the hands of br. Charles Hall." Hall was from Parowan and a longtime associate of Smith and Dame.[5]

When Amasa Lyman delivered the funeral discourse the following morning, Rufus's parents were not there to mourn. His mother and three of his brothers had perished in Iowa after the Latter-day Saints fled Nauvoo. His father, Samuel Adair, was visiting Payson at the time of the shooting. By the time Samuel reached Washington, Rufus was buried.[6]

A South Carolina native, Samuel Adair moved with his surviving family members to the banks of the Virgin River in the spring of 1857. Adair and his in-laws, the Mangums of Alabama, were among several families from the Southern states whom Young called to start a cotton-raising mission on the Virgin. The massacre at Mountain Meadows occurred just six months after the cotton missionaries' arrival. Samuel Adair, his son George Washington Adair, his brother John Wesley Adair, and his nephews John and James Mangum would each be accused of participating in the atrocity.[7]

After Rufus's funeral, Haight piloted Smith away from Washington, through Toquerville, then up the rough road towards Fort Harmony. Smith noted that Harmony's range furnished grazing for hundreds of sheep and goats and "some 1000 head of cattle."[8]

Though not the bishop of Harmony, "Lee is the master spirit of this Fort," Smith recorded. Lee had eight wives and some forty children there. Lemuel, one of Lee's five "adopted" Indian children and "the first Piede bought in this country," Smith said, "lives with his owner, br. Lee, and is married." Lemuel's wife was expecting a baby. Years later, Lee would claim that Lemuel was just a little boy when he interpreted for him at the 1857 massacre.[9]

As Smith recorded his observations, Harmony's young and single school-teacher, Marion Shelton, jotted down his own. "A. Lyman, and G. A. Smith arrived here from Tokerville, put up at Br Lee's," he wrote in his journal, adding cryptically in shorthand, "There was several girls come with them." While Smith spoke yet again on home manufacture, Lyman broke the mold to speak "on marriage relations, and how th[e]y aught to be sustained by the Saints."[10]

When Smith's group headed back to Cedar City on Friday, August 6, Lee claimed in his diary that he went with them at their request. He wrote that on that day and the next, Smith, Lyman, and apostles Erastus Snow and Charles C. Rich conducted an inquisition of complaints brought against himself, Haight, and Klingensmith. Other contemporary sources, however, show the ecclesiastical trial did not take place on August 6 and 7 as Lee claimed, but later that month, after details of the massacre leaked in Parowan.[11]

In reality, Lee did leave Harmony, but not for Cedar City. Though Lee's journal claimed he attended a two-day inquisition in Cedar then returned to preach in Harmony the following Sunday, Shelton recorded that he met Lee at Pinto that day, "with a wagon load of women." Lee, Shelton, and others from Pinto then headed to Pine Valley, where Lee held a dance until 2 a.m.[12]

Smith spent August 6 at Haight's house. He and McKnight drew up what they called a "history paper," titled "The Emigrant and Indian War at Mountain Meadows, Sept. 21, 22, 23, 24 and 25, 1857." After they mailed the brief to the Historian's Office in Salt Lake, a clerk there filed it under the label, "An Account of the battle by the Piedes and Emigrants at Mountain Meadows, Sept 21, 22, 23, 24, 25; 1857—by George A. Smith and James McKnight, Cedar City, August 6, 1858; from the most authentic sources." Those "authentic sources" likely included Dame, Haight, and Johnson, the only three men mentioned by name in the paper. Curiously, the report did not mention Lee, even though Smith had just spent time with him. Like Lee's September 29, 1857, account to Young, and Hamblin's June 22, 1858, account to Jacob Forney, Smith and McKnight's version placed full blame for the massacre on vengeful Indians.[13]

Their paper reflected false motives and half-truths, tied to an only partially accurate chronology that portrayed the Mormon settlers' involvement as purely benevolent, even heroic.

On Tuesday, September 22, 1857, the paper began, Native runners carried rumors to Cedar City that Indians had attacked an emigrant camp at the Mountain Meadows the day before. "The Indians were gathering in from

various parts, in considerable numbers," the rumors asserted, "with a determination to exterminate the emigrants, being exasperated in consequence of
the poisoning of springs by those emigrants, thus causing the death of several
Indians." Monday's daybreak attack left several emigrants and Indians killed
or wounded.

Immediately after this intelligence reached Cedar City, "efforts were
made to raise men to go and, if possible, conciliate the Indians," Smith and
McKnight's paper recited. The group, including interpreter Nephi Johnson,
left Cedar at 9 p.m. on Tuesday. When the men arrived at the Meadows
Wednesday morning, "they found the Indians in a great state of excitement
in consequence of the killing and wounding of some of their men." Johnson
tried to placate them, but "they threatened him and his party with instant
death if they did not either leave immediately or turn in and help them." If
Johnson's men "attempted to go to the emigrants' camp," the Indians warned,
"they would kill every one of them" too. "Finding that their services could
avail the emigrants nothing," the party "returned to Cedar and reported the
condition of the camp."

"On Friday evening, Wm. H. Dame, Isaac C. Haight and a party of men
started out for" the Meadows themselves, "to endeavor to put a stop to the
fight." But by the time they arrived "about daylight on Saturday morning," it
was too late. "The Indians had killed the entire company, with the exception
of a few small children, which were with difficulty obtained from them. The
Indians were pillaging and destroying the property and driving off the cattle
in every direction, . . . with the most unremitting energy, till everything was
cached."

Dame and Haight's group "found the bodies of the slain, stripped of their
clothing, scattered along the road about half a mile." The men borrowed "a
few spades from Hamlin's Ranch and buried the dead as well as they could."
But "the ground was hard and, being destitute of picks, and having but a limited number of spades, the pits could not be dug to very great depth."

"From the appearance of the camp ground" further south, the emigrants
had parked their wagons randomly until they were attacked, when they
quickly "gathered most of them into a close circle and dug inside two
rifle pits."

"It appears that, on the fifth day, the Indians withdrew from the siege
and that, towards evening, the emigrants left their camp and started back
towards Hamlin's Ranch and, after proceeding about a mile and a half, were
again attacked and all slain except the children above mentioned. . . . A large

number of the dead were killed with arrows—the residue with bullets," Smith and McKnight recounted, "the Indians being armed with guns and bows." The report said "it was supposed that there must have been some 200 Indians engaged in this fight."

"The Indians had also killed a large number of horses, mules and cattle, which were laying scattered over the plain," Smith and McKnight wrote. "Which was done in accordance with their tradition, requiring a sacrifice to be sent along with their departed warriors."[14]

Though based on what they said were "the most authentic sources," Smith and McKnight's report was full of holes. It did not explain how, if the massacre had been a "fight" between emigrants and Indians, no Indians were killed in the final battle. It did not say why, if the Indians had killed many horses, mules, and cattle, which lay scattered over the ground, no witnesses mentioned seeing animal bones along with the human remains. Nor did Smith and McKnight seem to understand that Paiutes did not practice a tradition of slaughtering beasts of burden to send to the afterworld with their departed warriors. The mistaken dates given for the siege and massacre, September 21–25, were the same ones Lee gave Young on September 29, 1857, so that Lee's report to Young appeared to come as an express rather than eighteen days after the atrocity.

In spite of its many incongruities, this version of events, told and retold by massacre perpetrators and others, became the basic story many Latter-day Saints accepted for generations.

As Smith prepared his massacre report, Jacob Hamblin was away from home. In early August, Hamblin met Jacob Forney in Salt Lake, responding to the Indian Affairs superintendent's request to return to him there if Forney had not reached southern Utah by late July. Skirmishes between emigrants and Native peoples on the northern route had detained the superintendent.[15]

As Forney's subagent, Hamblin reported he had located ten of the massacre's surviving children but believed there were more. Forney instructed Hamblin to recover all the survivors, "whether among whites or Indians, at any sacrifice," and shelter them at his Santa Clara home until Forney came to collect them.[16]

Though he left their meeting with a written authorization from Forney to recover the children, Hamblin also felt he needed a letter from Young. Latter-day Saints were more likely to heed their ecclesiastical leaders than government officials. The church president wrote him one on August 3. "I wish to have Brother Jacob Hamblin make arrangements to gather up those children that were saved from the Indian Massacre at Mountain Meadows last fall, with a view of delivering them over to Dr Forney, the Superintendent of Indian Affairs for this Territory," Young wrote stake presidents Dame and Haight. "Aid brother Hamblin in effecting this purpose. He has seen and conversed with Dr. Forney upon the subject, and will therefore be able to advise you in what manner you can assist him in the matter. The object of obtaining the children is to return them, so far as possible, to their friends in the States."[17]

After meeting with Hamblin, Forney went to work on his plans for recovering the children. He wrote Commissioner of Indian Affairs Charles Mix, asking for a leave of absence to escort the survivors to wherever Mix directed. He proposed picking them up in southern Utah, transporting them to northern California, then sailing with them for the East Coast via Panama.[18]

Meanwhile, Arkansas senator William Sebastian wrote Mix on August 22, reporting that he had asked William C. Mitchell, his constituent who first wrote him about recovering the survivors, to send "a list of the names and ages of the children, that they may be identified and restored." Sebastian hoped the children could be brought home before winter made travel infeasible. Not knowing all the families in the combined train, it was difficult if not impossible for Mitchell to ascertain the identity of all the surviving children. On September 1, Mix wrote Sebastian that he had not yet heard from Mitchell. "I have delayed action in the matter," Mix said, "hoping daily to receive the list of names referred to in your letter, so that there may be no mistake as to the identity of the parties."

On September 11, 1858—coincidentally the first anniversary of the massacre—Sebastian responded to Mix, quoting a letter just received from Mitchell, who was hoping to find his "little grandson" and other surviving children. "My two brothers-in-law, L. D. and Jesse Dunlap, each had two little daughters, under six years old." George Baker "had two daughters, under six. Mr. Jones had one or two; Alexander Fancher had ———." Sebastian presumed these details were "amply sufficient to identify the children," but the vague information Mitchell was able to provide would lead to confusion and guesswork about the children's identities.[19]

By early September, Hamblin committed to help Forney escort the children "to San Francisco in December or January, and have good talks with the Indians on the route. He felt anxious I should go with him," Hamblin wrote.[20] By December 11, seventeen surviving children had been identified and were "safe and well provided for." Though Hamblin was ready to help carry them north as soon as Forney came for them, the Indian Affairs superintendent did not arrive in January as planned. After finishing business in the north, Forney wrote "the weather was too inclement to travel, with so many little children, northwardly."[21] The friends and relatives of the surviving children would have to continue their anxious wait.

18

An Inquisition

Southern Utah, August 1858

On August 7, 1858, as George A. Smith's party returned to Parowan, Smith thought he had finished his paper on the massacre. But this version of events was about to be challenged.[1] Though he and Amasa Lyman preached as usual during Parowan's Sabbath services on August 8, a council meeting that night proved far from typical. Nearly every local leader signed a list of complaints against their stake president, William Dame, and requested an investigation.[2]

"Dame was a man that wished to push off all the responsible things that were not agreeable for him to shoulder on to those of others," one Parowan resident later wrote. "For instance, if a person was cut off from the Church he never would present the case or call the vote" but would have some other leader do it. "He would always have a loop hole for everything that was not agreeable for him to meet. This appeared to be one of President Dame's weak points."[3]

The list of grievances presented to Smith and Lyman did not explicitly mention the massacre. Most took aim at Dame's honesty, impartiality, and uprightness, mostly citing financial disputes over the preceding several years. But one item on the list was "the case of William Leaney who was brutally assaulted, and the man who assaulted him justified" by Dame. In a reminiscence thirty years later, Leany maintained that Dame ordered an attack on him for selling onions to the ill-fated emigrant company and for hosting at his home his old acquaintance from Tennessee, William Aden. Young Aden had joined the train hoping to reach California.[4]

Responding to the complaints, Smith and Lyman called an ecclesiastical hearing. "Br. Dame was much cast down when he showed me the charges against him," said James H. Martineau, a member of the Parowan stake high council, the stake historian, and Dame's adjutant in the local militia. Martineau was one of only two local leaders who did not sign the complainants' list against the stake president.[5]

Dame confided to Martineau that "although he was innocent, no one would believe it with so many names against him." Martineau noted that the list of complainants contained the names of one of Dame's two counselors in the stake presidency, all three members of Parowan's bishopric, and "all the High Council but myself."

Martineau responded to Dame that he "knew he was innocent and would stick to him to the last. And "if he fell," Martineau promised, he "would go with him."[6]

The stake historian meant what he said. Nearly twenty years later, when Dame faced federal charges for his role in the massacre, Martineau still contended that "he is innocent, and I know it."[7]

Smith and Lyman began their investigation of Dame at 2 p.m. on August 9 in the Parowan church's council room.[8] "I was clerk at this trial taking down every man's testimony in full," Martineau asserted.[9] But the finalized minutes that survived do not include any details of the testimony.[10]

The ecclesiastical council included Smith, Lyman, local Parowan leaders, John Higbee of Cedar City, Nephi Johnson of Johnson's Fort, and Samuel White of Sidon. Higbee, Johnson, and White had participated in the massacre. Whether any of these three spoke up is unclear, but something said that afternoon made the council want to question Isaac Haight. By the time the first day's hearing concluded at sunset, a rider headed south with a summons for the Cedar City stake president.[11]

"Received a note from John M. Higby by the request of Elders Lyman & Smith to go to Parowan," Haight wrote in his journal. When he arrived the next morning, he "was Surprised to find that Several charge[s] had been prefered against Br Dame President of Parowan by the High Council togather with his council."[12]

The inquiry continued from morning until sunset over the next three days.[13] Smith and Lyman deemed it "one of the most laborious and intricate case[s] they had sat on since the days of Joseph [Smith]."[14] George A. Smith said he felt "nearly sick from confinement of [the] Council Room."[15]

In the end, Smith and Lyman upheld Dame. "After a most searching investigation," Martineau said, "Br Dame came out unscathed. Br. G. A. Smith saying Br. Dame had not made half as many mistakes in the last five years as he himself had. And Br. Amasa Lyman said he had always thought well of Br. Dame but this had raised him 100 per cent in his estimation."[16]

The two apostles concluded that the charges against Dame were merely "the result of evil surmising backbiting & talking." They determined that "the rumors and statements made out doors, would not bear investigation when they came into Council," and, they asserted, "the Complainants were ashamed."[17] Martineau wrote that "much valuable instruction was given by Presidents G. A. Smith and A. Lyman, who exhibited throughout the whole proceedings, the greatest patience and impartiality."[18]

Though he included no record of the investigation's testimony in his finalized minutes, Martineau did incorporate the text of a document drawn up at the proceeding's end: "We have carefully and patiently investigated the complaints made against President William H. Dame, for four successive days," it read, "and are fully satisfied that his actions as a saint, and administration as a President, have been characterized by the right spirit, and are highly creditable to his position in the priesthood; and that the complaints presented before us are without foundation in truth."[19]

Though Martineau's minutes stated that Smith and Lyman gave "privilege . . . for all to sign it who felt disposed," he recorded in his personal journal that "all were required to sign it, which they did, finally."[20] Smith, Lyman, and Martineau were the first of the twenty-three men to sign the statement. Twenty-three-year-old Jesse N. Smith, a cousin to both Lyman and George A., signed last.[21] In early September 1857, after riding as far as Pinto to investigate the ongoing siege at the Mountain Meadows, Jesse had reported to Dame rumors that "John D. Lee and other white men were assuming a very hostile attitude toward the emigrants in connection with the Indians."[22]

Three days after Dame's trial, George A. called Jesse "to start a new settlement for cotton growing" on the Rio Virgin.[23]

On August 17, the day before George A. left Parowan for Salt Lake, he borrowed from his August 6 paper on the massacre as he wrote a report to Brigham Young. Though Smith excerpted some portions of his August 6 history, the substance and tenor of his account changed markedly after the Parowan hearing. While his August 6 history was titled "The Emigrant and Indian War," his August 17 letter referenced "the difficulties between the emigrants and Indians, which terminated in the horrible massacre at the Mountain Meadows."[24]

Smith's August 6 paper claimed a simple motive for the massacre: the attacking Indians were "exasperated in consequence of the poisoning of springs by those emigrants."[25] His August 17 letter to Young claimed the emigrants "conducted themselves in a hostile manner" not only "towards the Indians," but also "the [white] citizens," threatening to destroy the town of Fillmore, boasting of their participation in the murderous mobs of Missouri and Illinois, and poisoning a spring and ox at Corn Creek that killed Proctor Robison. In the settlements further south, the letter claimed, the emigrants planned to "fatten their stock" to sell to the approaching troops, then "help to kill every 'God damned Mormon.'"

Most significantly, George A. echoed the words of his cousin Jesse when he added, "It is reported that John D. Lee and a few other white men were on the ground during a portion of the combat, but for what purpose, or how they conducted, or whether indeed they were there at all, I have not learned."

While Smith's letter acknowledged that Lee and other settlers may have been involved, it also cited arguments for Dame's innocence, including his efforts to help the Turner, Dukes, and Collins trains—information that Smith likely gleaned from the Parowan trial.[26] Dame and Martineau also could have testified that when Haight came to a Parowan council meeting during the siege at the Meadows, asking Colonel Dame's permission to call out Cedar's militia, Dame and his council told Haight to assist the beleaguered emigrants on their way.[27]

Haight likely omitted from his church court testimony that Dame reversed that decision in a critical meeting with him immediately afterward, which later became known as the "tan bark council" because the participants met at a pile of bark for tanning hides. Following that private consultation, Haight sent a large group of Cedar City militiamen to the Mountain Meadows, where they helped carry out the massacre. Haight knew that pointing the finger at Dame during the ecclesiastical trial would mean implicating himself, and he almost certainly remained silent on that damning point. Finally, to defend himself during the church trial, Dame could claim that on the Friday of the massacre, he and Haight rode to the Mountain Meadows to resolve the siege there, only to find that they were too late.[28]

Martineau, who witnessed most of these events but none of the incriminating ones, "defended Br. Dame warmly during the whole trial."[29]

The inquisition did not seem to end as well for Haight as it did for Dame. "After a Patient but Painful investigation for three and a half days," Haight wrote, "most of the Charge[s] proved not true Much good Counsel & instructions were given and some severe chastisement by Elders Smith & Lyman."[30] Within two weeks of the Parowan hearing, Lyman and two other apostles would conduct a separate investigation of Haight, Klingensmith, and Lee.[31]

George A. Smith began his journey back to Salt Lake on August 17. Two days after he passed north through Lehi, a farmer there recorded, "Report says that J. D. Lee and others are taken on suspicion of participating in the massacre of an emigrating company at Mountain Meadows in Autumn of 1857." The rumor could have originated with Smith or with soldiers at Camp Floyd west of Lehi.[32]

Smith reached Salt Lake City on August 26 and spent the next day "journalizing."[33] He corrected the dates he originally gave for the atrocity. Though his August 6 account stated that the siege spanned from September 21 to 25, 1857—as Lee originally reported to Young—a Historian's Office clerk added an amendment that "this statement is doubtless incorrect as to the dates, as the massacre must have occurred earlier in the month, say about fifteen days." Smith signed his name after the amendment.[34]

Smith also met with Brigham Young two days after his return and with Governor Alfred Cumming a few days after that. Though no details of Smith's conversation with Young were recorded, the Historian's Office journal shows that Smith "conversed with [the governor] upon his (G A S's) recent visit to the Southern portion of the Territory." The journal entry mentioned only the two men's discussion of raising cotton, but there may have been more to their conversation.[35]

Amasa Lyman remained in the south. He returned to Harmony on August 23, accompanied by Latter-day Saint apostles Charles C. Rich and Erastus Snow. The three apostles "requested me to go as far [as] ceder with them," John D. Lee said. "Spoke of an investigation of some things." The investigation began in a Cedar City schoolhouse on the afternoon of August 24.[36] Bishop Philip Klingensmith's clerk wrote that the three apostles were there "to examine how matters stood between the Authorities and People, and to set things right."[37]

Lee added that "quite a no. of complaints were enterd against Pres. Haight & Bishop [Klingen]Smith." (Philip Klingensmith often went by P. K. Smith.) Lee admitted he too was accused, charged with "having used an influence against Pres. Haight[,] but was exhoneratd." The charge, he claimed, was found to be made "in blind Prejudice only." Yet Snow may have been distrustful since he told Lee to remain "with him where ever he tarried" that night. The two of them stayed at John Higbee's and breakfasted at Klingensmith's before the trial picked up again the next day.

"The investigation continued till near Night," Lee wrote. The apostles "heard the complaints of the Brethren, then reproved the authorities for the un[w]ise policy which they had adopted to govern the People & told them that they should never over rate their influence amoung the People,"

Lee summarized. "In turn reprove[d] all, gave good council, blessed & dismissed."[38]

Though Lee's journal entry struck an upbeat tone, another Harmony diarist, schoolteacher Marion Shelton, recorded that Lee was exhausted and fractious when he returned from the trial after dark that night. The following day, Lee exchanged words with Shelton, who promptly moved out of Lee's home to board with another family. "Brother Lee has been very cross for several days past," Shelton wrote in his diary a week after the ecclesiastical investigation.[39]

It is not clear whether Jacob Hamblin participated in the trial. By August 27 he had returned home from his visit to Jacob Forney in Salt Lake City. After his return, members of Tutsegavits's band confessed that in his absence they had killed an elderly Mormon in retaliation for a local Mormon's killing of a Paiute. "They broak his head with a stone," they told Hamblin.

Hamblin quickly wrote of the incident to George A. Smith. The letter also alluded to another unnamed crime he and Smith had recently discussed— likely the massacre. "I wish you would ask bro. Brigham about the affair we was talking of in Paroan," Hamblin wrote, obliquely. The two men must have spoken when Hamblin passed through Parowan en route from Salt Lake City. Referring to that conversation and Forney's charge to gather the massacre survivors to his home, Hamblin now wrote Smith, "My family is perfectly willing to take the childrin[.] it mite be better to doe so under present circumstances."

Hamblin's next words emphasized, "I [f]eel anxious for the time to come when we can punish offenses her[e] whether among Indians or white men. thare is some few scampes that runn over the writes of others with impunity. I believe it could be done this winter. I would like to here from you as soon as convienant."[40]

Smith's reply did not mention Hamblin's talk of offenses by "white men" but focused only on Indians, lamenting they were "so slow to implement principles church missionaries sought to teach them." Smith did not think it wise to "retaliate" or punish the implicated Paiutes but instead to instruct them "with unceasing and untiring patience to cease from shedding blood." Smith told Hamblin that Young agreed with this policy.[41]

19

Bring to Light the Perpetrators

Northern Utah, November 1858–March 1859

In early November 1858, a tall, well-built stranger, his face pale against his dark hair and beard, stepped into Ephraim Hanks's way station at the foot of Big Mountain pass. The pass, part of the trail that led into the Salt Lake Valley, later became known as Emigration Canyon. Hanks thought the sojourner bore "the appearance of being an ox driver," being "very roughly dressed" and having only one eye.[1]

Hanks fixed up a bed for the exhausted traveler, who asked if his host could "do something for his frozen fingers." Camping the previous night atop Big Mountain had left them frostbitten.

Hanks, who helped rescue hundreds of frostbitten Latter-day Saint emigrants stranded in 1856 snowstorms, applied a poultice to the man's fingers. He soon discovered his guest was no ox driver, but John Cradlebaugh of Ohio, recently appointed judge of Utah's second judicial district, which included southern Utah.[2]

Cradlebaugh continued his trek toward Salt Lake the next morning, hitching a ride on a lumber wagon. Hanks climbed on his horse and followed after him, convincing the judge to take supper with him after reaching Salt Lake. The two men, both in their thirties and both from Ohio, had plenty to talk about. Cradlebaugh told Hanks "he had met Judge Eckles" and, according to Hanks's retelling, found Eckles to be "very much prejudiced against us."[3]

Hanks quickly told church leaders about his positive experiences with Cradlebaugh. They were impressed with Hanks's report of the new judge who so unceremoniously entered their city. "Unlike many judicial officers," he "is a man who does not assume airs, and has no occasion for the feudal appendage of a squadron of dragoons to impress the citizens with a due appreciation of his dignity," George A. Smith wrote. "We hope that the Southern district will find in him the upright citizen judge, which he appears to be."[4]

The Saints' favorable first impression lined up with others'. In 1852 an eastern observer wrote that although Cradlebaugh, then serving as an Ohio state senator, was "a very decided partisan, he manages so as not to make himself disagreeable to his opponents" and "will usually make more friends than enemies," his only flaw being that "his organ of language is a little too active."[5]

Cradlebaugh, a widower, took a room in U.S. Marshal P. K. Dotson's boarding house. His fellow boarders were twenty-nine-year-old Judge Charles E. Sinclair of Utah's third district, two transient men deputized as marshals, and "a number of Grand Jurors."[6] The day after Cradlebaugh's arrival, newly appointed U.S. district attorney Alexander Wilson of Pennsylvania also rode into town with his wife and a letter of introduction from Thomas L. Kane.[7]

By the time Cradlebaugh and Wilson arrived, an apprehensive Brigham Young "had the watch box moved from the Temple lot to his own yard for the convenience of his own private watchmen."[8] Young's fears were not unfounded. Judge Sinclair reopened his third district court in Salt Lake's city hall, where he tried to resurrect the treason indictments that Judge Eckels's Camp Scott courts brought against Young and other Latter-day Saints for resisting the U.S. Army.[9]

"Congress has declared *death* to be the punishment for treason," Sinclair informed the grand jury. Sinclair argued that although Buchanan's April 1858 presidential pardon was "a public fact," he could not consider it as a judge since he had not been informed about it "judicially."[10]

New district attorney Wilson disagreed with Sinclair's position, arguing before the grand jury that it was unnecessary to reintroduce treason indictments for actions in the Utah War because of Buchanan's pardon.[11]

A few weeks later, Sinclair's court ruled that federally appointed U.S. marshals and attorneys, rather than the territorial marshals and attorneys elected by Utahns, should be the ones to execute Utah Territory's laws.[12] Sinclair and his fellow federal judges "adopted a rather austere and restricted policy," a *New York Times* correspondent observed, "virtually ignor[ing] the existence of the offices of Territorial Marshal and Sheriff. . . . The Mormon Judges, lawyers, and politicians urged that the United States Marshal was the proper officer in United States cases, and the Territorial Marshal and Sheriffs the proper officers in all Territorial cases." The judges' action "developed a great amount of bad talk and bad blood."[13]

Two days after the ruling, George A. Smith, reversing his earlier positive attitude towards Cradlebaugh, complained that although the judge had been in Utah for two months, he "has never been into his district," whose northern border was only about twenty miles south of Salt Lake City. Instead, he had been working "as alderman and prosecuting attorney in this city," Smith wrote, "to the exclusion of the [territorial] officers appointed by law to perform these duties."[14]

The brewing conflict between the federal courts and local rule heated up again in January 1859 when Utah's territorial legislature passed acts restricting those who could serve as jurors to men who had lived in Utah for at least a year—preventing recently arrived non-Mormon soldiers and teamsters from serving. "I cannot conceive how Gov. Cumming was induced to sign" the bill, a correspondent complained to the *San Francisco Daily Evening Bulletin*. The new rules would "paralyze . . . the power of the U. S. Court, and give it to Brigham Young and the Church, who seem determined to throw every obstacle in the way of Uncle Sam's jurisdiction in the Territory." An army officer recorded that Judge Cradlebaugh considered leaving come spring, believing he could accomplish nothing in Utah.[15]

The legislature also redrew judicial districts "at my suggestion," Governor Cumming wrote Secretary of State Lewis Cass, "and with the approval of Judges Sinclair and Cradlebaugh," Eckels being "absent from this Territory." Beginning May 1, Cradlebaugh's new district would encompass what later became western Nevada. But before then, Cradlebaugh would hold one court session in Utah's second district.[16]

Meanwhile, Cumming and Indian Affairs superintendent Jacob Forney continued their inquiry "into the circumstances of this horrible massacre," District Attorney Wilson wrote Secretary of the Interior Jacob Thompson, trying "to ascertain the truth concerning it, and the cause which prompted, as well as the parties engaged in it."[17]

Forney interviewed Isaac Haight in January while the Cedar City representative was in Salt Lake for the legislative session. Though neither man recorded the details of their conversation, Forney would soon come to doubt the story of an all-Indian massacre motivated by poisoning at Corn Creek.[18]

Later that month and again in early March, Forney wrote the U.S. commissioner of Indian Affairs about his planned trip south to retrieve the surviving children and bring them to northern Utah. He sought a leave of absence in the spring to take them "to Washington, or elsewhere as may be directed."[19]

After Sinclair adjourned his third district court in Salt Lake in mid-January, Cradlebaugh, recently moved to Camp Floyd in his second judicial district, announced he would open his court in Provo on March 8.[20]

Shortly before the court's opening, Wilson concluded there was not yet sufficient evidence to successfully prosecute those responsible for the Mountain Meadows Massacre or even procure grand jury indictments. Though Cumming and Forney had been investigating the crime, Wilson wrote Secretary Thompson on March 4, "as yet they have been unable to obtain any clew, either satisfactory or of a kind to warrant proceedings of a public nature."

Instead, Wilson could only summarize for Secretary Thompson what had been learned via hearsay:

> The massacre, it appears, is laid to the charge of the Indians to whom, it is said, [the emigrants] became obnoxious while passing through their settlements in the southern part of this Territory. The first attack was made on them on the 8th of September, at which time a number were killed and wounded. Shortly after, either on that or the next day, the emigrants made a corrall with their wagons which afforded protection and enabled them to keep at bay their enemies. But owing to the absence of water in the corrall they were soon victims to great distress and suffering.
>
> After remaining in this condition for several days, being continually surrounded by their enemies, and several having been killed in the attempts to get water, it appears that an offer was made to spare their lives and let them go on their journey, if they would give up their arms and property.
>
> This proposition, it appears, was accepted, because, for the want of water, they were reduced to the last extremity. But after they had parted with their arms, and were marching out of the corrall, they were treacherously murdered—every living soul,—all cut off, save only seventeen children [now] ranging from 3 to 7 years of age, but who are unable to tell their names or kindred. There were 119 killed. A more cold blooded butchery I have never heard of.

Though Wilson did not list the source of this account, it was strikingly similar to the information Jacob Hamblin shared with Superintendent Forney in June 1858. Wilson explained that Forney and Cumming's inquiries had thus far "been conducted with secrecy, as this is thought to be the best and only method of securing reliable information." Forney, in his capacity as

Indian Affairs superintendent, was about to visit southern Utah, where he planned to "make every effort in his power to ascertain the real facts in the case," Wilson wrote. "A mystery seems to shroud this wholesale butchery, but I entertain the hope that an avenging God will speedily bring to light the perpetrators."[21]

Two days before opening his court in Provo, Cradlebaugh requested army officials to place a force near the courthouse. Absent a proper jail in Provo, he wanted the military to guard prisoners on trial and to help execute arrest warrants that U.S. Marshal Dotson swore he could not serve "without military aid."[22] General Albert Sidney Johnston had previous instructions from Secretary of War Floyd that his military command could "act as a *posse comitatus* to enforce the execution of civil process" if necessary."[23] Believing Judge Cradlebaugh's request to be within this authority, Johnston sent a detachment of seventy infantry from Camp Floyd to Provo without notifying Governor Cumming.[24] The soldiers escorted four prisoners with them from Camp Floyd.[25]

Meanwhile, Utah attorney general Seth Blair and territorial marshal John Kay, along with George A. Smith, defense attorney Hosea Stout, and court reporter John V. Long, headed south for the Provo court, laboring through snow and mud.[26] With the exception of Smith, the men put up at Isaac Bullock's tavern, a hotel near the courthouse. That evening, Cradlebaugh and two deputy U.S. marshals also arrived at Bullock's, and the company of U.S. infantry camped next to the recently constructed school building called the Seminary, which doubled as the courthouse. The presence of the military in their community provoked fear and anger among Provo's citizens. "You may expect something rich, rare, and exciting," a newspaper correspondent wrote.[27]

On the cloudy morning of March 8, clusters of men streamed towards the seminary-turned-courthouse.[28] Nearing the entrance, they eyed the tent-camp of the infantrymen parked on the building's grounds. The soldiers' presence at the court evoked a range of emotions from onlookers. Some felt indignant, some intimidated. A few felt reassured.[29]

By 11 a.m. the courtroom was crowded with people. The county clerk called out the names of those chosen as jurors, and the twenty-three men—all Utah County Latter-day Saints—were sworn in.[30] Finally, Judge Cradlebaugh began. Though he addressed his charge to the "Gent[lemen] of the Grand Jury," he clearly aimed his words at others, both in and outside the courtroom.

"It has been some time since a Court having Judicial cognizance in your District was held," he commenced. "No person has been brought to punishment for some two years; and from what I have learned I am satisfied that crime after crime has been committed." In fact, he charged, Utah's territorial legislature had created laws "to prevent the Judiciary from bringing such offenders to justice."[31]

Only a few minutes into his opening speech, the new judge had offended Latter-day Saints in the courtroom. He "impugned the motives of the Legislature," defense attorney Stout thought incredulously, "accused them of legislating for the purpuse of tramiling the District Court &c for the purpose of preventing the punishment of crimes."[32]

A former state legislator himself, Cradlebaugh explained his perspective. Under U.S. law, he maintained, only territorial district courts like his could investigate and try criminal cases. But Utah's legislature had extended criminal jurisdiction to local probate courts, which Cradlebaugh insisted were only supposed to handle matters such as estates, private debts, and civil disputes.

In fact, Utah was not the only territory to provide broad powers to probate courts. Utah was unusual, however, in that most probate judges were Latter-day Saint bishops or other local church leaders.

Probate courts, Cradlebaugh argued, had no more legal authority to try criminal cases than did a "vigilance committee." He accused Utah's legislature of extending this power to probate courts to prevent U.S. district courts from trying criminal cases, thus undermining federal authority.[33]

Cradlebaugh also accused Brigham Young and other church leaders of destroying the district court's effectiveness by publicly impugning the reputation of the court and its judges. "There is no question about this; I read it in the Deseret News," he said. In that "organ of the Church," judges and attorneys were "abused in all kinds of language." Even jurors were "abused and spoken of in language that is calculated to influence their minds." Cradlebaugh admonished the grand jury "not to be governed by these outside influences."[34]

Stout fumed as he sat listening. The judge was taking "occasion to display his venom and prejudice against the people of Utah & particularly the church authorities and the laws of the Territory," he thought. "He denounced the Probate Courts in the bitterest terms."[35]

Cradlebaugh was just getting started. Next, he described several unprosecuted crimes committed in the second district since 1857, beginning with "the mountain meadow murder," in which "a whole train was cut off, except a few children who were too young to give Evedence in Court. It has been claimed that this offence was commited by Indians, but there is evidence that there were others who were engaged in it besides. . . . There are persons who know that there were others engaged in the crime."

The judge said he had brought a witness to court who saw "a large body of persons leaving Cedar City" before the massacre. Some rode armed in wagons, some on horseback. A day or two later, they returned with spoil. "The Indians complain that in the distribution of the property they did not get their share," Cradlebaugh said. "They seem to think that the parties engaged with them kept the best and gave them the worst."

Cradlebaugh told the grand jury he could provide names of those "engaged in assisting to exterminate the hundred persons that were in that train," adding that "a great number of them I have had named to me." He urged the grand jury to look into the case, "and if it is a fact that they have been guilty of that offence indict them, send for them and have them brought before this court."

The judge then discussed several unprosecuted cases of murder in the nearby villages of Springville and Pond Town (later Salem). Cradlebaugh said he brought witnesses to court in these cases too, who could identify those involved. One of the murdered men had supposedly "commited some offence," Cradlebaugh said, but the public has "no right to take persons and punish them" in acts of vigilante justice. In the Springville case, the judge said, witness testimony would show "an effort to cover up instead of to bring to light and punish."

Cradlebaugh may have sensed discomfort among the jurors. "It is not pleasant to talk about these things," he acknowledged, "but the crimes have been commited." He hoped the grand jury would investigate and bring forward indictments. "The question is with you whether you will bring those persons to trial," he said.

"To allow these things to pass over gives a colour as if they were done by authority," Cradlebaugh insinuated. "Such a case as that of the mountain meadows shows that there was some person high in the estimation of the people, and it was done by that authority; and this [Springville] case shows the same, and unless you do your duty such will be the view that will be taken."

Cradlebaugh said he had read in the *Deseret News* "of some higher law. It is perhaps not proper to mention that, but such teachings will have their influence upon the public mind." The people of Utah could know no law but that of the United States, he told them. "No person can commit crimes and say they are authorized by higher authorities, and if they have any such notions they will have to dispel them."

The judge concluded by telling the grand jury that District Attorney Wilson would be with them for their examination of witnesses, and that the court would afford them any aid needed.[36]

A din must have erupted as the court adjourned for lunch and the grand jury filed out of the crowded room. Stout felt Cradlebaugh had "referred to every thing that had happened or been falsly reported in the District for the last 3 or 4 years and charged the whole to the authorities of the church and in the plainest terms declared that he was now ready to do anything he could against both the church & people. The whole charge was a tirade of crimination."[37]

As the drama unfolded in the courthouse, another escalated outside. To local residents, the sight of soldiers stationed outside the court and within their community suggested the kind of oppression Latter-day Saints suffered in Missouri and Illinois.[38] Someone, most likely George A. Smith, circulated a petition to Provo's mayor and city council demanding the troops' removal and sent the manuscript version of the petition to Smith's Church Historian's Office in Salt Lake City.[39]

More than five hundred Provo citizens signed the petition, "aggrieved & outraged by the appearance of a Military force" in their city, pronouncing it "a high handed outrage, a direct infringement upon the rights of American citizens, & a gross violation of our liberties & municipal immunities." The petition declared Cradlebaugh's requisitioning of the troops "an attack upon the fidelity of our civil officers," who could adequately "secure & take care of prisoners" without military assistance. The petition charged that Cradlebaugh's real motives were "judicial terrorism . . . to coerce a grand jury to find presentments under fear of bristling bayonets."[40]

Cradlebaugh may have heard complaints about the troops during the lunch recess, because he explained their presence after court resumed. "Perhaps it is an unusual thing for them to be here," he acknowledged. Knowing the court needed to transport several witnesses and prisoners from Camp Floyd, and expecting to make arrests near Provo, Cradlebaugh explained he had requested General Johnston to send troops "to take care of the prisoners" after he learned Provo had no jail. The only "authority of the troops is to detain those persons in custody that may be taken prisoners, until they are called for by the Court," Cradlebaugh tried to reassure his audience. "They have no power beyond that."[41]

Privately, Camp Floyd's deputy quartermaster claimed, "Besides, past associations have shown the Mormon Officers of Justice, such as Sherriffs, Constables &c., could not be trusted, when the *Saints* were to be presented. Nor are they to be relied on for the administration of the laws, when those laws conflict with those of the Church."[42]

Cradlebaugh concluded his instructions to the grand jury by noting that their only duty was to bring indictments against persons accused of a crime, "and not to try them." "The same kind of evidence, therefore, that is required at [a] trial is not required before a Grand Jury." To issue an indictment, only twelve of the jury's twenty-three members had to agree that the evidence warranted a trial. Finally, he urged the jurors to "be expeditious." Cradlebaugh adjourned court and gave the grand jury two days to examine witnesses with District Attorney Wilson.[43]

Though the courthouse sat as silent as the snow that fell upon it the next day, "there was a knock down or so between the soldiers and citizens," Stout recorded. "The Judge has taken no steps to remove the troops who are very annoying."[44] Smith wrote a summary of the previous two days, which express riders delivered to church headquarters that night, along with church stenographer John V. Long's nearly verbatim report of Cradlebaugh's opening speech.

"On receipt of the news brought by your messengers we felt a little excited and indignant at the course being pursued by Justice C—gh," Historian's Office clerk Robert L. Campbell wrote back to Smith, "but as the Saints have learned that they need not expect any mercy at the hands of the world, we feel to exercise our faith that God may inspire you with wisdom to dictate, and the Mormon legal corps with policy and ability to pursue a course which shall cause the overrulling hand of the Lord to be visibly displayed in the fizzling out of Justice C's court. It has been remarked in the office that it is lucky that you are *happening* at Provo at this particular juncture; even as it was lucky that Judge Douglass *happened* to be at Monmouth on a certain occasion."[45]

Campbell was referring to an 1841 incident in which Judge Stephen A. Douglas had agreed to hear a case against Joseph Smith at a courthouse in Monmouth, Illinois. The hearing was to determine whether Smith should be extradited to Missouri to face criminal charges stemming from the 1838 Mormon-Missouri conflict. Douglas, who was stumping for Mormon votes in Nauvoo just before he agreed to hear Smith's case, voided the extradition writ on a technicality.[46]

Governor Cumming felt peeved that General Johnston had sent troops to Provo without his knowledge. Young charged that Cradlebaugh and others "have evidently gone to Provo designing to raise a muss," and believed that if the local people endured the troops' presence peacefully, Cradlebaugh's actions would "work its own curse" against him. Cumming also believed the judge had overreached in his charge to the jury and in bringing soldiers to court. He and church leaders began to document grievances against Cradlebaugh and Johnston, building a case against them.[47]

In the meantime, Young cautioned his people to be peaceful. If the soldiers did not keep "to the locality and duties which Judge Cradlebaugh has set forth in his charge and other remarks and letters," Young wrote Smith in Provo, counsel the people to "enter complaint, properly authenticated, to the proper officers and exercise the utmost forbearance till the nuisance can be removed."[48]

20

Nothing but Evasive Replies

Northern Utah, March–April 1859

March 11, 1859, was not a good day for Judge John Cradlebaugh. After two and a half days of hearing testimony about the various killings highlighted in his opening charge, the grand jury returned to court without a single indictment for murder. Instead, the jury brought indictments against two Indians accused of rape, Pangunts and Namowah. Frustrated, Cradlebaugh instructed the jury that they must regard the advice of District Attorney Alexander Wilson in their meetings with him and the witnesses. The judge then dismissed one juror because witnesses accused him of being an accessory to two of the murders under investigation.[1]

That same day, Provo mayor B. K. Bullock wrote Cradlebaugh on behalf of the city council and citizens who had petitioned him. Bullock said the troops were creating tensions with citizens, intimidating persons who needed to attend court, and becoming "a direct interference with the municipal regulations of American Citizens." He asked the judge to move the troops outside the city.[2]

Then "another knock down" erupted that evening when a wrestling match between a soldier and "one of the Provo boys [who] proved the bully" turned ugly. Several soldiers ran for their weapons but did not end up using them; the infantry's commander, Captain Henry Heth, and Provo town marshal William Wall came between the two groups before more violence broke out. But the political damage was done.[3]

That night, George A. Smith left Provo for the nearby town of Spanish Fork. Soon after, Cradlebaugh received another petition requesting the troops' removal, this one from Spanish Fork citizens. Responding to Mayor Bullock's petition, Cradlebaugh reasserted that Provo had no jail for prisoners, making the small force of soldiers necessary, and that he would dispense with their services as soon as he could. "As to your remark about intimidation," he wrote, "allow me to say that good American Citizens have no cause to fear American troops."[4] Thus began a series of charges and countercharges between Provo officials and Judge Cradlebaugh that would interfere with the pursuit of justice for years to come.

Though the majority of Utah County citizens wanted the troops gone, not all petitioners sought their removal. The judge also received petitions from several prosecution witnesses, "praying that the troops might be kept here for their protection." These petitioners said their knowledge of crimes in the community, which they believed had church sanction, put their "lives and property in imminent peril from the Mormon communists, should we appear and testify." They could only be protected, they believed, by keeping the troops near.[5] George A. Smith later recorded the names of ten Springville men who signed one of these petitions.[6]

Governor Cumming soon arrived in Provo, hoping to cool growing tensions. Looking for compromise, Cumming asked about "a good camping place for the soldiers out side the town."[7]

Along with Cumming came Indian Affairs superintendent Jacob Forney en route "to visit the southern Indians, and to bring the seventeen children" to northern Utah.[8] Cradlebaugh detained Forney in Provo so the superintendent could tell the grand jury what he knew of the "Mountain Meadow affair." While in Utah County, Forney met with Henry Higgins, a young man from Cedar City who had fled to the army's garrison at Camp Floyd. Higgins was the anonymous witness Cradlebaugh mentioned in his opening charge who had seen armed Cedar City men heading to the Meadows and returning with spoil.[9]

Higgins testified that while working as a community herdsman in September 1857, he saw about twenty-five settlers, some on horseback and some in two wagons, leaving Cedar at sundown. Higgins recalled the names of several—John M. Higbee of Cedar City's stake presidency, William Bateman, William Stewart, Samuel Pollock, Ezra Curtis, and Alexander Loveridge. Higgins asked where the men were going but got no answer. He saw the same men return with twelve to fourteen wagons "loaded with plunder," each drawn by four or five yoke of oxen. The wagons "were driven to Bishop P. K. Smith's" and "there unloaded," Higgins confided, the spoils later "sold at the Tithing office." Higgins also saw "cattle and other property in the possession of persons in Cedar City and Harmony, which he believed had belonged to the murdered emigrants."[10]

In a church meeting two weeks after the massacre, stake president Isaac Haight publicly "dismissed" Higgins as community herdsman, saying "there were many complaints of the herdsman cutting of[f] the cow tails to make" saddle cinches.[11]

Higgins's account of settlers' involvement differed from the statement that Jacob Hamblin gave Forney in June 1858, in which Hamblin claimed that only Indians committed the massacre, leading Forney to remark how "exceedingly convenient" it was "to implicate the Indians in all such cases." While still in Provo, he wrote the new U.S. commissioner of Indian Affairs, James Denver, that over the last twenty days, he had "received highly important and reliable information of the Mountain Meadow butchering affair." His talk with Higgins made Forney think he might be able to recover some of the emigrants' property. He estimated about "$30,000 worth" was distributed among southern Utah's "leading church dignitaries" within a few days of the massacre.[12]

Forney soon continued his journey south. Knowing Higgins's circumstantial evidence was insufficient to ensure convictions, District Attorney Wilson asked Forney to share any information he gained "from Indians and others" during his trip.

Wilson also recommended that Cradlebaugh go to southern Utah to investigate the massacre after concluding his Provo court. "In view of the great distance, and the difficulty of getting witnesses," Wilson wrote, "the best method of promptly and efficiently investigating and trying this case would be for a court to be held in that vicinity for that special purpose, or for a judge to go down there, and, in the capacity of a committing magistrate, make all the necessary preliminary investigations."

A committing magistrate could examine evidence, decide if charges should be brought, and issue warrants for the arrest of criminals. Cradlebaugh agreed that would be "the proper course, to make the investigations at the scene of the massacre, or as near there as practicable."[13]

In the meantime, with Forney on his way to handle Mountain Meadows affairs, Cradlebaugh continued to focus on murders committed near Provo. The judge, Indian Affairs agent Garland Hurt, and Springville resident Elvira Parrish secluded themselves for two hours, discussing the murders of Elvira's husband, William, and twenty-two-year-old son Beason. Two years earlier, the pair were brutally murdered as they attempted to leave Springville for California during the Mormon Reformation hysteria.[14]

"There had been public preaching at Springville, to the effect that no apostates would be allowed to leave," Elvira Parrish told Cradlebaugh. "If they did, hog-holes in the fences would be stopped up with them. I heard these sermons." Apostle Orson Hyde "and others preached that way," she said. "My husband was no believer in the doctrine of killing to 'save' as taught."

Elvira went to see the bodies of William and Beason laid out in Springville's schoolhouse the day after their murders, feeling "so prostrated" that she needed help walking. She saw four bullet holes in her son's left side, her husband's throat "cut from ear to ear" and the back of his head gashed. Elvira counted forty-eight piercings in his coat.

A few days before the vicious murders, someone stole the Parrishes' carriage and four horses. The family located two of the horses in Mayor Bullock's stable in Provo. Bullock returned them, saying he did not know how they got there.[15]

Elvira Parrish testified that when she reported the murders to Young, he responded that what happened in Springville "was done unbe-known to him," and that "if he had been apprised of the matter he would have used his influence to have prevented it."[16]

Parrish may have requested the private interview with Cradlebaugh because she feared testifying before the Provo grand jury. Two of the grand jurors were among the Springville men whom witnesses named as accessories to the crime. One of these two had sat on the Springville tribunal, which quickly closed the case, ruling that the murdered men "came to their death by the hands of assassins to the jurors unknown."[17]

After his interview with Parrish, Cradlebaugh subpoenaed seventeen Springville residents to appear before the grand jury, including Alexander McDonald, Hamilton Carnes, John Daly, Wilber Earl, Abraham Durfee, Joseph Bartholomew, and Aaron Johnson, all identified by Parrish and other witnesses as accessories.[18]

When they came to court to testify, McDonald and Carnes were immediately arrested on a private bench warrant from Cradlebaugh. The others "took the hint," wrote Hosea Stout. Unrecognized by U.S. marshals, they slipped out of the courthouse and disappeared. A posse soon started for Springville to search for them. A marshal also placed Mayor Bullock under military guard in the same tent with the other prisoners.[19]

"There was much feeling manifested by the citizens of Provo at this wonton piece of treachery and double dealing of the court," Stout recorded.[20] Though Bullock may have been arrested because of the stolen Parrish horses found in his stable, rumors spread that the mayor's arrest signaled the beginning of a purge. An angry crowd surrounded the courthouse and infantry encampment, throwing stones at soldiers and threatening to free the Mormon prisoners.

Provo sheriff Wall doubled "the police force to keep the boys in order." In response, infantry commander Henry Heth sent to Camp Floyd for reinforcements and ordered his guards to shoot anyone who stoned the Provo camp.[21]

According to the Historian's Office journal, George A. Smith immediately called on District Attorney Alexander Wilson in Provo, asking if he had Cradlebaugh subpoena the Springville men. Wilson replied he had not and considered it "wrong for the Judge to subpena men, & then arrest them and detain them as prisoners, under the false color of calling on them as witnesses."[22]

A few days after the arrests, Cradlebaugh discharged the grand jury. He chided the jurors, noting that two weeks had passed since their impaneling, "sufficient time" for them to examine the cases brought to their attention, yet they had issued no murder indictments. He asserted that the Springville murder case had been hindered by local church and civil officers colluding to protect the guilty and avoiding arrest.

He told the jurors they were mistaken if they expected to use his court only to protect "against the pec[a]dillos of Gentiles & indians." Only "when this people come to their reason and show that they will punish their own murderers & high offenders" will it "be time to enforce the law," he said. "If [the court] can bring you to a proper sense of duty in no other way it will turn the savages in custody loose upon you."[23]

Cradlebaugh then announced he had received word from General Johnston that he had dispatched more troops south. "He desires that I shall state to the court that they are not here to interfere with the citizens," Cradlebaugh added, unless their conduct "should make it necessary that such interference should take place, in self-defence."[24]

Wilson soon complained about Cradlebaugh's actions to Attorney General Jeremiah Black in Washington. While Wilson and the grand jury were investigating the Parrish murders, Cradlebaugh "commenced the examination of witnesses in the same case, as a committing magistrate." Cradlebaugh also dismissed the grand jury "while I had business before them," Wilson wrote, "and before they had an opportunity of acting upon other important business which I would have brought before them." The judge also discharged defendants "against whom I would have sent up indictments."[25]

Trying to calm the growing frenzy, Governor Cumming requested General Johnston to withdraw the troops from within Provo's city limits, telling Johnston he felt satisfied "the presence of the military force in this vicinity is unnecessary."[26]

Johnston wrote Cumming about his understanding of his federal orders. "I am under no obligation whatever to conform to your suggestions with regard to the military disposition of the troops of this Department," he wrote, "except only when it may be expedient to employ them in their civil capacity as a posse."[27]

As reports of Cradlebaugh's actions and the mobilizing army reached Salt Lake City, Latter-day Saint leaders assumed the worst. Wilford Woodruff recorded that Young, the Quorum of the Twelve Apostles, and "Bishops & Military Men" met late into the night of March 21, mulling over concerns. Young spoke against what he saw as Cradlebaugh's misuse of the courts. "They Pretend they want to arest men & want witnesses & when the Judge gets a witness at the Court He arests him with a Bench warrant & puts him into the Hands of the Soldary," he said. "I am willing to go to Court if necessary, but not while there is an Armey stationed to put me to death or to imprision me without Cause."

Rumors suggested the additional troops dispatched from Camp Floyd were actually on their way to Salt Lake to arrest Young. He sent messengers to watch the army's movements, declaring, "We will not submit to Mobocracy."[28]

Guards were stationed outside Young's home and office, and an alarm bell attached to his gate.[29] Young instructed Wells to tell Cumming that he and his people "would not tamely submit to a repetition of the Carthage Jail massacre," in which Joseph and Hyrum Smith were murdered, and that if Cumming "stepped forward in the present emergency, to see the laws faithfully executed, and peace preserved, he might depend upon being supported by the people."

Meeting with Cumming, Wells shared Latter-day Saint leaders' fear that the army's "intention is to try and harras and arrest Brigham Young" and "were he in their hands he would be massacred." Wells was adamant that the Saints would not allow their prophet to be "dragged into a military court and murdered."[30]

For their part, grand jury members protested that Cradlebaugh suddenly dismissed them "with a slanderous and insulting harangue." They asserted that soldiers had intimidated them and potential witnesses. They maintained they had in fact "presented indictments," which "were treated with contempt, and the prisoners indicted . . . liberated without trial."[31]

Local citizens prepared another petition to Cumming, criticizing Cradlebaugh's behavior and disputing his court's legality. Referencing the federal administration's efforts to restore peace with Utah Territory, the petition accused Cradlebaugh of intending "to force an angry collision between the citizens and troops" in "utter disregard" of Buchanan's policy. The petition asked the governor to have the troops removed from Provo and urged him to report Cradlebaugh's behavior to Washington. Copies of the petition circulated throughout Utah, with one garnering nearly 3,500 signatures.[32]

When Cumming received Johnston's letter refusing to withdraw the troops, he "was the mad[d]est man he ever saw," Wells reported. Johnston did "not recognize the Governor's authority."[33]

Cumming sent a flurry of reports to Washington, describing the volatile situation in Utah, Cradlebaugh's court, Johnston's dispatch of troops, and his futile efforts as governor to calm tensions.[34]

Cumming shared his belief that the troops had been ordered out "without sufficient cause." He acknowledged that some summoned witnesses had fled but blamed Cradlebaugh's arresting of witnesses called to testify. They fled in fear, he believed, "preferring to be branded as criminals" instead of "being dragged to camp, and confined in a guard house, until it shall please the Judge to release them, or to give them a trial." In short, Cumming told Secretary of State Lewis Cass, "It is my belief that the system now pursued will lead to much bloodshed, and is as much the result of hatred of Mormons as such, as of a love for justice." He asked the administration to remove the discrepancy between instructions issued to himself and Johnston and to order "that all requisitions for troops, be made by or through the Governor."[35]

Cumming also issued a proclamation declaring that the military companies still "stationed within sight of the Court House" in Provo had "a tendency not only to terrify the inhabitants, and disturb the peace of the Territory, but also to subvert the ends of justice, by causing the intimidation of witnesses and jurors." He sent a copy to Washington.[36]

Cradlebaugh promptly shot back, saying his "court has yet to learn that it is subservient to, and cannot act except under executive dictation."[37] He saw Cumming's proclamation as a protest against judicial use of military aid and believed it would only have an ill effect "upon the Mormon people, the army, and the judge."[38] He thought it was "designed to exasperate the people of this Territory against the troops, to obstruct the course of public justice, and to excite insubordination in the army."[39]

As rumors persisted that Young would be arrested by soldiers, Cumming insisted that if "Young had a writ issued against him he could do no other way ownly to give himself up," though the governor offered some protection. The scenario echoed the events prior to the assassination of Joseph Smith, when Illinois governor Thomas Ford encouraged Smith to give himself up for trial, promising his protection. Young once more considered flight for his people. "We must now go to work and find good hiding places to hide up old men women & Children and provisions," he instructed his associates. "We want some place that Cannot be taken."[40] To the Saints, again the war seemed far from over.

After dismissing the grand jury, Cradlebaugh continued his investigations as a magistrate, taking affidavits for the Utah County murders.[41] While Cradlebaugh examined witnesses, Marshal Dotson and a company of dragoons scoured Springville for the accused local men, but their search proved fruitless. A San Francisco correspondent recorded that the deputies could "obtain nothing but evasive replies, to their inquiries relative to the residences of any one; and but few of the inhabitants seem to know even who their next door neighbor is."[42]

Cradlebaugh's futile 1859 court session contributed to the failure to try the Mountain Meadows Massacre case for many years. His use of troops outside the courtroom and the arrests of subpoenaed witnesses reinforced the Latter-day Saint belief that they could not get a fair trial from federal courts. The judge's conclusion that the Mormon people were not willing to "punish their own murderers & high offenders"—and that until they were, the law was unenforceable in Utah—would be picked up and touted by other judges and non-Mormon politicians for nearly two decades.

21

Diligent Inquiry

Southern Utah, March–April 1859

As Judge Cradlebaugh continued his investigations of the Utah County crimes, Indian Affairs superintendent Jacob Forney drove his wagon to southern Utah, visiting Indian farms along the way. The Easterner made slow progress after leaving Provo, finding the road "exceedingly bad, in consequence of snow, mud, tremendous hills, and innumerable rocks and stones." More than once his wagon broke down or his mules wandered off, always, it seemed, in the middle of nowhere.[1]

Forney got some help at Nephi, bringing on William H. Rogers as his assistant. Born in Virginia in 1824, Rogers had come to Utah in the summer of 1858, perhaps as a teamster with the Utah Expedition. He had been sworn in as a deputy U.S. marshal during Cradlebaugh's Provo court.[2]

Heading south, Forney and Rogers hit Fillmore and Corn Creek, where they investigated the alleged poisoning of the spring and ox by the Arkansas emigrants. It was this incident, Hamblin told Forney in June 1858, that provided the primary motive behind the Mountain Meadows Massacre. Fillmore resident John Ray confirmed to Forney "that one of his oxen died" when the emigrants passed through, adding that while harvesting "the tallow of the dead ox," his wife "became suddenly ill." Her hand swelled and blackened, but she recovered.[3]

The boy who helped her skin the carcass was not so fortunate. Fourteen-year-old Proctor Robison's face became so swollen and bloated that he was unrecognizable when he died a few days later. Forney could see that people in Fillmore and other southern settlements, trying to make sense of the inexplicable, sincerely believed the emigrants poisoned the spring and ox.[4]

But he and Rogers dug deeper. They confirmed that one or two Pahvants "died from eating of the dead ox," Forney said, but this did not lead Pahvants to participate in the massacre as some claimed. "I have not been apprised that this excited any of them against the emigrants," Forney wrote, "and after strict inquiry I cannot learn that even one Pah-vant Indian was present at the massacre." He could not find evidence of trouble between the emigrant company and the Pahvants, nor a motive behind the alleged poisoning.[5]

"Why an emigrant company, and especially farmers, would carry with them so much deadly poison is incomprehensible," Forney reasoned. Even if they had been able to identify a motive, Rogers did not think even a barrel of arsenic could sufficiently poison the spring at Corn Creek to kill the cattle that drank from it. Forney surmised that the ox must have eaten "a poisonous weed," then died while the Arkansas train camped at Corn Creek.[6]

With no understanding of germ theory in mid-nineteenth-century America, people could only guess what caused the mysterious Corn Creek illness and deaths of cattle and the people who handled the carcasses. Along the trail from Utah to southern California during the mid- to late 1850s, people died or became seriously ill after handling cattle carcasses. After reviewing the circumstances and symptoms in Proctor Robison's and other documented cases from the 1850s, modern medical experts concluded that anthrax—a disease borne by cattle and passed to humans—was the likely culprit.[7]

Though Forney was wrong about a poisonous weed being the cause of the Corn Creek deaths, he was right when he concluded that some used the incident to shift motive and blame from the actual massacre perpetrators to the Pahvants and the massacre victims themselves. "*In my opinion,*" he reported to Washington, "*bad men,* for a bad purpose, have magnified a natural circumstance."[8]

At Corn Creek, Pahvant leader Kanosh joined Forney and Rogers for the rest of their journey. As they made their way south through Beaver, Parowan, Cedar City, and Pinto, they made "diligent inquiry concerning the massacre of this party of emigrants," Rogers said, but no one reported any incidents related to the emigrants' journey through these towns. Though settlers estimated the emigrants' numbers at 120 to 140, "no one professed to have any knowledge of the massacre, except that they had heard it . . . was done by the Indians."[9]

Jacob Hamblin's adopted Shoshone son, Albert, met Forney's group at Pinto about April 12, 1859. His father had sent him, Albert told them, to lead them to the crime scene at the Meadows, then on to Hamblin's home in Santa Clara.[10]

Several miles west of Pinto, the valley of the Mountain Meadows opened up before the travelers, beckoning them forward. "I was anxious to see the spot where the massacre took place," Forney said, "and also where the dead were buried." Beholding the valley's beauty for the first time, Forney and Rogers observed that it was some six miles long and at least a mile wide, covered with "luxuriant grass," the last grassy respite on the road to California.[11]

The men rode past Hamblin's ranch, where the homestead sat silent, its residents not yet moved there for the summer. Soon they came to "a few acres of oak brush and sage" jutting out thickly to the road, "the only thing of the kind I saw in the valley," Forney said.[12] Here the allure of the lovely Meadows came to a shocking end.

The scene, Rogers wrote, was "too horrible and sickening for language adequately to describe." Now, more than eighteen months after the crime, human vestiges still covered the ground "for a distance of more than a hundred yards around a central point," he wrote. "In places the bones of small children were lying side by side with those of grown persons, as if parent and child had met death at the same instant and with the same stroke." Strewn among the "skeletons and bones" were "rolls or bunches of tangled and matted hair, which from its length, evidently belonged to females." Faded "small bonnets and dresses, and scraps of female apparel" littered the ground, their forms, "in many instances, entire." The clothing fragments were, "like the bones of those who wore them, bleached from long exposure." Rogers did not mention seeing any male clothing.[13]

"The cries of women and children almost sound[ed] in one's ears," Forney felt as he walked the killing field. Though remains lay scattered over the ground, Forney saw three places where burials had been attempted, now nothing more than "imperfect holes." Rogers identified only one burial spot, "in a gulch or hole in the ravine by the side of the road," he said. "A large number of leg and arm bones, and also of skulls, could be seen sticking above the surface, as if they had been buried there, but the action of the water and digging of the wolves had again exposed them to sight." Taking in the horror, Rogers predicted that "the small valley known as the Mountain Meadows . . . will hereafter impart to its appropriate and once inviting name a sad and horrible history."[14]

Forney's party nooned at the spring near where the emigrants camped. Here, Forney and Rogers concluded, the company had "corraled the wagons and made a protective fort, by filling with earth the space under the wagons." They could still see the earthen evidence of the emigrants' digging in.[15]

After leaving the Meadows, Forney and Rogers met a young man driving his wagon south. The man, who was headed home to Fort Clara after purchasing flour in Cedar City, introduced himself as David Tullis. Forney began questioning him along with Albert Hamblin. Both were living at Hamblin's ranch in September 1857, Albert as part of the Hamblin family and Tullis as a hired hand. Forney was dubious when the two young men repeated the story of a solely Indian massacre. The pair knew better—Tullis had participated in the crime, and Albert had at least witnessed it. Although the two lived "within three and a half miles of the spot where the killing was done," Forney wrote, "neither were there, if one is to believe them."[16]

Forney's group reached Fort Clara on a mid-April evening. There, with images of the remains of murdered families fresh in his mind, he met thirteen child survivors of the Mountain Meadows Massacre.[17]

Though "poorly clad" and suffering from "sore eyes," the youngsters "were well" and "in a better condition than children generally in the settlements in which they lived," Rogers and Forney observed.[18] Many settlers of southern Utah were living in poverty, "destitute of clothing" as one woman put it.[19]

The "sore eyes," Rogers explained, "prevailed at the time as an epidemic."[20] The ailment, identified as "the terrible sore-eyes of Southern Utah" by a later observer, was common in the area for decades.[21]

Forney's group remained in Santa Clara for the next two days, distributing blankets, shirts, and other goods to the Santa Clara Paiutes, professing to them the friendship of the federal government. "Quite a number of Indians came in from the country on account of Forneys [arrival]," recorded schoolteacher Marion Shelton, who had recently left Harmony to work in Fort Clara. Forney also spent time talking with local settlers, including Shelton, who worked as Forney's clerk during the superintendent's visit. "Jacob Hamblin and others, of Santa Clara, expressed much anxiety to bring the guilty to justice," said Forney.[22]

On Sunday, April 17, thirteen surviving children once again bid farewell to the families they lived with. This time the wagon that carried them away headed for northern Utah. Jacob Hamblin joined Forney on his way. They would soon retrieve three more surviving children.[23]

At sunset four days later, Forney's suite reached Harmony. They "took Supper" with John D. Lee's family that night, though he was nowhere to be seen. Forney's party camped nearby for the night.[24]

The following morning, Lee showed up at the Indian Affairs superintendent's tent. Hamblin made introductions, and Lee invited Forney to breakfast. Forney declined the invitation, telling Lee he preferred "to Eat in his Tent."

Lee responded that it was "a free Country," and that Forney "Could Suit himse[l]f." Lee then turned and walked away.

Perhaps persuaded by Hamblin, Forney soon changed his mind. He and Hamblin emerged from the tent and followed Lee to his lodgings. The three men began again, exchanging the usual pleasantries while settling themselves into one of Lee's sitting rooms.[25] Forney's recent investigations had "led him to believe that Lee had a portion of the property belonging to these murdered emigrants," Rogers explained, "and his object on calling on him was to demand a surrender of the property."[26]

Forney asked his host if he "knew anything about the Mountain [Meadows] Massacre, & of the Property?"

"I would be willing to give all the information cheerfully that I [am] in possession of," Lee answered, "provided I could be Satisfied that it was with a good & honest intent that Such information was Sought."

Forney responded that "he did not wish to take the advantage" of Lee. He had no arrest warrant, nor did he have the authority to serve one even if he wanted to, he said. With this assurance, Lee launched into a diatribe as Forney sat and listened, dumbfounded.

Lee declared he was "an American Citizen & was tenatious of the constitutional rights & liberties that belonged to American citizens." But, he said, he and other Utahns had been deprived of these rights.

"Rotten heartd officials have been fourced upon us by Military Power, contrary to our wishes," Lee told the official. "For this & various other causes we forsook our homes & fire sides, desolating our Touns & cities, & would have committed them to ashes, chosed rather to roam the Mountains, where we could breathe the pure air of Freedom rather than to live in bondage & oppression," Lee said, omitting the fact that only northern Utah settlers had temporarily abandoned their homes with the army's arrival. Governor Cumming had called them back to their homes with President Buchanan's pledge that all charges of treason—or "of any other Nature" during wartime, Lee claimed—would be "forgiven & buried in an oblivion."

Under those conditions "we returned," Lee said, "hoping to enjoy our constitutional rights. . . . But, to our astonishment," as soon as the district courts opened, writs were issued and "armed Bodies of Troops were on the heels of every Man in authority, swearing that they Should be punishd for their offinces, thus dishonoring the Treaty of Peace that had been made between this People & the Government of the u.states." As for the men now "trying to

Serve writs & prying into any thing that had been done" prior to that treaty, Lee insisted, "it is none of their damm buisiness."

The Mormon policy had always "been to give way & suffer insults, abuse, & oppression," Lee said, which was why, even now, their men were merely trying "to keep out of the way of the officrs, leving their homes & farms & take to the Mountains" rather than fight, he said. The accused were not evading arrest because they were guilty of crime, Lee tried to convince Forney, but because they were sparing the U.S. troops.

"I confess that Brigham Young has more patience & for bearance then I have. If He felt as I do," Lee went on, the people "would Stand their ground," and when officers "come with their writs, Just Send them cross lots to Hell."

"That is my feelings, Mr. Forney," Lee said, "& you & Goverment May thank Brigham Young for the lives of that army. Had it not been for the re- spect that this People had for him[,] that army would have been used up & not a grese spot of them would have been found now. They were in our Power & so are they now."[27]

Lee might have tempered his braggadocio had he known who was headed his way. As he sat with Forney making threats against the U.S. Army, Captain Reuben Campbell led his command of Second Dragoons and two infantry companies south from Camp Floyd. Campbell's orders were to meet army paymaster Henry Prince at Santa Clara and escort him—and the substantial payroll he carried—safely back to Camp Floyd. Campbell was also instructed "to inquire into certain depredations said to have been committed by the Indians in that vicinity."

Judge Cradlebaugh traveled with the troops. After ending his investigation of the Utah County crimes, he headed for Mountain Meadows "as a court of inquiry or investigation," Rogers said. Based on Alexander Wilson's recom- mendation, Cradlebaugh intended "to see if he could obtain any evidence against persons who had been charged with participating in the massacre, that would justify him in arresting and holding them for trial." If needed, Cradlebaugh had General Albert Sidney Johnston's permission to use troops for protection or to enforce arrest warrants and other orders.[28]

Simultaneously, Brevet Major James Henry Carleton rode with his First Dragoons out of Fort Tejon in southern California. Carleton's command was to escort Paymaster Prince until meeting Captain Campbell's men at Santa Clara.[29] Like Campbell, Carleton also carried an additional order. His was "to bury the bones of the victims of that terrible massacre" at Mountain Meadows.[30]

22

Approach of the Troops

Santa Clara to Nephi, Spring 1859

Jacob Forney walked out of John D. Lee's house disgusted. When he reached his tent, he described their breakfast meeting to his assistant William Rogers. "Lee denied having the possession of any of the property," Forney reported, "or any knowledge concerning it, farther than that he had heard that the Indians took it." He also claimed "he was not at the massacre," Forney said, "but reached there just after it ended," and that Cedar City stake president Isaac Haight arrived soon after him.

"Lee applied some foul and indecent epithets to the emigrants," attempting to justify the killing. He alleged "they were slandering the Mormons, while passing along."[1] The story Lee told Forney was essentially the same one he told Brigham Young on September 29, 1857.[2]

The day after interviewing Lee, Forney, Rogers, and their wagon party set off for Cedar City, the next stop on their journey north with the surviving children. Lee set out with them on horseback, saying he would join the interview Forney planned to conduct with stake president Haight and his counselor, John Higbee. Forney wanted to discuss "the suspicions which had been expressed" that these two local leaders were involved in the massacre, Rogers said, "either as actual participants in the deed itself, or as inciting the Indians to the crime, and then sharing with them the spoils of the slain."

About halfway between Harmony and Cedar City, Lee suddenly spurred his horse ahead of the group. "We did not see him afterwards," Rogers said. When their party reached Cedar, "he was not there, or if he was, he kept secreted."[3]

Forney retrieved three more massacre survivors at Cedar, whom Hamblin had left there in their adoptive homes until the superintendent came. These three children brought the total number in the superintendent's care to sixteen. Forney had expected to find seventeen, but local settlers assured him he had "all that were saved."[4]

Though Lee was nowhere to be found, Forney interviewed Haight and Higbee. He "made of those ecclesiastics the same demand" he had of Lee, Rogers said, "and received about the same replies from them that Lee gave," with one exception. "They did not . . . attempt to justify the massacre, on the ground of [the emigrants] slandering the Mormons."[5]

The expanding federal investigations shook Cedar City's leaders. Stake president Haight chastised his congregation on Sunday, April 24, 1859—the day Forney, Rogers, and Hamblin reached Cedar. "There is actually more union & integrity amongst the Piede tribe than there is in this Church," Haight lectured. "There are men who have made covenants &c. &c and will for a little pay or a smile from a Gentile betray there brethren and cause there blood shed &c. There are many a Judas amongst us as a people We have got to become so perfect that we will lay [down] our lives before we reveal anything to our enemies & betray one another."

Another massacre participant, Joel White, spoke to the congregation about his recent visit to northern Utah. "The Gentiles are hunting almost for all the brethren in authority," he claimed. Massacre accomplice Ira Allen spoke next. "Those who were honest & upright . . . will be more likely to stand the trials," he said. "Damn the man that will deliver his brethren to the Gentiles."[6]

As Forney's party continued northward, Pahvant headman Kanosh, who had traveled with Forney south from Corn Creek, shared startling news. "Some Indians had told him on the way," Rogers said, "that there were two more children saved from the massacre than Mr. Hamblin had collected."

Though dubious about the rumor, Forney thought the possibility of finding additional survivors important enough to attempt another search. When his group camped at Corn Creek, he found Captain Reuben Campbell's Santa Clara–bound command stopped at the nearby Meadow Creek camp. Forney decided to send his assistant with them. He "directed me to return south again with the troops," Rogers said, to "see if I could ascertain anything about the two children spoken of by Kanosh."

John Cradlebaugh, traveling south with Campbell's command, asked Rogers if he would take the place of his deputy marshal, who had pulled out of the expedition because of illness. "As the duties of this post could in no way interfere with my search for the two children said to have been left," Rogers said, "and might enable me better to find them, I acceded to Judge Cradlebaugh's request."[7]

Forney shared his massacre investigations with Cradlebaugh, and the judge and Second Lieutenant William Kearny of the Tenth Infantry visited

Forney's Corn Creek camp to interview the survivors. Within two months, both Forney and Kearny published separate articles about what they learned from the children. Forney published his in two Salt Lake newspapers, while the southbound Kearny published his in Los Angeles. Before the articles appeared, Forney also sent Acting Commissioner of Indian Affairs Charles E. Mix similar information about the survivors. These accounts provide the earliest known documentation of the recovered children's identities, as stated by the children themselves.[8]

Both Forney and Kearny listed a boy named "John Calvin" or "Calvin," between seven and eight years old, who did not remember his surname. The boy told Forney his family came from Horse Head, Johnson County, Arkansas, and that his parents were "Joseph." Kearny's report said Calvin "was near his mother when she was killed," that he "pulled arrows from her back until she was dead," and that he did "not know what became of his father." Jacob Hamblin retrieved John Calvin from the home of E. H. Groves of Harmony. Harmony's blessing records show that a boy was given the name of John Groves on November 1, 1857. E. H. Groves claimed he purchased the boy from Indians for a horse, but Calvin assured Kearny "he never lived among the Indians."[9]

Calvin told the investigators he had brothers named Henry, James, William, and Larkin, and sisters Mary, Nancy, and Martha. Family members later identified the boy as John Calvin Miller, the son of Joseph (or Josiah) and Matilda Cameron Miller. Besides his parents, Calvin's nine-year-old brother, James William, was killed. Calvin apparently misremembered his young aunts and uncles on the Cameron side—Henry (16), James (14), Martha (11), and Larkin (8), and cousin Nancy (12)—as his siblings. None of the Cameron children; their adult brothers, Isom (18) and Tillman (24); nor parents Martha and William Cameron (both 51) survived the massacre.[10]

But Calvin thought his sister Mary was saved. According to Kearny's report, Calvin identified a girl, supposed to be four years old at the time of the massacre and retrieved from John Morris of Cedar, as Mary. Morris claimed to have ransomed the girl from Indians for blankets and flour. This girl was later identified as Calvin's sister, Mary Miller.[11]

Another child told investigators his name was "Ambrose Miram Taggit." He remembered coming from a place called Johnson County, about a week's travel from the house of his grandparents, who were still living when his wagon train left home. The boy said he had parents and two older brothers "killed by the Indians," but that he and a younger brother were spared and taken to Cedar City. Ambrose was "obtained of John M. Higby" who claimed he "purchased" him from Indians for a horse.[12]

Besides information from the children, Forney also shared a list of perpetrators. "I gave Judge Cradlebaugh," Forney wrote General Johnston on May 1, "the names of such persons who, I have reason to believe, participated in the affair, and when brought to trial can furnish the evidence to convict them." Forney believed that "with proper caution all the men can be arrested" and sent Rogers and Cradlebaugh *with a business letter* to some of the church dignitaries," perhaps as a ruse for Cradlebaugh to meet leaders like Haight, Higbee, Klingensmith, and Lee. The Indian Affairs superintendent told the general he believed that perpetrators would be in custody by the time he read his letter. Campbell's command, Forney wrote, should go as far as the Mountain Meadows, *"for reasons you will learn by and by."*[13]

Forney also informed General Johnston he had recovered "sixteen children, all, it is said, that remain of the butchering affair." The children seemed "contented and happy," though "poorly clad," he said. He intended to "get them fixed up as soon as possible." They appeared to be from three to nine years old, he wrote, all "intellectual and good looking."[14]

Forney wrote Johnston that most of the children were able to provide their first and last names—though later it became unclear whether some of these names were their original ones or names received from their adoptive families. A handful of children had some recollection of their former homes, Forney said.[15]

"More important than all, is, that at least four of the oldest of the children *know,*" Forney wrote, "enough of the material facts of the Mountain Meadow affair, to relieve this world of the white hell-hounds, who have disgraced humanity by being mainly instrumental in the murdering [of] at least one hundred and fifteen men, women and children." The Indian Affairs superintendent situated the children with families at the Spanish Fork farm, then returned to Salt Lake to find suitable quarters for them until they would return east.[16]

Forney was wrong when he told Johnston he believed massacre perpetrators would soon be in custody. He did not realize that many Mormons would close ranks to protect their own—even criminals among them—from outside forces they saw as unfair and anti-Mormon, particularly federal forces. As Lee put it, "true harted Saints will not go to law before Gentile Courts."[17]

As Lieutenant Kearny and Judge Cradlebaugh continued south, rumors spread through the southern settlements that Cradlebaugh and some two hundred U.S. troops were headed to southern Utah "to make arrests of the authorities," recorded James Martineau, William Dame's clerk in Parowan. The troops' approach sent local authorities scurrying "into the mountains, to avoid being taken," Martineau said. "We had been privately notified before, that they were coming to arrest leading Saints, but *they* gave out that they were merely coming to meet the Army paymaster, who was coming from California." From his mountain hiding place, Dame wanted someone to "find out the real object of their coming."[18]

The large procession—and the judge traveling with it—intimidated the settlers. "Accompanied by Judge Cradlebaugh," Martineau wrote, the entourage of seventy-five mounted dragoons, one hundred foot soldiers, and nearly three hundred mules hauling forty-seven baggage wagons passed through Parowan on May 2. Camping less than a mile outside town, "many of them kept up a drunken row nearly all night," Martineau said, "to the alarm of the citizens who are not used to such things." The townsmen "kept up a strong guard" through the night.

Martineau volunteered to seek out the information Dame wanted. "I spent the evening among" the troops, Martineau said, "and wormed from a Sergeant Healy the true object of their coming, which was not only to meet the paymaster, but to make the arrest of such leading mormons as they could, especially any concerned in the Mountain Meadow affair." Healy told Martineau that the judge would prosecute the Mormons before a non-Mormon jury "composed of camp followers, teamsters, &c. Trial before such a tribunal means condemnation," Martineau recorded, "and I for one will not appear before any such a court, if I can help it."[19]

"Sergeant Healy" was actually a nineteen-year-old private who lied about his age to join the army. An Irish immigrant, John J. Healy was a master storyteller who later helped start a whiskey trading post called Fort Whoop-Up in Alberta, Canada.[20]

Stories of misbehavior about the troops and camp followers flew in every direction. At Fort Clara, Dudley Leavitt reported that troops stole a mule, burned fences, and threatened to hang a man. Lee and another man claimed soldiers shot at a settler. Marion Shelton said the troops cursed "everything in the shape of mormons."[21]

The troops were "coming South, with the sworn intention of taking me and some other of the Breathren," Isaac Haight wrote in his journal, adding the assertion that they would "hang us without trial for a Supposed crime, taking the Law into their own hands in violation of the Consti[tu]tion." The following day, "not wishing to fall into their hands as I considered them nothing better than a Mob," Haight wrote, "I left home in company with J. M. Higbee . . . and others." The fugitives headed north, circumventing the troops by taking a less-traveled route through lower Beaver, where massacre participant William Stewart joined them. On May 7 they arrived at Salt Creek (Nephi), where they slept in the tithing office before heading east into the mountains. "We went in the Evening," Haight said, "to a Camp Called Balleguard where quite a number of Breathren who were prescribed by our ennemies had fled for Safety[.] we remained with them untill the last of the month."[22]

Even the innocent took to the hills at the army's approach. "To day Pres[t] Dame told me to send to the mountains," Martineau wrote on May 6. The troops, Dame told his clerk, intended "to take every man that is or has been in authority and I, having been one of the presidency here, must flee or be in danger of my life." Martineau lamented that he had "broken no U.S. Laws, but must be hunted like a felon by U.S. soldiers, apostates and indians, But after all, I am not the first one so treated, and will not, probably, be the last." Before fleeing, he buried "the public records and papers in a large stone Churn."[23]

Traveling south with Cradlebaugh and the troops, Deputy William Rogers felt baffled by the Mormons' behavior. "A large portion of the male inhabitants of the different Mormon towns and settlements through which we passed, either fled or secreted themselves on the approach of the troops. The cause of this I do not know," Rogers wrote. "The troops were certainly on no hostile expedition against the inhabitants," he said, "but were simply on their way to act as an escort to a paymaster of the army. And Judge Cradlebaugh did not seek to interfere with the rights or liberty of any man unaccused of crime."

Apparently unaware of the flying rumors and the Latter-day Saints' fear and distrust of U.S. troops and judges, Rogers concluded that the "large portion of the male inhabitants" of the Mormon settlements must have fled "from a consciousness of guilt of some kind."

At the troops' camping ground several miles south of Cedar City, Cradlebaugh issued arrest warrants for Haight, Higbee, and Lee and gave them to Rogers. The warrants, Rogers said, were based on affidavits "charging these men with being concerned in the Mountain Meadows massacre." Since Haight and Higbee could not be found in Cedar, Rogers "thought it best to proceed first to Harmony and try to secure Lee."

Rogers formed a posse of men traveling with Captain Campbell. As the nine men made their way to Harmony, they paused at a small settlement of several houses. The curious occupants came out when the posse rode in. Seeing the men, women, and children, Rogers asked if any of them knew anything of two massacre survivors still in southern Utah. No one "professed to know anything about any children besides those that Hamblin collected."

If additional survivors were still in the area, Rogers warned the small crowd, "every house would be searched if they were not given up."

Rogers's bold statement rattled Alexander Gordon Ingram, who confessed "his wife had one of the children." Alexander and his wife, Agnes, were the childless couple in their mid-thirties who adopted a baby boy in Harmony, a boy they named Louis Gordon. The Ingrams had recently moved to Pocketville, a village about forty miles away. Ingram begged Rogers to let his wife keep the toddler.[24]

"The child was very young," he told Rogers. Agnes was "very much attached to it," and the child "would give [Rogers] much trouble if [he] took it away."

"I ha[ve] no power to give the child away," Rogers replied, though he could see Ingram was anxious to keep the baby. "I w[ill] send and get it in a few days."[25]

Though Rogers continued to inquire about an eighteenth child through the remainder of his journey, neither he nor anyone else identified another. Though speculation about an eighteenth child continued for generations, only seventeen children were likely spared. The earliest known documentation, recorded just sixteen days after the massacre, has John D. Lee stating in a Provo meeting that "seventeen children was saved."[26]

After talking with Alexander Ingram and discovering the whereabouts of the seventeenth survivor, Rogers reached Harmony. With his posse backing him up, he approached Lee's house. One of Lee's wives came to the door.

"Mr. Lee had been absent two or three days in the mountains," she told Rogers, "looking for copper with the Indians."

Others at Harmony gave Rogers the same story. Realizing Lee had "played the same dodge" as Haight and Higbee, Rogers "deemed it useless to wait for his return." Instead, he returned to Captain Campbell's command and "proceeded on with it to the Mountain Meadows." There they camped near the same spot where the Arkansas emigrants had corralled their wagons.[27]

Campbell soon led his men south to their last camp, on the Santa Clara River, to await the arrival of Paymaster Prince from California. Before leaving, he ordered army surgeon Charles Brewer, along with a detachment of soldiers, to investigate and inter remains of the massacre victims. Near Brewer's camp in the Mountain Meadows, the men examined the trenches the emigrants made during their wagon-fort siege. The soldiers hoped to discover some written account hidden there. Instead, they found bed feathers and a few human bones, which told their own tale. Scattered about the area, the men also found remnants of bedding, clothing, and bodies—skulls, bones, and hair "bearing the appearance of never having been buried," Brewer said. He directed his men to bury the eight skulls and other bones discovered there at the base of a nearby hill, "upon the hill-side of the valley."[28]

Some twenty-five hundred yards to the northwest and fifty yards from the road, Brewer investigated a ravine bordered by a few scrub oak bushes. In what appeared to be a mass grave—matching a description Forney and Rogers gave—he found clumps of matted hair, skulls, and bones protruding from the ground, "most of which, on examination, I concluded to be those of men," said Brewer. "The relative positions and general appearance of the remains seemed to indicate that the men were there taken by surprise and massacred," Brewer concluded. "Some of the skulls showed that fire-arms had been discharged close to the head. I here buried eighteen skulls and parts of many more skeletons found scattered over the space of a mile towards the lines, in which directions, they were no doubt dragged by the wolves."

"Three hundred and fifty yards further on, and in the same direction," Brewer came to "another assembly of human remains . . . which, by all appearance, had been left to decay upon the surface." Some of these bones had "a little earth partially covering them," Brewer said. "Masses of women's hair, children's bonnets, such as are generally used upon the plains, and pieces of lace, muslin, calicoes, and other material" used in "women's and children's apparel" littered the ground. Brewer concluded that the remains found here were those of women, as well of children ranging in age from six to twelve years.

Here the soldiers buried "thirteen skulls, and many more scattered fragments" in another mass grave. "Many of the skulls" Brewer and his men found "bore marks of violence, being pierced with bullet holes, or shattered by heavy blows, or cleft with some sharp-edged instrument. The bones were bleached and worn by long exposure to the elements, and bore the impress of the teeth of wolves or other wild animals."

The men examined each article of clothing for a name and looked at each bone for a peculiarity—some clue which might identify a victim. All they found of this nature was an upper jaw with one extra tooth and closely crowded teeth.

Dr. Brewer and the troops made sure most of the remains they discovered were well buried, marking the mass graves with large mounds of stone.[29] As specimens of the crime scene, he took away with him "a sunbonnet, fragments of dress, locks of hair and bones," including the skulls of two young persons.[30]

Meanwhile, Captain Campbell and his men made their next camp on the Santa Clara River. There they awaited the arrival of Major Carleton and Paymaster Prince while Cradlebaugh and Campbell interviewed Santa Clara Paiutes.[31]

Several miles away at Fort Clara, Jacob Hamblin dispatched Ira Hatch to interpret for the troops. Campbell sent for Paiute headman Jackson, leader of a band "charged with massacreing the emigrants." In the presence of his bandsmen, Jackson "acknowledged that he had committed some outrages on the people of the United States," Campbell said. "He made the most humble protestations of future good conduct, in which I put some reliance if he is not encouraged to commit acts by the Mormons."[32]

Cradlebaugh said Santa Clara Paiutes "admitted that a portion of their men were engaged in the massacre, but were not there when the attack commenced." After the initial attack on the emigrants at their wagon corral, Jackson told Cradlebaugh, a white man visited his camp on the Clara. He brought with him "a piece of paper," which he claimed "Brigham Young had sent, that directed them to go and help to whip the emigrants." Some of the band went, Jackson said, but were afraid to venture near the encircled wagons because "the emigrants had long guns, and were good shots." His brother "was killed by a shot from the corral at a distance of two hundred yards." Jackson also said that "the Mormons who had killed the emigrants were painted so as to resemble Indians."[33]

The Paiutes told the investigators that "Nargutz" was there, but like them he dared not venture too near the emigrant camp. "Nargutz" was Paiute for "crying man," the name the Paiutes gave John D. Lee. Years later, Lee said the Indians called him this because he cried when he begged them to cease their attack on the emigrant corral at the Mountain Meadows. But the Santa Clara Paiutes said they called Lee "Nargutz" because he cried when some of his stock were lost or stolen.[34]

According to Rogers, the Indians told their interrogators that two other leaders on Cradlebaugh's wanted list, Haight and Higbee, were also present during the attack. Though other witnesses confirm Higbee did directly participate in the massacre, Haight did not appear at the Meadows until shortly after the atrocity. He played his part in Cedar City, directing the offensive.[35]

Learning that the Santa Clara Paiutes did not go to the siege until after the initial attack, the investigators concluded that the first attack must have been carried out by white men alone, painted as Indians.[36] This conclusion would contribute to belief that Mormons painted as Indians were the sole perpetrators of the massacre. But these investigators did not communicate with the Ash Creek or Coal Creek bands who lived near Harmony and Cedar City. After non-Mormon Indian agent Garland Hurt did so in September 1857, he concluded that it was these Indians, directed by Lee, who made the first attacks on the emigrants. After they "were repulsed on three different occasions," Hurt wrote, "Lee and the bishop of Cedar city [Klingensmith], with a number of Mormons, approached the camp of the emigrants under pretext of trying to settle the difficulty, and with lying, seductive overtures, succeeded in inducing the emigrants to lay down their weapons of defence."[37]

23

Catching Is Before Hanging

Santa Clara, May 1859

After interpreting for the federal troops at their Santa Clara camp on May 8, 1859, Ira Hatch returned to Fort Clara at dark. Local Paiutes were "much alarmed about the Soilders coming," a resident recorded. They "came and talked to us late in the evening." They were not the only ones upset. Hatch said "the soldiers had taken his horse, and treated him very badly. This caused the men here to be very much enraged," Marion Shelton wrote. They "talked like they wanted to go and fight the troops—thought it would be a good plan to kill them all. I thought this was nonsense."[1]

The next day, "Jacob Hamblin left for Pocketville," Shelton wrote, "in search of a child." John D. Lee and Philip Klingensmith also happened to be in that area. Fleeing Harmony, Lee headed south towards Toquerville, where Klingensmith had recently moved. The two men ended up a few miles further west near Pocketville, a new settlement on the Virgin River, surrounded by rugged mountains. The town was later renamed Virgin.[2]

Retrieving the seventeenth survivor was likely challenging. Now in her late thirties, the childless Agnes Ingram had been "happy to death to get this child," and the two had grown "very much attached." Now Hamblin asked her to turn over the toddler she had raised since infancy. Agnes's agony in giving up the "bright eyed and rosy cheeked boy" can only be imagined. But he was not hers to keep.[3]

On May 12, "Jacob Hamblin returned from Pocketville and brought a little child with him," Shelton wrote at Fort Clara. Hamblin then went to Captain Campbell's camp on the Clara to tell Deputy William Rogers that he had retrieved the seventeenth survivor. He also reported "that he had heard more, and learned more about the massacre during his absence after the child, than he ever knew before," Rogers said, "that he had been told of a number of men that he knew, who were concerned [in] it, that he never dreamed or suspected" would be involved.[4]

Rogers asked for the men's names, but Hamblin declined to provide them. "He informed me," Rogers said, "that he was under a promise of secresy not to divulge them to any one but Gov. Cumming." Rogers instructed Hamblin to take the seventeenth child to Jacob Forney in Salt Lake. Cumming later told Rogers that Hamblin "revealed nothing to him in regard to the massacre or those concerned in it."[5]

The additional information Hamblin learned in Pocketville may have come from Klingensmith and Lee, or from Pocketville residents Agnes and Alexander Ingram, Nephi Johnson, or Don Carlos Shirts. Whatever the case, it was likely Hamblin who shared news that spooked Lee and Klingensmith from their hiding place near Pocketville. Lee's journal entry states that someone brought word that Judge Cradlebaugh and the troops were now camped on the Clara. "They are waiting the arrival of [paymaster] Prince with 200 cavalry, escort and guard," Lee wrote.

Lee heard that upon Prince's arrival, Cradlebaugh planned to head back to Camp Floyd with Campbell's command. "But before they return my scalp they want, let it cost what it may," Lee wrote. He also heard they wanted to arrest him even more than they wanted "all the Piedes, Haight, Bishop [Klingen]Smith and all other criminals, but catching is before hanging and my trust is in God."

Klingensmith and Lee headed for the hills, their horses kicking up sand as they rode north along La Verkin Creek into the majestic mountains of what later became Zion National Park's Kolob Canyons.

Staying in the canyons east of the well-traveled route that passed through southern Utah, the pair traversed "rough, rugged and steep, limestone." At one point a rattler startled Lee. "According to tradition," killing your first snake of the year was equivalent to conquering your enemies that year, Lee wrote. "So I blowed his brains out."

For a day or two of their journey, Klingensmith deserted his companion, but Lee managed to find him. The two fugitives eventually camped near a summit six miles east of Harmony. From there, they could see the whole area. Looking through his spyglass, Lee did not see any troops, but felt awed by the "lovely and beautiful landscape." A snow-capped mountain lay to the south, its pine-green slopes descending into the verdant valley below. "My residence and farm appeared more dear and lovely to me than ever," Lee wrote. His heart ached when he spied, working in the pasture, his family, "from whom whose society I was deprived by wicked and corrupt men, for the gospel's sake."

Lee stealthily rode into the fields to converse with two family members. They shared rumors from Salt Lake. "Gov. Cummings notified Pres. Young to prepare to defend himself against the troops," they told Lee. "The Judge was determined to hold court," arrest Young, the twelve apostles, "and every other man that they wished," and "Gov. Cummings could not control them."

Returning to his camp, Lee relayed the rumors to "my partner" Klingensmith, he said. "The way things were shaping, it looked like bringing us to the test," Lee wrote. The pair "blessed each other and parted," with Klingensmith heading north. They would not see each other again for nine days. "Troubled in spirit," Lee did not sleep well. "The cogitations of my mind through the night plainly indicated that I in connection with others were threatened with trouble."

Lee again ventured down to the edge of his fields the next day, where he spoke with three of his wives, Aggathean, Rachel, and Sarah Caroline. He learned of fears "that should the troops visit Washington [Utah] in search of men, that one-half would turn traitors and go over to the soldiers," Lee said. "But such men are to be pitied and can only be looked upon as fair weather Mormons and not to be depended upon in the day of trial."[6]

As Lee and his wives talked, Paymaster Prince and Major Carleton's First Dragoons reached Captain Campbell's camp on the Santa Clara after their three-week trudge through the Mojave Desert. Carleton and Campbell both moved their camps to the Mountain Meadows. Judge Cradlebaugh and Deputy Rogers left them there and headed back to Cedar City.[7]

With the troops nearby at the Meadows and Deputy Rogers at his side, the judge intended to remain in Cedar some time to investigate the massacre. The town was now nearly desolate, with few people to be seen. Poverty-stricken by the Iron Mission's failure, and unhappy with their local leaders, large numbers of residents had left. Cradlebaugh and Rogers found "a good many vacant houses in the place," Rogers said, and secured one of them to stay in and use as a courthouse.[8]

Word spread through the area that Cradlebaugh intended to hold a court of investigation, backed by "troops to ensure protection, and enforce his writs." As soon as this was known—and with Haight, Higbee, and other massacre leaders away in hiding—the judge began getting late-night knocks at his door. Under cover of darkness, several informants shared what they knew, asking him not to reveal their identities for fear their lives would be endangered. They asked Cradlebaugh not to acknowledge them "if he met them in public," Rogers said.[9]

Figure 23.1 John D. Lee with wives Rachel and Sarah Caroline. Courtesy Utah State Historical Society.

Though Cradlebaugh, while working in Provo, had already heard "complaint after complaint" of robbery and murder, he said the "worst, and darkest in this appaling catalogue of blood" was the "cowardly, cold-blooded butchery and robbery at the Mountain Meadows." The informants at Cedar corroborated much of what the Santa Clara Paiutes and the oldest surviving children said, Cradlebaugh wrote. They "gave me every assurance that they would furnish an abundance of evidence in regard to the matter, so soon as they were assured of military protection." At least one informant had even participated in the massacre and agreed, if protected, to be a witness.[10]

Based on the testimonies of the Cedar City informants and Jackson of the Santa Clara Paiutes, the judge pieced together his own interpretation of the crime.

"The first attack," Cradlebaugh wrote, "was made by going down [a] ravine" near the emigrants' camp, "then at daylight firing upon the men who were about the camp-fires; in which attack ten or twelve of the emigrants were killed or wounded." To repel "the assailants," the emigrants created a wagon fort, and a five-day siege set in. Hiding behind a stone barricade along the crown of a nearby hill, "the besiegers appearing in the garb of Indians" fired at any "emigrants that exposed themselves."

"The Mormons seeing that they could not capture the train without making some sacrifice of life on their part," Cradlebaugh continued, "resolved to accomplish by strategy what they were not able to do by force." A wagon carrying white men and a white flag approached the besieged corral. The emigrants welcomed the wagon's occupants inside, including "John D. Lee," Cradlebaugh wrote, "little suspecting that they were entertaining the fiends that had been besieging them."

Professing "to be on good terms with the Indians, and represent[ing] the Indians as being very mad," the Mormon negotiators "proposed to intercede." During "several hours of parley, they having apparently visited the Indians, gave the ultimatum of the Indians, which was that the emigrants should march out of their camp, leaving everything behind them, even their guns." The Mormons promised "to bring a force and guard the emigrants back to the settlements."

"The terms were agreed to," Cradlebaugh wrote, "the emigrants being desirous of saving the lives of their families." The Mormon negotiators left the wagon fort and returned "with thirty or forty armed men. The emigrants were marched out, the women and children in front and the men behind, the Mormon guard being in the rear." After walking up the trail "about a mile, at a given signal the slaughter commenced. The men were most all shot down at the first fire from the guard."

Cradlebaugh recorded that the women and children were slaughtered a few hundred yards further north "with the aid of the Indians. Seventeen only of the small children were saved, the eldest being about seven years." Most of the spoils were taken to Cedar City. "The bed clothes upon which the wounded had been laying, and those taken from the dead, [were] piled in the back room of the tithing office" until they were sold. When Cradlebaugh visited it, he found the stench "still offensive."[11]

Based on the timing of the secret interviews in Cedar, the insider details shared, and subsequent events, Philip Klingensmith was likely one of Cradlebaugh's informants. Klingensmith later became the first perpetrator to file an affidavit about the massacre and testified as state's evidence in exchange for immunity from prosecution. Cradlebaugh and Rogers never included Klingensmith as a perpetrator in their accounts, even though Jacob Forney and numerous other sources pointed to him as a key participant. Nine days after he had parted ways with Lee near Harmony and "bent his way northward" towards Cedar, Klingensmith returned to Lee at his camp. Lee believed Klingensmith had simply been hiding in the mountains north of him.[12]

As Cradlebaugh conducted his investigations, Jacob and Rachel Hamblin started north from the Santa Clara fort, bringing to Forney the seventeenth survivor Jacob recently obtained from the Ingrams. Jacob's clerk, Marion Shelton, joined them. On May 19 they reached the Mountain Meadows, where they encountered Major Carleton. Carleton brought the Hamblins and the child to his encampment, where they spent the night. "He is a pretty little boy," Carleton noted, "and hardly dreamed he had again slept upon the ground where his parents had been murdered."[13]

Describing Jacob Hamblin as "a shrewd, intelligent, thinking man" despite his "little education," Carleton interviewed him and recorded his statement, the substance of which Hamblin said he had already given to Cradlebaugh.[14] Although Hamblin had told Deputy Rogers he was eager to see the massacre's leaders brought to justice, he was reticent to supply information to Major Carleton and army troops.[15]

Hamblin recited only what Indians told him they had done, saying little about white participation. Carleton was not impressed, and later called Hamblin "a consummate knave and villain."[16] Hamblin did, however, provide important clues. He described in veiled terms the fate of the emigrant men who left the wagon siege before the day of the massacre. He also told Carleton "that to his certain knowledge in [18]55, there were but three guns" among the Paiutes—a clear suggestion that they could not have carried out the massacre on their own. And he showed one of Carleton's men "a spot on the right hand side of the road where he had partially covered up a great many of the bones" the year after the massacre.[17]

Carleton interviewed Rachel Hamblin the next morning. Coached by her husband, she named Lee and other settlers as being at the Mountain Meadows during the week of the massacre, purportedly as bystanders or "to stop the fighting." Carleton described her as "a simple minded person" who "evidently looks with the eyes of her husband at every thing." But noting that "her own mother-heart was touched" by the traumatized orphans brought to her door after the massacre, Carleton felt "she at least deserves kind consideration for her care and nourishment" of the surviving children.[18]

The Hamblins left Carleton's camp on May 20, taking the seventeenth survivor on to Salt Lake.[19] That day, they sent their adopted Shoshone son Albert to Carleton's camp to share his testimony.[20] Carleton described Albert's account as "artfully made up; evidently part true and part falsehood." Ascertaining that the young man had "been trained in his statement," Carleton easily tripped him up under cross-examination. Reflecting both anti-Native and anti-Mormon bias, Carleton thought Albert "had engrafted upon his native viciousness all the bad traits of the community in which he lives."[21]

Besides conducting the three interviews, Carleton carried out his assignment to bury the massacre victims' bones.[22] From Campbell's troops he learned how the detachment under Dr. Brewer had recently buried some of the remains. Carleton "took a wagon and a party of men" to collect the bones from Hamblin's burial site of the previous summer. They also scoured the ground for others, finding a large number "up the slope of the hill, and in the ravines, and among the bushes."

"The scene of the massacre," Carleton wrote of the search, "even at this late day, was horrible to look upon. Women's hair in detached locks, and in masses, hung to the sage bushes, and was strewn over the ground in many places. Parts of little children's dresses, and of female costume, dangled from the shrubbery, or lay scattered about. And among these, here and there, on every hand, . . . there gleamed, bleached white by the weather, the skulls and other bones of those who had suffered. A glance into the wagon, when all these had been collected, revealed a sight which can never be forgotten." Marion Shelton, who saw the wagon, described it as "loaded with bones."[23]

While Dr. Brewer said the bones in his two mass burials were "pierced with bullet holes, or shattered by heavy blows, or cleft with some sharp-edged instrument," Carleton reported "that nearly every skull" he saw "had been shot through with rifle or revolver bullets." More than a century later, after the bones Carleton buried were accidentally unearthed, a forensic anthropologist analyzed them and concluded that the majority of adult male victims were shot in the head, while most of the women and children were "bludgeoned to death."[24]

Brewer showed Carleton one of two skulls he would carry away from the crime scene, "probably of a boy of eighteen," split on top "by two blows of a bowie knife, or other instrument of that character." The other skull was that of a seven- or eight-year-old child, shot through the back of the head, the ball "coming out near the right temple."[25]

Carleton "saw several bones of what must have been very small children." Brewer told him that "some infants, even, were butchered. The mothers doubtless had these in their arms, and the same shot or blow may have deprived both of life."[26]

Carleton estimated that the bones his men found came from thirty-two persons, based on "the number of pairs of shoulder blades, and of lower jaws, skulls and parts of skulls, etc." He found "the remains of two others, gotten in a ravine to the east of the spring where they had been interred at but little depth." All of these bones, he said, "I buried in a grave on the northern side of the ditch."[27]

"Around and above this grave" Carleton's men used nearby stones to build "a rude monument, conical in form, . . . fifty feet in circumference at the base, and twelve feet in height." At the pinnacle, they planted "a cross hewn from red cedar wood" whose top stood twenty-four feet from the ground. On the horizontal crossbar, the men carved an inscription from the New Testament: "VENGEANCE IS MINE: I WILL REPAY SAITH THE LORD." On the north side of the monument the soldiers erected a slab of granite that proclaimed, "HERE 120 MEN, WOMEN AND CHILDREN, WERE MASSACRED IN COLD BLOOD, IN SEPT., 1857. THEY WERE FROM ARKANSAS."[28]

Reflecting on how the horrendous crime should be punished, Carleton first cited Cradlebaugh, who thought "that with Mormon juries, the attempt to administer justice in this territory, is simply a ridiculous farce. He believes the territory ought at once to be put under martial law."

Carleton took it even further, charging that the execution of a few "Latter Day Devils" would be "inadequate . . . for this crime which nearly the whole Mormon population, from Brigham Young down, were more or less instrumental in perpetrating." To him, the Mormon people were "an ulcer on the body politic . . . which needs more than cautery to cure." He demanded "excision; complete and thorough extirpation."[29]

During his return to Fort Tejon, Carleton sent ahead a letter reporting on his trip. "I would to God," he wrote, that his commander,

> with an adequate force, and with his hands unfettered by red tape, could have the management of those *damned* Mormons just one summer, and that "I could be there to see." . . . It is no use to talk or split hairs about that accursed race. All fine spun nonsense about their rights as citizens, and all knotty questions about Constitutional Rights should be solved with the sword. Self preservation, the *first* law, demands that this set of ruffians *go*

out from amongst us as people. . . . No exorcism but that of *force* will ever banish [the]m from our midst. Give them one year, no more; and if after that they pollute our soil by their presence make literally *Children of the Mist* of them.[30]

24

Precious Legacies from the Departed Ones

Northern Utah to Northwest Arkansas,
May–October 1859

Not long after returning to Salt Lake City in early May 1859, Jacob Forney learned of a new plan for the surviving children's return home.[1] William H. Russell of the freighting firm Russell, Majors & Waddell had volunteered to transport the children from Salt Lake to the firm's supply center at Fort Leavenworth, Kansas. Russell would furnish two ox teams and wagons to bring the children east with one of the firm's returning caravans. "We esteem this an act of humanity," Russell explained.

In a letter explaining the plans, U.S. Indian Affairs commissioner Charles Mix instructed Forney to hire a few women to go with the caravan to "give these little ones all needful supervision and attention upon the road." Another agent would meet the children at Leavenworth and deliver them to their relatives and friends in Arkansas. With these new arrangements, Mix said, there was no need for Forney to leave his post in Utah.[2]

Forney soon transported the sixteen recovered children from Spanish Fork to Salt Lake, where he boarded them in the care of Ann Eliza Worley, a Latter-day Saint convert from Yonkers, New York. "My constant endeavor," Forney said, was to make the children "comfortable and happy." He busied himself preparing everything they would need for the journey, including plenty of clothing and blankets. He also requested that the ox wagons for the children be sent to him so he could "fix them up comfortably." Forney, the *Valley Tan* newspaper noted, was "a very kind protector."[3]

As Forney worked toward returning the children home, people in Arkansas eagerly awaited their arrival. That spring, former Arkansas congressman A. B. Greenwood, who had worked for well over a year to secure the children's recovery, replaced Charles Mix as commissioner of the Office of Indian Affairs. On June 7, Greenwood wrote William C. Mitchell, the former Arkansas state senator who had initiated inquiries into recovering the children. Explaining the new arrangements to transport the children east, Greenwood asked Mitchell to pick them up at Leavenworth and convey them to Carrollton, Arkansas, in two wagons. Mitchell willingly accepted.[4]

Though the sixteen survivors were supposed to begin their journey east in May, snowmelt from a late and heavy winter made the roads too rough for young children to travel.[5] The delay proved fortunate. In early June, Jacob and Rachel Hamblin arrived in Salt Lake with the seventeenth child, the last and youngest survivor recovered. When eight-year-old survivor Calvin saw the toddler, he reportedly "ran up to it, and kissing it remarked that it was his litt[l]e brother," adding that he had been wondering where he was.[6]

Increasingly concerned about the delayed and arduous journey that such young children would have to make in slow-moving ox wagons driven by "sundry ox-drivers," Forney made an intrepid move. Though his instructions from Washington were to accept Russell's offer, Forney risked proposing a different plan to General Johnston at Camp Floyd. "These unfortunate fatherless, motherless, and penniless children certainly demand more than an ordinary degree of sympathy," Forney entreated the general. Thus, "after mature reflection and consultation with several gentlemen," he wrote, "I am induced to assume the responsibility of changing the direction of this matter." His plan would work if he could obtain from Johnston two or three fast-moving and comfortable light-spring wagons, a baggage wagon, mules, and a military escort. He asked Johnston "whether this arrangement can be made without subjecting the service to any important inconvenience," and requested a rapid response given that Russell's next commercial caravan was soon to leave.[7]

Forney's bold and humane move, ignoring a direct order from his Washington superiors, put his career at risk and exposed him to possible reprimand from Johnston.[8] Within twenty-four hours of receiving Forney's letter, Johnston's adjutant, Fitz John Porter, responded from Camp Floyd. The general, Porter wrote, takes "great pleasure in aiding you to the full scope of his authority here, and on the road, in your humane efforts to transmit in comfort and safety those children."[9]

A company of dragoons was soon to depart Camp Floyd for a new assignment at Fort Kearny, Nebraska. Johnston said the children could travel under their protection as far as Kearny. From there, another escort would go with them to Fort Leavenworth. Johnston also directed his deputy quartermaster to furnish "three light spring-wagons, and one baggage-wagon" for transporting the little survivors, each of the carriages to be equipped with seats and arranged for the children's comfort.[10]

"I can hardly find language to express my thankfulness," Forney wrote in response to Porter. "Say to General Johnston that I appreciate his kindness, and return to him, in behalf of the unfortunate children, sincere thanks for the generosity in aiding me to convey those little ones in comfort and safety to Leavenworth." Forney promised to visit Camp Floyd the following day.[11]

Talk of the surviving children soon circulated in the army camp. "One of them is represented as being an interesting girl of eleven years, with drooping eyelids and a pale complexion. What an aspect of the world she has thus far seen!—bloody Indians and Mormons, and American[s] whose interests in her she can hardly yet understand," Captain John W. Phelps wrote the day after Forney's planned visit.[12]

After securing Johnston's assistance, Forney wrote the commissioner of Indian Affairs in Washington to solicit approval of his new plan. "One as familiar as I am with the extraordinary history of these unfortunate children," Forney explained, "cannot help feeling more than an ordinary degree of interest in their welfare." The three carriages provided by the army "are certainly much more comfortable than the large, heavy wagons" of a freighting caravan. The new plan, Forney wrote, would also shorten the children's journey by thirty to forty days.[13]

Forney petitioned probate judge Elias Smith, a Latter-day Saint, "for letters of Guardianship" for the massacre survivors. Forney was granted guardianship so that he, acting as agent for the children, could "use his best endeavors to recover the property of which they [and their families] have been despoiled."[14]

On June 26, companies A and C of the Second Dragoons rode out of Camp Floyd, beginning the trek to their new stations at Fort Laramie and Fort Kearny. "A considerable number of persons" traveled with them, Captain Phelps wrote, including "the children saved from the Mountain Meadow Massacre." The number included several officers going east on leave and a chaplain. "All will pay more or less attention to those unfortunate children, who really demand the sympathy of all persons who have proper feelings," Forney wrote.[15]

Also traveling with the party were disaffected Saints wanting to leave Utah, including the family of Frederick Gardiner. Gardiner, the owner of a Salt Lake City drugstore, was assigned as the company's medic and supplied it with a medicine chest for the trip.[16]

Forney secured five women to accompany the children as their nurses. "Mrs. Worley," the woman who had been caring for the children since their arrival in Salt Lake, was "*chief* nurse," Forney clarified. Another caretaker was Janet Hardie, a Scottish midwife who emigrated to Utah by ship and hand-cart in 1856. Hardie was ideal to attend to the children's medical needs. She had practiced at the University of Edinburgh, where she studied under James Y. Simpson, who became the first person knighted for contributions to medicine. Hardie's services were in high demand both in Scotland and Utah. Among those who received her care was the family of Brigham Young.[17]

Forney engaged three men to be "camp assistants." He directed them to do everything possible for the children's comfort, "especially to assist the women, put up the tents, get wood and water, and, in fact, anything that may become necessary."[18]

Finally, like a doting parent, Forney wrote Major D. P. Whiting, who, heading east on a leave of absence, had promised Forney "to take general supervision" over the whole children's party. "See that the children are properly fed," Forney dictated, "with properly arranged and well-cooked food. They should have little or no bacon or beans, but little fresh meat, plenty of rice, sugar, milk, butter, and eggs when they can be obtained." Forney had sent butter, a hundred pounds of crackers, and both dried and canned peaches as treats for the children.

Forney added that one of the three camp assistants, "Robert B. Jarvis, Esq., ex-Indian agent" and "a kind-hearted, clever gentleman," would "travel in the ambulances with the children, and has kindly promised to take special care of them." Forney "requested Mr. Jarvis to render the major some assistance, in addition to his other duties—to observe that the children got enough and of the proper kind of food." General Johnston provided an order for additional provisions at military posts along the route.[19]

Finally, on June 28, 1859, the entourage left Salt Lake City, all three of the children's carriages and their baggage wagon pulled by fast-moving teams of six mules apiece. Recording the news of the day, a Church Historian's Office clerk wrote that "the names of the children are as follows: John Calvin, Lewis, and Mary Sorel, their father being held in remembrance as 'Joe Sorel'; Ambrose Miram, and William Taggett; Frances Horn; Charles and Annie Francher; Betsey & Jane Baker; Rebecca, Louisa, & Sarah Dunlap; Sophronia or Mary and Ephraim W. Huff; Angeline & Annie, (surname unknown) and a little boy of whom there is no account."[20]

But in a late turn of events, not all of the seventeen survivors actually departed that day. U.S. Attorney Alexander Wilson asked Forney to hold back two of the children—the two boys who seemed to remember the most about the massacre. "I deem it important to the cause of justice," Wilson wrote Forney on the day the company departed, "that John Calvin Sorel and Ambrose Miram Taggit, being orphans, rescued from the Mountain Meadow massacre, should be detained, and by you held subject to my order, to testify in such legal proceedings as may be instituted against parties charged with molesting and killing" the emigrants. Forney acceded to Wilson's request and would personally care for the two boys for the next several months.

After leaving Salt Lake, the fifteen survivors and their company traveled east twelve miles before camping. Still concerned about their welfare, Forney rode out that evening to check on them. He felt "pleased to find all in fine spirits."[21]

Though fifteen of the surviving children were now on their way home, an anxious father kept up his long search for his missing son. Dr. Sidney B. Aden's son William had left his parents' house in St. Louis, Missouri, in the spring of 1857, striking out for the West. Around July 20 of that year, William reached South Pass, where he wrote his last letter home. William's letter said "he was going to spend the winter in *Provo*," his father wrote, where he "had engaged a job of *painting* scenery for a *theater*." William planned to go on to California the following spring.

In January 1859, Dr. Aden wrote Utah governor Alfred Cumming, saying he had news of William from Missouri ex-governor Lilburn W. Boggs, now in California. Boggs had learned that a Napa, California, merchant had dropped off William at Devil's Gate mail station, on the Sweetwater River in what was then part of Utah Territory.[22]

"Put yourself to a little trouble to ascertain the fate of my son," Aden begged Cumming, and "confer a lasting favor on anxious relatives, and afflicted parents, brothers & sisters." Aden acknowledged that his son may have "fallen by the hands of either Mormons or Indians," but he held out hope that his son "may yet live." Perhaps he "joined the Army & can't write," he conjectured, or "joined the Mormons & wont write."[23]

Sidney Aden also wrote Brigham Young, asking him to look into a "flying report" that William had "become a member of your Church." Aden described his son as "well grown, quite sprightly," and "pretty good looking." He was "a good Sign Painter" who "writes Poetry & sometimes Prose pretty well, makes a pretty good speech" and "picks the *Banjo* tolerably well." The father considered his missing son "one of the most injenius men of his age." He asked for Young's help. "By so doing," Aden pled, "you will confer a great favor upon a distressed family."[24]

Young soon responded that he had not "known either your son or his whereabouts, nor have I as yet found any one who has seen him or knows where he is." But he promised to send the distraught father any word he received.[25] The church president immediately ran a notice in the *Deseret News,* asking anyone with information to reply "to Pres. B. Young's office, or directly to Mr. S. B. Aden." Soon the *Valley Tan* began running a notice sent earlier, directing informants to William's brother Felen in St. Louis, who would reimburse expenses incurred in determining William's "whereabouts, or probable fate."[26]

In late March 1859, the Provo postmaster wrote Dr. Aden, saying that a William D. Roberts, an acquaintance of William Aden's from Provo, had just returned from a trip to California and "learned, by a man in one of the extreme Southern settlements, that a certain Indian is now wearing a peculiar buck skin coat, like one your son wore when he left here." Aden presumed from this news that his son "was either murdered or taken prisoner by the Indians."[27] Hanging onto hope for the latter possibility, he "published and scattered over Utah and California" an expanded notice, offering a thousand-dollar reward for delivering William, "if a prisoner, to Governor Cumming, of Utah, or Ex-Governor Boggs, of Napa Valley, California."[28]

Aden enclosed a copy of the circular in his letter back to Young. "Although I have great fears that he has been murdered," he wrote, "yet I have a hope, therefore, I have offered the reward; hoping it might elicit something in reference to him."[29]

Six weeks later, on July 12, Young wrote Aden again, this time with news about his missing son. "From all I can hear," he said, "I am induced to believe that he joined the emigrant company that was massacred at the Mountain Meadows. As all the reports that I have heard, or seen published, agree in the statement that none of that company were saved, except some sixteen very young children, it becomes my painful duty to inform you that, in case your son was in that company, I know of no reliably stated fact or even report upon which to ground the least hope that he is now alive."[30] Though Young's letter induced Aden to believe his son was murdered, the grieving father continued to hold out faint hope for the rest of his life.[31]

Though Dr. Aden's efforts to find his missing son proved futile, families of the long-absent surviving children were soon to be reunited with their loved ones. On July 4, 1859, the famed *New-York Tribune* editor Horace Greeley was traveling west on an overland tour when he encountered an eastbound train on the trail. "We met several wagonloads of come-outers from

Mormonism on their way to the states in the course of the afternoon," he wrote. In the company were "the children of the Arkansas people killed two years since, in what is known as the Mountain Meadows massacre."[32]

Eleven days later, a handcart company of Latter-day Saints was making its way west when it met "10 Wagons of returning Emigrants from the Valley," including the venerable "Sister Hardie," who "has charge of the children saved from the Mountain Meadow Massacre."[33]

When the children had been on the road for nearly a month, Commissioner Greenwood again wrote William C. Mitchell, the relative of many of the massacre victims who had led the efforts to retrieve them from Utah. Greenwood authorized him "to start upon the mission" to retrieve the children at Leavenworth. Knowing Mitchell's personal ties in the matter, Greenwood wrote, "I need not urge you to use all practical haste in setting out, as the children may reach that city" soon.[34]

Mitchell received Greenwood's letter on August 9 and set out for Leavenworth the next day "with a couple of two-horse wagons and a nurse." Eager to reach Leavenworth, Mitchell himself struck out on horseback ahead of the slower-moving wagons. Though his two sons and daughter-in-law had been massacred, he hoped his young grandson might be among the survivors.[35]

Mitchell arrived at the fort on August 22 and there received mistaken "intelligence from the department that the children were not expected at that point before the 1st or 5th September."[36] He may have turned back to find his wagons, for he was not at the fort when the children arrived on the morning of August 25.

Now stationed at Fort Leavenworth, a puzzled Stewart Van Vliet—the same man who was visiting Salt Lake City at the time of the massacre—telegraphed a message to the quartermaster general in Washington. "Fifteen Mountain Meadow children arrived this morning from Utah," he signaled. "No arrangements have been made and no one is here to receive them. What shall I do with them?"[37]

Fortunately, Mitchell's wagons arrived later that day. He "took charge of those children—five males and ten females," and telegraphed Greenwood in Washington that he had "received the children of Mountain Meadow massacre."[38] Mitchell found the children "comfortably clothed, in good health, and fine spirits."[39] He hired "an additional wagon and team for thirteen days," paid the Utah nurses, then escorted the children on their final leg home.[40]

On September 14, a Carroll County, Arkansas, resident reported that Mitchell had arrived home with the children and would "deliver them to their nearest relatives on to-morrow, at Carrolton. . . . It almost chills the blood in my veins to think of the horrible affair, and how those little fellows have suffered," said the anonymous writer, who had personally known many of the victims. The writer called on the government "to make ample provision for the education and raising of those children."[41]

On September 15, "a large concourse of the people of Carroll County assembled together in the Court House in Carrollton for the purpose of receiving the Mountain Meadow children who have just arrived under the charge of W. C. Mitchel." Colonel James Fancher "was called to the chair," and on a motion, "the children 15 in number were placed before the people on the President's stand; and Col. Mitchel pointed them out severally by name and parentage and gave the brief, but eventful and touching history of each child." He described how "the Mormons and Indians wantonly assailed" the emigrants and explained that two of the children had been retained in Salt Lake to give evidence in the case.[42]

The children were greeted "by old neighbors, friends and kinsfolk as though coming from the dead." People at the meeting later described it "as one of the most affecting spectacles ever known." Even decades later, they could hardly describe it "without shedding tears." According to those witnesses, "Some of the children were recognized by their relatives and claimed at once. Others could not be clearly identified, as they were so young."[43]

Mitchell thanked "the people of Carroll, Marion and Newton Counties, for their cooperation in arousing the attention of government to the forlo[rn] condition of said children while in captivity, and the terrible deed by which they were rendered orphans." Another man then led the group "in prayer and the offering of thanks and praises to God for the safe deliverance of said children, and their restoration to their relatives and friends."[44]

Though Mitchell had hoped his infant grandson had survived, each of the youngest boys was claimed by other families. His dashed hopes and the horseback journey to Leavenworth and back took a toll on the aging Mitchell's health. When he filed a brief report with Greenwood on October 4, he apologized that "protracted sickness which I have had, prevented me from making out my report at an earlier day."[45]

The three daughters of Jesse and Mary Dunlap—Rebecca, Louisa, and Sarah—soon went to live with their uncle, James D. Dunlap.[46] The three surviving children of George W. and Manerva Baker—Mary Elizabeth, Sarah

Frances, and William Twitty—went home with their grandmother, Mary Baker, widow of massacre victim John Twitty Baker.[47]

"The survivors found homes among kindred or the friends of their parents, and each one of them became an object of especial interest to all the people of the surrounding country," a journalist reported at a reunion of the survivors some forty years after the massacre. "The older children were talked to constantly for days about the massacre, and no doubt the little ones learned to believe some of the stories which fancy created where memory failed in trying to recall the details of the tragedy and its consequences."[48]

Shortly after the children's return, a committee that included relatives of the victims drafted resolutions memorializing "the success which has crowned the efforts of those who undertook to have reclaimed and restored to their native country and to their relations the little children that survived the mountain meadow massacre in Sept. 1857."

In the hearts of the relatives and friends of the victims, those whose "humane and philanthropic exertions" finally arrested "the attention of government" to do something about the case "saved these children from extreme wretchedness and ruin, and brought consolation to dear relations in Arkansas who were bowed in anguish and in fear." The resolutions particularly thanked Mitchell, Greenwood, Arkansas's two senators, and "Senator Guinn of California" for their "services rendered in discovering the place where said children were held in captivity and contributing to their releif and redemption." It also expressed "heartfelt thanks" to "Dr. Forney" and other "government agents for recapturing and delivering said children."

The resolutions "condole[d] with those of our fellow citizens, who mourn the loss of children and relation[s] who fell in the Mountain Meadow Massacre," and also "congratulate[d] some of those who thus mourn that these little children who survived said Massacre are here now restored to them and may be regarded as precious legacies from the departed ones."[49]

25

Unwilling to Rest Under the Stigma

East Coast and Utah, May–August 1859

In 1859 as the massacre survivors traveled north from southern Utah and then east to Arkansas, trouble over the territory again brewed in the nation's capital. Responding to Governor Cumming's earlier complaints about Judge Cradlebaugh's requisitioning of troops to assist him in his judicial duties, the *New York Daily Tribune* reported that Washington had instructed General Johnston "to hereafter wait the orders of the Governor before calling out the troops to act as a *posse comitatus* to assist the civil authorities."[1] Washington also revoked these rights from the U.S. district court judges and U.S. marshal. The government considered that "the prominent if not the only blame attached to [Cradlebaugh] is in calling on Gen. Johnston for troops."

Meanwhile, some of Utah's federal appointees shared their side of the story. "The Government dispatches and officers," the *New York Daily Tribune* reported a few days later, "state that Governor Cumming is as much under the influence of Brigham Young as any Mormon in Utah."[2] For his part, Cumming urged Young to prepare to go to court.[3]

Young responded in a May 12 filing in the probate court for Salt Lake County. His affidavit declared "that on or about the time between" September 9 and 30, 1857, a company of California-bound emigrants "were, as he was informed, attacked by a party of armed men, and by them murdered in the region of Country known as the Mountain Meadows." Because of "the disturbed state of affairs in this Territory during the fall and winter subsequent to the aforesaid murder," Young's affidavit related, "no court, to the knowledge of deponent was held in the County or Judicial District in which said murder was said to have been committed," and early the following spring he was succeeded as governor by Cumming and as superintendent of Indian Affairs by Jacob Forney.

Young noted that Cradlebaugh's grand jury speeches had "directly charged" him "with interfering with the courts of Justice, and preventing the punishment of offenders, thereby charging him as being accessory after the fact, to the murder aforesaid and other crimes," and "indirectly" charged him "with instigating the committal of the murder," thus "being accessory before the fact."

"Owing to the aforesaid charges having been made and published to the world by men in high authority, doubtless thereby acquiring more or less credence, and feeling unwilling to rest under the stigma of such infamous charges and accusations," Young in his affidavit requested "the privilege of a fair and impartial investigation and trial and the rendition of a Just Verdict on the Judgment of his peers."[4]

Upon receiving the affidavit, county probate judge Elias Smith, a Latter-day Saint, issued a warrant to arrest Young until the matter could be investigated and "dealt with according to law." The next day, county sheriff Robert T. Burton returned the warrant to the judge, reporting he had arrested Young and had him in "custody subject to the Court."[5] Young's submission shifted the burden to his accusers to prove their accusations and removed their purported need to use the military to make arrests.[6]

Young also encouraged others implicated in the massacre to stand trial. On May 25, 1859, five days after word of Washington's reprimand of Cradlebaugh reached Salt Lake, a clerk recorded Young's telling George A. Smith that "so soon as the present excitement subsided, and the Army could be kept from interferring with the Judiciary, he intended to have all the charges investigated that Judge Cradlebaugh has made such a stink about. And he would try to get the Governor & Dist. Atty. to go to Washington County, and manage the investigation of the Mountain Meadow Massacre, themselves."[7]

Six years later, Young recounted, "I told Governor Cumming that if he would take an unprejudiced judge into the district where that horrid affair occurred, I would pledge myself that every man in the regions round about should be forthcoming when called for, to be condemned or acquitted as an impartial, unprejudiced judge and jury should decide; and I pledged him that the court should be protected from any violence or hindrance in the prosecution of the laws; and if any were guilty of the blood of those who suffered in the Mountain Meadow massacre, let them suffer the penalty of the law."[8]

In late May 1859, the letter from Washington clarifying Governor Cumming's authority over the military reached Camp Floyd. As the *New York Daily Tribune* had reported, Secretary of War Floyd wrote General Johnston, "You will therefore only order the troops under your command to assist as a posse comitatus in the execution of the laws, upon the written application of the Governor of the Territory, and not otherwise. . . . The fidelity with which you have obeyed the instructions of this Department heretofore given you, is the fullest guarantee that you will with the same zeal and efficiency conform to these."[9]

General Johnston directed Captain Reuben Campbell to return to Camp Floyd from southern Utah with "all the troops in his command," as "the objects of the expedition were accomplished." Johnston's orders came just as Judge Cradlebaugh was making major progress in his southern Utah investigation. Though Cradlebaugh was not subject to the military order, he believed that without soldiers to protect witnesses and make arrests, it was "useless to attempt to hold a court." He and Deputy William Rogers left Cedar City for Camp Floyd with Campbell's command.[10]

The men returning to Camp Floyd did not know they were about to have a close encounter with the chief suspects they had been trying to arrest for weeks. Since the troops had arrived in southern Utah in early May, Isaac Haight's sparse journal recorded that he, John M. Higbee, William Stewart, and others were hiding in a mountain camp "where quite a number of Breathren who were prescribed by our enemies had fled for safety." There they stayed "untill the last of the month."[11]

Hearing that Captain Campbell's men had passed north of where they were hiding, Haight and his companions—assuming the road to be clear—decided "to get in the rear of the hounds" and started south for home. But as Haight recounted in his journal, when they reached the road they were accosted by a "sentinel and taken into a camp of the troops and compelled to remain until Daylight." Campbell's command had lost horses when eight or ten soldiers deserted, taking their mounts with them. The soldiers merely wanted to examine the Mormon men's animals to see if any were the stolen horses.[12]

Though the captured men were not the horse thieves the soldiers sought, Haight and his companions suddenly found themselves in what he called "the tightest place that ever he had been in." However nervous the arrested men felt, they managed to keep their cover. "I have certainly seen you before," remarked some of the men in camp when the detainees arrived. "Quite likely," William Stewart lied coolly, "we live in Provo City and are in pursuit of stolen horses, and are losing time every moment you detain us."[13]

Despite Stewart's ploy, the soldiers kept the men overnight. "After Daylight," Haight wrote, "they Examined our Horses and found them all right and let us go on our way." Haight and his men were "right glad . . . to get away from there as some of our bitterest Enemies were in the camp among which was Judge Cradlebaugh." Haight claimed it was a miracle from God. "Their Eyes were blinded so they did not know us although some of them had seen us at Cedar City[.] We felt that the Lord had delivered us from their grasp."[14]

Happy to be free, the four men continued south. On June 3, they "returned to Cedar City from their hiding places." Two days later, John D. Lee recorded their return in his journal.[15]

With Judge Cradlebaugh and Captain Campbell's men on their way back north, and Major James Henry Carleton's return to California, Lee and others rejoiced at their success in eluding their would-be captors. On May 28, Lee wrote, "Moquetas, chief, and a number of Indians came in search of me at dawn, 5 mi. from home. They felt warm and greeted me with a cordial welcome. Related the bribes that had been offered them by Cradlebaugh for my head. $5,000.00 reward, a considerable reward for a man that is endeavoring to obey the gospel requirements." Lee presented the Indians with ammunition and other gifts over the next few days.

Lee also wrote that he "received a letter from a friend informing me that Cradlebaugh has offered a reward of $5,000.00 for my person or head, and that he intended to make an example of Haight, Higbee, [Klingen]Smith and Lee." Of those willing to turn him in, Lee felt that "the spirit of apostasy is so appalling I scarcely know in whom to confide save God, the arm that cannot be broken."[16]

On June 1, Marion Shelton, Jacob and Rachel Hamblin, and the seventeenth child survivor of the massacre arrived in Salt Lake. There, Shelton "met br G. A. Smith and took supper with him then went with him to Pres. B. Youngs and remained until bed time." Over the next few days, Shelton enjoyed himself in the territorial capital, where his knowledge of recent events in the south made him a subject of curiosity among those interested in the motives of the officers and soldiers who went south. Shelton provided information that fueled their interest.[17]

On June 3, he testified by affidavit that "Enos, an Indian freebooter, . . . said that he had been offered, by the U S. Officers, money, blankets, shirts, drawers, and other goods . . . valued at about one thousand dollars, for the head of John D. Lee."[18] Shelton reported to the Historian's Office "that he traveled part of the way with Judge Cradlebaugh's escort" and that Carleton had disinterred from shallow graves "the bones of the emigrants, massacred at Mountain

Meadows, and buried them in one hole and built a monument over them of rough stones, fifteen feet high."[19]

For his part, Jacob Hamblin reported to Indian Affairs superintendent Jacob Forney.[20] Two days later, on June 18, he and George A. Smith "had an interview with Prest. Young." Hamblin undoubtedly told Young what he had learned at Pocketville. A clerk recorded that Young "told Br. Hamblin that as soon as a Court of Justice could be held, so that men could be heard without the influence of the military he should advise men accused to come forward and demand trial on the charges preferred against them for the Mountain Meadow massacre."[21]

The next day, George A. Smith wrote William Dame. He told Dame that the *New York Herald* had been "publishing a great many letters from this Office, we think they are rowsers." One of the letters was Smith's April 15 missive written from southern Utah, "making a defense of the Mt. Meadow charges." Smith thought "it was a good one."

Smith's April "defense" had discounted charges of white participation as mere persecution. Having met with Young and Hamblin, however, Smith seemed to take the charges more seriously. Still, he thought it a mistake that southern Utah men had fled from Cradlebaugh and the soldiers. Smith wrote, "I think the boys missed it in not securing the services of good lawyers, & paying them enough to enable them to follow the track." Smith wrote that "some day the charges will have to be investigated & the charges are of to[o] grave a character to be fooled with, a long and carefull legal preparation is necessary."

When such a trial might occur Smith did not know. He felt "it may be years before the blood thirsty rage for Mormon blood will be so abated as to render the existence of an impartial tribunal possible & it may be sooner." Regardless, Smith recommended, "If I was personaly concerned, I would be willing to pay a thousand dollars of the best property I have, to secure the services of competent Attorneys & have them preparing for the general issue which I would plead at the proper time."[22]

On July 5, Young discussed "reaction to the Mountain Meadow Massacre" with Smith, Albert Carrington, and James Ferguson. Young noted that District Attorney Alexander Wilson had called "to consult with him about making some arrests of parties accused of being engaged in that offense."[23] Young soon sent Smith and apostle Amasa Lyman south to urge those accused of the crime to prepare for trial and to try to put down crime in the settlements.[24]

Preaching in local towns as they traveled south, Lyman condemned "various notions and opinions which were our principle evils." He charged that some had distorted church doctrine, resulting in "delusion." He "refered to the eagerness of some to avenge the blood of inocence and that with too much Zeal, so that they delight in blood."

Repeating the main theme of his southern Utah tour a few weeks earlier, and reflecting racial prejudices, he urged the people to "not shed blood with the Spirit of Indians." He asked, "How was the blood of inocent to be avenged"? He answered, "We were not now in circumstances to accomplish this." The Saints were not to be "the ministers of death; it was only a Barbarians Spirit to have blood for blood." He denounced the notion "that one wrong repayed another."

Yes, "God designed that *all* the righteous that ever had been killed should be avenged," he said, but not "blood for blood." Instead, "the blood of the inocent was to be avenged by the righteous continueing righteous." If any Latter-day Saints "suppose the kingdom is to be built up by sheding blood," Lyman chided, they "were mistaken tho some that had great taste for sheding blood might have gratification; but they never would gain Salvation by such a Course; the best way to avenge the blood of the Prophets was to take a course to diminish the power of the Devil; . . . we had to wait as others had done, for the blood of the inocent to be avenged."

Lyman also condemned the "consecrateing of Gentile property." Though he said scriptures proclaimed that the righteous would inherit the property of the wicked, "this would be done when God placed the world into the hands of the Saints; and not by a Mormon stealing. . . . The Wicked was sometime swept off to make room for the righteous, but yet blood did not build up the kingdom; but the progress of 'the *pure in heart*'; we had to cultivate virtue and love for each; God wishes to save not to distroy his workmanship; he would fight our battles; we had to avenge the blood of the Prophets by casting the Devil from our fire sides and subdue every ill feeling."[25]

When Smith and Lyman reached Toquerville, they were visited by "A. J. Stratton . . . from Virgin City," the place where Jacob Hamblin had learned that participation in the massacre by local whites was far more extensive than he had imagined.[26]

The following Sunday, Smith and Lyman shook up the leadership of the church in Cedar City. According to Lee, who was not present, George A. Smith "returned to cerder, called a conference, disorganized the Stake, droped the presant Bishop P. K. Smith, Pres. I. C. Haight, Higbee & Mor[ri] ss."[27] The roles formerly played by the stake leaders and bishop were merged in Henry Lunt, assisted by two counselors. Lunt was returning to Salt Lake from England at the time of the massacre and unquestionably did not partic-ipate in it.[28]

Cedar City's plummeting population "was undoubtedly a contributing factor in the decision to combine normally separate offices into one."[29] Yet the massacre was also a factor.[30] Haight wrote in his journal that "in conse-quence of the persecution of our enemies I solicited to be released from the presidency of this Stake as my Enemies Swore they would destroy me if they could get me and there was little prospect of my being at home much for a time to come, to attend to the duties of my office, accordingly the organiza-tion of the Stake was suspended for the present."[31]

Lunt's version of events was that Smith stood up at the meeting and announced, "President [Young] has instructed me to come and disorganize this Stake of Zion and to make a Bishop and President out of one man and I nominate brother Henry Lunt as that man."[32]

The next day, after Smith and Lyman had moved northward, Klingensmith wrote a letter to Smith requesting that he and Hosea Stout defend him in forthcoming "proceedings . . . against me in a case of alleged murder at the Mountain Meadows in this neighborhood in Sept[r]. 1857."[33]

A few days later, Lyman traveled to Harmony and sent for Lee. "I came & had an interview with him upon Special business," Lee wrote. "Adressed a line to G. A. Smith & H. Stout, Lawers to defend my case, providd I should be arrested & brought before the Destrict court upon the charge of aiding in the Massacre at the Meadows." Lee maintained that "although I am innocent of the crime, yet I am compelld to employ council in to dirrect the case in the prope[r] channel."

Though proclaiming his innocence, Lee began to worry that the proceed-ings would turn against him. Soon after his interview with Lyman, he awoke one morning troubled by "visions of my Head through the past Night as well as that of My Family." Concluding that the dreams were "ominous of Evil plotting against me," he decided to go southward to "be out of the way."[34]

26

The Course Adopted Will Not
Prove Successful

Utah; Washington, DC; Arkansas, June–August 1859

When Captain Reuben Campbell and his party returned to Camp Floyd in early June 1859, they brought with them ghastly accounts and evidence from the Mountain Meadows. Captain John Phelps wrote of bones, fragments of female clothing, and locks of hair brought back by army doctor Charles Brewer. "Saw two skulls today from the scene of the Mountain Meadow Massacre," Phelps wrote. "One of them was shot through," the ball entering "the back part of the head and coming out near the right temple." The other skull "had two gashes on the top as if from a sharp knife." Both skulls "were of young persons."[1]

Judge John Cradlebaugh found a letter waiting for him from U.S. Attorney General Jeremiah Black, censuring him for his Provo court actions in March. "When we consider how essentially peaceable is the whole spirit of our judicial system," Black chided, and how it operates "by the arm of civil power, it can hardly be denied that the employment of military troops about the courts should be avoided."

Black did not absolve criminals. "It is very probable that the Mormon inhabitants of Utah have been guilty of crimes," he said, "for which they deserve the severest punishment." But he made it clear to Cradlebaugh that it was the district attorney's responsibility—not the judges'—to prosecute criminals.[2]

Black wrote Alexander Wilson on the same day he wrote Cradlebaugh, urging the district attorney to "carry on all public prosecutions," while "opposing every effort which any judge may make to usurp your functions." Black believed that if the judges "insist upon doing the duties of prosecuting attorney and marshal as well as their own, everything will be thrown into confusion, and the peace of the Territory may be destroyed."

Focusing on the massacre, Black called the crime "one of the most atrocious" in human history. He acknowledged that "the Mormons blame it upon the Indians," while a federal judge and others "declare their unhesitating belief that the Mormons themselves committed this foul murder." He directed Wilson to not "let any opportunity escape you of learning all that can be known upon this subject."[3]

Reacting to Black's censure, Cradlebaugh immediately wrote President Buchanan, expressing regret "that there is not more coincidence of view and harmony of action" between Utah's federal judges and Governor Alfred Cumming. Warrants for forty of the "eighty or more white men" engaged in the massacre, all forty of whom held "high civil & church offices," he alleged, were "now in the hands" of U.S. Marshal P. K. Dotson.[4] Cradlebaugh told Buchanan that while he hoped these suspects might somehow be brought to trial, Dotson had no plans to arrest them. In explanation, he enclosed a letter Dotson wrote him that same day.[5] Someone also sent a copy of the missive to the *San Francisco Evening Bulletin*, which soon published it.

Dotson's letter acknowledged receipt of arrest warrants for Lee, Higbee, Haight, "and thirty-six others" for the Mountain Meadows murders but expressed regret that "it is not in my power to execute any of these processes." Though he had not tried to arrest massacre suspects, Dotson said, he believed any attempts would be futile, as shown by his prior attempts to arrest suspects of other crimes, which failed because the suspects' communities shielded them. Six months earlier, Dotson added, he had requested Governor Cumming's permission for a military posse to help arrest these Utah Valley murder suspects, but Cumming declined. "I therefore do not feel warranted," Dotson wrote, "in again troubling his Excellency with another application."[6]

Attorney General Black's critical letter to Cradlebaugh also angered others at Camp Floyd. "Instead of breaking up this nest of thugs" in Utah, Captain Phelps objected, "our government seems to be cherishing them."[7] Another Camp Floyd writer described the "Mormon swine" as "ungodly, beastly and irreligious fanatics, a people semibarbarous." The anonymous writer praised Cradlebaugh while calling Cumming "a puppet" and "a mere cipher in the hands of Brigham Young." The letter, published in the *Fayetteville Arkansian*, called for "a Military Government" in Utah with "a man of nerve at [its] head, with power to declare martial law and try, by a drum head court, all offenders."[8]

Adding to the gridlock was Judge Delana Eckels's late June return to Utah and Camp Floyd from a lobbying trip he had taken to the east.[9] "Judge Eckels has returned," Captain Phelps documented, "not so much as a judge as a politician. He has arranged every thing for the election of General Johns[t]on to the presidency in 1860." Phelps explained that Eckels planned to use national animosity against the Mormons as a tool to win support for the general, whose troops were then occupying Utah. Eckles "considers this dirty Mormonism a hobby large enough to ride into the presidency upon," Phelps wrote. "Who would ever have thought that a set of murderers, whores and thieves would become the instruments for making a president? They are preserved for that purpose as carefully as a carpenter preserves his tools."[10]

Independent of the designs at Camp Floyd, District Attorney Wilson, Governor Cumming, and Utah superintendent of Indian Affairs Jacob Forney kept up their efforts to prosecute the massacre perpetrators. U.S. Commissioner of Indian Affairs and Arkansas congressman A. B. Greenwood—long an advocate of obtaining justice in the Mountain Meadows case—urged Forney to "make every effort consistent with your position and official duties to discover those persons who were actually engaged in, or accessory to it," not knowing Forney had already done that.[11] Greenwood also sent Wilson a copy of the letter, requesting he do all he could to assist Forney.[12]

Even before receiving Greenwood's letter, Wilson called on Brigham Young, seeking his help in "making some arrests of parties accused of being engaged in" the massacre. As recorded that day in the Historian's Office Journal, Young responded "that if the judges would open a court at Parowan or some other convenient location in the south, and would go there and hold a court, unprejudiced and uninfluenced by the presence of the army, so that men could have a fair and impartial trial He would go there himself, and he presumed that Gov. Cumming would also."

If these circumstances were met, Young promised Wilson "he would use all his influence to have the parties arrested and have the whole matter investigated thoroughly and impartially and justice meeted out to every man." But if a military posse were to be used "to arrest men to be treated like dogs and dragged about by the army, and confined and abused by them as has been the case here to fore," Young said, he would not use his influence or "crook his finger to arrest any person." Instead, the judges and military "must hunt them up themselves." Wilson agreed that "he did not consider it fair to drag men and their witnesses 200 or 300 miles to trial."[13]

Instead of working with Cumming, Forney, Wilson, and Young to see the massacre prosecuted, Utah's federally appointed judges made them subjects of a negative letter-writing campaign. In mid-July Judges Cradlebaugh and Sinclair fired off another letter to President Buchanan, declaring that Wilson "is not our teacher; appeals from our judgment do not go to him; nor is he our trier or impeacher." They also accused Wilson of indolence and conflict of interest. "His relations with the Mormons have been so objectionably manifested by his acts that he has lost our confidence in his willingness and ability to discharge properly and firmly the duties of a public prosecutor in this Territory." Nor were they willing to work with Cumming or Young, they said, because that would mean consorting with the enemy.[14]

In spite of the urging of Wilson, Cumming, and Forney to hold court in southern Utah near the massacre site—and Young's promise to help bring in suspects and witnesses if they did—Judge Eckels decided to hold court in Nephi, a relatively short distance from Camp Floyd but a long distance from key witnesses, suspects, and evidence of the massacre.[15]

Forney made clear his concerns to Greenwood. "The course adopted for the legal investigation of this matter will not prove successful at the contemplated court" because of its "great distance from where the really guilty and witnesses are living," Forney wrote. "Nephi is two hundred miles from Cedar City," where "nearly all the perp[e]trators and witnesses reside." It would be "very difficult indeed almost impossible, to bring all the parties to Nephi," he said. "Cedar City is the proper place to hold a court to successfully try those concerned in the Mountain Meadow affair. I suggested to Judge Eckels, indeed urged the propriety of going to Cedar City with his court. He seemed determined not to do so."[16]

Compounding the geographical roadblock was Dotson's refusal to attempt the arrest of massacre suspects without a military posse. Preparing for Eckels's court, Wilson asked Dotson if he had made any arrests on the forty warrants Judge Cradlebaugh had given him, "and if not, state whether you can make said arrests, and have the parties named in said warrants before the district court" at Nephi. But Wilson "received no reply" nor "answer of any kind whatever."[17]

Frustrated, Wilson and Cumming suggested that U.S. Marshal Dotson assign the arrest warrants to territorial marshal John Kay, a Mormon who "had a knowledge of the country and of the people, and expressed a determination, if legally deputized, to make arrests." With Young's promise to help if the military wasn't involved, Kay stood a good chance of apprehending them. Dotson, however, "declined to appoint Kay his deputy, on the ground that he was a Morm[o]n."[18]

Wilson asked Eckels to intervene with Dotson, but the judge refused, calling Kay "a notorious Mormon." To Eckels, accepting the church's help meant acknowledging its power. "I never will acknowledge," he wrote to Secretary of State Lewis Cass, "a power over the law and above the law."[19]

Governor Cumming protested to Cass that he had wanted Kay deputized because, as "the *territorial marshal*," he could "receive these writs from marshal Dotson, who had declined to serve them, unless accompanied by a military posse." Cumming reasoned, "I could perceive no material difference between the arrest and delivery of criminals by one person rather than another—whether Mormon or Gentile."[20]

In spite of these obstructions, Wilson did what he could to gather evidence. Forney provided him with "names his investigation led him to believe were guilty of the massacre," including Isaac Haight, John D. Lee, Philip Klingensmith, John M. Higbee, David Tullis, and Carl Shirts. Forney also listed Jacob and Rachel Hamblin as witnesses who could testify against key participants.[21]

Forney detailed the findings of his investigations to Greenwood about the same time he shared them with Wilson. "From various sources during the last twelve months, I am enabled to give you a reliable account of the emigrant company," he wrote, "and also some of the causes and circumstances of the inhuman massacre." Forney recounted the events leading up to the massacre and cleared the emigrant families of the charges Lee and some others had made against them.

"From the evidence in my possession," he concluded, "I am justified in the declaration that this massacre was concocted by white men and consummated by whites and Indians. The names of many of the whites engaged in this terrible affair have already been given to the proper legal authorities. I will in due time take the necessary steps for the recovery of the property, which was sold and divided among certain parties."[22]

Since May, Wilson had battled the serious tick-borne illness known as Mountain Fever. On August 18, he was well enough to dismiss, consistent with direction from Washington, "two indictments charging Brigham Young and others with treason" during the Utah War, indictments handed down by Eckels's grand juries at Camp Scott but rendered moot by Buchanan's pardon.[23]

But too ill to attend Eckels's court in Nephi, Wilson asked Stephen DeWolfe "to accept the appointment of deputy United States attorney for that court."[24] DeWolfe practiced law in Lexington, Missouri, before moving to Salt Lake in 1859 as agent and counsel for the freighting firm of Russell, Majors & Waddell. He would become well known for his efforts to expose the Mountain Meadows Massacre in the pages of the *Valley Tan* newspaper.[25] DeWolfe accepted the appointment.[26]

Wilson then directed Forney to furnish "DeWolfe with all the *evidence* you may have in your possession, or under your command, or within your knowledge, in relation to the Mountain Meadow massacre." Wilson also asked Forney to provide his personal testimony at the Nephi court.[27]

Having put the case and evidence into the hands of someone he felt would prosecute it well, the ailing Wilson planned to return home to the east. Not only were his health and finances poor, but his wife's health was also declining.[28] They left the territory on September 20.[29]

For his court, Judge Eckels assembled most of his grand jurors from Camp Floyd in Cedar County, claiming citizens of Nephi's Utah County had fled before his arrival.[30] Although some had fled, Utah County included the highly populated Provo, where jurors could easily have been obtained.[31] Eckels enjoyed another advantage over Cradlebaugh's earlier court—the choice of prosecutors. If Cradlebaugh considered Wilson to be soft on the Saints, the federal judges could not make the same charge of DeWolfe.[32] Despite having Forney's substantial evidence, Young's offer to help bring in suspects and witnesses, and a prosecutor and grand jury demonstrably unsympathetic to Mormons, Eckels's court did not attempt to indict a single massacre suspect.[33]

"Nothing has yet been done before the grand jury in regard to the Mountain Meadow massacre," DeWolfe explained in a letter to Wilson. "I presume, none of the witnesses in regard to it, are here, and I have called for no subp[o]enas against any of them," thinking it "altogether foolish and useless to institute any investigation into the matter, unless it could be gone into fully and thoroughly." DeWolfe thought this was "impossible to do at the present term of this court, with all the witnesses so far away, and the difficulty, if not impossibility, of bringing them before the court in any reasonable time."[34]

Wilson was disappointed but not surprised. He had feared it would not result in massacre indictments because it was "some 260 miles distant from the Mountain Meadow." Even after leaving Utah, he continued to urge Washington to adopt his previous proposal to hold court in Cedar City, which he believed "to be the only practicable way of thoroughly and successfully investigating and trying this horrible case."[35]

After the failed court, a devastated Forney wrote his superior Greenwood again, complaining that some federal appointees talked loudly about the horror of the massacre yet undermined efforts to bring the killers to justice. "I gave several months ago to the Attorney General and several of the United States judges the names of those who I believed were not only implicated, but the hell-deserving scoundrels who concocted and brought to a successful termination the whole affair," Forney lamented. Those "most guilty," he believed, were Haight, Klingensmith, Lee, Higbee, "Bishop Davis," David Tullis, and Ira Hatch. "These were the cause of the massacre," he charged, "aided by others."

Regretting "that nothing has yet been accomplished towards bringing these murderers to justice," he complained to Greenwood that "no well-directed effort has been made to catch them."

Most exasperating to Forney was the judges' refusal of Latter-day Saint cooperation in bringing suspects to trial. "Certain parties here who talk loudest did not make a proper effort to bring to trial the Mountain Meadow offenders," he wrote, "by refusing to hold court within a reasonable distance of the parties and witnesses; said court refused to accept the services of the territorial marshal who proposed to apprehend the supposed guilty, and refused fifteen hundred dollars, which were offered by Hon. William H. Hooper, delegate to Congress from Utah, to aid in defraying the expenses; and I had the assurance of several leading Mormons that the supposed guilty should be arrested, and I had no reason to doubt their sincerity."[36]

"I fear, and I regret to say it," Forney told Greenwood, "that with certain parties here there is a greater anxiety to connect B. Young and other church dignitaries with every criminal offense, than diligently endeavor to punish the actual perpetrators of crime."[37] Like Cradlebaugh, Eckels succeeded in gaining notoriety for his court but did little to achieve justice. "The prospect appears utterly hopeless of the courts accomplishing any thing worth speaking of, touching the administration of justice," wrote a Latter-day Saint observer.[38]

Forney also had eyewitnesses to the crime whose testimony was not used in court: two of the oldest massacre survivors, John Calvin Miller and Milum Tackett, whom he had kept in Salt Lake at Wilson's request so they could testify.[39] Newspaper editor Horace Greeley, who visited Salt Lake while the boys were there, wrote that they "distinctly remember that their parents surrendered to white men, and that these white men at best did not attempt to prevent their perfidious massacre. These children, moreover, were all found in the possession of Mormons—not one of them in the hands of Indians; and, though the Mormons say they ransomed them from the hands of Indians, the children deny it, saying that they never lived with, nor were in the keeping of savages; and the Indians bear concurrent testimony."[40]

Despite hopes that the boys might testify in a Utah trial, the prosecution's floundering in Eckels's court led Forney to make a new plan.[41] He headed for the nation's capital with the boys in hopes of seeking justice there. Greenwood telegraphed him to hurry to Washington "as there is an opportunity of sending them to Arkansas at a small expense, if brought at once." Besides hearing the boys' testimony, Greenwood was eager to return them to their anxious relatives in Arkansas. Forney and the boys reached Washington on December 12.[42]

Meanwhile, George A. Smith urged massacre suspects to prepare for the possibility of a future trial. "My feelings are of the best kind towards you," Smith assured Isaac Haight on November 6. "I appreciate your unpleasant position in consequence of the persecution, that the enemies of all righteousness have waged against you, and shall ever be ready to render you any aid that may be within my reach to enable you to repel the vile and unfounded charges alledged against you by Judge Cradlebaugh."

Smith shared with Haight his belief that the anti-Mormon "clique" was pressuring the White House "to secure a military government for the Mormons." To do this, "they have avoided an investigation by the Judiciary, of the charges against you and others, as it would dispell the phantom." By claiming, "We cannot do any thing," they hoped to receive "extraordinary powers" over Utah. "Not knowing what instructions may come to the Army," Smith urged the accused to make "arrangements for defence and should military despotism not succeed be prepared [f]or the first opportunity to exon[e]rate themselves, before an impartial tribunal."[43]

Despite Forney's efforts to drum up support in Washington for a massacre prosecution, his arrival there with the two survivors proved ill-timed. As Utah territorial delegate Hooper wrote Young on December 7, "The late difficulties at Harper's Ferry"—a precursor to the Civil War—"and the feelings growing out of them, had completely overshadowed Utah and her difficulties."[44]

Eager to return the two boys to relatives in Arkansas after their long stay in Utah, Greenwood arranged for them "to be conveyed to Carrollton and delivered to W. C. Mitchell, Esq., to be delivered to their relations."

They finally reached Carrolton in January 1860.[45] There they were "examined by the government authorities" and adjudged "too young to be used as legal witnesses"—just as the massacre perpetrators had expected they would be when they spared their lives.[46]

PART 5
INTERLUDE

27

Vengeance Is Mine

Southern States and Utah, 1860-62

On November 7, 1860, South Carolinians poured into the streets of Charleston for a torchlight parade. The procession featured an effigy of a man hung from a scaffold and set afire. Cheers erupted as the flames licked at the placard the effigy held in its hands: "Abe Lincoln, First President Northern Confederacy." The violent display was a reaction to the Republican president's election the day before.[1]

Southern states had threatened secession if the anti-slavery Republican Party won the presidency, and they soon showed they meant it. In December, South Carolina delegates voted to secede. "The United States . . . are bound to be destroyed," Brigham Young reacted. "Those things which [they] wished to bring Upon us shall come upon them." By February, six more states followed South Carolina's lead—Mississippi, Georgia, Florida, Alabama, Louisiana, and Texas—in what was called the "Great Secession Winter."[2]

"There is no more a United States," Young declared in his Sunday address on February 10. James Buchanan, still the president, "is not so prompt now as he was three years ago, when he sent troops to Utah" based on reports of a Mormon rebellion. But when "South Carolina comes out and boldly declares her secession from the compact of States, and takes possession of all the public property within her borders, except Fort Sumter," Young said, Buchanan's response was only, "Do not infringe upon them: they have the right to do this."

Young preached that it made no difference what Buchanan or incoming president Lincoln did. "God has come out of his hiding-place," he said, "and has commenced to vex the nation that has rejected us," never to unite again, while " 'Mormonism' will live, and God will promote it."[3]

In 1857, Latter-day Saints feared that the "scene of blood" prophesied by Joseph Smith referred to the coming of U.S. troops to Utah. Now, they believed it meant the conflict brewing in the states. "I have heard Joseph say," Young remembered, " 'You will see the sorrows and misery of the world and the misery that will be upon this land, until you will turn away and pray that your eyes may not be obliged to look upon it.' Said he, 'There are men [here] that will live to see the affliction that will come upon this nation.' "[4]

The nation was catapulted into civil war in April 1861 after Confederate troops attacked Fort Sumter—the last federal stronghold in South Carolina.[5] Captain Henry Heth, who commanded troops in Provo during Judge Cradlebaugh's court, painfully resigned his commission on April 18, the day after his home state of Virginia seceded. He headed east from Camp Floyd in Colonel Edmund Alexander's conveyance to "cast his lot with Virginia."[6]

Like Heth, others who marched to Utah to put down a "rebellion" became soldiers in "the Great Rebellion." The next time Heth met his regiment and company in the East, they were the enemy. Heth's fellow Tenth Infantry captain during the Utah War, Jesse Gove, became a Union colonel. Though Heth would live to witness the Confederacy's final surrender at Appomattox Courthouse, Gove died in battle in Virginia a year into the war.[7] Not long before Gove's death, General Albert Sidney Johnston, beloved by both Northern and Southern men at Camp Floyd, was mortally wounded while commanding Confederate troops at Tennessee's bloody Battle of Shiloh.[8]

Utah governor Alfred Cumming and his wife, Elizabeth, left Utah near the end of his term in May 1861. A Georgian, Cumming knew Lincoln would not reappoint him. Within weeks of Cumming's departure, the last states to join the Confederacy seceded—Arkansas, North Carolina, and Tennessee.[9]

As the conflict heated up, Latter-day Saints came to view their earlier expulsion from the United States with gratitude. "I rejoice that we are at peace and not obliged to fortify Great Salt Lake City, as the people are obliged to do in Washington," Wilford Woodruff preached. "We are safe." Isaac Haight wrote that "while war and Commotion is abroad in the Land and the wicked are Slaying the Wicked according to the Revelations of the Lord[,] the Saints are Enjoying the Blessings of peace and prosperity in the vallies of the mountains."[10] The Civil War certainly brought a season of peace to massacre perpetrators like Haight. With Washington absorbed in a deadly national conflict, federal officials' attention was diverted from the Utah crime.

With most of the U.S. troops now gone, Young felt secure enough to venture from Salt Lake again. On May 15, a group of sixty men, women, and children, including Woodruff, climbed into twenty-three carriages and left for a preaching tour of Utah's southern settlements. Young often made a spring-time excursion after his people began settling southern Utah. But this trip was different—it was the first time he ventured that far south since the army occupied the territory in 1858, and this time he would assess the status of southern Utah's cotton industry. With the war's onset, he knew that access to southern cotton would likely cease.[11]

Along the way, Young preached in American Fork, Springville, Nephi, Round Valley, Fillmore, Beaver, Parowan, Cedar City, and Pinto, the village just northeast of the Mountain Meadows.[12] When the travelers prepared to head south to Santa Clara on the morning of May 25, Woodruff pulled on his great coat and mittens, noting that Pinto Creek was still thick with ice.

After the group traveled a few miles through the Meadows, a landmark appeared on the horizon. It was Major Carleton's stone cairn, standing "about 12 feet high, but beginning to tumble down," Woodruff wrote in his diary. "A wooden Cross was placed on top." As the entourage watered their horses at the nearby spring, Young and others climbed from their carriages to visit "the Mountain Meadow Monument put up at the burial place of 120 persons killed by Indians in 1857," Woodruff recorded.[13]

Woodruff described the inscriptions chiseled into the two stone slabs that lay against either side of the cairn's base. The one on the north read, "120 Men, women, & Children, Murdered in Cold Blood Early in Sept 1857 From Arkansaw," he wrote. The one on the south declared, "Erected by Company K 1st Dragoons May 1859." The visitors also looked up to read the biblical inscription on the north-facing side of the cedar cross's horizontal plank: "Vengence is mine and I will repay saith the Lord." After reading the statement, Woodruff recorded, "Prest Young said it should be Vengence is mine and I have taken a little."[14]

When Lee reported the atrocity as an Indian massacre to Young in late September 1857, he claimed the emigrants "belonged to the mob in Missouri & Illinois." He said they had done "all the evil they Could," and had "poisoned Beef & gave it to the Indians & some of them died. They poisoned the springs of water several of the saints died."[15] Now this demonized view of the emigrants echoed in Young's words. If the emigrants had committed the crimes that Lee and others claimed, then in Young's view, God had taken vengeance on them, as promised by the biblical scripture.[16]

According to Woodruff's May 25 journal entry, after watering their horses and visiting the monument, Young's group continued south. Nearly a century later, in her book *The Mountain Meadows Massacre*, Juanita Brooks recorded a story passed down in her family. She wrote that her father and uncles said they had heard their father, massacre participant Dudley Leavitt, say that after Young made his statement about vengeance, "He didn't say another word. He didn't give an order. He just lifted his right arm to the square, and in five minutes there wasn't one stone left upon another. He didn't have to tell us what he wanted done. We understood."[17]

Contemporaneous and early descriptions of the visit do not support this Leavitt family lore. Though the monument was later destroyed, none of the eyewitness accounts—from Woodruff, Parowan resident Calvin Pendleton, and George D. Watt (later writing as an excommunicated Mormon)—mention the cairn's desecration at the time of Young's visit or his giving a signal or order for its destruction.

Instead, after Young's stop at the site that spring, non-Mormon mail agent Edwin R. Purple passed through the area and described the monument as still standing. Detailing his journey from Los Angeles to Salt Lake for a California newspaper, Purple wrote that when his mail company "passed near the place that four years ago was the scene of the Mountain Meadow massacre, I left the train and rode down to the spot." Purple described the scene, including the spring near the emigrants' campsite and the monument that now marked the spot. "About two years ago," Purple wrote, "Major Carrolton . . . collected the bones and placed a pile of stones over them, surmounting them with a cross, on which is the inscription *Vengeance is mine and I will repay saith the Lord.*"[18]

Some days before Purple's arrival, Young's group left the massacre site, continuing on the road south into the Santa Clara canyon, passing Dudley Leavitt's town of Gunlock, and camping after a long day's journey of thirty-five miles. Over the next four days, the party continued its loop tour, moving east and then northward through the settlements of Santa Clara, Tonaquint, Washington, Toquerville, Pocketville, Grafton, and, in Woodruff's words, "Harmony or John D. Lees Fort."

At Harmony, Lee heard that when Young "came to the Monument that contained [the emigrants'] Bones, he made this remark, Vengeance is Mine Saith the Lord, & I have taken a little of it." Like other contemporary accounts, Lee's diary mentions nothing about tearing down the cairn. But he did write that in a "private conversation," Young told him "the company that was used up at the Mountain Meadowes were the Fathers, Mothe[rs], Bros., Sisters & connections of those that Muerders the Prophets; they Merritd their fate, & the only thing that ever troubled him was the lives of the Women & children, but [this] could not be avoided."[19]

Lee claimed Young "said this was the best Fort that had ever been built in this Territory," though Woodruff recorded that the group found Harmony in a dilapidated and lonely condition. Lee "spent about $30,000" on the fort, Woodruff wrote, "& now the roof was all falling in & it was Entirely deserted except by J. D. Lee" and his "6 wives, 26 Children, [and] 10 Hiered men total 42 souls. He was about to abandon the place for the want of water."[20]

After their tour through Utah's southernmost settlements, Young's party returned to Salt Lake on June 8. In his regular Sunday address the next day, he shared a detailed account of the trip. Of his visit to the massacre site, he said, "We . . . pass[ed] through the Mountain Meadows, a place you have heard of where the massacre was, We saw the monument, watered our horses, passed through to the divide, over the divide or rim of the [Great] basin, and down . . . until we came to the waters of Santa Clara."[21]

Six weeks after Young's return, Colonel Philip St. George Cooke, a non-Mormon who commanded the Mormon Battalion during the U.S.-Mexican War, led the last columns of U.S. soldiers out of what had been Camp Floyd, headed for the conflict in the East.[22]

Near the head of Echo Canyon, an eastbound camp of sixty soldiers from Camp Floyd—probably Colonel Cooke's command—met a westbound stage-coach carrying the secretary of the recently created Nevada Territory, thirty-five-year-old law clerk Orion Clemens, and his younger brother. Clemens had sought a job from his St. Louis mentor, Edward Bates, after Lincoln made Bates his attorney general. Hoping for an appointment in the new adminis-tration, Clemens asked for "the post of Secretary of a Territory," Bates said, "any Territory except *Utah*." In recommending him, Bates told Secretary of State William Seward that he considered Clemens "an honest man of fair me-diocrity of talents & learning—more indeed of both, than I have seen in sev-eral Territorial secretaries."[23]

Clemens's brother, a Mississippi steamboat pilot, headed west with Orion to avoid being conscripted to captain gunboats in the erupting Civil War. The Clemens brothers departed from St. Louis on July 18. Traveling by stage-coach, they reached Salt Lake City on August 5.[24]

"Here we laid over two days," Orion Clemens wrote the *Missouri Democrat* two weeks later, "and while there visited Brigham Young, the portly, jolly, and talkative First President of the Mormon Church; Heber C. Kimball, Second President, and [Daniel H.] Wells, Third President."

Clemens reported a conversation he had with Kimball during the meeting.

"I'd like to see the South give the North a grubbing," Kimball said, "and I'd like to see the North give the South a good grubbing."

Figure 27.1 Samuel Clemens. Courtesy University of Nevada, Reno, Special Collections.

Though the Saints had been "run out of both North and South," Kimball wanted the South "to grub a little the hardest," because Senator Stephen A. Douglas, "a Northern man," had urged repealing Utah's territorial status shortly before the Utah War. It was "the duty of Congress," Douglas had said, "to apply the knife and cut out this loathsome, disgusting ulcer."[25]

Now Douglas, recently passed away, has "gone to hell," Kimball said, "and old Buchanan will follow after him."

"Will Lincoln go that way, too?" asked Clemens, a supporter of the Union and Lincoln.

"Well," Kimball said, turning to look at his brethren, "he's trying to draw me out."

"I am," Clemens said, "I want to know your sentiments."

"Well," Kimball shared his belief, "if Lincoln hadn't got his hands so full with the South, he would have pitched into us."

Of the war, Kimball said that "you won't see peace any more; the United States will go all to pieces, and the Mormons will take charge of and rule all the country; republicanism will be overthrown, but I won't say what will take its place, nor when, nor at what time the Mormons will commence their rule."

Then, apparently remembering that he was speaking to a Lincoln appointee, Kimball changed his tune. "But mind, I am a Union man, we are Union men, we are going to stand by the country," he said. "Now, tell it just as I say it."[26]

Young's office journal confirms that the meeting took place on August 7. A man "introduced Mr Clements Secr of the Territory of Nevada who was on his way to Carson, accompanied by his Brother," a clerk recorded. "They conversed with Pres. Young & Well[s] principally about this Territory" and "the health of the Country. Opinion of Mr. [Jim] Bridger who said he would be willing to give $50 for the first bushel of wheat raised in this barren Country. The improvements in the Valley far exceeded their expectations, after the conversation they politely took their leave."[27]

Though no one in that meeting knew it yet, Young and the other Latter-day Saint leaders had just met a man who would become an American icon. Orion Clemens's brother, who barely received mention in Young's office journal, was twenty-five-year-old Samuel Clemens. Sam would begin his writing career soon after reaching Nevada, publishing stories in Western newspapers under the penname "Mark Twain."

Twain later wrote about his 1861 journey through Utah in his bestselling travel narrative *Roughing It*, published in 1872. Of his and his brother's visit to Young, he wrote that the man "seemed a quiet, kindly, easy-mannered, dignified, self-possessed old gentleman of fifty-five or sixty."[28]

The Clemens brothers stayed at the Salt Lake House, located just south of the Pony Express and Overland Stage stations on Main Street and frequented by non-Mormons. Twain remembered Utah as "a luscious country for thrilling evening stories about assassinations of intractable Gentiles. I cannot easily conceive of anything more cosy than the night in Salt Lake which we spent in a Gentile den, smoking pipes and listening to tales [about] how heedless people often come to Utah and make remarks about Brigham, or polygamy, or some other sacred matter, and the very next morning at day-light such parties are sure to be found lying up some back alley, contentedly waiting for the hearse."[29]

Despite these characterizations, the Clemens brothers did not need a hearse when morning came. "We were well treated in Salt Lake," Orion said. "At the end of our two days' sojourn," Samuel later wrote, "we left Great Salt Lake City hearty and well fed and happy—physically superb but not so very much wiser, as regards the 'Mormon question,' than we were when we arrived."[30]

"We had a deal more 'information' than we had before," he wrote, "but we did not know what portion of it was reliable and what was not—for it all came from acquaintances of a day—strangers, strictly speaking. We were told, for instance, that the dreadful 'Mountain Meadows Massacre' was the work of the Indians entirely, and that the Gentiles had meanly tried to fasten it upon the Mormons; we were told, likewise, that the Indians were to blame, partly, and partly the Mormons; and we were told, likewise, and just as positively, that the Mormons were almost if not wholly and completely responsible for that most treacherous and pitiless butchery."[31]

The celebrated British ethnographer Sir Richard Francis Burton stayed in the Salt Lake House the year before the Clemens brothers while he wrote a book about the Latter-day Saints. He found himself as perplexed as Samuel Clemens by conflicting tales of the massacre. "The horrible 'Mountain Meadow Massacre,'" Burton wrote, "was, according to the anti-Mormons, committed by the Saints to revenge the death of an esteemed apostle—Parley P. Pratt—who, in the spring of 1857, when traveling through Arkansas, was knived by one Hector M'Lean, whose wife he had converted and taken unto himself. The Mormons deny that the massacre was committed by their number, and ask the Gentiles why, if such be the case, the murderers are not brought to justice?"[32]

Though massacre participants were not brought to justice during the Civil War, they were subject to the hand of nature. On Christmas Day 1861, heavy rains began pummeling southern Utah. In late December and early January, the Harmony branch record reported "the storms still raging; prospects dark and gloomy; . . . the face of the country is deluged in water." The rains—like the biblical Noah's flood—reportedly lasted for some forty days, making "the Earth . . . a sea of water."

In mid-January 1862, rivers and tributaries became violent torrents, carving the landscape and destroying buildings, farms, orchards, vineyards, dams, and canals throughout the region. In the Mountain Meadows, the springs that ran along the east of the emigrant siege site and mass grave widened and deepened, forming a chasm that threatened to erode the monument site. The deluge may have made more rocks tumble from the monument—if human hands had not leveled them already.[33]

The floods came "as a thief in the night," remembered Santa Clara witnesses, a "wall of water" more than ten feet high that "looked like the sea as it came out of the kanion and spread over the bottoms from hill to hill." Settlers never forgot the "spectacle of dreadful magnificence": giant logs and cottonwood trees shooting down the Santa Clara "like arrows upon the current," "great trees and boulders battering . . . down" the two-feet-thick and eight-feet-high rock walls of the Santa Clara fort, the "mad river slashing into the bank, carving out pieces as big as a house."[34]

As the flood transformed the landscape, it also altered the lives of the local people, including massacre perpetrators. At a settlement called Adventure near today's Zion National Park, former Cedar City bishop Philip Klingensmith lost his "house, Cane mill, Blacksmith shop, 150 Gals. of molasses," and most of his belongings "down the flood."[35] At Gunlock, Dudley Leavitt's polygamous families abandoned their houses and watched as their possessions went downstream.[36] Ira Hatch, the interpreter who helped track and kill at least one emigrant who escaped from the Meadows, lived in the first portion of Santa Clara's fort to fall. "Suddenly," wrote one witness, "the southwest corner of the fort, Hatch's home, fell into the flood, sweeping away everything he owned. Other families suffered, but he, taken by surprise, lost all."[37]

No one suffered greater losses than John D. Lee. Though his fortunes had dramatically improved after the Mountain Meadows Massacre, the flood of 1862 marked a reversal of those fortunes. Lee experienced a financial setback from which he never recovered, losing horses, cattle, sheep, his mill in Washington, and the entire Harmony fort as its adobe walls melted. Worst of all, on January 31, a severe wind gust sent a second-story wall of the fort crashing through the ceiling of his wife Sarah Caroline's home, crushing

Figure 27.2 The five fingers of Kolob rise above ruins of old Fort Harmony. Wally Barrus, Courtesy Church History Library.

two of their children, five-year-old Margarett Ann and six-year-old George Albert.[38]

Lee buried his children in higher ground west of the destroyed fort. He made a small monument to them, carving into a sandstone marker their names, birthdates, cause of death, and poetic verse he composed. He placed the headstone so it faced west. Behind it to the east, the five-fingered cliffs of Kolob, like the hand of God, towered on the horizon. Poetic lines inscribed in the marker asked:

Was it for sins that we have done
Death snatched from us those little ones[39]

28

In the Midst of a Desolating War

Western United States and Washington, DC, 1862-65

The epic flood of 1862 also impacted southern California, where the Santa Ana River rose twenty-five feet. Sometime before March, a group of Union Army volunteers at San Bernardino took into custody two Utah men, one from Santa Clara and one from Pinto, when the traveling duo tried to sell the soldiers butter and cheese. Four days later, the two learned the reason for their arrest when James H. Carleton, now a colonel and the army volunteers' leader, was finally able to cross the engorged Santa Ana to reach the camp.

"Who pulled down the monument at the Mountain Meadows?" Carleton interrogated the prisoners.

One of them answered "he didn't think it was any body" in southern Utah, because people already "had too much work of their own to do, and [even] if they hadn't they did not like work well enough to do that."

"I guess that brother Brigham and John D. Lee Isaac C. Haight John M Higbee and Prime Coleman had a hand in it," Carleton shot back. "We are coming to learn them to leave dead folks's bones alone."

Carleton told the prisoners he intended "to repremand for the insult to him and his Nation (U.S.) in tearing down that Monument which he erected at . . . the Mountain Meadow Massacre g[ro]und."

Carleton apparently only meant to frighten the Latter-day Saints with this threat, because he and his California Column of volunteers were actually on their way to drive Confederate troops out of New Mexico.[1] For the region's Paiutes, however, Carleton's march spelled doom. His soldiers "killed quite a number" of Paiutes from the Muddy River region of Nevada as they passed through. Once in New Mexico, Carleton marked his infamous place in history through his campaign to kill and drive the Navajo, culminating in the 1863-64 Long Walk to the reservation of Bosque Redondo that brought death to hundreds of men, women, and children.[2]

That summer, with the Southern "states rights" representatives gone from Congress, Republicans pursued their 1856 planks against polygamy and slavery, making both practices illegal in all U.S. territories. President Abraham Lincoln signed Congress's Morrill Anti-Bigamy Act on July 2, 1862.[3] "Congress had no Constitutional right to pass such an act," protested Brigham Young, who considered plural marriage a religious principle.[4]

The Saints' desires to let local values prevail over those imposed by the federal government had led Utah Territory to make another bid for statehood and the independence that came with it.[5] Besides polygamy, the Mountain Meadows Massacre stood as an obstacle to statehood. "This atrocious affair has done us, and still continues to do us as a people, incalculable injury, and will prove a serious obstacle to our admission into the Union as a sovereign and independent State," Utah congressional delegate John M. Bernhisel wrote Young. "The miscreants who were engaged in this cold blooded and diabolical deed, will have a fearful account to render in the judgment of the great day."[6]

Three days after Lincoln signed the Anti-Bigamy Act, the U.S. Army's Department of the Pacific ordered Colonel Patrick Edward Connor and his California Third Volunteer Infantry to command military operations in its District of Utah. Connor and his regiment felt disgruntled with the assignment. "The men enlisted to fight traitors" in the Civil War, Connor explained to the Union Army commanding general. Instead, Connor and his men were told to establish a military post in Utah and protect telegraph, mail, and emigration routes from Indian attacks.[7] If he could not "fight traitors" in the East, Connor determined to make the territory's Native people and Mormons the enemies he would oppose. He called the Saints "a community of traitors" and "murderers, fanatics, and whores." Rejecting the army's assumption that he would station his troops outside Utah's settlements at the former Camp Floyd, he established a new garrison in the foothills just three miles east of Salt Lake City, much to the consternation of interim Utah governor Stephen S. Harding, Young, and the city's residents. He named the new garrison Camp Douglas after Stephen A. Douglas, the Illinois senator who stated in 1857 that it was Congress's duty "to apply the knife and cut out th[e] loathsome, disgusting ulcer" of Mormonism.[8]

Colonel Connor also turned his ire on local Native populations. On the bitter-cold morning of January 29, 1863, following several conflicts between Shoshone Indians and settlers and miners, Connor and his men assailed a winter camp of Shoshone on the Bear River just across Utah's northern border in present-day Idaho.

The troops slaughtered hundreds of men, women, and children, many of them as they tried to escape. The soldiers left the Shoshone bodies where they fell, the remains seen by travelers for years. They plundered the camp and auctioned off stolen items at Camp Douglas. Rather than being prosecuted or even investigated for his role in the massacre, Connor was widely praised and promoted to brigadier general as a reward for his role in what he reported as a "battle." For several years afterward, Camp Douglas held celebrations of the "glorious victory" on the massacre's anniversary.[9]

The irony in the opposing perceptions of Utah Territory's two major massacres, occurring within six years of each other, is striking. While the Mountain Meadows Massacre was widely condemned, the significantly larger Bear River Massacre was hailed as a victory. In one case, U.S. troops carried out the slaughter and left the bodies to rot. In the other, U.S. troops buried the victims, built monuments to them, condemned the massacre, and assisted in the crime's investigation. The difference lay largely in who the victims were. The Mountain Meadows victims were white emigrants fulfilling the expansionist belief of "Manifest Destiny," while the Shoshone were among Indigenous peoples who stood in the way of that vision.

The Mountain Meadows Massacre continued to go unpunished throughout the Civil War, with wartime strains on the federal budget partly to blame. On January 28, 1863—the day before the Bear River Massacre—Utah associate justice Charles B. Waite complained to U.S. Attorney General Edward Bates that neither the territorial legislature nor the federal treasury was paying court expenses.[10]

The Union government balked at sending scarce funds to a sparsely populated western territory.[11] Utah's legislature, controlled by Mormons, withheld financial support, believing the federal government should pay the expenses of courts over which federally appointed judges presided. Besides, many legislators were polygamists who could lose their freedom if prosecutors and courts enforced the Morrill Act.[12]

Caught in the middle, Utah's federal judges tried using the Mountain Meadows Massacre to win federal support. "No lapse of time," Justice Waite wrote, "should shield the perpetrators from punishment. The murder of over . . . a hundred persons in cold blood, without any provocation, and for purposes of plunder only, is a circumstance that may well attract attention even in the midst of a desolating war."[13]

As was the case in the immediate aftermath of the Utah War, federal appointees in Utah were divided in their attitudes toward the Mormons, with some supporting a call from Colonel Connor for martial law and others opposing it. Utahns found non-Mormon territorial chief justice John F. Kinney—who had mellowed in his opposition to the Saints—so much to their liking that they elected him their delegate to Congress, replacing John Bernhisel, a Mormon.[14] But on March 3, 1863, the day before Congress opened its session, Young gave a fiery speech at a mass meeting in Salt Lake condemning other federal appointees. The next day, Latter-day Saint representatives visited Utah governor Stephen S. Harding and two judges, asking them to resign and leave the territory.[15]

The two judges, in turn, wrote President Lincoln, declaring that "the administration of justice is suspended in this Territory" and refusing to hold court until "properly supported by the military power of the government, which we consider, as at present advised, to be at least Five Thousand men."[16] The same scenario that led to the Utah War in the 1850s seemed to be playing out again. Governor Harding wrote Lincoln's secretary of state, William H. Seward, saying that the "most ghastly crimes" had occurred in the two judges' districts, traceable "to men of high standing in the Mormon Church," adding that one district was "the scene of the ever to be remembered 'Mountain Meadow Massacre.'"[17]

Amid this turmoil, a pamphlet titled *Utah and the Mormons. Speech of Hon. John Cradlebaugh, of Nevada, on the Admission of Utah as a State* reached the territory. Cradlebaugh had become congressional delegate of the new Nevada Territory, and he aimed to prevent Utah statehood. Cradlebaugh didn't actually deliver his speech before Congress, as the pamphlet claimed, but he did circulate it.[18] The pamphlet included a withering personal account of his 1859 investigation of the Mountain Meadows Massacre.

The Constitution does not protect "every class of persons who may assume to themselves a religious faith at war with the most cherished sentiments of virtue and morality throughout the Christian and civilized world," he wrote, alluding to polygamy and blood atonement, which, he contended, inspired the massacre. "As a duty to manifest our disapprobation of practices and doctrine so odious," Cradlebaugh argued, the Mormon people must be kept "under the general jurisdiction of the Government" as a territory rather than receiving the independence statehood provided.[19] Cradlebaugh realized his aim. The next year, Congress denied Utah's bid for statehood, while Nevada, with its badly needed flow of silver to the U.S. Treasury, became a state.

After Young heard about and likely read Cradlebaugh's pamphlet—a copy with Young's name on it survives today—he spoke publicly about the thousands of troops and hangers-on who had occupied the territory during the Utah War. He explicitly referenced Cradlebaugh's efforts to investigate the Mountain Meadows Massacre. Young claimed Cradlebaugh had "wanted *the whole army* to accompany him to Iron county to try the whites for the murder of that company of emigrants." In fact, Cradlebaugh had tagged along with the army's planned excursion to southern Utah in 1859. But he ended his Cedar City investigations when the troops returned to Camp Floyd.

"I told Governor Cumming," Young said, "that if he would take an un-prejudiced judge into the district where that horrid affair occurred, I would pledge myself that every man in the regions round about should be forth-coming when called for, to be condemned or acquitted as an impartial, un-prejudiced judge and jury should decide." Young promised "that the court should be protected from any violence or hindrance in the prosecution of the laws; and if any were guilty of the blood of those who suffered in the Mountain Meadow massacre, let them suffer the penalty of the law." Despite his offer, Young said, "to this day they have not touched the matter, for fear the Mormons would be acquitted from the charge of having any hand in it, and our enemies would thus be deprived of a favorite topic to talk about, when urging hostility against us. 'The Mountain Meadow massacre! Only think of the Mountain Meadow massacre!!' is their cry from one end of the land to the other."[20]

Years more would pass before a federal prosecutor finally accepted Young's proposal.[21]

By the spring of 1863, Young's attitude toward John D. Lee had changed, perhaps influenced by the Cradlebaugh pamphlet, which accused Lee of di-rect complicity in the massacre.[22] He may also have read an equally damning document that included multiple sources he could not easily dismiss. A year earlier, Bernhisel had written Young, asking if he had received "Senate Executive Document No. 42," an 1860 compilation containing substantial "information in relation to the massacre at Mountain Meadows."[23]

Young replied he had "neither received nor seen" the document but requested a copy, which arrived in August 1862, fifteen months after Young visited the Mountain Meadows monument and spoke with Lee at Harmony.[24] Lee had consistently maintained that Indians were solely responsible for the massacre, but the Senate publication clearly showed they did not act alone, pointing to Lee as a party to the killings. The report was one more item in the growing public evidence challenging massacre leaders' version of the story. Young soon had a chance to confront Lee about it.[25]

In April 1863, Young, George A. Smith, and other church officials left Salt Lake for their annual springtime tour of southern Utah. When the entourage reached the community of Washington, where Lee had a home, the church leaders held a public meeting.[26]

According to a journal account, Young and others visited Lee before the meeting. Young "spoke to him, about the 'Mountain Meadow.'"[27] Mormon doctrine proclaimed that those who shed innocent blood were damned from reaching the highest heaven, where God and Jesus Christ dwelt.[28] In his confrontation with Young, Lee again "tried to blame the Indians for the massacre," said the account, "but Pres Young, would not accept his testimony and at last said, 'John D. Lee, do all the good you can, while you live, and you shall be credited, with every good deed you perform, but" in heaven, "where God and the Lamb dwell, you shall never be.'" This severe chastisement from his spiritual leader made Lee weep bitterly.[29]

After Cradlebaugh published his pamphlet, he entered the Civil War with a regiment from his native Ohio. During a charge at Vicksburg, Mississippi, he took a Minié ball in the mouth, effectively ending his public career. He returned to his home in Eureka, Nevada, where he died several years later, before anyone was formally indicted for the massacre.[30]

James Carleton never got his chance to rebuild the monument his troops erected in 1859. Instead, that honor went to soldiers under Patrick Connor's command. In May 1864, Captain George Price and the troops of Company M, Second California Cavalry, paused at the site on their way north to Camp Douglas. Price reported that the memorial's cedar cross was gone and its stones "scattered around the springs" adjacent to the site. The grave that lay underneath the former cairn showed "evidence of much decay." Price surmised that both grave and monument had been "defaced by impious hands."

Price's men built a new memorial fourteen feet high, with a square base from which rose a "pyramidal column." They again topped the cairn with a cross bearing the scripture, "Vengeance is mine, I will repay saith the Lord." A man who helped rebuild the monument said it "appears well from the road, and will stand for years, if no impious hand destroy it."[31]

But within two months, vandals began their work. On July 1, a passing Latter-day Saint noted that someone had written on the cross, "Remember Hauns mill and Carthage Jail"—two massacres of Mormons for which no one was ever punished, as if either justified the massacre at Mountain Meadows.[32] By the end of 1864, a Camp Douglas newspaper reported that the new monument had been torn down, an "inhuman, damnable act," the editors wrote, "worse than Sacrilege."[33]

Soon a dramatic series of events changed the state of national and local affairs in the United States. On April 9, 1865, Confederate general Robert E. Lee surrendered to Union war hero Ulysses S. Grant at Appomattox Court House. Six days later, Abraham Lincoln died of a point-blank gunshot to the head inflicted by John Wilkes Booth at Ford's Theatre in Washington, plummeting much of the nation into mourning.

29

Too Horrible to Contemplate

Utah, 1865–70

After visiting Utah in 1860, renowned British explorer and ethnologist Richard F. Burton wrote of Brigham Young, "Where occasion requires, he can use all the weapons of ridicule to direful effect, and 'speak a bit of his mind' in a style which no one forgets. He often reproves his erring followers in purposely violent language, making the terrors of a scolding the punishment in lieu of hanging for a stolen horse or cow."[1] Young's predecessor, Joseph Smith, taught his followers to reprove "with sharpness" and then show "an increase of love toward him whom thou hast reproved, lest he esteem thee to be his enemy."[2] Young often coupled that approach with giving his people the benefit of the doubt.

"I would rather think my brethren innocent than guilty any time, as there is more pleasure in such a thought," he wrote in 1865 to a man charged with misconduct. "You have it in your own power to vindicate your character, and to prove to your brethren that you are as innocent as you assert." That power, Young said, was to pursue "a right course."[3]

Young's 1863 tongue-lashing of John D. Lee over the Mountain Meadows Massacre left Lee feeling he had been cut off from the church, though no formal or public action was taken against him at the time. But Lee sought to work his way back into Young's good graces by pursuing "a right course" and being a model citizen. "He always attended church, he was the first to fill the assignment made by Brigham Young to get out poles for the new telegraph line, he was prompt in paying his tithe," wrote Lee's biographer, Juanita Brooks.[4]

"I allways feel that you have been a Father & a friend to me espesially in my weakness," Lee wrote Young a few months after his 1863 rebuke, "and was it in my Power there is no good that I would withold from you."[5] Lee kept up his efforts over the next several years. After sharply chastising Lee and seeing he steadfastly denied guilt, Young seemed to back off.[6] Lee maintained enough good standing in the church to be sealed to his last plural wife in 1865.[7]

By that year, as the Civil War wound to its close, federally appointed judges began holding court in southern Utah, though none chose to take up the Mountain Meadows Massacre. The case was now eight years old and growing colder with each passing year. The atrocity might never have been prosecuted but for the fact that some came to see it as a political weapon.[8]

John Titus, a well-educated, politically ambitious, Pennsylvania lawyer, became chief justice of the Utah Supreme Court in 1863. Titus was appointed U.S. attorney for the newly formed Arizona Territory before he accepted the Utah judgeship instead.[9]

Because Latter-day Saints tended to vote as a bloc, Titus and other non-Mormon newcomers found it difficult to advance politically in Utah unless they could either receive Mormon leaders' endorsement or figure out ways to disfranchise the majority population. By late 1865, Titus had joined with Patrick Connor to form a loose organization that later coalesced into the Liberal Party, sometimes called the "Anti-Mormon" party. Before the group had a formal name, Mormons labeled it "the clique."

The group met in the cellar of the Gilbert & Sons store on Salt Lake's Main Street, where store employee James Dwyer listened to the discussions and summarized them in letters to Latter-day Saint leaders. "As I have a capital chance of hearing a great many things that is said," Dwyer explained, "I shall keep you posted in all . . . their future movements." He wrote that "their greatest aim is, to destroy Polygamie," swearing "that if it takes the whole strenth of the army[,] the Goverment would send [troops] to crush out Polygamie."

"They are doing their utmost by letters to Washington and secret combinations in this city with Gen Connor at the Head, . . . to wrest the power of Goverment from" Brigham Young, Dwyer wrote. Though Young had held no official government position for years, they recognized what Utah governor Alfred Cumming had said: although Cumming was governor of the territory, "Brigham Young was Governor of the people."[10]

Titus traveled to Washington, DC, and soon called for Connor to join him there in lobbying against the Latter-day Saints.[11] "They feel confident of their success in bringing trouble on Utah," Dwyer reported, "and they believe before next fall Polygamie will be wiped out."[12]

Dwyer concluded the men cared less about polygamy than getting lucrative contracts for provisioning troops the government might send. "As one of the Gilbert boys said in my hearing . . . I dont care a d—n what they do with polygamie if I only can get the contracts," Dwyer wrote. "They feel determined to l[o]se none of the contracts and prevent them from falling into the hand of Brigham."[13]

In a letter to the U.S. attorney general, Judge Titus wrote, "The people of Utah . . . are wholly actuated by a fanaticism, which claims to be intensely religious, and which involves much of malignity impurity, avirice, hypocricy, falsehood treachery and violence, both in its faith and practice." He said this fanaticism put them "in absolute hostility to all other persons" and that the U.S. Constitution "*affords no protection to these Mormon abuses.*" He called for the removal of all Latter-day Saints holding federal positions.[14]

Titus's group hoped that attracting public attention at the national level would lead to federal legislation against the Mormons. The focus on polygamy aroused the public's curiosity and indignation. Coupled with the Mountain Meadows Massacre and other instances of Utah violence, they hoped to make a convincing case that the Saints were incapable of self-rule.[15]

Though moderate attitudes toward Utah prevailed during the Lincoln administration and the Civil War, in the Reconstruction period following the war, opinion in the country divided. Some people wanted to leave Utah alone, while others wished to reconstruct the territory like the southern states. Rhetoric like Titus's was part of the latter campaign.[16]

In a May 1866 meeting with three army officers—including Captain George F. Price, who helped rebuild the Mountain Meadows monument—Young explained why, in his view, a massacre investigation had not yet happened. Young told the officers he had urged judges "to go south and investigate" the massacre and "pledged my all to protect them with my life in so doing, but they would not do it."

Young believed that by leaving "the matter in an unsettled condition," his critics could "reflect evil on me no matter how unjustly." He said he "anxiously desired the matter thoroughly cleared up and investigated," saying, "if there were Mormons guilty in that act it was one of the most dastardly things that ever occurred, and let them be brought to justice."

"They will not clear it up," he said, "for [the] sake of loosing it off [on] me."

Captain Price replied that he had never heard Young directly charged with the massacre. Instead, he heard that Young "sent some letters down that way to prevent such an occurrence. It is usually charged on John D. Lee, the Bishop there," Price said.

"John D. Lee is not the bishop there nor ever was," Young chafed. "I wish and have wished it investigated and cleared up, that [the] guilty might be punished."

"If they escape earthly punishment," Price concluded, "they can never escape eternal punishment."

"That is so," Young concurred, "they never can."[17]

Speaking in the Salt Lake Tabernacle later that year, Young again denounced the massacre. "There are some things which transpire that I cannot think about," he lamented. "There are transactions that are too horrible for me to contemplate," and "the Mountain Meadows massacre" was one of them. Young could not "think that there are beings upon the earth . . . who could be guilty of such atrocities."[18]

By that time, Utah settlers were experiencing Indian raids on their livestock in what became known as the "Black Hawk War." Conflicts between the settlers and Utes, along with their allies, led to atrocities on both sides, including settlers' senseless massacre of peaceful Paiutes in Circleville, Utah, in April 1866.[19]

That summer, a *Salt Lake City Union Vedette* correspondent spoke with Indians in the vicinity of southern Utah about the Mountain Meadows Massacre. "These Indians," he reported, "do not hesitate to acknowledge their connection with the massacre, but charge the Mormons with being the instigators and chief actors in the tragedy." Because Mormon-Indian relations had deteriorated, the reporter believed the Saints' influence over the Indians was slipping, and that they might be willing to share information leading to "the arrest and punishment of the white miscreants who planned the indiscriminate slaughter of men, women and children at Mountain Meadows."[20]

That summer, John D. Lee went to St. George to confer with resident apostle Erastus Snow, who was directing efforts in the south to protect settlers from raids during the Black Hawk War. Snow told Lee "that in almost every Instance our troubles with the Natives were brought on by imprudent & rash conduct on the part of some of our brethern."[21]

Snow's statement may have made Lee wince. Snow was gradually uncovering evidence of Lee's and others' participation in the Mountain Meadows Massacre.[22]

In March 1867, thirty-seven-year-old George Spencer of Washington, Utah, wrote Snow confessing, "I was in that horrid 'Mountain Meadow affair.'" He pleaded, "What can I *now* do? . . . Many are willing to *die* for salvation; but how few will *live* for it. Oh that God may direct me through his servants how to be of *some* use in His Kingdom!"[23]

Snow forwarded the letter to Young, adding, "There are numbers more in this region who were engaged in the same affair, some applying for their [temple] Endowments[,] for Wives Etc. I have hitherto refrained from saying much on the subject to any one. If you deem it wisdom to give me any advice as to the Course I ought to pursue with them, it would be very thankfully received."[24]

"That is an affair about which I wish I could never think," Young responded, "and about which I wish I had never heard. But men will act independent and they must endure the consequences of their actions. I can give no encouragement to any man who was engaged in that transaction, and can only say let them remain as they are." Though Young instructed Snow not to extend further temple blessings to them, he did not report Spencer or other purported massacre participants to civil authorities.[25]

Another Utahn struggling with the massacre—though not a participant in the crime—was George A. Hicks, a Harmony Latter-day Saint who abhorred Lee. Hicks "accused Lee of misquoting scriptures," wrote one historian, "laughed at his faith-promoting stories," and "branded Lee as a swindler, a liar, a sensual brute, and a hypocrite."[26]

In October 1867, Hicks wrote Young about the sermon the church president gave the previous December condemning the massacre. Hicks complained that Lee "said publick[ly] and Privately that you did Not mean what you sayed but Mearly Sayed it to blind the eyes of the Gentiels and to Satsfy a few individuals." Hicks wanted to know Young's "real intentions," writing, "If you are in favor of the Mountain meadows massacre I would like to know."

Hicks felt disturbed that Lee had not been publicly disciplined. "Lee is in full felow ship" in Harmony, Hicks complained, "and is frequently Called upon to pr[e]ach much to anoyance of Good men." He wrote that Lee received a recommend from Harmony's bishop "to Get another wife." Believing Lee was damned because of his participation in the massacre, Hicks asked Young to respond and "dispose all my dark fears."[27]

Hicks was right—Lee's new bishop did issue him a recommend of worthiness, but before Lee reached Salt Lake City to be sealed to another plural wife, his marriage plans unraveled. Never again would Lee marry polygamously, which required being of good standing in the church in the nineteenth century.[28]

At first, Young did not answer Hicks's letter or further discipline Lee as Hicks wanted, though he eventually did both. The historical record is silent on why Young hesitated to conduct a church investigation of Lee and other massacre perpetrators at this time, even as evidence of their participation mounted. He may have been subject to confirmation bias—the tendency to embrace evidence that reinforces one's view and reject what doesn't. He didn't want to believe Lee and other church members had a hand in such a horrific act, especially when they denied it. And one of Young's trusted advisors, apostle George A. Smith, who conducted his own investigation of the massacre in southern Utah in 1858, continued to maintain that Indians were primarily if not solely responsible for the atrocity.

Young lacked civil authority to investigate the crime and, with all the conflicting accounts, preferred to have government authorities do it anyway. But he did not want suspects prosecuted until he could be assured they would receive a fair and unbiased trial.[29] History provided ample examples in which courts were stacked against the Latter-day Saints and other groups who fell outside the American norm. Finally, even if the perpetrators escaped earthly punishment, Young believed, they could never escape divine retribution.

Young may have also accepted what Lee had insinuated in his September 1857 report to him—that Indians had massacred the emigrants as a result of Young's strategy of encouraging Indian cattle raids during the Utah War, and thus as a consequence of his wartime leadership. All wars have unintended consequences, but leaders rarely dwell on them.[30]

In April 1868, Lee wrote in his journal that he had received "a Ficticious Letter . . . proporting to have been written at camp Douglass, the author styleing himself Maj. Burt, commander of 2000 gurrilers, giving me 10 days to make my escape in or I should be hung up in that old Fort Harmony for being in the Mountain Meadow Massacre."

Lee's wife Emma believed the fake letter was from two southern Utah Saints who had chided Lee about the massacre: John Lawson (with whom he had a long-standing water dispute) and George Hicks. Emma considered Hicks "a poor sneaking, pusylanimous Pup" who was "always Medling with other men's Matter[s]." She said, "he had better sing low & keep out of her Path or she would put a load of salt in his Backside, this being the 3rd letter of the kind."

Continuing to blame Natives for the massacre, Lee described Hicks as "a Traitor" who pointed out to gentiles "all the Brethrn who he thought had been at Mountain Meadow when Indians killed" the emigrants.[31]

When he did not hear from Young, Hicks wrote him again, saying that only Young could resolve "the matter which rests with such weight upon my mind." Reminding Young of how he condemned the massacre in his December 1866 sermon, Hicks hoped "that the perpitrators of that bloody deed would soon be punished for their crimes or if they were not punished, their names would be stricken from the Church books."

Hicks said he carried a copy of Young's sermon in his pocket and "read it to a great many people"; he also sang a massacre ballad to anyone who would listen. He was surprised that this "conduct made some excitement." When people asked him "to desist," he wrote Young, he "continued to read and quote your remarks and to sing the song" until "at length I was *gently* warned that my course of conduct would be punishe[d] if I continued."

Hicks repeated Lee's claim that Young publicly condemned the massacre only "to *blind* the eyes of the gentiles and to satisfy a few individuals" who would not be silenced. Hicks said that although Lee's claim was "not generaly believed," still, "doubts and fears are beginning to rise in my mind in relation to the matter, in short, my peace of mind is almost gone." Hicks asked if Lee's claim was true. He had been advised to pray about the matter, which he did, "but," he wrote, "the bloody scene passes before my minds eye day and night."[32]

Young finally replied to Hicks in February 1869. In handling his voluminous correspondence, Young typically had a clerk read a letter to him, after which he explained how to answer the writer. The clerk often jotted notes to record Young's thoughts, then expanded them into a response, which Young signed.

Clerical notes written on the last page of Hicks's letter show that Young told the clerk to "send him comfort." This was followed by "did you have a hand therein[?] if not—why is your peace broken?" Then Young counseled, "you need not concern yourself." The final note assured Hicks that Young also wanted "judgment had on the matter."[33]

But "comfort" never made it into the reply the clerk wrote Hicks, which asserted that if " 'the bloody scene passes before you day and night,' " then Hicks "must have been a participator in the horrible deed." If so, "one can readily imagine why 'it rests with such weight upon your mind', and 'why you cannot sleep at nights'; the surprise would be that you could." If true and "you want a remedy," the letter advised, then a "rope round the neck taken with a jerk would be very salutary." The letter directed Hicks to the "courts of law and officers in the Territory," who "would be happy to attend to your case."

On the other hand, if Hicks was innocent, the letter counseled, then he was giving himself "a great deal of foolish trouble." It asked, "Why do not all the Latter day Saints feel as you do? Simply because it does not concern them." As to Hicks's questioning his faith, the letter affirmed, "If the Gospel was true before the 'Mountain Meadow Massacre', neither that nor any other event that may transpire can make it false."

Finally, the letter stated that Young had offered Governor Cumming extensive aid "to thoroughly investigate that matter, but he declined to take any action." Young had continued to offer assistance in the case, "but it has never been accepted."

Despite that failure, "the perpetrators of that tragedy will meet their reward" in the afterlife. "God will judge this matter and on that assurance," the letter said, "I rest perfectly satisfied." It concluded, "If you are innocent, you may safely do the same; if you are guilty, better try the remedy."[34]

That summer, Hicks was named orator of the day for Harmony's July Fourth celebration, a choice Lee found annoying. Lee took the speaker's stand after Hicks, snubbing Hicks's oration in his remarks and refusing to participate in the day's festivities, claiming he "did not Strike hands with the Enemies of this Kingdom, neither Make Merry with those who defamed the Character of the Prophet Brigham." Lee's comments left "a strange sensation on the Minds of Many."

In August, Lee participated in a muster for militia members in the southern settlements, a military exercise in which most men in the area were required to take part. Lee "took coma[n]d of a Portion of the Bat[talion]."[35]

Colonel William Dame should have commanded a regiment that included Lee's nemesis, Hicks, but Dame became "sick, and it was thought that a large part of it was a timid and nervous fear to enter into such a conflict." Hicks also refused to take part in the exercise, claiming "he had talked so bitterly against John D. Lee that he was afraid that some of Lee's friends would take advantage of the conditions in the conflict and shoot him." After hearing the evidence in Hicks's case, a court martial "found him guilty of cowardice."[36] In spite of growing criticism from Hicks and others, Lee continued to enjoy fellowship among some Latter-day Saints, including massacre participants like Isaac Haight and those who accepted the story they had been telling since 1857.[37]

The year 1869 marked the end of the "pioneer" period in Utah Territory's history. The May completion of the nation's transcontinental railroad in northern Utah meant that emigrants and other travelers to the territory no longer needed to come by foot, wagon, or handcart but instead could glide along metal tracks. The railroad's completion brought an influx of non-Mormon residents, observers, and lecturers into what had been the relatively isolated home of the Latter-day Saints, resulting in increased Mormon efforts to shape transcontinental audiences' perceptions of their church.[38]

In the fall of 1869, George A. Smith maintained that Indians were solely responsible for the massacre—in spite of evidence to the contrary—repeating the claim Lee made to Young shortly after the atrocity that white men went to the Meadows to aid the emigrants but "arrived too late."

Writing to the husband of a woman who mentioned the massacre in a lecture, Smith claimed that "the massacre was charged upon the Mormons, as an excuse for keeping an army in the territory, and that those particularly interested in depleting the U.S. Treasury of its gold were most zealous in urging

Figure 29.1 George A. Smith. Courtesy Utah State Historical Society.

this charge." Federal officials like Alfred Cumming and Alexander Wilson wanted to accept Young's help, but the army followers and federal judges "were interested in prolonging the difficulty." The lack of an investigation, he asserted, proved "the charge is false." Smith said, "There has never been a time when President Brigham Young and his brethren were not ready to give every aid in their power to discover and bring to Justice the participants in this massacre."[39]

Now, nearly thirteen years after the massacre, Young wanted Lee, the man whose name was becoming synonymous with the atrocity, to move far from the center of Latter-day Saint civilization, out on the frontier where his zealousness could be translated into practical pioneering—and where his presence would be less likely to attract the gaze of outsiders flooding the territory.[40]

In early 1870, Young passed through the southern Utah settlements, traveling as far south as Kanab, a new Latter-day Saint settlement just north of the Arizona border and the Grand Canyon. During that trip, according to Lee, Young "advised Me to Sell & Select a location in the South for My self & Boys."[41] Though Lee did not initially take the hint, events later that year would force him from his comfortable homes and fields into exile on a new and challenging frontier.[42]

30

Cut Off

Utah and Nevada, 1870-71

In 1869, naturalist John Wesley Powell catapulted to national fame by leading the first exploration down the Colorado River through the Grand Canyon. Afterward, he wanted to repeat the feat with fewer risks and better scientific results, relying on Utah settlers for assistance. In September 1870, he met Brigham Young, Jacob Hamblin, and some forty others at Parowan for another expedition. Powell hoped to identify spots where packers could deliver supplies to his crew, and Young wanted to find places to expand Mormon settlement and preserve access across the Colorado that would allow his people to migrate further south.[1]

John D. Lee and William Dame were employed in the expedition—Lee as the "road commissioner," and Dame as "commissary" in charge of a "Traveling Tavorn" to assure expedition members enjoyed a "sumpteous Table." Lee, known for his capacity to work under harsh conditions, had ingratiated himself again to Young, and Dame had successfully masked his role in the massacre, maintaining his image as a dependable and trustworthy local leader.

During part of the journey, Lee accompanied Young, who again advised him to take his family and settle in a new frontier region.[2] A few days southeast of Parowan near the Paria River, a tributary of the Colorado, Young asked Lee what value he saw in the area. Lee replied he "would want no greater punishment" than to be sent to the inhospitable desert region.[3]

After exploring the Paria River, the two parts of the expedition split. Hamblin and Powell's party headed south into northern Arizona, while Young's group went to Kanab.[4] There Lee's old friend Levi Stewart and Young discussed the idea of a community sawmill. Young doubted the venture would succeed, but Stewart thought it might if Lee took charge.

"I replied," Lee wrote, "that if the Prest. wanted Me to Run that Mill, I was willing to do for the best, for the advance of kingdom, yet I was aware that unless Energetic Men took hold & Run the Mill, it would be a sinking buisiness."

Figure 30.1 Paiute leader Tau-gu (Coal Creek John) and John Wesley Powell. Courtesy American Antiquarian Society.

Lee agreed to "return home, Sell out & haste back & take charge of the Mill" in what was called the Skutumpah Valley.[5]

At some point during the trip, Lee's name came up in conversation between Young and southern Utah's resident apostle, Erastus Snow. Over the years, Snow had gleaned information about the Mountain Meadows Massacre, aided by Lorenzo Roundy, bishop of the Mormon settlement of Kanarra eight miles northeast of Harmony. For the most part, Snow had "refrained from saying much on the subject to anyone," including Young.[6] But he now broke his silence, perhaps bothered by the kindly manner in which Young treated Lee during the expedition or Young's praise of Lee's energy and pioneering skills.

Whatever the reason, Snow later testified that he and Roundy "communicated to President Young the facts" about the massacre "as we had learned them, and the sources of our information."[7] Roundy felt Young "did not know the truth" and bluntly told him he had "been misled and deceived" about the matter. "If you want to know the truth about it," Roundy suggested, "ask Nephi Johnson, & he will tell you."[8]

Young's company arrived back in Salt Lake City on September 24. Decades later, Nephi Johnson testified that he was called to Salt Lake, where Young "requested me to tell him all I knew of the whole affa[i]r." Young had read non-Mormon investigators' accounts of the massacre but chose to ignore them in favor of what his own trusted men told him of the atrocity. Now Johnson, a Mormon witness to the crime, stood before him, backing up much of what non-Mormon investigators had said.

Johnson knew the prime movers in the crime were not Indians. He could testify that Lee played a leading role in the massacre from the first attack to the final slaughter, and that Lee was not alone. Militiamen sent by Isaac Haight had gathered Paiutes to the Meadows and orchestrated the final attack. As Johnson relayed his version of events, Young paced the floor, "deeply impressed," several times interjecting, "Why did Lee lie to me?"

Believing Johnson's statement that many who took part in the massacre did so under duress and at their militia leaders' orders, Young said he would not hold the younger men responsible but would punish the ringleaders. He soon acted on what he learned.[9]

Between the church's general conference sessions on October 8, "we held a Council at noon at Presidet Youngs office," Wilford Woodruff wrote. The First Presidency and Quorum of the Twelve Apostles "by unanimous vote Cut of[f] Isaac Haight, John D Lee & [George] Wood, for Committing a great Sin & they were not to have the Privilege of Returning . . . to the Church again in this life."[10] Apostle Joseph F. Smith wrote of the meeting, "John D. Lee and I. Haight and Geo. Wood, were cut off the Church because of extreem wickedness, or for having been engaged in the M. M. M."[11]

Though no evidence exists that Cedar City resident George Wood participated in the massacre, he murdered Olive Coombs Higby and attempted to kill her teenaged daughter in 1862. In her 1950 book on the massacre, Juanita Brooks wrote that Olive's granddaughter, Olive Millburn, believed her grandmother had been murdered because she was gathering information about the massacre that she intended to publish. But contemporary sources show that Wood confessed immediately after committing the crime that he believed Olive was running a brothel in Cedar City and that her daughter had seduced his son.[12]

Unaware of his excommunication, Lee went about setting up his new home and sawmill in Skutumpah.[13] Visiting Kanab on November 17, Lee was "informed," he wrote, "that Myself, I. C. Haight, & Geo. Wood had been expelled from the Church, but for what cause it [was] not Stated." Though Lee must have known the massacre was the reason, he wrote that his conscience was clear and that he "had not done anything knowingly or designedly wrong," adding, "I borrowed no trouble about the Matter."[14]

In Lee's mind, his accusers, Erastus Snow and Lorenzo Roundy, were the wrongdoers. "I was aware that Satan was working through certain Persons to injure Me," he wrote. He dismissed the excommunication as a ruse, a public move on Young's part to throw off detractors.

But Lee's excommunication soon hit home. Though some Kanab residents, like massacre participant George W. Adair, treated Lee sympathetically, others now "turned a cold shoulder upon Me & kept out of My way," wrote Lee. "Now is the time to find out who are your true friends."[15]

On a visit to the Washington settlement, where three of Lee's wives still lived, he heard whisperings in his family. When he asked his wife Lovina "what was up," she confessed she had gone to see Young to learn the truth about her husband's rumored excommunication. Young had not only confirmed the news but declared Lee would never be "rebaptised again by his consent." Because Lee was no longer a church member authorized to practice polygamy, Young counseled Lovina to leave Lee, "to take her children & do right & look to her oldest Son to take care of her."

Wounded, Lee called Lovina "an ungratefull woman," adding that she "or any other of My wives who do not wish to live with Me can be free."[16]

The next day, Lee went to see Young, who was wintering at his home in nearby St. George. "Met Me quite warmly at [fir]st," Lee recorded of his encounter with the church president, "But afterwards apeared a litle cool." According to Lee's journal, he asked Young why "all of a sudden I Must be cut off from this church" after thirteen years of fellowship following the massacre. "If it was wrong now, it certainly was wrong then," Lee protested.[17]

Young "replied that they had never learned the particuelars until lately."

Lee remonstrated that he told Young the truth in 1857, "with the Exception of one thing & that was that I suffered the blame to rest on Me, when it should rest on Persons whoes Names that has never been brought out."

In reality, when Lee reported the massacre to Young in 1857, he blamed Indians for the murders, claiming no white men participated. Most importantly, he concealed that he conspired with other local leaders to orchestrate the attack and the final slaughter.

But now Young had learned more information from Latter-day Saints he trusted, like Nephi Johnson and Erastus Snow. Unable to conceal the extent of his participation from Young any longer, Lee pivoted, attempting to justify his participation on moral or religious grounds.

He was innocent "of doeing any thing designedly wrong; what we done was by the mutual consent & council of the high counsellors, Presidents, Bishops & Leading Men, who Prayed over the Matter & diligently Sought the Mind & will of the Spirit of Truth to direct the affair," he told Young. "Our covenants & the love of Righteousness alone prompted the act. My concience is clear before God& I know that I have a reward in Heaven." Lee begged for a rehearing of his case.

"You can have a rehearing," Young conceded after Lee's emotional display, but "I want you to be a Man & not a Baby."

Young arranged a meeting between Lee and Erastus Snow to schedule the rehearing, which was set for the following week.[18]

Lee visited Isaac Haight in Toquerville to commiserate with his fellow excommunicant. Haight "felt ready to despare," Lee wrote, because no notice of a rehearing "had been sent to him & he feared that he would never get a hearing until there would be a change of Dynasty."

"Do not suffer such a thought to enter your heart," Lee replied, "for there was Justice in the rulers of Iseral yet."[19]

But while Lee was away, Snow visited his home in Washington to cancel the rehearing. "They, the council, had concluded not to have an investigation at present," Snow told Lee's family, because "the least Said at presant, the better."[20]

Lee received this news when he returned to Washington, along with an anonymous letter delivered by Snow's son. "If you will consult your own safety & that [of] others," the letter reportedly read, "you will not press your self nor an investigation on others at this time least you cause others to become accessory with you & thereby force them to inform upon you or suffer. Our advice is, Trust no one. Make yourself scarce & keep out of the way."[21]

Lee needed no further warning. He began traveling through the local towns, settling his affairs and buying supplies before departing. While visiting Kanarra for a New Year's celebration, he ran into Bishop Lorenzo Roundy. Still steaming about what Roundy and Snow had told Young about his role in the massacre, Lee intentionally joined a dance formation that placed him in the same group with Roundy.

"You are as Rough as an old Grisley," Roundy said when the two clasped hands.

"Lorinzo, Every Dog will have his day," Lee growled back. "Now is your day. By & by it will be my day."[22]

Lee faced more opposition as he tried to settle up and leave Harmony. "Many who owed me refused to pay," he wrote. What was more, Harmony bishop W. D. Pace "used a heavy & wicked influence to break up My Family, & had persuadd My Family not to go with Me, as I was droped from the church." Lee left with only one of his two Harmony wives, Sarah Caroline, though the other, Emma, later decided to join him.[23]

As Lee made his final trek to the remote Skutumpah ranch, he once again stayed with Haight in Toquerville, selling his host a breech-loading firearm.[24] Later, Lee sold his interest in the sawmill, reasoning, "My Position is rather P[r]ecarious & unsafe."[25]

He was not the only massacre perpetrator moving towards the outskirts of Latter-day Saint society. Since leaving Cedar City in 1860, Philip Klingensmith had become something of a nomad.[26] After losing his home in the 1862 floods, he accompanied Hamblin on a visit to Native peoples south of the Colorado River.[27] Following a brief attempt to start a new community in central Utah with local Indians, Klingensmith moved to Nevada, where he farmed, mined, and freighted.[28]

Living in the non-Mormon mining regions of Nevada was risky for a Mormon of Klingensmith's background. He had a falling out with a son who turned informant, telling Nevadans his father participated in the Mountain Meadows Massacre. The revelation "caused considerable excitement among the settlers."

Charles Wesley Wandell, a former Mormon who served as prosecuting attorney for Nevada's Lincoln County, told Klingensmith "what his son had exposed, and hurried him out of town."[29] Klingensmith shared his story of the massacre with Wandell, who persuaded him to make a public statement about the crime.[30]

Wandell had launched a series of "Open Letters to Brigham Young" in the *Daily Corinne (Utah) Reporter*, using the pen name "Argus."[31] When he received "the startling and unexpected information" that Young had excommunicated Haight and Lee for their roles in the massacre, he began to focus on the atrocity.[32]

As Wandell had urged, Klingensmith swore out an affidavit about the massacre before the Lincoln County clerk on April 10, 1871, making him the first participant to give an official written statement about the atrocity in his own name. When asked whether Young authorized the massacre, Klingensmith said he didn't know. Haight had told him "he had orders from headquarters to kill all of said company of emigrants except the little children." But Klingensmith swore he did not "know whether said headquarters meant the regimental headquarters at Parowan"—where William Dame was commander—"or the headquarters of the Commander-in-Chief at Salt Lake City," Daniel H. Wells.[33] Importantly, Klingensmith acknowledged that he "discharged" his firearm at the massacre—a tacit confession.[34]

In the early 1870s, two disaffected Mormons, William S. Godbe and E. L. T. Harrison, started the *Mormon Tribune*, later renamed the *Salt Lake Tribune*. The paper's editorial policy was to "know no such distinctions as 'Mormon' or 'Gentile,'" and its editor promised that the "TRIBUNE shall not express any opinion as to the guilt or innocence of any persons accused of crime until such cases are decided by the courts."[35]

But the *Tribune*'s proprietors soon determined that to succeed financially, their paper would have to engage, as one newspaper historian put it, in "a gloves-off fight on ecclesiastical as well as economic, political and social issues." Religion and politics being highly polarized in Utah, there were too few subscribers in the neutral class "to make such a newspaper as they had pledged to publish economically viable."[36] Though this would change in modern times, the early *Tribune* soon settled into a successful niche as a boldly anti-Mormon newspaper.

On August 10, 1871, the *Tribune* printed a letter by E. C. Brand, a missionary for the Reorganized Church of Jesus Christ of Latter Day Saints, who made a preaching tour through southern Utah.[37] The Reorganized Church was a smaller rival of the Utah-based church, and its members believed their organization—not the one led by Brigham Young—was the rightful successor to the church formed by Joseph Smith.[38] "At the Mountain Meadows," Brand wrote of his tour, "I re-erected the cross, torn down from the monument, and wrote another inscription."[39]

He also interviewed John D. Lee, hoping to persuade the excommunicant to join his church. In his journal, Lee wrote that Brand said "9 Tenths of the People believe that Brigham has Treacherously . . . Made Me a scape Goat, to bear of[f] his sins." Lee said Brand told him to "come to them & I would find Friends & protection. . . . All we ask of you is to tell us that Brigham Young counceld it, which almost every body believd."

Lee acknowledged he might never be readmitted to his own church. "But," he stressed, "let this, My Testim[on]y, suffice from troubling Me on the subject any More: Brigham Young knew nothing of the Mountain Massacre until it was all over; & verry Much regretted it when he heard of it, & I am satisfied that he never would have suffered it, could [he] have prevent d."

"I believe in even-handed Justice," Lee told Brand. "I would never betrey an innocent Man to Save my own Neck, no, I would hang a thousand times first."[40]

When Brand returned to Salt Lake, he reported his interview to the *Tribune*, which quoted Lee as saying "that the greater portion of 'Argus' letter was very true; but that Brigham Young had nothing to do with the bloody deed." Lee also "disclaimed playing anything more than a subordinate part himself in the affair, and said he would be glad to see the responsibility of the murder fixed on the real authors."[41]

But the next day, the *Tribune* published a letter from Brand reasoning that Lee would not have done what he did unless ordered. Brand asserted that Lee affirmed much of Argus's account of the massacre, saying "that the 'saddle was on the right horse' "—implying that Lee charged the massacre to Young. Brand said Lee "made the same statement at Parowan, at the Post office."[42]

Weeks later at the Parowan post office, Lee saw Brand's letter and fumed that Brand used his name "in clandistine Manner to falsely try to establish his wicked purpose." Lee told the postmaster the account "was false as hell & Mr. B[rand] knew it."[43]

In October 1871, Lee hosted Major John Wesley Powell and his party at the Skutumpah ranch when they passed through en route to the north. Powell had just completed his second trip down the Colorado to the Crossing of the Fathers, where he and expedition photographer Jack Hillers left the river for the season, sending the rest of Powell's crew further downstream to the Paria's mouth. Powell and Hillers rode back to civilization with a pack train that Jacob Hamblin had led to the ford with Powell's supplies. Hamblin had then gone on to Fort Defiance in Arizona Territory with Isaac Haight and George Adair.[44]

Hillers, whose photographs of Powell's expedition soon made him famous, wrote that Lee "entertained us hugely" at his ranch.[45] Neither Powell nor his men, though funded by Congress, sought to turn in Lee. Later, they would even use federal funds to pay him.[46]

Figure 30.2　Men of second Powell expedition. Courtesy Utah State Historical Society.

"About this time," however, Lee recorded in his journal, word of threatened arrests reached Skutumpah. "I had to dodge to keep out of the way of the officers, who had writs for all who practiced Polygamy &c."[47]

31

Boiling Conditions

Utah and Arizona, 1871

After Civil War general Ulysses S. Grant was inaugurated as U.S. president in 1869, anti-polygamy sentiment heated up again in Washington. Unenforceable in practice, the 1862 Morrill Anti-Bigamy Act had little effect on the Latter-day Saints, who believed their plural marriages were sanctioned by the Bible and protected by the Constitution. But other Americans felt just as strongly that polygamy was immoral. Hoping to stamp out the practice, they urged the Grant administration to reconstruct Utah as the federal government was reconstructing southern states after the war.[1]

Washington responded by appointing James B. McKean of New York as Utah's new chief justice. McKean accepted his appointment with a sense of mission as strong as that of the Mormons, believing he had been commissioned by God to root out polygamy.[2]

McKean was a distinguished public servant, both a U.S. congressman and a Civil War colonel of volunteer troops.[3] On receiving news of McKean's judicial appointment, Utah's congressional delegate, William H. Hooper, wrote George A. Smith that he "considered him a very good man." But given Washington's new get-tough policy toward Utah, Hooper thought McKean would be expected to show "his teeth toward us."[4]

In the anti-polygamy campaign that followed, the now thirteen-year-old Mountain Meadows Massacre case and other instances of extralegal violence from the Utah War period became political ammunition. McKean focused his anti-polygamy campaign on seventy-year-old Brigham Young. To many Americans, plural marriage evoked both curiosity and rancor.[5] By combining polygamy with old murder charges, prosecutors focused on sex and violence, a surefire formula for attracting public attention. In his zeal, however, McKean violated jury laws, a mistake for which the U.S. Supreme Court would later reverse his decisions.[6]

Utah's U.S. attorney, Charles H. Hempstead, told his superiors that it would take far more money than he received to prosecute "'Mormon outrages' and murders committed years agoe, such as the 'Parrish murders, Mountain Meadow Massacre' &c."[7] Hempstead resigned, and McKean appointed Robert N. Baskin, a non-Mormon resident of Salt Lake City, to serve until Washington named a replacement.[8] Baskin, partly trained at Harvard, was described by one Salt Lake visitor as "a lawyer of shrewdness and coolness" who was "inflamed against Mormonism."[9]

Utah's anti-Mormon political machine of the 1860s solidified into the Liberal Party in the 1870s, and Mormons derisively labeled its leaders "the Gentile Ring." If Justice McKean was its "organizing spirit," wrote one commentator, Baskin was its "executive arm."[10] Baskin had personal reasons for wanting to pursue old murder cases in Utah. He had vowed to seek justice after a client, Dr. J. King Robinson, was called out one night to attend a patient, then beaten to death in Salt Lake City. The brutal murder had never been solved.[11]

Like Judge John Cradlebaugh before him, Baskin believed there was "an irrepressible conflict between the system established by the Mormons and the republican institutions of the United States which would preclude the admission of the Territory into the Union as long as that conflict continued, and that it could only be ended by destroying the temporal power" of Latter-day Saint leaders.[12]

To go after Young and polygamy effectively, McKean and Baskin felt they needed more than the toothless Morrill Act. They decided to try polygamists under a Utah territorial law against lewd and lascivious cohabitation—a clever gambit that turned the law against its polygamous drafters, who did not intend it to apply to plural marriages.[13]

Between September and November 1871, Brigham Young was charged with multiple counts of lascivious cohabitation—and with murder. The latter charge stemmed from the notorious axe bludgeoning of an arms dealer by William "Bill" Hickman, a Mormon, during the Utah War.[14]

Latter-day Saints, horrified at the prospect of seeing their church president behind bars, wanted to protect him from what they thought was certain death, remembering the murder of Young's predecessor, Joseph Smith.[15] Apostle John Taylor, wounded during Smith's assassination, protested Young's "putting himself into the hands of the Marshal," afraid of seeing the tragedy repeated. Young assured Taylor and others "that things were entirely different to what they were then." Shifting from his 1850s stance, Young "did not consider that he would be exposed to assassination . . . as Joseph was in

Carthage jail." He "intended to meet and fight the opposition in the court room," and he defied "the world to prove aught against him."[16]

In October, Young and other Latter-day Saint leaders submitted to arrest. In the highly publicized proceedings that followed, McKean said the case pitted "the government of the United States" against "another government— claiming to come from God."[17] In a letter to Overland Stage magnate Ben Holladay, a long-time friend and a non-Mormon, Young pointed to McKean's declaration "that it is not Brigham Young and others—for murder or un-lawful co-habitation,—that are being tried," but "'Federal Authority against Polygamic Theocracy.'"[18]

However sensationally the case started, Young simply posted bail on his cohabitation charge and, assured the murder charge was not imminent, left to spend the winter in the warmth of southern Utah.[19]

News of McKean's efforts whizzed to both coasts by telegraph and passed throughout Utah Territory and the West. As John Wesley Powell and his overland party continued north from Skutumpah after staying with John D. Lee, they felt the growing tension as rumors spread that polygamous Mormon leaders faced arrest. When the party reached Manti on October 23, "We heard of the trouble at Salt Lake," Jack Hillers wrote. The local bishop "was all in a flurry. Indians came in and told him that soldiers were on their way to arrest him. We left him in a state of boiling conditions."[20]

Just a few weeks before, as Powell left the Colorado River at Crossing of the Fathers with Hillers, he sent the rest of his crew downstream to the mouth of the Paria in Arizona. There the men concluded their 1871 expedition and waited for a pack train to bring them supplies and guide them to their winter quarters.[21] As time passed, Powell's men worried about starving if the supply train went missing.[22]

As the men camped on the north side of the Colorado, they were sur-prised to see Indians and horses on the other side. Soon another figure appeared, calling out, "G-o-o-d m-o-r-n-i-n-g," in "long drawn out" tones. When Powell's men rowed across to investigate, they "were met," Frederick Dellenbaugh wrote, "by a slow-moving, very quiet individual, who said he was Jacob Hamblin."[23]

Hamblin was returning from a visit to the Hopi—accompanied by nine Navajos and Mountain Meadows Massacre participants Isaac Haight and George Adair. Powell's crew ferried Hamblin's group across the river. Near its bank, with their campfire illuminating the red sandstone cliffs, this odd assortment of men cast together by fate—government explorers, Navajos,

Jacob Hamblin, and massacre participants—shared a meal, tobacco, and conversation. The whites asked their Navajo companions to sing Native songs.

"Some of their chants were rather pretty," wrote Clem Powell, Major Powell's cousin, "and [we] persuaded all of the Indians to dance while the chief paddled away on the bottom of an inverted camp kettle. All of us, white and red, joined hands and danced around the fire." When the men finally slept, a full moon passed overhead, lighting the desert landscape with ghostly hues as the nearby waters of the Paria and Colorado mixed, tumbled over rocks, and plunged into the canyons below.[24]

When Hamblin's party left the next day, Powell's men urged Hamblin's crew "to hurry our train up," emphasizing they "were wearily waiting for it."[25] Their situation became desperate when the train still had not arrived a few days later. "If we are compelled to leave here on foot with but one day's rations," John F. Steward confided to his diary, "I do not know how it will end." Nursing a leg injury from the river trip, Steward feared he would "probably not survive." Powell's men placed their hope in Hamblin's party, reasoning that on reaching Kanab, they would quickly send the supply train if it had not yet started.[26]

When Hamblin's party got to Kanab, they learned the train had left days earlier and might be lost.[27] Worried, Isaac Haight gathered up food and, with another man, drove "furiously" to the Paria. Powell's men were awestruck when the two "large-hearted gentlemen" arrived at their camp two days later. Their "prompt and generous efforts in our behalf," said Clem Powell, was something he and the other crew members would "long remember."[28]

The rescued men found Haight's sacrifice to save their lives incompatible with what they had heard of his role in the massacre. "He is an agreeable man," wrote Stephen Vandiver Jones, assistant topographer. "It is hard to believe him guilty of the crimes laid to his charge. Can it be that he would sanction and assist in the murder of women and children?"[29]

After Powell's men left for their winter quarters at Kanab, Hamblin sought to secure ownership of the river crossing where the men had camped.[30] The site would be valuable to the Saints in interacting with tribes across the river, as well as in further settling Arizona. If unfriendly parties preempted the site, they might cut off access to the crossing just when polygamy prosecutions had rekindled talk of yet another Mormon migration.

In the meantime, Judge McKean's campaign accelerated, prompting polygamists to flee their homes to avoid prosecution. Receiving word that "writs were out for My self, Haight & others," John D. Lee took steps to defend himself. "I obtained some cartridges," he wrote, then hid with other fugitives in a mountain dell. The general stampede of polygamists provided good cover for the massacre perpetrators. Lee went to Kanab, and Haight went to Toquerville. Lee heard "that Spies were out in every Setlements, & writs for every Man that had More wives then one."

Lee soon met Hamblin, who directed him to "join a company & make a Road to the crossing of the Colerado River" at the mouth of the Paria. Hamblin invited Lee to settle the crossing site and build a ranch there, hoping to retain a small interest in it himself. "So if you have a woman that has Faith enough to go with you," Hamblin instructed Lee, "Take her along & some cows." Hamblin thought Lee could support two hundred head of cattle there and volunteered to provide seeds and fruit trees.[31]

Though Hamblin temporarily sheltered Lee, Haight, and other massacre participants swept up in the polygamists' flight, he had long deplored the atrocity.[32] Frederick Dellenbaugh of Powell's expedition believed Hamblin when he said "that if he had been at home [at the Mountain Meadows] that day the crime would not have happened."[33]

Hamblin was willing to testify against massacre participants if the case came to trial. Young felt that time might soon be at hand. Anticipating that McKean might charge him as an accomplice in the massacre, Young asked Hamblin to record what he knew about the crime.[34]

In November 1871, Hamblin signed a letter to Young about the massacre of the Arkansas company and the raid on the Dukes train. On November 28, Hamblin signed an affidavit containing similar information.[35] The letter and affidavit stated that Hamblin was in Young's office in September 1857 when a messenger from southern Utah arrived seeking counsel on what to do with the besieged emigrants. Hamblin reported that "the spirit of the Express" was that "they [the emigrants] ought to be chastised," and that Young answered, "*No!* they have a perfect right to pass, let them go on."

In some ways, Hamblin's 1871 version of events differed from what he had reported to Major James H. Carleton in 1859. Hamblin told Carleton that while returning from Salt Lake to his ranch at the Meadows in September 1857, he encamped near Fillmore "with a company from Iron county," who told him only that a party of emigrants "had all been killed off at Mountain Meadows, except seventeen children."

Now, fourteen years after the massacre, Hamblin wrote that it was John D. Lee who told him the "immigrants were all wiped out excepting a few children," and that when Hamblin asked why, Lee answered, "They were enemies to us, and that this was the beginning of great and important events."

According to his 1871 account, Hamblin next ran into William Dame, to whom he "spoke emphatically against such proceedings." Dame countered, "Lee, and the Indians had commenced a bad job and it had to be disposed off, for if it should come to the ears of President Buchannen it would endanger the lives of the breth[re]n." Hamblin answered, "I had rather that Jas Buchannen and all of his cabinet would know the indians had killed and wounded a few men, than for the Lord Almighty to know that I had consented to the death of women and children."[36]

While wintering in southern Utah, Young learned that the charge of murdering the arms dealer had come down in McKean's court. Young could have crossed the territorial border to hide in Arizona but resolved instead to return to Salt Lake to face the charges. Again fearing he would be assassinated, Latter-day Saints tried to dissuade him as he traveled home. Undeterred, he assured them, "God would overrule all for the best good of Zion."[37]

While Young hurried north to face his accusers, John D. Lee went further south into hiding. In late November, he set out driving cattle to the Colorado River crossing—cattle perhaps descended from stock owned by massacre victims.[38] Lee decided to drive the animals down the Paria River, where narrow canyons would help keep the cattle from straying. The treacherous course required both man and beast to wade through icy water at a time when flash floods could engulf and drown them all.

The ordeal took Lee, a son, and two friends "some 8 days of toil, fatuige, & labour," Lee wrote. "Some of our animals Mired down" in quicksand. The men could pull themselves free from the muck, but they had to rescue cattle, whose weight made them sink.

When one cow sank beyond help, Lee and his companions shot and butchered it in place, surviving on the beef. Ten miles or so above the mouth of the river, they finally left most of the cattle to graze in an open area before reaching the confluence of the Paria and the Colorado in Arizona. The trip took much longer than expected. Two of Lee's wives, Rachel and Emma, and their children soon joined Lee at the mouth of the Paria, where they began building a settlement they called Lonely Dell.[39]

Young reached Salt Lake on December 26, 1871.[40] By then, newly appointed U.S. district attorney George C. Bates had arrived in Utah to replace interim appointee Robert Baskin.[41] Bates, a New York native, had served as U.S. attorney for Michigan, where he prosecuted James Strang, leader of a

Mormon schismatic group.[42] Bates then moved to Illinois, where he suffered severe financial losses in the Great Chicago Fire of 1871.[43]

When Bates took over responsibility for prosecuting Young, Latter-day Saint leaders believed he would treat them fairly.[44] One man reported to Young after visiting the new prosecutor, "I am decidedly pleased with him. From such gentlemen no good man has aught to fear."[45]

As Young prepared for his trial, Bates received a copy of Philip Klingensmith's April 1871 affidavit from Nevada, which had not yet become public. Though Klingensmith's affidavit stated he did not know whether orders for the massacre originated in Salt Lake or Parowan, Bates wrote his superior in Washington that he believed it showed the emigrants "were murdered, under the written orders . . . of Brigham Young himself."

Bates proposed to prosecute the massacre case in Beaver, Utah, the following May. He requested additional funding and "two companies of soldiers there to aid the US Marshal, to arrest Defendants, defend jurors and witnesses from assault, and to Enable a United States court to Enforce its mandates." Bates concluded his letter, "Please read this to the new Atty General; and if possible to [President] Grant himself, and direct me how to act."[46]

At long last, Bates thought, the stage was set for the massacre case to come to trial.

32

Zeal O'erleaped Itself

Utah, Arizona, and Washington, DC, 1871-72

George C. Bates hoped to convict Brigham Young, but bickering over finances and infighting among federal appointees slowed the process. "A small ring of Politicians" in Utah, Bates wrote his superiors in Washington, wanted "to have Brigham Young and other Mormons *persecuted* and harassed in Every form and Shape." Bates incurred their wrath "because," he said, "I will do nothing except 'calmly, justly, and fairly,' without fear favor or affection."[1]

Hoping to try the Mountain Meadows Massacre case, Bates negotiated to get Philip Klingensmith as a witness. Klingensmith agreed to testify if offered protection. Bates believed that with evidence from Klingensmith, corroborated by others, "we can convict the crowd of murderers."

Bates proposed holding court in Beaver with the aid of U.S. Army soldiers—the strategy Judge John Cradlebaugh tried in 1859. But Bates needed more funds to pay witnesses, jurors, and courtroom expenses. Eager to secure justice for the massacre victims, he sought federal funding, asking Washington: "Can the US Government; afford to leave their murder unavenged??"[2] Washington, however, refused to allocate funds, seeing the crimes as local in nature.

At the same time, Bates found himself pinched between suspicious Mormons and hardline officials, including Judge McKean, who wanted to replace him with Robert Baskin. Both Bates and McKean went to Washington to plead their cases. McKean's faction had the ear of President Ulysses S. Grant, who offered to accept Bates's resignation. Bates refused and had the U.S. attorney general and solicitor general on his side. Both sides presented petitions signed by non-Mormons in Utah to endorse their positions. McKean's group had three hundred signatures, while Bates's had at least five times that number.[3]

Eager to break the stalemate, both sides watched for the decision of the U.S. Supreme Court in the case of *Clinton v. Englebrecht*, which tested whether McKean's judicial decisions against Latter-day Saints would hold up. In deciding the *Englebrecht* case, which dealt with overreaching by Salt Lake City police, McKean disregarded an 1859 Utah law requiring that juries be chosen from pools selected by county courts. Given Utah's overwhelmingly Latter-day Saint population, McKean knew such juries would be made up mostly, if not exclusively, of people he assumed would favor the Mormon parties in the case.[4]

The problem McKean noted was a longstanding one in American law. Both judges and jurors tended to come from whatever group made up the majority voting population, making it difficult for those in the minority to get equal justice.[5] The Saints had experienced such discrimination before settling Utah and becoming the majority. Now they saw the Utah jury law as a way of preserving their rights, especially against federally appointed judges who they felt were biased against them.

Judge McKean, on the other hand, recognized the importance of preserving minority rights in a territory where Latter-day Saints were the majority. Rather than balance the rights of the majority and minority populations, however, he sought to exclude Mormons entirely.[6] In the end, the U.S. Supreme Court ruled against McKean, declaring he had "wholly and purposely disregarded" Utah's 1859 jury law.[7] Unless the law changed, the court said, McKean was bound to follow it.

Though the 1859 jury law would eventually change, the decision meant that every case in which McKean disregarded the law was effectively overturned.[8] As the Chicago *Post* editorialized, "McKean's zeal o'erleaped itself."[9]

"A telegram announced that the U.S. Supreme Court had decided that the trials in the territorial court over which Judge McKean presided were illegal," John Wesley Powell's brother-in-law, then in southern Utah, recorded. "Consequently all the Mormon prisoners, from Brigham Young down are released. A jubilee was being held in Washington," Utah.[10]

Before the Supreme Court's *Englebrecht* decision, John D. Lee nervously kept his vigil at the Lonely Dell. But soon a rush for precious minerals on the Colorado made even Lonely Dell not lonely enough for the man whose name was frequently on the public's lips when discussing the Mountain Meadows Massacre. Regardless of his tenuous situation, the garrulous Lee could not refrain from talking to passersby, though he often used his middle name—Doyle—as an alias.[11]

Most passing miners, it turned out, had little interest in seeing Lee arrested. At Lonely Dell, he invited one group to supper, which they gratefully accepted. After eating, one man proposed a game of cards. Latter-day

Saint society frowned on card playing, but Lee accepted the invitation, saying that "for pasttime," he "would do [so] with pleasure." The night "passed of[f] quite agreeably, & prejudices began to give way," Lee wrote.

In spite of his friendliness to the miners, he overheard an Englishman trying to stir up others to take him "to Salt Lake City [for] the reward." A Canadian snapped back, "You had better dry up your damed noise or you [will] get sent cross lots to Hell." The Canadian warned the Englishman that Lee "was armed to the teeth . . . & as for his part he did not want to make his Money by betraying a man . . . who had been kind to him."

Another said he had been "prejudiced against Lee . . . & was once the Man to have helped to take him." But after meeting Lee, he decided, "Whether he is guilty or not, that is none of My buisiness. He has treatd Me like a gentleman."

The night before the company left, a miner told one of Lee's hired hands that some of the miners "think More of the reward for his Skelp, then th[e]y would of a gold Mine." He warned that they might return with a posse to catch Lee.

Stirred by the warnings, Lee left his wife Emma and their children at the Lonely Dell and moved his wife Rachel and their children to Jacob's Pools, an even more remote spot along the Vermillion Cliffs road. There they built a rock-and-stick dwelling for her and their children, and "pased off the lonely hours of the day as best we could," he wrote—a bitter contrast to earlier times.[12]

On June 8, 1872, Lee wrote in his journal that he received a "confidential Letter," which promised that if he "continued faithful & true to that Mission," he "never should be captured by My Enemies." The letter, from an unnamed source, said "to take no further trouble on that Point, that I should have timely warning of the approach of Danger & that I should be remembered for My integrity & interest in the welfare of this People & Kingdom." Concerns about the miners eventually abated, and Lee started back toward Lonely Dell.[13]

At Lonely Dell and the Pools, the Lee families received visits from current and former members of John Wesley Powell's survey crew. One was Francis Marion Bishop, who became a friend of massacre perpetrator Nephi Johnson when Johnson worked for the survey. Bishop had also met Ira Hatch, the interpreter who helped track and kill the emigrant "Baker" at the Muddy River shortly after the massacre.[14]

With these acquaintances, Bishop was well situated to meet "the celebrated John D. Lee of Mountain Meadow Massacre fame." According to Bishop, Lee talked "very freely and said he could prove that he was not on the ground at

Figure 32.1 John D. Lee family members at home at Jacob's Pools. Courtesy Utah State Historical Society.

the time and that he opposed the whole affair in the council. Gave me considerable information regarding the unfortunate occurrence." Bishop felt "that some part of his statement don't sound right in connection with the statements of other parties," and he recorded Lee's damning acknowledgment "that there were a majority of the council who decided to help destroy the train thinking it the only course to be pursued, and that some of them were actually present and stained their hands with the blood of men, women, and children."[15]

Former Powell employee E. O. Beaman, who accompanied Bishop on one visit with Lee, left a brief account of the massacre from Lee and other locals. "Although the majority of the immigrants were well-to-do, respectable people, and inclined to pass the Mormons by without molesting them," Beaman recorded of their assertions, "there were among them a few incendiary spirits; and to these may be attributed the tragedy that followed." Beaman observed, "This hellish deed is generally attributed to the Indians, but that the leaders were Mormons is generally asserted," with Lee blamed as "the prime instigator."

Beaman wrote that according to Lee, "a messenger was sent to Brigham during the siege, asking counsel; and the answer was: 'Let the immigrants go; they have been sufficiently punished for the indignities offered us.' This answer arrived too late." Beaman remarked that although Lee was "a fugitive from justice with a price set on his head," he was very hospitable to Bishop and him, though "his manner was marked by that eternal vigilance which is the price of safety."[16]

The next month, John H. Beadle, special correspondent for the *Cincinnati Commercial*, reached Lonely Dell. There he met Emma and "eight or ten children." When he asked about John D. Lee and the ferry, Emma feigned ignorance, answering that "Major Doyle lived there, and she knew of no Lee's Ferry, and no such man as John D. Lee."

Emma's denials made Beadle think he had arrived at the wrong location. When Major Doyle returned, the journalist wrote, they passed the afternoon "quite sociably, and I had not the slightest idea whom I was talking to when in relating some incident my host inadvertently spoke of himself as 'Lee.'"

Catching the slip, Beadle asked if he knew "any such man as John D. Lee."

"That's what some folks call me," Lee admitted.

"You!" Beadle exclaimed. "Why, I thought your name was Doyle."

Lee said his name was John Doyle Lee, but around there he was known as "Major Doyle."

Avoiding mention of the massacre, Lee chalked up his false identity to McKean's efforts to prosecute polygamists. He confessed to being a polygamist and asked, "Suppose you've heard of me?"

Beadle saw this as a smokescreen for "the real reason of his seclusion" but said nothing more until Lee "made a slight reference" to the massacre. Beadle then delicately proposed that, "if it was not disagreeable" to his host, he "should like to hear the *true* account of that affair."

Lee nervously cleared his throat, shifted his chair, then "broke suddenly into a perfect torrent of speech," Beadle said.

"I unbosomed My feelings to him freely," Lee later acknowledged.

Lee denied consenting to the massacre or being present when it occurred. He said he knew who was responsible but refused to betray those "whose motives at first were pure," though "bad as it *turned out*." Lee complained that "my name's heralded all over the country as the biggest villain in America."

As the shadows crept down the massive cliffs surrounding Lonely Dell, Lee "rattled off" his latest version of events that led to the massacre. Even more vehemently than before, he blamed the federal government, Pahvant Indians, and the victims themselves for the massacre.

"Buchanan had sent his army to destroy us," Lee said. Not wanting the army to "find any spoil," the Saints intended "to burn and destroy everything and take to the mountains and fight it out guerilla." The people were "all hot and enthusiastic."

Into this scenario came the emigrants, whom Lee vilified as "the worst lot I ever saw." He said "the company had quarreled . . . and separated, but the biggest half got here first" just as the Mormon militiamen were "going out to war." Lee called the emigrants' conduct "scandalous" and dehumanized them, saying "they acted more like devils than men."

Over the years, the litany of accusations against the emigrants to jus- tify the massacre had grown far beyond Lee's 1857 accounts, as accusatory as they were. Now Lee told Beadle the emigrants had "boasted openly that Buchanan's whole army was a coming right behind 'em, and would kill every g— d—n Mormon in Utah, and make the women and children slaves."

They whipped two bulls through the settlements, calling them Brigham and Heber, "yelling, singing, blackguarding and blaspheming." At Spanish Fork, "one of 'em stood on his wagon tongue, and swung a pistol, and swore that was the pistol that helped kill old Joe Smith, and by the bloody—it was for Brigham Young."

When they reached the Pahvant Indians, "they shot one dead," crippled another, and poisoned a spring. South of Corn Creek, he averred, they used "big Missouri whips" to "snap off the heads of chickens and throw them in their wagons." To a widow who objected, they replied, "Shut up, you G—d d—n Mormon —, or I'll shoot you." Her relatives then came out with their guns "and swore revenge on the whole outfit."

Lee told Beadle that Indians followed the emigrants to the Mountain Meadows. They planned to "make a rush right into the camp," Lee said, "but the dogs got to barking in the corral and let the emigrants know Indians was about. Then one fool Indian off on the hill fired his gun, and spoilt the whole plan." Hearing the gunfire, attackers in the ravine opened fire, killing "six or eight."[17]

After the siege began, "the Indians killed all their cattle and nearly all their horses," Lee asserted. When a council of Mormon militiamen met, Lee was asked what to do. "Persuade the Indians away," he claimed to have said. One man at a second council asked why the settlers should help the emigrants when they "will only go on to California, and bring back a lot to murder us—they must all die!" Lee said he spoke against this plan until younger militiamen said they had killed an emigrant at a spring outside the emigrants' besieged corral. That news sealed the doom of the rest because, as Lee later explained, the murdered man's companion made it back to the corral and reported that Mormons were the killers. "Now we've killed one," the council members said, "we can't let any go, or it will be worse for us."[18]

"I will not betray those men," Lee told Beadle. "They were enthusiastic, but their motives were pure. They knelt and prayed fervently to be guided, then decided the emigrants must die. The country was at war, you know, and those men were their enemies, and had forfeited their lives by their own folly."

Lee maintained that "before the last charge was made I went and tried to persuade the Indians to save the women. But they said 'all was mean and all had to die.'" The other settlers "joined the Indians and the emigrants was killed." Though Lee knew fifty to sixty militiamen were involved, he told Beadle "there was but twenty white men in it." Then backpedaling, he clarified, "I don't believe any one of them was killed by a white man actually." He claimed the emigrants had "eighty men able to fight—and they fought well, and did the best that could be done—and about forty or fifty women," significantly inflating the number of adults killed to obscure that dozens of the victims were children. Instead, Lee boasted that he saved seventeen children by purchasing them from the Indians.

When darkness fell over Lonely Dell, Lee's talk finally became more composed. He described the distribution of the surviving children, Indian Affairs superintendent Jacob Forney's retrieval of them, and Judge John Cradlebaugh's efforts to arrest suspects, which Lee said violated President James Buchanan's peace treaty with the Mormons.

Lee concluded by referring to his interview with Brand, the preacher with the Reorganized Church of Jesus Christ of Latter Day Saints. Still vexed at how the interview was reported, Lee lamented that some people "keep saying . . . that I should come out and might criminate President Young."

"If I was to make forty confessions," Lee avowed, "I could not implicate Brigham Young." Lee said Young had sense "enough to see that such a thing" would "damage him and this people." Lee related that "a messenger was sent first thing to ask his counsel, and he sent back word 'By all means, and as you expect salvation, let them go on.'" Before the rider returned, however, "the whole thing was over—brought to a head by the killin' of the man at the spring." Lee thought it a "pity" that the rider didn't return with Young's order in time, "for those enthusiastic men, they will obey counsel."

Beadle did not believe all of Lee's account, but he gave him a platform to share his story. Although Lee admitted "the complicity of white men" in the massacre, Beadle said "all the Mormons in that section" gave a much higher number of white men involved than Lee did at that time. Beadle also quoted a Mormon who showed him "cattle in his own herd sprung from stock captured at Mountain Meadow." This man "avowed his belief" that the massacre was committed "only for spoil."

By the time Beadle left Lonely Dell, he felt certain Lee would resist arrest. "He often repeated the words, 'I'll die like a man and not be choked [hung] like a dog.'" Besides, "his house is a perfect arsenal in the way of loaded guns." If Lee's whereabouts were not generally known before, they would be when Beadle's account appeared in the *Salt Lake Tribune* on July 29, 1872.[19] After reading it, Lee wrote that "although the account given was far from being correct, nevertheless it was nearer true then any other written account previously brought to light."[20]

Despite Lee's infamy and excommunicated status, both Mormons and non-Mormons who saw him showed little desire to turn him in. Not long after Beadle's departure, Lee hosted more of Powell's men, rendezvousing at his ferry to begin their 1872 river trip through the Grand Canyon.[21]

Frederick Dellenbaugh had been part of Powell's crew that was rescued at the mouth of the Paria in 1871. Now returning to that spot with this year's crew, he noticed something had changed. "We discovered that some one had come in here since our last visit," Dellenbaugh wrote, "and built a house."[22]

Signaling to the owner that he was there, Dellenbaugh fired three shots into the air but got no reply. He slung his Winchester over his shoulder and walked up the Paria towards the house. Spotting Dellenbaugh, a woman slipped inside. Further on, Dellenbaugh found a man plowing a field. The plowman, Dellenbaugh learned, was John D. Lee. As soon as the man "understood who I was he was very pleasant and always was while we were there," Dellenbaugh said.[23]

The two eventually became friendly enough to discuss the massacre. Lee claimed "he really had nothing to do with it and had tried to stop it, and when he could not do so he went to his house and cried." Lee told Dellenbaugh that was why "the Pai Utes ever after called him Naguts or Crybaby."[24]

During their stay, Powell's men exchanged goods with Lee, assisted with the farm, built a bridge across the Paria, and helped improve an irrigation dam.[25] Grateful, Lee and his family invited the men to join them in celebrating the July 24 holiday commemorating the arrival of Mormon pioneers in the Salt Lake Valley.[26]

"Had a good dinner," Clem Powell recorded. "The Old Gent regaled us with sermons, jokes, cards, &c." Lee's enthusiasm and frequent sermonizing led Clem to conclude that "Lee is a little crazy."[27]

Despite Lee's reputed role in the massacre, Dellenbaugh found him "a pleasant enough man," he wrote, "and I feel sure that, ordinarily he would have had no murderous intentions." Although Powell's men had no plans to apprehend Lee, "yet he sometimes thought we might be trying to capture him."[28]

When Lee delivered "a lengthy dissertation on the faith of the Latter-day Saints," the company's mischievous cook, Andy Hattan, "delighted to get behind him and cock a rifle. At the sound of the ominous click Lee would wheel like a flash to see what was up. We had no intention of capturing him, of course, but it amused Andy to act in a way that kept Lee on the *qui vive*."[29]

The Lees took pity on sickly James Fennemore, whom Powell hired as a photographer from the leading Salt Lake gallery of Savage & Ottinger. They nursed a grateful Fennemore back to health. Years later, Fennemore would be present at Lee's death.[30]

As Powell's men waited at the Lonely Dell, Major Powell was searching for a reprovisioning spot far downstream, led by massacre participant George W. Adair and two Indian guides.[31] Adair was on the Powell expedition payroll, continuing his duties on and off for a year and a half.[32]

"Adair is our Indian interpreter, a late acquisition to the party," Clem Powell wrote. "He abounds in jest and anecdotes; his yarns about the campfire would set up a Dime Novel Company for a twelve-month."[33]

Dellenbaugh spoke with Adair about the massacre. "George Adair, whom I knew well, a young fellow at the time, said he joined the [massacre] crowd without knowing what it was all about." Dellenbaugh concluded that Haight, Lee, and Klingensmith "were the real perpetrators" of the crime.[34]

In mid-August 1872, while on his way to Latter-day Saint settlements to buy winter supplies, Lee ran into John Wesley Powell, Adair, and others on their way to the mouth of the Paria. Lee led them back to Lonely Dell, where the group enjoyed "a super of vegitables." Powell and his crew soon set off down the Grand Canyon.

Lee resumed his supply trip to the settlements with wife Rachel until they reached Harmony. The scenery of "the pleasant home of our former abode, brought forcibly to our Minds the many hapy Scenes as well as sorrows, of by gone days," Lee wrote. He spent his sixtieth birthday and a Sabbath there, attending and addressing a public meeting just as he had done on his forty-fifth birthday in 1857, the day before he led an "expedition" to the Mountain Meadows.

On September 11, 1872—the fifteenth anniversary of the massacre—Lee went to Parowan, where he "had an interesting interview with Prest. W. H. Dame who invited us to Dine with him." Sometime that day, a U.S. marshal showed up. Before the *Englebrecht* decision, the marshal's appearance would have made them flee. Now, Lee wrote, "I Made Myself known to him & had quite a chat with him & took a glass to geather as a Matter of Policy."[35]

The meeting punctuated the impasse that kept the massacre from being investigated and prosecuted. After *Englebrecht,* Utah's federal appointees had no confidence in Mormon juries or territorial officers, and in any case they lacked funding to do their work. They put off making arrests and waited for a time when they would have tougher laws and better funding to tackle the case.[36]

PART 6

PROSECUTION

33

The Time Has Come

Utah, Arizona, and Washington, DC, 1872-74

While Utah's federally appointed officials declined to prosecute massacre perpetrators until the territory's jury laws changed, they took actions that would leave them better prepared for that day. They lobbied Washington to build a military installation in Beaver, Utah, a bustling mining town with a significant non-Mormon population, arguing that a fort there would not only protect settlers from Indian raids, but also shelter witnesses and the court in a future trial on the massacre.[1]

Brigham Young protested the building of another military fort in Utah, offering instead to help bring those responsible for the massacre to justice. Although his repeated offer "has not yet been accepted," Young told Secretary of War William W. Belknap in 1872, "I have neither doubt nor fear that the perpetrators of that tragedy will meet their just reward."[2] Despite Young's protests, Congress appropriated $120,000 to build Fort Cameron in Beaver.[3]

By then, a team of Latter-day Saints had helped John D. Lee build a ferry boat at Lee's Lonely Dell outpost on the Colorado River in Arizona.[4] The ferry was soon put to use by Mormon pioneers sent by Young and guided by Jacob Hamblin to settle along the Little Colorado River.[5] Lee ferried them across the Colorado, but not for free.[6] Though he showed friendship to members of his former church, he remained outside the fold.

Travelers were curious about the outcast they saw at Lonely Dell and Jacob's Pools.[7] In May 1873, a Mormon missionary met "a family belonging to John D Lee of Mountain Meadow fame"—Rachel and their children—subsisting in a rock structure at the Pools, "the most wild and romantic" spot he had ever beheld. When the eastbound missionary reached Lonely Dell, he found Lee running the ferry, living with Emma and their youngsters. Lee told him "he was the Father of 62 children."[8]

The following month, Lee's old adversary Lorenzo Roundy passed through Lonely Dell, saying soldiers would arrive in a few days to establish a military post there. The next day, two of Lee's children came, sharing the rumor that the soldiers threatened to "hang old Lee & every child that had a drop of his Blood runing in its veins." Lee decided to "get out of the way to Parts unknown."[9]

He fled south across the Colorado, pressing into the desert. After a grueling journey, he encountered Jacob Hamblin, Ira Hatch, and other Indian missionaries.[10] "Nearly f[ri]ghtened to de[a]th" at the reported approach of six hundred soldiers, Lee "was a regular mooving Arsenal," wrote one missionary, "loaded down with guns, Pistols and Amunition" and intent to "fight to the last." Lee told two inquisitive missionaries "that President Brigham Young knew nothing about the Mountain Meddow Masecree until after it was perpetrated," confirming "by an oath" that Young "was inocent in the affair."[11]

Hamblin and the missionaries were helping Hopi Indians establish a farm at an Arizona spring called Moenave. Hamblin told Lee he could stay at Moenave and help with crops. In turn, Hamblin agreed to look after Lee's properties and family north of the Colorado River, including Emma, who was expecting a baby.[12]

Lee spent weeks waiting for Hamblin's promised return, battling severe illness and anxiety. Thinking a blackbird on a cornstalk mocked him, he drew his gun and shot the creature.[13] Rachel finally came to her husband's rescue in late July, reporting that soldiers had not, in fact, come to Lonely Dell.[14]

Though Lee's role in the massacre and freeness in discussing the crime made him a high-profile target, lesser-known perpetrators circulated more freely. Massacre participant George Adair still worked for John Wesley Powell. Returning from Washington, DC, Powell welcomed two renowned guests to Salt Lake—New York Times correspondent Justin E. Colburn and artist Thomas Moran. Powell took Moran to meet Brigham Young, George A. Smith, George Q. Cannon, and "all the leading Mormons." A surprised Moran wrote, "They are very much like the rest of mankind and all smart fellows."[15]

Powell accompanied his visitors to Fillmore, stopping to transact business while his guests continued on. "Powell does not leave here with us," Moran wrote in Fillmore, "but gives us a man who has been with him a long while. So we are all right."[16] That man, George Adair, guided the visitors on a journey chronicled both by Colburn in the Times and in sketches and paintings by Moran. Adair guided the men from Fillmore to Kanab, taking them on a side trip through Kolob Canyon in what later became Zion National Park.[17]

Adair then went on another trip for Powell's survey while Moran made sketches at the Grand Canyon from which he later painted his famous *Chasm of the Colorado*, for which Congress paid the princely sum of $10,000.[18] Though Adair talked about the massacre with Powell's men, Colburn never mentioned Adair's name or the atrocity in his *Times* articles.[19]

Not long after Colburn and Moran visited the region, Lee left Moenave for Lonely Dell, where Emma presented him their newborn daughter. But Lee's joy turned to anger when he learned Emma had given birth with only their young children to attend her. Though Lee had asked Hamblin to arrange a midwife for Emma, Hamblin said nothing of that to her. Instead, Hamblin told Emma "she had no buisiness hav[ing] any young Lees," John D. wrote, "seeing I was disfellowedshiped."[20] Excommunicants were not authorized to have polygamous marriages.[21]

"Through the Night," Lee wrote in his journal, he and Emma "talked over M[any] things, till I was horror stricken at the low Mean depravity & treachery of [a] Man of the Experience & standing of Hamblin." Lee managed to convince Emma to stay with him, but the episode launched a lifelong feud between him and Hamblin.[22]

Lee soon went north to Pahreah for supplies. Despite the risk, he could not resist speaking at a meeting and attending a party. Some Latter-day Saints still befriended Lee. But "on the other Extreme," Lee wrote, he received "a nasty, filthy, insulting Note & without provication" from a former acquaintance.[23]

On January 28, 1874, Lee received a telegram from Young and George A. Smith, addressing him as "Dear Sir" instead of "Dear Brother," a tacit reference to his excommunication. They had heard about his ferrying church members across the Colorado. "We are Glad to hear you are still interested in the advancement of our Set[t]lements," they wrote politely.

They gave Lee permission to use the new Mormon-built boat at Lonely Dell if he would "see that this Ferry is kept up." But they asked no favors of him and "never contempl[a]ted" anyone crossing the river without paying Lee—not even themselves.[24]

On March 2, Young left his winter home at St. George to tour the settlements along the Virgin River. Smith traveled with him. That evening, Young preached in a church meeting at Toquerville.[25]

Isaac Haight was then living in Toquerville with his plural wife Eliza Ann Price and their youngest children. Like Lee, Haight languished under the weight of excommunication for his role in the massacre. One man said that sixty-year-old Haight "looked to be the most miserable and unhappy man

I ever saw." Concerned for Haight's welfare, Toquerville's newly called bishop asked Young about Haight's spiritual standing. Decades later, the bishop remembered Young responding that "Isaac Haight will be damned in this world and will be damned throughout eternity."[26]

But according to an account of Haight's son-in-law C. J. Arthur, Young was of a different mind the next day. Arthur's wife Caroline—Haight's daughter—died in childbirth at 2 p.m. on March 3. Arthur telegraphed the news of her death from Cedar City to her father at Toquerville. "He read the telegram a few moments after entering his house from returning thither from the waters of baptism," Arthur wrote in his 1877 private memoirs.[27]

Young and Smith had already left Toquerville for their next stop, but Haight was rebaptized "by instruction of Prest B. Young," Arthur recalled, "he having been cut off the Church on account of a misunderstanding of the President about his course in the M.M.M." Haight's priesthood and temple endowment were afterwards "restored in full by the instructions of Prest. B. Young," Arthur added. It was "generally believed" that Caroline died about the same time her father was rising up out of the baptismal water.[28]

No other record has been found of this rebaptism. But five days later, Haight was elected to serve as an appraiser for his Toquerville Ward's communal society—possibly a sign of his renewed fellowship in the church.[29]

If Arthur's account is accurate, someone—perhaps Haight himself—convinced Young that Lee was responsible for the massacre, and that Haight's only fault was failing to control him.[30]

On March 15, Lee wrote an ingratiating letter to Young, hoping to bridge the gulf that stood between them since Young excommunicated him more than three years earlier. Lee thanked Young for the January telegram about the ferry, which revived "new hopes" that he "was not altogether Fatherless cast of[f] & forsaken." He also offered "to Explore the regions of AZ or any other Place" while Emma ran the ferry at Lonely Dell.[31]

When Young did not respond, Lee resolved to face him. Lee reached Washington, Utah, on April 5, where he washed and shaved before riding to Young's St. George residence. There he "found Prest. B. Y." enjoying dinner with friends and family before returning to Salt Lake the next morning. Young "recieved me with the kindness of a Father," Lee wrote in his journal, and "had Me partake of a splendid supper with him & the guest[s]."[32]

During the evening, Lee "drew out" from Young his plans for Latter-day Saint settlement of Arizona. Though Lee hoped to play a role in that expansion, he learned Young's plans did not include him.

Lee kept up his efforts the next morning, falling in with Young and his entourage as it traveled north. He rode alongside "them as far as [K]anarah to hear them talk & Preach," Lee wrote.[33] Lee's old nemesis George A. Hicks felt furious to see him "riding on horse back on the right hand side of [Young's] carriage." After Hicks shared his criticism in the *Salt Lake Tribune*, Cedar City church leaders excommunicated him for "apostacy."[34]

At Kanarra that night, Young and Smith stayed with Bishop Lorenzo Roundy, while Lee stayed with a brother-in-law. The following day, however, Young had stern words for Lee, perhaps prompted by conversation with Roundy the previous night. "This Morning," Lee wrote, "Prest. Young implicit[ly] enjoined it upon Me" not to let the ferry "go into the hands of our Enimies, not to hire gentiles to tend it. Said that he had been told that I associatd with genti[l]es, & played cards, that I eat & drank with them, & that I swore as th[e]y did." Young said "he was sorry to hear that I was on the back grounds, that I once was a faithful Man & Sought the interest of this kingdom & that he could trust Me to do anny thing on Earth that was wanted to be done, & he hoped that these reports were false."

Though Lee acknowledged drinking and playing cards "with gentiles," he denied "cursing & going back on the church." Lee wrote that Young counseled him to "be careful & stand to your integrity," then blessed him and "drove on."[35]

Young's recollection of their meeting differed from Lee's account. Three years later, Young said he told Lee, "If you killed these emigrants my advice to you is to get a big strong rope, ride into a cedar swamp, and hang yourself just close enough to the ground to let the wolves strip the meat from your carcas[s]."[36]

Whatever transpired, it was the last time the two ever met. Though Lee wrote Young again the following month, Young did not write back, and he never restored Lee's membership in the church.[37]

Meanwhile, the stalemate that had halted prosecution of polygamists and massacre participants was unraveling, in part prompted by Young's former plural wife Ann Eliza Webb, who launched a sensational lecture tour after leaving Young. The lectures, attended by President Ulysses Grant and members of Congress, helped fuel the drive for legislation to resolve Utah's legal confusion and prosecute polygamy.[38]

Grant urged Congress to act. He "called out certain prominent members of the Judiciary Committees of the two houses," a news source reported, telling them "he desired some practical legislation before adjournment with regard to Utah matters." Feeling "tired of the contest out there between the federal officials and those claiming to be acting under the Territorial laws," he wanted jurors selected "in the federal courts in such manner as will take that power out of the hands of the Mormon authorities."[39]

Four months later, on June 23, 1874, Congress passed the Poland Act, obligating U.S. authorities to prosecute offenses against both federal *and* territorial laws in Utah and directing that court costs for territorial offenses "be paid out of the treasury of the Territory." The act limited probate court jurisdiction, as earlier federal judges including John Cradlebaugh had advocated, and directed that in creating jury pools, the U.S. district court clerk and local probate court judge should choose names alternately so that "one-half of the two hundred names selected would be Mormons and the other half would not."[40]

Conditions finally seemed ripe to prosecute perpetrators of the Mountain Meadows Massacre.

In September, Judge Jacob S. Boreman of Utah's second district held the first court under the Poland Act. "It is the first time in the history of this Territory," proclaimed the *Salt Lake Tribune*, "when a Federal Court convened wi[t]h the prospect of being able to me[t]e justice impartially and reach high-handed criminals."[41]

Because of the act, Boreman's initial grand jury was a mix of Latter-day Saints and non-Mormons. "You are part on one side, and part on the other," Boreman told his jurors. "If you do not do your duty as you have solemnly sworn to do," he warned, "it will only give cause for further legislation, and a much more rigorous law wil[l] be enacted."[42]

Recognizing the court's newly confirmed jurisdiction over both federal and territorial matters, Boreman charged grand jurors to first investigate "offences against the United States, and when through with these, turn your attention to Territorial matters." Under violations of federal law, he focused them particularly on polygamy, which he called "not only a crime, but a loathsome ulcer upon the body politic," quoting former senator Stephen A. Douglas.

When Boreman turned to territorial crimes, he directed jurors to the massacre. "The blood of those innocent victims cries out to you to-day for justice," he said, "and the stain of that innocent blood will forever rest upon the people of this Territory until they wash their hands of the awful crime and bring to justice the cowardly villains who had the cruelty to commit such a black and bloody deed."[43]

On September 24, the Mormon and non-Mormon grand jurors indicted nine men—William Dame, Isaac Haight, John D. Lee, John Higbee, Philip Klingensmith, George Adair, Ellott Willden, Samuel Jewkes, and William Stewart—for "feloniously wilfully premeditatedly designedly and of their malice aforethought" killing men, women, and children at the Mountain Meadows.[44]

The record does not state why only these nine men and not others were indicted. The reasons can only be deduced. Dame, Haight, Lee, Higbee, and Klingensmith all played key roles in planning or carrying out the massacre. Stewart killed William Aden on the first day of the massacre, using a weapon borrowed from Ellott Willden. Adair was at the massacre and recounted the crime to John Wesley Powell's men. Jewkes's role in the killings is unclear, but like some of the other indicted men, his family took in one of the surviving children—Prudence Angeline Dunlap.[45]

In early October, Deputy Marshal William Stokes, acting under U.S. Marshal George Maxwell, quietly received arrest warrants based on the indictments. Maxwell told Stokes "that Lee was the most important one of all those indicted, and that he wanted him arrested first," though he believed "Lee would never be taken alive."[46]

Over the previous weeks, seventy-three-year-old Brigham Young's health had declined markedly. According to the *Salt Lake Tribune*, a surgical procedure left him "in a semi-comatose state" and "rapidly sinking."[47] Young managed to attend his church's general conference in early October. " 'How very feeble Bro. Brigham looks,' was the frequent remark of the Saints, after leaving the Tabernacle yesterday morning," the *Tribune* reported.[48]

Later that month, feeling "sick nigh unto death," Young escaped the cold in Salt Lake for his southern home in St. George. The *Tribune* reported he had difficulty eating, required medical attention along the way, and would soon need to "have his measure taken" for a coffin.[49]

One *Tribune* article noted that the Mormon-dominated legislature, while calling for an investigation of the massacre and other crimes, had said "all these stories about Mountain Meadows" and other murders were "Gentile inventions," and an investigation "would show the hands of the Mormon leaders to be unstained with blood." Now, the article challenged, the Poland Act gives the Mormons "an opportunity to prove their innocence" of those crimes. "The day of reckoning, so long wished for, has at length arrived; and we ask that the search be honestly and thoroughly made no matter whose head goes into the basket."[50]

George W. Adair

William H. Dame

Isaac C. Haight

John M. Higbee

Samuel Jewkes

Philip Klingensmith

John D. Lee

William C. Stewart

Ellott Willden

The nine men indicted for the massacre are shown in Figures 33.1–33.9.
Figure 33.1 George W. Adair. Public Domain; **Figure 33.2** William H. Dame.
Public Domain; **Figure 33.3** Isaac C. Haight. Public Domain; **Figure 33.4**
John M. Higbee. Public Domain; **Figure 33.5** Samuel Jewkes. Public Domain;
Figure 33.6 Philip Klingensmith. Public Domain; **Figure 33.7** John D. Lee.
Courtesy Sherratt Library, Special Collections, Southern Utah University
and Jay Burrup; **Figure 33.8** William C. Stewart. Courtesy FamilySearch;
Figure 33.9 Ellott Willden. Courtesy Jay Burrup.

Among the Saints, apostle John Taylor, who would succeed Young as church president, spoke out against the massacre. "Do you deny it?" Taylor asked. "No. Do you excuse it? No. There is no excuse for such a relentless, diabolical, sanguinary deed," Taylor declared. "That outrageous infamy," he said, "is looked upon with as much abhorence by our people as by any other parties in this nation or in the world."

As much as Taylor wished the massacre had never happened, he recognized it "cannot be undone." He called on the public to "blame the perpetrators," not the entire Latter-day Saint community. Taylor had been in the council that excommunicated Lee and Haight, and he publicly called the massacre "a disgrace to humanity."[51]

In an October 1874 interview with a California newspaper correspondent, George A. Smith confirmed that "Mormon leaders are desirous of having the charges investigated and the perpetrators brought to justice," denying that "Mormon leaders were implicated in any manner in the massacre." Lee and Haight, he pointed out, were not "leading Mormons," and "it would be possible for them to be guilty with out implicating in any manner the Mormon Church."[52] The *Salt Lake Tribune* responded by accusing top church leaders of responsibility for the massacre and excoriating them for "deserting John D. Lee."[53]

As Young was traveling through southern Utah in late 1874, so was Deputy Stokes, looking for Lee. The deputy was on his way to Lonely Dell when he heard rumors "that Lee had come from the Colorado River, and was then in the southern counties of Utah." Stokes sent two posse recruits, Thomas Winn of Beaver and Franklin Fish of Parowan, to Panguitch to see if Lee was visiting his wife Sarah Caroline's home there.[54]

Stokes was riding from Beaver to Parowan on November 7 when a carriage overtook him. "Four of the best fighting men of Beaver City" guarded the conveyance, Stokes said, "armed with Henry rifles"—prized for their repeating-fire capabilities. As the suite passed by, the guards rode between Stokes and the carriage, which the deputy realized carried Young. But there was "no reason for alarm," the deputy wrote. "Brigham Young was not the man that I was after at *that* time."[55]

Not long after Young's carriage passed, Stokes ran into Winn and Fish, emerging from a canyon on their return from Panguitch.

"Your man is there!" Winn reported.

"Very much surprised," Stokes brought the two men into Parowan, where they made new plans. Iron County sheriff D. P. Clark, a lapsed Mormon who lived in the town, soon got wind of the news. "I do not see things as you do or as I used to," Clark told Collins Hakes, his brother-in-law who was visiting Parowan, "but you can go and tell Prest. Young of it and if [he] does not want him [Lee] arrested I will have two as good horses as are in Town all ready and you and I can beat any Marshall to Lee and prevent his arrest."[56]

Sometime between 9:00 and 10:00 p.m., Hakes went to William Dame's place, where Young and his party were sleeping. Young roused members of his party and gave them Hakes's news. "Some talk was indulged in about it," Hakes later recalled, "when Prest Young looked up and said Brethren it is all right[.] The time has come when they will try J. D. Lee and not the Mormon Church and that is all we have ever wanted."[57]

Unaware of these events, Stokes added more men to his posse. On November 9, he and his men galloped full speed into Panguitch. After trying in vain to get adults on the street to help them locate their man, Winn finally found "a little boy" and asked "where Lee's wife lived." The child pointed out a house.[58]

As Stokes and Winn approached it, the deputy spied a woman talking into a log henhouse a few feet from the home. He told Winn to keep an eye on the log pen as he searched the home. Moving towards the house, he encountered a young man who told him his name was Sam. Stokes ordered him to help search the premises and arrest Lee.

"John D. Lee is my father, sir," Sam objected.

Stokes replied he did not care if Lee was Sam's *grandmother*, the young man was going in with him to search the house.

After finding several women inside but not his suspect, Stokes—with Sam in tow—stepped out towards the henhouse. By then, Lee's son-in-law Henry Darrow was also on the scene. Sam and Henry became agitated as the marshal circled the pen. Peering into a small opening between two logs of the henhouse, Stokes spied a man peeking out from under the straw.[59]

Winn crept near to Stokes and whispered, "There is some one in that pen."

Winn positioned himself, "holding his Henry rifle ready for instant use." Stokes hesitated, wondering if he and Winn could pull off an arrest on their own. Just then Stokes spotted deputy Fish approaching on horseback.

"Mr. Lee," an emboldened Stokes shouted, "come out and surrender yourself." Though Stokes repeated the demand several times, the fugitive did not move. Stokes motioned Fish to come closer, but Fish sat frozen in his saddle, his gun pointed at the house.

Two guns were pointed through the logs of the house, Stokes observed, "aimed directly at me."

Stokes whipped two pistols from his overcoat and shoved one of them, a dragoon pistol with a sawed-off barrel, into the pen, eighteen inches from Lee's head.

"You go in there and disarm Lee," Stokes ordered Winn. "I promise you that if a single straw moves, I will blow his head off."

Lee's son-in-law begged Stokes not to shoot, saying Lee was just an old man.

"I would not hurt a hair of Lee's head if he surrendered peacefully," Stokes answered, but neither "would I permit Lee to get away alive."

"Hold on boys," Lee's voice finally came from the henhouse. "Don't shoot. I will come out." Lee rolled off his back, holstered his pistol, and crawled out of the pen. Covered in bits of straw, he stood and coolly said, "Well, boys, what do you want of me?"

"I have a warrant for your arrest," Stokes said, "and must take you to Beaver."

All the men went into the house, where family members "seemed wild with excitement, some of them crying." Lee tried to calm his family, saying "the time had come when he could get a fair trial."

Stokes made his own effort to calm them, offering each a glass of wine. When he held out a glass to one of Lee's weeping daughters, she took it and said, "Here is hoping that father will get away from you, and that if he does, you will not catch him again till h—l freezes over."

"Drink hardy, Miss," Stokes replied.

Oddly polite, as if Stokes and his men were paying a social call, Lee apologized that he had not yet offered them something to eat. He asked the women to make breakfast.

Steeling themselves for the long ride ahead, the men who had just pointed guns at each other sat down to share a meal. Lee's son Alma was also there. The sons told their father that if he didn't want to go to Beaver, "to say so, and they would see that he didn't go."

Lee asked Stokes how to answer them.

"I told him to tell the boys to turn themselves loose," Stokes said, "that I knew I had no friends in that place, except those who came with me, but we were well armed, and when trouble commenced we would shoot those nearest to us" first "and then continue to make it lively while we lasted."[60]

Hearing that, Lee agreed to go with Stokes, promising to "see that the boys behaved themselves." By then a crowd of some 150 had gathered around the house. "The excitement became intense" throughout town, many indulging in "considerable loud talking." One of Lee's wives said "she would rather see him dead than in the hands of the U.S. Marshal." Yet in the end, no one interfered. "Had a gun been fired," one witness said, "a massacre would have ensued."[61]

Putting a positive spin on his arrest, Lee said "he had been hunted and hounded long enough, and was glad that he was captured. He intended to make a clean breast of it" and was pleased at the opportunity "to unbosom himself to the world."[62]

Stokes rented a team and a wagon from his prisoner and hired Lee's son-in-law Darrow to drive the outfit. Lee, his wife Rachel, and two posse members climbed into the tightly covered wagon. Stokes and the rest of his posse mounted their horses and guarded the wagon out of Panguitch. Despite apprehensions that Mormons would try to free Lee, the trip was uneventful.

"When we reached Beaver," Stokes said, "the people were almost thunder-struck with astonishment to know that John D. Lee had been arrested." The prisoner was placed under guard in the town jail, and the telegraph sent word of the arrest nationwide.[63]

34

Do You Plead Guilty

Utah, 1874-75

Deputy Marshal William Stokes's arrival in Beaver with John D. Lee "caused considerable excitement." Crowds flocking to glimpse the infamous prisoner saw a sixty-two-year-old man "of ruddy complexion," with "a mild blue eye," a reporter wrote, "and not unpleasant countenance, though his gaze is somewhat unsteady."[1] Lee was in fine spirits despite his arrest. "He is very fond of liquor," the correspondent noted, "and after arriving in town he got a drink which seemed to revive him and unloose his tongue. He talked freely to all, and quoted scripture, and related funny incidents in his life."[2]

Lee's arrest catapulted him and Rachel into the public eye. Demand for their photographs ran high, and news writers painted word portraits of them for a curious public.[3] Rachel was depicted admiringly as the devoted companion of her husband—or more sensationally as a shotgun-toting fighter with "fiery eyes" who "no doubt wore the clothing and jewelry" of massacre victims and stuck to her spouse "like a leech to a sick man."[4] John D. was portrayed at once as "an animal" with a "villainously low and receding" forehead and as a man whose remarkable life, "aside from the terrible massacre," had "no parallel in America."[5]

Lee basked in the limelight, and one California correspondent wrote that "no one can talk with him without being impressed with the idea that he does not expect to meet the punishment of a murderer."[6] Utah's U.S. marshal, George Maxwell, thought it unsafe to keep the prisoner in the Beaver jail while rumors of escape or assassination circulated. The marshal had Lee whisked in irons from the low-security town jail to a military cell at Fort Cameron, three miles east.[7]

Before being confined there, Lee "expresse[d] himself anxious to tell what he knows about the massacre, and to expose the responsible parties." Some speculated "that Brigham Young or George A. Smith, is in for it," but a *Salt Lake Tribune* correspondent concluded Lee was "hinting at Isaac C. Haight or William H. Dame." Haight was in hiding, but Dame peacefully surrendered to Deputy Stokes in Parowan. Journalistic portraits of Dame also cut a wide swath, from bloodthirsty killer to law-abiding citizen whose peaceful submission signaled innocence.[8]

About thirty minutes after his arrest, Dame, a former missionary, received another mission assignment sent by George A. Smith, who was in southern Utah. Dame wrote Smith, apologizing that because of his arrest "on indictment . . . for 'Murder,' " he couldn't fill the assignment. "But," he added, "trust I will be able to fulfill [the] next call"—implying he would be found innocent. "I suppose the 'Meadows' is [the] cause of my arrest," Dame wrote casually, and "if so I suppose I must prepare." He wanted the help of former U.S. attorney George C. Bates and his partner, Jabez G. Sutherland. Not knowing them personally, Dame asked Smith to "represent my wish to them."[9]

Dame had long ago persuaded Latter-day Saint leaders that he was not responsible for the massacre, and Smith agreed to contact Bates for him.[10] During Bates's term as U.S. district attorney, he sought to prosecute those responsible for the massacre, promising them a fair trial. But his fairness cost him professionally, distancing him from Judge McKean and other Liberal Party leaders. Financially desperate after leaving office, Bates turned to church leaders for help.

"I am *poor*," he wrote Smith in 1873, "and have suffered in my business from the course that I have taken." He asked for legal work.[11] Smith promised to do what he could, eventually retaining Bates as a church attorney at five hundred dollars a year.[12]

On November 22, Smith received Dame's letter. Maxwell had Dame spirited by stage to Salt Lake for safekeeping.[13] Learning that Dame was coming, Smith "telegraphed Bates and Sutherland to meet him on his arival."[14] They consulted briefly with the prisoner before he was locked in the territorial penitentiary.[15]

Convinced of Dame's innocence but not of Lee's, Smith saw the whole legal proceeding as a political ploy. He knew Liberal Party leaders wanted to tie him and Brigham Young to the massacre, and he heard there was a warrant for his arrest. "They will probably find me at the Saint George House, where I have taken rooms," Smith wrote Bates. "It seems so incredible to me that I have not given the rumor Credence."

Smith had a lung condition that would soon take his life. He told Bates he "would sincerely regret" being removed from mild St. George to frigid Beaver. "The difference in climate is immense," he shuddered.[16] Even if he were found innocent, imprisonment might kill him. Besides, Smith wrote, "I cannot conceive how they can mix me up with the affair."[17]

When Lee's case was called in court on December 1, a former New Yorker named Wells Spicer—a non-Mormon lawyer, miner, and former *Salt Lake Tribune* correspondent—announced himself as Lee's attorney.[18] Lee wrote Smith that Spicer offered his services "as a Friend without money or price."[19] In the end, Lee got what he paid for, Spicer being better suited to handle mining claims than criminal defense. But for Spicer, the case offered a coveted moment of fame.[20]

Spicer told the court he and his client wanted to go to trial as soon as possible.[21] The prosecution was not ready, however, and both Lee's case and Dame's were postponed until the February 1875 term of the second district court.[22]

Months before the trial, Utah governor George L. Woods told President Ulysses S. Grant that Lee "can be convicted," even with Mormon jurors. "The general sentiment is that the Church have abandoned him, and will seek his conviction."[23] Utah district attorney William Carey also wrote to Washington, reporting that a grand jury composed "of both Mormons and Gentiles" indicted sixty to seventy persons of crimes, and that all but one had eventually been found guilty. The only major problem remaining was "the want of funds in the Marshals office."[24]

As Lee and Dame languished in prison, the defense and prosecution worked on their cases. Enos D. Hoge, a former Utah Supreme Court justice, joined Spicer in Lee's defense.[25]

On January 2, 1875, Jacob Hamblin wrote Smith from Kanab, reporting that Spicer had met with him. The defense lawyer wanted Hamblin to testify *for* his client at trial.[26] Hamblin had long wanted to testify *against* Lee for his massacre role, but in the Saints' battle with Liberal Party members over polygamy, he and Lee became temporarily allied again, leaving Hamblin uncertain what to do.[27]

"I think I could goe thare and tell Some things that mite favor Mr. Lee," Hamblin volunteered, but only "if I did not tell all I hurd." Hamblin asked Smith if he should go to Beaver. He ended up not going.[28]

Dame, meanwhile, was eager to go to trial. Brigham Young Jr. visited him in the Salt Lake penitentiary and reported that Dame's "most intimate friends know [him] to be innocent."[29]

Dame wasn't innocent, but it was easy for him to pretend he was and for people to believe him. Two days before the massacre, he voted with his

Parowan council to help the besieged emigrant company "continue their journey in peace." Only after that meeting, when Haight cornered him privately in the "tan bark council," did Dame relent to Haight and authorize the atrocity. Dame himself did not reach the Meadows until the day after the killing ended.[30]

Lee, Dame, and the public wanted speedy trials—the defendants because they didn't want to stay in jail, and the public because justice had been too long coming.[31] At first, Liberal Party members also demanded speedy justice to show weakness in the Poland Act. Doubtful a mixed jury would convict the defendants, they hoped an acquittal would bring harsher jury laws to exclude Latter-day Saints entirely.[32]

Though Lee and Dame were behind bars, the seven other indicted defendants remained at large: Haight, Philip Klingensmith, John M. Higbee, William Stewart, Ellott Willden, Samuel Jewkes, and George Adair.[33] Klingensmith, who planned to turn state's evidence when giving his affidavit in 1871, presumably would appear when summoned.[34]

Latter-day Saint leaders previously offered to help bring the suspects to court, provided they were treated humanely, and on December 6, George A. Smith suggested to George Bates that he represent the fugitives.[35]

Three days later, Bates received a letter from the uncaptured defendants. "We wish to engage you as our counsel," they wrote. "We have never evaded nor sought to evade a fair investigation of the crimes with which we are charged," they claimed, "but, on the contrary, have ever been willing and anxious to have such an investigation before a fair-minded and impartial court and jury." They were willing to appear in court if they could post bail and be free while awaiting trial, unlike Dame and Lee, who had been imprisoned for months.

Bates considered the legal landscape. Murder was a territorial offense, and all the free defendants purportedly resided outside the territory. Efforts to arrest them were unlikely to succeed; the men's voluntary surrender would save the prosecution time and money. Bates conferred with Assistant District Attorney David P. Whedon, who reminded Bates the law prohibited bail for suspects arrested on capital crimes. Bates said the defendants had not yet been arrested, and so a deal to have them appear voluntarily would be legal. Whedon told him "to apply to Judge Boreman."[36] Bates did, and the proposition irked the judge, who ordered Bates and Sutherland to appear in court for "professional misconduct" in asking him to negotiate with indicted felons.[37]

In the meantime, one correspondent reported that Lee planned to turn state's evidence. According to the writer, Lee "denies the ravishing and murder of helpless women, and asserts that Haight, Higby and others have charged their enormities upon him."[38] Although his interests were at odds with Haight's and Higbee's, Lee opted to add Bates and Sutherland to his defense team. Lee hoped to reconcile with church leaders, and he sent an ingratiating note to George A. Smith on February 20 about his expanded defense team.[39]

Smith replied with an empathetic yet distant letter. "You stated that you have employed Judges Spicer[,] Sutherland and Genl. Bates to defend you," Smith wrote formally. "I dont believe that you can find more reliable or better qualified Attorneys in the Ter[ritor]y. I hope that you may obtain a fair and speedy trial which you & your friends so much desire."[40]

On Friday, April 2, 1875, the *Salt Lake Tribune* announced Lee and Dame would be tried the next week in Beaver.[41] On Saturday morning, Marshal Maxwell started south with Dame for court, arriving the next evening.[42] Earlier, Deputy Stokes reached Beaver after a long but futile hunt for the fugitive defendants. The newest member of Lee's legal team—non-Mormon William W. Bishop of Pioche, Nevada—also arrived.[43]

Lee's lawyers were "determined, if possible, to bring the case to trial this term, as it is fully believed the court . . . does not intend to bring up the case at this term, through lack of evidence," newspapers reported. Lee himself was reportedly "anxious for trial . . . declar[ing] his innocence" and "confident of acquittal."[44] But the prosecution's star witness, Philip Klingensmith, still hadn't shown up.[45]

On Tuesday morning, April 6, guards escorted Lee into the courtroom. As the court clerk read the charges against him, Lee seemed to take in every syllable, staring attentively at the clerk.

"To this indictment do you plead guilty or not guilty?" asked the clerk.[46]

Lee pled "not guilty."[47]

William Dame's arraignment came later that week. Like Lee, Dame pled "not guilty" and—citing the Sixth Amendment—"demanded a speedy trial."[48] Prosecutors did not expect to try Dame until after Lee, and ultimately, Boreman denied Dame bail and sent him back to the Salt Lake penitentiary.[49]

In Lee's case, prosecutor Whedon explained that the marshal had not located key witnesses, despite valiant efforts. Whedon expected Lee's trial to take at least two weeks, cost hundreds or thousands of dollars, and "require the summoning of a large number of additional Jurors and witnesses."

Lee responded with an affidavit insisting on a trial at the present court term. His legal team was ready, and his confinement, especially "the irons on his limbs," harmed his health and might "endanger his life." Lee declared himself innocent and wanted a chance to prove it. Besides, many defense witnesses might later "be unable to attend" court because of death or disability, being "very old and infirm."[50]

On Wednesday, April 14, the court convened to hear arguments on postponing the trial. Lee, escorted by Marshal Maxwell and accompanied by wives Rachel and Sarah Caroline, entered the courtroom looking "depressed and unwell."[51] Prosecutor Whedon argued that investigating a massacre of some 118 people took time. The prosecution needed more witnesses and more money to round them up. He believed they were "absent through fear" but could be procured before the July court term. Whedon assured the court his motion was "not made for delay but for justice."[52]

Spicer scoffed at the prosecution arguments. The court could make witnesses attend, "money or no money," he asserted. As Spicer spoke, "Lee wept [and] looked around" the courtroom.[53]

Defense attorney William Bishop arose and appealed to the court to uphold the law requiring a speedy trial. Under a well-settled legal rule, the prosecution should not be entitled to postponement unless it showed the impossibility of proceeding, which the prosecution had not, Bishop argued.[54] If the prosecutor couldn't get witnesses for this court term, what made him think he would have them next term? "Call your troops from the Fort Cameron," Bishop challenged, "and send them as the agents of the government to bring these witnesses in irons if needs be."[55]

Despite the defense's arguments, Judge Boreman was swayed to postpone the trial again, but with a warning. All along, Boreman said, "I told everybody I wanted this case tried [at the] very first opportunity. . . . The law says a man shall have a speedy trial."

"I will grant the application this time," Boreman ruled for prosecutor Whedon. But "I expect the prosecution to be ready in July if it takes all next summer."

"Let the case be continued," the judge ordered.

"Let the case be continued," Bishop echoed dejectedly.[56]

35

Open the Ball

Utah 1875

On April 15, 1875, George A. Smith walked into the Church Historian's Office in Salt Lake City with a telegram announcing that although John D. Lee's attorney had "pushed a speedy trial," the court had delayed the trial "without any just cause." A clerk recorded, "Every one indignant." Judge Jacob Boreman's decision to postpone Lee's and Dame's cases struck many Latter-day Saints as yet another denial of their constitutional right to a speedy trial.[1]

Beaver's newspaper reported that Lee was "rapidly declining" and had "endured too much out-door life to maintain good health in close confinement."[2] Lee soon gained a measure of freedom "through sympathy." The May 7 *Salt Lake Tribune* announced that Lee "now has the liberty of Camp Cameron."[3] Almost two weeks later, a Beaver source reported that Lee "makes his headquarters at the post trader's store, and is visited by Saint and sinner without passes."[4]

One of Lee's visitors found him eager for company, "and, if approached in a spirit of kindness, . . . quite talkative." Lee's chattiness led the visitor to conclude "that were it not for his attorney he would convict himself." Asked if he felt justified in covering up the massacre, Lee objected to the question, adding that "he would never stretch hemp." The visitor left feeling that "if a proper course could be pursued," Lee would "make a clean breast of it."[5]

When Marshal George Maxwell ordered Lee back to the Beaver jail to cut costs,[6] the fort surgeon requested that the prisoner "be allowed to remain at large" for his health. The *Tribune* marveled that a federal official "should show such a tender regard for the foremost criminal of the age." Lee pleaded, "My health is feeble, . . . and I fear confinement will prove fatal." Lee promised that if he could remain free at the fort, newfound friends there would pay for "a special guard to be with me night and day till the Court sits."[7] But Maxwell remained firm and returned Lee to jail.[8] A month and a half later, Lee had once again managed to acquire liberties. The *Tribune* reported he was "no longer ironed" and even marched in Beaver's July 4 parade.[9]

Meanwhile, Dame's attorneys applied additional pressure, informing U.S. Attorney William Carey that on the first day of the court term, they would demand a trial and that the indicted defendants who remained at large would appear and demand trials too.[10] The prosecution had subpoenas issued for numerous witnesses, and deputies traveled great distances looking for the missing defendants but still had not found them.[11] They couldn't even find the prosecution's star witness, Philip Klingensmith, who had claimed Dutch Flat near Pioche, Nevada, as his home.[12]

Among the witnesses served, only one filed a formal deposition to excuse himself from appearing. Claiming heart palpitations and a lack of transportation kept him from court, James M. Mangum went before a Kanab justice of the peace and testified about the massacre. Mangum claimed "John D. Lee wanted him to go to the Mountain Meadows as interpreter" because "the Indians were mad." Lee asked him and Jacob Hamblin's brother Oscar "to come and try and pacify them." They went and, he asserted, "found about two hundred Indians at the Meadows, who were very mad."

"They immediately disarmed us, and threatened to kill us," Mangum claimed. "I saw John D. Lee there, he was trying to pacify them, but they would not listen to him or us, and I verily believe that had it not been for an Indian boy that John D. Lee raised, the Indians would have killed John D. Lee, Oscar Hamblin and myself." He averred that "he did not see W. H. Dame at that time, or during that year." Mangum's testimony was couched to absolve both Lee and Dame, foisting the blame entirely on Native people.[13]

As the court's opening approached, the *Salt Lake Tribune* proposed a strategy for the trial. "No matter how convincing the evidence," the paper forecasted, Lee would not be convicted since a jury made up partly of Mormons would not meet the unanimous vote required for conviction. The most that could be expected is that the non-Mormon jurors might vote to convict, resulting in a hung jury. The prosecution's duty, therefore, should be to try the case in the press.

"The punishment of Lee—however richly he may deserve punishment— is not so much an object as to elicit the whole truth," the writer suggested. "Several leading newspapers of the East and West will be represented at the trial, and full reports will be published which will be read by millions of our citizens." Should the jury acquit Lee, "the utter inadequacy of the Poland Bill to execute the law and award justice to red-handed offenders, will be made apparent to the country, and Congress, in the face of this disgraceful fact, cannot well avoid at the next session, enacting a law that shall remedy existing defects."[14]

Beaver soon became crowded as all the players in the courtroom drama converged on the town. Representing the prosecution were U.S. Attorney Carey and his deputy, David Whedon. Supporting them as U.S. marshals were Maxwell and his deputies.[15] Representing Lee was William W. Bishop of Pioche, Nevada; Wells Spicer; and Enos D. Hoge.[16] Representing Dame and the uncaptured codefendants was George Bates and his partner Jabez Sutherland, both of Salt Lake City, and St. George lawyer John M. Macfarlane, brother of massacre participant Daniel Macfarlane and son-in-law to Isaac C. Haight.[17]

William Dame had been transported from Salt Lake and confined at Fort Cameron pending trial. He was reportedly in good health, pleased that his trial would finally begin, and "apparently certain of an acquittal."[18]

Lee, now said to be "in fair health," was accompanied by wives and children "giving all the aid they can to the counsel to prepare for the trial." Besides them, Lee had been abandoned. "Lee has no aids, comfort or support from any of the Latter Day Saints in Utah," wrote a Nevada correspondent. "It seems that he is deserted by all but his family and his attorneys."[19]

The prosecution had two key allies in town, Mormon dissenters Bill Hickman and Amasa Lyman. Hickman, who bludgeoned an arms dealer to death with an ax during the Utah War, had earlier turned state's evidence in an unsuccessful effort before the 1871 McKean court to tie Brigham Young to the murder. A *Tribune* editor referred to Hickman as the marshal's "chief of staff." His job in Beaver, according to one wry correspondent, was "giving aid to the prosecution and comfort to the wavering witnesses."[20]

Of even greater relevance for the trial was Lyman, spiritual leader of a group called the Godbeites that opposed Young. Once a Latter-day Saint apostle, Lyman had been among the church leaders who investigated the massacre in 1858. He knew southern Utah and its people, and his role during the court session was to help prosecutors "expose those guilty of aiding in the slaughter." A newspaper correspondent wrote that Lyman's appearance "created no little excitement" in town. Some conjectured "that many of those who acted under a mistaken idea of duty at the time of the tragedy, and aided in carrying out the orders of those in authority, will now, under the advice of Lyman, make a full confession of what they know of the affair, laying the responsibility properly where it belongs."[21]

Witnesses who responded to subpoenas and arrived for the trial felt rest-less, not knowing when they would be allowed to return to their farms. With all the lawyers, witnesses, journalists, family members, and curious spectators in town, Beaver brimmed with people, and the pending court pro-ceedings were on everyone's lips.[22]

Monday morning, July 12, found the courtroom "crowded to suffoca-tion." Reporters for several newspapers and the Associated Press perched on seats that Marshal Maxwell had reserved for them. About 11:15 a.m., Judge Boreman, described by a reporter as an "energetic man" with "no fears of the Church of Jesus Christ of Latter-day Saints, nor of anything else," assumed the bench as Deputy Stokes proclaimed the court open. Adam Patterson was sworn in as the official court reporter. A second shorthand reporter, Josiah Rogerson, was also on hand to record the trial, requested by Latter-day Saint leaders.[23]

Lee's and Dame's cases were first on the court calendar. In spite of the an-ticipation in the courtroom, neither the prosecution nor Lee's defense was ready to begin, and the case was continued to the next day.[24]

Fred Lockley, one of the *Tribune*'s owners and its correspondent for the Lee trial, wrote that marshals were still "having an exceedingly lively time getting in their witnesses." Two key prosecution witnesses, Klingensmith and Joel White, were "still out," and prosecutors hesitated to proceed without them.[25]

Lee was also struggling to get witnesses. He declined the marshal's help and sent three of his sons in search of friends to testify in his favor. The friends' reluctance to appear left Lee in tears. Though indignant that their client's associates deserted him, Lee's lawyers put on the best face they could.[26]

After court adjourned that afternoon, the lawyers were "busy as bees." Prosecutors grilled their witnesses "to see what force of testimony they have to produce in Court." Meanwhile, defense lawyers, in the words of the *Tribune*'s Lockley, had "long and loving interviews" with Lee.

Lockley heard Lee had "been quite free" in condemning his co-conspirators. "To use the slang phrase here," Lockley wrote, Lee felt "that the Church has thrown off on him." Though Dame, "the pet," had "been soothed in the penitentiary by pleasant attentions," Lee had "been let severely alone in his solitary cell." In spite of this, Lee's lawyers spoke confidently of his ac-quittal, and "no one," Lockley assured his readers, "expects his conviction, whatever force of evidence may be produced." Instead, observers simply wondered, "How much will he tell?"

If Lee could implicate "those higher in the everlasting priesthood than himself," Lockley urged, then the prosecution could "place him on the witness stand and give him immunity for his past crimes." Lockley looked for "thrilling developments" and predicted that prosecutors Carey and Whedon were "likely to come out with laurels."[27]

Despite the hype about going to trial, attorneys on both sides worked behind the scenes to hammer out a plea deal instead.[28] As negotiations with Lee and his counsel heated up, Lockley, who previously had been "admitted to the confidence of court, prosecution and marshal," was suddenly asked to stay outside.

Lockley watched as people came and went into the negotiating room. Behind closed doors, a prosecutor grilled witnesses. One defense attorney passed into an antechamber with Lee's wife Rachel, while another wife waited in the hall. "In an adjoining office," Lockley scribbled, "Lee is closeted with the remainder of his counsel."

As Lockley sat writing outside earshot of the negotiations, he faced an ethical dilemma. On the one hand, he had been entrusted with "many secrets" about the case. On the other hand, he ruminated, "I am here as a newspaper man . . . to gather news." He knew it was "not well to blab too much" and wondered how much he should say. Ultimately, he chose to publish what he had learned.

"The lawyers on both sides," he revealed, "are diligently killing time." Prosecutor Carey had announced himself ready for trial the next day. The witnesses and jurors were restless. Lee's lawyers—Hoge, Bishop, and Spicer—urged their client to confess fully. Dame's counsel—Bates, Sutherland, and Macfarlane—worried about how a full confession would affect their client. Lockley thought they "seem[ed] to be acting in the interest of the Church." The six lawyers, Lee, and two or three of his wives held "a final counsel of war," Lockley reported. "The issue of their deliberations will be laid before the prosecution this evening, and will be treated as their ultimatum."[29]

Inside the negotiating room, prosecutors offered not to prosecute Lee on the existing indictment if he simply agreed to give a written confession, though he would have "to take his chances as to future indictments." If the written confession proved "satisfactory," prosecutors promised to drop all charges against Lee, making him a free man. Lee's lawyers finally concurred with the deal and implored him to accept it.[30]

The press soon relayed a rumor conveying the essential terms of the deal with Lee. The prosecution's goal, the report said, was to discover whether he and Dame had led the massacre under anyone's orders.[31]

On Tuesday evening, Bates sent a telegram to Latter-day Saint leaders, reporting that Lee had agreed "to testify against Dame Higbee Haight and some eighteen others" in exchange for Carey's agreeing not to prosecute him. "Lee's testimony," Bates reported, "defends President Young[,] Geo A Smith[,] and all others in the north." Lee put "the entire responsibility on the People at Parowan and Cedar City—who visited and aided the Indians in slaughtering the emigrants." Bates said Lee's testimony was consistent with that of 105 witnesses in town, "who all speak just as Lee does."[32]

Bates reported that Dame's trial would start the next day or so. He felt satisfied Dame would go free despite Lee's testimony. "We expect to win," he wrote. Prosecutors had charged Dame with murder by gun, and it would be easy to prove he was not at the massacre.[33]

Court convened again on Wednesday, July 14, in the thickly crowded courtroom. After chiding Bates "like a Teutonic uncle" and fining him fifty dollars, Boreman finally vacated his contempt order against the defense lawyer.[34] The Lee and Dame cases were called up, and again they were delayed. Prosecutor Carey said he was still missing a key witness or two but believed they would arrive by the following Monday.[35]

The main witness Carey still expected was Klingensmith. Just an hour after Boreman granted the delay, Marshal Maxwell received a dispatch from Deputy Cross, saying he had finally apprehended the prisoner. Equipped with a hired team, provisions, shooting-irons, and "some rough mountaineer as a guide," Cross had tracked his man through the deserts of Nevada to southern California. The heat turned his guide "crazy as a bed-bug," and exhaustion made his team give out, forcing Cross "to rustle around quite lively to procure other animals." But when he finally located Klingensmith in San Bernardino County, he found him "willing to come and give all the testimony in his possession." They expected to reach Beaver the next day. "This witness," reported the *Tribune*, "will enable Carey to go to trial, and Monday will open the ball."[36]

36

A Means of Escape

Beaver, July 14–19, 1875

On Wednesday, July 14, 1875, after Judge Boreman again continued John D. Lee's trial, news that Lee planned to turn state's evidence spread "with the rapidity of a prairie fire."[1] A widely circulated report from Beaver said Lee would become a prosecution witness, telling "all he knows of the Mountain Meadow massacre." Lee agreed to talk, the report stated, because he believed "he was to have been sacrificed to appease the wrath of the government and shield more guilty parties." Sources believed witnesses would "corroborate all of Lee's statements, which will convict W. H. Dame and many other high Mor[mo]n authorities and explain fully everything connected with the massacre."[2]

Yet the reporter detected "a strong feeling in favor of Dame on the part of the people from Southern Utah who are here as witnesses, many of whom were concerned in the massacre, and they evince great animosity toward Lee." Latter-day Saint sentiment generally condemned Lee, with his 1870 excommunication carrying great weight. Deputies "have had the greatest difficulty in getting witnesses for Lee's defense," the reporter noted. "Quite a number have positively refused and defied the Marshal, while all those on Dame's behalf are present, which is attributed to the fact that Dame is a Mormon in full fellowship and Lee is not."[3]

That evening, Beaver's newspaper editors interviewed defense attorneys William Bishop and Enos Hoge. The lawyers claimed there was "a fixed determination on the part of all—even those who professed to be Lee's friends at one time, to let him be sacrificed that justice may be appeased and the clamors of the people stilled for ever." In addition to strong public feeling against Lee, they faced a prosecution that reportedly had a wide array of witnesses. Facing such obstacles, Lee's attorneys counseled him to take "advantage of the means of escape which the government holds out to him—and turn State's evidence."[4]

George Bates telegraphed church headquarters in Salt Lake, reporting that although the trials for Dame and Lee were set for the following Monday, Lee would not be tried because he planned to take a plea deal. Lee was "making charges against large numbers of individuals in southern Utah who," according to Bates, "were not there at all." But Bates also reported that after examining witnesses in Dame's case, he felt convinced Dame would be acquitted.

Bates surmised that the prosecution's strategy was not to convict anyone but "to obtain evidence to show that the Indians were incited and aided by Mormons and that although the Leading men of Salt Lake have no active part in it yet that it was done under the influence of their teachings." By failing to obtain a conviction in Utah in such an infamous case, Bates predicted, the prosecution hoped to "create prejudice against the [M]ormon Church."[5]

A *Salt Lake Tribune* article suggested that Lee should be freed if he would indict Brigham Young, George A. Smith, or Daniel H. Wells. The pro-Mormon *Ogden Junction* exclaimed, "This has been the grand object in view of all the prosecutions that have been attempted in connection with that bloody affair. Lee's long confinement and the course taken with him in a military prison, were designed to squeeze out of him something that would appear to criminate the above named gentlemen." Ultimately, the writer opined, the prosecution hoped to trace the crime all the way up to Brigham Young, whose conviction alone would "satisfy the blood-yearning of the hounds who are yelping about 'excitement' and 'disclosures' and 'important developments.'"[6]

The public eagerly waited in anticipation, and the marshal issued an order to protect Lee from interruption while he dictated his confession to a scribe. "From the nods and winks of counsel and Marshal's deputies," *Salt Lake Tribune* owner and reporter Fred Lockley concluded, "startling developments [were] in store." Witnesses closely connected with the massacre reportedly became "alarmed and left town."[7]

Assisted by his defense team, Lee described his reasons for confessing. "The entire blame has rested upon the Mormon people in Utah," his statement said. "Now, in justice to humanity I feel it my duty to show up the facts as they exist according to the best of my ability, though I implicate myself by so doing. I have no vindictive feelings whatever against any man or class of individuals. What I do is done from a sense of duty to myself, to my God and to the people at large, so that the truth may come to light and the blame rest where it properly belongs."[8]

The complete version of this confession was never made public, but Bishop allowed reporters to copy several of its opening and closing paragraphs. "Most of those engaged in this unfortunate affair," the statement said, "were led on by religious influences, commonly called fanaticism, and nothing but their devotion to God, and their duty to him, as taught to them by their religion and their church leaders, would ever have induced them to have committed the outrageous and unnatural acts, believing that all who participated in the lamentable transaction, or most of them, were acting under orders that they considered it their duty—their religious duty—to obey."

Because he believed in "the sincerity of their motives," Lee continued, he had "suffered all kinds of ill-treatment and injury, as well as imprisonment, rather than expose these men." Now he believed the government and the court did not intend "to punish those men, but rather to protect them and let the b[l]ame rest on their leaders, where it justly and lawfully belongs." Those leaders, he said, were "Isaac C. Haight and Jno. M. Higbee, commanding officers."[9]

This was the first time Lee publicly identified Haight and Higbee as massacre participants. But unlike Dame, they had evaded arrest.[10]

The closing paragraphs of Lee's confession stated that "a few days after the massacre, I was instructed by Major Isaac C. Haight, next in command to W. H. Dame, in Iron military district, to carry a report of what had been done to President Brigham Young, at Salt Lake. Haight directed me to give my report and stand up with manly courage, and shoulder as much of the blame as possible." Lee said he obeyed. "I went to Salt Lake and reported to Brigham Young the exact facts connected with the transaction," the statement claimed, "shouldering a greater share of responsibility than justly belonged to me."[11]

In fact, Wilford Woodruff's September 29, 1857, diary account of Lee's report to Young and himself showed the opposite. Lee blamed the massacre entirely on "the Indians" and even on the emigrants themselves for deserving their fate. The only thing he did at the Mountain Meadows, Lee reported to Young, was to help bury the emigrants' bodies.[12]

"In justice to Brigham Young," Lee's 1875 confession added, "I must say that when he heard my story he wept like a child, walked the floor and wrung his hands in bitter anguish and said it was the most unfortunate affair, the most unwarranted event that had ever happened to the Mormon people. He said this transaction will bring sorrow and trouble upon us in Utah. I would to God it had never happened."[13] This part of Lee's confession is supported by

Woodruff's journal entry, which documented that Young told Lee his story of the massacre was "heart rending."[14]

Bishop did not allow reporters to see the pages of Lee's confession that detailed the massacre itself. This may have been because they might have affected the trial's outcome, or because Bishop planned to later publish Lee's confession for profit. Whatever the case, the defense attorney did permit reporters to state the "character" of these pages "as follows": The emigrants were "decoyed out of their stronghold by [a] flag of truce" and "the wounded were hauled out and dispatched." The killing was carried out by "thirty white men and a large number of Indians." The descriptions of "the killing of the men, women and children surpass in horror all that has ever been written concerning the massacre, and are more terrible, atrocious and bloody than the most vivid imagination can conjure."

Lee said that "seventeen children were saved" and that no children were killed later. The mass killing occurred under "military orders" during the Utah War when an army was approaching from the east, an invasion was expected from the west, and "the Mormon people were in a state of excitement, and acted as desperation dictated."

Though Lee had earlier said he did not want to expose the rank-and-file participants of the massacre because they were simply following their leaders' orders, Bishop said Lee "offered to give the prosecution the names of twenty-five of the murderers and where they could be found."[15]

Some court watchers had hoped Lee's confession would support the theory "that the massacre was instigated by Brigham Young as a means of revenge upon the people of Arkansas" for the murder of apostle Parley P. Pratt in Arkansas.[16] Instead, reports from Mormon and non-Mormon newspaper writers thought Lee's testimony and that of "other important witnesses" would "entirely refute all charges which have been made against Brigham Young and the leaders of the Mormon Church in Salt Lake City." The testimonies would prove that Young "sent emphatic command that the Mountain Meadow massacre should not be committed."[17] Lee had implicated only his southern Utah co-conspirators for planning and carrying out the massacre.[18]

Ben Holladay, America's famous "Stagecoach King," wrote Young from Washington, DC, on July 19. Holladay, a non-Mormon, had long since sold his holdings to Wells, Fargo & Company but retained fond memories of early freighting days in Utah. Holladay defended Young's innocence and read with optimism news reports of the impending trials. He congratulated Young that "*you will* soon be *exhonerated* from all *possible knowledge* or *blame* of the 'Mountain Meadow Massacre'."[19]

After prosecutors received Lee's statement, U.S. Attorney William Carey promptly rejected it, pronouncing it "unsatisfactory" because Lee did "not tell enough." The *Salt Lake Tribune* reported that the prosecution rejected it because, while it criminated "Haight and Higbee, who are not in custody," it "tells nothing to implicate Dame, who is in custody" and in whose trial Carey hoped to use it. While waiting for Lee's statement, Carey had agreed with defense counsel to try Dame first. But after finding that the statement contained nothing to incriminate Dame, he reversed his decision and decided to try Lee first.[20]

When Lee learned that prosecutors rejected his confession and would still try him, he protested to Lockley that "he had told the truth, and no power on earth could compel him to tell more than the truth." Prosecutors "had not fairly dealt with" him, he complained. "He had been prevailed upon to tell all he knew about the affair," he said, "and now they refused to accept it, and were making public use of his facts."[21] Defense attorney Bishop asserted that "the real reason for their refusal to discharge Lee and accept his statement" was "that John D. Lee shows, beyond the possibility of a doubt, that Brigham Young is innocent."[22]

For non-Mormon Liberal Party leaders in Utah, having Young and George A. Smith cleared of wrongdoing would defeat the party's strategy to usurp political control of the nearly all-Mormon territory. For them, Lee's statement exonerating Young could not have come at a worse time. Washington had recently sacked Judge McKean, who had so intrepidly gone after Young in Salt Lake.[23] Robert Baskin had helped coach William Carey in winning a conviction of George Reynolds, a polygamist chosen by Latter-day Saint leaders for a test case on the constitutionality of anti-polygamy laws. But to the dismay of Liberal Party leaders, the conviction was overturned just before Lee's trial date.[24]

With the loss of McKean and the overturning of Reynolds's conviction, Liberal Party members turned to Baskin to join the prosecution in the Lee case.[25] Accepting the challenge, he hurried to Beaver.[26] The *Salt Lake Tribune* billed Baskin as "the distinguished criminal lawyer of Salt Lake" and drummed up interest in the pending trial by calling it "the most important criminal case ever tried in the United States."[27]

37

Hope for a Hung Jury

Beaver, July 20-28, 1875

Crowds pressed into Judge Jacob Boreman's courtroom on Tuesday morning, July 20, to witness at long last the official opening of Lee's trial.[1] The room hushed as Boreman took the bench, the marshal proclaimed the court open, and the clerk called for "the case of the People against John D. Lee."[2]

The prosecution immediately blindsided defense attorneys with a new indictment against all nine massacre defendants. The original indictments, which charged each suspect with shooting a single victim, had two weaknesses. First, William Dame and Isaac Haight could prove they didn't shoot anyone since they weren't at the massacre. Second, prosecutors struggled to find witnesses who saw Lee shoot anyone.[3]

The first count of the new indictment charged the nine defendants jointly, making each responsible for murders committed by any of them. Under this count, prosecutors no longer had to prove a defendant shot anyone, only that he acted with others in perpetrating the massacre. The second new count charged that defendants conspired with Indians to commit murder.[4]

The prosecutors moved to try Lee initially on just the first count.[5] This tactic meant they could try him twice, once on each count. They could also turn to their advantage one of Lee's defenses—that Indians committed the crime. If Lee's defense blamed Indians during the first trial, prosecutors could use that evidence against him in a new trial under the second count.

The new indictment also offered political advantages for prosecutor Robert Baskin and his Liberal Party. Since the party's goal was getting Congress to pass legislation to disfranchise Latter-day Saints, keeping the massacre case in the public eye was essential, and two trials—one for each count of the new indictment—would double the publicity. Also, Baskin was the party's choice for Utah's congressional delegate, and if trial publicity led to disfranchising the Mormons—including Mormon women, who had received voting rights in Utah five years earlier—his odds of winning the seat would greatly increase.

Figure 37.1 John D. Lee, his legal team, and the judge: Left to right: (seated) William W. Bishop, John D. Lee, and unidentified man; (standing) Jacob Boreman, Enos Hoge, and Wells Spicer. Courtesy Utah State Historical Society.

"The most we can hope for is a divided jury," Liberal Party member Fred Lockley reported in his *Salt Lake Tribune*. "Strange to say we are all hoping this will be the result, as the attention of the whole country is directed to this trial." If the jury failed to convict Lee, he wrote, "Congress cannot fail to give us additional legislation" that excluded Latter-day Saints from juries and voting.[6]

The Baskin team's new indictment caused "a lively skirmish," forcing defense lawyers to scramble. Shortly before the trial, Lee's attorneys had ousted Jabez Sutherland and George Bates from their defense team, anticipating that Lee's confession would shift the blame to other defendants, including Dame, whom Sutherland and Bates represented. But now that prosecutors planned to prosecute Lee and Dame on joint murder charges, the two defense teams reunited.[7]

That prosecutors wanted a hung jury in the first trial started to become clear during jury selection. Defense lawyer William Bishop expected to spend the entire court term battling the prosecution over jurors. Instead, prosecutors put up only a weak fight before declaring themselves satisfied. Stunned again, Lee's lawyers stepped into the court clerk's office to discuss this second surprise move.[8]

Conviction required a unanimous verdict. Though some men on the jury would likely vote to convict Lee, if even one Mormon juror voted to acquit him, as prosecutors expected, the outcome would be a hung jury, the ideal result for the Liberal Party. To defense lawyers, a hung jury was not as good as an acquittal. But it was better than a conviction, especially given the evidence against Lee. When defense counsel emerged from the clerk's office, they accepted the jury as it was.[9]

Thus, before a single piece of evidence was introduced or a single witness examined, both sides tacitly conceded that Lee would not be convicted in the first trial.[10] Defense lawyer Bates telegraphed church headquarters in Salt Lake, showing he believed the trial was no longer about convicting Lee, but casting aspersions on church leaders: "All efforts to implicate Geo A Smith."[11] The trial was no longer about justice for the massacre victims. It was about winning political power.

When court reopened on Friday, July 23, a reporter wrote that "the interest of the people is at fever heat."[12] Though Smith and Brigham Young were not on trial, prosecutor William Carey focused on the two men in his opening argument. Carey said the doomed emigrants' inability to get needed supplies while passing through Utah was the result of a high order—not mentioning that church leaders' direction not to trade or sell supplies to any passing emigrants was an edict issued throughout the territory in the face of possible war.[13]

At the Corn Creek campground, Carey continued, the southbound Arkansas emigrants encountered northbound George A. Smith and his party. When the emigrants asked for good places along the trail to graze stock, the answer was "at the Mountain Meadows," Carey said, implying that Smith sent the emigrants there to be massacred. In reality, Jacob Hamblin, encamped with Smith, told the emigrants about all the major campsites from Corn Creek to the Muddy River, not just Mountain Meadows, where traveling parties had typically camped since even before Mormon settlement.[14]

"What became of the gold and silver?" Carey asked, referring to any money the emigrants had. "We have not been able to trace [it]," he said. Then, contradicting himself, he alleged that Brigham Young decided its disposition.[15]

Finally, Carey said the prosecution would prove local militia units were ordered to the massacre scene. Though Smith had not served in the Iron County militia since 1854, when he became church historian in Salt Lake City and Dame replaced him as commanding colonel, Carey asserted that Dame, Haight, and Higbee "were the officers immediately under" Smith. In sum, Carey said the prosecution intended to trace "if possible" the massacre order to its "real source."[16]

From an evidentiary perspective, Carey's arguments were faulty and did not even point to Lee, the man on trial. But to succeed politically, Carey only needed to try Smith and Young in the court of public opinion. His speech kept the courtroom spellbound, his insinuations of guilt titillating journalists and, through them, the wider public.

The prosecutors' first task in the trial was to prove that murder had in fact been committed. To do so, they called two witnesses who traveled through the Mountain Meadows after the massacre. The first soberly described seeing the remains of victims who had been stabbed, slashed, or shot.[17] The second testified to seeing skeletons of women and children, tresses of hair, and scraps of calico, all in roughly the same location midway between the north and south ends of the valley.[18]

The prosecution's next task was to prove who committed the crime. For that, prosecutors turned to their star witness, co-conspirator Philip Klingensmith, who had turned state's evidence. Like Lee, Klingensmith had become a pariah.[19] Shunned by neighbors for his role in the massacre and dropped by the church from his position as bishop, he had gradually moved to the margins of Latter-day Saint society and slipped over the edge.[20]

The *Tribune*'s Lockley tried to redeem Klingensmith by describing him as not "a naturally bad man," but "a stolid Pennsylvania Dutchman, . . . a plodding, hardworking man."[21] Other journalists were less charitable. "He seems to be as great a villain as any of them," the *Pioche Daily Record* declared, "and on the principle of rats deserting a sinking ship, he hastens now to tell the bloody tale."[22]

Klingensmith's gruesome testimony about the massacre came out in spurts over the course of three days as both prosecution and defense attorneys grilled him. Emigrants passing through Cedar City clashed with local people, he said. At a Sunday council in Cedar, local leaders debated having Indians attack the company. Some opposed the plan, and the discussion ended when Haight "jumped up and broke up the meeting."[23]

Though much of Klingensmith's testimony is corroborated by other sources, he lied about his own role in the crime. He claimed Haight sent him and another Cedar City militiaman, Joel White, to Pinto with a letter telling people there to "try and pacify the Indians" so the emigrants could pass safely.[24]

In fact, Klingensmith and White had gone to Pinto, but that was before the Sunday council, meaning they were likely trying to advance the attack on the company, not stop it. White was with William Stewart on September 7, 1857, when Stewart killed emigrant William Aden between Cedar City and the Meadows, and White wounded Aden's companion—hardly the work of a peacemaker.[25]

Klingensmith testified that after the emigrants fought back and dug in, Haight went to Parowan to confer with militia commander Dame about what to do next. Haight returned to Cedar saying he had orders to "decoy" out the emigrants and "spare nothing but the small children that could not tell the tale." Major John M. Higbee led a Cedar City militia company that included Klingensmith to the Meadows, where they arrived in the night, meeting Lee and others already there. When Lee learned they had been ordered to destroy the emigrants, he protested that they had "strong fortifications" and "there was no possible chance to get them out." Higbee said to decoy them out "the best way you can," turning command over to Lee to execute the scheme.[26]

Cedar City militiamen joined others who had come north to the Meadows from Washington, Utah. Lee told the combined group of some fifty men about the plan to kill the emigrants. Klingensmith said he and militiaman William Slade briefly stepped aside to discuss "the horrible thing that we was about to enter into," an act "that ran contrary to our natural feelings."

"What can we do?" Klingensmith claimed to have said.

Slade replied there was nothing they could do, "and directly the order was given to march down" towards the emigrants' corral.

The men waited while Lee went into the emigrants' wagon fort under a white flag, pretending to negotiate for their safe passage. Eventually, he came out walking near two baggage wagons that carried children and the wounded. The rest of the emigrants emerged on foot, and militiamen lined up side by side with the emigrant men as though to protect them from Indians. After moving northward, supposedly to safety, Higbee shouted "Halt!," signaling the militiamen to turn and shoot the emigrant men. Men on horseback chased down a few who tried to flee. Except for small children, no emigrants from the wagon fort escaped the slaughter.[27]

The suspense in the courtroom "was terribly painful" as Klingensmith recounted "the horrible details of the bloodshed," wrote a reporter. Lee's wives hardly breathed as they strained forward to catch every word. "Lee's square, hard, low, bronzed face and neck became fairly purple-black" as he listened to his old friend turn on him.[28]

Under grilling, Klingensmith admitted to possibly shooting one man. He gave details of finding homes for the surviving children, of how the emigrants' property was handled, and about Lee reporting the massacre to Young. Klingensmith implicated many participants in the slaughter. He incriminated Lee, but since Lee and the baggage wagons were out of his sight when the killing began, he couldn't say he saw Lee kill anyone.[29]

Trying to tie Smith to the crime, Baskin asked, "Was George A. Smith down there about that time?"

"Not that I recollect," the witness replied.

"Did you see him before this occurrence?"

"No, sir," Klingensmith answered.

"Do you know," Baskin pressed, "whether any of these orders which led to that massacre emanated from George A. Smith, and if so, state what it was."

"No, sir," the witness replied. "Not that I know about."[30]

Defense attorney Jabez Sutherland, a non-Mormon, objected to Baskin's frequent attempts to implicate Smith instead of the man on trial. "Lee is only a figurehead in this prosecution," Sutherland protested. The prosecution's primary intent was "to convict somebody else."

Baskin countered that prosecutors' intent was "simply to arrive at the truth, let it implicate whom it will."[31]

The prosecution's efforts to blame top church leaders hit their mark. "The testimony of Klingensmith was telegraphed to all the leading papers in the United States," reported the *Salt Lake Tribune*. It "was the town talk," creating "intense excitement among all classes." The *Tribune* quoted the *Virginia Enterprise*, which called Young "the real criminal" in the massacre. "Even if he is beyond the reach of a legal indictment," it urged, "he ought to be arraigned and condemned to death in every honest heart in the world."[32]

Prosecutors freely admitted "their desire is to get the facts before the people and a popular verdict against the powerful Mormon Church," wrote a reporter, hoping the trial would "break the backbone of this priestly con-federacy." Lee's lawyers remained confident their client would escape conviction, publicly saying they expected a hung jury.[33]

On July 26, a flurry of other prosecution witnesses took the stand. Joel White's testimony confirmed portions of Klingensmith's and undercut Lee's claim that vengeful Indians drove the massacre. White said the Indians who participated were initially friendly with the Mormons and only forty or fifty in number—far too few to force local militiamen into participating as Lee claimed.[34]

Former Fort Harmony resident Annie Elizabeth Hoag testified how before the massacre, Lee spoke of Haight's plan to have Lee and some Indians attack the train. The reason, Lee told his Harmony congregation, was that emigrant men got drunk, went to Haight's place, "called him out," and threatened to "send an army of soldiers to attack Brigham Young[,] Dame[,] Haight[,] and every other damn Mormon in the country."[35]

After the massacre, Hoag testified, Lee returned with Indians and called the fort's residents together again, reporting the massacre. As Lee spoke, Hoag said, a messenger came into the meeting with a message that stopped Lee's speech. It was a "dispatch . . . from Brigham Young to let the emigrants go, not to hurt them."[36]

Thomas Willis, a Cedar City teenager at the time of the massacre, said Haight visited his father's house and "wanted to know which would be the best way to make an attack on the train." Thomas said local Paiutes did not seem upset. His older brother John took the stand next, saying he saw Indians from outside the area in town. Thomas was then recalled, testifying about the tithing house auction of spoils from the massacre.[37]

William Young, an ailing witness in his late sixties, took the stand on July 27. He had witnessed the massacre from the hillside militia camp. While he acknowledged Lee was present on the final day of slaughter, he didn't say white men killed emigrants but had no trouble testifying of "excited" Indian participation.[38]

Samuel Pollock testified he was at the Meadows during the massacre but, like William Young, claimed to have watched from a distance. He named some whites present on the ground—including Lee, Higbee, Klingensmith, and William Stewart—but mostly focused on Indian participation.[39]

That afternoon, Sutherland addressed Judge Boreman. "If your honor please," he began, "we desire to examine as witnesses in this case, Brigham Young and George A. Smith." Explaining both were "too feeble to travel," Sutherland asked the court's and prosecutors' consent to depose Young and Smith in Salt Lake.[40]

"We do not consent to that," Baskin objected. "We want them to appear on this stand."[41]

Boreman denied Sutherland's request, and a new witness took the stand. John W. Bradshaw lived in Cedar City during the massacre. Like other militiamen, Bradshaw said he was mustered to go to the Meadows to help bury emigrants already killed. When he showed up with a spade and not a gun, he claimed, Haight berated and dismissed him, telling him he was a fool who didn't understand what was happening. The militiamen who went to the Meadows, Bradshaw said, brought guns but no spades.[42]

Witness testimony continued the next day with Robert Kershaw, who lived in Beaver when the Arkansas emigrants passed through. He testified that George A. Smith had been through town earlier and "forbid us to trade any produce with them whatever, under penalty of being cut off from the Church." Prosecutor Carey asked when Smith was there. "Not more than three days" ahead of the train, Kershaw claimed, inaccurately.[43]

The defense objected to Kershaw's testimony as irrelevant. "This evidence is pointed to some person not in the indictment," Spicer protested. "In this indictment," Sutherland added, the "mode of killing is specified with guns, not by starvation."[44]

Judge Boreman overruled the objections, saying the prosecution could show a conspiracy. "The prosecution is anxious to convict the Mormon Church if no one else," the *Pioche Daily Record* observed.[45]

Cross-examining Kershaw for the defense, Spicer asked why Smith preached against trading with the emigrants. Kershaw explained that with "Johns[t]on's army being on the road" for Utah, "we should want all the grain we had here for supplies." If they retreated into the mountains as expected, "the people might not be able to raise any more bread for years; that is the only reason he stated."[46]

Witness James Pearce was just eighteen when he went to Mountain Meadows with other men from the Washington settlement. En route, he heard "talk of stopping them emigrants" because, he recalled, they "said they would exterminate the Mormons when they got to California." He claimed to have stayed behind with William Young in the militiamen's camp when others went to meet the emigrants. When the men got back, he reported, "they said all the emigrants was killed." Pearce saw a lot of Indians friendly with Mormons around camp. They, like the militiamen, left camp on the morning of the massacre.[47]

Pearce said Klingensmith appeared to be "one of the officers" at Mountain Meadows and had "a good deal to say" about what was going on there. Though Klingensmith was technically only a private on the militia rolls, Pearce said Klingensmith was "looked up to as being kind of a captain" at the Meadows.[48] Pearce's description of Klingensmith's leadership role undercut the ex-bishop's portrayal of himself as a reluctant, minor player in the massacre, eroding his credibility.[49]

The next prosecution witness was E. W. Thompson, a Beaver resident in 1857 who was now a disaffected Mormon. According to his brother-in-law, Thompson had "nothing good to say about the Church" and was "great friends" with Judge Boreman. Asked by prosecutors if he recalled hearing anything about the emigrants before they arrived in Beaver, Thompson said he didn't. A letter was read that forbade trading, he remembered, but it "applied generally to emigrants" and wasn't specifically directed toward the massacred Arkansas company. Although Thompson knew George A. Smith was "down through this country at that time," he didn't remember seeing him in Beaver.[50]

"Did you hear him speak during the month of September?" prosecutor Whedon asked.

"I could not say that I did," Thompson answered.[51]

Finally, a man named William Roberts testified. He had lived near Parowan for the previous twenty-two years. Long after the massacre, Lee confused him with another William Roberts who, Lee said, had been "abusing him" over the killings. At the time, Lee mistakenly confronted the William Roberts now on the stand, telling him, "I was there, and what I done I done by orders." Lee excused the massacre, Roberts said, by claiming the emigrants "were bad men," some of whom "had murdered the prophet" Joseph Smith.[52]

After Roberts left the stand, the prosecution surprised Lee's lawyers once again by abruptly resting its case.

Sutherland then submitted a telegram confirming the poor health of Brigham Young and George A. Smith and announcing he would depose them in Salt Lake. He offered to cover prosecutors' travel costs if they would attend. They refused, again insisting they wanted to examine the church leaders in court.[53]

From a legal perspective, prosecutors had been unable to tie Smith or Young directly to the massacre. But their allegations, combined with salacious details of the crime, accomplished the goal of inciting public sentiment against the Saints and their leaders.

"If civil law will not reach these blood thirsty fanatics," the *Daily Nevada State Journal* demanded, "let martial law or lynch law be invoked, not alone to execute justice upon the men actually engaged in the massacre, but upon the arch fiend who inspired them."[54] The *San Francisco Post* called for "stern vengeance," not only on those who carried out the massacre but also on the Mormon prophet. "If civil law will not reach Brigham Young," it proclaimed, "martial law or lynch law should."[55]

"Jury trials seem too slow for such barbarians," wrote Nevada's *Gold Hill News*. The writer damned Young "and his lecherous apostles and proselytes" and condoned having them "arrested by the military and hanged in rows upon the public streets of Salt Lake."[56] The *Salt Lake Tribune* reprinted the articles, including one that called for genocide: "We should deal with these Mormon savages as we would with the Indians, their allies and tools in the work of butchery. No Mormon should be left in the United States."[57]

The *Deseret Evening News* condemned the threats: "An impartial journal would say calmly, 'Let justice be done;' not 'Let vengeance rule, law or no law.' "[58] The *Tribune* responded that the Latter-day Saint papers were merely excusing the massacre and shielding the murderers.[59]

Despite assurances he would not be convicted, Lee grew worried enough to concoct a back-up plan. When guards conducted a surprise search of his cell, they found a large butcher knife, a long-handled axe, a stone chisel, a saw-toothed knife for cutting bars, and other tools. Marshal Maxwell responded by placing Lee in chains, adding two more guards to watch him, prohibiting all visitors except attorneys, and ordering the prisoner "searched every time he is moved from jail."[60]

That evening, Lee's wife Emma "appeared at the jail and demanded admission to her husband's cell." When the jailor refused, she pelted him with rocks. "When the deputy marshal interfered," she put up her fists and "invited the officer to come on." Emma's actions got her into the jail, but not the way she wanted. "To-night," newspapers reported, "she will occupy a neighboring cell to that of her husband."[61]

38

The Curtain Has Fallen

Beaver, July 29–August 7, 1875

John D. Lee's face was wet with tears as he entered the courtroom on July 29, 1875. His show of emotion may have been part of a plan to prove an argument his lawyers were soon to make.[1]

A major weakness in the prosecution's evidence worked in the defense's favor. "No witness has sworn that Lee was engaged in the killing," the *Pioche Daily Record* emphasized.[2] Not even star Philip Klingensmith could say he saw Lee kill anyone.

"A large and interested audience" listened with "marked attention" to defense attorney Wells Spicer's opening statement, though he struggled to present a coherent defense.[3] At times he said Lee did not participate in the massacre, and at other times he said Lee did, though under coercion.[4]

Countering Klingensmith's testimony that Lee was a leader at the massacre, Spicer claimed that the Paiutes called Lee "Yahguts," meaning "cry baby," because he refused to participate, instead running away "with tears in his eyes, offering to risk his own life if anyone would stand by him."[5]

Spicer directed blame for the crime on Indians and even the victims themselves. He also accused Isaac Haight and John Higbee, still at large. They were the ones "active in perpetrating this great murder," Spicer argued. As militia major, Haight was "the one man and the only man" Klingensmith was "compelled to obey."[6]

Haight had sent Lee to report the massacre to authorities in Salt Lake, there "to take as much of the responsibility" on himself as he could. Lee's mission, Spicer said, was to "arrange it there so that they should not themselves be punished for that crime"—to "shield themselves by their own stories"—including the story "that Indians done it" on their own.[7] When church leaders in Salt Lake condemned the massacre, "the participators in this act" endeavored even more to "defend themselves and to ward it off their own shoulders and throw it onto somebody else."[8]

Spicer next tried to blame Indians in league with Haight and Higbee for the crime, though he conceded that Lee negotiated with the emigrants to leave their wagon fort. But instead of taking the emigrants up the road where Indians lay in wait, Spicer claimed, Lee went cross country to avoid them, hoping greed for the emigrants' property would draw the Indians into the abandoned wagon corral. Then Lee could guide the emigrants safely to Cedar City.[9]

While Lee was on his "errand of mercy," Spicer claimed, others "were plotting to thwart that treaty." Now, seventeen years later, the jury was being asked to convict Lee, the "only man that set to resist this tide, this scheme, this council of destruction," on "the testimony of these men who counseled planned and compelled it."[10]

Spicer's long and rambling opening address soon lost the audience's rapt attention. The *Salt Lake Tribune* called it "incoherent and illogical." Reporter Fred Lockley dubbed it "Spicer's Boomerang," suggesting the lawyer's admissions and contradictions might come back on his client.[11]

After a long lunch break, Spicer gave up his extemporaneous speech in favor of reading from a prepared script. Now, he said, Lee benevolently "went to the scene of the conflict as soon as he learned that the Indians had threatened to attack the emigrants." Lee tried "to draw off the Indians and save the lives of the emigrants," but the Indians "demanded that Lee and the whites around there" help "capture the corral and the emigrants." If they refused, the Indians threatened to kill Lee and exterminate the local settlers. Lee sent Higbee from the Meadows to Haight in Cedar City, asking for reinforcements to help "save the emigrants," and the Indians agreed to wait for a response. Haight's answer, Spicer claimed, was to work out a compromise—to let the Indians have the emigrants' property if they would spare their lives.[12]

According to Spicer, the Indians and the emigrants agreed to these terms. But as Lee went to the emigrants' corral "to carry out the terms of the treaty," the Indians rushed the emigrants, killing them without the aid of any of the whites except P. K[lingen] Smith."

Spicer concluded that the prosecution had not proved Lee guilty. "There never were any orders issued, such as K[lingen]smith has sworn to," Spicer insisted. "The killing of the emigrants was an act of Indian atrocity and not chargeable to the defendant nor any white man or men."[13]

Spicer's contradictory opening statement, Lockley wrote, "left the gentlemen of the jury in a hapless state of mystification."[14]

Court reconvened the next morning with a smaller audience. "Every day the crowd in the court room is becoming thinner, the people generally losing interest in the trial," reported one correspondent. "It is dragging along at such length that all are tired of it."[15]

The four witnesses that Friday—Jesse N. Smith, his older brother Silas, Elisha Hoops, and Philo Farnsworth—underwent grilling by both sides about events before the massacred company reached Mountain Meadows.[16] The defense tried to prove that the emigrants had angered Indians at Corn Creek by poisoning an ox, but Baskin browbeat Hoops, the witness with the most elaborate poisoning story, until he destroyed his credibility.

"You are abusing me," Hoops protested to Baskin.

"I plead guilty to the charge," Baskin quipped.

The witness begged Judge Boreman for relief, but to no avail.[17]

While Friday's defense was again underwhelming, Baskin's performance exceeded expectations. A *Pioche Daily Record* correspondent observed that the witness examination excited "the deepest interest."[18]

When court resumed Saturday morning, July 31, so did the struggle among attorneys. Philo Farnsworth finished testifying, followed on the stand by John Hamilton Sr. and Jr., who told of seeing emigrant property in the hands of painted Indians after the massacre. The testimonies of Richard Robinson and Samuel Jackson gave lawyers more chances to argue but provided little evidence to bolster either side's position.[19]

The public generally believed Lee guilty and had little interest in his defense, which a Pennsylvania newspaper described as "hopelessly thin."[20] It reported, "No evidence was offered to clear Lee of his connection with the massacre."[21]

When court convened on August 2, defense attorney Jabez Sutherland created a stir by producing a sealed package addressed to the court clerk. Opening it, Sutherland announced that depositions of Young and Smith had arrived. Boreman quelled the excitement, ordering Sutherland not to read them aloud but to file them with the court.[22]

Sutherland then called fellow defense lawyer John M. Macfarlane to the stand, drilling him on the location of persons tied to the massacre. On cross-examination, Baskin established that much of Macfarlane's testimony was based on his belief or hearsay.[23]

When Macfarlane stepped down, the defense rested its case.

This time prosecutors were surprised.

"Have you any further witnesses?" the prosecution asked.

"No, sir," came the reply.[24]

With the evidence phase of the trial now over, newspapers again offered their own verdicts. "There seems to be little room to doubt that Brigham Young inspired the whole business," one paper concluded.[25] Some called again for retribution. "Common justice demands that the Mormon leaders be apprehended, rigidly tried and made [to] suffer the full penalty of their enormous crimes; that the common herd of blinded serfs be disenfranchised and the Territory reorganized altogether," the *Pioche Daily Record* insisted. "Extermination is necessary and justifiable by the facts of the case."[26]

The *Salt Lake Tribune* reprinted an article from a Nevada newspaper that predicted the trial's political outcome. "Congress will meet, the atrocity will be told on the floor of the National council chamber . . . and Mormonism will be considered as a felony, and not a religion." Congress could repeal the act that made Utah a territory, "disfranchise all Mormons and disqualify them from sitting upon juries, and thus place the entire control of the Territory in the hands of the Gentiles." The paper concluded that no matter the verdict of the trial, "it will place before the people facts upon which Congress must and will act, and Mormonism[,] hemmed in on all sides, must perish."[27]

Noting that not a single Indian was asked to testify, a Los Angeles reporter interviewed a local Paiute leader called Beaver by local settlers. Beaver said the story of emigrants poisoning an ox and spring was a lie. He knew Moquepus (or Moquetas), a Paiute leader who was at the Mountain Meadows Massacre with his band. Moquepus told Beaver that "Lee came and asked them to help kill the emigrants," promising the Indians horses, clothing, and cattle in return. "Lee led the Indians at the massacre," Beaver said, "and Moquepus always said Lee was chief over him in that fight."

"I know that what I tell is true," Beaver avowed. "I tell it because these cowards have thrown all the blame on the Indians." Lee "got caught, and when brought here he got scared" and "said the Indians did it."[28]

With the evidence phase of the trial ended, Judge Boreman ordered the jury sequestered, and lawyers on both sides spent the rest of the day arguing over proposed jury instructions.[29]

When Boreman reappeared the next afternoon, the courtroom was jammed with spectators "manifest[ing] the most excited and intense interest." Boreman delivered the jury instructions, charging jurors to look to the evidence, disregard outside influence, and remember their duty was "not only to the prisoner at the bar but also to the people" and their own consciences.

"Your action will be looked to with great interest, far and near," he warned, "and it behooves you to act candidly, carefully and conscientiously."[30]

William Carey delivered the closing argument for the prosecution, re-emphasizing prosecutors' theory of a top-down conspiracy for the massacre. "Everything connected with it," he said, "shows how carefully and how well it was planned." After reviewing evidence supporting this theory, he pointed to Lee.

Though Lee was now an old man, "whenever I . . . feel any sympathy for him," Carey reflected, "my mind immediately reverts to the Mountain Meadows[. T]here I see old men[,] young men[,] women[,] children[.] I see them murdered in cold blood and I see this man [as] one of the principal executors of that foul deed."

"It is a mercy to punish him," Carey offered. "If I were he . . . I would ask that I might be punished for committing such a heinous crime. . . . If any one is ever to be punished this man is one that should be."

Jabez Sutherland then stood to give the defense's closing argument. Unlike the inexperienced Spicer, Sutherland—a former prosecutor, judge, and congressman—was a fine orator.

"Death under any circumstances," he intoned, "is a solemn event." The jurors' role is "to decide whether John D. Lee is such a moral monster as to imbrue his hands in the blood of men, women and children in a cold blooded massacre."

"In this solemn and responsible function," he counseled, "I feel assured you will proceed with caution . . . ; that you will form no hasty judgment; that you will not suffer your decision to be influenced by any fanatical party zeal."

"Any mistake which you commit by proceeding too hastily," he warned, "would expose you to the same moral condemnation as though you had taken human life like an assassin."

Klingensmith, by his own admission, was only "one of the murderers," Sutherland charged. Why had not prosecutors brought in other participant witnesses to testify? he asked. "They have no right[,] gentlemen[,] to ask 12 intelligent men . . . to take any man's life on the testimony of any such witnesses as Klingen Smith or Joel White" when there were witnesses who had not been heard.

Without the testimony of these other witnesses, Sutherland asked, can you say "that you have not any . . . rational doubt of the truth of [Klingen]smith's testimony or White's testimony[?] Do you feel a moral certainty that they have told the truth[?]"[31]

The next morning, Sutherland again urged the jury not to decide his client's fate without hearing all potential witnesses.[32] "The law presumes a prisoner [to] be innocent until such a quantity of evidence has been submitted to the jury as removes all rational doubt[,] all reasonable doubt," he said. "You want to be so sure that the prisoner is guilty that you would be justified before God and you could go and lay your own hands upon that man."

"There is no reason," Sutherland argued, why Lee's name "should be added to the list of the slain in order to appease anybody" or satisfy "the public conscience[.] For that destruction you should be as careful of the life of John D. Lee as you would be of any other man's life."[33]

Defense lawyer Enos Hoge next took his turn to reinforce Sutherland's arguments.

"Look at this man [Klingen] Smith," Hoge directed the jurors. "Look at him and see if a felon[,] coward[,] murderer[,] [and] assassin is not seen written upon every line and lineament of his features. Not even old age or the soothing influence of time," he said, could erase "the damning lines of crime upon his countenance[.] He stands before you a confessed perjurer, a confessed assassin[,] . . . a moral coward and a confessed murder[er]."

"God hates a coward," Hoge preached, and "this man Smith confesses himself to be a coward." During the massacre, he "did not have hardihood to raise his finger and check this damnable outrage." Instead, he admitted "he imbrued his hands with the blood of these innocent men women [and] children. I ask you gentlemen, how much credit is due to such a man?"

After discrediting the witnesses against his client, Hoge pointed at Lee and asked, "Will you make an example of this old man and shed his blood simply to appease public clamor?"[34]

William Bishop closed for the defense. Speaking for hours, he sought to strip the trial of political pressures.

"What are you trying this case on[?]" Bishop asked the jury. "Popular rumor[,] newspaper reports[,] or upon the testimony[?]"

He warned jurors they would someday have to answer to God for their decision in this case.

"You must be convinced beyond a reasonable doubt," he insisted. "You must be satisfied to a moral certainty of the guilt of this defendant or else you must acquit him."

Bishop charged that the prosecution's real motive in the trial was to make a case "against Brigham Young, George A. Smith, and the Mormon Church. . . . If there was no question of politics or religion connected with it," he said, "you never would [have] seen my friend Carey or Baskin within 250 miles from here." They came for a "chance here to blacken[,] vilify[,] the character of" Young and Smith.[35]

That morning's *Tribune* echoed Bishop's assertions. "It must be apparent to every unprejudiced thinker," the writer said, "that Brigham Young is guilty in the matter of Mountain Meadows." The paper called for a federal commission to try Young and Smith, warning that without such action, "the memory of this Administration will only survive in infamy."[36]

As the trial wrapped up, George A. Smith lay dying in Salt Lake City. After visiting Smith, his friend Robert Burton sent a note to the dying man's cousin, Latter-day Saint apostle Joseph F. Smith. "You know how little it takes when a man is in such a low state to [a]ffect him," he wrote. Burton called the prosecutors "*infernal hounds*" for trying to implicate Smith and Young in the massacre. To console the dying man, Burton wrote, "I said what I could to comfort him and drive from his mind any thought of those things."[37]

Following Bishop's closing arguments, only prosecutor Robert Baskin's concluding argument remained before the jury retired.

Late in the trial, one newspaper predicted that Lee, having given a written confession, "may get little sympathy from either Mormon or Gentile." After hearing the prosecution's evidence, a reporter wrote that local people were "all siding with the prosecution." One source claimed that even "the partner of one of Lee's attorneys has asserted that Lee will be convicted."[38]

But a quick conviction of Lee would not benefit Baskin and fellow Liberal Party members as much as a hung jury. They needed to continue stirring public sentiment to drive Congress to adopt additional legislation to disfranchise the Mormons. "This is really the trial of Brigham Young and the Mormon system at the bar of the civilized world, and not merely the trial of some murderers before a jury," offered the *Tribune*.[39] Instead of trying to sway Mormon jurors to his side during his closing speech, Baskin made statements that alienated them, arraigning Brigham Young as accessory to the massacre, and his church's doctrine as motivating the crime.[40]

"It seems to me," Baskin charged, alluding to blood atonement, "that a part of the Mormon Religion is to kill[,] . . . to shed human blood for another." The church, he said to the jury, eight of whom were Latter-day Saints, "is a blasphemous expression, and one that should be obliterated throughout all times." Though the prosecution had presented no reliable evidence that implicated Brigham Young, Baskin claimed the order for the massacre went from "the prophet of God, to one of his abject adherents; and the evidence and all the circumstances show that the order made by Brigham Young was actually carried out."[41]

After Baskin closed, the jury deliberated while the nation waited. Fred Lockley declared he could not find anyone in town "who has the slightest belief that a verdict will be found." A report out of Beaver now went so far as to say that "if one be reached, it will disappoint everybody."[42]

Early Saturday morning, August 7, the jury sent for Judge Boreman, who convened court. Lee was ushered in "looking rather pale and agitated."

"Have you agreed upon a verdict?" Boreman asked jurors.

"We have not," the foreman replied. "It is impossible for us to agree."

Boreman ordered a recess until 5:00 p.m., advising the jury to try again.[43] When court reconvened, the foreman reported they still could not reach a verdict. Nine jurors had voted to acquit, three to convict. Boreman then discharged the hung jury.[44]

"The Mormons voted for solid acquittal," and "one Gentile"—the jury's elected foreman—"voted with the Mormons," a *Tribune* correspondent wrote.[45] The paper reprinted a *San Francisco Chronicle* article that proposed, "If justice fails vengeance should be invoked, and they who killed without law should also suffer without law."[46] Calling Mormonism "a festering sore in the great body politic," "a foul stain on the national honor," and "a species of compound felony," the *Pioche Daily Record* proposed that Congress "repeal [Utah's] Territorial charter, indict Brigham Young, reorganize the Territory and inaugurate a new form of government."[47]

The *London Times*, which had no political dog in the fight, reached a different conclusion. "The question of responsibility for the Mountain Meadow massacre has been a source of long contention in the territory of Utah. It was at one time supposed that Brigham Young would be implicated in the affair, but the evidence on this trial has shown that he had no connexion with it."[48]

Despite the political rhetoric, both sides knew Lee's case had not closed. A hung jury meant prosecutors could try him again.

"The curtain has fallen on the first act in this great drama," the *Pioche Daily Record* declared.[49]

The second act would be more dramatic still.

39

Coerce Me to Make a Statement

Salt Lake and Washington, DC, August 1875–April 1876

Two days after Lee's trial, Marshal George Maxwell, along with Bill Hickman and other deputies, placed the prisoner in an open carriage for transport to the territorial penitentiary in Salt Lake, there to await his second trial. Lee's family members bid him a hasty farewell, weeping bitterly as the carriage drove away into the night. Despite the late hour, spectators thronged Beaver's streets and nearly every stop along the journey, "anxious to se[e] that wonderful Man, John D. Lee, of whom so Much is said," Lee wrote in his journal.

Along the route, Lee "met several warm Friends," he wrote, "who all advisid Me to come out & tell the whole story" about the massacre and "let the blame rest where it Justly belongs." They, like the prosecuting attorneys, believed he had held back.[1]

Meanwhile, William Dame was moved from the penitentiary to Beaver's Fort Cameron for his trial.[2] Prosecutors issued subpoenas for several witnesses in his case, including Isaac Haight and massacre participants Ira Hatch and Carl Shirts. But the potential witnesses were nowhere to be found.[3]

The witnesses' disappearance worked to Dame's advantage.[4] Haight was one of the few men who knew firsthand the key role Dame played in the crime. Meeting with his Parowan council and Haight during the week of the massacre, Dame had advised peace toward the emigrants besieged at Mountain Meadows. Only when Haight pulled him aside afterward in the "tan bark council" did Dame relent and authorize their destruction instead.[5] With Haight and other witnesses hiding, Dame had little to fear. Friends unaware of his about-face decision just before the massacre defended him, believing him innocent.

With none of the witnesses available to testify, Judge Jacob Boreman granted the prosecution's motion to delay Dame's trial. He was returned to the Salt Lake penitentiary where, for the first time since their arrest, he and Lee were permitted to interact.[6] Previously, Lee and Dame had been kept separate, giving them no chance to compare stories. The change in policy made Lee ask Deputy U.S. Marshal William Stokes "why he brought Col. Dame here."

Lee seemed worried that having his old friend Dame around might make it hard for him to tell prosecutors what he knew about the Parowan leader's role in the massacre.

Stokes replied "that he had spoken to Maxwell on the Subject," and if Lee wished to make another statement, they would see that Dame's presence didn't hinder him.

Pressure mounted on Lee to tell prosecutors more than he had in his previous written confession. Though Lee's attorneys pressed for a speedy second trial, prosecutor William Carey objected to trying Lee at the next term, thinking it pointless "unless the Jury law was so amended as to Exclude Mormons from sitting as Juriors."[7]

Lee was in limbo, it seemed, unless Congress acted or he gave prosecutors something to change their minds—like a confession that implicated leaders higher than Haight.

Visitors screened by prosecutors soon paraded through Lee's cell, urging him to tell more. One was Jason W. Briggs, an apostle of the Reorganized Church of Jesus Christ of Latter Day Saints, whose members had long challenged Brigham Young's claim as the rightful successor of founding prophet Joseph Smith.[8] Briggs, serving as a missionary in Salt Lake, "paid me a friendly visit of about two hours," Lee wrote, "advis[ing] me to Make a statement in truth of that unfortunate affair, the M. Meadows, & let the blame rest where it should."[9]

Marshal Maxwell described the political landscape to Lee and encouraged him to talk before it changed. "I could not possibly get a Trial till next spring," Lee summarized, "& by that time Congress will most likely amend the Jury act, granting the power to the Marshal [to] sumons a Jury indepen[dent] of Mormons."

"Your chances," Maxwell stressed, "will then be worse then Ever."

Maxwell also reminded Lee that his finances "will be waisting away & your Family suffer still more." But if Lee turned state's evidence and testified against "Dame & others," he could avoid further prosecution.

Lee answered that he had "reflected Much of late over this subject, & had Made My Mind that should an offer be Made again to Me that I would accept it, provided I could be assured of My liberty."

The marshal promised him he would be set free on those conditions.[10]

George Bates, a member of Lee's legal team during the first trial, complained to one of Young's sons that prosecutors had aimed for a hung jury so they could "ask Congress for a special Act to draw special juries to try the 'Mountain Meadow Massacre.'" At the September term of the district court, prosecutors planned to seek indictments against George A. Smith as an accessory before the fact and Young as an accessory after the fact, Bates asserted.[11]

Plans to indict Young and Smith, however, never materialized. Smith died on September 1, 1875.[12]

In its "Memorium" article on Smith, the *Salt Lake Tribune* again sought to link Smith to the massacre. "It was shown by testimony at the Lee trial that this man rode through the Territory in advance of the doomed emigrants," prohibiting trade with them. "Although the fact was not clearly brought out" that Smith was a massacre accomplice, the writer said, "the impression remained upon the mind of the hearer, that his visit to the southern settlements influenced the councils at Cedar City, Parowan and Fort Harmony to decree the destruction of the train."[13]

Those who wanted to connect Young to the massacre saw their hopes fade with Smith's death. The *Tribune* went so far as to suggest that Young had Smith killed because "he was the direct link connecting the massacre of the emigrants with Brigham Young."[14]

Meanwhile, the hunt continued for the indicted massacre suspects still at large. On the morning of September 12, after riding 125 miles nonstop, Deputy Marshal Stokes and a hand-picked posse surrounded the St. George home of Haight's stepson John MacFarlane, expecting to make arrests. But Salt Lake newspapers prematurely posted stories of the impending arrest, confirmed by an overexcited Marshall Maxwell, who indiscreetly wired money to Stokes on the public telegraph line. Tipped off, Haight, John Higbee, William Stewart, and Ellott Willden rode off before the posse closed in.[15]

Hearing of the fugitives' escape, Lee lamented "that Higbee and Stewart would Soon be out of the country where they would not be found."[16] Lee had decided to testify against his co-conspirators, as Philip Klingensmith had done against him, but his testimony would do little good unless they were in custody. He could tell what he knew about Dame, but his strongest testimony was against Haight, the massacre's lynchpin, the man who hid his own guilt while making Lee the scapegoat.

Yet what prosecutors undoubtedly wanted most was for Lee to accuse Young. Lee was willing to testify against his co-conspirators but not Young, whom he repeatedly said had nothing to do with the crime. On September 20, he wrote in his journal, "Matters have & are being delayed with design of Cohearce me to Make a statement beyond what I know." Lee resolved "by the help of God" not "to bear false witness against My Neighbour."[17]

In the view of many people of his day, Lee faced an eternity in hell for his role in the massacre.[18] But he had long rejected the traditional Christian view of an afterlife in favor of the multitiered heaven that Joseph Smith preached. Lee hoped to reach the highest heaven, but according to Smith's revelations, anyone who committed "murder whereby to shed innocent blood" forfeited that chance.[19]

In Lee's mind the only question was whether he had "shed innocent blood." In his various massacre accounts, he rationalized that the victims were not innocent, and that as a soldier simply following orders, he had done nothing "knowingly," "adversely," or "designedly wrong."[20] Bearing false witness against Young to save himself, however, could trigger the church leader's execution. This, Lee felt, would make him responsible for an innocent person's blood, subjecting him to eternal damnation.

In another "long talk with Dupt. M. Stokes," Lee recorded on September 23, "he advised Me to avail myself of the offer of the court & become a Witness."

"I could not in Truth testify to what they wanted," Lee told Stokes. "I would rather take chances then to do so."

"That would not sattisfy the court," Stokes answered, saying there was no advantage in letting Lee go unless he "would give more information then they already had."

"You Must take your own course then," Lee replied.[21]

Lee's intractability irritated the federal marshal. "Gen. Maxwell was quite gruff," Lee wrote. "Said that he had never tried to befriend a Man more then he had Me with a litle Sucess, that I did not nor would not apreciate their kindness, but would stick to the g.d. Mormon[s] instead of My friends, until it will be too late for Me, that they intended to have let Me go, as they had . . . Clingingsmith if I would only tell what I knew."

But "the Truth they did not want & as for lies, they Must call on Some other Person to tell them besides Me." That decision, Lee said adamantly, "was setled with Me" and would be "from this time fourth."[22]

In late October, Deputy Bill Hickman visited Lee in the penitentiary. Hickman, who robbed and murdered an arms dealer during the Utah War, had bought his freedom from prosecution by saying Young ordered the killing. Now Hickman encouraged Lee to "make a clean sweep of all & be free." Catching Hickman's hint, Lee responded, "I would Stand by Record." Though Lee had lied about his own role in the crime, he would not falsely blame the innocent to win his freedom, believing that would damn him.

And "thus we parted," Lee wrote.[23]

After the arrests of Lee and Dame in November 1874 and the subsequent capture of Klingensmith, George W. Adair was the next of the nine indicted suspects apprehended, captured while sleeping in Marysvale, a small town northeast of Beaver.[24] Newspapers labeled Adair "one of the instigators and leaders" in the massacre, though the only witness in Lee's trial who implicated him was William Young, who said he saw him "one time in the camp" at the Meadows.[25] Adair might have been indicted because, like Lee, he talked openly about the massacre, including to men of the John Wesley Powell expedition.

Though Marshal Maxwell told Lee that Deputy Hickman was tracking Samuel Jewkes and "would get him certain," Jewkes proved elusive.[26] He resided in a small central Utah town called Fountain Green, and as the *Tribune* noted, Jewkes had "been absent for several months—in fact ever since Bill Hickman made a call for him to answer to an indictment for participation in the Mountain Meadows murders." Again the local people shielded their own. "Every stranger is closely scrutinized lest he be a marshal in disguise."[27]

While the lawmen pursued fugitives, Liberal Party leaders believed they were on the cusp of success in the battle for political control of Utah. Their efforts to sway national opinion were bearing fruit.[28] At a conference that fall, for example, Methodists declared that "Mormonism is an institution entirely hostile to Republican institutions," and that "under the present jury system the law is absolutely without force, as proven in the late trial of Lee." They encouraged Congress "to deal more firmly" with the Saints through "an amended jury law and the suppression of polygamy." They also urged the nation's press "to keep the matter before the people till these reforms are secured."[29] In October, a Salt Lake grand jury again indicted prominent Latter-day Saint George Reynolds for polygamy.[30] William Carey, fresh from the Lee trial, successfully prosecuted Reynolds.[31]

With news of Reynolds's conviction and Lee's trial spreading across the land, accompanied by cries for punishing Young and the Mormons, Liberal Party members believed the time was ripe to lobby Congress. Robert Baskin set out for Washington to "lend his aid towards the passage of useful legislation for Utah," and to contest Latter-day Saint leader George Q. Cannon's seat as Utah's congressional delegate.[32]

Baskin drafted bills to punish polygamy and exclude Mormons from juries, attempting to revive portions struck by Congress from the original 1874 Poland Bill. At the time of that bill's passing, Vermont representative Luke Poland, after whom the bill was named, said the committee reviewing the bill thought it best to draw juries "from the body of the people" and not just "persons who were not Mormons and who might be hostile to them."[33]

Though Baskin lobbied for his bills, Congress hesitated to take them up. Curtailing the constitutional rights of an entire people because of the crimes of a few seemed wrong.[34]

Baskin's 1876 efforts in Washington failed. "There is a God in Heaven who controls the actions of the wicked for the glory of His name," Young exulted.[35]

With no federal legislation to change jury composition in Utah, those who tried to wield Mountain Meadows as a political tool saw decreasing value in their strategy. Prosecutors faced a choice: either proceed in trying the only two massacre suspects in custody or release them.

Dame's legal expenses mounted to almost three thousand dollars, a large sum in 1876, but it looked less and less as though he would be prosecuted.[36] He was not at the massacre, and witnesses had heard him publicly instruct Haight to help the besieged emigrants on their way, before he privately reversed course. Dame was eventually released. On March 22, Lee—still in the Salt Lake penitentiary—received a letter from Dame announcing he was home and no longer anticipated being tried.[37]

Lee struggled to keep up with his own legal expenses. His defense attorney E. D. Hoge "complain[ed] biterly of the neglect of my sons & sons in law," Lee wrote, "that not a cts. had been paid to him by any of them & that he did not see how he could attend court at Beaver."[38] One visitor advised Lee to solve his financial problems by writing a "a small Book containing a skitch of my life," thereby amassing "a fortune in a short time."

Lee shared this money-making scheme with the one lawyer who still stood by him, William Bishop.[39] The idea would stick with Bishop as a way to receive compensation for his unpaid legal services.

Meanwhile, the officers responsible for holding and prosecuting Lee were replaced. After a grand jury found that Marshal Maxwell mishandled fees appropriated for witnesses and jurors, he was replaced by William Nelson, "a firm-set, quick-motioned, deep-thinking man, who minds his own business, performs his duty fearlessly and impartially, and withal is a jovial, social, approachable being."[40]

U.S. district attorney William Carey was sacked after a disgruntled deputy accused him of "being derilect in his duties as prosecuting Officer."[41] Carey had lost all favor with the Liberal Party, whose members, paradoxically, now accused him of being "owned, body and soul, by the Mormon Church, and . . . carried about in the breeches pocket of Brigham Young."[42] In truth, the party may simply have lost patience with Carey's limited legal skills.[43]

With Dame's case dismissed and no second trial for Lee on the horizon, William Bishop believed a dismissal was plausible for his client. Lee hoped he might be freed "on a writ of heabeas corppeas."[44] Despite the evidence of his role in the massacre, it looked as though the infamous prisoner might escape further prosecution. But Bishop and Lee did not know yet that President Ulysses S. Grant had just appointed a Michigan prosecutor, one of that state's best trial lawyers, as the new U.S. attorney for Utah. Sumner Howard would change the course of the Mountain Meadows Massacre prosecution.[45]

40

Mr. Howard Gives Promise

Utah, May–September 1876

Though William Dame had been freed temporarily, he had not been cleared of responsibility for the massacre. As the May 1876 term of the second judicial district court convened in Beaver, interest grew in trying not only John D. Lee and George W. Adair, but also Dame. "Considerable interest is taken in reference to the trial of Lee, Dame and Adair," reported the *Salt Lake Tribune*, "and what disposition will be made of these cases."[1]

Despite his guilt, Dame could be confident he would not be convicted. On September 9, 1857, Isaac Haight and his counselor Elias Morris had visited Dame about the ongoing siege at Mountain Meadows. When they arrived in Parowan, Dame convened a council of local leaders. "The decision, which was finally arrived at was to the effect that the company should be protected, if possible, from Indian violence," Morris later recounted. Had he been called as a witness for Dame, that undoubtedly would have been his testimony.[2] Dame's reversal in the "tan bark council" was known only to Haight and Morris, and Dame no doubt knew Morris could not implicate him without incriminating himself.

People like James Martineau, who only witnessed Dame publicly or in writing advise Haight to let the emigrants pass unmolested, were willing to testify on his behalf. Dame could provide evidence of his written order to that effect.[3]

Martineau and Morris were subpoenaed to testify on Dame's behalf at the May 1876 term of court and made the long trip from northern Utah.[4] But they never got the opportunity. The recent change in prosecuting attorneys led an assistant district attorney to move for a delay on behalf of the prosecution. As justification, he pled that witnesses, including Philip Klingensmith, who testified in Lee's first trial, could not be found.[5]

Defense attorney Sutherland objected on behalf of the defendants and pressed for the trials to proceed, noting Lee and Dame had been imprisoned for eighteen months. He had no objection to the prosecution's using transcripts of testimony from Lee's first trial as evidence. He even "pledged the defense to bring the other defendants in ten days."[6]

Judge Boreman scowled at the prosecution's meager efforts, censuring "the neglect of United States District Attorney Carey in not subpœnaing witnesses." Defense attorney Sutherland—together with Enos Hoge, who showed up at court despite his complaints about not being paid by Lee—then petitioned the court to grant the prisoners bail. Their arguments prevailed, and the following day, Lee, Dame, and Adair all went free.[7]

The *Salt Lake Tribune* lamented "that men charged with so he[in]ous a crime should be turned loose upon society again to imbrue their hands with more innocent blood," though it also acknowledged that Lee, Dame, and Adair had been in custody for months despite the constitutional guarantee of a speedy trial.

The *Tribune* blamed William Carey for the lack of further trials in the case. "We find the Prosecuting Attorney totally indifferent about the matter, and no witnesses subpœnaed to be present to testify." The *Tribune* also bemoaned the lack of financial support of the "general government to aveng[e] the blood of the victims." Even "if Mr. Carey had wished to do anything useful for his country we do not see how he could have succeeded," the paper concluded. "As we understand the matter, the U.S. Marshal is without funds to pay the heavy costs of the trials."

The *Tribune* editor was pessimistic about future legal action. "We fully expect this is the last we shall hear of these much talked of Mountain Meadows prosecutions," he wrote.[8]

Not long after Lee, Dame, and Adair's release, Utah's newly appointed U.S. district attorney, Sumner Howard, arrived in Salt Lake City and immersed himself in his work. He found "the office in a *most wretched condition*," he soon wrote, "no files—no history of any of the many important cases to be attended to and every one of these old matters to be looked up and put in shape for trial."[9]

The *Salt Lake Tribune* welcomed Howard's arrival, seeing him as better than the sluggish Carey. Howard, it announced, "has the reputation of an able lawyer" and, unlike Carey, was "in the full vigor of his powers." The *Tribune* writer felt hopeful. "Mr. Howard gives promise that he will perform his duty though it may make things uncomfortably hot for many persons." The paper portrayed Howard as the Liberal Party's chief legal weapon against the Mormons: "He leads the attack upon this horde of law-defying priests and their perverse and misguided followers."[10]

But Howard wanted to avoid political entanglements and focus simply on bringing indicted criminals to justice. He reviewed the available evidence in his office to determine what legal action it justified. There was virtually no information to convict Dame, and Adair's case had not yet been well developed. The testimony from the previous year's trial, however, showed substantial evidence of Lee's guilt.

That trial demonstrated two major problems. First, the mixed jury of Mormons and non-Mormons virtually assured Lee would not be convicted. Second, despite strong evidence that Lee was part of a conspiracy leading to the murders, the prosecution failed to present clear evidence that he personally killed anyone.[11]

Howard devised simple ways to solve the two problems. First, rather than create another polarized jury, as his predecessors had, he would cooperate with the defense in having Lee tried by a jury of his peers—local Latter-day Saints. Second, he would find witnesses willing to testify that Lee was a killer.

To do that, he accepted the offer Brigham Young had repeatedly made to prosecutors and the court since 1859: to cooperate in bringing those guilty of the massacre to justice.[12] Until now, prosecutors had never asked Young to make good on his offer.[13] Why Howard chose to cooperate with Young and Latter-day Saint leaders became a matter of speculation—and controversy.

Those politically aligned against the church cried foul, suspecting bribery.[14] Others had already concluded that George A. Smith's death had doomed the Liberal Party's hopes of tying Young to the crime.[15] For his part, Howard, after reviewing the evidence, quickly realized that accepting Young's assistance with bringing in witnesses could help him win Lee's conviction.[16]

On September 4, 1876, Howard—accompanied by Marshal William Nelson, court reporter Adam Patterson, and *Tribune* reporter John C. Young, a nephew of Brigham Young—left Salt Lake City and made his way to southern Utah.[17]

Despite predictions that the defendants in the massacre case would all skip bail, when Howard's party stopped in Beaver, Lee and Adair were already there, ready for trial. So was another indicted coconspirator, Ellott Willden, recently apprehended. Before the court's opening, Howard and company went on to visit the Mountain Meadows. Howard thought it was important to see the site, "feeling that to intelligently conduct the prosecution it was necessary to visit the scene of the butchery."[18]

Before Howard left Salt Lake, Young's counselor Daniel H. Wells wrote a letter of introduction for him and Marshal Nelson, instructing a local

Latter-day Saint leader to find someone well acquainted with the area to guide them to the Mountain Meadows. "We wish you to extend to them such courtesies and assistance as they may need in carrying out this programme in as agreeable a manner as possible." In case the recipient was skeptical of the new prosecutor because of his predecessor, Robert Baskin, Wells assured the reader that "Mr. Howard has dispensed with the services of Mr. Baskin in the prosecutions; so we trust that the prosecutions will henceforth simmer down from whole communities to individuals. All is right."[19]

While in 1859 Judge John Cradlebaugh had declined to investigate or try the case in southern Utah without the nearby presence of U.S. troops, Howard trusted he would be safe simply with the presence of a Mormon guide, as promised by Wells.

Howard's party arrived at the Meadows on September 8, 1876, nineteen years after the Arkansas emigrants were besieged on the same ground. The area was no longer lush with green grass. "Now," wrote a journalist, "not a spear of grass can be seen, hills and hollows are alike overgrown with sage brush, and deep gullies come from every side." But fragments of human remains still bore witness to the tragedy, "a rib as white as snow, a shoulder-blade half buried in the sand." The monument marking the emigrants' resting place was "now simply a heap of stones three feet wide and a rod long."[20] After seeing the killing field, Howard returned to Beaver.

Wells, a counselor to Brigham Young in the First Presidency and former commander of the Nauvoo Legion militia, also made his way to Beaver, arriving before Lee's second trial began. On Sunday, September 10, Wells "preached a red hot Mormon sermon . . . on 'duty.'" John D. Lee, still free on bail, was in the audience and heard the address.[21]

The next day—September 11, exactly nineteen years after the final blood-bath at the Meadows—Lee was surrendered by the men who had put up bail for him and placed in Marshal Nelson's custody.[22] Lee's bondsmen, the *Tribune* reported, "are leading men in the Mormon Church here, and they claim they withdrew from the bond because they heard he meant to take leg bail." "He feels extremely gloomy," a reporter noted, even though his lawyer William Bishop "assures him of an acquittal."

Meanwhile, George Adair tried to turn state's evidence. The prosecutors, however, deemed his testimony "not needed."[23] Later, Adair "asked Mr. Howard what he would advise him to do in his case."

Howard told him to plead guilty.

"I'll see you in h—l first," Adair reportedly replied.[24]

By the end of the month, Adair lost his legal advisor when Sutherland withdrew as his attorney.[25]

Though Lee was again in custody, the prosecution was not quite ready for his trial because Klingensmith had not yet arrived.[26] Securing Klingensmith's appearance at the second trial was not any easier than for the first. Just a few days earlier, he had been "captured in a lumber camp on the Mohave Desert," the *Daily Alta California* reported. "The Deputy Marshal got a band of Indians to assist in his capture."[27]

As Lee's second trial approached, the *Salt Lake Tribune* reminded readers why the first one had ended in a hung jury. "The conviction of the prisoner was not so much an object with the prosecution, as the procurement of such testimony as would fix the crime of this wholesale assassina[t]ion upon men higher up in the Church." The writer noted changes in the political landscape that had occurred since then. George A. Smith had died, "and a prosecution of Brigham Young for murder or being accessory thereto, is decreed inexpedient. The weight of evidence, then, as we understand it, will be directed against the criminals placed on trial."[28]

In sum, while in the first trial Baskin and others aimed to attract public opinion in hopes of garnering federal legislation to change jury laws and disfranchise Mormons, in the second trial Sumner Howard aimed simply to try the guilt or innocence of the prisoner at the bar, John D. Lee.[29]

Since nine men had been indicted for the crime and it was clearly a case of group violence, some observers grew concerned when, on September 14, Howard offered a motion not to prosecute Dame, arguably the most powerful defendant in custody. Howard's rationale was not unusual for district attorneys; most successful prosecutors did not try cases they were unlikely to win. As the *Tribune* reported, "Mr. Howard says he has been unable, up to this stage of the game, to get any evidence of a competent character," and therefore had Dame discharged.[30] The dismissal did not exonerate Dame, and if evidence later arose—including in Lee's trial—to prove his guilt, he could be charged again.

A *Tribune* writer chafed at Dame's release. He repeated the long-held view of leading Liberal Party members that Dame "likely received word from George A. Smith that it was the will of their master, Brigham Young, that the emigrants should be made away with as an act of war." More accurately, he accounted for the lack of evidence against Dame by surmising that he carried out the massacre "through the aid of others." The article expressed confidence that eventually the truth would surface, proving that Dame "took an active part in plotting the hellish tragedy."[31]

Young's other First Presidency counselor, George Q. Cannon, who believed Dame's claims of innocence, welcomed the news of his release. "I was very glad to see Bishop Dame at liberty," Cannon wrote. "He has been most cruelly treated by our enemies, having been arrested as a participator in the Mountain Meadows Massacre and kept for nearly 2 years in prison, without a chance to vindicate himself." Cannon attributed Dame's imprisonment as persecution meant "to frighten him so that he would implicate innocent men."[32]

Dame's release was heralded by Parowan's citizens, who welcomed his return from Beaver with a brass band and choir singing celebratory songs, including a Latter-day Saint favorite, "Hard Times Come Again No More." When time arrived for the party to retire, "all expressed their pleasure and joy at his being with us in freedom and safety again."[33]

41

The Responsibility Before You

Beaver, September 14-15, 1876

Like William Dame, John D. Lee repeatedly asserted his innocence, claiming "he went to the Mountain Meadows on an errand of mercy and not of death." But given everything he had already disclosed about the massacre—including in his "confession" to prosecutors—his claims rang hollow. At the beginning of this new court term, he admitted "things look mighty gloomy for me now."[1]

With Lee's lack of funds to pay for legal counsel, only two members of his original defense team—lawyers William Bishop and Wells Spicer—remained. At the last minute, J. C. Foster, a lawyer from Bishop's town of Pioche, Nevada, joined them. Bishop—the best lawyer of the three—superseded Spicer as Lee's lead counsel for the new trial.[2]

On the prosecution side, Presley Denny—the only holdover from the prosecutors in Lee's first trial—joined the new U.S. district attorney, Sumner Howard.[3]

On Thursday, September 14, 1876, it took only an hour to impanel a jury—all of them Latter-day Saints. Adopting the same strategy he used in the first trial, defense lawyer Bishop aimed for Mormon jurors, assuming they would favor his client. But Lee wasn't so sure. According to the *Salt Lake Tribune*, he wanted a few gentile jurors. If true, Lee's counsel ignored him. "Four Gentiles were called," the *Tribune* reported, "but all were peremptorily excused by the counsel for the defense, contrary to the prisoner's wishes."[4]

When prosecutor Howard accepted the all-Mormon jury, it "startled the defendant's counsel" and the courtroom audience. "Everybody stared at his neighbor and asked if the Church of Jesus Christ of Latter-day Saints and the District Attorney had entered into a conspiracy to hang Lee for appearance sake," wrote the *Tribune*'s John C. Young, "or had the prosecution sold out?"[5]

In fact, Howard was outmaneuvering the defense. His strategy was simple. He hoped to convict one suspect at a time, beginning with Lee. If sufficient testimony developed during the proceedings against Lee, he would use it to prosecute others, including Dame.[6] He would avoid alienating Mormon jurors as prosecutors Robert Baskin and William Carey had in the first trial when they repeatedly argued that Lee's crimes were motivated by his religion. Instead, Howard would contend that Lee violated his faith by participating in the killings, and that it was the Mormon jurors' responsibility to condemn him or share guilt for the crime. Thus, while Lee's defense was "very anxious to get every gentile off the jury," Howard later explained to the jurors, "I let them do it because I wanted to put right before you the responsibility."[7]

In his opening statement, Howard told the jury that "he intended to try John D. Lee for acts committed by Lee personally." He proposed to prove that Lee acted "without any authority from any council or officer, but in direct opposition to the feelings of and wishes of the officers of the Mormon church." Howard also promised to prove that Lee had personally killed at least four massacre victims.[8]

In his opening defense statement, Bishop attacked the prosecution's case the way he had in the first trial, disparaging its witnesses, beginning with Klingensmith. To Bishop's surprise, Howard interjected that Klingensmith would not testify. The unexpected announcement made Bishop flounder "like a fish out of water." He rambled for twenty minutes, disparaging "all others whom the prosecution would have testify, declaring that no one save actual participants could tell anything" and arguing that they, being guilty, could not be trusted.[9]

Lee's defense did not know yet that Howard had two witnesses willing to testify they saw Lee kill emigrants. Using their testimony, Howard promised to show "that Lee shot one woman with his rifle, clubbed the rifle, and brained another woman; then drawing his pistol, shot another, and seizing a man by the collar and drawing him out of a wagon cut his throat."[10]

On Friday, Howard called as his first witness Brigham Young's counselor Daniel H. Wells, whose presence and demeanor signaled to jurors and the public that Latter-day Saint leaders were cooperating with the prosecution. Wells had helped the prosecution by encouraging eyewitnesses, including Nephi Johnson, to testify. Now forty-three, Johnson had hidden until Wells sent one of Johnson's sons for him. Wells introduced him to Howard in Beaver and requested that he relate to the prosecutor what he knew of the massacre.[11]

Wells also wrote Jacob Hamblin, encouraging him to come to court at Beaver and to bring Samuel Knight, who was living at Hamblin's ranch at the north end of the Mountain Meadows in September 1857 and who drove one of the two wagons transporting emigrants out of their wagon fort during the final massacre.[12] Prosecutors Carey and Baskin had sought Hamblin's testimony at Lee's first trial, but without success.[13]

Wells wrote Hamblin he wanted him to bring key witnesses in with "the utmost secrecy." Secrecy would preserve the prosecution's strategy to catch the defense off guard and keep Lee—then free on bail—from fleeing if he became aware that eyewitnesses of his crimes planned to testify.

Aware of Howard's strategy of trying one defendant at a time, but not entirely trusting the prosecutor yet, Wells wrote Hamblin that he wanted the indicted men not on trial to stay out of sight. It was "not desirable to have any more arrests as it may embarrass matters more than they are already," Wells explained. The church had taken a beating in the national press during the first trial. "We want the cases now in hand disposed of before any more shall arise."[14]

When Wells took the witness stand in Lee's second trial, his testimony aimed to undermine the false defense argument that the emigrants' conduct enraged Indians, who attacked them in revenge, while local settlers were powerless to stop them. Wells confirmed that Lee "was a man of influence with these Indians, a man popular with them," suggesting Lee could have stopped—or led—an Indian attack.[15]

Howard put seven more witnesses on the stand, including three who did not participate in the slaughter—Laban Morrill, Jacob Hamblin, and James Haslam. Using their testimony and that of participant Joel White, he asserted that Lee's orders were to restrain Indians from hostility but that Lee violated those instructions. Although Lee in fact was following orders from Isaac Haight and William Dame, Howard did not attempt to prove that. Instead, he sought to place the blame squarely on the man then on trial—Lee.

Morrill described the Cedar City church council the Sunday preceding the massacre in which Isaac Haight described the plan to attack the emigrants. Shocked by the plan, which violated their religious principles, Morrill refused to support it and "demanded a written letter or order from [Dame] before [he] would act." Morrill remembered that "Klingensmith was the most obstinate of any in the council, and was determined on the emigrants being massacred."[16]

Morrill argued in the council meeting that Brigham Young's advice should be sought before taking drastic measures. The council agreed. Haight sent express rider James Haslam to Salt Lake the next day, seeking Young's guidance.[17]

Haslam testified that before he left Cedar City the next day, Haight told him of a message from Lee "that the Indians had got the emigrants corraled on the Mountain Meadows." Haight told Haslam he would send a message to Lee "to quiet the Indians and keep them in check until" Haslam's return. Haslam left on Monday, arrived in Salt Lake on Thursday, started back the same day, and reached Cedar on Sunday, September 13, with Young's response. The response ordered that the emigrants "be protected," Haslam remembered. But the message arrived too late.[18]

Unlike his lengthy testimony in the first trial, Joel White's direct examination focused narrowly on his interaction with Lee, suggesting Lee was a proponent of killing the emigrants.[19]

Howard next turned to three witnesses who had participated in the crime—Samuel Knight, Samuel McMurdie, and Nephi Johnson. Like Knight, McMurdie drove one of the two wagons that carried the wounded and some children from the emigrants' besieged wagon fort. Knight and McMurdie were with Lee during the killing. Howard used the testimonies of these participants both to establish Lee's leadership role in the massacre and to prove he had personally murdered emigrants.

Knight testified that Lee and Klingensmith ordered him to bring his team and wagon from Hamblin's ranch down to where the emigrants were under siege. They said they needed his assistance to "haul away the sick and wounded . . . to take them back to the settlements where they could care for them." Knight related how Lee directed the loading of his wagon with the emigrants' guns and some of the wounded. When the final massacre began, he said he saw Lee strike one of the women in McMurdie's wagon ahead of his, killing her.[20]

Knight also testified about Lee's actions during the week of the massacre. Lee told him he was present during the initial attack on the emigrants, showing him the "holes in his hat and shirt, where he had narrowly escaped being shot."[21]

McMurdie testified that he went to Mountain Meadows expecting to help "preserve the emigrants from the Indians." When asked who gave him orders at the Meadows, McMurdie identified Lee. He testified that when the massacre began, he "saw Lee draw his pistol and shoot from two to three in the head, of those that was in my wagon," including at least one woman.[22]

"The evidence of McMurdy," a *Deseret News* correspondent reported, "was very clear and positive as to Lee having shot and killed four or five wounded men and women, lying helpless in the wagon that witness was driving."[23]

On cross-examination, the defense tried to implicate others besides Lee.

"Will you please tell me then, sir," Bishop asked, "the names of any that were of the parties that were there present on the ground at the time you started to drive down to the emigrant camp?"

"It is impossible for me to do it," McMurdie responded.[24]

Seeking to discredit McMurdie, the defense probed his statement that he went to rescue the emigrants. "You didn't know," the defense asked, "that anyone was to be killed?"

"No, sir," McMurdie replied.

"You thought you were on an errand of mercy?"

"Yes, sir."

"Thought you had gone there in good faith to help those emigrants back to Cedar City?"

"Yes, sir, that was my understanding."[25]

The defense asked McMurdie if he had done anything to prevent "any of the killing of those people?"

"I believe," McMurdie replied, "I am not on trial, sir."[26]

William Bishop would return to McMurdie's testimony again during his closing argument, portraying him as a willing participant in the massacre, a man with blood on his hands. "The fact that for 1[9] years he has remained in cowardly silence shows you that he comes here to swear and to swear for his life and not for justice." Bishop told jurors they should "not hang a dog upon the evidence of that man."[27]

Prosecutor Howard put Nephi Johnson on the witness stand next. Johnson, who had a view of nearly the entire massacre scene as it unfolded, portrayed Lee as a leading figure in the crime. Asked who carried the false flag of peace to the emigrants' corral, Johnson testified, "It was John D. Lee had the management of the concern." Asked who directed the wagons to go to the emigrant camp to carry away the emigrants' guns and wounded, Johnson responded, "it was Klingensmith and John D. Lee; they seemed to be engineering the thing."[28]

Johnson also said that when the killing began, he saw Lee "fire his gun and saw a woman fall as I looked down to the wagons." Asked if Lee assaulted other emigrants, Johnson answered, "I can't swear, but from the motions, I should say that he cut a mans throat."[29]

John D. Lee had painted himself to family members as a heroic figure who tried to protect the emigrants. Now Johnson's testimony corroborated Knight's and McMurdie's, all portraying Lee as a brutal killer. Johnson's testimony proved particularly persuasive. "His cross examination, which was scorching, showed that he could tell sufficient to hang every man who took part in the massacre," the *Salt Lake Tribune* reported. "All he said damaged Lee materially."[30]

During direct examination, prosecutor Howard asked Johnson if he had "anything to do in any way, shape or manner, with that massacre."

"No, sir," he claimed.[31]

The defense challenged Johnson's assertion that he witnessed much of what happened at the Meadows yet took no part. "Was you present at any council that was held there on the field previous to the massacre, and he[a]rd any agreement as to the killing of the emigrants, anything of that sort?" Bishop asked.

"No, sir," Johnson hedged. "I didn't."

"You didn't hear that anybody was to be killed until after you heard shooting?"

"Yes, sir."[32]

The defense finally got Johnson to admit that Lee had asked him "to talk to the Indians in a way I didn't want to."

"Tell me how he wanted you to talk to the Indians?"

"He wanted me to tell them that they would get the emigrants out some way so they could have their guns and horses."

"You refused to tell the Indians that, did you?"

"Well, I talked to them," Johnson admitted.[33]

The response tainted Johnson's claims of innocence. But it also added to the mounting evidence of Lee's guilt.

Defense lawyer J. C. Foster pounded at the witnesses' refusal to talk about massacre participants besides Lee. "There appears to have been an intention on the part of those witnesses to disclose nothing more than was absolutely necessary to convict John D. Lee and at the same time give no clue to any other person," Foster told the jury. "This is a conspiracy among these witnesses to clear themselves and their friends and to sacrifice John D. Lee to the law."[34]

If you believed the prosecution's witnesses, defense attorney Spicer mockingly told the jury, it appeared that Lee singlehandedly killed all the emigrants. Everyone else was "hunting and running after their horses, while John D. Lee in 3 minutes killed 119 men with his own hands."[35]

In a letter to his wife Emma, Lee seethed, "Knights & McMurdy, swore that I committed the awful deeds, that they did with their own wicked

hands, I own that I am perfectly whiped out & have come to the conclusion that some men . . . will swear black is white if the good Brethren only
say so." Lee added that Nephi Johnson "was the last man that I could have
believed . . . would have sealed his damnation by bearing false testimony
against me his neighbor . . . to take away my life."[36]

Though Knight, McMurdie, and Johnson each played a role in the atrocity,
they were not legally obliged to incriminate themselves while testifying in
Lee's trial; they were only required to tell the truth about the defendant. In
spite of the defense's attempts to discredit them, their eyewitness testimonies
proved withering to Lee.

42

Sufficient to Warrant a Verdict

Beaver, September 15-20, 1876

Jacob Hamblin took the stand next. Samuel Knight, Samuel McMurdie, and Nephi Johnson all testified they saw John D. Lee kill emigrants, but because they were accomplices, prosecutors needed someone innocent of the crime to bolster their testimonies. As Judge Jacob Boreman later explained to the jury, "Accomplices are not to be disbelieved, simply because they were accomplices," and if their testimony is "corroborated in any material point by other evidence," it is "entirely sufficient to warrant a verdict."[1]

In May 1859, army investigator James H. Carleton interviewed Hamblin, who said he shared a camp near Fillmore in late September 1857 "with a company from Iron county." The company told him a train of emigrants "had all been killed off at Mountain Meadows, except seventeen children." Hamblin didn't mention John D. Lee being part of that group.[2]

"These people from Iron County" didn't share details about the massacre. A year and a half later, after retrieving the seventeenth surviving child in Pocketville, Hamblin told Deputy William Rogers "he had heard more, and learned more about the massacre during his absence after the child, than he ever knew before."[3]

Now, testifying in Lee's trial nearly two decades later, Hamblin asserted he camped near Fillmore in late September 1857 with Lee, who there told him the full details of the crime, including his own murderous role. Hamblin claimed Lee told him the emigrants "came through there and behaved very rough, saying that they helped kill old Joe Smith" and threatened to aid the approaching federal army during the Utah War. Believing the army came "with the intention of exterminating them or compelling them to abandon their religion," Lee "was asked by authority—Bishop Haight or Dame—to go and watch those emigrants and see that they didn't molest these weak settlements."[4]

Hamblin testified that Lee told him he gathered Indians who, not content with merely watching the emigrants, "made the first attack." Lee said he tried to stop the attack, but "he could not keep the Indians back." Afterwards, the Indians became "so mad because one of their men had got killed, and another wounded," that they compelled Lee to lead more attacks, "which he did once or twice."[5]

Hamblin also testified that Lee told him about three emigrant men outside the besieged corral. One was killed by Mormons, but the others "got back to camp," telling fellow emigrants that white men were attacking them, not just Indians. With that knowledge, Lee told Hamblin, the emigrants would cause problems "if they was permitted to go" on to California.[6]

Hamblin said that during the week of the massacre, Lee received two messages. "One message came to not disturb the emigrants." Later, when it was learned "that they had [already] been attacked" before the first message arrived, the next message "was that they should be used up or killed."[7]

Hamblin claimed Lee told him an Indian "chief of Cedar City" brought two emigrant girls to Lee after the main slaughter and asked what to do with them. Hamblin said Lee told the Indian to shoot one and that Lee slit the other's throat.[8]

Lee felt furious as he listened to Hamblin's testimony, later calling him "the fiend of Hell" for it. Hamblin "testified under oath that I told him that two young women were found in a thicket where they had secreted themselves, by an Indian chief," Lee wrote his wife Emma. Hamblin claimed the chief "brought the girls to me & wanted to know what was to be done with them," and "that I replied that they was too old to live & would give evidence & must be killed [that] the Indian said they were to pretty to kill [but] that I . . . then cut her throat . . . & the Indian killed the other."

Lee protested he had "never heard of" such a thing before, "let alone committing the awful deed." He charged "the old hypocrete" Hamblin with using the trial "to reek his vengeance on me, by swearing away my life."[9]

Despite what he wrote to Emma to retain her devotion, Lee had heard the story about the girls before. In his 1872 interview with journalist John H. Beadle, Lee related that "a set of d—d villains told to all the country that I violated two of the girls," a story Lee called "an infernal lie." Lee was likely referring to Carleton's report of the massacre published in 1860.[10]

Though Hamblin's testimony helped establish Lee's murderous role in the massacre, it also helped the defense. An essential element of first-degree murder was malice, which Judge Boreman defined as "a wrongful act done intentionally and without good cause or excuse."[11] Hamblin's testimony raised the question, Did Lee's compliance with alleged orders to carry out the massacre constitute malice?

Describing that day's proceedings, Daniel H. Wells reported to Salt Lake a skirmish between Bishop and Howard during Hamblin's testimony. "During the examination of Jacob Hamblin this morning," Wells wrote, "Lee's attorney tried to implicate authorities."

Roles from the first trial had reversed. Now the defense wanted to implicate Brigham Young and other Mormon leaders to clear their client, and the prosecution wanted to focus solely on the man on trial—Lee.

"Bishop got off bitter speech saying that Lee was . . . sacrificed" and that he "intended to show from Hamblin's testimony that Lee was aided by other white men and was acting under orders," Wells explained. "Howard replied in a brilliant and telling speech in which he defied the defense and the whole world to produce one particle of evidence connecting any authorities or any Church with the atrocities of this case."[12]

The *Salt Lake Tribune* also flip-flopped. Lee, whom the newspaper previously labeled "Butcher Lee," now became Lee the martyr. The paper depicted Hamblin as a scoundrel, "one of Daniel H. Wells' witnesses, and . . . a party to the plot to sacrifice Lee in order that the Mormon priesthood may be whitewashed."[13]

Hamblin testified that he previously reported what he knew about the massacre to Young and George A. Smith, giving them more details than he related in his trial testimony because he "recollected more of it" then, telling them "everything I could." Young told him "as soon as we can get a court of justice we will ferret this thing out," Hamblin said, "but till then don't say anything about it."[14]

During cross-examination, Bishop asked Hamblin if there were not courts of justice in Utah before. "I have never seen the effects of it yet," Hamblin answered.[15]

The defense tried to capitalize on Hamblin's statement that Lee received orders from Haight or Dame to kill the emigrants. The testimony contradicted Howard's opening argument, in which he claimed, "Lee is alone responsible for the crime."[16] Howard countered by calling Nephi Johnson back to the stand and asking about the Dukes company that traveled immediately behind the massacred party. Johnson testified that Lee "asked me to take the company into the mountains in Santa Clara and he would follow with the Indians and kill them."

"Did he tell you that he had authority to do that?" Howard asked.

"No, sir."[17]

After Johnson's testimony, the prosecution announced it had finished presenting evidence. To nearly everyone's surprise, so did the defense, offering no separate evidence of its own.[18]

The next time the court convened, prosecution lawyer Presley Denny presented his closing argument. Denny confined himself to Lee's "inciting Indians to attack the emigrants before the answer to the message sent to President Young was received, and acting in opposition to the directions of the council at Cedar, showing that Lee was the main leader of the massacre from beginning to end."[19]

J. C. Foster gave arguments for the defense. He sought to raise doubts about the testimony of the prosecution's witnesses. "These witnesses [h]ave testified to conversations t[h]at occurred 19 years ago," he said. "19 years ago, gentlemen!" He asked the jurors, "Who of you, in that box can remember any one conversation . . . that occurred that leng[th] of time ago?"[20]

Foster relied on a legal treatise that said jurors must take "verbal testimony . . . with the greatest of caution unless they are perfectly satisfied beyond any doubt that the conversation was perfectly narrated and the whole truth told."[21]

Though this challenged Hamblin's recollection of a conversation with Lee nearly two decades before, Foster also tried using Hamblin's testimony in Lee's defense. Hamblin said Lee "told him he had orders" to carry out the massacre. "Now gentlemen," Foster reasoned, "if there were orders given there is somebody responsible for those orders." If Lee was simply following them, then that "shows no malice, shows no evil intent here on the part of John D. Lee to commit this crime."[22]

Foster argued that if Lee made the first attack on the emigrants "under compul[s]ion from the Indians, fearing his own life, he is no more responsible for it than I am to day."[23] The defense had tried the self-defense argument in the first trial, only to have prosecutors point out that compulsion does not absolve someone of taking human life.[24] Foster now argued that compulsion would, however, reduce the severity of the crime to "either manslaughter or murder in the second degree."[25]

Wells Spicer followed, again for the defense. He begged the jury not to convict Lee on the testimony of "actual assassins" in the massacre, then addressed Hamblin's testimony. "I do not think that Jake Hamblin would go on the witness [stand] and tell a single thing but what he believes is true," Spicer said. But nearly twenty years had passed since Lee purportedly confessed to Hamblin, and his memory could be mistaken.[26]

William Bishop presented the defense's final closing argument. He played to the sympathies of the Latter-day Saint jurors, rehearsing their church's history of persecution, the murder of Joseph Smith, and the threat of an approaching army in 1857. He read Young's 1857 martial law proclamation, emphasizing "that at that time war existed in Utah."[27]

Bishop played on stories about the slain emigrants. "Here is a force that comes determined to oppress and oppose the Mormon people," he told the jury. "Here is an emigrant train saying that they assisted in the massacre and the death of Joseph Smith. People that will sit upon our southern borders while an army from the north brings death and destruction along this land." Haight and the Cedar City council, Bishop claimed, "had made up their minds that the people were enemies; that they had come as warriors[;] that they were a hostile force[;] that they had come with armies, well equipped marching through the territory."[28]

Bishop also assailed the prosecution's witnesses, saying all had "come here to sacrifice John D. Lee, in order to save other parties that took a hand in that transaction." They "come here," he said, "with the blood of other men trickling down from their faces, smearing their countenances and damning their souls." How could such men be trusted? Bishop "would rather take Satan[']s excuse for his rebellion in heaven," he said, "than the statement of one of those men concerning any affair in life."[29]

Like the other defense attorneys, Bishop sought to undermine Hamblin's credibility by criticizing his nineteen-year silence. "This is [t]he first time he has ever seen a proper chance," Bishop mocked. "Why I wonder if he means that this is a good time because the prosecution has concluded not to hang Brigham Young."[30]

Bishop also took aim at Latter-day Saint leaders' cooperation with the prosecution, portraying it as a political move. Of Young's deposition, which Howard introduced earlier in the proceedings, Bishop said, "I can see an intended conviction of John D. Lee and a shifting of the responsibility of the Mountain Meadow massacre from the shoulders of the people of southern Utah and fastening it upon John D. Lee."[31]

Bishop asked the jury if they thought convicting Lee could really "raise the black cloud that has hung over the Mormon Church." People will simply say they have "taken a few of the guilty wretches and let them testify to just enough to hang Lee," Bishop asserted. "That will be the way the people will talk."[32]

The defense offered options other than first-degree murder to the jurors. If they believed the testimony of the accomplices and Hamblin that Lee killed people under orders, then Lee acted out of duty, without malice, and was guilty of a lesser crime than first-degree murder. If they believed the community feared the emigrants' threats and perceived real danger of violence, then the massacre was justified as self-defense, in which case they should acquit Lee.

Sumner Howard then rose to present the prosecution's final argument. He had agreed to an all-Latter-day-Saint jury, he explained, so the case would rest on the shoulders of Mormons. He did not use Klingensmith as a witness because Klingensmith had testified to save his own life and had not personally seen Lee kill anyone. Though Johnson, Knight, McMurdie, and White took part in the massacre, none of them had been indicted and therefore had nothing to gain from testifying.[33]

Taking on Bishop's argument that he "would not hang a dog upon the evidence of" massacre participants, Howard maintained that Johnson and McMurdie were unwilling accomplices, led to participate "by false pretenses and deceit."[34]

Howard also reviewed the documentary evidence. The approaching army was not expected until the following spring, and Young had written, "Keep quiet. Let there be no excitement." Howard argued Lee's motive was not about protecting the territory from the emigrants but "plunder and nothing else."[35]

Ignoring contrary evidence, Howard returned to his original assertion that Lee alone was responsible, challenging anyone to show "an iota of evidence that points to the Church at Cedar City or to any officer of that Church and makes them responsible for the commission of this offense." He claimed, "There is not a shadow of evidence except the assertion of John D[.] Lee that he was ordered to do this great crime."[36]

Like Bishop, Howard played to the jurors' emotions, recalling the murder of the emigrant girls as described by Hamblin. "Tell me in the name of humanity, in the name of Christianity," Howard asked, "how can any man do such a crime and shield himself under any orders in any necessity."[37]

Howard spoke so loudly that his "voice and argument [were] plainly heard in the residences around the court house," wrote one reporter.[38] He insisted that the jury bore the responsibility to remove the odium of the massacre from Utah. "This Mountain Meadow Massacre," he averred, "has been a great bugbear ever since its occurrence by which you have been characterized as a people unworthy of political power and the sooner you remove that bugbear and let the daylight into the facts the sooner the world at large will know where you stand."[39]

Howard wanted the world to know that Latter-day Saints as a people were not responsible for the massacre. The blame rested on the shoulders of individuals like Lee. "Then you may ask me why I introduced these documents," he said of the materials he got from church leaders. Because "this is documentary evidence that the hands of the authorities of this territory were clean. . . . I am told that I am not trying this case but am trying to vindicate the character and integrity of the people. I say to you that that is true."[40]

People packed the courtroom the next morning to witness the final scenes of the famous trial.[41] Judge Boreman first instructed the jury, defining the degrees of unlawful killing. "To constitute murder, the killing must have been with malice aforethought," he said. "Malice is a wrongful act done intentionally and without good cause or excuse," he explained. "If the killing alleged was done or participated in by the prisoner, and done with malice aforethought and was wilful, deliberate and premeditated, he is guilty of murder in the first degree."

If the jury determined "the killing was with malice aforethought," but was "not wilful, deliberate and premeditated, it would be murder in the second degree. And if the killing was unlawful, but there was no malice, the crime would be manslaughter." Though Lee's attorneys had tried to justify the massacre, Boreman said he could see no evidence "that the assailants were doing a lawful act when the killing occurred; nor that they who did the killing were acting in defense of themselves, their families or property."[42]

The jurors retired to deliberate at 11:45 a.m. Just under four hours later, the twelve men re-entered the packed courtroom. Despite great excitement in the crowd, "not a feature of [Lee's] face moved" as the jury announced its verdict.[43]

PART 7

PUNISHMENT

43

The Demands of Justice

Utah, September–December 1876

"Guilty of murder in the first degree."

Though Lee would soon boast of his stoicism in hearing the words that "stamped him a murderer and recommended him to the hangman," his family members in the courtroom "were so terror stricken," he wrote, "that they could not bear to talk with me."[1]

No records were made of the private jury deliberations that produced the groundbreaking verdict, but second-hand accounts surfaced. The first, published by the *Salt Lake Tribune* several days later, said the first jury ballot stood "seven for murder in the first degree, four for murder in second degree and one for manslaughter."[2]

Decades later, juror Andrew Corry said he was the one who voted manslaughter. In the early 1930s, a Lee granddaughter recorded that Corry told her, "I . . . disliked very much to give in to the jury for I know that Lee was not the only one responsible." But another jury member convinced Corry that "some one had to be sacrificed" to spare others, "so at last I gave in."[3]

The *Tribune* article attributed a change in the second ballot to prayer. "The juryman highest up in the priesthood," the paper asserted, "brought his brethren to time by a well said prayer."[4]

Lee gave his own explanation. "The Jury was selected also & instructed to bring in a verdict of guilty of murder in the first degree," he wrote his wife Rachel, claiming that "the names of each Jury man on the list was marked with an X and some with two," and that "leading men of the church told my attorney W. W. Bishop to select the Jury from the Names that were marked . . . promising him that if he would do so . . . that Jury would acquit me."[5]

Lee's memoirs, posthumously edited and published by an embittered Bishop, echoed these claims. The defense attorneys "had been furnished a list of the jurymen, and the list was examined by a committee of Mormons." The unnamed committee marked potential jurors who would convict with a dash, those who would prefer not to convict with a star, and those who would certainly acquit with two stars. Lee's attorneys selected jurymen who "were marked with *the two stars* in the list." Bishop charged "that the Mormons, who gave us the list so marked, had shown it to Howard before they gave it to us, and informed him that he had nothing to fear!"[6]

Depending on the accuracy of the details, what Lee and Bishop described was either normal jury selection or illegal jury tampering. Trial lawyers always try to pick jurors sympathetic to their positions. It would not have been illegal for both the prosecution and defense in Lee's case to seek opinions about how potential jurors might vote. But it would be illegal for jurors to commit in advance to vote a specific way.[7]

Bishop's actions in the immediate wake of the trial suggest there was no jury tampering. When prosecutor Sumner Howard was accused of malfeasance in dealing with Lee and his confession, Bishop announced that he considered Howard "an honest, efficient man in every respect," and admitted "that he was fairly beaten by Howard, who is justly entitled to the credit of the victory" in the trial.[8] When Bishop appealed Lee's conviction to the territorial supreme court, he listed numerous reasons that the court should grant his client a new trial. None of them included jury tampering.[9]

Finally, evidence about the jury's deliberations weighs against the charge. The first jury ballot was seven for first-degree murder, four for second-degree murder, and one for manslaughter—hardly a solid "unit in rendering a verdict of murder in the first degree," as Lee claimed.[10]

Immediately after the jury announced its verdict to the crowded courtroom, Daniel H. Wells telegraphed the news from Beaver to Salt Lake.[11] For Wells, the trial provided a better, though still not complete, understanding of the massacre—exploding some myths, exonerating Pahvants, and showing that southern Paiutes who participated did so under white persuasion. "I never knew before," Wells telegraphed, that "Indians from Corn Creek did not follow that company & that the Indians who were engaged in the massacre were exclusively those who lived below this point who I now believe would never have interrupted the emigrants had they not been incited to the deed by Lee."[12]

Journalists soon reported Lee's unhappy state. "At times," the *Salt Lake Daily Herald* published, "he warmly threatens to expose the whole story of the killing at the Meadows, and how it was brought about, and again he is sullen and uncommunicative. He is mad and sad by turns."[13]

In letters to his wives Emma and Rachel, Lee angrily blamed his conviction on fellow massacre participants Samuel Knight, Samuel McMurdie, and Nephi Johnson, who testified against him, while obscuring their own roles to protect themselves, just as Philip Klingensmith had done in the first trial. He asserted that Wells came to Beaver "to advise & council & direct" the all-Mormon jury to convict him, "sent here to have the thing cut & dried which he did to perfection."[14]

Latter-day Saint leaders had, indeed, cooperated with prosecutors, as they had expressed a desire to do since 1859.[15] Coincidentally, on September 11, 1859—the second anniversary of the massacre—Lee had learned that if he and other perpetrators were apprehended, "we need not expect . . . Sucour, Simpathy, or Pity from our Brethren."[16]

Howard suffered swift political criticism for accepting church leaders' help in securing witnesses and winning Lee's conviction with an all-Mormon jury, which undermined Liberal Party leaders' efforts to disfranchise Latter-day Saints.[17] Yet one Liberal Party member defended Howard. U.S. Collector of Revenue O. J. Hollister had worked with Robert Baskin and James McKean in lobbying Congress against the Mormons.[18] But now Hollister implored *Salt Lake Tribune* readers to see whether Howard's methods might result in changes the Liberal Party wanted. "Howard has taken a new departure," he argued, "allow[ing] the Church to use the court to try and convict one of its own long-cherished assassins." If "the Church has concluded to deliver over all of its assassins to justice," he asked, "are not the ends of justice reached in this way as well as another?"

"Is it an object worthy of all our efforts to demonstrate further that Mormon juries won't convict a Mormon murderer or bigamist, in the hope of getting Congress to exclude Mormons from the jury box?" he inquired. "Congress has never come within gunshot of excluding Mormons from the jury box," he reminded readers.[19]

The *Tribune* took Hollister to task. "The Mormon Church cannot purge itself of its offenses, it cannot denounce murder as a crime, and conform its habits to the teachings of the age, without falsifying Latter-day revelation, and admitting its entire system of preposterous pretension to be a lie," the newspaper argued.

As the debate raged, Howard and Marshall Nelson shared their perspective with their superior, U.S. Attorney General Alphonso Taft. "Those whose thunder is stolen by this conviction and the fixing of the crime where the evidence places it, and who failed in the same prosecution before, are exceeding angry, and are making to the public such misrepresentations as their malice suggests," they wrote.

Howard and Nelson lambasted the prosecutors' strategy in Lee's first trial. "Their public boast," they wrote, was "that the former trial of John D. Lee in July 1875 was not for the purpose of convicting the prisioner, but to fix the odium of the Mountain Meadow butchery upon the Mormon Church." They then used the trial to "call for a large amount of public money," with "no result except the advancement of certain schem[e]s and aspirations of local politicians." Howard's obtaining Lee's conviction in the second trial brought them "disappointment and envy, together with the loss of political capital."[20]

Bishop's and Lee's claims that Lee was a scapegoat offered up so no other Mormons would be prosecuted became a myth passed down for generations. In reality, Lee's conviction was only the first that Howard sought. Even before Judge Boreman set Lee's execution date, Howard set his sights on capturing and prosecuting other massacre participants, specifically Isaac Haight, John Higbee, and William Stewart. Haight and Higbee "were 'high up' in authority and were leaders and instigators of the bloody tragedy," Howard wrote Taft, while Stewart "killed the first Emigrant"—William Aden—outside the besieged emigrant corral.[21]

But catching the suspects proved daunting. Haight moved from place to place, often living under assumed names.[22] Local people kept suspects "posted in regard to all movements of our officers and cannot be taken by them," Howard explained. He asked Taft for "one or more first class Detectives who can be sent among them to work up the case and devise means to arrest them." Despite what he averred in Lee's trial, Howard aimed to obtain convictions as high up in the Mormon hierarchy as possible. Haight and Higbee were "nearer the 'seat of power' than Lee ever was," and their capture would enable prosecutors to "gradually work our way to the core of rottenness," he assured Taft.[23]

Meanwhile, Lee's attorneys drafted a motion for a new trial, but Judge Boreman denied it.[24] On October 10, 1876, Lee appeared before the judge for sentencing. "Have you anything to say why the sentence of death shall not now be pronounced against you?" Boreman asked.

"I have not," Lee answered.

Consistent with his Liberal Party leanings, Boreman gave a long speech declaring the massacre "to have been the result of a vast conspiracy extending from Salt Lake City to the bloody field" and accusing Mormon leaders of obstructing justice. "They have suddenly changed their policy," Boreman said, "and seem no[w] to be consenting to your death." Like Bishop and Lee, Boreman asserted that church leaders "hoped by your conviction to appease the public indignation throughout the country, and that your conviction and death would end the further investigation of the matter."

Boreman insisted that if this were the case, "they are greatly mistaken. This dread crime will not down and your conviction is but the beginning of the end. The demands of justice will not be satisfied until the guilty leaders in planning or executing that crime are known and brought to the bar of justice and their cases investigated in the courts and passed upon by impartial juries."

Judge Boreman asked Lee to choose the mode of execution, "by hanging, by shooting or by beheading."

"I would rather be shot," Lee answered.

Boreman set Lee's execution date for January 26, 1877, when "you [will] be taken from your place of confinement and anesthetized by public shot until you are dead. And may Almighty God have mercy upon your soul."[25]

After the sentencing, Lee poured his energy into preserving his life and his family's waning faith in him. "In this affair," he assured Rachel, "I plead innocent, as I always have done before." Though he could no longer deny the evidence of his participation in the massacre, he clung to the excuse that he had lacked malice. "I used my best arguments with weeping against the commission of that crime but all to no avail," he claimed. "Further resistance would have endangered my life."

He hoped his life might be spared if he furnished officials more details of the massacre. "Though the Truth has slumbered, for many years," he wrote Emma, "it must now come to my deliverance." He implored Emma and Rachel to "hunt up all my Journals & records."[26]

Even if the records proved inadequate to save him from the executioner, Lee wanted "to have a History of [his] life published to the world." In it, he hoped "to remove that foul odium & dark cloud of callumny that has so long beclouded the atmosphere of myself & Family," he told Emma, "& let the blame rest where it justly belongs."[27] He also hoped proceeds from his story's sales would pay his legal fees.[28]

Lee lacked funds even to pay for transcribing documents required for an appeal of his conviction. According to his affidavit, he had "been so long confined in prison and put to such great expense by reason of his arrest and trial that he is wholly insolvent and unable to pay."[29]

Before his second trial, Lee had resolved "not to betray his friends." But with his death sentence looming, he changed his mind.[30] He hoped his sons could buy his freedom by delivering the three fugitives Howard wanted—Haight, Higbee, and Stewart. Knowing he would soon be transferred from Beaver to the Salt Lake penitentiary, he urged his sons at Panguitch to come to him quickly to discuss this tactic "that may be the means of my obtaining my liberty."[31]

He wrote Rachel to "get some trusty Indians . . . to find out the retreat of the 3 men Haicht, Higbee & Stewart," then have "the Boys with the Indians . . . slip up on their camp at night . . . get good positions & lay there till light in the morning," allowing them to "get the drop on them." It was only fair that his co-conspirators "should come up & face the music as I have."[32]

Lee wrote his son Harvey that he had enlisted help from "Idaho Bill," a convicted highway robber Lee met in prison. Idaho Bill had falsely convinced Lee he was Christopher "Kit" Carson Fancher, the surviving emigrant boy Lee took into his home after the massacre. Idaho Bill offered to help Lee's sons capture Haight and the others if he could gain his own freedom.[33]

When Marshal Nelson transported Lee back to the Salt Lake penitentiary, Howard and others greeted him warmly, giving him preferential treatment in hopes of extracting useful disclosures. Lee learned he "would have a room bunk & Mattress furnished me on the outside of the Penetentiary," as well as "stationary & a chance to write."[34]

Owing William Bishop a considerable financial debt, Lee gave him the rights to his life story, his only potentially lucrative asset. Racing against time to finish his manuscript, Lee wrote Bishop, "I wish you to . . . publish to the world the history of my life and of my connection with the affair for which I have been tried." Knowing he might not finish before his death, Lee promised, "my journals and private papers will be furnished you by my family, the same to be returned when examined."[35]

In his letters to family, including his wife Sarah Caroline, he begged all who had any regard for him "to wake up" and raise funds to pay his lawyer for an appeal.[36] To daughter Sara Jane, Lee explained that without funds, Bishop could not travel from Nevada to appeal his case to Utah's supreme court. "My case will have to lay over or I be executed according to the decission of Judge Boreman."[37]

To Emma, Lee expressed particular interest in her sending "the Journal that I carried in my pocket when Chas Hopkins came to Harmony . . . when Judge Cradleba[ug]h was after him." Lee asserted in his letter that Hopkins,

a massacre participant, "said to me Bro. Lee if I was in your place I would expose the whole thing, I know that you opposed it, & argued against, in tears,
& I will swear to it." Though Hopkins had long since died, this type of information supported Lee's line of defense. He hoped his journals would verify
this story and contain other "facts that may be of much value to me."[38]

On December 20, 1876, Bishop wrote Marshal Nelson, complaining that
Lee's "family have not paid me a dollar yet, and I shall not go to Salt Lake"
to appeal his case. Instead, Bishop would "send a *Brief*—and do what I can
for him without going," but "I am financially *cramped* just now, and cannot
afford the few hundred dollars it would cost to go there to attend Supreme
Court—Tell Lee that I am sorry to quit him—but necessity knows no law."[39]

44

Allow the Law to Take Its Course

Utah, January–March 1877

Sumner Howard sought to make political hay from his success in the Lee case. In early January 1877 he asked Utah's congressional delegate, George Q. Cannon, to use his influence to appoint him as a judge. Howard promised Cannon "if he got the office, that he would administer the law fairly." He said he had no ill feelings towards Mormons but would treat them justly "as citizens of the United States." Cannon assured him he would do what he could.[1]

Judge Jacob Boreman's term was drawing to a close, and Howard knew there was animosity between him and the Latter-day Saints.[2] Though Cannon viewed Howard as an improvement over Boreman, the judge had no intention of retiring and was reappointed. In the end nothing came of Howard's overtures.[3]

Meanwhile, Lee finally came up with funds to appeal his case. "I got Col Nelson to have me taken to the city twice to try & raise the money," he wrote. After weeping and pleading, "I at last prevailed with Capt [William H.] Hooper and Bp John Sharp to loan me $250." William Bishop then agreed to travel to Salt Lake to represent Lee before the territorial supreme court, which granted a stay of Lee's January execution pending the appeal.[4]

Bishop challenged nearly everything, from the 1874 grand jury that indicted Lee to Judge Boreman's 1876 closing charge.[5] Bishop argued that the indictment filed before the first trial was not lawfully presented to the grand jury and that the guilty verdict in the second trial was based mainly on "the evidence of confessed accomplices."[6]

Howard and his co-counsel responded that "the verdict was supported on the testimony of unimpeached witnesses," reading in full the testimonies of Nephi Johnson, Samuel Knight, Samuel McMurdie, and Jacob Hamblin. Following this counterargument, Bishop declared "that the whole Mormon Church was accessory either before or after the fact."[7]

The territory's supreme court—made up of Utah's three U.S. district court judges, including Boreman—ruled that "the defendant was fairly and impartially tried," affirming the lower court's judgment.[8]

Defeated, Bishop complained to Lee that "we had the prejudice of civilization to contend with—the united press of the nation opposed us, and no one was found who would speak a word of kindness in your behalf." Bishop also blamed Latter-day Saint leaders. "We found the so-called *Head of the Church* furnishing evidence against you and the members all arrayed as willing tools. . . . The whole people it appeared demanded a victim. Under such circumstances we could only fail."

Bishop assured Lee he had done his best. "Men of greater ability could have been secured to defend you," Bishop wrote him, but no one "would have been more truly devoted to your interests than I." He would have succeeded were it not for so much "outside pressure and prejudice."

Since Lee had no more money, Bishop let the period expire for appealing to the United States Supreme Court.

"I am sorry that you were unable to raise the money," the defense attorney wrote, "for I do think we could have reversed the case in that court—But," he added callously, "it is useless to speak of what might have been—it is existing facts that now demand attention—I do most certainly wish and expect the remainder of your manuscript."[9]

Lee promised to send his life history "without delay."[10] Others tried moving in on Bishop's literary turf, but Lee loyally fended them off. As he explained to one suitor, "My worthy attorney W. W. Bishop held that right by previous arrangement made at my trial at Beaver."[11]

Bishop's expectations were deflated when the manuscript arrived in early March. Lee had written extensively about his early years but nothing about his life in Utah or the massacre. This was "the most material part of it all," Bishop complained to him—and the part most likely to sell books. Knowing his client was about to face a firing squad, Bishop asked for Lee's journals and other writings he could use that might "throw light on the work" posthumously.[12]

Lee kept up his writing and went to great lengths to have his family collect his journals for Bishop.[13] Bishop and Nelson received the journals but did not return them to Lee's family as agreed. Decades later, Bishop and Nelson descendants still had some of Lee's journals and sold or donated them to California's Huntington Library. The others somehow disappeared.[14]

Bishop later acknowledged that Lee left his manuscript in an "unfinished state" but claimed Lee "had previously dictated a full confession to me."[15] Although Lee did make a confession to Bishop prior to his first trial when he was plea-bargaining with prosecutors, they declared the confession incomplete and unsatisfactory. "The real reason for their refusal to discharge Lee and accept his statement," Bishop had written in July 1875, "is that John D. Lee shows, beyond the possibility of a doubt, that Brigham Young is innocent and knew nothing of the transaction until many days after the massacre occurred."[16]

As Lee languished in prison, lawmen hoped to apprehend other massacre perpetrators. Deputy William Stokes—who arrested Lee and William Dame—believed he could capture Haight, Higbee, and Stewart if he could just get financing for his efforts. Stokes feared that if they were "not arrested soon, . . . they will all be gone to New-Mexico."[17]

Howard wrote Attorney General Alphonso Taft again, requesting a five-hundred-dollar reward for the capture of each fugitive. "No ordinary method will secure them," he implored. They were "desperate men" who had "the sympathy and assistance" of many others.[18]

The mercurial George C. Bates, one-time prosecutor and erstwhile Lee defense lawyer, also wanted in on the action. He felt these men, who were once his clients, had betrayed him. "They have sold me out, turned their backs upon me, and put their case into the hands of [Jabez] Sutherland," Bates's former partner, "who intrigues with others to let them escape," he asserted. The fugitives "are as guilty as old John D. Lee himself," he told Judge Boreman, "and they can be, and ought to be captured, brought into Court, tried, convicted and sentenced to-death."

Bates claimed friendship with men in President Rutherford Hayes's cabinet and wanted to use his connections to get an investigator to help him.[19]

But Judge Boreman shot down Bates's appeals. "It would be very unfortunate if M[r] Bates should get from the Department any recognition in the respect he refers to," Boreman wrote the new U.S. attorney general Charles Devens. "He cannot be trusted with the arrest of any one" and "is totally unreliable."[20]

In early March, Howard and Nelson prepared to transport Lee from Salt Lake back to Beaver to await his execution. The prosecutor confided he "felt very keenly the uncomfortable outlook of the proposed journey over a wild, mountainous, and almost uninhabited country of 150 miles with a man like Lee in charge, and only Marshal Nelson and myself to guard him."

Howard worried about a possible rescue attempt, hearing Lee had "40 sons who had sworn that he never should be executed." In reality, Lee had twenty-four living sons, some of whose mothers had long ago left him and ten of whom were still children.

The only foe Howard and Nelson ended up facing was mud. They had to get out of their coach when it got stuck, and Howard observed that his overshoes became buried "so deep in the muddy soil of Zion that the Latter-Day Saints . . . will need a revelation to find them."[21]

When the trio reached Beaver, "the only relatives awaiting [Lee's] arrival were a son and son-in-law. All men appear to have forsaken him," wrote a *Deseret News* correspondent.[22]

Howard and Nelson turned Lee over to U.S. soldiers stationed at nearby Fort Cameron.[23] The prosecutor and marshal reported they had reason to believe Lee's wife Rachel "has been in active communication with certain Indian warriors, evidently with a view of securing their co-operation in an effort at rescue."[24] Rachel may have only been fulfilling her husband's plea to find Indians to help capture Haight, Higbee, and Stewart. Still, Howard requested "an order on the commander of Fort Cameron, Beaver, for guard to prevent the rescue of John D. Lee."[25]

Lee was accordingly placed in solitary confinement.[26]

Two sentinels stood continual duty at the guardhouse, instructed to "allow no communication whatever with the prisoner by soldiers or citizens" unless "provided with a pass by the U.S. Marshal, countersigned by the Comd'g Officer; and then only in the presence of the Officer of the Day."

Fort Cameron's commanding officer even ordered that until the day after Lee's execution, no passes would be issued for "men to leave the post" because "the probability of an attempted rescue demands the presence of all the men at the Garrison."[27]

The tight security frustrated members of the press, who wanted access to the infamous prisoner. A *New York Herald* reporter speculated that Lee's seclusion stemmed from Howard's "hopes to obtain from the prisoner a sworn statement with regard to the participation of Haight, Higbee and Dame in the Mountain Meadows massacre." But Marshal Nelson told the reporter "Lee has no statement to make," claiming Lee's contract with Bishop "to publish a book containing Lee's statement of the origin and development of the movement which resulted in the massacre" precluded the prisoner's communication with the press.[28]

Despite such claims, a writer for the *Salt Lake Tribune* believed that with Lee "left alone, and in the hands of cussed Gentiles, as the dread Everlasting opens its portals before him, it is more than likely that he will make a clean breast of it."[29]

Soon after his arrival, Lee was taken before Judge Boreman, who had also traveled south from Salt Lake City. The prisoner appeared "utterly broken down."[30] Over the previous few weeks, his favorable treatment in the Salt Lake penitentiary had ended, and he had been locked up with other prisoners. "The foul air & filthy stench" of the chamber pots and the cold, rock floor "was near taking my Life," Lee had complained. "My Lungs was fearful."[31] When Judge Boreman asked if he had anything to say about his sentence, Lee said no. Boreman set his new execution date for March 23, 1877.[32]

Lee spent his last days focused on writing his life history. "He eats and drinks little, is cool and firm, and seems to have given up all hope of a reprieve, and says he will die bravely, making no new revelations."[33]

A few months earlier, Lee's second-oldest son Joseph had written him, "If you have don rong ignorantly then there is not so much sin attributed to you but if you did rong with your eyes open then is the greater sin upon you." If Lee was guilty, Joseph told his father, his execution would be an atonement for his sin. "If god suffer the wicked to slay you the debt is payed and you are honerable in the site of god & richeous men."[34]

Other Lee descendants were not as willing to accept Lee's sentence. A granddaughter circulated a petition to commute his death sentence to life imprisonment.[35] In Beaver, one son passed around a petition for his pardon.[36]

Some took a dim view of these efforts. "Our dispatches say that attempts were made by Lee's friends and some Gentiles to have his sentence commuted," a Nevada newspaper reported. These "lily-hearted, cowardly and imbecile Gentiles" should have their names "covered with execrations as thick as a Mormon's hide is plastered with fanaticism."[37]

Utah governor George W. Emery received at least three petitions to pardon Lee—from Beaver, Panguitch, and Greenville, Utah—though the *Salt Lake Daily Herald* doubted a petition "would have any influence on his excellency."[38] The first signature on the Beaver document was from Lee's former defense attorney Wells Spicer, who may have authored it. Portions closely resembled arguments defense attorneys used during the second trial, including that Lee "is but one of many who are equally guilty" and was convicted by the testimony of co-conspirators, thus being "made a sacrifice to atone for the whole crime."

Unlike arguments used at Lee's trials, the petitions also asserted—as Lee tried to do in 1858—that the massacre was covered by President James Buchanan's pardon and Governor Alfred Cumming's clemency after the Utah War. The petitions falsely claimed the massacre had "been condoned & pardoned" following "an investigation by the authorities of the U.S. and by his Excellency governor A. Cumming."[39]

Governor Emery thoughtfully considered the petitions. "If I consulted only my feelings in the premises I should yield to your entreaties," he responded. "But when I reflect upon the horrible crime Mr. Lee committed and the unmistakable evidence of his guilt, there is nothing left to me but to allow the law to take its course."[40]

Emery also called it "a lame excuse" to claim "it was necessary to sacrifice those emigrants for the reason that an army was about to invade this Territory." He emphasized that they "were a peaceable company of travelers... seeking homes still further west" and should have been protected instead of "foully murdered."

Neither was the governor swayed by the argument that Lee was just one of many participants. "Mr. Lee is to be punished for the part he personally bore in the terrible affair," he explained, "and all participants with him are to be punished as soon and as fast as the officers of the law can apprehend and bring them to trial."[41]

Most Utahns agreed with Governor Emery. Though more than five hundred people signed the petitions to have Lee pardoned, the vast majority of Utah citizens did not. Instead, noted the Mormon-owned *Salt Lake Daily Herald*, there seemed an "almost universal feeling that he should be made to atone for his crime."[42]

On March 22, 1877, the day before Lee was to be shot, Emery received a telegram "from the United States Marshal at Beaver, inquiring if he had anything further to communicate relating to Lee."

"Nothing whatever," the governor replied.[43]

45

Under Sentence of Death

Beaver to Mountain Meadows, March 20-23, 1877

On Tuesday, March 20, 1877, Army Second Lieutenant George T. T. Patterson received his orders. He and a detachment from his company at Fort Cameron were to proceed secretly to the "appointed place," there to thwart any interference "with the proper execution . . . of John D. Lee, a convict under sentence of death." They slipped out of the fort that evening after twilight.[1]

Nearly twenty-four hours after the departure of Patterson's detachment, Marshal William Nelson drove to Fort Cameron to tell Lee to prepare for a "journey." Knowing what that meant, Lee showed little emotion, surprised only by the timing. The court had set his execution date for Friday, and it was just Wednesday evening. Lee laid down his pen, leaving his autobiography completed only through 1847. Wanting "to die clean," he asked for a bath and fresh clothing.[2]

The nation that had followed Lee's trials now awaited news of his death. Reporters from coast to coast returned to southern Utah, this time to cover his execution. Tipped by Marshal Nelson that Lee was about to be moved earlier than planned, the journalists scurried to join the entourage that soon strung out on the road.[3]

About a dozen troops led the way, followed by Nelson driving his covered carriage. Inside, Lee sat uncharacteristically quiet, facing a deputy holding a "double barrelled gun." On the flanks and to the rear rode more than two dozen other cavalrymen. Wagons of reporters followed behind the main cluster, hurrying to catch up.[4]

"The low rumbling of the carriages and wagons on the highway; the constant tramping of the horses' feet against the hard ground, and the crack of the whips and encouraging 'get up' of the impatient drivers resounding in the still night, made strange and weird impressions upon the mind and foreboded the terrible mission that the Marshal and trusted retinue were going upon," wrote one reporter. "Every noise was as a funeral dirge and every sound as a death knell for the old man, hoary-headed and gory-handed."[5]

With only a new moon to light "the darkest hours of the night," wrote another, "the strange forms of the mountains took on stranger shapes in the darkness." Would there be a rescue attempt? Some last-minute rumors swirled around Rachel Lee. One even claimed she would kill her husband herself to deny federal authorities the satisfaction.[6]

The suspense made good newspaper copy for a public riveted on Lee and the massacre.

Though only the lawmen knew where Nelson's party was headed, Lee's suspicions were aroused the moment they took the road west at Cedar City. He had thought the place of his execution was to be Fremont Pass, northeast of Parowan, where famous explorer John C. Fremont and his party almost starved during the winter of 1854. But justice officials chose a more notorious site.[7]

During the ride along Leach's Cutoff, Lee ventured a confession. Methodist minister George Stokes, father of the deputy who arrested him, accompanied Lee on the journey. "Before reaching this point," wrote a reporter, Lee admitted to the reverend that he had personally murdered people at the massacre, killing "five emigrants and possibly six."[8]

Lee's escort stopped at Leach's Spring—near the spot where William Stewart had shot emigrant William Aden—to rendezvous with Patterson's slower-moving detachment. There, many reporters saw Lee up close for the first time. Emerging from the covered wagon and now certain of where they were headed, Lee exclaimed, "What, going to take me to the old ground—to the old ground" where the massacre took place? Some reporters thought "he showed considerable disappointment."[9]

Perhaps spurred by that tinge of emotion, Lee astonished listeners with his chatter. He talked about "the condition of the horses and teams" and told yarns unusual for a man about to die. Next, "with a relish and appetite quite amazing," Lee ate a meal of crackers, bologna sausage, bacon, and whiskey, served on the pine boards that would form his coffin. He then rolled up in blankets and slept soundly, just as he had done within hours after the massacre.[10]

"A more composed and imperturbable human being in such a trying ordeal we never wish to see," wrote one newspaperman.[11]

Sometime after 3:00 p.m., the party started on its final leg to the Mountain Meadows. For their next campsite, Lee guided his captors to a spring halfway down the Meadows, near where the Mormon militiamen camped before the massacre. Though he said he had not stopped at the site since the crime two decades earlier, his memory of the place remained sharp.[12]

Officials never explained their surprising decision—kept secret until the final hours—to end Lee's life at the Meadows. Rarely in U.S. jurisprudence had a convict been taken to the scene of the crime for execution.[13] The effort required major expense and inconvenience—Mountain Meadows was nearly a hundred bone-rattling miles from Beaver. Perhaps part of the reason was moral example. Crime and punishment would go together, a perfect stage for any tragedian.

Hope also lingered that Lee might finally implicate Brigham Young. For many Americans, it had become almost an article of faith that Young had a hand in everything that occurred in Utah.[14] Though now deeply embittered towards the church president, Lee still denied that he ordered the massacre. The chance he might say more was almost certainly a reason for taking the condemned man to the scene of the crime.[15]

The location did nearly break Lee, though not with the result his captors sought. He begged Marshall Nelson to end the awful suspense and "shoot him then and there." When Nelson refused, something Lee said to a deputy made the camp fear he planned to flee and force sentinels to shoot him. Lieutenant Patterson ordered that the prisoner be taken alive if he tried.[16]

Lee spent the last night of his life there in the Meadows, placed in a wagon alone with Reverend Stokes in what was likely another attempt to get him to tie Young to the massacre. Instead, Lee merely argued with the minister about religion, defending his Mormon faith with a torrent of scripture.[17] When the discussion ended, he slept heavily.[18]

Waking on Friday morning, March 23, Lee "broke silence . . . and conversed with the utmost freedom with the Marshal and reporters."[19] Word spread that Lee confessed to Stokes of killing emigrants "with his own hand," though not specifying "what their sex or age were." A reporter asked Lee if it were true he ravished two emigrant girls before he "cut their throats." The question soured Lee, who now "denied having killed anybody" or even having been "instrumental in accomplishing the destruction of any person."[20]

After breakfast, Lee "pointed out various places of interest in connection with the massacre," at the same time "being careful not to state anything antagonistic to his recently assumed innocence."[21] The party then divided up and traveled another mile south to the lower end of the Meadows. Fulfilling his orders, Patterson sent one group to scout the eastern foothills and protect the flank from the rumored rescue attempts. The main party, with Lee in tow, continued south on the old trail. The two groups met just north of the springs where the massacre victims had warded off their attackers by circling and chaining together their wagons. When carpenters began nailing together the pine boards of his coffin, Lee kept talking, as if to ward off his death knell.[22]

The quick march of Patterson and Nelson surprised most would-be spectators hoping to witness the execution. Once alerted, they streamed out of Beaver and other points farther south, trying to make up for lost time.[23]

Brigham Young—feeble in the last months of his life—was attending a church conference in St. George, and he too wanted to know how the final scene would play out. He asked some men to ride through the night to witness the execution and give him a report.[24] Josiah Rogerson, a stenographer and telegrapher who reported Lee's first trial, followed the entourage from Beaver so he could capture Lee's last words.[25]

By midmorning as many as three hundred onlookers were at the Meadows, many of them Latter-day Saints from nearby settlements. With Patterson's men keeping spectators at a distance, some climbed the surrounding hills for a view.[26]

The official party, closer in and new to the area, seemed surprised by what they saw. Instead of the legendary lush grasses of the Meadows, they saw deep gullies, scrub oak, and sage. Near the old springs—or what remained of them—was "a sunken pool of slimy, filthy water." The rivulet that once ran through the southern end of the valley had been replaced by an ugly wash 20 feet deep and about 150 feet wide. Some thought the change a natural result of erosion. Others thought "the cu[r]se of God" had "fallen upon it."[27]

Lee's life was now measured by minutes. He fully appreciated his situation, he said, having "full faith in the pure principles of Mormonism," though lacking belief in some of its current practices. That comment was probably aimed at Young and his policies. Lee repeated a famous phrase uttered by Joseph Smith before his death: that he would die "as calm as a summer's morning."[28]

The cairn marking the burial place of many massacre victims was again "a crumbling mass of rocks and dirt." Lee asked Marshal Nelson not to take him near it. Nelson, Prosecutor Howard, and Reverend Stokes pulled him aside elsewhere in a final attempt to procure accusations. Lee signed a document implicating "two or three others" in the massacre—but not the man they wanted most. The prisoner seemed to grow weak as he walked back to the main party, leaning heavily on the reverend's arm and faltering just before reaching his coffin, set twenty-five feet west of three government wagons. Lee sat down to rest on the pine box. In front of him, screened by blankets hung from the wagons, five executioners awaited the order to fire.[29] Officials took care to conceal the members of the firing squad, fearing retribution from Lee's family.[30]

"I wish to speak to that gentleman," Lee replied when asked if he had any last words. He pointed to James Fennemore, the young photographer of the John Wesley Powell expedition whom John D. and Emma had nursed back to health at the Lonely Dell a few years before. Fennemore was setting up his camera nearby to document Lee's execution.[31]

"I wish to ask a favor of you," Lee said. "I want you to furnish my three wives a copy."

Over his lifetime, Lee had married nineteen women, who bore him more than sixty children. Though three of his wives had died faithful to him, most had left him years ago. Only three stood by him to the end: Rachel, Emma, and Sarah Caroline.

Fennemore promised to give the three their husband's final portrait. Satisfied, the condemned man arose to give his last speech.[32] Lee spoke deliberately at times, with few gestures, "then rushed off into a humid style."[33]

Twice he said he had done nothing "designedly" wrong, repeating the phrase that had been his salve for nearly twenty years. "My Conscience is clear before God and man. I am ready to meet my Redeemer." When he spoke of his family, his eyes moistened.[34]

Toward the end of his five-minute speech, his voice became stronger. "I do not believe everything that is now taught and practised by Brigham Young, I do not care who hears it, it is so. I believe he is leading the people astray, downward to distruction, but I believe in the gospel that was taught in its purity and introduced by Joseph Smith in former days."[35]

In the final moments of his life, unable to undo the atrocity that played out on the same site two decades before—or to face fully what he and his co-conspirators had done—Lee clung to what, in his mind, was a last vestige of integrity. Even as he faced the firing squad, he resisted the pressure to charge Young with the massacre.

His speech ended, Lee knelt beside the coffin with Reverend Stokes while the minister offered a prayer.[36] The marshal then stepped forward to blindfold Lee with a white handkerchief near the spot where Lee had used a white swag to convince the besieged emigrants to let him into their wagon fort.

"Let them shoot the balls through my heart," Lee urged the officer. "Don't let them mangle my body," he begged, at the site where beasts tore the victims' bodies after the massacre.[37]

His hands left free, Lee clasped them above his head and braced for the impact. Those standing near the condemned man stepped aside, and Marshal Nelson moved a short distance southwest. At exactly eleven o'clock, he gave the command.

"Ready—aim—fire."

Guns flashed, sending hot lead into Lee. Some of the bullets passed clear through, cutting ridges into the ground behind him. Lee fell back against his coffin, into his final oblivious sleep.[38]

"It was altogether the most remarkable spectacle ever witnessed," wrote a reporter, "to see this old man suffer the death penalty on the very spot were twenty years ago he made for history the Mountain Meadows Massacre."[39]

Figure 45.1 John D. Lee's execution. Lee is seated on his coffin left, surrounded by reporters and government officials. To the right are the wagons from which the executioners fired. Courtesy Church History Library.

46

Failure to Arrest These Men

United States, Late Nineteenth and Early Twentieth Centuries

The month before his execution, John D. Lee had tried to win his freedom by giving prosecutor Sumner Howard a new "statement of the Mountain Meadows massacre." As prosecutors had done with Lee's earlier statement, Howard rejected this confession as grounds for staying the execution because every man Lee implicated had died or was in hiding, or prosecutors had better evidence against him. Still, Howard received Lee's permission to publish the document after his execution. He arranged with the *San Francisco Daily Bulletin* to print the confession the day after Lee's death.[1]

William Bishop was angry at Lee for giving his confession to Howard. He knew Howard's publication of Lee's confession could undermine the changes he was making to his own copies of Lee's confession and in his book on Lee's life. To outdo Howard, Bishop published his version two days before Howard's—and the day before Lee's execution—in two major newspapers on both coasts, the *San Francisco Chronicle* and the *New York Herald*.[2]

The biggest difference between Howard's and Bishop's published versions was in describing the roles played by Brigham Young and George A. Smith. By vilifying church leaders, Bishop could take revenge for the loss he suffered at Lee's second trial after they assisted the prosecution in securing witnesses, while also making his version more appealing for book sales.

In the Bishop version, Lee supposedly said, "My journals and private writings have been destroyed by order of Brigham Young. I have nothing left but my memory."[3] Bishop knew that was not true because he himself was in possession of Lee's journals and other writings.[4]

In the Howard version, Lee wrote that someone—presumably Isaac Haight—sent a messenger to Young before the massacre "asking his advice about interfering with the company," but the messenger "did not return in time." Though Lee knew Haight was a militia major like himself in 1857, the Bishop version has Lee saying, "I still think Lieutenant Colonel Haight had his orders from the heads of the Church." Both versions have Lee conversing with George A. Smith before the massacre about how to handle passing emigrants. In the Howard version, Lee warned Smith of the need for orders to protect emigrants from molestation. In the Bishop version, Smith "taught the people that it was their duty to kill all emigrants."[5]

Shortly after publication of the two versions, former Utah prison guard Edwin Gilman filed an affidavit saying he had heard Lee read his confession aloud and that it "charged Brigham Young with direct complicity" in the massacre. Gilman claimed Howard had suppressed that portion because he was paid by "Young's confidential clerk."[6]

Gilman's allegations infuriated Howard and ignited a firestorm. U.S. Attorney General Charles Devens called Howard to account. Howard swore he had not "erased, altered or 'suppressed'" a word of the confession, which was in Lee's "own handwriting from date to signature." A *New York Herald* correspondent examined the document and confirmed Howard's assertion. Even Bishop came to Howard's defense, calling Gilman's charge "as foolish as it is false."[7]

The *Herald* correspondent concluded that Gilman's "assault on Mr. Howard" was "cowardly" and "unwarrantable." The correspondent interviewed Gilman and asked "whether he believed that Mr. Howard ever saw or knew of the passages" alleging that Young ordered the massacre. "Well," Gilman admitted, "I can't say that I honestly believe he did."[8]

If Lee really had said Young ordered the massacre, he could have bought his freedom with this information, or at least a stay of execution pending a trial of the church leader. Despite offers from law enforcement officials, Lee had consistently refused to accuse Young, believing that in doing so he would damn himself in the afterlife. Lee went to his death instead.

William Bishop had no such concerns. He wanted payback for the embarrassment he felt in losing Lee's second trial and profit from the time he had invested in his client. He expanded Lee's statement even further when he published it as *Mormonism Unveiled; or the Life and Confessions of the Late Mormon Bishop, John D. Lee; (Written by Himself)*, a sensational book that shaped historical interpretation of the Mountain Meadows Massacre for generations.[9]

Still eager to convict more massacre perpetrators, Howard reminded Attorney General Devens that massacre victims' relatives also had an interest in the capture of the indicted fugitives. They wanted "someone, well recommended, to be appointed by the President of the United States, to arrest the Mountain Meadows Murder[er]s." Some officials in Utah had already recommended Deputy U.S. Marshal William Stokes, the man who arrested Lee.[10]

The family of massacre victim William Aden hoped Jerome Cross—the deputy who brought in Klingensmith—could help capture perpetrators. Cross wrote them that Isaac Haight was in southern Utah but "not expected to live long" due to "heart-disease!" John M. Higbee was teaching school in southern Arizona, and William Stewart was "in hiding at the Bull Mountains near the Rio Virgin River."[11]

But Howard opposed the idea of anyone "known to be connected with the Marshal's force" trying to make the arrests. They could never succeed because local telegraph lines were "owned and operated exclusively by parties interested in the escape of these men," Howard explained. "W$^{m.}$ Stokes could not take a days journey towards the place of their concealment but what his movements would be heralded in advance." The only way to achieve success, Howard insisted, was by authorizing a reward "privately to parties not known to be acting with the officers."[12]

Observing Howard's continued efforts to prosecute other massacre perpetrators, the Salt Lake Tribune recanted its previous criticisms of him: "THE TRIBUNE unreservedly condemned District Attorney Howard's strategy in the trial of Lee, believing he was giving everything away for a barren victory. But we take it all back."[13]

Meanwhile, massacre participants continued to make themselves scarce. "I fear they will be getting out Indictments against all who had anything to do with the Mountain meadow matter," Nephi Johnson's father warned his son, advising him to flee "to new or old Mexico" with his family, "where there is none but faithful saints that understand all about your trouble and dificulty." If Nephi would shave his face clean "and take some other name," his father advised, "I think you will be out of their reach."[14]

By 1877, the ailing, seventy-five-year-old Brigham Young had grown calloused to public criticism. On August 29, he died in Salt Lake City. An estimated twenty-five thousand people filed past his body as it lay in state in the Salt Lake Tabernacle.[15] The Salt Lake Tribune ran a lengthy obituary, which, though far from respectful, employed a muter tone than usual about the man who had been the paper's favorite target.[16]

One month later, Howard decided to resign his post as Utah district attorney. He had found no evidence that Young ordered the massacre. The

Figure 46.1 Brigham Young late in life. Courtesy Church History Library.

church leader was now gone, and Howard had grown weary of political battles and federal government apathy toward pursuing the fugitives. He returned home to Michigan, the last federal officer to seriously prosecute the atrocity.[17]

Two years after Young's death, a frustrated Judge Boreman was still writing to Washington for help in capturing the fugitives. Like Howard, he recommended offering a five-hundred-dollar reward, appointing special agents familiar with the country, and covering their expenses while they tracked the fugitives. He admitted the search might require months and still end in failure, but that was a necessary risk. "The failure to arrest these men," Boreman warned, "is discouraging to officers and encouraging to criminals."[18]

Attorney General Devens responded that he favored the reward but still balked at covering expenses.[19]

Because Young's and George A. Smith's deaths had diminished the political value of the case, Liberal Party members' desire to pursue and prosecute the fugitives also waned. Instead, Robert Baskin and other party members finally achieved their goal of disfranchising Mormons, not by focusing on the massacre but through anti-polygamy legislation. The 1887 Edmunds-Tucker Act replaced local judges sympathetic to polygamy with federally appointed ones, disfranchised Utah women of the suffrage rights they had exercised since 1870, and prohibited all men who would not sign an anti-polygamy oath from voting and serving as jurors or public officials. The legislation led to the Liberal Party's clean sweep of Salt Lake City's February 1890 elections.

Liberal candidates took all council races and, for the first time, the capital city had a non-Mormon mayor.[20]

Wilford Woodruff, who became the Latter-day Saint president in 1889, issued a manifesto in October of that year, eventually ending the practice of plural marriage among the church's faithful.[21]

Robert Baskin was elected Salt Lake City's mayor two years later. By instituting municipal improvements, including cleaner water, he won the respect of Latter-day Saints. The man who had been their chief nemesis became a renowned leader of their church's headquarters city and later chief justice of the Utah Supreme Court.[22] He joined church leaders in publicly celebrating the centennial of Brigham Young's birth in 1901. The assembled throng greeted him "with uproarous applause."

"It gives me pleasure to be present on this memorable occasion," Baskin said. "The fact that I have been asked to make a speech is the best evidence that conditions have changed, and I think for the better. If we go back twenty-five years ago we find wormwood in the mouths of both sides," he admitted. "But that wormwood has been taken out and now we meet each other as brothers."

"Although I differed with Brigham Young," Baskin recalled with considerable understatement, "I think he possessed qualities that no other man ever had. It was his power over men and his great common sense. He was not great in classical learning," but "brought his people together from all nations. . . . If 'Mormonism' has the elements of perpetuity," proclaimed the man who previously fought the faith, "it will survive all opposition and commend itself more than it does today. If it stands the test it will come out brighter because of the opposition."[23]

When Baskin died in 1918, the *Deseret News* observed, "The News and the Judge having learned something from experience—this paper found itself able conscientiously to support him for high public office and to commend his official acts and policies."[24]

As theocracy and polygamy waned, Utah's political fortunes changed. In 1896, it became the forty-fifth state in the Union, and the majority population of Latter-day Saints—including women—were finally free to choose their own candidates for all political offices instead of Washington's appointees. As a federal requirement for statehood, the pro-Mormon People's Party and the anti-Mormon Liberal Party that dominated territorial politics were dissolved in favor of national Democratic and Republican parties, and Utahns were woven into the political fabric of America.[25]

Over the years, it became increasingly easy for massacre perpetrators and their families to shift all blame to Lee—the only man convicted of the crime—even though Isaac Haight recruited Lee, William Dame authorized the final killings, and dozens of other men participated in the mass murder.[26]

Lee was not the only scapegoat. From the beginning, the men who orchestrated the massacre planned to saddle Paiutes with the crime. Although the vast majority of the region's Paiutes played no role, they and their posterity suffered under the burden of being blamed for the atrocity.[27]

Though the beautiful Mountain Meadows had been an ancestral camping ground for Paiute bands, anthropologist Isabel Kelly could find no Paiutes who claimed connection to that land in the 1930s.[28] Instead, it was a haunted place. "My grandmother told us if you have to go through there, you better hurry and get through before it gets dark," recounted tribal member Eleanor Tom. "She said you could hear crying and screaming at night. Gramma would say, 'Those people are still alive there, crying. Ghosts might jump into you.'"[29]

As for the Indian missionary Jacob Hamblin, Lee never forgave him for testifying against him. The animosity was mutual. Before their deaths, "each warned his children against those of the other, each issuing a solemn edict that none of his descendants should ever marry any from the opposite family," wrote Lee biographer Juanita Brooks. "The net result, as might be expected, was a great many intermarriages, with mixed loyalties" for generations.[30]

To Lee, Hamblin was a traitor and a gadfly. Another gadfly, Lee's long-time critic George A. Hicks, wrote Brigham Young a few months before the church president died, saying his local bishop had unjustly excommunicated him.[31] In 1901, Hicks appealed to the Parowan Stake High Council to reverse his 1874 excommunication, which he said was due to his publicly criticizing Young in the *Salt Lake Tribune* after he saw Lee riding alongside his carriage that year. "I hope that public sentiment has sufficiently changed—that I do not ask in vain."[32] But sentiment had not yet changed enough. Hicks was not rebaptized into the church until 1923.[33]

Meanwhile, in other parts of the United States—mainly the Ozark states—the survivors of the massacre lived out their lives. The children who might have enjoyed prosperity with their parents and older siblings in California instead endured the horrors of the Civil War, which was brutally hard on the areas to which they returned. Some of the children lived long lives despite traumatic memories of the massacre. Others had little to no memory of what

Kit Carson Fancher

Sarah Baker Mitchell ·

Elizabeth Baker Terry

Nancy Saphrona Huff Cates

Some survivors of the massacre are shown in Figures 46.2–46.5.

Figure 46.2 Kit Carson Fancher. Public Domain; **Figure 46.3:** Sarah Baker Mitchell. Public Domain; **Figure 46.4:** Elizabeth Baker Terry. Public Domain; **Figure 46.5:** Nancy Saphrona Huff Cates. Public Domain.

happened.[34] Not surprisingly, the children and their families harbored resentment toward Mormons generally and the killers particularly.

Many Latter-day Saints felt collective guilt for the atrocity, even if they didn't participate in it. Though some perpetrators and those close to them tried to justify their wrongdoing, the vast majority of Saints deplored the massacre.[35] "From the 'First Presidency' down to the humblest farmer," a non-Mormon journalist wrote in 1875, "I have diligently sought out reasons" for the massacre from the Latter-day Saints. "I must bear witness that the Mormons repudiate the crime. From no one have I obtained a single word of approval, or aught that could be construed into a sanction of the massacre." But the crime became a lasting stain on the church's history, its infamy dogging church members and at times plaguing its missionary work.[36]

Massacre participant Daniel S. Macfarlane went to Europe as a missionary in 1877. Calling Macfarlane out as "one of the redhanded villains who was at the Mountain Meadows," the *Salt Lake Tribune* suggested that "pamphlets of the LEE TRIAL" be scattered "among the people where he will preach." If "some non-Mormon will take the trouble to ascertain this tramp's field of labor," the editors promised to supply them with literature "to make matters uncomfortable for McFarlane."[37]

John Morgan, a Latter-day Saint missionary in the South who had nothing to do with the massacre, received a Ku Klux Klan threat. "We are well acquainted with the doings of your people in Utah; also with their history," the note read. "The fate of your Bishop Lee should be another warning to you. Be it as it may, we will not suffer you any longer to impose upon Some of the ignorant men of this mountain." Then came the ultimatum: "This is our last warning[;] quit or take the consequence." Morgan ignored the threat and safely completed his mission.[38]

Others were not so fortunate. In 1884, masked vigilantes at Cane Creek, Tennessee, attacked Mormon missionaries, killing two, along with two local Mormons, in what became known as the "Cane Creek Massacre." One of the missionaries murdered in the attack had earlier listed Mountain Meadows as a topic he had to confront whenever addressing crowds in the region.[39]

Visiting the Mountain Meadows forty years after the massacre, Latter-day Saint leader J. Golden Kimball—who served in Tennessee when his fellow missionaries were murdered there—reflected on the impact of "the terrible crime" not only on the victims and their families, but also his people. "It was with peculiar, and solemn feelings when I comprehended the enormity of the crime and the injury done the Church of Christ. The persecution Elders had passed through, and that I had during five years missionary experience in the Southern States," he wrote, "was quite an experience."[40]

A Mormon missionary who visited Carroll County, Arkansas, in 1900 recorded a conversation he had with a local man. "Members of the emigrant train killed in Utah," the Arkansan told the missionary, "had gone from this neighborhood," and "their relatives still lived here." He warned that because of the "deadly hatred against" Mormons there, "should we attempt to hold meetings we would last no longer than 'a powder keg in torment.'"[41]

47

Haunted

Western United States and Northern Mexico, Late Nineteenth and Early Twentieth Centuries

Dozens of militiamen who played a role in the massacre lived out their lives by successfully hiding their connection to it. But avoiding prosecution did not mean they escaped all consequences for what they had done.

Some, like George Spencer, agonized under their guilt.[1] "Oh! what a life I have led," Spencer wrote in torment to apostle Erastus Snow ten years after the massacre.[2] Journalists wrote that "young Spencer wasted to a skeleton" and "became quite a monomaniac on the subject."[3] Suffering mental anguish, Spencer passed away in 1872 at the age of forty-two, dying in "grief and remorse for his share in the act."[4] Joseph Clewes, who played only a minor role as Isaac Haight's courier during the week of the siege, left Utah and Mormonism but suffered the rest of his life under "a horrible remembrance of those five days."[5]

Of the nine indicted for the massacre, five were arrested—John D. Lee, William Dame, Philip Klingensmith, Ellott Willden, and George Adair.[6]

After buying his freedom by testifying against Lee, Klingensmith pursued the lonely life of a prospector.[7] A family tradition said he became ill and went to an Indian camp in Arizona, where he died and was buried by his hosts.[8] A newspaper report, published in Nevada in 1881, said "his body was found in a prospect hole" in Sonora, Mexico. Some thought Mormons had murdered him, although a Pioche, Nevada, journalist expressed doubt. "If he was really killed by the Mormons," he wrote, they "waited an unconscionable" time to do so, missing "many a good and more convenient opportunity."[9]

Dame escaped further prosecution by keeping quiet. In 1884, he received a visit from court reporter Josiah Rogerson—who was preparing a transcript of Lee's trials. Rogerson knew that evidence implicated Dame as the highest-ranking militia leader of the massacre. Dame, who had suffered a stroke, "winced and weakened" under these charges, Rogerson noticed. The visitors urged Dame to give a statement under oath—to be kept confidential until his death—explaining his side of "all that took place," including "what was said between Haight and he on that pile of posts near his barn" two nights before the final massacre in the "tan bark council."

"He sat confused and somewhat thoughtful for a few moments," Rogerson wrote, and "sad to relate, he replied to all of our pleadings, like the reserved Dame that we had always known him to be."

"My days are numbered," Dame answered, "and I do not care to say anything more about this matter, than I have said on one or two occasions[:] that Bro. Haight mis-understood me, and that John. D. Lee, was advised and requested to do all that he could to keep the Indians off till the answer came back from Governor Young. I am willing to be tried when I get across the River, and am willing that Our Father be the Judge."

"We could not get another word of admission from him," Rogerson wrote. "A month or so after our interview," a second stroke "took him across The River."[10]

The cases against the two other men indicted and arrested for the massacre—George Adair and Ellott Willden—were dropped for lack of evidence. Though both men talked to others about the atrocity, they portrayed themselves as minor players and did not mention their killing anyone.[11]

Of the remaining men indicted but not arrested, Samuel Jewkes may have been charged only because he was rumored to have had two surviving children living with his family, one of whom supposedly "disappeared" after she pointed out her father's killer. Contemporary evidence, however, showed the Jewkes family only had one survivor, Prudence Angeline Dunlap. Jewkes avoided arrest, and authorities lost interest in him.[12]

The other three men at large—Isaac Haight, John Higbee, and William Stewart—continued to run from the law.[13] For a time, they lived under aliases at the isolated Mount Trumbull sawmill in Arizona, the source of lumber for the Latter-day Saint temple in St. George, Utah. "I was impressed with the uneasiness of these men whenever strangers would drive up to the house," recalled one witness. "They would invariably run to hide. I remember one of them had a hut built out in the lava bed to which he would invariably flee if a stranger came in sight."[14]

A few months before Brigham Young died, Stewart wrote him from Cedar City. "I am getting tired of being hunted by Government Officials," he said, describing himself as "an outcast" and seeking Young's help in selling a one-third share in a Cedar grist mill.[15] Within a few weeks of this letter, the San

Francisco *Daily Morning Call* reported, "Stewart still lives, lurking about the vicinity of Cedar City, but hidden from the authorities."[16]

Stewart fled, leaving his family behind.[17] "I Started For A[rizona] T[erritory]," Stewart wrote of his subsequent ordeal. "Got My Leg Mashed & Lay 3 years under it." As he recuperated, "26 peices of bone Came out of it."[18] In October 1881, he was carried back to his Cedar City home. "I have been a confirmed invalid and prisoner in my own home, shut out from the society of all save my family," he wrote Erastus Snow, while still failing to acknowledge his guilt. "It was for no fault of my own I was suffering."[19]

After Snow's death, Stewart wrote church president Wilford Woodruff, detailing his woes.[20] Lamenting that "Prest. E[rastus] Snow my Old Friend & Councler is gone," Stewart told Woodruff that the last time he saw Snow, "he asked me if Eli[a]s Morris Sent Me any Money. I Said No. he Said if he would Send you $1000 it is nothing but what he aught To do." Stewart wrote Morris for help, but "he was not Kind Enough to awnser me," Stewart told Woodruff. "To Save him & others, I am An Exile. he was I[saac] C. H[aight's] Councler & onley for him & a few more [I] would not bee here."

The First Presidency authorized Stewart to receive $150.00 from his local tithing office. He bought a used carriage and started for Mexico. He got only as far as Taylor, Arizona, where he wrote the Presidency. "My hurt Pained Me So bad I had To Stop. It Comenced to Snow & Rain it Stoped all travel over The Mountains. Am Sorey I Could Not Go On."[21]

Who, other than himself, did Stewart feel he was shielding by staying a fugitive as late as 1891? An associate reported that Stewart often said "he did not think the Church ordered" the massacre "or knew of it until after it occurred," though "he considered it [a] natural result of doctrines that had been promulgated."[22] Stewart likely blamed Haight and Higbee, though they too were fugitives. But Haight's former Cedar City counselor Elias Morris had largely managed to escape blame for the crime.

Stewart eventually reached Mexico, where in late 1894 "while cutting wood," he wounded the leg he broke previously. The sore "turned to gangrene and resulted in his death."[23]

Around that time, John Higbee returned to Cedar City and public life after nearly two decades of hiding.[24] He issued a self-serving and inaccurate account of the massacre under the pseudonym of Bull Valley Snort, grossly exaggerating the number and role of Indians in the massacre.[25]

Following Utah statehood in 1896, Higbee was able to have the charges against him dropped on grounds that time and witnesses' deaths rendered a fair trial impossible.[26] Several years later, as he had done with Dame, court reporter Josiah Rogerson asked him for a statement "that the truth might be known after he was gone."

Higbee "repeatedly affirmed" that no blame rested on Brigham Young, George A. Smith, or anyone else "in authority north of Iron County." Instead, "he charged the weight of the mistake on Dame, yet laid a goodly portion of blame on Lee's assumption of authority." Higbee did not mention Haight, probably because their close association at the time of the massacre would implicate himself.[27]

Higbee died from "a lingering illness in December 1904."[28] "The latter part of his life," a former Mormon asserted, "was a hell on earth. He was partially insane most of the time, and his fears of imaginary foes and the shrieks of murdered women and children ringing in his ears made an awful Nemesis which pursued him to his grave."[29]

By mid-1880, Haight had moved to the new Latter-day Saint settlement of Manassa, Colorado.[30] He wrote his wife Eliza Ann that he craved reuniting with her in Utah but saw no chance of returning there "until the [federal] Hounds leave."[31] Haight later moved in with a son and daughter in a Mormon settlement near the San Juan River in New Mexico until he felt safe enough to return to Toquerville, Utah.[32]

Just days after his arrival in Toquerville, Latter-day Saint newspaper editor Charles W. Penrose gave a speech in Salt Lake about the Mountain Meadows Massacre that evoked a response from the *Salt Lake Tribune*. Both accounts featured Haight's name and revived public feeling against him.[33] Now seventy-one years old, Haight had begun participating in ceremonies in the St. George Temple.[34]

According to his granddaughter, some Latter-day Saints recognized him in the temple and threatened him if he did not vacate the sacred edifice. "As there was considerable buzzing" in St. George, he wrote under a pseudonym to a daughter, he decided to flee to Cedar City "for a few days until things quiet down."[35]

Hostility among the people of St. George eventually drove Haight to Thatcher, Arizona, where he joined a nephew, Hyrum Brinkerhoff, on a colonizing mission to Mexico. To obscure his identity, he continued to use aliases.[36] The mission proved difficult and lonely. "I think that most of those in this country have felt sorely tried to part with those that are dear to them as their lives and wander as fugitives in a strange land and people," Haight

wrote, "but when they have tried it as long as I have they will not feel so impatient[;] yet I feel it very sorely."

"I am lookin for a change of officials in Utah that I can have a fair & impartial and speedy trial," he wrote in July 1885. "Then I hope to be on hand to
have my trial, and spend the rest of my days with my Dear Family."[37]

Later that month, George Calvin Williams encountered Haight, going
by his mother's maiden name of Horton, at a church meeting in Mexico.
Williams, a former Baptist preacher and Latter-day Saint convert who claimed
thirteen relatives among the massacre victims, could not believe Haight still
found fellowship in the church. Haight was even serving as clerk to apostle
George Teasdale, who was living in Mexico. Williams approached Teasdale,
saying the country "wasn't big enough" for both him and Haight and warning
"that one of us better get out of Mexico and do it quick." Teasdale relayed the
conversation to Haight, who fled back to his nephew's in Thatcher, Arizona.[38]
There Haight died of pneumonia on September 8, 1886.[39]

The nephew kept Haight's body in a casket he stowed in the cellar of his
home and inn, expecting immediate family members to claim it. But no one
came. After lying in the cellar for many years, Haight's remains were finally
buried in a Thatcher cemetery. In more recent times, a relative erected a
gravestone reading: "IN MEMORY OF ISAAC C. HAIGHT . . . A NOBLE MAN
HAS GONE TO HIS REST. HE PAID THE HIGH PRICE OF LEADERSHIP."[40]

George Calvin Williams stewed about Haight for a decade, writing the
First Presidency about him. "With reference to Isaac C. Haight," Wilford
Woodruff and his two counselors replied, "we can, in some degree, we believe, sympathize with the feelings that filled your heart on meeting him."
But now he had "gone to his God to meet his deserts; and for his sake we
hope that he was not as guilty as common rumor charges," they wrote. "Some
things in relation to that terrible act will never be known until the secrets of
all hearts are revealed."[41]

Forty years after the massacre, Elias Morris, Haight's counselor who was
with him and Dame during the "tan bark council," died after falling down
an elevator shaft in Salt Lake, striking a beam on the way to the basement.
A tribute described his death as "shocking."[42]

Sixty years after the massacre, only a few of its perpetrators remained
alive, among them Nephi Johnson, the Paiute-language interpreter Haight
summoned to the Meadows. Of all who witnessed the massacre, he perhaps
saw more than any other. Perched where he could take in the entire killing
field, he watched the butchery of men, women, and children.[43]

Figure 47.1 Nephi Johnson. Courtesy Church History Library.

Though Johnson's testimony helped secure Lee's conviction, Johnson never got over his burden of guilt. Throughout his life, he told pieces of his story again and again, perhaps trying to salve his conscience.[44] At eighty-five, he approached a nineteen-year-old schoolteacher he knew from church, visiting her classroom at the end of a school day.[45]

"Leaning with both hands on his cane," and peering at her with "his sharp black eyes and long beard," the young woman remembered, "he said impressively, 'I want you to do some writing for me. My eyes have witnessed things that my tongue has never uttered, and before I die, I want them written down. And I want YOU to do the writing.'"

Busy with other concerns, and not knowing Johnson's past, the schoolteacher put him off. The old man seemed disappointed—he had come ready to talk. "OK, then," he said. "We'll do it another time. Maybe if you could come down to the ranch after school has closed."

"Silly, foolish me!" the teacher, Juanita Leavitt (later Brooks), would lament the rest of her life. "Why didn't I just reach for a pencil and pad, settle

Figure 47.2 Juanita Leavitt Brooks. Courtesy Utah State Historical Society.

myself and say, 'Go ahead?'" Years later she would gather all the information she could to uncover her community's dark secret and, in 1950, publish the first scholarly book on the subject, *The Mountain Meadows Massacre*.

But after that school year of 1919, young Juanita Leavitt forgot to visit Johnson until a messenger came looking for her. "Grandpa Johnson is down," the courier said. "He's really quite sick—looks like he might not get up again. But he keeps calling for the little schoolteacher."

Early the next morning, Leavitt rode her horse to Johnson's Mesquite, Nevada, ranch, where his daughter Maggie escorted her into his bedroom.

"The little schoolteacher is here, Father," Maggie said, touching her father's head. "She has come to do your writing for you."

"Good! Good!" he said, opening his eyes.

"Rest awhile," Leavitt said, seeing his condition, "Then we can talk." She promised not to leave.

But the old man never did regain his faculties.

"He seemed troubled," Leavitt observed. "He rambled in delirium—he prayed, he yelled, he preached."

Amidst his hallucinations, Johnson suddenly opened his eyes "wide to the ceiling" and screamed, "Blood! BLOOD! BLOOD!"

"He acts like he is haunted," Leavitt fretted to a man at the ranch.

"Maybe he is," the man replied. "He was at the Mountain Meadows Massacre."[46]

Acknowledgments

The expansive research for this book could never have been accomplished by just two persons. We owe an immense debt of gratitude to the many people and organizations whose contributions have made this book possible. Given how much time has passed since we started this work and how memories fade, we regret that we will inevitably leave out some who deserve recognition. But with apologies to some we might inadvertently omit, we acknowledge those to which we are indebted as this book goes to press.

Because the research for this book grew out of that for *Massacre at Mountain Meadows*, we thank again the many individuals and institutions listed on pages 233 to 241 of that volume. In addition, we thank the numerous colleagues who have provided specific research assistance for this book, helped to source-check our manuscript, and read versions of it to provide comments and suggestions. They include Thomas G. Alexander, Matthew Brown, Jay Burrup, LaJean Purcell Carruth, LeGrand R. Curtis Jr., Diann Fancher, Harley Fancher, Chad Foulger, Alison Kitchen Gainer, Matthew J. Grow, P. Jane Hafen, Janiece L. Johnson, William P. MacKinnon, Andrea Maxfield, Brandon Metcalf, Darren Parry, W. Paul Reeve, Brian Reeves, and Frank Rolapp.

In addition, we thank the Church of Jesus Christ of Latter-day Saints History Department and the Ensign Peak Foundation for providing funding that aided in the book's research and source-checking. For our research on Samuel Clemens's experience in Utah, we thank Elmira College's Mark Twain Archives and the Center for Mark Twain Studies for extending its Quarry Farm writer-in-residence fellowship to Barbara.

To the many friends we have made among descendants of the massacre victims as we worked on this project, some no longer with us, we express special appreciation for opening your hearts and homes to us. Hearing your stories and feelings about your ancestors; seeing with you their artifacts, images, and places they lived; grieving together at the Mountain Meadows; and rejoicing with you in achieving National Historic Landmark status for the site have made telling this story profoundly meaningful and important to us. We hope this book offers a measure of healing to you and your families.

Finally, we extend deep appreciation to our spouses and children, who patiently sacrificed our attention as we worked for a combined total of more than forty years to bring this story to light. We could not have done it without their support.

Abbreviations

AHCJ	Abraham Hoagland Cannon, Journal, BYU.
AJ-DHM	Richard E. Turley Jr. and Ronald W. Walker, eds., *Mountain Meadow Massacre: The Andrew Jenson and David H. Morris Collections* (Provo, UT: Brigham Young University Press; Salt Lake City: University of Utah Press, 2009).
AMLC	Amasa M. Lyman Collection, CHL.
Arrington	Leonard J. Arrington, *Brigham Young: American Moses* (New York: Alfred A. Knopf, 1985).
AV	Authorized (King James) Version of the Bible.
Baskin	R. N. Baskin, *Reminiscences of Early Utah* ([Salt Lake City]: R. N. Baskin, 1914).
BC	Jacob S. Boreman Collection, HL.
Beadle	J. H. Beadle, "Interview with Jno. D. Lee, of Mountain Meadows Notoriety," *Salt Lake Daily Tribune*, July 29, 1872.
Beaman	E. O. Beaman, "The Cañon of the Colorado, and the Moquis Pueblos," *Appletons' Journal* 11 (1874): 481-84, 513-16, 545-48, 590-93, 623-26, 641-44, 686-89.
Bigler	David L. Bigler, *Fort Limhi: The Mormon Adventure in Oregon Territory, 1855–1858* (Spokane, WA: Arthur H. Clark, 2003).
"Bishop"	"Captain Francis Marion Bishop's Journal," ed. Charles Kelly, *UHQ* 15 (1947): 159-238.
BL	Bancroft Library, University of California, Berkeley.
BOM	The Book of Mormon (Salt Lake City, UT: The Church of Jesus Christ of Latter-day Saints, 2013).
Brooks1	Juanita Brooks, *John Doyle Lee: Zealot, Pioneer Builder, Scapegoat* (Logan: Utah State University Press, 1992).
Brooks2	Juanita Brooks, *The Mountain Meadows Massacre*, 2nd ed. (Norman: University of Oklahoma Press, 1991).
Brooks3	Juanita Brooks, *On the Ragged Edge: The Life and Times of Dudley Leavitt* (Utah State Historical Society, 1973).
"BY"	"Brigham Young: Remarkable Interview with the Salt Lake Prophet," *New York Herald*, May 6, 1877. Reprinted in "Interview with Brigham Young," *Deseret Evening News*, May 12, 1877.
BYOJ	Brigham Young, office journal, CR 1234/1-2, CHL.
BYU	L. Tom Perry Special Collections, Harold B. Lee Library, Brigham Young University, Provo, UT.

Cactus   Cactus, letter to the editor, July 13, 1875, in "The Lee Trial," *Pioche*
                (NV) Daily Record, July 17, 1875.
Carleton   James H. Carleton, *Report on the Subject of the Massacre at the*
                Mountain Meadows in Utah Territory, in September, 1857, of One
                Hundred and Twenty Men, Women and Children, Who Were from
                Arkansas (Little Rock, AK: True Democrat Steam Press Print, 1860).
"Cates"   "The Mountain Meadows Mas[s]acre: Statement of Mrs. G. D. Cates,
                One of the Children Spared at the Time," *Dardanelle Arkansas*
                Independent, Aug. 27, 1875. Reprinted in "The Mountain Meadow
                Massacre: Statement of One of the Few Survivors," *DAG*, Sept. 1,
                1875.
CCF   Utah Second District Court, Criminal Case Files, 1874–77, Series
                24291, USARS, copy at CHL. Number following abbreviation is case
                file.
CCSR   Cedar City Stake, Record of children blessed, 1856–63, CHL.
CCWR   Cedar City Ward Relief Society Minute Book, CHL.
CD   Richard S. Van Wagoner, ed., *The Complete Discourses of Brigham*
                Young, 5 vols. (Salt Lake City: Smith-Pettit Foundation, 2009).
CHC   B. H. Roberts, *A Comprehensive History of The Church of Jesus Christ*
                of Latter-day Saints, 6 vols. (Salt Lake City: Deseret News Press,
                1930).
"Children"   " 'Children of the Massacre' May Meet in Reunion," *Arkansas Sunday*
                Post Dispatch, 1895. Also found in JH, 1857, Supplement, 5–8.
CHL   Church History Library, The Church of Jesus Christ of Latter-day
                Saints, Salt Lake City, UT.
Christian   J. Ward Christian, letter, Oct. 18, 1857, in "Late Outrages on the
                Plains—Another Account," *Los Angeles Star*, Oct. 31, 1857.
CM   Collected Material concerning the Mountain Meadows Massacre,
                CHL.
Compton1   Todd M. Compton, *A Frontier Life: Jacob Hamblin, Explorer and*
                Indian Missionary (Salt Lake City: University of Utah Press, 2013).
Compton2   Todd Compton, "Civilizing the Ragged Edge," *JMH* 33, no. 2
                (Summer 2007).
CP   Alfred Cumming Papers, Duke University, Durham, North
                Carolina.
CPWC   Caroline Parry Woolley Collection, Gerald R. Sherratt Library,
                Southern Utah University, Cedar City, UT.
Cradlebaugh   *Utah and the Mormons: Speech of Hon. John Cradlebaugh, of Nevada,*
                on the Admission of Utah as a State (Washington, DC: L. Towers,
                1863).
Crampton   C. Gregory Crampton, "F. S. Dellenbaugh of the Colorado," *UHQ* 37
                (Apr. 1969): 214–43.

CSM	Cedar Stake, minutes, William R. Palmer Collection, Special Collections, Gerald R. Sherratt Library, Southern Utah University, Cedar City, UT.
D&C	Doctrine and Covenants (Salt Lake City: The Church of Jesus Christ of Latter-day Saints, 2013). Citations include section and page numbers, separated by a colon.
DAC	*Daily Alta California* (San Francisco, CA).
DAG	*Daily Arkansas Gazette* (Little Rock, AR).
Darrah	William Culp Darrah, "Beaman, Fennemore, Hillers, Dellenbaugh, Johnson and Hattan," *UHQ* 16–17 (1948–49): 491-503.
DBY	Everett L. Cooley, ed., *Diary of Brigham Young, 1857* (Salt Lake City: Tanner Trust Fund, University of Utah Library, 1980).
Dellenbaugh	Frederick S. Dellenbaugh, *A Canyon Voyage* (New York: G. P. Putnam's Sons, 1908).
DEN	*Deseret Evening News* (Salt Lake City, UT).
DJ	William H. Dame, journal, microfilm, CHL.
DN	*Deseret News* (Salt Lake City, UT).
DNSJ	*Daily Nevada State Journal* (Reno, NV).
DUV	*Daily Union Vedette* (Camp Douglas, UT).
EOM	Daniel H. Ludlow, ed., *Encyclopedia of Mormonism* (New York: Macmillan, 1992).
"Extract"	"Extract from a Letter to the Editor, Dated Carroll Co., Jan. 5, 1858," *Arkansas State Gazette and Democrat* (Little Rock, AR), Feb. 13, 1858.
FALG	Federal and local government files, YOF.
FELC	Frederic E. Lockley Collection, HL.
FHL	Family History Library, The Church of Jesus Christ of Latter-day Saints, Salt Lake City, UT.
Fish	Joseph Fish, *The Life and Times of Joseph Fish, Mormon Pioneer*, ed. John H. Krenkel (Danville, IL: Interstate Printers & Publishers, 1970).
Forney1	J. Forney to Kirk Anderson, May 5, 1859, in *VT*, May 10, 1859.
Forney2	J. Forney to A. B. Greenwood, Sept. 29, 1859, in *Report of the Commissioner of Indian Affairs, Accompanying the Annual Report of the Secretary of the Interior, for the Year 1859* (Washington, DC: George W. Bowman, 1860).
Fowler	Don D. Fowler, ed., *"Photographed All the Best Scenery": Jack Hillers's Diary of the Powell Expeditions, 1871-1875* (Salt Lake City: University of Utah Press, 1972).
FRU	United States Department of Justice, United States files relating to Utah, 1855–1912, CHL.

Furniss   Norman F. Furniss, *The Mormon Conflict, 1850–1859* (New Haven, CT: Yale University Press, 1960).

GASLC   George A. Smith, Letterpress Copybook, GASP, CHL.

GASP   George A. Smith papers, CHL.

GIC   General incoming correspondence, YOF.

Genteel   Ray R. Canning and Beverly Beeton, eds., *The Genteel Gentile: Letters of Elizabeth Cumming* (Salt Lake City: Tanner Trust Fund, University of Utah Library, 1977).

GOF   General office files, President's office files, YOF.

Gordon   Sarah Barringer Gordon, *The Mormon Question: Polygamy and Constitutional Conflict in Nineteenth-Century America* (Chapel Hill: University of North Carolina Press, 2002).

Gove   *The Utah Expedition, 1857–1858: Letters of Capt. Jesse A. Gove, 10th Inf., U. S. A., of Concord, N. H., to Mrs. Gove, and Special Correspondence of the New York Herald*, vol. 12, New Hampshire Historical Society Collections, ed. Otis G. Hammond (Concord: New Hampshire Historical Society, 1928).

Grow   Matthew J. Grow, *"Liberty to the Downtrodden": Thomas L. Kane, Romantic Reformer* (New Haven, CT, & London: Yale University Press, 2009).

H&H   LeRoy R. Hafen and Ann W. Hafen, eds., *The Utah Expedition, 1857–1858: A Documentary Account of the United States Military Movement under Colonel Albert Sidney Johnston and the Resistance by Brigham Young and the Mormon Nauvoo Legion*, vol. 8 of The Far West and the Rockies Historical Series, 1820–1875 (Glendale, CA: Arthur H. Clark, 1958).

Hafen   Arthur Knight Hafen, "A Sketch of the Life of Samuel Knight, 1832–1910: Frontiersman, Indian Missionary, Early Dixie Pioneer and Churchman," typescript, 1960, Daughters of Utah Pioneers, Salt Lake City, UT.

Haslam   James Haslam, interview by S. A. Kenner, reported by Josiah Rogerson, Dec. 4, 1884, typescript, in Josiah Rogerson, Transcripts and Notes of John D. Lee Trials, CHL.

Hawley   John Pierce Hawley, autobiography, 1885, Community of Christ Archives, Independence, MO. Published as John Pierce Hawley, *Autobiography* (Hamilton, MO: Robert Hawley, 1981).

HBM   Harmony Branch, minutes, HL, sometimes misidentified as Rachel Lee's journal.

HDoc29   *Accounts of Brigham Young, Superintendent of Indian Affairs in Utah Territory*, H.R. Ex. Doc. No. 37-29 (1862).

HDoc71   *The Utah Expedition*, H. Ex. Doc. 35-71 (1858).

HDT   *Helena Daily Independent* (Helena, MT).

HI	Thomas Ford, *A History of Illinois* (Chicago: S. C. Griggs, 1854).
HL	Huntington Library, San Marino, CA.
HOCHD	Historian's Office, Collected Historical Documents, ca. 1851–69, CHL.
HOGCM	Historian's Office, General Church Minutes, 1839–77, CHL.
HOHC	Historian's Office, History of the Church, CHL.
HOJ	Historian's Office, Journal, 1844–1997, CHL.
HOLC	Historian's Office, Letterpress Copybooks, CHL.
"Horrible"	"The Late Horrible Massacre," *Los Angeles Star*, Oct. 17, 1857.
Huntington	Dimick Baker Huntington, journal, 1857–59, CHL.
IC	Incoming correspondence, YOF.
ICHC	Isaac C. Haight Correspondence, CHL.
ICHJ	Isaac C. Haight Journal, CHL.
JD	*Journal of Discourses*, 26 vols. (Liverpool: F. D. Richards, etc., 1854–86).
JDL1-BT	*United States v. John D. Lee*, First Trial, Jacob S. Boreman Transcript, BC, available at mountainmeadowmassacre.org. The numbers that follow this abbreviation stand for the book and page number, which are separated from each other by a colon.
JDL1-PS	*United States v. John D. Lee*, First Trial, Adam Patterson Shorthand Notes, BC, available at mountainmeadowmassacre.org. The numbers that follow this abbreviation stand for the book and page number, which are separated from each other by a colon.
JDL1-RS	*United States v. John D. Lee*, First Trial, Josiah Rogerson Shorthand Notes, Josiah Rogerson, Transcripts and Notes of John D. Lee Trials, 1875–85, CHL, available at mountainmeadowmassacre.org. The numbers that follow this abbreviation stand for the book and page number, which are separated from each other by a colon.
JDL1-RT	*United States v. John D. Lee*, First Trial, Josiah Rogerson Transcript, Josiah Rogerson, Transcripts and Notes of John D. Lee Trials, 1875–85, CHL, available at mountainmeadowmassacre.org. The numbers that follow this abbreviation stand for the book and page number, which are separated from each other by a colon.
JDL2-BT	*United States v. John D. Lee*, Second Trial, Jacob S. Boreman Transcript, BC, available at mountainmeadowmassacre.org. The numbers that follow this abbreviation stand for the book and page number, which are separated from each other by a colon.
JDL2-PS	*United States v. John D. Lee*, Second Trial, Adam Patterson Shorthand Notes, BC, available at mountainmeadowmassacre.org. The numbers that follow this abbreviation stand for the book and page number, which are separated from each other by a colon.
JDLC	John D. Lee Collection, HL.

Jenson1   Andrew Jenson, *Encyclopedic History of the Church of Jesus Christ of Latter-day Saints* (Salt Lake City: Deseret News, 1941).

Jenson2   Andrew Jenson, ed., *Latter-Day Saint Biographical Encyclopedia*, 4 vols. (Salt Lake City: Andrew Jenson History, 1901–36).

JFLB   Jacob Forney Letter Book, CHL.

JH   Journal History of The Church of Jesus Christ of Latter-day Saints, CHL.

JH-BY   Jacob Hamblin to Brigham Young, Nov. 13, 1871, GOF.

JHJ   Jacob Hamblin, journal, JHP.

JHM   James Henry Martineau, Autobiography and Journal, original in HL, photocopy in CHL.

JHM1907   James Henry Martineau to F. E. Eldredge, July 23, 1907, "The Mountain Meadow Catastroph[e]," CHL, also located at BYU.

JHP   Jacob Hamblin Papers, CHL.

JHS   Jacob Hamblin, statement, Nov. 28, 1871, in Depositions, 1858–77, GOF.

JMH   *Journal of Mormon History*.

JNSJ   Jesse N. Smith, journal, CHL.

"Jones"   "Journal of Stephen Vandiver Jones, April 21, 1871–December 14, 1872," ed. Herbert E. Gregory, *UHQ* 16–17 (1948–49): 19-174.

Journals   John D. Lee, *Journals of John D. Lee, 1846–47 and 1859*, ed. Charles Kelly (1938; Salt Lake City: University of Utah Press, 1984).

JRS   Josiah Rogerson, "Speech of John D. Lee at Mountain Meadows," Mar. 23, 1877, CM. Rogerson's shorthand of Lee's final words is not extant.

Kearny   [Lt. Kearny], "List of the Children Saved from the Mountain Meadows Massacre," *Los Angeles Southern Vineyard,* June 3, 1859. Also reprinted in "The Mountain Meadows Massacre—List of the Children Saved," *SFDEB,* June 11, 1859, copy in Historian's Office, Newspaper Scrapbook, 12:70, CHL.

Kingdom   Benjamin E. Park, *Kingdom of Nauvoo* (New York: Liveright Publishing, 2020).

KS   "Klingensmith," *SLT,* Aug. 4, 1881.

LAS   *Los Angeles Star* (Los Angeles, CA).

LADS   *Los Angeles Daily Star* (Los Angeles, CA).

"LC"   "Lee's Confession," *Sacramento Daily Record-Union,* Mar. 24, 1877.

LCLO   Letters from Church leaders and others, YOF.

LDU   Letters from District of Utah, SCF.

Little   James A. Little, *Jacob Hamblin, A Narrative of His Personal Experience, as a Frontiersman, Missionary to the Indians and Explorer* (Salt Lake City: Juvenile Instructor Office, 1881).

"LLC"   "Lee's Last Confession," *SFDEB Supplement,* Mar. 24, 1877.

LOC   Library of Congress, Washington, DC.

Lockley L[ockley], letter to the editor, July 12, 1875, in "Lee's Trial," *Salt Lake Daily Tribune*, July 15, 1875.

LPCB Letterpress copybooks, YOF.

LRS Letters received, SCF.

LSDOJ Letters sent by the Department of Justice, Instructions to U.S. Attorneys and Marshals, 1867–1904, RG 60.

Lyman1 Francis M. Lyman, journal, Diary Excerpts of Francis M. Lyman, 1892–96, typescript, in *New Mormon Studies CD-ROM: A Comprehensive Resource Library* (Salt Lake City: Smith Research Associates, [1998]).

Lyman2 Edward Leo Lyman, *Amasa Mason Lyman: Mormon Apostle and Apostate, a Study in Dedication* (Salt Lake City: University of Utah Press, 2009).

MACF Membership and court files, Ecclesiastical files, YOF.

MacKinnon1 William P. MacKinnon, ed., *At Sword's Point, Part 1: A Documentary History of the Utah War to 1858*, vol. 10 of Kingdom in the West: The Mormons and the American Frontier (Norman, OK: Arthur H. Clark, 2008).

MacKinnon2 William P. MacKinnon, ed., *At Sword's Point, Part 2: A Documentary History of the Utah War, 1858–1859*, vol. 11 of Kingdom in the West: The Mormons and the American Frontier (Norman, OK: Arthur H. Clark, 2016).

Marcy R. B. Marcy, *Thirty Years of Army Life on the Border* (New York: Harper & Brothers, 1866).

MatMM Ronald W. Walker, Richard E. Turley Jr., and Glen M. Leonard, *Massacre at Mountain Meadows: An American Tragedy* (New York: Oxford University Press, 2008).

MB1 Minute Book 1, 1874–77, District Court (Second District) Minute Books, Series 5319, USARS, microfilm copy at FHL.

MBB Minute Book B, 1869–81, District Court (Second District) Minute Books, Series 5319, USARS, microfilm copy at FHL, photocopy at CHL.

MC John D. Lee, *A Mormon Chronicle: The Diaries of John D. Lee, 1848–1876*, ed. Robert Glass Cleland and Juanita Brooks, 2 vols. (San Marino, CA: Huntington Library, 2003).

McGlashan C. F. McGlashan, "The Mountain Meadow Massacre," *Sacramento Daily Record*, Jan. 1, 1875.

MCOP Wm. H. Dame to "Majors, Commandants of Posts and Captains of Companies," Sept. 14, 1857, copied in PSHR, first section, 27.

MJRY *Memoirs of John R. Young* (Salt Lake City: Deseret News, 1920).

"Meeting" "Public Meeting of the People of Carroll County," *Arkansas State Gazette and Democrat* (Little Rock, AR), Feb. 27, 1858.

MMM	Mountain Meadows Massacre.
MMM-CLP	Richard E. Turley Jr., Janiece L. Johnson, and LaJean Purcell Carruth, eds., *Mountain Meadows Massacre: Collected Legal Papers*, 2 vols. (Norman: University of Oklahoma Press, 2017).
MMML	Mountain Meadows Massacre Letters, 1874–77, LRS.
MMMRF	Mountain Meadows Massacre Research Files, CHL.
Moorman	Donald R. Moorman and Gene A. Sessions, *Camp Floyd and the Mormons: The Utah War* (Salt Lake City: University of Utah Press, 1992).
MS	*Latter-Day Saints' Millennial Star* (Liverpool, England).
MU	William W. Bishop, ed., *Mormonism Unveiled; or The Life and Confessions of the Late Mormon Bishop, John D. Lee; (Written by Himself)* (St. Louis: Bryan, Brand & Co., 1877).
NAMP32	Letters Received by the Office of the Adjutant General (Main Series) 1871–80, National Archives Microfilm Publications, Roll 32, 1871, NARA.
NARA	National Archives and Records Administration, Washington, DC.
Nauvoo	Glen M. Leonard, *Nauvoo: A Place of Peace, a People of Promise* (Provo, UT: Brigham Young University Press, 2002).
Novak1	Shannon A. Novak, *House of Mourning: A Biocultural History of the Mountain Meadows Massacre* (Salt Lake City: University of Utah Press, 2008).
Novak2	Shannon A. Novak and Derinna Kopp, "To Feed a Tree in Zion: Osteological Analysis of the 1857 Mountain Meadows Massacre," *Historical Archaeology* 37, no. 2 (2003): 85-108.
NYDT	*New York Daily Tribune* (New York, NY).
NYH	*New York Herald* (New York, NY).
NYPL	New York Public Library, New York, NY.
NYT	*New York Times* (New York, NY).
OC	Outgoing Correspondence, YOF.
OCR	*Oregon City Enterprise* (Oregon City, OR).
OJ	*Ogden Junction* (Ogden, UT).
Outrages1	"More Outrages on the Plains," *Los Angeles Star*, Oct. 24, 1857.
Outrages2	"The Late Outrages on the Plains—Another Account," *Los Angeles Star*, Oct. 31, 1857.
Outrages3	"The Late Outrages on the Plains—Further Particulars," *Los Angeles Star*, Nov. 7, 1857.
PDR	*Pioche Daily Record* (Pioche, NV).
Penrose	Charles W. Penrose, *The Mountain Meadows Massacre: Who Were Guilty of the Crime* (Salt Lake City: Juvenile Instructor Office, 1884).

Peterson	Charles S. Peterson, "A Historical Analysis of Territorial Government in Utah, under Alfred Cumming, 1857–1861" (master's thesis, Brigham Young University, 1958).
PGM	Provo Utah Central Stake, general minutes, CHL.
Phelps	John Wolcott Phelps, diary, NYPL.
PDJ	*Pioche Daily Journal* (Pioche, NV).
PKS	Philip Klingon Smith [Klingensmith], affidavit, Apr. 10, 1871, in "A Mormon Monstrosity," *New York Herald*, Sept. 14, 1872, also in "A Massacre by Mormons," *New York Times*, Sept. 14, 1872.
"Powell"	Charles Kelly, ed., "Journal of W. C. Powell, April 21, 1871–December 7, 1872," *UHQ* 16–17 (1948–49): 257–478.
PSHR	Parowan Stake Historical Record, 1855–60, CHL.
Reeve	W. Paul Reeve, *Religion of a Different Color* (New York: Oxford University Press, 2015).
Reilly	P. T. Reilly, *Lee's Ferry: From Mormon Crossing to National Park*, ed. Robert H. Webb (Logan: Utah State University, 1999).
RG 60	Record Group 60, NARA.
Rogers	Wm. H. Rogers, "The Mountain Me[a]dows Massacre," *Valley Tan* (Salt Lake City, UT), Feb. 29, 1860.
Rusho	W. L. Rusho, *Lee's Ferry* (Salt Lake City: Tower Productions, 1998).
SDR	*Sacramento Daily Record* (Sacramento, CA).
SDRU	*Sacramento Daily Record-Union* (Sacramento, CA).
SFDEB	*San Francisco Daily Evening Bulletin* (San Francisco, CA).
SCF	Source-chronological files, General Records of the Department of Justice, RG 60, NARA.
SDoc1	*Message of the President of the United States to the Two Houses of Congress at the Commencement of the Second Session of the Thirty-Fifth Congress*, S. Doc. No. 35-1 (1858).
SDoc32	*Message of the President of the United States, Communicating, in Compliance with a Resolution of the Senate, the Correspondence between the Judges of Utah and the Attorney General or President, with Reference to the Legal Proceedings and Condition of Affairs in that Territory*, S. Doc. No. 36-32 (1860).
SDoc42	*Message of the President of the United States, Communicating, in Compliance with a Resolution of the Senate, Information in Relation to the Massacre at Mountain Meadows, and Other Massacres in Utah Territory*, S. Doc. No. 36-42 (1860).
SDoc67	*Message of the President of the United States, Communicating, a Dispatch from Governor Cumming, Relative to the Termination of the Difficulties with the Territory of Utah*, S. Doc. No. 35-67 (1858).
SDU	*Sacramento Daily Union* (Sacramento, CA).

Shelton   Marion J. Shelton, diary, Marion J. Shelton Papers, CHL. Transcriptions by LaJean Carruth.

Shirts   [Peter Shirts], statement, ca. 1876, Bureau of American Ethnology, manuscript 3141, Smithsonian Institution, National Anthropological Archives, Suitland, MD.

SLC14   Carol Holindrake Nielson, *The Salt Lake City 14th Ward Album Quilt, 1857* (Salt Lake City: University of Utah Press, 2004).

SLT   *Salt Lake Tribune* (Salt Lake City, UT). This abbreviation includes years when the paper operated under other similar names.

SLDH   *Salt Lake Daily Herald* (Salt Lake City, UT).

SLH   *Salt Lake Herald* (Salt Lake City, UT).

Stenhouse   T. B. H. Stenhouse, *The Rocky Mountain Saints: A Full and Complete History of the Mormons, from the First Vision of Joseph Smith to the Last Courtship of Brigham Young* (New York: D. Appleton, 1873).

SLGD   *St. Louis Globe-Democrat* (St. Louis, MO).

Stout   Hosea Stout, *On the Mormon Frontier: The Diary of Hosea Stout, 1844–1861*, ed. Juanita Brooks, 2 vols. (Salt Lake City: University of Utah Press, Utah State Historical Society, 1964).

T&S   *Times and Seasons* (Nauvoo, IL).

TAR   Edward Leo Lyman and Larry Lee Reese, *The Arduous Road* (Victorville, CA: Lyman Historical Research, 2001).

TF   Morris A. Shirts and Kathryn H. Shirts, *A Trial Furnace: Southern Utah's Iron Mission* (Provo, UT: Brigham Young University Press, [2001]).

"Thompson"   Herbert E. Gregory, ed., "Diary of Almon Harris Thompson," *UHQ* 7 (1939): 3-140.

TLKC   Thomas L. Kane Collection, CHL.

TM   LaJean Purcell Carruth and Janiece Johnson, Trial matrix comparison, mountainmeadowmassacre.org.

Turner   John G. Turner, *Brigham Young, Pioneer Prophet* (Cambridge, MA: Belknap Press of Harvard University Press, 2012).

Turner2   *Nicholas Turner v. United States*, U.S. Court of Claims, Indian Depredation Case Files, Box 592 (9696–9720), Case File no. 9702, RG 123, entry 31, NARA.

UDF   Utah delegate files, YOF.

UHQ   *Utah Historical Quarterly.*

UofU   Special Collections, J. Willard Marriott Library, University of Utah, Salt Lake City, UT.

USARS   Utah State Archives and Records Service, Salt Lake City, UT.

USBIA   U.S. Bureau of Indian Affairs, Letters Received by the Office of Indian Affairs, Utah Superintendency Papers, Microfilm Publications 234, NARA. Microfilm copy located at CHL.

USHS	Utah State Historical Society, Salt Lake City, UT.
"Visit"	"Visit of the Superintendent of Indian Affairs to Southern Utah," *DN*, May 11, 1859.
VT	*Kirk Anderson's Valley Tan* (Salt Lake City, UT).
WBDRT	*Wilkes-Barre Daily Record of the Times* (Wilkes-Barre, PA).
Welch	Peyton Y. Welch, letter, Oct. 26, 1857, in "More Trains Destroyed by the Mormons and Indians," *Hornellsville (NY) Tribune*, Jan. 21, 1858. Reprinted from the *Missouri Expositor*, Jan. 5, 1858.
Welch2	Peyton Welch, testimony, Feb. 28, 1896, *Peyton Y. Welch v. United States and Utah Indians*, U.S. Court of Claims Indian depredation case files, claim nos. 9239 & 9702, RG 123, entry 31, NARA.
WHDP	William H. Dame Papers, CHL.
Woodruff	Wilford Woodruff, journals, 1833–98, CHL.
Woolley	Caroline Keturah Parry Woolley, *"I Would to God": A Personal History of Isaac Haight*, ed. Blanche Cox Clegg and Janet Burton Seegmiller (Cedar City: Southern Utah University Press, 2009).
Worster	Donald Worster, *A River Running West: The Life of John Wesley Powell* (New York: Oxford University Press, 2001).
WWGC	Wilford Woodruff General Correspondence files, CHL.
YOF	Brigham Young, Office Files, CHL.
ZIC	Edwin Brown Firmage and Richard Collin Mangrum, *Zion in the Courts: A Legal History of the Church of Jesus Christ of Latter-day Saints, 1830–1900* (Urbana: University of Illinois Press, 1988).

Notes

Preface

1. Brooks2, v, xix, xx.
2. Will Bagley, *Blood of the Prophets: Brigham Young and the Massacre at Mountain Meadows* (Norman: University of Oklahoma Press, 2002), xviii.
3. Brooks2, 217; *MatMM*, x.
4. "First Presidency's Mountain Meadows Massacre anniversary statement," *Salt Lake Tribune*, Sept. 11, 2007; Jessica Ravitz, "LDS Church Apologizes for Mountain Meadows Massacre," *Salt Lake Tribune*, Sept. 11, 2007; Carrie A. Moore, "LDS Church Issues Apology over Mountain Meadows," *Deseret News*, Sept. 12, 2007.
5. Peggy Fletcher Stack, "Mountain Meadows Now a National Historic Landmark," *Salt Lake Tribune*, July 5, 2011.
6. Chad J. Flake and Larry W. Draper, *A Mormon Bibliography, 1830–1930*, 2nd ed. (Provo, UT: Religious Studies Center, Brigham Young University, 2004), 1:627–29; Brian D. Reeves, "'Divert the Minds of the People': Mountain Meadows Massacre Recitals and Missionary Work," in *Go Ye into All the World: The Growth & Development of Mormon Missionary Work*, ed. Reid L. Neilson and Fred E. Woods (Provo, UT: Religious Studies Center, 2012), 291–315; Richard E. Turley Jr., "Problems with Mountain Meadows Massacre Sources," *Brigham Young University Studies* 47, no. 3 (2008): 147–51.

Chapter 1

1. Endowment House sealings, living couples, vol. 1 (1856–61), 226–27, CHL; Compton2, 168; Myrl Tenney Arrott, "Sarah Priscilla Leavitt Hamblin: A Pioneer Midwife," typescript, 27, CHL; Elwin C. Robison, "Historic Structures Report of the Brigham Young Estate" (Report for Historic Sites Group, Church History Department, Salt Lake City, UT, Jan. 15, 2011), 9–10, CHL.
2. Robison, "Historic Structures Report," 9–10; Randy Dixon, research on Brigham Young offices, CHL; Endowment House sealings, living couples, 1:226–27.
3. Compton2, 160, 166, 170–71; Endowment House sealings, living couples, 1:226–27; Compton1, 96–97; Nicholas L. Syrett, *American Child Bride: A History of Minors and Marriage in the United States* (Chapel Hill: University of North Carolina Press, 2016), 1–76; Cynthia Culver Prescott, "'Why She Didn't Marry Him': Love, Power, and

Marital Choice on the Far Western Frontier," *Western Historical Quarterly* 38, no. 1 (Spring 2007): 29.

4. JHJ, 1850–54, 46; Mary Henderson, "History of Utah: Historic Sites and Landmarks," vol. 2, 142–43, typescript, CHL; Washington County Court Records, Book A, 1854–72, 7–8, film 484840, FHL; Compton2, 165, 170.

5. Arrott, "Sarah Priscilla Leavitt Hamblin," 24–26; Compton2, 165, 168–71; Compton1, 96; LPCB 3:737.

6. Endowment House sealings, living couples, 1:226–27; *MatMM*, 193–94, 197.

7. *MatMM*, 160–61, 194, 197; TM, 418–21, 513–15, 646–48, 1090–93; Rogers; Shirts.

8. *DBY*, 78; H&H, 36–38; Editorial, *DN*, Sept. 16, 1857. On the Utah War, see MacKinnon1; MacKinnon2; H&H; Furniss.

9. Editorial, *DN*, Sept. 16, 1857; H&H, 36.

10. Carleton, 11; *MatMM*, 208–9, 244–49; *AJ-DHM*, 150, 161; "The Emigrant Children Were Brought First to My Parents' Home," typescript, CPWC.

11. *MatMM*, 104, 208–9, 243–49; Carleton, 11, 14; TM, 444–45; Basil G. Parker, *Recollections of the Mountain Meadow Massacre* (Plano, CA: Fred W. Reed, 1901), 4.

12. Carleton, 11–12, 14, 485–87; *MatMM*, 196, 208–9, 243–49; JH-BY; TM, 442, 444–45, 666.

13. "LLC."

Chapter 2

1. *SLC14*, 27–29, 70–71; "List of Prizes," *DN*, Oct. 21, 1857; Laurel Thatcher Ulrich, "An American Album, 1857," *American Historical Review* 115, no. 1 (Feb. 2010): 1–25.

2. *SLC14*, 71; *EOM* 1:290; Larry C. Porter, "A Study of the Origins of The Church of Jesus Christ of Latter-day Saints in the States of New York and Pennsylvania, 1816–1831" (PhD diss., Brigham Young University, 1971); Lyman D. Platt, "Members of the Church of Jesus Christ of Latter-day Saints Baptized by September 26, 1830," *Nauvoo Journal* 1 (1989): 19; Richard Lyman Bushman, *Joseph Smith: Rough Stone Rolling* (New York: Alfred A. Knopf, 2005).

3. Joseph Knight Sr., reminiscences, 9, CHL; William G. Hartley, *Stand by My Servant Joseph* (Salt Lake City: Deseret Book, 2003); http://josephsmithpapers.org/person/polly-peck-knight, accessed Sept. 17, 2014; Hafen, 1, 3.

4. *MatMM*, 7–16; Patricia Nelson Limerick, *The Legacy of Conquest* (New York: W. W. Norton, 1987), 282–83.

5. Joseph Knight Sr., reminiscences, 9; Polly Peck Knight, biography; *SLC14*, 70–71; Family group record for Joseph Watkins Johnson and Elizabeth Knight, familysearch. org, accessed Oct. 13, 2014; *MatMM*, 13–14; *Nauvoo*, 54–61, 380–98; *Kingdom*, 236–38; *HI*, 353–54; "A Proclamation, to the Saints Scattered Abroad," *T&S*, Jan. 15, 1841.

6. *HI*, 357; Turner, 111–18.

7. See HOHC, May 4, 1842, 10:473; *JD*, 2:31; *Nauvoo*, 258–60; *Kingdom*, 96–97.

8. D&C 132:18; *Nauvoo*, 261, 463–64, 474–76; Heber C. Kimball, journal, Dec. 24, 1845, CHL; Lisle G. Brown, ed., *Nauvoo Sealings, Adoptions, and Anointings* (Salt Lake City: Smith-Pettit Foundation, 2006), vii–viii, 159.

9. Jennifer Ann Mackley, *Wilford Woodruff's Witness* (Seattle, WA: High Desert Publishing, 2014), 168.

10. George D. Smith, ed., *An Intimate Chronicle* (Salt Lake City: Signature Books, 1995), 224.

11. AHCJ, Dec. 6, 1889.

12. Alma 37:30–31, 3 Nephi 9:5, 8–11, BOM.

13. 2 Kings 9:6–7, AV.

14. Luke 11:50–51, Revelation 6:9–11, AV.

15. "Awful Assassination of Joseph and Hyrum Smith," *T&S* 5, July 1, 1844; *Nauvoo*, 398–401.

16. Woodruff, Apr. 15, 1856.

17. *HI*, 411, 413; *Kingdom*, 265–66.

18. Smith, *An Intimate Chronicle*, 223.

19. *HI*, 412.

20. ICHJ, Apr. 11, 1846.

21. "To Our Patrons," *Nauvoo Neighbor* (Nauvoo, Illinois), Oct. 29, 1845.

22. Richard E. Bennett, *Mormons at the Missouri: 1846-1852*, 2nd ed. (Norman: University of Oklahoma Press, 2004), 131–41; Genealogical information for Elizabeth Knight Johnson and Joseph Watkins Johnson Jr. family, familysearch.org, accessed July 17, 2017.

23. *SLC14*, 71; Hafen, 3–4.

24. "Abraham O. Smoot—George B. Wallace Company, 1847," Pioneer Database, churchofjesuschrist.org, accessed Jan. 21, 2021; Hafen, 4; "Remarks," *DN*, Sept. 23, 1857; Turner, 144.

25. Walter Nugent, *Habits of Empire* (New York: Vintage Books, 2009), 131, 155–56; Limerick, *Legacy of Conquest*, 82.

26. Nugent, *Habits of Empire*, 131, 153–56.

27. George W. Cullum, *Biographical Register of the Officers and Graduates of the U. S. Military Academy at West Point, N.Y.*, 3rd ed., vol. 2 (Boston: Houghton, Mifflin, 1891), 30; "Death List of a Day," *NYT*, Mar. 29, 1901.

28. Will Bagley, *So Rugged and Mountainous* (Norman: University of Oklahoma Press, 2010), 374.

29. Cullum, *Biographical Register*, 2:30–31; "Remarks," *DN*, Sept. 23, 1857.

30. *SLC14*, 71; "Brigham Young Company (1848)," Pioneer Database, churchofjesuschrist.org, accessed July 17, 2020.

31. Susa Young Gates, *Lydia Knight's History* (Salt Lake City: Juvenile Instructor Office, 1883), 90–92.

32. Arrington, 224–26; Thomas G. Alexander, *Things in Heaven and Earth* (Salt Lake City: Signature Books, 1991), 154; *EOM* 4:1503–4.

33. *MatMM*, 20.

34. Orson Pratt, address, Aug. 29, 1852, in *DN—Extra*, Sept. 14, 1852. For the history of the "kingdom of God," see Matthew J. Grow, Ronald K. Esplin, Mark Ashurst-McGee, Gerrit J. Dirkmaat, and Jeffrey D. Mahas, eds. *Council of Fifty, Minutes, March 1844-January 1846*, vol. 1, Administrative Records series of *The Joseph Smith Papers*, edited by Ronald K. Esplin, Matthew J. Grow, and Matthew C. Godfrey (Salt Lake City: Church Historian's Press, 2016).

35. Bigler, 21, 37; *MatMM*, 47, 50, 102, 107; David Rich Lewis, "Native Americans in Utah," in *Utah History Encyclopedia,* ed. Alan Kent Powell (Salt Lake City: University of Utah Press, 1994), 389; Robert S. McPherson, "Setting the Stage: Native America Revisited," in *A History of Utah's American Indians*, ed. Forrest S. Cuch (Salt Lake City: Utah State Division of Indian Affairs/Utah State Division of History, 2000), 2, 3–21.

36. See *EOM* 3:981–82; 3 Nephi 21:1, BOM; D&C 49:24.

37. 3 Nephi 16:15, 20:15–17, 21:12–13, BOM.

38. Dennis R. Defa, "The Goshute Indians of Utah," in Cuch, *A History of Utah's American Indians*, 93; Hafen, 5–6; James G. Bleak, Annals of the Southern Utah Mission, Oct. 1853, 20–21, manuscript, CHL; JH, Oct. 7, 1853, Apr. 14, 1854.

39. JHJ, 1854–58, June 10, 1854; Reeve, 77, 91; McPherson, "Setting the Stage," 17; Ned Blackhawk, *Violence over the Land* (Cambridge, MA: Harvard University Press, 2006); Brian Q. Cannon, "'To Buy Up the Lamanite Children as Fast as They Could': Indentured Servitude and Its Legacy in Mormon Society," *JMH* 44, no. 2 (Apr. 2018): 1–35.

40. JHJ, Dec. 24, 1854.

41. Brigham Young, discourse, July 8, 1855, HOGCM, shorthand transcribed by LaJean Purcell Carruth; Turner, 244–46; *JD*, 3:258; *MatMM*, 20–21; William P. MacKinnon, "Sex, Subalterns, and Steptoe," *UHQ* 76 (Summer 2008): 227–46.

42. "The Mormons and their Customs," *Washington D.C. Republic*, Nov. 25, 1852, quoting the *St. Louis Intelligencer*.

43. *JD*, 3:259; Young, discourse, July 8, 1855, HOGCM; Turner, 245–46.

44. Gordon S. Wood, "Rhetoric and Reality in the American Revolution," *William and Mary Quarterly* 23 (Jan. 1966): 3–32.

45. D. J. Mulloy, "'Liberty or Death': Violence and the Rhetoric of Revolution in the American Militia Movement," *Canadian Review of American Studies* 38, no. 1 (2008): 119.

46. Brigham Young, remarks, Mar. 17, 1848, Sept. 23, 1849, HOGCM; *JD*, 5:97; Turner, 31, 177.

47. Woodruff, Mar. 2, 1856; *MatMM*, 24–25; Turner, 254–55.

48. Turner, 256–57; *JD*, 4:56.

49. Hafen, 6.

50. *JD*, 4:54; Woodruff, Sept. 21, 1856; Turner, 258; Leviticus 1:1–17, AV.

51. *JD*, 4:53; Turner, 258.

52. Woodruff, Sept. 21, 1856; Turner, 258.

53. Turner, 258.

54. *JD*, 4:219–20.

55. I. C. Haight to Brigham Young, Oct. 29, 1856, IC; LPCB 3:461–62; Turner, 258; *MatMM*, 59.

56. Turner, 13, 20, 31, 41; HOJ, Oct. 23, 1859; *MatMM*, 16–17.

57. CSM, Dec. 9, 1855.

58. I. C. Haight to Brigham Young, June 11, 1857, Ecclesiastical files, MACF; Fish, 153–54.

59. LPCB 3:641.

60. TM, 595–99, 605.

61. Hawley, 14; *MatMM*, 25, 27; 3 Nephi 24:2, BOM.

62. LPCB 3:690; Turner, 263; *MatMM*, 23–24.

Chapter 3

1. Howard R. Lamar, *The Far Southwest, 1846–1912* (Albuquerque: University of New Mexico Press, 2000); "Memorial and Resolutions to the President of the United States, Concerning Certain Officers of the Territory of Utah," Executive files, Governor's office files, YOF; "Expedition against Utah," *DN*, Oct. 7, 1857; MacKinnon1, 68–73, 107–11; *MatMM*, 27–28.

2. "Memorial and Resolutions to the President of the United States"; "Expedition against Utah"; MacKinnon1, 68–73; *MatMM*, 27.

3. JHM, Jan. 5, 1857; "Territory of Utah Legislative Assembly Rosters," 2007, http://archi ves.utah.gov, accessed Sept. 25, 2014. Latter-day Saints had been discussing the possibility of forming their own nation since the 1840s. Matthew J. Grow, Ronald K. Esplin, Mark Ashurst-McGee, Gerrit J. Dirkmaat, and Jeffrey D. Mahas, eds. *Council of Fifty, Minutes, March 1844–January 1846*, vol. 1, Administrative Records series of *The Joseph Smith Papers*, edited by Ronald K. Esplin, Matthew J. Grow, and Matthew C. Godfrey (Salt Lake City: Church Historian's Press, 2016).

4. *MatMM*, 28.

5. MacKinnon1, 106–11; *MatMM*, 28.

6. John M. Bernhisel to Brigham Young, Apr. 2, 1857, UDF; MacKinnon1, 87, 103–7; *MatMM*, 28.

7. William P. MacKinnon, "Hammering Utah, Squeezing Mexico, and Coveting Cuba: James Buchanan's White House Intrigues," *UHQ* 80 (Spring 2012): 133.

8. HDoc71, 7; *MatMM*, 30.

9. Woodruff, July 24, 1857; *DBY*, 54–59; *MatMM*, 36–38, 45; MacKinnon1, 408; Turner, 271.

10. *MatMM*, 45, 49.

11. *MatMM*, 47–48; Daniel H. Wells, General Orders, Aug. 1, 1857, Letter Book, 93, Nauvoo Legion (Utah), Adjutant General Records, CHL.

12. LPCB 3:732.

13. *MatMM*, 49–73; HOJ, Aug. 3, 1857; Historian's Office Diary of George A. Smith, Aug. 2–Sept. 10, 1857, CHL.

14. *MatMM*, 74–76; HOJ, Aug. 3–5, 8, 10–12, 28, 1857; Novak1, 52–53.

15. Outrages1.

16. Compton1, 96, 98; Hafen, 6–7; LPCB 3:737.

17. LPCB 3:737.

18. HDoc29; *MatMM*, 94–95.

19. Lorenzo Snow to Brigham Young, Aug. 7, 1857, IC; Lorenzo Snow to Brigham Young, Aug. [13]. 1857, IC; Verulum Dive to Brigham Young, Aug. 8, 1857, IC; *MatMM*, 94–95.

20. HDoc29, 21.

21. John Benson, account, 1849, in "Nicholas Turner's First Wagon Trip to California in 1849," https://www.wikitree.com/wiki/Turner-8738; *MatMM*, 92.

22. Welch; *MatMM*, 102–3.

23. Huntington, Aug. 10, 1857; *MatMM*, 96–98.

24. Huntington, Aug. 11, 1857.

25. Brigham Young, discourse, Aug. 16, 1857, reported by George D. Watt, in Historian's Office Reports of Speeches, CHL.

26. *DBY*, 58.

27. Young, discourse, Aug. 16, 1857; MacKinnon1, 484–85; Will Bagley, *So Rugged and Mountainous* (Norman: University of Oklahoma Press, 2010), 354–55, 369.

28. Daniel H. Wells to A. Johnson, Aug. 13, 1857, Letter Book, 97, Nauvoo Legion (Utah) Records, 1851–70, CHL. The circular also went to Major Evans (Lehi), W. B. Pace (Provo), Allen Weeks (Cedar Valley), G. W. Bradley (Nephi), W. S. Snow (Manti), L. W. McCullough (Fillmore), W. H. Dame (Iron County), and P. C. Merrill (Davis County).

29. Woodruff, Aug. 13, 1857; *MatMM*, 45–46, 98.

30. *DBY*, 62; Young, discourse, Aug. 16, 1857.

31. Young, discourse, Aug. 16, 1857; HOJ, Aug. 16, 1857; Richard E. Turley Jr., "The Murder of Parley P. Pratt and the Mountain Meadows Massacre," in *Parley P. Pratt and the Making of Mormonism*, ed. Gregory K. Armstrong, Matthew J. Grow, and Dennis J. Siler (Norman, OK: Arthur H. Clark, 2011), 297–313.

32. Young, discourse, Aug. 16, 1857.

33. William C. Staines, journal, Aug. 21, 1857, CHL; Turner, 272.

34. *DBY*, 61.

35. Outrages1.

36. Huntington, [Aug.] 30–[31], 1857; HDoc71, 203–4; *MatMM*, 146.

37. J. W. Dunn, diary, Sept. 9, 1857, typescript, University of Texas, Austin, TX; "From Carson Valley," *San Joaquin Republican*, Nov. 4, 1857, copied from *Placerville Argus*, Nov. 1, 1857.

38. George A. Smith to William H. Dame, Sept. 12–13, 1857, WHDP.

39. HOJ, Aug. 31, 1857.

40. Huntington, Sept. 1, 1857; Woodruff, Sept. 1, 1857; BYOJ, Sept. 1, 1857; HOJ, Sept. 1, 1857; *DBY*, 71; JHJ, 1854–58, 81–82; *MatMM*, 118, 146; Compton1, 98–99.

41. *MatMM*, 116–18.

42. *MatMM*, 118–19.

43. *MatMM*, 119.

44. *MatMM*, 80–81, 246–47.

45. *MatMM*, 77–79, 244, 248; Novak1, 13–14, 62.

46. *MatMM*, 79, 245–46.

47. *MatMM*, 81, 247–49; Novak1, 62–63.

48. *MatMM*, 81–82, 248.

49. Huntington, Sept. 1, 1857; Woodruff, Sept. 1, 1857; BYOJ, Sept. 1, 1857; HOJ, Sept. 1, 1857; *DBY*, 71; JHJ, 1854–58, 81–82; *MatMM*, 118, 146; Compton1, 98–99.

50. Huntington, Sept. 1, 1857.

51. Huntington, Aug. 16, 18, Sept. 1, 1857; LPCB 3:737.

52. *DBY*, 71.

53. JHJ, 1854–58, 82.

54. HDoc29, 85.

55. Compton1, 99; HDoc29, 86, 93; George A. Smith to William H. Dame, Aug. [Sept.] 12[–13], WHDP. Dimick Huntington's oft-retrospective journal puts Tutsegavits's ordination on September 10. Huntington, Sept. 10, 1857. Wilford Woodruff recorded the ordination on September 16. Woodruff, Sept. 16, 1857. Smith's account—written "Sunday evening," September 13—recounts, "We ordained Tutsegabbotts an Elder this Evening." The letter, which chronicles the events of that day, provides the best-documented date for the event.

56. Welch; *MatMM*, 116; Haslam, 4–5.

57. Outrages1; Outrages3; *MatMM*, 105–6, 120.

58. "Horrible"; "Our Los Angeles Correspondence," *DAC*, Oct. 27, 1857; *MatMM*, 119–20.

59. *MatMM*, 175; Outrages1; Welch.

60. Outrages1; *AJ-DHM*, 127; Welch; Fish, 60.

61. *MatMM*, 175–76; Outrages1.

62. Outrages1.

63. *MaMM*, 137, 159–60.

64. "Remarks," *DN*, Sept. 23, 1857; *DBY*, 76–78; HOJ, Sept. 8, 1857.

65. *DBY*, 76–78, 76n78; "Remarks," *DN*, Sept. 23, 1857.

66. George A. Smith to William H. Dame, Aug. [Sept.] 12[–13], 1857, WHDP; Andrew J. Allen, reminiscences and journal, Sept. 13, 1857, CHL; LPCB 3:827.

67. *DBY*, 79.

68. HOJ, Sept. 10, 1857.

69. *MatMM*, 182; Haslam, 9–11.

70. "The Utah Expedition," *NYT*, Feb. 4, 1858; Haslam, 9–12; TM, 3452; *MatMM*, 182–83.

71. Haslam, 10–12; *MatMM*, 183.

72. Brigham Young to Isaac C. Haight, Sept. 10, 1857, draft, OC; LPCB 3:827–28; *MatMM*, 183.

73. LPCB 3:827–28; Young to Haight, Sept. 10, 1857, draft, OC; *MatMM*, 183–86.

74. Haslam, 10–12; *MatMM*, 183.

75. TM, 3454; Hamilton G. Park, statement, Oct. 1907, typescript, CM; Hamilton G. Park, statement, ca. 1910, CHL; *MatMM*, 186; Haslam, 13.

Chapter 4

1. *MatMM*, 212; "Horrible."
2. *MatMM*, 56, 59, 211–12.
3. "LLC"; "LC."
4. PKS; *MatMM*, 150, 212–13, 259.
5. AHCJ, June 13, 1895.
6. "LLC"; "LC"; JDL2, 72-73; *MatMM*, 213.
7. JDL1-BT 3:14; *MatMM*, 244–49; "Horrible."
8. JDL1-PS 5:40; *MatMM*, 178, 213; "LLC"; "LC."
9. *MatMM*, 198–201, 214; SDoc42, 16–17; TM, 1100–1101; "LLC"; "LC."
10. *MatMM*, 214; "LLC"; AJ-DHM, 150, 161; Woodruff, Sept. 29, 1857.
11. Woodruff, Sept. 29, 1857; "LLC"; "LC"; TM, 1100–1101; *MatMM*, 214.
12. Hamilton Wallace, Reminiscence, undated, Collection of Mormon Diaries, LOC, microfilm copy at CHL; *MatMM*, 214.
13. *MatMM*, 160, 213–14; SDoc42, 16.
14. *MatMM*, 164, 180, 259; AJ-DHM, 324–25.
15. JDL2-BT 1:68, 70–72; *MatMM*, 208, 213, 216; TM, 994–95.
16. *MatMM*, 208, 213, 216; TM, 1122, 3646.
17. Carleton, 11; Rogers; "LLC"; "LC"; *MatMM*, 216–17.
18. Rogers; Carleton, 11–12; *MatMM*, 217, 245–46; Compton1, 485–86.
19. Carleton, 11–12, 14; *MatMM*, 217.
20. "Cates"; *MatMM*, 218–21; TM, 942–45.
21. JDL1-BT 3:22.
22. TM, 449, 3517–30.
23. TM, 424–46; *MatMM*, 198–99.
24. TM, 3567.
25. *MatMM*, 202, 208, Appendix A; "Cates"; "Butchery"; Sallie Baker Mitchell, 11.
26. "LC"; "LLC."
27. TM, 449, 3524-28, 3547.
28. TM, 449; *MatMM*, 217; Forney1; Biography of James Whittaker, c. 1947, carbon copy of typescript, HL.
29. "Horrible"; TM, 1249–51.
30. "Horrible"; Mathews to Judson, Oct. 8, 1857, in *San Diego Herald,* Oct. 17, 1857.
31. TM, 1251.
32. Mathews to Judson, Oct. 8, 1857.
33. "Horrible."
34. TM, 449–50.
35. "Horrible." Some have surmised that "young Baker" was the *youngest* Baker man in the train, nineteen-year-old Abel. But Warn's early account points to the other "young Baker" of the train, twenty-seven-year-old George, who had traveled to California before and knew the terrain. Decades later, Sarah Frances Baker, two years old in 1857, remembered her father, George, holding her in his arms in one of the two lead wagons when he was shot, while then five-year-old Martha Elizabeth Baker remembered

their father placing her and Sarah in the wagons. "Butchery." The conflicting accounts exemplify the complications of memory.

36. "Horrible."
37. TM, 1255–57.
38. Lyman, *Biography, Francis Marion Lyman,* 37; *MatMM,* 223.
39. "Horrible"; TM, 1009–10.
40. Brigham Young to Isaac C. Haight, Sept. 10, 1857, CHL.
41. Haslam; *MatMM,* 225–26.
42. CSM, Sept. 13, 1857.

Chapter 5

1. JDL1-BT 5:311, 318.
2. TM, 2090–97; JDL1-RS 9:14.
3. *AJ-DHM,* 55; CCWR, Dec. 10, 1857; Mary Hannah Burton White entry, "Pedigree Resource File," familysearch.org, accessed Oct. 6, 2017.
4. HBM, Sept. 13, 1857; TM, 934–35; Benjamin Platt, autobiography, typescript, HL. Hoag remembered that most white men from Harmony went to the Meadows, but contemporaneous and later sources contradict her, saying only Carl Shirts and Lee went. *MatMM,* 190.
5. JDL1-PS 5:17; "Gilbert Morse," *SLT,* Sept. 28, 1876; Shirts; Platt autobiography.
6. *AJ-DHM,* 279; TM, 925–28; *MatMM,* 153.
7. TM, 929–32; *MatMM,* 139, 142–44, 153; Benjamin Platt, reminiscence, 1899–1905, typescript, CHL; Platt autobiography; Carleton, 20.
8. TM, 932.
9. TM, 932–33; "Gilbert Morse"; *MatMM,* 153.
10. *AJ-DHM,* 279; Shirts.
11. Shirts; "Gilbert Morse"; Platt reminiscence; Platt autobiography; TM, 935; McGlashan.
12. JDL1-RS 4:13; Shirts; Platt reminiscence; Platt autobiography.
13. Shirts.
14. Shirts; Cates.
15. JDL1-PS 5:18; Shirts.
16. Shirts; *MatMM,* 160.
17. TM, 936.
18. Shirts.
19. TM, 937–39; *MatMM,* 194.
20. Shirts; TM, 939–40.
21. See, e.g., Deuteronomy 19:10, 13, 21:8–9, 1 Samuel 19:5, Jeremiah 7:6, 22:3, Matthew 27:4, AV; Alma 39:5, BOM; D&C 132:19, 26–27.
22. TM, 940–41; Shirts; *AJ-DHM,* 149, 161.
23. TM, 941–42, 944.

24. Shirts.

25. TM, 943, 945–46. On Calvin, see Kearny; SDoc42, 57; Carleton, 26, 27.

26. TM, 944–45; HBM, Nov. 1, 1857; *MC* 1:199; Carleton, 27.

27. *AJ-DHM*, 46.

28. CSM, Sept. 13, 1857.

29. *AJ-DHM*, 45, 55; CCWR, Dec. 10, 1857; Mary Hannah Burton White entry, "Pedigree Resource File," familysearch.org, accessed Oct. 6, 2017; McGlashan.

30. Hawley, 16; John Hawley to "Bro. Joseph," June 12, 1884, in *Saints' Herald* (Lamoni, IA), June 28, 1884.

31. Hawley, 14.

32. Hawley to "Bro. Joseph"; Hawley, 16.

33. Hawley, 2, 16; *MatMM*, 258.

34. Hawley, 16; Hawley to "Bro. Joseph"; *MatMM*, 264.

35. Hawley, 16; Hawley to "Bro. Joseph."

36. Parowan Utah Stake, Melchizedek Priesthood minutes and records, Sept. 13, 1857, CHL; *MatMM*, 211–14.

37. PSHR, first section, p. 26, second section, p. 41; Outrages1; *MatMM*, 105–6, 175.

38. Outrages1.

39. PSHR, first section, Sept. 10, 1857, 26–27; JHM, Sept. 14, 1857; Fish, 60.

40. MCOP.

41. "Horrible."

42. "Horrible"; Carleton, 17.

43. "Horrible"; Outrages1. The Young brothers were no relation to Brigham Young. *MatMM*, 225, 379n100.

44. "Horrible."

Chapter 6

1. LPCB 3:827, 844–48; *DBY*, 79–80; Andrew J. Allen, journal, Sept. 14, 1857, typescript, CHL.

2. LPCB 3:844–48; *JD*, 5:98–99.

3. LPCB 3:834–38, 844–48.

4. LPCB 3:840–41.

5. Brigham Young to James W. Denver, Sept. 12, 1857, Governor's office files, Executive files, Governor's Letterpress copybook, 648–51, YOF.

6. LPCB 3:849–53; Grow, 47–66; H&H, 263–65.

7. *DBY*, 80; George Laub, journal, Sept. 13, 1857, CHL; Allen journal, Sept. 13, 1857; *JD*, 5:231–35.

8. Laub journal, Sept. 13, 1857; *JD*, 5:236.

9. Laub journal, Sept. 13, 1857.

10. *DBY*, 68–69, 80; Elias Smith, journal, Sept. 14, 1857, CHL; Woodruff, Sept. 14, 1857; HOJ, Sept. 14, 1857.

11. *DBY*, 80–83.

12. Gove, 59; Furniss, 109.

13. *DBY*, 80; PSHR, second section, Sept. 26, 1857; JHM, Sept. 26, 1857.

14. LPCB 3:858–60; *A Letter from Brigham Young and Daniel H. Wells, Great Salt Lake City, Sept. 14, 1857, to Brother Philo Farnsworth* (Provo, UT: Brigham Young University Library, 1963); Brigham Young and Daniel H. Wells to James W. Cummings and Robert T. Burton, Sept. 18, 1857, Nauvoo Legion Letterbook, 105, Nauvoo Legion (Utah) Records, CHL.

15. LPCB 3:858–60; *A Letter from Brigham Young and Daniel H. Wells.*

16. Myrl Tenney Arrott, "Sarah Priscilla Leavitt Hamblin: A Pioneer Midwife," typescript, 28, CHL; JH-BY; PGM, Sept. 20, 1857; American Fork Ward Historical Record, Sept. 20, 1857, CHL; PSHR, second section, Sept. 26, 1857, 36; JHM, Sept. 26, 1857.

17. HBM, Sept. 20, 1857; *TF*, 492.

18. "LLC."

19. JHM, Sept. 24, 1857.

20. Homer Brown, journal, Sept. 20, 1857, Homer Brown Papers, CHL.

21. Volney King, "Millard County, 1851–1875," *Utah Humanities Review* 1, no. 3 (July 1947): 261; Thomas Waters Cropper, autobiography, 1926, 35, CHL; Proctor Robison grave marker, Fillmore, Utah, cemetery.

22. Carleton, 7.

23. Carleton, 7; Janet Burton Seegmiller, *A History of Iron County* (Salt Lake City: Utah State Historical Society, 1998), 64. In 1871 and 1876, Hamblin gave longer accounts of this visit. See chapters 31 and 42 of this book; JH-BY; JHS; TM, 3665–86, 3689–98, 3702–35, 3745–46.

24. Arrott, "History of Sarah Priscilla Leavitt Hamblin," 27; Carleton, 7; TM, 3748–49; JHM, Sept. 24, 1857; William H. Dame to George A. Smith, Sept. 21, 1857, GASP.

25. Carleton, 7; JH-BY; JHS; TM, 3748–49; JNSJ, Sept. 25, 1857; TM, 3748–49.

26. MCOP; Carleton, 7.

27. MCOP; JHM, Sept. 14, 1857.

28. Carleton, 7; TM, 3748–49.

29. Carleton, 7; PSHR, second section, Sept. 26, 1857, 36; JHM, Sept. 26, 1857; TM, 3747–48.

30. TM, 482, 3686–87, 3746–47; Carleton, 6.

31. Carleton, 7.

32. Outrages1; Welch2; Christian.

33. Carleton, 7; Brooks3, 78.

34. Carleton, 7–8; Arrott, "History of Sarah Priscilla Leavitt Hamblin," 28.

35. Carleton, 7–8.

36. JHS.

37. JH-BY; JHS.

38. SDoc42, 79; Carleton, 8–9.

39. JHJ, 41–42.

40. JHJ, 41; Carleton, 8.

41. Carleton, 8; TM, 3698–99.

42. "Last Will and Testament of John T. Baker," Apr. 1, 1857, typescript, Chancery Court Record Book A, 75–76, copy in family information and research materials of Cheri Baker Walker, Boone County Historical and Genealogical Society, Boone County, AR; *MatMM*, 79.

43. Carleton, 8.

44. Arrott, "History of Sarah Priscilla Leavitt Hamblin," 31.

45. Christian; Mrs. M. E. Wilson, deposition May 30, 1903, in *Nicholas Turner v. United States* and *Peyton Y. Welch v. United States and Utah Indians*, U.S. Court of Claims Indian depredation case files, nos. 9702 & 9239, RG 123, entry 31, NARA.

46. Outrages1.

47. Outrages1; J. Ward Christian to Benj. Hayes, Oct. 25, 1857, Letters received by the Office of Indian Affairs, 1824–81, California Superintendency, 1858, Records of the Office of Indian Affairs, RG 75, microfilm publication M234, reel 36, NARA.

48. Outrages1; Mrs. M. E. Wilson; Christian to Hayes, Oct. 25, 1857; Christian; Welch.

49. Welch; Welch2; "William A. Wilson," biographical sketch, in *An Illustrated History of Los Angeles County, California* (Chicago: Lewis Publishing, 1889), 676–77; Outrages1; Christian; "Horrible."

50. Outrages1; Welch2; *TAR*, 64.

51. Outrages1.

52. Honea, Outrages1; Welch2; Welch; Brooks3, 78.

Chapter 7

1. PGM, Sept. 27, 1857; Carleton, 7; JH-BY; JHS; TM, 3665–66, 3682, 3702–5, 3745–46; "Died," *DN*, Feb. 22, 1865.

2. PGM, Sept. 27, 1857; JH-BY; JHS.

3. PGM, Sept. 27, 1857.

4. Susan Tate Laing, ed., *Andrew Hunter Scott* (Provo, UT: Andrew Hunter Scott Genealogical Association, 2001), 530; Samuel Pitchforth, diary, Sept. 30, 1857, photocopy of typescript, CHL.

5. HOJ, Sept. 28, 1857.

6. Penrose, 56–57; HOJ, Sept. 29, 1857.

7. Woodruff, Sept. 28–29, 1857.

8. Woodruff, Sept. 28, 1857; John M. Bernhisel to Brigham Young, Nov. 2, 1857, UDF; Gove, 68.

9. HDoc71, 33; Gove, 69, 73.

10. Penrose, 56–57; Woodruff, Sept. 29, 1857; Thomas G. Alexander, *Things in Heaven and Earth* (Salt Lake City: Signature Books, 1991), 21, 34–37, 179; Frank J. Cannon and Harvey J. O'Higgins, *Under the Prophet in Utah* (Boston: C. M. Clark, 1911), 84; *MatMM*, 60.

11. Huntington, Sept. 20, 1857.

12. Woodruff, Sept. 29, 1857; HOJ, Sept. 28–29, 1857; George A. Smith and James McKnight, "The Emigrant and Indian War at Mountain Meadows," Aug. 6, 1858, HOCHD.

13. Woodruff, Sept. 29, 1857; *MatMM*, 14.

14. Woodruff, Sept. 29, 1857; PGM, Sept. 27, 1857.

15. Woodruff, Sept. 29, 1857.

16. Woodruff, Sept. 29, 1857; *MC* 2:164.

17. Woodruff, Sept. 29, 1857. A forensic anthropologist who later studied the bones of at least twenty-eight massacre victims found no evidence of venereal or congenital syphilis. Novak1, 107–9.

18. Woodruff, Sept. 29, 1857. In 1870, Lee claimed he told Young "the Truth & the Whole Truth" during the meeting—except that he had not let responsibility rest on "Persons whoes Names . . . has never been brought out." *MC* 2:152.

To his life's end, Woodruff maintained Lee "did not at the time implicate himself or any white Men but said it was Done by the Indians." Wilford Woodruff, statement, ca. 1882, CM; Wilford Woodruff, in "The Law of Adoption," *Deseret Weekly*, Apr. 21, 1894; "Discourse by President Wilford Woodruff," *MS* 56, no. 22 (May 28, 1894): 338. John W. Young, who said he was also present during Lee's report, affirmed Lee said nothing of white involvement. Penrose, 56–57; "BY." Massacre participant Nephi Johnson had "no doubt . . . that John D. Lee, in reporting the affair to Governor Young, lied to him and laid it on the Indians." *AJ-DHM*, 330.

19. BYOJ, Sept. 29, 1857. On Young's using the mill as a retreat, see HOJ, Dec. 24–25, 1850; Alice Merrill Horne, "One of the Pioneers," *Young Woman's Journal* 15, no. 4 (Apr. 1904): 165; *DBY*, 36.

20. LPCB 3:915, 4:101. Although Young continues to tell Indians, "The enemies of this people can never be your friends," he does not ask them to fight. MacKinnon2, 243.

21. BYOJ, Sept. 29, 1857; LPCB 3:863; MacKinnon1, 330; Woodruff, Sept. 27, 1857.

22. LPCB 3:863–64; Woodruff, Sept. 29–30, 1857.

23. Joseph Smith to N. C. Saxton, Jan. 4, 1833, Joseph Smith Letterbook 1, 17–18, CHL; Woodruff, Sept. 29–30, 1857.

24. Woodruff, Sept. 30–Oct. 1, 1857.

25. Woodruff, Sept. 30, 1857; "List of Prizes," *DN*, Oct. 21, 1857; *SLC14*, 28, 70–71.

26. Louisa Barnes Pratt, journal and autobiography, 369, CHL; "Rumored Massacre on the Plains," *LAS*, Oct. 3, 1857.

27. "Rumored Massacre on the Plains"; "Horrible."

28. Pratt, journal and autobiography, 369.

29. Francis M. Lyman to Amasa M. Lyman, Oct. 6, 1857, AMLC.

30. "Horrible."

31. Pratt, journal and autobiography, 369; "Horrible."

32. "Horrible."

33. "Horrible"; "Public Meeting," *LAS*, Oct. 17, 1857.

34. "Horrible."

35. "The Federal Government and the Mormons," *SFDEB*, Oct. 27, 1857; "The Immigrant Massacre," *DAC*, Oct. 17, 1857; "For the East," *DAC*, Oct. 20, 1857.

36. "Federal Government and the Mormons."

Chapter 8

1. George W. Armstrong to Brigham Young, Sept. 30, 1857, Report B432, USBIA.
2. Armstrong to Young, Sept. 30, 1857.
3. *JD*, 5:293.
4. LPCB 3:869–71.
5. Gove, 69–70, 73; HDoc71, 33.
6. LPCB 3:858-60; *A Letter from Brigham Young and Daniel H. Wells, Great Salt Lake City, Sept. 14, 1857, to Brother Philo Farnsworth* (Provo, UT: Brigham Young University Library, 1963); MacKinnon1, 347–48.
7. *Genteel*, 10n3; MacKinnon1, 348.
8. MacKinnon1, 415, 420.
9. Outrages1; Christian; Welch; Shirts. Although the train's members give various dates for the attack, "on or about" October 3, 1857, seems the most accurate. Turner2; Welch2.
10. Outrages1; *An Illustrated History of Los Angeles County, California* (Chicago: Lewis Publishing, 1889), 676–77; Marion F. Turner, deposition, Dec. 20, 1906, in Turner2.
11. Welch; Welch2; Mrs. M. E. Wilson, deposition, May 30, 1903, in Turner2 and Welch2; Outrages1.
12. Outrages1; Shirts.
13. Outrages1; Christian; Shirts.
14. Welch.
15. Wilson deposition, May 30, 1903.
16. Outrages1; Welch; Fish, 60–61.
17. Outrages1; Christian.
18. *TAR*, 64; Welch2; Christian; "Further News from Utah," *Stockton Daily Argus*, Nov. 14, 1857.
19. Outrages1.
20. JHM1907.
21. Brooks3, 78.
22. Outrages3; George F. Hendry to Brigham Young, June 25, 1860, MACF.
23. Jacob Hamblin to Brigham Young, [Oct.] 14, 1857, IC.
24. "From Southern California," *SDU*, Nov. 14, 1857; "Further News from Utah."

Chapter 9

1. HBM, Oct. 17, 18, 1857.
2. Woodruff, Sept. 29, 1857; *MC* 1:148; TM, 492, 690.

3. George K. Bowering to Edward Hunter, Oct. 12, 1858, Edward Hunter Collection, CHL.

4. TM, 811–16, 3570–71, 3687, 3746–47.

5. Haslam, 17; *AJ-DHM*, 55, 282; *MC* 2:3–4.

6. *MC* 1:148; TM, 3571.

7. CCSR, entries 199–201, 206, 213; *EOM* 1:129.

8. HBM, Nov. 1, 1857; "LC"; "LLC"; Woodruff, Sept. 29, 1857; *AJ-DHM*, 49. The parents of other children blessed in Harmony on this date were Harmony residents. Brooks1, 382–83.

9. HBM, Nov. 1, 1857; *AJ-DHM*, 49; *MatMM*, 220; Kearny.

10. *MatMM*, 220; TM, 677–78.

11. *MatMM*, 217–20; Kearny.

12. TM, 452–53; CCSR, entry 173; *MatMM*, 219.

13. CCSR, entries 194, 196.

14. *AJ-DHM*, 45; CCSR, entry 213; *MatMM*, 219.

15. Samuel McMurdie, journal, Nov. 2, 1857, photocopy, CHL; TM, 405, 494, 3518–21.

16. TM, 494–95, 743–45, 991, 1132; Leonard J. Arrington, "The Mormon Tithing House: A Frontier Business Institution," *Business History Review* 28, no. 1 (Mar. 1954): 24–58; Leonard J. Arrington, *Great Basin Kingdom: An Economic History of the Latter-day Saints, 1830–1900* (Urbana: University of Illinois Press, 2005), 141–42.

17. BYOJ, Sept. 18, 1858; TM, 991–97. On the iron industry, see *TF*, 371–419.

18. Louisa Barnes Pratt, journal and autobiography, 382–83, CHL; Louisa Barnes Pratt, *Mormondom's First Woman Missionary*, ed. Kate B. Carter (n.p., n.d.), 331; *MatMM*, 47.

19. CCWR Nov. 12, Dec. 10, 1857; *AJ-DHM*, 55.

20. TM, 991–96; *AJ-DHM*, 49; McGlashan.

21. McGlashan.

22. "Cates."

23. Outrages3.

24. Carleton, 8.

25. Outrages3; "Horrible"; Edward Leo Lyman, *San Bernardino* (Salt Lake City: Signature Books, 1996), 259; Jenson2 3:417.

26. Outrages1; Outrages2; Outrages3.

27. *AJ-DHM*, 64, 191; JH-BY.

Chapter 10

1. "Interesting from Utah," *NYH*, Feb. 23, 1858; BYOJ, Oct. 10, 12, 1857; "Later from Salt Lake City," *LAS*, Dec. 12, 1857; "More Important Items from the Mormon Country," *DAC*, Dec. 13, 1857; "Late and Important from Utah," *NYT*, Jan. 14, 1858; "The Mormon War," *NYH*, Jan. 14, 1858; "From Work to Rest," *Burlington Hawkeye Weekly* (Burlington, IA), Aug. 11, 1887.

2. "Married," *DN,* Apr. 2, 1856; JH, June 8, 1856, 14; *Portrait and Biographical Album of Lee County, Iowa* (Chicago: Chapman Brothers, 1887), 387.

3. Woodruff, Mar. 3–4, 1840; Wilford Woodruff letter, Apr. 29, 1840, *T&S,* June 8, 1840; "Elder Woodruff's Letter," *T&S,* Mar. 1, 1841; "Discourse by President Wilford Woodruff," *MS* 48 (Nov. 28, 1895): 754; *Nauvoo,* 78, 105.

4. LPCB 3:899; "More Important Items"; "Interesting from Utah"; John [I.] Ginn, "Mormon and Indian Wars," undated typescript, 28–29, CHL.

5. "Interesting from Utah"; "Later from Salt Lake City"; "More Important Items"; "Late and Important from Utah"; "The Mormon War"; "From Work to Rest."

6. LPCB 3:909, 912–13; Ginn, "Mormon and Indian Wars," 23–24; O. W. Willits, *The Story of Oak Glen and the Yucaipa Valley* (Yucaipa, CA: Cobbs Printing Enterprise, 1971), 23; LPCB 3:912–13.

7. "Later from Salt Lake," *DAC,* Dec. 11, 1857; "Later from Salt Lake City"; "Late and Important from Utah"; "More Important Items."

8. "Biographical Sketch and Diary of Isaac Chauncey Haight, 1813–1862," copied by Brigham Young University Library, 1940, 123, microfilm, FHL.

9. "Position of the Mormon Army," *New York Tribune,* Jan. 15, 1858; PSHR, second section; Samuel McMurdie journal, Nov. 23, 1857, CHL; JHJ, Nov.–Dec. 1857; Edward Partridge journal, Dec. 1, 1857, CHL.

10. Partridge journal, Dec. 16, 1857; JHJ, 44; Brooks2, 132.

11. Jacob Hamblin to Brigham Young, Dec. 26, 1857, YOF.

12. MacKinnon1, 408–11; Grow, 159.

13. LPCB 3:852–53.

14. John M. Bernhisel to Brigham Young, Nov. 13, 1857, UDF; "Army for Utah," *Fayetteville Observer* (Fayetteville, TN), June 18, 1857.

15. MacKinnon1, 411.

16. MacKinnon1, 415; "The Mormon War," *Preble County Democrat* (Eaton, OH), Nov. 26, 1857; "House of Representatives," *Washington Union* (Washington, DC), Dec. 24, 1857.

17. "Latest Intelligence," *NYT,* Nov. 20, 1857.

18. Gene A. Sessions and Stephen W. Stathis, "The Mormon Invasion of Russian America: Dynamics of a Potent Myth," *UHQ* 45 (Winter 1977): 24; MacKinnon1, 440.

19. MacKinnon1, 442–43.

20. Buchanan, "Message of the President of the United States," Dec. 8, 1857, in Cong. Globe Appendix, 35th Cong., 1st Sess. 5–6 (1857); MacKinnon1, 484; John M. Bernhisel to Brigham Young, Dec. 17, 1858, UDF.

21. John B. Floyd, "Report of the Secretary of War," Dec. 5, 1857, in Cong. Globe Appendix, 35th Cong., 1st Sess. 33 (1857); MacKinnon1, 484–85.

22. Floyd, "Report of the Secretary of War."

23. Grow, 161–62; MacKinnon1, 486–87.

24. MacKinnon1, 442, 497–502, 504–5.

25. SDoc42, 42–43; Roger Logan Jr., "DuBuque Once a Thriving Boone County Town Dates Back to 1814," *Harrison Daily Times,* Apr. 30, 1969; Boone County Historical

and Railroad Society, *History of Boone County, Arkansas with a Narrative by Roger V. Logan, Jr.* (Paducah, KY: Turner, 1998), 307.

26. SDoc42, 42–43; *MatMM*, 244–46, 248.
27. "Emigrant Massacre," *San Francisco Herald*, Oct. 15, 1857; SDoc42, 42–43.
28. MacKinnon1, 500, 504–5, 508.
29. MacKinnon1, 498, 509; Grow, 165.
30. Grow, 41; MacKinnon1, 510–11.

Chapter 11

1. Gove, 77; H&H, 19; MacKinnon1, 339.
2. HDoc71, 56–57; Arrington, 255; Marcy, 270–71; *Genteel*, 28–30; Gove, 67, 71, 79.
3. H&H, 19–20; Gove, 89, 92–93; *Genteel*, 13–14; Furniss, 115–16, 148–49.
4. Brigham Young to A. S. Johnston, Nov. 26, 1857, OC; *Genteel*, 20–23.
5. Marcy, 224–63; "Our Utah Correspondence," *NYH*, July 8, 1858, reprinted in *Utah Expedition*, 314–18; "The Utah Expedition," *NYT*, Mar. 9, 1858; "From the West: Interesting Letters from Captain Marcy," *NYT*, July 1, 1858; "Interesting from Utah," *NYT*, July 8, 1858; "Captain Marcy's Winter Expedition on the Plains," *NYT*, Nov. 30, 1858; SDoc1, 182–83; Furniss, 154–56.
6. MacKinnon2, 39, 51, 89, 133, 136, 234n34, 241, 271, 286–87, 354, 395.
7. Furniss, 149–50; Moorman, 30.
8. H&H, 20; Furniss, 150; *Genteel*, 6nn1–2, 19–24.
9. HDoc71, 205; A. Cumming to Lewis Cass, Nov. 28, 1857, Letterpress Copybook, 2:5, CP.
10. A. Cumming to Lewis Cass, Jan. 3, 1858, Letterpress Copybook, 2:12, CP; G. Hurt to A. Cumming, Dec. 17, 1857, enclosed in A. Cumming to Lewis Cass, Jan. 30, 1858, U.S. Department of State, Utah Territorial Papers, 1853–73, CHL.
11. A. Cumming to Brigham Young, Nov. 21, 1857, FALG; *Genteel*, 13.
12. Cumming to the People of Utah Territory, Nov. 21, 1857, FALG; *Genteel*, 5n7, 8–9.
13. Scribal notation on A. Cumming to Brigham Young, Nov. 21, 1857.
14. Stout, 1:646.
15. Furniss, 114–15, 124–25, 145, 168; HDoc71, 66–67; Moorman, 30; Arrington, 274; Peterson, 28.
16. Peterson, 16; Nels Anderson, *Desert Saints* (Chicago: University of Chicago Press, 1966), 188.
17. *Genteel*, 5n7, 37n1; Arrington, 274–76; Furniss, 158; Moorman, 41; A. Cumming to Lewis Cass, Dec. 13, 1857, Letterpress Copybook, 2:11, CP.
18. A. Cumming to Lewis Cass, Jan. 3, 1858, Letterpress Copybook, 2:13, CP.
19. Peterson, 9–10, 29–30; *Genteel*, xii; Furniss, 190–91.
20. Peterson, 21.
21. Cumming to Cass, Nov. 28, 1857; Peterson, 22–23.
22. Peterson, 20, 29–30, 56–59; *Genteel*, 60.

23. Furniss, 166–67; *Acts, Resolutions and Memorials Passed by the Legislative Assembly of the Territory of Utah, During the Seventh Annual Session, for the Years 1857-58* (Salt Lake City: Shepard Book Co., 1919), 5, 8–9, 11–17, 20–21; "An Act," *DN*, Dec. 23, 1857; Everett L. Cooley, "Journals of the Legislative Assembly, Territory of Utah, Seven Annual Session, 1857-1858," *UHQ* 24 (1956): 113–14.

24. Peterson, 25.

25. Cong. Globe, 35th Cong., 1st Sess. 428 (1858).

26. Grow, 165–67; Richard D. Poll, "Thomas L. Kane and the Utah War," *UHQ* 61 (Spring 1993): 124–26; Albert L. Zobell Jr., *Sentinel in the East* (Salt Lake City: Nicholas G. Morgan Sr., 1965), 107–17; Oscar Osburn Winther, *A Friend of the Mormons* (San Francisco: Gelber-Lilienthal, 1937), 65–77; Fish, 62.

Chapter 12

1. "Extract"; Outrages1.

2. "Meeting"; Novak1, 1, 63.

3. "Meeting."

4. "Meeting"; Novak1, 1.

5. "Meeting."

6. "Meeting in Newton County," *Arkansas State Gazette and Democrat*, Apr. 17, 1858; Carleton, 6.

7. "Meeting in Newton County."

8. Salmon River Mission journal, Feb. 25, 1858, CHL; T. S. Smith to Brigham Young, Feb. 28, 1858, IC; Bigler, 220–36; William G. Hartley, "Dangerous Outpost: Thomas Corless and the Fort Limhi/Salmon River Mission," *Mormon Historical Studies* 2 (Fall 2001): 152–55.

9. Milton D. Hammond, journal and life sketch, Feb. 25, 1858, USHS.

10. Salmon River Mission journal, Feb. 25, 1858; Smith to Young, Feb. 28, 1858; Bigler, 223–24.

11. Salmon River Mission journal, Feb. 25–28, 1858; Thomas Sasson Smith, journal, Feb. 25–28, 1858, CHL; Smith to Young, Feb. 28, 1858; Bigler, 224–32.

12. Woodruff, Feb. 25, 1858; LPCB 4:67.

13. Thomas L. Kane to Brigham Young, Feb. 25, 1858, copied in Thomas L. Kane to [James Buchanan], Mar. 5, 1858, Utah War Correspondence, TLKC.

14. Brigham Young to Thomas L. Kane, Feb. 25, 1858, OC.

15. Kane to [Buchanan], Mar. 5, 1858.

16. Woodruff, Feb. 25, 1858; Kane to [Buchanan], Mar. 5, 1858; Andrew J. Allen, journal, Feb. 27, 1858, CHL.

17. Woodruff, Feb. 25, 1858.

18. LPCB 4:76; John M. Bernhisel to Brigham Young, Dec. 31, 1857, Utah War Correspondence, TLKC; "Rush Valley Military Reservation, Utah," H.R. Ex. Doc. 43-96, at 2.

19. LPCB 4:76, 79, 234; DJ, Apr. 7, June 15, 1858; JHM, Apr. 13–July 23, 1858; HOJ, June 24, 1858; Lovinia Dame to William H. Dame, May 30, 1858, William H. Dame Collection, BYU.

20. Grow, 155, 160; Woodruff, Feb. 25, 1858.

21. Woodruff, Feb. 25, 1858.

22. Cong. Globe, 35th Cong., 1st Sess. 861, 864, 867-70 (1858).

23. Reeve, 90–91.

24. "The Emigrant Massacre," *San Francisco Herald*, Oct. 15, 1857; SDoc42, 42–43; Cong. Globe, 35th Cong., 1st Sess. 870.

25. Cong. Globe, 35th Cong., 1st Sess. 872–73; Alfred M. Williams, *Sam Houston and the War of Independence in Texas* (Boston: Houghton Mifflin, 1893), 353.

26. Cong. Globe, 35th Cong., 1st Sess. 873-75.

27. "Interesting from Utah," *NYH*, Feb. 23, 1858. Excerpts from a letter in *LAS*, Dec. 12, 1857, also reprinted in "The Mormon War," *NYH*, Jan. 14, 1858.

28. "By Authority," *Washington Union* (Washington, DC), Apr. 10, 1858; HOJ, Nov. 4, 1858; "The Defeat of the Army Bill," *National Era* (Washington, DC), Mar. 4, 1858.

29. Furniss, 193; SDoc1, 203–4; Kane to [Buchanan], Mar. 5, 1858.

30. SDoc1, 10.

Chapter 13

1. Brigham Young to Thomas S. Smith, Mar. 8, 1858, OC; David L. Bigler, *Fort Limhi: The Mormon Adventure in Oregon Territory, 1855–1858* (Logan: Utah State University Press, 2004), 260–61, 278.

2. BYOJ, Mar. 8, 1858; Brigham Young to Thomas L. Kane, Mar. 9, 1858, OC.

3. Peterson, 28.

4. On the changing political atmosphere in Washington and its causes, see Furniss, 168–75; Peterson, 25.

5. Peterson, 30–31; Arrington, 262.

6. H&H, 21; Peterson, 31.

7. *Genteel*, 33.

8. See George A. Smith to William H. Dame, Feb. 24, 1858, in WHDP; BYOJ, Apr. 12, 1858.

9. History of the Church, 28:270, Mar. 21, 1858, manuscript, CHL.

10. *A Series of Instructions and Remarks by President Brigham Young, at a Special Council, Tabernacle, March 21, 1858* (Salt Lake City, 1858), 5.

11. BYOJ, Mar. 30, 1858.

12. *Genteel*, 40, 41; Furniss, 190–91.

13. *Genteel*, 41–42.

14. *Genteel*, 43.

15. Furniss, 190–91.

16. History of the Church, 28:341–42, 349; BYOJ, Apr. 12, 13, 14, 1858; SDoc67, 2–7. For details on Cumming's trip, see *Genteel*, 47–49; HOJ, Apr. 13, 1858.

17. Bigler; David Bigler, "Mormon Missionaries, the Utah War, and the 1858 Bannock Raid on Fort Limhi," *Montana* 53 (Autumn 2003): 30–43; HOJ, May 4, 1858.

18. HOJ, Apr. 14, 1858.

19. SDoc67, 2–3.

20. *Genteel*, 49–50.

21. Brigham Young to Governor Cumming, Apr. 16, 1858, OC.

22. LPCB 5:143.

23. LPCB 5:135.

24. SDoc67, 4–6.

25. SDoc67, 5–6. Stenographers' copies of the speeches of Cumming and the others are found in FALG.

26. See Alfred Cumming, address, Apr. 25, 1858, FALG; Gilbert Clements, address, Apr. 25, 1858, FALG.

27. See transcript of Cumming's responses, Apr. 25, 1858, FALG.

28. HOJ, Apr. 25, 1858; Woodruff, Apr. 25, 1858.

29. Brigham Young, address, Apr. 25, 1858, FALG.

30. SDoc67, 6.

31. Cumming address, Apr. 25, 1858.

32. HOJ, Apr. 25, 1858; Woodruff, Apr. 25, 1858; Young address, Apr. 25, 1858.

33. SDoc67, 5.

34. SDoc67, 7.

35. HOJ, May 4–5, 1858; LPCB 4:143; *Genteel*, 42.

36. Jacob Forney to C. E. Mix, May 21, 1858, Jacob Forney Letterbook II, confirms that "Governor Cuming visited the Indian farm during his trip through the Mormon settlements." HOJ, May 5, 1858.

37. Thomas L. Kane, diary, 1858, 16–20, BYU. Will Bagley, *Blood of the Prophets: Brigham Young and the Massacre at Mountain Meadows* (Norman: University of Oklahoma Press, 2002), 197–98, dates the interview in the Kane journal to earlier in the year as Kane traveled north to Salt Lake from California. We date it to May 5, 1858, however, because it mentions Armstrong by name and because details on the Saints' move south in the following entry, dated the "6th," parallel details in the HOJ for May 6. For example, on page 28 of the diary, Kane describes how many wagons he saw, "800 in one day's ride!" HOJ notes, "Kane and Gov. Cumming arrived in G.S.L. City having met 800 wagons between Springville and that City."

38. Thomas L. Kane, diaries, 1858, microfilm, CHL; Kane diary, 1858, 25–28, BYU; Albert L. Zobell Jr., *Sentinel in the East: A Biography of Thomas L. Kane* (Salt Lake City: Nicholas G. Morgan Sr., 1965), 151–53; Gove, 159; Grow, 172.

Chapter 14

1. LPCB 4:144.
2. BYOJ, May 13, 1858; HOJ, May 13, 1858.
3. Alfred Cumming to Brigham Young, May 12, 1858, IC.
4. *Genteel*, 54, 62; Peterson, 34.
5. Furniss, 193.
6. SDoc1, 10.
7. SDoc1, 203–4.
8. Furniss, 190, 194.
9. Gove, 159-60, 164.
10. A. S. Johnston to A. Cumming, May 21, 1858, IC.
11. A. Cumming to Edward Hunter, May 23, 1858, IC.
12. *Genteel*, 59–60, 63, 69.
13. Gove, 167–68, 170; SDoc1, 208.
14. BYOJ, May 25, 1858; Furniss, 172.
15. BYOJ, May 26–June 5, 1858.
16. BYOJ, June 5, 1858.
17. Woodruff, June 7–8, 1858.
18. BYOJ, June 7, 1858; Bigler, 260–65.
19. George D. Grant, et al., to Brigham Young, June 6, 1858, IC.
20. James Ferguson to Daniel H. Wells, June 6, 1858, IC.
21. Ferguson to Wells, June 6, 1858.
22. LPCB 4:224.
23. SDoc1, 210; LPCB 4:234; *Genteel*, xv, 67, 73, 76.
24. *Genteel*, 76–78.
25. *Genteel*, 78–79.
26. BYOJ, June 9, 1858; LPCB 4:234.
27. SDoc1, 211–12.
28. Woodruff, June 11, 1858.
29. SDoc1, 213.
30. Stewart Van Vliet to Brigham Young, Apr. 25, 1858, IC.
31. Arrington, 273.
32. SDoc1, 213–14. See also BYOJ, June 12, 1858; Arrington, 274; H&H, 23.
33. Woodruff, June 13, 17, 1858; BYOJ, June 17, 20, 1858.
34. Woodruff, June 11, 1858.
35. Furniss, vii.
36. *NYDT*, July 3, 1858.
37. Gove, 175.

Chapter 15

1. HOJ, June 19, 1858; Woodruff, June 19, 1858; J. D. Lee to Brigham Young, June 19, 1858, IC.

2. Woodruff, June 19, 1858; BYOJ, June 19, 1858; Brigham Young to A. Cumming, June 19, 1858, YOF; HOJ, June 19, 1858.

3. Woodruff, June 19, 1858; BYOJ, June 19, 1858; HOJ, June 19, 1858; Jenson2 1:127.

4. Little, 57; *Genteel*, 76; HOJ, June 21, 1858.

5. Jacob Forney to Chas. E. Mix, June 22, 1858, JFLB; SDoc42, 44–45; Jacob Forney to C. E. Mix, Aug. 6, 1858, JFLB.

6. SDoc42, 42–44, 46; Forney to Mix, June 22, 1858, JFLB.

7. Forney to Mix, June 22, 1858; Forney to Mix, Aug. 6, 1858.

8. "Report of J Hamblin," June 22, 1858, JFLB.

9. "Interesting from Utah," *NYT*, July 8, 1858; HDoc71, 203.

10. "Interesting from Utah."

11. Forney to Mix, Aug. 6, 1858; Forney to Mix, June 22, 1858.

12. Forney to Mix, June 22, 1858.

13. LPCB 4:262–63.

14. HOJ, June 24, 1858; BYOJ, June [24], 1858; DJ, June 15, 1858.

15. LPCB 4:234; DJ, Apr. 7, June 15, 1858.

16. DJ, Apr. 7, June 15, 1858; JHM, Apr. 13–July 23, 1858; HOJ, June 24, 1858; Lovinia Dame to William H. Dame, May 30, 1858, William H. Dame Collection, BYU.

17. Jacob Hamblin to Brigham Young, Feb. 14, 1858, IC; MacKinnon1, 425–26; Compton1, 117–22; BYOJ, June [24], 1858; Joseph C. Ives, *Report upon the Colorado River of the West, Explored in 1857 and 1858 by Lieutenant Joseph C. Ives, Corps of Topographical Engineers, Under the Direction of the Office of Explorations and Surveys, A. A. Humphreys, Captain Topographical Engineers, in Charge* (Washington, DC: Government Printing Office, 1861).

18. BYOJ, June [24], 1858.

19. Woodruff, June 24, 1858.

20. JDL2-BT, bk. 1, 113–24.

21. Forney to Mix, Aug. 6, 1858; Forney to Mix, June 22, 1858.

22. Gove, 177, 184, 371; Fitz-John Porter, journal, July 2, 1858, Fitz-John Porter Papers, LOC, photocopy at CHL; HOJ, June 26, 1858; Carleton, 11–15.

23. Marcy, 264.

24. *MJRY*, 115; Leo J. Muir, comp., *The Life Story of George William McCune* (Los Angeles: Westernlore Press, 1959), 65; Porter journal, July 2, 1858.

25. Porter journal, July 2, 1858.

26. *MJRY*, 115; LPCB 4:271.

27. *Genteel*, 81, 176, 371; A. S. Johnston to A. Cumming, June 19, 1858, microfilm, CP.

28. James Ferguson to Brigham Young, June 26, 1858, IC.

29. *Genteel*, 83–84; Gove, 185.

30. Porter journal, July 2, 9, 1858.

Chapter 16

1. Gove, 176–79; George P. Hammond, ed., *Campaigns in the West, 1856–1861: The Journal and Letters of Colonel John Van Deusen Du Bois* (Tucson: Arizona Pioneers Historical Society, 1949), 69–70; *Genteel*, 76, 81.

2. *Campaigns in the West*, 69–70, 117–18; "Special Correspondence of the Herald," *NYH*, July 30, 1858, in *Utah Expedition*, 371.

3. Elizabeth Cumming to Anne Smith, July 9, 1858, CP, CHL; *Genteel*, 77–78, 82–84.

4. *Campaigns in the West*, 69–70, 117–18; *Genteel*, 84.

5. *Genteel*, 83.

6. Isaiah Moses Coombs, journal, July 3, 1858, Isaiah Coombs Collection, CHL; Gove, 178, 371; Andrew J. Allen, journal, July 1–6, 1858, CHL.

7. HOJ, July 6, 1858.

8. HOJ, July 7–9, 1858.

9. Allen, journal, July 18, Aug. 7, 1858; *Campaigns in the West*, 72; "The Utah Expedition: Its Causes and Consequences," *Atlantic Monthly* 3 (May 1859): 570.

10. JHM, July 2, 1858; *MC* 1:174.

11. *MC* 1:171, 173; Shelton, June 26–30, July 1–3, 1858; ICHJ, July 4, 1858; Fish, 65.

12. *MC* 1:174; Shelton, July 6, 1858.

13. *MC* 1:174–76.

14. JHM, July 19, 1858; Company E, 2nd Battalion 10th Regiment, journal, July 10, 1858, Territorial Militia Records, series 2210, USARS.

15. Sixty-Third Quorum of Seventy, minute book, June 6, July 11, 1858, microfilm, Seventies Quorum Records, 1844–1975, CHL; CSM, June 6, 1858.

16. Cedar City Ward, Relief Society minute book, June 10, 1858, CHL; *MatMM*, 257–59.

17. HBM, July 11, 1858; *MC* 1:176.

18. Marcy Barney to B. Young, Oct. 3, 1858, Files relating to divorce and family difficulties, Ecclesiastical files, YOF; R. Wilson Glenn to George A. Smith, Aug. 19, 1858, GASP.

19. HOJ, July 9, 11–15, 1858.

Chapter 17

1. HOJ, July 15–22, 1858; George A. Smith to Robert L. Campbell, July 19, 1858, in HOCHD; JHM, July 22, 1858; Lyman2, 272.

2. George A. Smith to Robert L. Campbell, July 24, 27, Aug. 2–6, 1858, HOCHD; HOJ, Aug. 6, 1858; ICHJ, July 25, 1858; HBM, July 21–24, 1858.

3. Smith to Campbell, July 27, 1858.

4. Lyman2, 272–73; ICHJ, July 25, 1858.

5. Smith to Campbell, July 27, Aug. 2–6, 1858; ICHJ, July 26, 28, 30–31, Aug. 1–2, 1858; Janet Burton Seegmiller, *A History of Iron County* (Salt Lake City: Utah State Historical Society, 1998), 49, 51, 53.

6. Smith to Campbell, Aug. 2–6, 1858; Samuel Newton Adair, autobiographical sketch, Sept. 15, 1919, in A. C. Chapman, comp., "Samuel Newton Adair: His Personal History," Jan. 2003, copy available at familysearch.org.

7. Adair, autobiographical sketch; *MatMM*, 256, 260–61.

8. Smith to Campbell, Aug. 2–6, 1858; ICHJ, Aug. 4, 1858; Shelton, Aug. 4, 1858.

9. Smith to Campbell, Aug. 2–6, 1858; "LC"; "LLC."

10. Shelton, Aug. 4, 1858; HBM, Aug. 5, 1858; ICHJ, Aug. 5, 1858; Smith to Campbell, Aug. 2–6, 1858.

11. *MC* 1:179; Shelton, Aug. 6–8, 23–25, 1858; Thomas G. Alexander, *Brigham Young, the Quorum of the Twelve, and the Latter-day Saint Investigation of the Mountain Meadows Massacre* (Logan: Utah State University Press, 2007).

12. Shelton, Aug. 6–9, 1858; *MC* 1:179; Smith to Campbell, Aug. 2–6, 1858.

13. George A. Smith and James McKnight, "The Emigrant and Indian War at Mountain Meadows," Aug. 6, 1858, in HOCHD; Smith to Campbell, Aug. 2–6, 1858. Juanita Brooks later described this document as "the first official report of the Mountain Meadows Massacre to Brigham Young." Brooks2, 165. The account, however, is not addressed to Young, nor do scribal notations on it confirm that it was ever sent to or received by him.

14. Smith and McKnight, "Emigrant and Indian War," Aug. 6, 1858.

15. Forney to Mix, June 22, Aug. 6, 1858, JFLB; Jacob Forney to Jacob Hamblin, August 4, 1858, JFLB; Little, 57.

16. Forney to Hamblin, August 4, 1858; SDoc42, 7.

17. LPCB 4:302, 316; Compton1, 128.

18. Jacob Forney to Charles E. Mix, Aug. 7, 1858, JFLB; SDoc42, 75.

19. SDoc42, 46–48.

20. JH, Sept. 10, 1858; SDoc42, 7.

21. Thales H. Haskell to Jacob Forney, Dec. 11, 1858, JFLB; *Report of the Commissioner of Indian Affairs* (Washington, DC: George W. Bowman, 1860), 371; SDoc42, 75, 79.

Chapter 18

1. George A. Smith to R[obert] L. C[ampbell], Aug. 2–6, 1858, HOCHD.

2. HOJ, Aug. 9, 1858; JHM, Aug. 10–12, 1858; "Minutes of an investigation held before Geo. A. Smith and Amasa Lyman, commencing Aug. 8, 1858," 1–2, manuscript, HOCHD.

3. Fish, 69.

4. "Minutes of an investigation," 1–2; William Leany, reminiscence, 1888, 21–22, CHL.

5. JHM, Aug. 10–12, 1858; HOJ, Aug. 9, 1858.

6. JHM, Aug. 10–12, 1858.

7. JHM, June 8, 1875.

8. "Minutes of an investigation," 2, 3; HOJ, Aug. 9, 1858.

9. JHM, Aug. 10–12, 1858.

10. "Minutes of an investigation." The summary of the meeting was also copied in PSHR, Aug. 13, 1858, 2nd sec., 43–44.

11. "Minutes of an investigation," 3; *AJ-DHM*, 52–53.

12. ICHJ, Aug. 10, 1858.

13. "Minutes of an investigation," 3–4; HOJ, Aug. 10–12, 1858.

14. HOJ, Aug. 12, 1858.

15. George A. Smith to Robert L. Campbell, Aug. 15, 1858, HOCHD.

16. JHM, Aug. 10–12, 1858.

17. HOJ, Aug. 12, 1858.

18. "Minutes of an investigation," 4.

19. "Minutes of an investigation," 4; Signed note clearing Dame of charges, Aug. 12, 1858, photocopy of manuscript, William Horne Dame, Papers, CHL; Brooks2, 169.

20. "Minutes of an investigation," 4; JHM, Aug. 10–12, 1858.

21. Signed note clearing Dame of charges, Aug. 12, 1858, photocopy of manuscript, WHDP; Brooks2, 169; Lyman2, 274.

22. *AJ-DHM*, 68; JNSJ, Sept. 8–9, 1857.

23. JHM, Aug. 15, 1858.

24. George A. Smith and James McKnight, "The Emigrant and Indian War at Mountain Meadows," Aug. 6, 1858, in HOCHD; George A. Smith to Brigham Young, Aug. 17, 1858, IC, copy in HOLC 1:885–91.

25. Smith and McKnight, "Emigrant and Indian War," Aug. 6, 1858.

26. Smith to Young, Aug. 17, 1858.

27. *MatMM*, 166–67, 175–78; Smith to Young, Aug. 17, 1858.

28. *MatMM*, 178–79; Smith and McKnight, "Emigrant and Indian War," Aug. 6, 1858; Smith to Young, Aug. 17, 1858.

29. JHM, Aug. 10–12, 1858; *MatMM*, 178–79.

30. ICHJ, Aug. 12, 1858.

31. Smith to Campbell, Aug. 15, 1858; HOJ, Aug. 17, 1858; *MC* 1:179.

32. Levi Savage Jr., journal, Aug. 26–28, 1858, CHL; HOJ, Aug. 17–26, 1858.

33. HOJ, Aug. 26, 27, 1858.

34. Smith and McKnight, "Emigrant and Indian War," Aug. 6, 1858.

35. HOJ, Aug. 26–31, 1858.

36. *MC* 1:179; Shelton, Aug. 23–25, 1858. Though Lee dates his journal to reflect that this trial took place on August 5–6 and that George A. Smith was present, Marion Shelton's journal and other contemporary sources establish that the investigation took place on August 24–25 after Smith returned north.

37. George K. Bowering, journal, 231, CHL.

38. *MC* 1:179.

39. Shelton, Aug. 25–Sept. 2, 1858.

40. Jacob Hamblin to George A. Smith, Aug. 29, 1858, GASP.

41. George A. Smith to Jacob Hamblin, Sept. 22, 1858, HOLC 1:559–60; Lyman2, 274.

Chapter 19

1. HOJ, Nov. 4, 1858.

2. Stout, 2:668, Nov. 4, 1858; HOJ, Nov. 4, 1858; BYOJ, Nov. 4, 1858, YOF; Editorial, *Circleville Herald* (Circleville, Ohio), Apr. 2, 1852.

3. JH, Nov. 4, 1858; BYOJ, Nov. 4, 1858.

4. HOLC 1:615; Stout, 2:668, Nov. 4, 1858.

5. Editorial, *Circleville Herald*, Apr. 2, 1852.

6. HOJ, Jan. 1, 1859; "Death of Mrs. Cradlebaugh," *Circleville Herald*, July 23, 1852.

7. BYOJ, Nov. 5 [6], 1858; HOLC 1:615; HOJ, Nov. 5, 6, 1858; Brigham H. Roberts, "History of the Mormon Church," *Americana (American Historical Magazine)* 8 (1913): 1116; *VT*, Nov. 6, 1858.

8. HOJ, Nov. 4, 1858.

9. *Charge of Hon. Chas. E. Sinclair, Judge of the Third Judicial District of the Territory of Utah; Delivered in Great Salt Lake City, Nov. 22nd, 1858* (Salt Lake City: n.p., 1858), 1–8; SDoc32, 21–44, 58–59; Stout, 2:668.

10. *Charge of Hon. Chas. E. Sinclair*, 1, 3, italics in original; SDoc32, 11–21.

11. SDoc32, 11–24, 58–59.

12. Stout, 2:669, 672.

13. "Affairs in Utah," *NYT*, Oct. 19, 1860.

14. HOLC 1:651–53.

15. "Letter from Great Salt Lake City," *SFDEB*, Mar. 17, 1859; John W. Phelps diary, Jan. 8, 1859, John W. Phelps Papers, CHL.

16. A. Cumming to Lewis Cass, Jan. 28, 1859, in Letterpress book 2:74–75, CP; "Letter from Provo City, U.T.," *SFDEB*, Apr. 19, 1859.

17. Alexander Wilson to Jacob Thompson, Mar. 4, 1859, Letters Received, Judiciary Accounts Utah, 1853–1900, RG 60, entry 58; SDoc42, 102.

18. Peter Boyce to J. Forney, Jan. 1, 1859, JFLB; ICHJ, Jan. 4, 1859; SDoc42, 52–53.

19. Two letters from Jacob Forney to James W. Denver, Jan. 28, 1859, JFLB; Jacob Forney to Jacob Hamblin, Jan. 28, 1859, JFLB; SDoc42, 42, 48–49, 51.

20. SDoc32, 21–24; Cumming to Cass, Jan. 28, 1859; "United States District Court, 2nd Judicial District," *DN*, Feb. 9, 1859.

21. Wilson to Thompson, Mar. 4, 1859.

22. SDoc32, 11–21.

23. SDoc1, 211–12.

24. F. J. Porter to Henry Heth, Mar. 9, 1859, James Buchanan file, Utah Appointment Papers, RG 60, entry 650, NARA; SDoc32, 6; "Letter from Provo City, U. T.," *SFDEB*, Apr. 12, 1859; H&H, 30–34.

25. SDoc32, 21–24; Stout, 2:689.

26. Stout, 2:688; SDoc32, 21–24.

27. "Letter from Salt Lake City," *SFDEB*, Mar. 24, 1859; Stout, 2:688; D. Robert Carter, *From Fort to Village: Provo, Utah, 1850–1854* (Provo City Corporation, 2008), 112.

28. Stout, 2:688.

29. Furniss, 215–16; "Letter from Provo City, U. T.," *SFDEB*, Apr. 12, 1859. Ironically, state militiamen accompanied Latter-day Saints to protect them when they sought redress for mob actions in Missouri in the 1830s, only to face local residents' outcry that soldiers near a courthouse stirred fear and were antithetical to civil justice. "The Mormon Difficulties" *New York Spectator*, Apr. 14, 1834.

30. John V. Long, "Judge Cradlebaugh's Charge to the Grand Jury," Mar. 8, 1859, manuscript, 1, Proceedings of Judge Cradlebaugh's court, FALG; J. V. Long, "Names of the Grand Jurors," Mar. 26, 1859, Proceedings of Judge Cradlebaugh's court, FALG; "Letter from Provo City, U. T.," *SFDEB*, Apr. 12, 1859; "Court Doings at Provo," *DN*, Apr. 6, 1859; Cradlebaugh, 53.

31. "Judge Cradlebaugh's Charge," 2–4.

32. Stout, 2:689.

33. "Judge Cradlebaugh's Charge," 2–4; James B. Allen, "The Unusual Jurisdiction of County Probate Courts in the Territory of Utah," *UHQ* 36 (Spring 1968): 133–34; Thomas G. Alexander, "Carpetbaggers, Reprobates, and Liars," *Historian* 70 (Summer 2008): 219.

34. "Judge Cradlebaugh's Charge," 4–5.

35. . Stout, 2:689.

36. "Judge Cradlebaugh's Charge," 4–12.

37. Stout, 2:689.

38. See William G. Hartley, "'Almost Too Intolerable a Burthen': The Winter Exodus from Missouri, 1838–39," *JMH* 18, no. 2 (1992): 40; "United States District Court," *DN*, Mar. 30, 1859.

39. "United States District Court," *DN*, Mar. 30, 1859.

40. Petition of the citizens of Provo to the mayor and city council, Mar. 10, 1859, manuscript copy, in HOCHD; "United States District Court," *DN*, Mar. 30, 1859; "More Trouble with the Mormons" and "Letter from Provo City, U. T.," *SFDEB*, Apr. 12, 1859, italics in original.

41. John V. Long, Report of court proceedings, second session, Mar. 8, 1859, 1–2, Proceedings of Judge Cradlebaugh's court, FALG; "District Court, 2nd Judicial District," *DN*, Mar. 16, 1859; "More Trouble with the Mormons"; Moorman, 109.

42. George Hampton Crosman to W. A. Gordon, Mar. 31, 1859, BL; "Army Supplies," *DN*, Dec. 29, 1858.

43. Long, Report of court proceedings, second session, Mar. 8, 1859, 1–3; "District Court, 2nd Judicial District," *DN*, Mar. 16, 1859.

44. Stout, 2:689.

45. Rob. L. Campbell to George A. Smith, Mar. 11, 1859, GASP.

46. Richard Lyman Bushman, *Joseph Smith: Rough Stone Rolling* (New York: Alfred A. Knopf, 2005), 425–27; Jeffrey N. Walker, "Habeas Corpus in Early Nineteenth-Century Mormonism," *BYU Studies* 52 (2013): 31–38.

47. Young to Smith, Mar. 10, 1859, GASP.

48. Brigham Young to George A. Smith, Mar. 15, 1859, GASP; LPCB 5:74.

Chapter 20

1. Stout, 2:689–90, Mar. 11, 1859; "Letter from Provo City, U. T.," *SFDEB*, Apr. 12, 1859; Will Bagley, ed., *The Whites Want Everything* (Norman, OK: Arthur H. Clark, 2019), 462–63.

2. B. K. Bullock to John Cradlebaugh, Mar. 11, 1859, in John Cradlebaugh Appointment Papers, RG 60, entry 350; "United States District Court," *DN*, Mar. 30, 1859; "Letter from Provo City," *SFDEB*, Apr. 12, 1859.

3. Stout, 2:689–90; Moorman, 111; HOLC 1:731–35.

4. John Cradlebaugh to the Mayor and City Council of Provo, Mar. 12, 1859, in Cradlebaugh Appointment Papers, RG 60, entry 350; "Letter from Provo City, U. T.," *SFDEB*, Apr. 12, 1859; "United States District Court"; Stout, 2:690.

5. "Letter from Provo City, U. T.," *SFDEB*, Apr. 12, 1859; "Letter from Provo City, U. T.," *SFDEB*, Apr. 19, 1859; T. W. Williams et al. to John Cradlebaugh, Mar. 14, 1859, in Cradlebaugh Appointment Papers, RG 60, entry 350.

6. HOJ, Apr. 18, 1859.

7. HOJ, Mar. 14–15, 1859; Stout, 2:690.

8. Stout, 2:690; SDoc42, 52–53.

9. John V. Long, "Judge Cradlebaugh's charge to the Grand Jury," Mar. 8, 1859, manuscript, 6, Proceedings of Judge Cradlebaugh's court, FALG.

10. Cradlebaugh, 42; SDoc42, 100–101.

11. CSM, Sept. 27, 1857.

12. SDoc42, 52–53; *MatMM*, 251–54.

13. SDoc42, 53, 100–101.

14. Cradlebaugh, 43–47; HOJ, Mar. 17, 18, 1859. For more on what came to be known as the Parrish-Potter murders, see Polly Aird, *Mormon Convert, Mormon Defector: A Scottish Immigrant in the American West, 1848-1861* (Norman, OK: Arthur H. Clark, 2009).

15. Cradlebaugh, 44–46.

16. "Court Doings at Provo," *DN*, Apr. 6, 1859; Cradlebaugh, 4; HOJ, Mar. 30, 1859.

17. Cradlebaugh, 45–53, 56–60.

18. Stout, 2:690; Cradlebaugh, 43–47.

19. Stout, 2:690–91; HOJ, Mar. 18, 1859.

20. Stout, 2:691.

21. Letterbook 2:86–89, CP; HOJ, Mar. 18, 1859; Moorman, 111; Stout, 2:691.

22. HOJ, Mar. 18, 1859.

23. John Cradlebaugh, Discharge of grand jury, Mar. 21, 1859, Proceedings of Judge Cradlebaugh's court, FALG; "Discharge of the Grand Jury," *DN*, Mar. 30, 1859; "Discharge of the Grand Jury," *VT*, Mar. 29, 1859; "More Trouble with the Mormons," *SFDEB*, Apr. 12, 1859.

24. "District Court, 2nd Judicial District," *DN*, Mar. 30, 1859; George Hampton Crosman to W. A. Gordon, Mar. 31, 1859, BL; SDoc32, 6–7.

25. Alexander Wilson to Jeremiah Black, Apr. 8, 1859, in John Cradlebaugh File, James Buchanan Administration, Utah Appointment Papers, RG 60, entry 350.

26. Letterbook 2:77–81, CP; SDoc32, 6; "Letter from Provo City, U. T.," *SFDEB*, Apr. 12, 1859.

27. A. S. Johnston to A. Cumming, Mar. 22, 1859, in Cradlebaugh Appointment Papers, RG 60, entry 350.

28. Wilford Woodruff, Historian's private journal, Mar. 21, 1859, CHL.

29. Davis Bitton, "The Cradlebaugh Court (1859)," in *Social Accommodation in Utah*, ed. Clark Knowlton (Salt Lake City: University of Utah, 1975), 81; Arrington, 276.

30. HOJ, Mar. 24, 27, 1859; JH, Mar. 24, 27, 1859; Arrington, 277.

31. "Protest of the Grand Jury," *DN*, Mar. 30, 1859; "Discharge of the Grand Jury," *DN*, Mar. 30, 1859. Cradlebaugh reportedly said he never received this protest. "Letter from Provo City, U. T.," *SFDEB*, Apr. 19, 1859.

32. "Memorial and Petition," *DN*, Mar. 30, 1859; HOJ, Mar. 25, 1859.

33. HOJ, Mar. 24–25, 1859; Letterbook 2:88, CP.

34. Letterbook 2:86–89, 91–92, 94–95, CP; F. J. Porter to A. Cumming, Mar. 30, 1859, in Correspondence: 1859, CP.

35. Letterbook 2:86–89, CP.

36. Letterbook 2:90–92, CP; "By Alfred Cumming, Governor, Utah Territory. A Proclamation," *DN*, Mar. 30, 1859; "Letter from Provo City, U. T.," *SFDEB*, Apr. 19, 1859; SDoc32, 7; HOJ, Mar. 28, 1859.

37. "Court Doings at Provo," *DN—Extra*, Apr. 2, 1859; "Court Doings at Provo," *DN*, Apr. 6, 1859; "Letter from Provo City, U. T.," *SFDEB*, Apr. 19, 1859.

38. SDoc32, 7.

39. "Court Doings at Provo," *DN—Extra*, Apr. 2, 1859; "Court Doings at Provo," *DN*, Apr. 6, 1859; "Letter from Provo City, U. T.," *SFDEB*, Apr. 19, 1859.

40. Woodruff, Historian's private journal, Apr. 2, 3, 1859.

41. Letterbook 2:86–89, 94–95, CP; Cradlebaugh, 43–67.

42. "The Court & the Army," *DN*, Apr. 6, 1859; "Letter from Provo City, U. T.," *SFDEB*, Apr. 19, 1859; Crosman to Gordon, Mar. 31, 1859; HOJ, Mar. 30, 1859.

Chapter 21

1. SDoc42, 53, 100–101; Forney1; "Visit."

2. Forney1; "Visit"; Rogers; Utah Territory, Great Salt Lake County, Great Salt Lake City, 13th ward, 1860 U.S. Census, population schedule, 18; HDoc29, 29; "That Butchery," *SLT*, Nov. 21, 1874; "Things at a Deadlock in Utah," *SFDEB*, June 24, 1859.

3. SDoc42, 75–78; Rogers; *MatMM*, 122–23; JFLB, 292.

4. SDoc42, 75–78; *MatMM*, 122–23.

5. SDoc42, 75–78.

6. SDoc42, 75–78, italics in original; Carleton, 17.

7. *MatMM*, 121-23.

8. SDoc42, 75–78, italics in original.

9. Rogers. James Lynch, a teamster at Camp Floyd in 1859, said he accompanied Forney and Rogers to southern Utah, where he helped retrieve the surviving children and bring them back to northern Utah. His accounts of the journey significantly contradict each other and other contemporary evidence, both Mormon and non-Mormon, making the veracity of his claims highly questionable. James Lynch, affidavit, [May 1859], microfilm, File 39.U, Letters Received, 1859, Office of the Adjutant General, RG 393, NARA; James Lynch, affidavit, July 27, 1859, enclosed in Samuel H. Montgomery to Alfred B. Greenwood, Aug. 17, 1859, microfilm, File M83, Utah Superintendency, 1849–80, Letters Received by the Office of Indian Affairs, 1824–81, U.S. Bureau of Indian Affairs, RG 48, NARA. After reading Lynch's first account reprinted in "The Mountain Meadows Massacre," *SFDEB*, May 31, 1859, Forney told Marion Shelton that "many of the statements made by Mr. Lynch were false." HOJ, June 25, 1859.

10. Forney1; "Visit"; Rogers.

11. Forney1; "Visit"; Rogers; SDoc42, 76.

12. SDoc42, 79; Rogers; Forney1; "Visit."

13. Rogers.

14. Forney1; "Visit"; Rogers.

15. SDoc42, 78; Rogers; Forney1; "Visit."

16. SDoc42, 76–77; Rogers; *MatMM*, 263, 267.

17. Shelton, Apr. 14, 1859; Forney1; "Visit"; Rogers.

18. SDoc42, 8; Rogers; SDoc42, 89.

19. Cedar City Ward, Relief Society, minute book, Nov. 12, Dec. 10, 1857, CHL; Sixty-Third Quorum of Seventy (Cedar City), minutes, Apr. 20, 1859, Seventies Quorum records, microfilm, CHL.

20. Rogers.

21. Norman R. Bowen, ed., *A Gentile Account of Life in Utah's Dixie, 1872–73: Elizabeth Kane's St. George Journal* (Salt Lake City: Tanner Trust Fund, University of Utah Library, 1995), 39, 39n52, 64; Henry Lunt to B. Young, Sept. 11, 1867, GIC; *MatMM*, 246.

22. Shelton, Apr. 15–16, 1859; Forney1; "Visit"; Rogers; Joseph Horne, journal, Apr. 16, 1859, CHL.

23. Shelton, Apr. 17, 21, 1859; Forney1; "Visit"; SDoc42, 57–58.

24. Shelton, Apr. 21, 1859; *MC* 1:210.

25. *MC* 1:210.

26. SDoc42, 100–101.

27. *MC* 1:210–11.

28. SDoc42, 14–15.

29. *MMM-CLP* 1:50–51, 59–61; Carleton, 3; Rogers.

30. Carleton, 3; *MatMM*, 3.

Chapter 22

1. Rogers.

2. Woodruff, Sept. 29, 1857.

3. Rogers.

4. SDoc42, 57; Forney1; "Visit"; SDoc42, 8, 48.

5. Rogers.

6. CSM, Apr. 24, 1859.

7. Rogers.

8. Rogers; SDoc42, 8; Carleton, 26; Gove, 407; Forney1; "Visit"; Kearny.

9. Forney1; "Visit"; SDoc42, 57; Kearny.

10. *MatMM*, 244–45, 248.

11. Kearny.

12. SDoc42, 57–58; Forney1; "Visit"; Kearny.

13. SDoc42, 8–9, italics in original.

14. SDoc42, 8–9; Forney1; "Visit."

15. SDoc42, 8.

16. "Return of Sup't Forney from the Mountain Meadows," *VT*, May 3, 1859; SDoc42, 8–9, 58; "Later from Salt Lake," *NYH*, June 16, 1859.

17. *MC* 1:208.

18. JHM, Apr. 29, May 2, 1859.

19. JHM, May 2, 1859.

20. William P. MacKinnon, "Loose in the Stacks: A Half-Century with the Utah War and Its Legacy," *Dialogue* 40, no. 1 (Spring 2007): 50; MacKinnon2, 645–46; Gordon E. Tolton, *Healy's West: The Life and Times of John J. Healy* (Missoula, MT: Mountain Press, 2014); "Captain John J. Healy, Western Pioneer, Dies," *San Francisco Call*, Sept. 19, 1908.

21. Shelton, May 6, 1859; *Journals*, 203; HOJ, May 11, 18, and 27, 1859.

22. ICHJ, May 1, 7–8, 1859.

23. JHM, May 6, 1859.

24. Rogers; HBM, Nov. 1, 1857; *AJ-DHM*, 49; *MatMM*, 220.

25. Rogers.

26. Rogers; PGM, Sept. 27, 1857.

27. Rogers.

28. SDoc42, 16–17. Carleton later reported slightly different numbers regarding Brewer's burials. Carleton, 28.

29. SDoc42, 16–17.

30. Phelps, June 10, 1859.

31. Cradlebaugh, 17–18; Rogers; SDoc42, 16–17; Carleton, 28.

32. *MMM-CLP* 1:59–61; SDoc42, 14–16; Rogers; Shelton, May 8, 1859.

33. Cradlebaugh, 17; Rogers; Carleton, 19.

34. Rogers; LLC; Frank A. Beckwith, *Indian Joe: In Person and in Background* (Delta, UT: DuWil Publishing, n.d.), 199–221.

35. Rogers; *MatMM*, 212–13, 257, 258.

36. Carleton, 19–20; Cradlebaugh, 18; Rogers.

37. HDoc71, 203.

Chapter 23

1. Joseph Horne, reminiscences and diary, May 8, 1859, CHL; Shelton, May 8, 1859.

2. Shelton, May 9, 1859; *Journals*, 201–3; *MC* 1:212.

3. *MatMM*, 220; Rogers.

4. Shelton, May 12, 1859; Rogers.

5. Rogers.

6. *Journals*, 203–9, May 11–15, 1859.

7. Cradlebaugh, 18–19; Carleton, 3, 28; Rogers.

8. Rogers; Shelton, May 23, 1859; Marc Ensign, "The Cache Valley Connection to Utah's Greatest Atrocity," Apr. 27, 2022, https://www.cachevalleydaily.com/news/archive/ 2022/04/27/commentary-the-cache-valley-connection-to-utahs-greatest-atrocity/ #.Yopp16jMLD4.

9. Rogers; Cradlebaugh, 20.

10. Cradlebaugh, 16–17, 20; Rogers.

11. Cradlebaugh, 18–20, 22.

12. *Journals*, 204–5, 207, 211; Cradlebaugh, 42; HDoc71, 203; *MMM-CLP* 1:38n27.

13. Shelton, May 18–19, 1859; Carleton, 27.

14. Carleton, 5–6, 9, 28.

15. See Forney2.

16. Carleton, 6–9.

17. Carleton, 24, 28.

18. Carleton, 11–12.

19. Carleton, 27.

20. Carleton, 12.

21. Carleton, 15–16.

22. Carleton, 3; J. H. Carleton to W. W. Mackall, June 24, 1859, in Letters and Telegrams Received, Department of the Pacific, RG 393, Part 1, Box 15, NARA.

23. Carleton, 28–29; Shelton, May 20, 1859.

24. SDoc42, 17; Carleton, 28–29; Novak2, 93–100, 102.

25. Carleton, 29; John W. Phelps to Dear General, June 12, 1859, John W. Phelps Letter Book, 1859–66, NYPL; Shannon A. Novak and Alanna L. Warner-Smith, "Assembling Heads and Circulating Tales," *Historical Archaeology* 54 (2020): 71–91.

26. Carleton, 29. Forensic anthropologist Shannon Novak reported her findings that in Carleton's burial, "no infant remains were identified . . . but three children were present." They were eight or nine, seven, and four years old. Novak2, 92.

27. Carleton, 28. When this grave was accidentally uncovered in 1999, bones from twenty-eight individuals were found in it. "The discrepancy could be explained

by miscounting, incomplete excavation and recovery, or erosion of the grave." Novak2, 87.

28. Carleton, 28–29; Shelton, May 20, 1859.

29. Carleton, 30–31.

30. Carleton to Mackall, June 24, 1859, in Letters and Telegrams Received, Department of the Pacific, RG 393.

Chapter 24

1. "Return of Sup't Forney from the Mountain Meadows," *VT*, May 3, 1859; SDoc42, 58.

2. SDoc42, 53–57.

3. SDoc42, 58–59, 66; 1880 U.S. Census, Salt Lake City Seventh Ward, Salt Lake County, Utah Territory, 18; Ann Eliza Worley entry, familysearch.org, accessed Oct. 13, 2013; Editorial, *VT*, May 24, 1859.

4. *Biographical Directory of the American Congress, 1774–1961* (Washington, DC: United States Government Printing Office, 1961), 973; SDoc42, 60, 67.

5. SDoc42, 59.

6. Rogers.

7. SDoc42, 10–12, 61–62.

8. SDoc42, 60.

9. SDoc42, 10–11.

10. SDoc42, 10–12.

11. SDoc42, 11–12.

12. Wolcott [John Walcott Phelps] to Dear Helen [JWP's sister], June 22, 1859, John W. Phelps Letter Book, 1859–66, NYPL; SDoc42, 65.

13. SDoc42, 60–61.

14. HOJ, June 25, 1859; Utah District Court, Salt Lake County, Probate Records, Book A, 126, June 27, 1859, film 425668, FHL.

15. SDoc42, 12, 65; Phelps, June 26, 1859.

16. Hugh Garner, ed., *A Mormon Rebel: The Life and Travels of Frederick Gardiner* (Salt Lake City: Tanner Trust Fund, University of Utah Library, 1993), 115; Henry Hobbs, journal, July 15, 1859, microfilm, CHL.

17. SDoc42, 62–65, 68–69; Editorial, *VT*, June 29, 1859; Audrey M. Godfrey, "Housewives, Hussies, and Heroines, or the Women of Johnston's Army," *UHQ* 54 (Spring 1986): 174.

18. Editorial, *VT*, June 29, 1859; SDoc42, 63, 65, 68.

19. SDoc42, 63–68.

20. "Departure," *DN*, June 29, 1859; Editorial, *VT*, June 29, 1859; "From Salt Lake City," *Missouri Republican* (St. Louis, MO), July 26, 1859; HOJ, June 28, 1859; Forney2, 371–72; Carleton, 32; Editorial, *VT*, July 6, 1859; Hester Elvira Nash, biographical sketch, 4, CHL.

21. SDoc42, 64–66.

22. S. B. Aden to Alfred Cumming, Jan. 27, 1859, CP; Sidney B. Aden entry, familysearch. org, accessed Apr. 19, 2015.

23. Aden to Cumming, Jan. 27, 1859.

24. S. B. Aden to Brigham Young, Mar. 14, 1859, IC.

25. LPCB 5:116.

26. "Information Wanted," *DN*, Apr. 27, 1859; "Information Wanted," *VT*, May 17, 24, June 1, 22, 1859.

27. "$1,000 Reward!," *VT*, July 6, 20, 27, August 3, 10, 1859.

28. "Lingering Hope," *SLT*, Dec. 24, 1874; "$1,000 Reward!"

29. S. B. Aden to Brigham Young, May 30, 1859, IC.

30. LPCB 5:185.

31. "Lingering Hope."

32. Horace Greeley, *An Overland Journey from New York to San Francisco in the Summer of 1859*, ed. Charles T. Duncan (New York: Alfred A. Knopf, 1964), 153, 158, 160.

33. Thomas McIntyre, journal, July 15, 1859, CHL; Ila May Fisher Maughan, *Joseph McKay-Martha Blair* (Salt Lake City: Utah Printing, 1967), 44.

34. SDoc42, 69–71.

35. SDoc42, 90.

36. SDoc42, 80, 90.

37. SDoc42, 85.

38. Carleton, 32; SDoc42, 90; William C. Mitchell, affidavit (first one on this date), Oct. 26, 1860, in Survivors Affidavits Collection, Territorial Papers, 1789–1873, RG 46, NARA. According to "Children," Mitchell was accompanied by "one Mrs. Railey of Arkansas."

39. "The 'Mountain Meadows' Children," *Washington, D.C. National Intelligencer*, Sept. 3, 1859; SDoc42, 90.

40. SDoc42, 90. Gardiner noted he too was "paid off" at Leavenworth. Garner, *Mormon Rebel*, 115.

41. "Extract from a Letter to This Office, Dated 'Mt Pleasant, Caroll Co., Ark., *September* 14, 1859,'" *Arkansas State Gazette* (Little Rock, AR), Sept. 24, 1859.

42. "Return of the Survivors of the Mountain Meadow Massacre," *Fayetteville Arkansian*, Oct. 7, 1859; SDoc42, 90.

43. "Children."

44. "Return of the Survivors of the Mountain Meadow Massacre."

45. SDoc42, 90, 98–99.

46. James D. Dunlap, affidavit, Oct. 26, 1860, in Survivors Affidavits Collection; William C. Mitchell, affidavit (second one on this date), Oct. 26, 1860, in Survivors Affidavits Collection.

47. Joseph B. Bains, affidavit, Oct. 23, 1860, in Survivors Affidavits Collection.

48. "Children."

49. "Return of the Survivors of the Mountain Meadow Massacre."

Chapter 25

1. Untitled Article, *NYDT*, May 10, 1859, 4.
2. "The Latest News, Received by Magnetic Telegraph," *NYDT*, May 14, 1859.
3. HOJ, May 9–10, 1859; Alfred Cumming to A. S. Johnston, May 9, 1859, CP; Alfred Cumming, proclamation, May 9, 1859, CP; "By the Governor," *DN*, May 11, 1859.
4. Brigham Young, affidavit, May 12, 1859, quoted in warrant issued by Elias Smith, May 12, 1859, in Robert Taylor Burton Papers, 1855–62, CHL.
5. Warrant issued by Elias Smith, May 12, 1859, and return of Robert T. Burton inscribed on the warrant, May 13, 1859, Burton Papers. A variant warrant is found in Salt Lake Probate Court, Warrant, May 1859, CHL.
6. BYOJ, May 22, 1859.
7. HOJ, May 25, 1859.
8. *JD*, 10:110.
9. John B. Floyd to A. S. Johnston, May 6, 1859, CP.
10. SDoc42, 16; Rogers.
11. ICHJ, May 8, 1859.
12. ICHJ, May 29, 1859; Phelps, June 3, 1859; *Journals*, 219.
13. *Journals*, 218–19.
14. ICHJ, May 29, 1859; *Journals*, 219.
15. ICHJ, June 3, 1859; *Journals*, 214. Lee marks their arrival as June 2.
16. *Journals*, 211–12.
17. Shelton, June 1–3, 1859.
18. Marion J. Shelton, affidavit, June 3, 1859, in HOCHD.
19. HOJ, June 1, 1859.
20. Jacob Hamblin, affidavit, June 16, 1869, HOCHD.
21. HOJ, June 18, 1859.
22. HOLC 2:127.
23. HOJ, July 5, 1859, transcription of Deseret Alphabet entry by LaJean Purcell Carruth.
24. HOJ, May 25, June 18, 1859; HOLC 2:127; *MC* 1:214.
25. Manti Ward General Minutes, July 13, 1859, CHL.
26. HOJ, July 27, 1859; Rogers. Virgin City was also called Pocketville.
27. *MC* 1:213. See also HOJ, July 31, 1859. Klingensmith's release as bishop became a turning point in his life. He later claimed he never attended another Latter-day Saint meeting after that day, though that was not true. TM, 694–95; PKS.
28. Henry Lunt, journal, Sept. 8, 14, 1857, typescript, CHL.
29. *TF*, 397.
30. Arrington, 279.
31. ICHJ, July 31, 1859.
32. Lunt journal, July 31, 1859. Brigham Young to Whom it may concern, Nov. 7, 1859, YOF.
33. Philip Klingensmith to George A. Smith, Aug. 1, 1859, GASP.
34. *MC* 1:214.

Chapter 26

1. Phelps, June 4, 10, 1859.
2. SDoc32, 2–4.
3. SDoc32, 9; SDoc42, 101–2; "Utah Affairs," *NYT*, June 4, 1859.
4. John Cradlebaugh to James Buchanan, June 3, 1859, in U.S. Dept. of Justice, UT appointment papers, Cradlebaugh folder, RG 60, entry 350, bx. 722; HOLC 1:817–18; "Things at a Deadlock in Utah," *San Francisco Evening Bulletin*, June 24, 1859.
5. Cradlebaugh to Buchanan, June 3, 1859.
6. "Things at a Deadlock in Utah"; HOLC 1:815–16.
7. Phelps, June 4, 1859.
8. "Letter from Utah," *Fayetteville Arkansian*, July 16, 1859.
9. Phelps, June 23, 1859; "Arrival," *DN*, June 22, 1859.
10. John Walcott Phelps to Dear Hickman, July 1–2, 1859, in John Walcott Phelps Letter Book, 1859–66.
11. A. B. Greenwood to Jacob Forney, July 2, 1859, in Letters Sent, 1824–81, Correspondence of the Office of Indian Affairs and Related Records, microfilm M21, RG 75, NARA; A. B. Greenwood to Jacob Forney, July 2, 1859, in Registers ("Abstracts") of Letters Sent, 1839–80, Record 61, p. 269, 11:453, NARA; SDoc42, 66.
12. A. B. Greenwood to Alexander Wilson, July 2, 1859, in Letters Sent, 1824–81.
13. HOJ, July 5, 1859; George D. Watt, notes for BYOJ, July 5, 1859, Watt papers, CR 100/665, box 15, fds 43&45, CHL. Transcriptions of both by LaJean Purcell Carruth.
14. John Cradlebaugh and Charles E. Sinclair to Buchanan, July 16, 1859, U.S. Department of Justice, Utah appointment papers, Cradlebaugh folder, RG 60, entry 350, box 722; SDoc32, 11–21.
15. Alexander Wilson to William H. Rodgers, Aug. 5, 1859, in Wilson to Black, Nov. 15, 1859, in U.S. Dept. of Justice, UT appointment papers, Cradlebaugh folder, RG 60, entry 350, box 722; SDoc32, 41; Wilson to Black, Nov. 15, 1859.
16. SDoc42, 74, 79.
17. Alexander Wilson to Peter K. Dotson, Aug. 18, 1859, in Wilson to Black, Nov. 15, 1859; SDoc32, 42.
18. Alexander Wilson to William H. Rodgers, Aug. 5, 1859, in Wilson to Black, Nov. 15, 1859; Wilson to Black, Nov. 15, 1859.
19. D. R. Eckels to Lewis Cass, Sept. 27, 1859, FALG.
20. Alfred Cumming to Lewis Cass, Feb. 2, 1860, in Letterpress Book 1:476–92 (reverse side) and 2:127–41, CP.
21. SDoc32, 29, 55, 58–59; Wilson to Black, Nov. 15, 1859.
22. SDoc42, 74, 79.
23. SDoc32, 29, 55, 58–59; Wilson to Black, Nov. 15, 1859.
24. Wilson to Black, Nov. 15, 1859.
25. Furniss, 210.
26. Wilson to Black, Nov. 15, 1859.
27. SDoc32, 55–56.

28. BYOJ, Aug. 22, 1859.

29. Wilson to Black, Nov. 15, 1859; BYOJ, Sept. 20, 1859.

30. Eckels to Cass, Sept. 27, 1859; "Federal Courts and Judges," *DN*, July 8, 1863; Albert Carrington to Jacob G. Bigler, Sept. 7, 1859, OC.

31. HOLC 1:837–38.

32. Cradlebaugh and Sinclair to Buchanan, July 16, 1859; SDoc32, 19–20; Furniss, 210.

33. "First Judicial District Court," *DN*, Sept. 7, 1859; Eckels to Cass, Sept. 27, 1859.

34. SDoc32, 61; Wilson to Black, Nov. 15, 1859.

35. Wilson to Black, Nov. 15, 1859.

36. SDoc42, 86–87.

37. SDoc42, 74.

38. HOLC 1:837.

39. Forney2, 372; Carleton, 32.

40. Horace Greeley, *An Overland Journey: From New York to San Francisco in the Summer of 1859* (New York: Alfred A. Knopf, 1964), 190.

41. Forney2, 372.

42. SDoc42, 98–99; Albert Watkins, ed., *Publications of the Nebraska State Historical Society*, vol. 20 (Lincoln: Nebraska State Historical Society, 1922), 339.

43. HOLC 1:845–46.

44. William Hooper to Brigham Young, Dec. 7, 1859, UDF.

45. SDoc42, 99; Carleton, 32.

46. "Children."

Chapter 27

1. *Charleston Courier*, quoted in *Richmond Enquirer*, Nov. 16, 1860; Doris Kearns Goodwin, *Team of Rivals* (New York: Simon & Schuster, 2005), 293.

2. Woodruff, Jan. 1, 13, 1861; E. B. Long, *The Civil War Day by Day* (Garden City, NY: Doubleday, 1971), 13; Henry Adams, *The Great Secession Winter of 1860–61 and Other Essays*, ed. George Hochfield (New York: Sagamore Press, 1958).

3. "Remarks," *DN*, Feb. 27, 1861; Woodruff, May 1, 1861.

4. Woodruff, Sept. 29, 1857, Jan. 1, 1861; "Remarks"; "Peace! Peace! When There Is No Peace!," *MS*, August 10, 1861. The first published version of the prophecy is in *The Pearl of Great Price* (Liverpool: F. D. Richards, 1851), 35. It is currently found in D&C 87. For early manuscript copies, see Robin Scott Jensen, Robert J. Woodford, and Steven C. Harper, eds., *Manuscript Revelation Books*, vol. 1 of The Revelations and Translations Series of *The Joseph Smith Papers*, ed. Dean C. Jessee, Ronald K. Esplin, and Richard Lyman Bushman, facsimile ed. (Salt Lake City: Church Historian's Press, 2009), 291, 381–83, 477–79.

5. "The Fulfilment of Prophecy," *MS* 24, no. 34 (Aug. 23, 1862): 529–33.

6. John Gary Maxwell, *The Civil War Years in Utah* (Norman: University of Oklahoma Press, 2016), 19, 28; James L. Morrison Jr., ed., *The Memoirs of Henry Heth* (Westport, CT: Greenwood Press, 1974), 148–49.

7. Maxwell, *Civil War Years in Utah,* 19; Gove, 404; Morrison, *Memoirs of Henry Heth,* 148–49.

8. George W. Cullum, *Biographical Register of the Officers and Graduates of the U. S. Military Academy at West Point, N. Y.* (Boston: Houghton, Mifflin, 1891), 1:368; Maxwell, *Civil War Years in Utah,* 132; Charles P. Roland, *Albert Sidney Johnston* (Austin: University of Texas Press, 1964), 221–22, 238–49.

9. Maxwell, *Civil War Years in Utah,* 63–64.

10. "Remarks," *DN,* June 26, 1861; ICHJ, Jan. 1862; "The Progress of Events," *DN,* May 22, 1861.

11. Woodruff, May 15, 1861; Furniss, 230; Juanita Brooks, *The Mountain Meadows Massacre* (Norman: University of Oklahoma Press, 1950), 182.

12. Woodruff, May 15–22, 24–25, 1861; *CD* 3:1822–23. In another contemporaneous account, Calvin Pendleton wrote William Dame that he traveled from Parowan through the southern settlements with Young's party. Pendleton wrote nothing about the destruction of the monument. Calvin [C. Pendleton] to William H. Dame, June 5, 1861, Dame-McBride family papers, UofU.

13. *AJ-DHM,* 19-22; Woodruff, May 25, 1861; "The Mountain Meadow Massacre," *Hutchings' California Magazine,* Feb. 1860, 347.

14. Woodruff, May 25, 1861; Carleton, 28–29; HOJ, July 18, 1860.

15. Woodruff, Sept. 29, 1857.

16. "Brigham Young: A Long Talk with the Prophet," *NYT,* May 20, 1877.

17. Woodruff, May 25, 1861; Brooks, *Mountain Meadows Massacre,* 183n16.

18. "Letter from Salt Lake," *Stockton Daily Independent,* Aug. 1, 1861; *In Memoriam: Edwin R. Purple* (New York: Privately Printed, 1881), 6–7. Though Purple did not give the exact date he visited the site, he was clearly traveling behind Young—his mail company arrived in Salt Lake eight days after Young's party returned there. He led his train out of Los Angeles on May 8, 1861, and reached Salt Lake on June 16.

19. *MC* 1:313–14.

20. Woodruff, May 25 to June 8, 1861.

21. LPCB 5:800; *CD* 3:1823.

22. Maxwell, *Civil War Years in Utah,* 70; Moorman, 276.

23. Philip Ashley Fanning, *Mark Twain and Orion Clemens* (Tuscaloosa: University of Alabama Press, 2003), 53; U.S. Statutes at Large, 1863, v. 12, 209–14.

24. Orion Clemens to Mollie Clemens, September 8 and 9, 1861, in "Supplement A," Harriet Elinor Smith and Edgar Marquess Branch, eds., *Roughing It* (Berkeley: University of California Press, 1993), 769–71; Fanning, *Mark Twain and Orion Clemens,* 54–55, 57; Jerome Loving, *Mark Twain* (Berkeley: University of California Press, 2010), xvii.

25. Maxwell, *Civil War Years in Utah,* 78.

26. Franklin R. Rogers, ed., *The Pattern for Mark Twain's* Roughing It (Berkeley: University of California Press, 1961), 47–48; Fanning, *Mark Twain and Orion Clemens,* 52–53.

27. BYOJ, Aug. 7, 1861, CHL.

28. Twain, *Roughing It*, 92–93.

29. Fitz-Hugh Ludlow, *Heart of the Continent* (New York: Hurd and Houghton, 1870), 315–17; Twain, *Roughing It*, 99.

30. Rogers, *The Pattern for Mark Twain's* Roughing It, 48; Twain, *Roughing It*, 116.

31. Twain, *Roughing It*, 116–17.

32. Richard F. Burton, *The City of the Saints* (New York: Harper, 1862), 339–40.

33. Jacob Hamblin to George A. Smith, Feb. 2, 1862, GASP; New Harmony Ward, Cedar City Utah West Stake, general minutes, Dec. 29, 1861, Jan. 1, 1862, CHL; *MC* 2:4–7; Angus M. Woodbury, "A History of Southern Utah and Its National Parks," *UHQ* 12, nos. 3-4 (July-Oct. 1944): 151; Brooks3, 101–3; James G. Bleak, Annals of the Southern Utah Mission, Dec. 25, 1861, Jan.–Feb. 1862, 113–14, 123a–123c, CHL.

34. Todd Compton, "The Big Washout: The 1862 Flood in Santa Clara," *UHQ* 77 (Spring 2009): 111, 113–15.

35. "Record of the Harmony Branch"; *MC* 2:6.

36. Brooks1, 271.

37. *MJRY*, 119; Compton, "The Big Washout," 118.

38. *MatMM*, 254; New Harmony Ward, general minutes, Jan. 4, 13, 17, 18, 31, and Feb. 6, 1862, 3, 5–8; *MC* 2:5–7.

39. *MC* 2:358; L. Douglas Smoot, "'Was It for Sins That We Have Done This': Two Grave Marker Poems by John D. Lee," *Mormon Historical Studies* 7 (Spring/Fall 2006): 103–12.

Chapter 28

1. Henry Lunt to George A. Smith, Mar. 5, 1862, and William S. Warren to George A. Smith, Mar. 12, 1862, GASP; Megan Kate Nelson, *The Three-Cornered War* (New York: Scribner, 2020), 124-35; Andrew Edward Masich, *The Civil War in Arizona* (Norman: University of Oklahoma Press, 2006), 38-39.

2. Nelson, *Three-Cornered War*, 188, 192, 198, 201-3, 205-13, 232; L. R. Bailey, *The Long Walk* (Los Angeles: Westernlore Press, 1964); Thom Hatch, *The Blue, the Gray, & the Red* (Mechanicsburg, PA: Stackpole Books, 2003), 117–37; Aurora Hunt, *Major General James Henry Carleton, 1814–1873* (Glendale, CA: Arthur H. Clark, 1958), 217, 273–93.

3. George P. Sanger, ed., *The Statutes at Large, Treaties, and Proclamations, of the United States of America* (Boston: Little, Brown, 1863), 12:501–2; *Journal of the Senate of the United States of America, being the Second Session of the Thirty-Seventh Congress* (Washington, DC: Government Printing Office, 1861), 748; Reeve, 164.

4. LPCB 6:336.

5. W. H. Hooper and George Q. Cannon to Brigham Young, June 24, 1862, and W. H. Hooper and George Q. Cannon to Brigham Young, July 13, 1862, UDF.

6. John M. Bernhisel to Brigham Young, July 11, 1862, UDF.

7. *The War of the Rebellion: A Compilation of the Official Records of the Union and Confederate Armies*, series 1, vol. 50, part 2 (Washington, DC: Government Printing Office, 1897), 5–6, 133; Kenneth L. Alford, "'It Was Not My Intention to Take Any Prisoners': Contemporary Views of the 1863 Massacre at Bear River," in *Proceedings of the South Carolina Historical Association* (Charleston: South Carolina Historical Association, 2019), 21; Charles E. Mix, Sept. 19, 1862, in Annual Report of the Commissioner of Indian Affairs (Washington, DC: U.S. Government, 1862), 215.

8. *War of the Rebellion*, 119; Kenneth L. Alford, "Camp Douglas: Keeping a Watchful Eye on Salt Lake and the Saints," in *Salt Lake City: The Place Which God Prepared*, ed. Scott C. Esplin and Kenneth L. Alford (Provo, UT: Religious Studies Center, Brigham Young University, 2011), 179-202; Alford, "Contemporary Views," 19; "Affairs in Utah," *NYT*, Nov. 15, 1862; *CD* 4:2076; Stephen A. Douglas, *Remarks of the Hon. Stephen A. Douglas, on Kansas, Utah, and the Dred Scott Decision, Delivered at Springfield, Illinois, June 12, 1857* (Chicago: Daily Times Book and Job Office, 1857), 11–15.

9. Alford, "Contemporary Views," 19–20, 24–29, 34.

10. C. B. Waite to Edward Bates, Jan. 28, 1863, Utah Appointment Papers, Abraham Lincoln Administration, RG 60, box 723.

11. There was no law requiring the federal treasury to pick up the tab, as shown by Waite to Bates, Jan. 28, 1863.

12. See HOLC 1:689–95.

13. Waite to Bates, Jan. 28, 1863.

14. HOJ, June 25, 1863.

15. Brigham Young, speech, Mar. 3, 1863, reported by George D. Watt, Reports of Speeches, 1845–85, CHL; HOJ, Mar. 4, 1863; Francis M. Long, affidavit, Mar. 5, 1863, enclosed in Thomas J. Drake and Charles B. Waite to Abraham Lincoln, Mar. 6, 1863, Abraham Lincoln Papers, LOC.

16. Drake and Waite to Lincoln, Mar. 6, 1863.

17. Stephen S. Harding to William H. Steward, Mar. 11, 1863, Lincoln Papers.

18. Cong. Globe, 37th Cong., 3rd Sess. 816 (1863); Cong. Globe Appendix, 37th Cong., 3rd Sess. 119–25 (1863); J. F. Kinney to Brigham Young, Mar. 23, 1864, UDF.

19. Cradlebaugh, 26–27.

20. *JD* 10:109–10; "Federal Courts and Judges," *DN*, July 8, 1863. The pamphlet with Young's name on it is in the CHL.

21. William Nelson and Sumner Howard to Alphonso Taft, Sept. 23, 1876, MMML.

22. Cradlebaugh, 20.

23. John M. Bernhisel to Brigham Young, Apr. 25, 1862, UDF.

24. Brigham Young to John M. Bernhisel, June 26, 1862, draft, and Brigham Young to John M. Bernhisel, Aug. 29, 1862, UDF.

25. SDoc42, 86, 88, 96; Carleton, 19; Rogers.

26. On Young's trip, see David John, journal, May 21, 1862 [Apr. 21, 1863]–May 19, [1863], in David John, diary, June 19–21, 1889, BYU; Alonzo H. Raleigh, diary, Apr. 19–May 19, 1863, CHL; L[yman] O. Littlefield, letters to editor, Apr. 22–May [19],

1863, in "Progress of President Young and Company," *DN*, Apr. 29, May 6, 13, 20, 27, 1863.

27. John journal, May 6, 186[3], in diary, June 19–21, 1889.

28. HOHC, 11:196, May 16, 1843; Revelation to Joseph Smith, July 12, 1843, Revelations Collection, CHL (current D&C 132:19, 26, 39). Richard F. Burton, *The City of the Saints* (New York: Harper and Brothers, 1862), 426, wrote of the Saints, "Their two mortal sins are: 1. Adultery; 2. Shedding innocent blood."

29. John journal, May 6, 186[3], in diary, June 19–21, 1889; TM 3336.

30. William M. Cradlebaugh, "William M. Cradlebaugh—Nevada Biography—1883," in *Nevada Historical Society Papers, 1913–1916*, vol. 1 (Carson City: State Printing Office, 1917), 175.

31. George F. Price to M. G. Lewis, May 25, 1864, in *DUV*, June 8, 1864; George F. Price, *Across the Continent with the Fifth Cavalry* (1883; repr., New York: Antiquarian Press, 1959), 442.

32. Lorenzo Brown, diary, July 1, 1864, typescript, 129–30, CHL.

33. "Worse Than Sacrilege," *DUV*, Dec. 24, 1864.

Chapter 29

1. Richard F. Burton, *The City of the Saints* (New York: Harper and Brothers, 1862), 239.

2. D&C 121:43.

3. LPCB 7:569.

4. Brooks1, 277.

5. John D. Lee to Brigham Young, Nov. 11, 1863, GIC.

6. David John, journal, May 6, 186[3], in David John, diary, June 19–21, 1889, BYU, microfilm copy available at CHL.

7. Endowment House sealings, living couples, vol. D (1853–73), July 18, 1863, June 10, 1865, CHL. Lee was sealed to two wives in 1863 but had already been married to them for several years.

8. James G. Bleak, Annals of the Southern Utah Mission, ca. 1898–1907, 287, CHL; J. F. Kinney to Brigham Young, Feb. 27, 1864, UDF; "Death Was Sudden," *SLH*, Sept. 29, 1900; "From South Utah, Silver Regions," *DUV*, Nov. 1, 1865.

9. John S. Goff, *The Supreme Court Justices 1863–1912*, vol. 1 of Arizona Territorial Officials (Cave Creek, AZ: Black Mountain Press, 1975), 52–53.

10. James Dwyer to John W. Young, Dec. 27, 1865, GIC; HOJ, Jan. 28, 1864.

11. James Dwyer to "Bro Cannon," Feb. 16, 1866, GIC.

12. James Dwyer to "Bro Cannon," Feb. 26, 1866, GIC.

13. James Dwyer to "Bro Cannon," Mar. 5, 1866, GIC.

14. John Titus to James Speed, Mar. 27, 1866, Utah Appointment Papers, Andrew Johnson Administration, RG 60.

15. Terryl L. Givens, *The Viper on the Hearth* (New York: Oxford University Press, 1997); Gary L. Bunker and Davis Bitton, *The Mormon Graphic Image, 1834–1914* (Salt Lake City: University of Utah Press, 1983); LPCB 8:193, 196.

16. Donna L. Dickerson, *The Reconstruction Era* (Westport, CT: Greenwood Press, 2003), 279–90.

17. "Conversation between Col Potter, Capt Grimes and Prest Young on establishment of liquor saloons," May 8, 1866, FALG; George A. Smith to W. H. Hooper, May 7–8, 1866, HOLC 2:533; "Mountain Meadows Massacre," *SLT*, Oct. 18, 1872.

18. "Remarks," *DN*, Jan. 9, 1867; Woodruff, Dec. 23, 1866.

19. John Alton Peterson, *Utah's Black Hawk War* (Salt Lake City: University of Utah Press, 1998); Sue Jensen Weeks, *How Desolate Our Home Bereft of Thee* (Melbourne, Australia: Clouds of Magellan, 2014); "Circleville Massacre Memorial Dedication," *UHQ* 84 (Summer 2016): 262–68.

20. "Mountain Meadow Massacre," *DUV*, July 27, 1866.

21. *MC* 2:18–19. In a public meeting in September, Snow "strongly vindicated the rights of the Red men." *MC* 2:28.

22. *MC* 2:20–21; Penrose, 67.

23. G. Spencer to E. Snow, Mar. 26, 1867, GIC; *MatMM*, 262.

24. Erastus Snow to B. Young, June 24, 1867, LCLO.

25. LPCB 10:331.

26. Davis Bitton, "'I'd Rather Have Some Roasting Ears': The Peregrinations of George Armstrong Hicks," *UHQ* 68 (Summer 2000): 214.

27. George A. Hicks to Brigham Young, Oct. 15, 1867, GIC.

28. *MC* 2:75–76, 87–89.

29. TM, 3750–52.

30. Kenneth J. Hagan and Ian J. Bickerton, *Unintended Consequences* (London: Reaktion Books, 2007); Marcus Schulzke, "The Unintended Consequences of War: Self-Defense and Violence against Civilians in Ground Combat Operations," *International Studies Perspectives* 18 (Nov. 2017): 391–408; MacKinnon2, 607–8; William P. MacKinnon, "'Lonely Bones': Leadership and Utah War Violence," *JMH* 33 (Spring 2007): 121–25.

31. *MC* 2:100–102.

32. George A. Hicks to Brigham Young, Dec. 4, 1868 (finished Jan. 21, 1869), GIC; Austin E. Fife, "A Ballad of the Mountain Meadows Massacre," *Western Folklore* 12, no. 4 (Oct. 1953): 229–41.

33. Clerical notations on Hicks to Young, Dec. 4, 1868.

34. LPCB 11:362–63.

35. *MC* 2:122–23.

36. Joseph Fish, autobiography, [ca. 1917–23], 95–96, typescript, Joseph Fish Collection, CHL; Iron Military District, record book, [ca. 1860–77], Utah Territorial Militia Records Series 2210, USARS.

37. *MC* 2:106–9.

38. "The Celebration Yesterday," *DEN*, May 11, 1869; David Walker, *Railroading Religion* (Chapel Hill: University of North Carolina Press, 2019), 288.

39. HOLC 2:941–49; JH, Nov. 25, 1869; "Mountain Meadow Massacre," *DN*, Dec. 1, 1869.

40. On the effect of the railroad, see Walker, *Railroading Religion*. In the press, as well as federal reports, Lee was mentioned often as a leader in the massacre. See "The Mountain Meadows Massacre—A Tale of Horror," *SFDEB*, Apr. 23, 1859; "Things at a Deadlock in Utah," *SFDEB*, June 24, 1859; "Revelation of Affairs in Mormondom," *SFDEB*, Aug. 25, 1859; Rogers; "The Mountain Meadow Massacre," *DUV*, July 28, 1866; HDoc71, 203; Carleton, 19; SDoc42, 86, 88; Cradlebaugh, 19–21.

41. *MC* 2:134.

42. Lee's biographer wrote that Lee "did not act upon the advice" because "his farms [were] so prosperous and his plans so promising." Brooks1, 288.

Chapter 30

1. Richard E. Turley Jr. and Eric C. Olson, "Fame Meets Infamy: The Powell Survey and Mountain Meadows Participants, 1870–1873," *UHQ* 81 (Winter 2013): 6; LPCB 12:341–42; John D. Lee to Emma B. Lee, Dec. 9, 1876, HM 31214, JDLC.

2. *MC* 2:136; Reilly, 14.

3. *MC* 2:138.

4. Worster, 210, 216–17; Little, 96; Compton1, 294–327.

5. *MC* 2:140–42.

6. Erastus Snow to B. Young, June 24, 1867, LCLO; Penrose, 67–68; LPCB 10:331; "Remarks," *DN*, Jan. 9, 1867; *CD* 4:2391.

7. Penrose, 67–68; *MC* 2:135.

8. John R. Young to Susa Y. Gates, June 1, 1927, John Ray Young Scrapbook, 1928–30, 109–10, CHL; John R. Young to W. S. Erekson, Feb. 1928, CM. John R. Young, writing many decades after the fact in 1927 and 1928, placed this event in 1865, a year in which Young did in fact visit southern Utah. The totality of the evidence, however, including Nephi Johnson's testimony, suggests the event occurred in 1870. In an 1877 interview, Young said of the massacre, "I never knew the real facts of this affair until within the last few years." "BY."

9. *AJ-DHM*, 328–31; "Local and Other Matters," *DEN*, Sept. 24, 1870; LPCB 12:396.

10. Woodruff, Oct. 8, 1870.

11. Joseph F. Smith, journal, Oct. 8, 1870, CHL. See also Andrew Jenson, "Lee, John D.," undated note, Andrew Jenson Collection, CHL. The minutes of the meeting in which Lee was excommunicated, along with other early minutes of the Quorum of the Twelve, burned in the Council House fire of June 21, 1883. William W. Taylor to the Presidency and Members of the High Council of the Salt Lake Stake of Zion, July 6, 1883, in Salt Lake Stake, Report Regarding Destruction of Stake Records, CHL; Jenson1, 161.

12. Henry Lunt to Brigham Young, Aug. 3, 1862, IC; Juanita Brooks, *The Mountain Meadows Massacre* (Stanford, CA: Stanford University Press, 1950), 136n4. For more on Olive Coombs Higby's background, see Laurel Thatcher Ulrich, *A House Full of Females: Plural Marriage and Women's Rights in Early Mormonism, 1835–1870*

(New York: Alfred A. Knopf, 2017), 319–20; Laurel Thatcher Ulrich, "Juanita Brooks's Footnote: History, Memory, and the Murder of Olivia Coombs," *UHQ* 90, no. 3 (2022): 180–95.

13. *MC* 2:142–45.

14. *MC* 2:143–44; Brooks1, 293–94.

15. *MC* 2:145–47.

16. *MC* 2:150–51.

17. *MC* 2:151–52. On Young in St. George, see Andrew J. Allen, reminiscences and journal, Nov. 20, 1870, CHL.

18. *MC* 2:152.

19. *MC* 2:153.

20. *MC* 2:152.

21. *MC* 2:153–54.

22. *MC* 2:154. *MC* transcribes Lee's diary as saying "Counsellor I. Willis" spoke with Lee. For John Willis as Roundy's counselor, see Kanarra Ward, Cedar West Stake, Manuscript history and historical reports, CHL.

23. *MC* 2:155–58; Brooks1, 297.

24. *MC* 2:155.

25. *MC* 2:158; Brooks1, 297, 383.

26. "St. George Stake Journal," in William R. Palmer, notes, typescript, William R. Palmer Papers, CHL.

27. "Report of a Journey . . . Performed in 1863, Compiled from the Journal of Jacob Hamblin," HOCHD.

28. Philip Klingen Smith to Brigham Young, Nov. 17, 1864, IC; Anna Jean Backus, *Mountain Meadows Witness: The Life and Times of Bishop Philip Klingensmith* (Spokane, WA: Arthur H. Clark, 1995), 205–8; Warren Foote to D. W. Sessions, Mar. 13, 1866, HOCHD; KS.

29. "Local Intelligence," *Pioche (NV) Weekly Record*, July 23, 1881; W. Paul Reeve, *Making Space on the Western Frontier* (Urbana: University of Illinois Press, 2006), 120; James G. Bleak to E. Snow, Jan. 29, 1870, copy of telegram, James G. Bleak Collection, CHL.

30. TM, 692; "Death of a Noted Mormon," *PDR*, June 15, 1875.

31. "Argus Letters," *Daily Corinne (UT) Reporter*, July 15, 1871.

32. "History of Mormonism," *Corrine (UT) Reporter*, Aug. 12, 1871; "An Open Letter to Brigham Young," *Corrine Daily Utah Reporter*, Feb. 24, Sept. 12, Nov. 5, 1870.

33. PKS. Daniel H. Wells commanded the Utah Territory militia in 1857. Jenson2 1:63.

34. PKS.

35. J. Cecil Alter, *Early Utah Journalism* (Salt Lake City: Utah State Historical Society, 1938), 349, 352, 353, 355; "Policy of the Tribune," *SLT*, Nov. 16, 1871. Like many newspapers, the *Tribune* underwent slight name changes over time but will be cited in the text throughout simply as the *Salt Lake Tribune*.

36. O. N. Malmquist, *The First 100 Years* (Salt Lake City: Utah State Historical Society, 1971), 18–19, 31; Ronald W. Walker, *Wayward Saints* (Urbana: University of Illinois Press, 1998), 237–38.

37. "The South from a New Standpoint," *SLT*, Aug. 10, 1871.

38. *EOM* 3:1211–16.

39. "The South from a New Standpoint."

40. *MC* 2:164.

41. "Elder Brand's Trip South," *SLT*, Aug. 9, 1871.

42. "The South from a New Standpoint."

43. *MC* 2:164–65.

44. Worster, 231–32; Fowler, 84–87; "Jones," 99; Beaman, 546; Little, 108.

45. Fowler, 87.

46. "Powell," 474.

47. *MC* 2:173.

Chapter 31

1. George P. Sanger, ed., *The Statutes at Large, Treaties, and Proclamations, of the United States of America, from December 5, 1859, to March 3, 1863*, vol. 12 (Boston: Little, Brown, 1863), 501; Baskin, 38; Thomas G. Alexander, "A Conflict of Perceptions: Ulysses S. Grant and the Mormons," *Ulysses S. Grant Association Newsletter* 8, no. 4 (July 1971): 31–33, 40; Gordon, 81.

2. Arrington, 371; Edward W. Tullidge, *Life of Brigham Young* (New York: Tullidge & Crandall, 1876), 420–21; *ZIC*, 137, 141.

3. "The Great Crusade," *DN*, Nov. 15, 1871; "McKean, James Bedell," Biographical Directory of the United States Congress, 1774–Present, accessed July 26, 2013, http://bioguide.congress.gov/scripts/biodisplay.pl?index = M000491; James B. McKean to A. J. Falls, June 20, 1871, in LRS.

4. W. H. Hooper to George A. Smith, June 5, 1870, GASP.

5. Terryl L. Givens, *The Viper on the Hearth* (New York: Oxford University Press, 1997), 144–45; Sarah Barringer Gordon, "The Mormon Question: Polygamy and Constitutional Conflict in Nineteenth-Century America," *Journal of Supreme Court History* 28 (Mar. 2003): 14.

6. *Clinton v. Englebrecht*, 80 U.S. 13 Wall. 434 (1871).

7. Chas. H. Hempstead to A. T. Akerman, Jan. 20, 1871, Letters Received, Utah, 1853–70, Records of the Attorney General's Office, RG 60.

8. *CHC*, 5:390–91.

9. George Alfred Townsend, *The Mormon Trials at Salt Lake City* (New York: American News, 1871), 17; "A Rattling Review of Affairs in Salt Lake," *DN*, Dec. 6, 1871.

10. Townsend, *Mormon Trials at Salt Lake City*, 18–19.

11. Baskin, 13–16; Stenhouse, 616–20. Young said it was never solved because the investigation got too close to exposing leading anti-Mormons in the murder. LPCB 9:250.

12. Baskin, 5, 17–18.

13. *ZIC*, 137–38; Baskin, 54.

14. Indictments against Brigham Young and others, enclosed in George C. Bates to attorney general, Dec. 4, 1871, LDU; Editorial, *DEN*, Oct. 3, 1871; Editorial, *DEN*,

Nov. 27, 1871; "Court Proceedings," *DN*, Nov. 29, 1871; HOJ, Sept. 26, 1871; Hope A. Hilton, *"Wild Bill" Hickman and the Mormon Frontier* (Salt Lake City: Signature Books, 1988), 124–25; "Local and Other Matters," *DN*, Oct. 12, 1870; Leonard J. Arrington and Hope A. Hilton, "William A. ('Bill') Hickman: Setting the Record Straight," *Task Papers in LDS History*, no. 28 (Salt Lake City: Historical Department of The Church of Jesus Christ of Latter-day Saints, 1979), 33; MacKinnon1, 146; William A. Hickman, *Brigham's Destroying Angel*, ed. J. H. Beadle (New York: Geo. A. Crofutt, 1872), 122–25, 204–5; Daniel W. Jones, *Forty Years among the Indians* (Salt Lake City: Juvenile Instructor, 1890), 129–30.

15. "Correspondence," *MS* 25, no. 19 (May 9, 1863): 301; Arrington, 297–98; HOJ, Sept. 26–27, 1871.

16. HOJ, Sept. 27, 1871.

17. "Opinion of Chief Justice McKean," *DN*, Oct. 18, 1871; Arrington, 372; *ZIC*, 137–38.

18. LPCB 12:884.

19. "Admitted to Bail," *DN*, Oct. 25, 1871; Editorial, *DEN*, Nov. 27, 1871; "Thomas Fitch Interviewed by a N. Y. 'Herald' Reporter," *DEN*, Nov. 23, 1871.

20. Fowler, 89.

21. Worster, 231–32; Fowler, 84–86; "Thompson," 56, 58–61; "Jones," 98–106; "Journal of John F. Steward," ed. William Culp Darrah, *UHQ* 16–17 (1948–49): 245–50.

22. "Powell," 341–44; "Letters of Captain F. M. Bishop to the Daily Pantagraph, 1871–72," *UHQ* 15 (1947): 249; Rusho, 24–25; Reilly, 22, 24.

23. Dellenbaugh, 153; "Powell," 357–58.

24. Frederick S. Dellenbaugh, *The Romance of the Colorado River* (New York: G. P. Putnam's Sons, 1909), 93n1; "Powell," 357–59; Little, 108; Compton1, 342–43.

25. "Powell," 359. October 28, 1871, was a full moon. U.S. Naval Observatory Astronomical Applications Department, accessed May 26, 2015, http://aa.usno.navy. mil/rstt/onedaytable?form=1&ID=AA&year=1871&month=10&day=28&state= UT&place=kanab.

26. "Journal of John F. Steward," 249–50.

27. *MC* 2:194.

28. "Powell," 361–62n81.

29. "Jones," 106. Earlier in the year, Haight had accompanied Hamblin on an unsuccessful journey to find a route to the Dirty Devil River for Powell. Isaac C. Haight, diary entries, in Jacob Hamblin, diary, 1871–73 and 1877, JHP.

30. Jacob Hamblin to Erastus Snow, Sept. 13, 1871, James G. Bleak Collection, ca. 1854–1927, CHL; Reilly, 21; Compton1, 489.

31. *MC* 2:173–76.

32. Jacob Hamblin to George A. Smith, Aug. 29, 1858, GASP; Forney1.

33. Crampton, 220, 242; Darrah, 497; Fredrick S. Dellenbaugh to Stites, May 24, 1933, Juanita Brooks Collection, USHS.

34. HOHC, 43:1754.

35. JH-BY; JHS.

36. JHS; JH-BY; Carleton, 7.

37. "Journal of Pres. Young & Party," Dec. 19, 21–22, 1871, in HOJ, between entries Dec. 23 and 24, 27 and 28, 1871.

38. *MC* 2:175–77; Beadle.

39. *MC* 2:175, 177–78, 180–81.

40. "Journal of Pres. Young & Party," Dec. 26, 1871, in HOJ, between entries Dec. 27 and 28, 1871; Brigham Young and George A. Smith to Daniel H. Wells, Dec. 15, 1871, Letters and telegrams, Communications, YOF; Robert T. Burton, diary, Dec. 26, 1871, CHL.

41. Lists of Chief Justices, Associate Justices, U.S. Attorneys, and U.S. Marshals for Utah Territory, 1850–90, James Buchanan Administration, Utah Appointment Papers, box 722, fd 1, RG 60.

42. Mary C. Graham and Marian J. Matyn, "Millard Fillmore, George C. Bates, and James Jesse Strang: Why Michigan's Only King Was Tried in Federal Court," *Court Legacy* 11, no. 2 (June 2003): 1–6.

43. Ross A. Webb, *Benjamin Helm Bristow* (Lexington: University Press of Kentucky, 1969), 101; *American Biographical History of Eminent and Self-Made Men*, Michigan vol. (Cincinnati, OH: Western Biographical, 1878), 16–17.

44. George Q. Cannon to B. Young and George A. Smith, Dec. 1, 1871, LCLO.

45. Frank Fuller to Brigham Young, Dec. 5, 1871, IC.

46. George C. Bates to B. [H]. Bristow, Dec. 27, 1871, SCF.

Chapter 32

1. George C. Bates to A. T. Akerman, Dec. 1871, LDU; George C. Bates to Attorney General, Dec. 4, 1871, LDU; George C. Bates to George H. Williams, Jan. 5, 1872, LDU.

2. George C. Bates to B. H. Bristow, Dec. 27, 1871, LDU.

3. Orson F. Whitney, *History of Utah*, 4 vols. (Salt Lake City: George Q. Cannon & Sons, 1892–1904), 2:675–80, 731; George H. Williams to George C. Bates, Mar. 2, 1872, Letters Sent by the Department of Justice, Instructions to Attorneys and Marshals, vol. C, Oct. 1871–Apr. 1873, 204, NARA.

4. *Acts and Resolutions of the Legislative Assembly of the Territory of Utah, Eighth Annual Session—For the Years 1858-9* (Great Salt Lake City: J. McKnight, 1859), 5; *Clinton v. Englebrecht*, 80 U.S. 13 Wall. 434 (1871); "Plea in Abatement in the Case of the People v. Brigham Young," *DN*, Oct. 18, 1871; "Opinion of Chief Justice J. B. McKean," *DN*, Nov. 22, 1871. Robert Baskin, when testifying of the Mormons before the Committee on Territories, moderately stated, "I must do them justice to say that the question of religion does not enter into their courts, in ordinary cases; I have never detected any bias on the part of jurors there in this respect, as I at first expected; I have appeared in cases where Mormons and Gentiles were opposing parties in the case, and saw, much to my surprise, the jury do what was right; but whenever this religion, or their peculiar institution, polygamy, comes in, then they are very sensitive,

and you may be very certain what will be their decision." *Execution of the Laws in Utah*, H. R. Rep. No. 21-41, at 15 (1870).

5. See, e.g., Chip Colwell-Chanthaphonh, *Massacre at Camp Grant: Forgetting and Remembering Apache History* (Tucson: University of Arizona Press, 2007); "Evidence Published," *Tucson Arizona Citizen*, Feb. 17, 1872; Karl Jacoby, *Shadows at Dawn: An Apache Massacre and the Violence of History* (New York: Penguin Press, 2008), 187–88.

6. LPCB 12:859, 883.

7. *Clinton v. Englebrecht*, 80 U.S. 13 Wall. 434 (1871); *ZIC*, 137–38.

8. "The Englebrecht Case," *SLT*, Apr. 16, 1872; *ZIC*, 138, 145, 147.

9. Whitney, *History of Utah*, 2:687.

10. "Jones," 119.

11. *MC* 2:184, 185, 187; Reilly, 25.

12. *MC* 2:188, 192–94, 196–99; Brooks1, 309–11; "Bishop," 227n46, 235–38; Darrah, 491–92; Beaman, 592.

13. *MC* 2:200–202.

14. "Bishop," 157, 212, 224–25, 227, 229, 232, 234–36; "Thompson," 79.

15. "Bishop," 237–38; *MC* 2:200, 259n80.

16. Beaman, 593; *MC* 2:200, 259n79.

17. Beadle; *MC* 2:202–3.

18. Beadle; *MatMM*, 189.

19. Beadle.

20. *MC* 2:210–11.

21. Darrah, 495; *MC* 2:204; Fowler, 129.

22. Frederick S. Dellenbaugh, *The Romance of the Colorado River* (New York: G. P. Putnam's Sons, 1909), 316.

23. Crampton, 235.

24. Dellenbaugh, 211.

25. Fowler, 129–30; *MC* 2:205–6; Frederick Samuel Dellenbaugh, Diary, Second Powell Expedition, 1871–73, July 13–20, 1842, 149, Frederick Samuel Dellenbaugh Papers, NYPL.

26. *MC* 2:206; "Powell," 434; Fowler, 130.

27. "Powell," 434; Fowler, 130.

28. Crampton, 235, 236.

29. Dellenbaugh, 212.

30. *MC* 2:206–7, 260n86; Darrah, 495; "Powell," 435.

31. Fowler, 131–33; *MC* 2:207.

32. Richard E. Turley Jr. and Eric C. Olson, "Fame Meets Infamy: The Powell Survey and Mountain Meadows Participants, 1870–1873," *UHQ* 81 (Winter 2013): 13–16, 22–23; "Powell," 422.

33. "Powell," 422. For references to Adair's interactions with Powell's men, see Fowler, 95, 96, 104, 107, 110n61, 111n63, 113, 117, 132; "Jones," 113–14, 120, 126–27, 131–33, 135–36, 138–39, 141; "Thompson," 74–82, 88, 90, 93, 98–99, 101, 105–6, 108n68; "Powell," 410, 413, 417, 422, 449, 453–54, 457–58, 471.

34. Crampton, 242.

35. *MC* 2:207–13.

36. Woods to Grant, Apr. 18, 1872, LDU; C. M. Hawley to George C. Bates, Nov. 9, 1872, enclosed in C. M. Hawley to George H. Williams, Nov. 20, 1872, LDU; *ZIC*, 145–48; M. T. Patrick to George H. Williams, Jan. 24, 1873, LDU.

Chapter 33

1. Will Bagley, ed., *The Whites Want Every Thing* (Norman, OK: Arthur H. Clark, 2019), and the following items in NAMP32: W[illiam] W. B[elknap], Jan. 21, 1871, note; C. M. Hawley to Major General Ord, Jan. 12, 1872, enclosed in George L. Woods to Major General Ord, Jan. 12, 1872; P. H. Sheridan to the Adjutant General, Feb. 25, 1872, enclosed in P. H. Sheridan to E. D. Townsend, Mar. 7, 1872; P. H. Sheridan to E. D. Townsend, Apr. 17, 20, June 3, 18, 1872; P. H. Sheridan to Assistant Adjutant General, Apr. 19, 1872; Quarter Master General to Secretary of War, May 8, 1872 (included in Sheridan to Townsend Apr. 20, 1872); P. H. Sheridan to Adjutant General, June 11, 1872; George H. Weeks to Adjutant General's Office, June 18, 21, 1872; and the following endorsements enclosed in Woods to Grant, Oct. 2, 1871: W. T. Sherman, Oct. 31, 1871; [President to Secretary of War], Oct. 25, 1871; E. D. Townsend, Nov. 1, 1871; P. H. Sheridan, Nov. 6, 1871. See also George L. Woods to U. S. Grant, Oct. 2, 1871, film no. 1065813, FHL; C. M. Hawley to U. S. Grant, Feb. 24, 1872, in Selected Documents Relating to the Mountain Meadows Massacre, 1857–76, NARA.

2. Brigham Young to William W. Belknap, May 21, 1872, NAMP32; LPCB 13:80–84.

3. Thomas G. Alexander and Leonard J. Arrington, "The Utah Military Frontier, 1872–1912," *UHQ* 32 (Fall 1964): 333–34.

4. *MC* 2:219–20; Rusho, 37.

5. *MC* 2:222, 224, 227; *MatMM*, 258; Compton1, 367–71.

6. Joseph Royal Miller and Elna Miller, eds., *Journal of Jacob Miller* (Elna Miller, 1967), 83; Horton D. Haight, "Copy of Report of the Arizona Mission as Made to Pres Brigham Young," Aug. 1873, CHL.

7. James Tempest, journal, Apr. 22, 1873, photocopy, CHL; Andrew Amundsen, diary, Apr. 22, 1873, CHL; Rusho, 39; *MC* 2:240–41.

8. Henry Holmes, journal, May 6, 9, 13, 1873, CHL.

9. *MC* 2:246, 263.

10. *MC* 2:263–64; Haight, "Copy of Report of the Arizona Mission," Aug. 1873.

11. Andrew Amundsen, autobiography and diary, typescript, p. 20, BYU; Samuel Rose Parkinson, journal, June 26, 1873, photocopy, CHL; Tempest journal, June 26, 1873.

12. Haight, "Copy of Report of the Arizona Mission," Aug. 1873; Holmes journal, June 23, 1873; *MC* 2:264; "The Arizona Mission," *DEN*, July 17, 1873; Little, 110.

13. *MC* 2:265–66, 269; Parkinson journal, June 30, 1873.

14. *MC* 2:272–73, 275, 277.

15. Amy O. Bassford, ed., *Home-Thoughts from Afar* (East Hampton, NY: East Hampton Free Library, 1967), 29–30; Worster, 298–301.

16. Bassford, *Home-Thoughts from Afar*, 33; Worster, 301.

17. Gaell Lindstrom, "Thomas Moran in Utah" (lecture, Utah State University, Logan, UT, Nov. 29, 1983), 3–5; "The Land of Mormon," *NYT*, Aug. 7, 1873; "The Colorado Canon," *NYT*, Sept. 4, 1873; "Thompson," 111–14; Bassford, *Home-Thoughts from Afar*, 135; Nancy K. Anderson, *Thomas Moran* (Washington, DC: National Gallery of Art/New Haven, CT: Yale University Press, 1997), 208; Anne Morand, *Thomas Moran: The Field Sketches, 1856–1923* (Norman: University of Oklahoma Press, 1996), 41–42, 108, 152–54.

18. "Thompson," 114; Anderson, *Thomas Moran*, 55–57, 60, 98–100.

19. Crampton, 242.

20. *MC* 2:306.

21. *JD* 4:165; Kathryn M. Daynes, *More Wives Than One* (Urbana: University of Illinois Press, 2001), 82.

22. *MC* 2:306, 341n31.

23. *MC* 2:308–9.

24. *MC* 2:327–28.

25. Historian's notes, Mar. 2, 1874, in St. George Utah Stake General Minutes, CHL; Brigham Young and George A. Smith, Mar. 3, 1874, telegram, YOF. Only page 4 of the document is extant.

26. John Bringhurst, statement, July 27, 1928, CM; Jenson2 4:678.

27. Christopher J. Arthur, autobiography and journals, 1875–1916, part 4, 33–34, typescript, CHL. Arthur wrote part 4 as a memoir in 1877.

28. Young and Smith, Mar. 3, 1874, telegram; Arthur, autobiography and journals, 1875–1916, part 4, 32–33. In the mid-twentieth century, Haight's granddaughter Caroline Parry Woolley wrote that Young himself rebaptized Haight in St. George on the night of March 3. Contemporary minutes show this was impossible, as Young left St. George on March 2. Arthur's 1877 account says Haight's baptism was performed in Toquerville on March 3 by instruction of Young, not by Young, which is possible. Blanche Cox Clegg and Janet Burton Seegmiller, eds., *"I Would to God": A Personal History of Isaac Haight* (Cedar City: Southern Utah University Press, 2009), 139–40, 209n52.

29. Historian's notes, Mar. 8, 1874, in St. George Utah Stake General Minutes, CHL.

30. *CHC*, 4:178n30.

31. J. D. Lee to Brigham Young, Mar. 15, 1874, IC.

32. *MC* 2:333, 335–36.

33. *MC* 2: 336–37.

34. George A. Hicks to B. Young, Feb. 18, 1877, MACF; "Some Startling Facts," *SLT*, Aug. 21, 1874; "Excommunications," *DN Semi-Weekly*, May 23, 1874.

35. *MC* 2:337–38.

36. "Brigham Young: A Long Talk with the Prophet," *NYT*, May 20, 1877. "In 1870 Pres B.Y. in his office investigated the extent of the guilt of John D. Lee and Isaac C Haight, who were both cut off the Church, Lee [both!] never to be allowed to return to the Church; Pres. Young told him to go and hang himself." John D. Lee Sketch, Biographical sketches, Andrew Jenson Collection, CHL.

37. J. D. Lee to B. Young, May 17, 1874, IC.

38. Gordon, 112–13.

39. "President Grant, Clagett and Merritt on Utah," *DN*, Feb. 26, 1873.

40. 43 Cong. Rec. 4466–68 (1874); *Utah Affairs. Congress and Polygamy* (Salt Lake City: Deseret News, 1874), 27–30; *ZIC*, 148–49.

41. "Judge Boreman's Charge to the Grand Jury," *SLT*, Sept. 13, 1874.

42. "Second District Court," *SLT*, Sept. 13, 1874; "Judge Boreman's Charge to the Grand Jury."

43. "Second District Court."

44. Joint Indictment, Sept. 24, 1874, CCF 31; Individual indictments for John M. Higbee, Samuel Jewkes, and William C. Stewart, Sept. 24, 1874, CCF 32, 33, 35; Individual indictments for John D. Lee, William H. Dame, Ellott Willden, George Adair, and Philip K. Smith, Sept. 24, 1874, in MBB, 287–89, 395, 431–33, 442–44, 572–73; Individual indictment for Isaac C. Haight, Sept. 24, 1874, BYU; *MMM-CLP* 1:407–45.

45. *MatMM*, 256–62; *AJ-DHM*, 49.

46. *MU*, 293. In *Mormonism Unveiled,* William Bishop included a transcript of an April 1, 1877, letter he received from William Stokes detailing his arrest of Lee. We cite Stokes's account as found in *Mormonism Unveiled* because, unlike Lee's "confession" in the book, there is no evidence that calls into question its veracity.

47. "The Prophet's Health," *SLT*, Sept. 30, 1874; "City Jottings," *SLT*, Sept. 30, 1874; Turner, 373–74.

48. "City Jottings," *SLT*, Oct. 8–9, 1874.

49. "The Mormon Murders," *SLT*, Oct. 30, 1874; "The Royal Cortege"; "City Jottings," *SLT*, Oct. 31, Nov. 3, 13, 1874.

50. "Investigation Asked For," *SLT*, Oct. 7, 1874.

51. John Taylor, "Blood Atonement and Mountain Meadows," [1874], manuscript, John Taylor Presidential Papers, 1877–87, CHL; "Correspondence," *DN*, Apr. 15, 1874; Penrose, 76–77.

52. "Interviewing the Mormon Apostles," *Sacramento Record Union*, Oct. 27, 1874.

53. "Going Back on John D. Lee," *SLT*, Oct. 31, 1874.

54. *MU*, 294–95; "The Butcher!," *SLT*, Nov. 13, 1874; "Vengeance Is Mine," *SLT*, Nov. 14, 1874; Royal, "Another Version," *SLT*, Nov. 14, 1874.

55. *MU*, 295.

56. Collins R. Hakes to F. M. Lyman, July 18, 1907, First Presidency Miscellaneous Documents, 1887–1918, CHL; Collins R. Hakes Sr. to W. Aird Macdonald, May 21, 1914, CM; C. R. Hakes, statement, Apr. 24, 1916, CM; Josephine to Susan, Feb. 5, 1874, and William Moroni West obituary, *DN*, Feb. 18, 1874, both accessed at www.geni.com/people/William-Moroni-West.

57. Hakes to Lyman, July 18, 1907; Hakes to Macdonald, May 21, 1914, CM.

58. *MU*, 296; Fish, 156.

59. *MU*, 296–99; Arrest warrant, Oct. 13, 1874, MBB, 289–90.

60. *MU*, 296–300; "The Butcher!"; "Vengeance Is Mine"; Royal, "Another Version"; Fish, 143, 153.

61. "The Butcher!"; "Vengeance Is Mine"; *MU*, 300; Royal, "Another Version."

62. Royal, "Another Version"; "Mountain Meadow Massacre," *SLDH*, Jan. 1, 1875.
63. "The Butcher!"; Royal, "Another Version"; *MU*, 300–301.

Chapter 34

1. "Vengeance Is Mine," *SLT*, Nov. 14, 1874; "Utah," *Sacramento Record Union*, Nov. 16, 1874; "A Mormon Tragedy," *NYT*, Nov. 23, 1874.
2. "Vengeance Is Mine"; "Utah."
3. "John D. Lee, of Mountain Meadows," *SLT*, Nov. 17, 1874; "City Jottings," *SLT*, Nov. 17, 19, Dec. 8, 1874; "The Old Butcher," *SLT*, Nov. 20, 1874.
4. "A Mormon Tragedy"; "John D. Lee, of Mountain Meadows"; "John in Durance Vile," *SLT*, Nov. 17, 1874; "City Jottings," *SLT*, Nov. 19, 1874.
5. "John D. Lee, of Mountain Meadows"; "The Prisoner Lee's Life in Jail," *NYH*, Nov. 24, 1874.
6. "A Mormon Tragedy."
7. George R. Maxwell to George H. Williams, Nov. 23, 1874, enclosing George A. Woodward to George R. Maxwell, Nov. 16, 1874, LRS; "The Old Butcher"; "Miscellaneous," *SLT*, Nov. 17, 1874; "Utah," *SDU*, Nov. 17, 1874; "Beaver City," *SLT*, Mar. 19, 1875; "Telegraphic!," *SLT*, May 5, 1875; "A Mormon Tragedy"; "John D. Lee," *SLDH*, Nov. 26, 1874.
8. "John D. Lee, of Mountain Meadows"; George A. Smith, journal, Nov. 18, 1874, GASP; "Mountain Meadow Massacre," *SLDH*, Nov. 19, 1874; "Miscellaneous," *SLT*, Nov. 19, 1874; "City Jottings," *SLT*, Nov. 19, 1874; "Arrest of Bishop Dame," *SLT*, Nov. 22, 1874; "Mountain Meadows," *SLT*, Nov. 24, 1874; "Col. William H. Dame," *SLT*, Nov. 28, 1874; "The Arrest of Col. Dame—Co-operative Store and Stock Herd," *DN*, Dec. 9, 1874.
9. William H. Dame to George A. Smith, Nov. 18, 1874, Incoming letters, GASP.
10. George A. Smith to Brigham Young, Aug. 17, 1858, LCLO; George A. Smith and James McKnight, report, Aug. 6, 1858, HOCHD; Josiah Rogerson, untitled typescript pages, ca. 1911, 7, in CM; *MC* 1:323–24n43.
11. George C. Bates to George A. Smith, Oct. 23, 1873, GASP.
12. LPCB 13:491, 493.
13. "Col. Dame En Route for This City," *SLDH*, Nov. 22, 1874; "Mountain Meadows," *SLT*, Nov. 24, 1874; Smith journal, Nov. 23, 1874, GASP; "The Arrival of Colonel Dame," *SLDH*, Nov. 24, 1874; "Utah," *SDR*, Nov. 26, 1874.
14. Smith journal, Nov. 22, 1874, GASP.
15. "The Arrival of Colonel Dame."
16. George A. Smith to George C. Bates, Nov. 26, 1874, GASLC; Smith journal, Nov. 22, 1874.
17. George A. Smith to George C. Bates, Dec. 6, 1874, GASLC.
18. "Our Beaver Letter," *SLDH*, Dec. 5, 1874; "City Jottings," *SLT*, Dec. 6, 1874; Lynn R. Bailey, *A Tale of the "Unkilled"* (Tucson, AZ: Westernlore Press, 1999), 11–22;

Utah Territory, Box Elder County, Corrine, 1870 U.S. Census, population schedule, 18; Advertisement, *SLT*, May 24, 1871; "Beaver," *SLDH*, Apr. 14, 1875; "Wells Spicer," *PDR*, June 8, 1875; *Utah, its Territorial Policy, and its Relation to the Federal Government* (s.l.: s.n., ca. 1872), [13], copy in FRU.

19. J. D. Lee to George A. Smith, Feb. 20, 1875, GASP.

20. Bailey, *Tale of the "Unkilled,"* 14, 18; Dan L. Thrapp, *Encyclopedia of Frontier Biography* (Glendale, CA: Arthur H. Clark, 1988), 1346–47; "Judge Spicer's Address," *SLT*, Aug. 3, 1875.

21. "Our Beaver Letter."

22. MB1, 110; MBB, 290, 397.

23. George L. Woods to U. S. Grant, Dec. 4, 1874, Records of the appointments division, Field office appointment papers, Utah—Governor, Governor—Woods, Geo., box 690, RG 48, NARA.

24. William Carey to George H. Williams, Dec. 29, 1874, LRS.

25. "Mountain Meadow Massacre," *SLDH*, Jan. 1, 1875; *History of the Bench and Bar of Utah* (Salt Lake City: Interstate Press Association, 1913), 102.

26. [Jacob Hamblin] to George A. Smith, Jan. 2, 187[5], Incoming letters, GASP.

27. See Jacob Hamblin to George A. Smith, Aug. 29, 1858, GASP; Forney1; JH-BY; JHS.

28. [Hamblin] to Smith, Jan. 2, 187[5].

29. James Jack to George A. Smith, Jan. 6, 1875, Incoming letters, GASP; Brigham Young Jr., journal, Jan. 20, 1875, CHL.

30. *AJ-DHM*, 64; *MatMM*, 177–79.

31. See, e.g., "The Mountain Meadows Massacre," *SLT*, Jan. 19, 1875.

32. "Amending the Poland Bill," *SLT*, Dec. 2, 1874; "Mocking at Our Griefs," *SLT*, Dec. 2, 1874; " 'Royal' and His Persecuters," *SLT*, June 20, 1875.

33. MB1, 57; Indictments, CCF 31–33, 35; MBB, 287–89, 395, 431–33, 442–44, 572–73; Individual indictment for Isaac C. Haight, Sept. 24, 1874, BYU; *MMM-CLP* 1:407–45.

34. "John D. Lee on Trial," *PDJ*, Apr. 6, 1875; "Telegraphic!," *SLT*, Apr. 6, 1875; "Second District Court," *SLDH*, Apr. 6, 1875.

35. BYOJ, Sept. 2, 1859; HOJ, July 5, 1859, transcription by LaJean Purcell Carruth; George A. Smith to George C. Bates, Dec. 6, 1874, GASLC.

36. "A Card," *SLDH*, Feb. 24, 1875; "A Card," *DEN*, Feb. 24, 1875; "A Card," *DN*, Mar. 10, 1875; "From Beaver," *SLT*, Feb. 24, 1875; "Parowan," *SLT*, Mar. 2, 1875.

37. "From Beaver"; "Another Judicial Movement," *DEN*, Feb. 24, 1875; "Another Judicial Movement," *DN*, Mar. 10, 1875.

38. "Utah," *SDR*, Feb. 6, 1875; "From Beaver."

39. J. D. Lee to George A. Smith, Feb. 20, 1875, Incoming letters, GASP.

40. LPCB 13:706.

41. "Utah Affairs," *SLT*, Apr. 2, 1875.

42. "The Mountain Meadows Trial," *SLT*, Apr. 3, 1875; "Telegraphic!," *SLT*, Apr. 6, 1875; "Second District Court," *SLH*, Apr. 6, 1875; "John D. Lee on Trial," *PDJ*, Apr. 6, 1875; "Territorial Dispatches," *DEN*, Apr. 6, 1875; "Territorial Dispatches," *DN*, Apr. 14, 1875; [Josiah] Rogerson to G. A. Smith, Apr. 6, 1875, telegram, Incoming letters, GASP.

43. "Beaver," *SLT*, Apr. 6, 1875; Rogerson to Smith, Apr. 6, 1875, telegram, Incoming letters, GASP; "Not So," *PDJ*, Apr. 10, 1875.

44. "Telegraphic!" *SLT*, Apr. 6, 1875; "Second District Court," *SLH*, Apr. 6, 1875; "John D. Lee on Trial," *PDJ*, Apr. 6, 1875; "Territorial Dispatches," *DEN*, Apr. 6, 1875; "Territorial Dispatches," *DN*, Apr. 14, 1875; Rogerson to Smith, Apr. 6, 1875, telegram, Incoming letters, GASP.

45. "Telegraphic!," *SLT*, Apr. 6, 1875; "Second District Court," *SLH*, Apr. 6, 1875; "John D. Lee on Trial," *PDJ*, Apr. 6, 1875; "Territorial Dispatches," *DN*, Apr. 14, 1875.

46. "Telegraphic!," *SLT*, Apr. 7, 1875; "Second District Court," *SLDH*, Apr. 7, 1875; "Territorial Dispatches," *DEN*, Apr. 7, 1875; "John D. Lee on Trial," *PDJ*, Apr. 7, 1875.

47. "Second District Court," *SLDH*, Apr. 7, 1875; "Territorial Dispatches," *DEN*, Apr. 7, 1875; "John D. Lee on Trial," *PDJ*, Apr. 7, 1875; "Telegraphic!," *SLT*, Apr. 7, 1875; HOJ, Apr. 6, 1875. For the official record of the arraignment, see MB1, 145; MBB, 291.

48. "Letter from Geo. C. Bates," *SLT*, Apr. 16, 1875; "Colonel Dame's Case," *SLDH*, Apr. 11, 1875; MBB, 400–405; MB1, 155–56.

49. "Beaver Notes," *SLT*, Apr. 14, 1875; HOJ, Apr. 14, 1875; "Local and Other Matters," *DEN*, Apr. 14, 1875.

50. MBB, 292–98.

51. "Journal Special from Beaver," *PDJ*, Apr. 15, 1875; "Territorial Dispatches," *DN*, Apr. 21, 1875.

52. MBB, 299–302; MB1, 166–67; "Journal Special from Beaver," *PDJ*, Apr. 15, 1875; "Lee's Case Continued," *SLDH*, Apr. 15, 1875; "Territorial Dispatches," *DN*, Apr. 21, 1875.

53. *MMM-CLP* 2:578; "Territorial Dispatches," *DN*, Apr. 21, 1875.

54. *MMM-CLP* 2:579–82; "Journal Special from Beaver," *PDJ*, Apr. 15, 1875; "Territorial Dispatches," *DN*, Apr. 21, 1875.

55. *MMM-CLP* 2:583; "Journal Special from Beaver," *PDJ*, Apr. 15, 1875; "Territorial Dispatches," *DN*, Apr. 21, 1875.

56. *MMM-CLP* 2:589.

Chapter 35

1. HOJ, Apr. 15, 1875; "Want Them Punished Anyhow," *DEN*, Apr. 17, 1875.

2. "City Jottings," *SLT*, Apr. 25, 1875; "Our Country Contemporaries," *DN*, Apr. 28, 1875; Editorial, *Weekly Nevada State Journal* (Reno, NV), May 15, 1875.

3. "Beaver Items," *SLT*, May 7, 1875.

4. "City Jottings," *SLT*, May 19, 1875.

5. "Mountain Meadows Massacre," *SLT*, May 12, 1875.

6. "Our Country Contemporaries," *DEN*, June 4, 1875; "Our Country Contemporaries," *DN*, June 9, 1875.

7. "John D. Lee," *SLT*, May 30, 1875.

8. "City Jottings," *SLT*, June 3, 1875; "Beaver City," *SLT*, June 4, 1875.

9. "City Jottings," *SLT*, July 13, 1875; "Lee's Trial," *SLT*, July 15, 1875.

10. MBB, 422–23.

11. See subpoenas at https://archives.utah.gov/research/inventories/24291.html and https://mountainmeadowsmassacre.com/subpoenas; "The Lee Trial," *SLT*, July 11, 1875; "Obedience to Counsel," *SLT*, July 31, 1875.

12. TM, 529–31; "John D. Lee on Trial," *PDJ*, Apr. 6, 1875; MBB, 574–75; "Our Beaver Letter," *SLT*, July 20, 1875.

13. MBB, 324–25.

14. "The Approaching Lee Trial," *SLT*, June 29, 1875.

15. Cactus; Lockley; "The Lee Trial," *SLT*, July 11, 1875; "The Lee Trial," *SLT*, July 13, 1875; "City Jottings," *SLT*, July 2, 1875.

16. "Our Country Contemporaries," *DEN*, July 12, 1875; Lockley; "The Lee Trial," *SLT*, July 11, 1875; "The Lee Trial," *SLT*, July 13, 1875; "For Beaver," *PDJ*, July 8, 1875; "Wells Spicer," *PDR*, June 8, 1875.

17. "Lee's Trial," *SLT*, July 16, 1875; Lockley; "Our Country Contemporaries," *DEN*, July 12, 1875; Woolley, 47, 56. The highly questionable *MU*, 232, 380, suggests John Macfarlane was at Mountain Meadows, though somewhat ambiguously.

18. Cactus; "Lee and Dame on Trial for the Mountain Meadow Massacre," *DAC*, July 13, 1875; "The Lee Trial," *SLT*, July 13, 1875; "Mountain Meadow Massacre," *DAC*, July 18, 1875.

19. Cactus; "Mountain Meadow Massacre," *DAC*, July 18, 1875.

20. Cactus; "Mountain Meadow Massacre," *DAC*, July 18, 1875; "City Jottings," *SLT*, July 13, 1875; Baskin, 36–38; HOJ, Sept. 26, 1871; Hope A. Hilton, *"Wild Bill" Hickman and the Mormon Frontier* (Salt Lake City: Signature Books, 1988), 124–25; "Murder in Rush Valley," *DEN*, Oct. 10, 1870; "Mountain Meadow," *Carthage (MO) Banner*, July 29, 1875; "Obedience to Counsel," *SLT*, July 31, 1875.

21. Cactus; "Mountain Meadow Massacre," *DAC*, July 18, 1875; Ronald W. Walker, *Wayward Saints* (Urbana: University of Illinois Press, 1998), 206–8; chapters 17-18.

22. Lockley; Cactus.

23. "Our Country Contemporaries," *DEN*, July 16, 1875; Cactus; Lockley; *MMM-CLP* 2:717–38.

24. "Lee and Dame on Trial for the Mountain Meadow Massacre," *DAC*, July 13, 1875; Lockley; "Our Country Contemporaries," *DEN*, July 16, 1875.

25. Lockley; "The Lee Trial," *SLT*, July 11, 1875; "Obedience to Counsel," *SLT*, July 31, 1875; MBB, 329, 428–29; MB1, 234–35; Robert Kent Fielding and Dorothy S. Fielding, eds., *The Tribune Reports of the Trials of John D. Lee* (Higganum, CT: Kent's Books, 2000), 103n4.

26. "The Lee Trial," *SLT*, July 11, 1875; Cactus.

27. Lockley.

28. "The Lee Trial," *SLT*, July 14, 1875; "Mountain Meadow Massacre," *SLDH*, July 21, 1875; "The Beaver Trial: Lee's Confession," *OJ*, July 20, 1875; "The Lee Trial," *PDR*, July 25, 1875.

29. "Lee's Trial," *SLT*, July 16, 1875.

30. "Mountain Meadow Massacre," *SLDH*, July 21, 1875; "The Beaver Trial: Lee's Confession," *OJ*, July 20, 1875; "The Mountain Meadow Horror," *OCR*, July 30, 1875;

"The Lee Trial," *PDR*, July 25, 1875. Prosecutors had little to lose in offering to drop the first indictment since it was reportedly defective. "The Mountain Meadow Horror," *OCR*, July 30, 1875.

31. "Lee to Make a Confession of the Mountain Meadow Massacre," *DAC*, July 14, 1875; "Salt Lake July 13—," *PDJ*, July 15, 1875.

32. LPCB 18:453–54. According to Bates, the plea deal had been reached "before Sutherland or myself got here."

33. LPCB 18:454.

34. "Mountain Meadows," *SLT*, July 17, 1875; "The Lee Trial," *SLT*, July 15, 1875; F. L., "Mountain Meadows: George C. Bates and His Contempt of Court," *SLT*, July 17, 1875; "Our Country Contemporaries," *DEN*, July 19, 1875; "Beaver: John D. Lee Still Writing His Statement," *SLDH*, July 17, 1875; MB1, [2179].

35. "Mountain Meadows," *SLT*, July 17, 1875; "The Lee Trial," *SLT*, July 15, 1875; "Mountain Meadows Massacre," *SLDH*, July 15, 1875; "The Mountain Meadow Massacre Trials," *NYH*, July 15, 1875; "The Lee Trial," *SLT*, July 15, 1875.

36. "Mountain Meadows," *SLT*, July 17, 1875; "The Mountain Meadow Massacre Trials," *NYH*, July 15, 1875; "The Lee Trial," *SLT*, July 15, 1875; "Our Beaver Letter," *SLT*, July 20, 1875; "The Mountain Meadow Massacre," *DAG*, July 18, 1875; "Pacific Coast," *PDJ*, July 18, 1875; "Utah," *WBDRT*, July 19, 1875; "Mountain Meadows Massacre," *SLDH*, July 15, 1875; "Beaver," *SLDH*, July 17, 1875; "Klingen Smith in Beaver," *DEN*, July 17, 21, 1875; "Mountain Meadow Massacre," *DAC*, July 18, 1875; LPCB 18:457–58.

Chapter 36

1. "Our Country Contemporaries," *DEN*, July 19, 1875; "Mountain Meadows Massacre," *SLDH*, July 15, 1875.

2. "The Mountain Meadow Massacre Trials," *NYH*, July 15, 1875; "The Beginning of the End—John D. Lee Turns State's Evidence," *Gold Hill (NV) Daily News*, July 15, 1875; "The Mountain Meadow Massacre," *DAG*, July 16, 1875; "Mountain Meadow Massacre," *Decatur (IL) Daily Republican*, July 16, 1875; "A Beaver (Utah) dispatch . . .," *Edwardsville (IL) Intelligencer*, July 21, 1875.

3. "The Mountain Meadow Massacre Trials," *NYH*, July 15, 1875; "The Beginning of the End—John D. Lee Turns State's Evidence," *Gold Hill (NV) Daily News*, July 15, 1875; "The Mountain Meadow Massacre," *DAG*, July 16, 1875; "Mountain Meadow Massacre," *Decatur (IL) Daily Republican*, July 16, 1875.

4. "Our Country Contemporaries," *DEN*, July 19, 1875; "Mountain Meadow Massacre," *SLDH*, July 18, 1875; "Our Beaver Letter," *SLT*, July 20, 1875; "The Beaver Trial," *OJ*, July 20, 1875; "Mountain Meadow Massacre," *SLDH*, July 21, 1875; "The Lee Trial," *PDR*, July 25, 1875.

5. [Bates] to Unknown, July 14, 1875, Telegram Book Nov. 7, 1873, to Aug. 6, 1875, 455–56, YOF.

6. "The Trial at Beaver," *OJ*, July 17, 1875; "The Beaver Trial," *OJ*, July 20, 1875; "Mountain Meadow Massacre," *SLDH*, July 21, 1875.

7. "Our Beaver Letter," *SLT*, July 20, 1875; "Lee and the Priesthood," *SLT*, July 18, 1875; "The following is extracted . . .," *PDR*, July 22, 1875; F[rederic] L[ockley], July 16, 1875, in "Our Beaver Letter," *Salt Lake Daily Tribune,* July 20, 1875; "The Lee Trial," *SLT*, July 17, 1875; "Mountain Meadow Massacre," *SLDH*, July 16, 1875; "Utah," *OCR*, July 23, 1875; "Pacific Coast," *PDR*, July 17, 1875.

8. "The Lee Trial," *PDR*, July 25, 1875; "Mountain Meadow Massacre," *SLDH*, July 21, 1875; "The Beaver Trial," *OJ*, July 20, 1875.

9. "Mountain Meadow Massacre," *SLDH*, July 21, 1875; "The Beaver Trial," *OJ*, July 20, 1875.

10. "The Lee Trial," *SLT*, July 20, 1875; "Progress of the Trial of the Mormon Murderers," *LADS*, July 21, 1875.

11. "Mountain Meadow Massacre," *SLDH*, July 21, 1875; "The Beaver Trial," *OJ*, July 20, 1875.

12. Woodruff, Sept. 29, 1857.

13. "Mountain Meadow Massacre," *SLDH*, July 21, 1875; "The Beaver Trial," *OJ*, July 20, 1875.

14. Woodruff, Sept. 29, 1857.

15. "Mountain Meadow Massacre," *SLDH*, July 21, 1875; "The Beaver Trial," *OJ*, July 20, 1875.

16. "Utah," *OCR*, July 23, 1875.

17. "Pacific Coast," *PDR*, July 17, 1875; "Beaver," *SLDH*, July 17, 1875; "Light on the Mountain Meadow Affair," *Elmira (NY) Daily Advertiser*, July 17, 1875; "Mountain Meadow Massacre," *DAC*, July 18, 1875.

18. George C. Bates to James Jack, July 16, 1875, two telegrams and translation, Telegram Book Nov. 7, 1873, to Aug. 6, 1875, 457–58, YOF.

19. B. M. Holladay to Brigham Young, July 19, 1875, Blair Family Papers, UofU. On Holladay, see J. V. Frederick, *Ben Holladay* (Glendale, CA: Arthur H. Clark, 1940); Ellis Lucia, *The Saga of Ben Holladay* (New York: Hastings House, 1959).

20. "The Lee Trial," *PDR*, July 25, 1875; "Our Beaver Letter." *SLT*, July 20, 1875; "Court at Beaver," *DEN*, July 17, 1875; "Pacific Coast," *PDJ*, July 18, 1875; "Mountain Meadow Massacre," *SLDH*, July 18, 1875.

21. "The Lee Trial," *SLT*, July 23, 1875.

22. "The Lee Trial," *PDR*, July 25, 1875.

23. George F. Prescott to U. S. Grant, Mar. 17, 1875, telegram, United States Department of Justice, United State Files Relating to Utah, 1855–1912, CHL. On McKean's character and dismissal, see *CHC*, 5:446–50; Baskin, 44–52; Arrington, 373; "Eastern," *DEN*, Mar. 17, 1875; "What a Change!," *DEN*, Apr. 2, 1875.

24. "*The United States*, Respondents, v. *George Reynolds*, Appellant," in *Reports of Cases Determined in the Supreme Court of the Territory of Utah* (San Francisco: A. L. Bancroft, 1877), 226–32; *ZIC*, 151–52; Baskin, 61–63.

25. Frederic E. Lockley, "Memoirs of an Unsuccessful Man," unpublished autobiography of Frederic Lockley, 1901, 209, FELC; Frederic Lockley to [Elizabeth Metcalf Campbell Lockley], July 17, 22, 1875, FELC.

26. "The Lee Statement," *DEN*, July 19, 1875; "The Lee Statement," *DN Weekly*, July 21, 1875.

27. "The Lee Trial," *SLT*, July 20, 1875. The *Tribune*'s verbiage was repeated in "Progress of the Trial of the Mormon Murderers," *LADS*, July 21, 1875; "Lee's Trial," *PDR*, July 23, 1875.

Chapter 37

1. "The Lee Statement," *DEN*, July 19, 1875; "Mountain Meadow Massacre: Lee's Statement 'Too Thin' for Use," *SLDH*, July 20, 1875; "The Lee Trial," *SLT*, July 20, 1875; "Will the Truth Come Out," *DAG*, July 20, 1875; "Utah," *DAC*, July 20, 1875; "Progress of the Trial of the Mormon Murderers," *LADS*, July 21, 1875; "The Lee Statement," *DN Weekly*, July 21, 1875; "The Beaver Trial: Lee's Statement 'Unsatisfactory!'," *OJ*, July 20, 1875; TM, 32, 34.

2. "The Lee Trial," *SLT*, July 23, 1875.

3. "The Lee Trial," *SLT*, July 23, 1875; CCF 31; "Latest from Beaver," *DEN*, July 20, 1875; "The Beaver Trial," *OJ*, July 20, 1875; "Mountain Meadow Massacre," *SLDH*, July 21, 1875; *MMM-CLP* 1:407–45; "Mountain Meadow Massacre," *SLDH*, July 16, 1875; "The Lee Trial," *SLT*, July 21, 1875. Utah law said accessories could be guilty of murder. See *Acts, Resolutions, and Memorials, Passed by the First Annual, and Special Sessions, of the Legislative Assembly of the Territory of Utah* (Great Salt Lake City: Brigham H. Young, 1852), 142; *Acts, Resolutions and Memorials, Passed at the Several Annual Sessions of the Legislative Assembly of the Territory of Utah* (Great Salt Lake City: Joseph Cain, 1855), 205.

4. CCF 31; "The Beaver Trial," *OJ*, July 20, 1875; *MMM-CLP* 1:407–45.

5. "Our Country Contemporaries," *DEN*, July 26, 1875.

6. F. Lockley to [Elizabeth Metcalf Campbell Lockley], July 31, 1875, FELC; "Mocking at Our Griefs," *SLT*, Dec. 2, 1874; "Amending the Poland Bill," *SLT*, Dec. 2, 1874; "'Royal' and His Persecuters," *SLT*, June 20, 1875; "Duty of Congress," *SLT*, Aug. 5, 1875.

7. TM, 48–49; "The Lee Trial," *SLT*, July 23, 1875; "The Beaver Trial," *OJ*, July 20, 1875; LPCB 13:767.

8. TM, 120–270, 285–87; "The Lee Trial," *PDR*, July 25, 1875.

9. TM, 267–68; MB1, 235–36; "The Lee Trial," *SLT*, July 23, 1875; "The Lee Trial," *DEN*, July 23, 1875; "The Lee Trial," *PDR*, July 25, 1875; "Mountain Meadows," *SLT*, July 27, 1875; "Our Country Contemporaries," *DEN*, July 27, 1875; "The Mountain Meadow Massacre," *Elmira (NY) Daily Advertiser*, July 27, 1875.

10. "The Mormon Massacre," *HDT*, July 25, 1875.

11. George C. Bates to James Jack, July 22, [1875], Brigham Young Telegram Book (Nov. 7, 1873, to Aug. 6, 1875), 461, YOF.

12. "The Mormon Massacre," *HDT*, July 25, 1875.

13. TM, 288–94; "The Lee Trial," *DEN*, July 23, 1875. On conserving grain, see *MatMM*, 47–49.

14. TM, 294–95; "The Lee Trial," *DEN*, July 23, 1875; *MatMM*, 119.

15. TM, 329–33; "The Lee Trial," *DEN*, July 23, 1875.

16. TM, 335–37; "The Lee Trial," *DEN*, July 23, 1875; Daniel H. Wells, Special Orders, May 21, 1854, order 442, Nauvoo Legion (UT), Records, ca. 1852–58, USARS, microfilm copy at FHL; PSHR, second section, entry of July 15, 1856; *MatMM*, 51.

17. TM, 357–68.

18. TM, 369–75.

19. TM, 710.

20. *MC* 1:213; HOJ, July 31, 1859; TM, 524–31, 694–97; Warren Foote, autobiography, 1865, 1:194, CHL.

21. "Obedience to Counsel," *SLT*, July 31, 1875.

22. Editorial, *PDR*, July 29, 1875; "Press Comments," *SLT*, Aug. 3, 1875; "Speaking Freely," *SLT*, Aug. 4, 1875; "The United States," *London Times*, Aug. 13, 1875.

23. TM, 383–93.

24. TM, 393–96.

25. *MatMM*, 141, 263–64, 343n70.

26. TM, 402–10.

27. TM, 410–28.

28. "Unveiled," *SLGD*, July 24, 1875; "A Tale of Horror," *Steubenville (OH) Daily Herald*, July 24, 1875; "Some Mormon History," *LADS*, July 25, 1875.

29. TM, 424–54, 480–507, 513–18, 521–769. Whether Klingensmith fired varies according to the shorthand reporter. Rogerson recorded, "I fired once." Patterson wrote, "Whether I did nor not I can't tell." TM, 424.

30. TM, 516–17.

31. TM, 468–69, 476; "A Tale of Horror"; "Unveiled," *SLGD*, July 24, 1875; "The Massacre," *DAG*, July 25, 1875.

32. "City Jottings," *SLT*, July 25, 1875. See also "The Mountain Meadows," *SLGD*, July 26, 1875.

33. "The Mormon Massacre," *HDT*, July 25, 1875; "The Lee Trial," *DEN*, July 23, 1875; "The Lee Trial," *LADS*, July 24, 1875; "Utah," *DAC*, July 24, 1875.

34. TM, 770–922.

35. TM, 923–32.

36. "The Lee Trial," *PDR*, July 29, 1875; TM, 934–45; "Mountain Meadow Massacre," *SLDH*, July 27, 1875; "The Lee Trial," *SLT*, July 27, 1875.

37. TM, 950–51, 957–59, 963–64, 973–74, 983–85, 991–97.

38. TM, 1015–46, 1055–61.

39. TM, 1076, 1088–108, 1121–29; "Beaver, U.T., July 27," *PDR*, July 28, 1875.

40. JDL1-BT 4:72.

41. TM, 1151.

42. TM, 1152–217; "The Lee Trial," *SLT*, July 28, 1875; "Incidents of the Trial," *SLT*, Aug. 1, 1875.

43. TM, 1218–27.

44. TM, 1227–29.

45. TM, 1229–30; "The Lee Trial," *PDR*, July 29, 1875.

46. TM, 1230–43.

47. TM, 1259–98. Though Pearce claimed he was only about fourteen at the time of the massacre, records show he was actually eighteen.

48. TM, 1317–19.

49. TM, 1324.

50. Fish, 144, 147, 156; TM, 1298–306.

51. TM, 1312–13.

52. TM, 1349–56.

53. TM, 1356–77; MB1, 242–43.

54. Editorial, *DNSJ*, July 25, 1875.

55. "City Jottings," *SLT*, July 27, 1875, quoting the *San Francisco Post*.

56. "The Massacre," *SLT*, July 27, 1875, citing the *Gold Hill News*. See also "City Jottings," *SLT*, July 27, 1875; "The Duty of Government," *SLT*, July 28, 1875; "Voice of the Press," *SLT*, July 30, 1875.

57. "Crime of the Priesthood," *SLT*, July 31, 1875, quoting *San Francisco Post*.

58. "Wants Extra-Judicial Measures," *DEN*, July 29, 1875.

59. "Covering It Up," *SLT*, July 29, 1875.

60. "Pacific Coast," *PDR*, July 29, 1875; "The Mountain Meadows Massacre," *LADS*, July 29, 1875; "The Massacre," *DAG*, July 30, 1875; "The Beaver Trial," *OJ*, July 29, 1875; "The Lee Trial," *DEN*, July 29, 1875; "Mountain Meadow Massacre," *SLDH*, July 29, 1875; "The Lee Trial," *SLT*, July 29, 1875; "The Mountain Meadow Massacre," *DAC*, July 30, 1875; "The Lee Trial," *PDR*, July 29, 1875.

61. "The Lee Trial," *DEN*, July 29, 1875; "Mountain Meadow Massacre," *SLDH*, July 29, 1875; "The Beaver Trial," *OJ*, July 29, 1875; "The Lee Trial," *SLT*, July 30, 1875; "The Massacre," *DAG*, July 30, 1875; "Pacific Coast," *PDR*, July 30, 1875; "Beaver, July 28," *PDJ*, July 30, 1875.

Chapter 38

1. "The Mountain Meadow Massacre," *DAC*, July 30, 1875; TM, 1511; "Judge Spicer's Address," *SLT*, Aug. 3, 1875; MB1, 243–44.

2. "The Lee Trial," *PDR*, July 29, 1875.

3. "The Lee Trial," *PDR*, July 30, 1875.

4. TM, 1383-573.

5. TM, 1505–12.

6. TM, 1515–16.

7. TM, 1517–21.

8. TM, 1521–22.

9. TM, 1563–67, 1569–70.

10. TM, 1569–72.

11. "The Lee Trial," *PDR*, July 30, 1875; "The Lee Trial," *SLT*, July 30, 1875; "Judge Spicer's Address," *SLT*, Aug. 3, 1875.

12. TM, 1573–79; "Judge Spicer's Address," *SLT*, Aug. 3, 1875.

13. TM, 1580–81.

14. "Judge Spicer's Address," *SLT*, Aug. 3, 1875.

15. "Mountain Meadow Massacre," *SLDH*, July 31, 1875; "The Beaver Trial," *OJ*, July 31, 1875; MB1, 245.

16. TM, 1702–2063.

17. TM, 1879–80.

18. "The Lee Trial," *PDR*, July 31, 1875.

19. TM, 1971–2138.

20. Editorial, *WBDRT*, July 31, 1875.

21. "Utah," *WBDRT*, July 31, 1875.

22. TM, 2148–54; MB1, 247–48; CCF 31. The affidavits were printed in "Depositions of Presidents Brigham Young and Geo. A. Smith Concerning the Mountain Meadow Massacre," *DEN*, Aug. 2, 1875; "Mountain Meadows," *OJ*, Aug. 3, 1875; "The Lee Trial," *SLT*, Aug. 3, 1875; "Brigham's Deposition," *NYT*, Aug. 3, 1875; "Depositions of Presidents Brigham Young and Geo. A. Smith Concerning the Mountain Meadow Massacre," *DN*, Aug. 4, 1875. In them, both denied having any knowledge of the massacre until after it occurred. Young described Lee's reporting of the massacre, acknowledged receiving a letter from Haight before the massacre, and said he instructed Haight "to let this company of emigrants and all companies of emigrants pass through the country unmolested, and to all[a]y the angry feelings of the Indians as much as possible." Smith said he was unaware of the Arkansas company before meeting it at Corn Creek on his return to Salt Lake in 1857 and first heard about the massacre when he was near Fort Bridger after it occurred.

23. TM, 2154–62.

24. TM, 2163.

25. "Mormon Butchery!," *SLT*, Aug. 1, 1875, quoting *San Francisco Chronicle*; "The Mountain Meadow Massacre," *NYH*, Aug. 3, 1875.

26. "The Necessity of the Day," *PDR*, Aug. 3, 1875.

27. "Duty of Congress," *SLT*, Aug. 5, 1875.

28. "What the Indians Say," *Los Angeles Weekly Herald*, Aug. 7, 1875.

29. TM, 2163–89; CCF 31.

30. "The Lee Trial," *DEN*, Aug. 4, 1875; "The Beaver Trial," *OJ*, Aug. 4, 1875; TM, 2228–29.

31. TM, 2271–78, 2304, 2318–21, 2374.

32. TM, 2380–86; MB1, 249–50.

33. TM, 2399–2400, 2502–3.

34. TM, 2570–72, 2583–93.

35. TM, 2602–973; MB1, 249–50; "The Lawyers at Work," *SLT*, Aug. 8, 1875.

36. "Equal and Exact Justice," *SLT*, Aug. 4, 1875.

37. R. T. Burton to Joseph F. Smith, Aug. 3, 1875, Joseph F. Smith Papers, CHL.

38. "Mountain Meadow Atrocity," *DNSJ*, July 29, 1875; "The Lee Trial," *PDR*, July 30, 1875; "The Mountain Meadow Massacre," *DAC*, July 30, 1875.

39. "Brigham's Testimony," *SLT*, August 1, 1875.

40. MB1, 250–51; "Beaver, August 5," *PDR*, Aug. 7, 1875; "Beaver, 5," *PDJ*, Aug. 7, 1875.

41. TM, 3074, 3083, 3213.

42. "The Case of the Defense," *SLT*, Aug. 3, 1875; "Beaver, Utah, August 6," *PDR*, Aug. 8, 1875.

43. MB1, 255; "The Verdict," *SLT*, Aug. 8, 1875.

44. "Mountain Meadow Massacre," *SLDH*, Aug. 8, 1875; "The Verdict," *SLT*, Aug. 8, 1875; HOJ, Aug. 6, 1875.

45. "The Verdict"; "The Mountain Meadow Massacre," *DAC*, Aug. 8, 1875.

46. "Justice or Vengeance," *SLT*, Aug. 8, 1875.

47. "Needful," *PDR*, Aug. 8, 1875.

48. "The United States," *London Times*, Aug. 9, 1875.

49. "Needful," *PDR*, Aug. 8, 1875.

Chapter 39

1. *MC* 2:343–44, 346.

2. "The Beaver Trial," *SLT*, Aug. 11, 1875.

3. CCF 34.

4. CCF 31.

5. *MatMM*, 136, 177–79.

6. Application for continuance, Aug. 5, 1875, in *United States v. William H. Dame*, CCF 34; *MC* 2:368.

7. *MC* 2:349–50, 368.

8. See Zenos H. Gurley, *The Legal Succession of Joseph Smith, Son of Joseph Smith the Martyr* (Plano, IL: True Latter-day Saints' Herald, [1866]), 4–8; *Brighamite Doctrines: A Delineation of Some of the False Doctrines of Brighamism . . .* (Plano, IL: True Latter-day Saints' Herald, [1864]).

9. *MC* 2:350; *The History of the Reorganized Church of Jesus Christ of Latter Day Saints*, vol. 4 (Independence, MO: Herald House, 1967), 7–8, 111.

10. *MC* 2:351–52.

11. George C. Bates to Brigham Young, Aug. 9, 1875, TLKC.

12. "Decease of President George A. Smith," *DEN*, Sept. 1, 1875; "Death of Geo. A. Smith," *SLT*, Sept. 2, 1875.

13. "In Memoriam," *SLT*, Sept. 2, 1875.

14. "Mountain Meadows," *Wilkes-Barre (PA) Record of the Times*, Apr. 10, 1877; "More Proof," *SLT*, Mar. 27, 1877.

15. "Higbee and Haight," *SLDH*, Sept. 9, 1875; "Haight and Higbee," *SLT*, Sept. 10, 1875; "Haight and Higbee," *SLT*, Sept. 14, 1875; "Our Beaver Letter," *SLT*, Sept. 19, 1875; *MC* 2:361.

16. *MC* 2:375.

17. *MC* 2:364–65.

18. See, for example, "Conviction of John D. Lee," *Colorado Chieftain*, Sept. 28, 1876.

19. D&C 131, 132:19.

20. Woodruff, Sept. 29, 1857; Wilford Woodruff, statement, undated, CM; Penrose, 51–53; "The Lee Execution," *NYH*, Mar. 25, 1877; *MC* 2:143–44, 151–53, 358; *MU*, 291; JRS.

21. *MC* 2:368.

22. *MC* 2:378.

23. *MC* 2:382; HOJ, Sept. 26, 1871; Daniel W. Jones, *Forty Years among the Indians* (Salt Lake City: Juvenile Instructor, 1890), 129–30; "Prisoners and Cases," *SLT*, May 2, 1872; J. H. Beadle, ed., *Brigham's Destroying Angel* (New York: G. A. Crofutt, 1872), 190–93.

24. "Reminiscences of John R. Young," *UHQ* 3 (July 1930): 85.

25. "Crime," *SLT*, Nov. 3, 1875; "Territorial Dispatches," *DN*, Nov. 10, 1875; "Arrest of Adair," *SLT*, Nov. 3, 1875; TM, 1019.

26. *MC* 2:361.

27. "Southern Utah," *SLT*, Dec. 24, 1875; "The Fountain Green Choir," in *Our Pioneer Heritage*, comp. Kate B. Carter, vol. 4 (Salt Lake City: Daughters of Utah Pioneers, 1961), 165, 167.

28. "The Lee Trial," *SLDH*, Aug. 8, 1875; "Verdict of the People," *SLT*, Aug. 12, 1875; "The Blindness of Hate," *DEN*, Aug. 14, 1875; "The Mormon Butchery," *SLT*, Aug. 14, 1875; "Endowment Robed Jury," *SLT*, Aug. 15, 1875; "How to Right the Wrong," *SLT*, Aug. 17, 1875; "The Republic's Shame," *SLT*, Aug. 19, 1875; *MC* 2:372.

29. "Utah Affairs," *SLT*, Sept. 8, 1875.

30. LPCB 13:954–55. This was the second indictment against Reynolds for practicing plural marriage. The first trial ended in conviction, but was "reversed, on the grounds that the grand jury had been improperly impaneled." Gordon, 115.

31. LPCB 14:60.

32. "A Word of Caution," *SLT*, Nov. 30, 1875.

33. "Utah Matters in Washington," *DN*, Dec. 29, 1875; 43 Cong. Rec. 4468, 5417 (June 2, 23,1874).

34. 44 Cong. Rec. 777 (Jan. 31, 1876).

35. LPCB 14:470–71, 473.

36. "Correspondence," *DEN*, Sept. 23, 1876.

37. *MC* 2:421–22, 445. Dame returned to Parowan before he was formally granted bail, which occurred in May 1876.

38. *MC* 2:436.

39. *MC* 2:452.

40. George Q. Cannon to Brigham Young, Feb. 4, 15, 1876, LCLO; "It Has Come," *SLDH*, Dec. 14, 1875; MB1, 343–46; LPCB 14:65–66; "Mountain Meadows," *San Francisco Daily Morning Call*, Mar. 10, 1877.

41. Benjamin A. Spear to [Edwards] Pierrepont, Jan. 20, 1876, MMML; George Q. Cannon to Brigham Young, Feb. 4, 1876, LCLO.

42. "Owned by Brigham," *SLT*, Apr. 29, 1876. Brigham Young and George Q. Cannon were not, in fact, eager for Carey's removal and tried to have him retained, but to no avail. George Q. Cannon to Brigham Young, Feb. 24, 1876, LCLO.

43. In spring 1875, when Carey first prosecuted George Reynolds for polygamy, Baskin saved the day by suggesting a vital witness, he later claimed. Baskin, 62–63. Before the beginning of Lee's trial later in the year, a reporter for the *Tribune* believed that without Baskin's aid, Carey "would have made a complete failure of the trial." Frederic Lockley to [Elizabeth Metcalf Campbell Lockley], July 22, 1875, FELC.

44. *MC* 2:450–52.

45. "Capital Topics," *National Republican*, Mar. 31, 1876; Geo. Q. Cannon to Brigham Young, Mar. 31, 1876; John S. Goff, *The Supreme Court Justices 1863–1912*, vol. 1 of *Arizona Territorial Officials* (Cave Creek, AZ: Black Mountain Press, 1975), 100-101.

Chapter 40

1. "Miscellaneous," *SLT*, May 10, 1876.

2. *AJ-DHM*, 248–49; *MatMM*, 178.

3. *MatMM*, 136, 178–79; James H. Martineau to Susan Martineau, May 3, 1876, James H. Martineau Collection, CHL. Higbee quoted Dame's initial order in his 1894 Bull Valley Snort, showing it may still have been in existence then. Bull Valley Snort [John M. Higbee], statement, Feb. 1894, 5, photocopy of manuscript, Juanita Brooks Collection, UofU.

4. JHM, May 2–7, 1876; Martineau to Martineau, May 3, 1876; *AJ-DHM*, 62–64, 68–69.

5. MBB, 334–37.

6. Continuance hearing, May 10, 1876, manuscript, in Josiah Rogerson, Transcripts and Notes of the John D. Lee Trials, CHL, transcription by LaJean Purcell Carruth; "The Mountain Meadows," *SLDH*, May 11, 1876.

7. "Miscellaneous," *SLT*, May 11, 1876; "Miscellaneous," *SLT*, May 12, 1876.

8. "Released on Bail," *SLT*, May 12, 1876.

9. Sumner Howard to T. W. Ferry, May 27, 1876, MMML.

10. "Our New District Attorney," *SLT*, May 30, 1876.

11. See pp. C37P8–C37P9, C37P28, C37P2.

12. LPCB 13:83.

13. See, e.g., Delana R. Eckels to Lewis Cass, Sept. 27, 1859, copy, FALG.

14. Frederic E. Lockley, "Memoirs of an Unsuccessful Man," unpublished autobiography, 228, FELC.

15. "Mountain Meadows," *Wilkes-Barre (PA) Record of the Times*, Apr. 10, 1877; "More Proof," *SLT*, Mar. 27, 1877.

16. "The United States," *London Times*, Aug. 9, 1875.

17. "Personal," *SLT*, Sept. 5, 1876; "Southward," *SLT*, Sept. 9, 1876; Lockley, "Memoirs of an Unsuccessful Man," 228. On John C. Young, see "Local and Other Matters,"

DN, Nov. 17, 1875; "Cancer of Stomach Claims Jno. C. Young," *DEN*, May 30, 1910; Baskin, 24.

18. "Beaver," *SLT*, Sept. 10, 1876; HOJ, Aug. 28, 1876.
19. Daniel H. Wells to John R. Murdock, Sept. 1, 1876, Daniel H. Wells Collection, CHL; Jenson1, 52–53.
20. "Mormon Perfidy," *Atlanta Constitution*, Sept. 23, 1876.
21. "The Lee Trial," *SLT*, Sept. 12, 1876.
22. Entry for Sept. 11, 1876, MB1; Commitment of John D. Lee into custody, Sept. 11, 1876, CCF 31.
23. "The Lee Trial," *SLT*, Sept. 12, 1876.
24. "Beaver," *SLT*, Sept. 24, 1876; "The Lee Trial," *PDR*, Sept. 29, 1876.
25. MB1, 496.
26. "The Lee Trial," *SLT*, Sept. 12, 1876.
27. "Southern Coast Notes," *DAC*, Sept. 10, 1876; "Batch of Items from the Southern Counties," *SDU*, Sept. 11, 1876; "City Jottings," *SLT*, Sept. 13, 1876.
28. "Mountain Meadows Trials," *SLT*, Sept. 9, 1876.
29. See F. Lockley to [Elizabeth Metcalf Campbell Lockley], July 31, 1875, FELC.
30. "The Lee Case," *SLT*, Sept. 17, 1876; MB1, 466; LPCB 14:494.
31. "Caught in the Toils," *SLT*, Sept. 21, 1876; *AJ-DHM*, 69; "LLC"; *MatMM*, 178–79, 212–13.
32. George Q. Cannon, journal, Nov. 6, 1876, CHL.
33. "Correspondence," *DEN*, Sept. 23, 1876.

Chapter 41

1. "Lee Interviewed," *SLT*, Sept. 14, 1876.
2. "Lee Interviewed"; "The Lee Case," *SLT*, Sept. 17, 1876; Notice, *PDR*, Sept. 13, 1876; TM, 3826.
3. Attorneys assisting Carey in the prosecution in Lee's first trial included D. P. Whedon, R. N. Baskin, Charles J. Swift, C. M. Hawley, and Presley Denny. MB1, 236.
4. "The Lee Trial," *SLT*, Sept. 15, 1876; J. D. Lee to Rachel Lee, Sept. 24, 1876, HM 31218, JDLC; "Territorial Dispatches," *DN*, Sept. 20, 1876; LPCB 14:498.
5. "The Lee Case."
6. See Sumner Howard to Alphonso Taft, Oct. 4, 1876, in LRS.
7. TM, 3916–17.
8. "Mountain Meadows," *PDR*, Sept. 17, 1876.
9. "The Lee Trial"; "The Lee Case"; "Mountain Meadow Massacre," *SLDH*, Sept. 15, 1876.
10. "Territorial Dispatches," *Deseret Weekly News*, Sept. 20, 1876.
11. TM, 3413–16; "The Lee Case," *SLT*, Sept. 19, 1876; *AJ-DHM*, 331.
12. Daniel H. Wells to Jacob Hamblin, Aug. 22, 1876, Letterpress Copybook, Daniel H. Wells Collection, CHL.

13. Editorial, *SLT*, Sept. 21, 1876; Amasa Lyman, journal, July 19, 1875, AMLC; "Merriment Misplaced," *SLT*, Oct. 18, 1876.
14. Wells to Hamblin, Aug. 22, 1876.
15. TM, 3415–16.
16. TM, 3432–49; "Territorial Dispatches," *DEN*, Sept. 16, 1876.
17. TM, 3433–37.
18. TM, 3451–53, 3466; "Territorial Dispatches," *Deseret Weekly News*, Sept. 20, 1876; Haslam.
19. TM, 3467–78.
20. TM, 3478–79, 3491–508.
21. TM, 3482–86.
22. TM, 3521–32.
23. "Territorial Dispatches," *DN*, Sept. 20, 1876.
24. TM, 3537–38.
25. TM, 3539–40. In the first trial, other witnesses claimed they had been called out to the Meadows to save the emigrants or help bury the dead. TM, 1161–63, 1584. But once at the Meadows, the men were instructed how to carry out the massacre.
26. TM, 3544–45.
27. TM, 3901.
28. TM, 3556–58.
29. TM, 3564–66.
30. "The Lee Trial," *SLT*, Sept. 16, 1876.
31. TM, 3562.
32. TM, 3630–31.
33. TM, 3638.
34. TM, 3839–40.
35. TM, 3864.
36. J. D. Lee to Emma B. Lee, Sept. 21, 1876, HM 31211, JDLC.

Chapter 42

1. Jacob S. Boreman, charge to the jury, Sept. 20, 1876, CCF 31.
2. Carleton, 7. Hamblin greatly expanded his original account in 1871 and in his 1876 trial testimony. See JH-BY; JHS; TM, 3748–49; JHM, Sept. 24, 1857; William H. Dame to George A. Smith, Sept. 21, 1857, GASP; JNSJ, Sept. 25, 1857.
3. Shelton, May 12, 1859; Rogers.
4. TM, 3717–20.
5. TM, 3690–91, 3718.
6. TM, 3731.
7. TM, 3676.
8. TM, 3692–97, 3705.
9. J. D. Lee to Emma B. Lee, Sept. 21, 1876, HM 31211, JDLC.

10. Beadle; Carleton, 26.

11. Boreman, charge to the jury, Sept. 20, 1876, CCF 31.

12. LPCB 19:288–89.

13. Editorial, *SLT*, Sept. 21, 1876; "The Butcher Lee," *SLT*, Jan. 24, 1875.

14. TM, 3750–52.

15. TM, 3752.

16. "Mountain Meadow Massacre," *SLDH*, Sept. 15, 1876; "The Lee Trial," *SLT*, Sept. 15, 1876.

17. TM, 3762.

18. TM, 3766–77.

19. "Territorial Dispatches," *DN*, Sept. 27, 1876; TM, 3769–79, 3781–826.

20. TM, 3827–28.

21. TM, 3829–30.

22. TM, 3857–58.

23. TM, 3837.

24. TM, 1143.

25. TM, 3861.

26. TM, 3866.

27. TM, 3872–76, 3881–84, 3886–87.

28. TM, 3876, 3889, 3890–91.

29. TM, 3893, 3899.

30. TM, 3903–4.

31. TM, 3884–85.

32. TM, 3910.

33. TM, 3914–17.

34. TM, 3901, 3921.

35. TM, 3922–25, 3933.

36. TM, 3937. Howard ignored Klingensmith's statement in the first trial that he was ordered to the Meadows "armed and equipped." TM, 404.

37. TM, 3963–64.

38. "Territorial Dispatches," *DEN*, Sept. 19, 1876.

39. TM, 3915, 3932.

40. TM, 3925.

41. "The Lee Trial," *SLT*, Sept. 21, 1876.

42. Boreman, charge to the jury, Sept. 20, 1876, CCF 31.

43. "The Lee Trial," *PDR*, Sept. 29, 1876; "The Lee Trial," *SLT*, Sept. 21, 1876.

Chapter 43

1. "The Lee Trial," *PDR*, Sept. 29, 1876; "The Lee Trial," *SLT*, Sept. 21, 1876; J. D. Lee to Rachel Lee, Sept. 24, 1876, HM 31218, JDLC.

2. "The Verdict," *SLT*, Sept. 26, 1876.

3. Andrew Corry, statement, Aug. 2, 1931, transcript, MMMRF.

4. "The Verdict," *SLT*, Sept. 26, 1876; Corry, statement, Aug. 2, 1931.

5. J. D. Lee to Rachel Lee, Sept. 24, 1876, HM 31218, JDLC.

6. *MU*, 33.

7. "The Lee Case," *SLT*, Sept. 17, 1876.

8. "Lawyer Bishop," *SLDH*, June 14, 1877; "Sumner Howard," *SLT*, Jan. 19, 1878.

9. *Reports of Cases Determined in the Supreme Court of the Territory of Utah from the January Term, 1877, to the June Term, 1880 Inclusive*, vol. 2 (Chicago: Callaghan, 1881), 442–45.

10. "The Verdict," *SLT*, Sept. 26, 1876; J. D. Lee to Emma B. Lee, Sept. 21, 1876, HM 31211, JDLC.

11. LPCB 19:299.

12. LPCB 19:298.

13. "Beaver," *SLDH*, Sept. 22, 1876.

14. J. D. Lee to Rachel Lee, Sept. 24, 1876, HM 31218, JDLC; J. D. Lee to Emma B. Lee, Sept. 21, 1876, HM 31211, JDLC.

15. See HOJ, May 25, June 18, July 5, 1859; George A. Smith to William H. Dame, June 19, 1859, HOLC 2:127–28; Jno. Cradlebaugh and Chas. E. Sinclair to James Buchanan, July 16, 1859, John Cradlebaugh file, James Buchanan Administration, Utah Appointment Papers, RG 60, entry 350, NARA; BYOJ, Sept. 2, 1859; George A. Smith to I. C. Haight, Nov. 6, 1859, HOLC 1:84; *JD*, 10:110; "Conversation between Col Potter, Capt Grimes and Prestd Young on establishment of liquor Saloons," May 8, 1866, FALG; LPCB 11:362–63; HOLC 2:944–45; LPCB 13:80–84; George A. Smith to John Codman, Dec. 4, 1874, GASLC.

16. *MC* 1:219.

17. "Caught in the Toils," *SLT*, Sept. 21, 1876; "A Barren Victory," *SLT*, Sept. 22, 1876.

18. George Q. Cannon to Brigham Young, May 16, 1872, LCLO.

19. "Howard's Course," *SLT*, Sept. 26, 1876.

20. William Nelson and Sumner Howard to Alphonso Taft, Sept. 23, 1876, MMML, copy in FRU.

21. Sumner Howard to Alphonso Taft, Oct. 4, 1876, MMML, copy in FRU.

22. [Isaac C. Haight] to [Eliza Ann Price Haight], Dec. 2, 1877, ICHC, typescript copy in Caroline Parry Woolley, Biography of Isaac C. Haight, draft, 205–6, CPWC; [Isaac C. Haight] to [Eliza Ann Price Haight], Oct. 14–15, 1877, ICHC, typescript copy in Woolley, Biography of Isaac C. Haight, draft, 205–6, CPWC; "The Answer to a Request Was No!," undated typescript, CPWC; "If There Is a Mission You Can Perform You Shall Be Called," undated typescript, CPWC; *MMM-CLP*, 1:506; Robert A. Slack, "A Biographical Study of Isaac Chauncey Haight, Early Religious and Civic Leader of Southern Utah" (master's thesis, Brigham Young University, 1966), 94; Woolley, 161; David E. Miller, *Hole-in-the-Rock* (Salt Lake City: University of Utah Press, 1966), 144; "Those Pioneers Went through the Hole in the Rock," undated typescript, CPWC.

23. Howard to Taft, Oct. 4, 1876.

24. LPCB 19:299; "Beaver," *SLT*, Sept. 22, 1876; MB1, 501.

25. Jacob S. Boreman, Sentence of John D. Lee, Oct. 10, 1876, BC; *MMM-CLP* 2:693; "The Sentence of Lee," *SLDH*, Oct. 15, 1876.

26. J. D. Lee to Rachel Andora Lee, Oct. 12, 1876, HM 31220, JDLC; J. D. Lee to Emma B. Lee, Oct. 10, 1876, HM 31212, JDLC.

27. J. D. Lee to Emma B. Lee, Oct. 10, 1876.

28. *MU*, 34.

29. John D. Lee, petition for transcript, Oct. 14, 1876, photocopy, CHL.

30. J[ohn] C. Y[oung], Sept. 13, 1876, in "The Trial," *SLT*, Sept. 16, 1876.

31. J. D. Lee to William Prince, Oct. 13, 1876, HM 31233, JDLC.

32. John D. Lee to Rachel Andora Lee, Oct. 17, 1876, HM 31221, JDLC.

33. John D. Lee to Harvey P. Lee, Oct. 17, 1876, HM 31208, JDLC; " 'Idaho Bill,' One of the Captive Children, Tells His Tale," *NYH*, May 17, 1877.

34. J. D. Lee to Joseph H. Lee, Oct. 26, 1876, HM 31216, JDLC.

35. *MU*, 34; William W. Bishop to William Nelson, Dec. 20, 1876, HM 31236, JDLC.

36. John D. Lee to Sarah C. W. Lee, Nov. 1, 1876, HM 31223, JDLC.

37. J. D. Lee to Sara Jane Lee, Nov. 16, 1876, HM 31227, JDLC.

38. J. D. Lee to Emma B. Lee, Dec. 9, 1876, HM 31214, JDLC; *MatMM*, 258.

39. Bishop to Nelson, Dec. 20, 1876.

Chapter 44

1. George Q. Cannon, journal, Jan. 8, 1877, CHL.

2. "Boreman's Balderdash," *OJ*, Oct. 11, 1876.

3. George Q. Cannon to Brigham Young, Jan. 11, 1877, LCLO; Sumner Howard to Alphonso Taft, Feb. 3, 1877, LDU.

4. John D. Lee to Joseph H. Lee, Feb. 24, 1877, HM 31217, JDLC; *MMM-CLP*, 765.

5. "The Lee Case," *SLT*, Feb. 1, 1877.

6. *Reports of Cases Determined in the Supreme Court of the Territory of Utah from the January Term, 1877, to the June Term, 1880 Inclusive*, vol. 2 (Chicago: Callaghan, 1881), 442–43.

7. "The Lee Case."

8. *Reports of Cases*, 2:456.

9. William W. Bishop to John D. Lee, Feb. 23, 1877, HM 31234, JDLC.

10. John D. Lee to William W. Bishop, Mar. 2, 1877, HM 31210, JDLC.

11. John D. Lee to O. A. Patton, Mar. 4, 1877, HM 31232, JDLC.

12. William W. Bishop to John D. Lee, Mar. 9, 1877, HM 31235, JDLC.

13. See the following in JDLC: John D. Lee to Rachel Lee, Sept. 29, 1876, HM 31219; J. D. Lee to Emma B., Oct. 10, 1876, HM 31212; J. D. Lee to Rachel A. Lee, Oct. 12, 1876, HM 31220; John D. Lee to Emma Lee, Oct. 26, 1876, HM 31213; John D. Lee to Jos. and Hellen Wood, Oct. 26, 1876, HM 31228; John D. Lee to Sara Jane Lee, Nov. 16, 1876, HM 31227; John D. Lee to Emma Lee, Dec. 9, 1876, HM 31214; John D. and Rachel Lee to "My Children at the Mow-E-yabba," Dec. 15, 1876, HM 31230; John

D. and Rachel Lee to Lehi and Amorah Smithson, Dec. 25, 1876, HM 31229; Nancy Lee Dalton to John D. Lee and Rachel Lee, Jan. 27, 1877, HM 31240; Emma Lee to John D. Lee, Feb. 1, 1877, HM 31243; Lehi and Amorah Smithson to John D. Lee, Feb. 9, 1877, HM 31247; William W. Bishop to John D. Lee, Feb. 23, 1877; John D. Lee to Joseph Hyrum Lee, Feb. 24, 1877, HM 31217; Sarah Lee Dalton to John D. and Rachel Lee, Feb. 24, 1877, HM 31241; John D. Lee to William W. Bishop, Mar. 2, 1877, HM 31210.

14. *MC* 1:vii, xxviii–xxix; *Journals*, xxii–xxiii.

15. *MU*, 212.

16. "The Lee Trial," *PDR*, July 25, 1875.

17. Jacob S. Boreman to S. Howard, Feb. 23, 1877, enclosed in Sumner Howard and William Nelson to Alphonso Taft, Mar. 3. 1877, MMML, copy in FRU.

18. Sumner Howard and William Nelson to Alphonso Taft, Mar. 3, 1877, MMML.

19. George C. Bates to Jacob S. Boreman, Mar. 9, 1877, enclosed in Jacob S. Boreman to Charles Devens, Apr. 25, 1877, MMML, copy in FRU.

20. Boreman to Devens, Apr. 25, 1877, MMML.

21. "Journeying with Lee," *NYT*, Mar. 31, 1877; Brooks, 379–84.

22. "Our Country Contemporaries," *DN*, Mar. 14, 1877; "Journeying with Lee."

23. William Nelson and Sumner Howard to Alphonso Taft, Feb. 21, 1877, telegram, MMML.

24. "John D. Lee," *NYH*, Mar. 21, 1877.

25. William Nelson and Sumner Howard to Alphonso Taft, Mar. 1, 1877, telegram, enclosed in George McCrary to Charles Devens, Mar. 23, 1877, MMML.

26. Edward D. Townsend to Commanding Officer, Fort Cameron [Henry Douglass], Mar. 3, 1877, and Henry Douglass to Edward D. Townsend, Mar. 9, 1877, both enclosed in McCrary to Devens, Mar. 23, 1877, MMML.

27. Henry Douglass, General Orders no. 8, Mar. 8, 1877, enclosed in McCrary to Devens, Mar. 23, 1877.

28. "John D. Lee," *NYH*, Mar. 21, 1877.

29. "John D. Lee Sentenced," *SLT*, Mar. 9, 1877.

30. "Our Country Contemporaries," *DN*, Mar. 14, 1877.

31. John D. Lee to Joseph H. Lee, Feb. 24, 1877.

32. MB1, 603.

33. "Lee Bravely Awaiting Death," *NYH*, Mar. 18, 1877.

34. Joseph H. Lee to John D. Lee, Jan. 31, 1877, HM 31244, JDLC; Brooks1, 379.

35. "John D. Lee," *SLDH*, Mar. 16, 1877.

36. "Will Be Executed," *SLT*, Mar. 18, 1877.

37. "To-Morrow's Execution," *Eureka (NV) Republican*, Mar. 22, 1877.

38. "John D. Lee," *SLDH*, Mar. 16, 1877.

39. Petitions for the pardon of John D. Lee, Mar. 1877, Secretary of Territory, Utah Territory Executive Papers, 1850–96, Series 241, USARS.

40. "Petition for Pardon," *SLT*, Mar. 28, 1877.

41. "Petition for Pardon"; "John D. Lee," *SLDH*, Mar. 16, 1877.

42. "John D. Lee," *SLDH*, Mar. 16, 1877; Petitions for the pardon of John D. Lee, Mar. 1877, Secretary of Territory, Utah Territory Executive Papers, 1850–96, Series 241, USARS; "The Mormon Murderer," *NYH*, Mar. 20, 1877; "Beaver," *SLDH*, Mar. 21, 1877.

43. "Pacific Coast Dispatches," *Eureka (NV) Republican*, Mar. 22, 1877.

Chapter 45

1. H. Douglass to George T. T. Patterson, Mar. 20, 1877, as cited in George T. T. Patterson, report, Mar. 26, 1877, enclosed in H. Douglass to E. D. Townsend, Mar. 28, 1877, microfilm, Correspondence Regarding John D. Lee Trial and Execution, file 1013, AGO 1877, RG 94, NARA.

2. *MU*, 203, 212; *MMM-CLP* 2:785; "Shooting of Lee!"; "Miscellaneous," *SLT*, Mar. 8, 1877; Patterson, report, Mar. 26, 1877; "Through the Heart."

3. "Lee and Young," *NYH*, Mar. 23, 1877.

4. "M. M. M.," *SLDH*, Mar. 25, 1877; "Lee and Young"; "Territorial Dispatches," *DEN*, Mar. 23, 1877; "Lee's Last Moments," *SFDEB*, Mar. 23, 1877; "The Last of Lee," *SLT*, Mar. 24, 1877; "Sight-Seeing," *Provo (UT) Semi-Weekly Enquirer*, Mar. 21, 1877.

5. "Shooting of Lee!"

6. "Lee and Young"; "John D. Lee," *SLDH*, Mar. 20, 1877; "Lee Bravely Awaiting Death," *NYH*, Mar. 18, 1877; "Beaver," *SLDH*, Mar. 21, 1877.

7. "The Lee Execution," *NYH*, Mar. 25, 1877; "Shooting of Lee!"

8. "Shooting of Lee!"; "Through the Heart." On the Stokes relationship and Lee's arrest, see JRS; "The Butcher!," *SLT*, Nov. 13, 1874; *MU*, 293–301; "Vengeance Is Mine," *SLT*, Nov. 14, 1874; "Another Version," *SLT*, Nov. 14, 1874.

9. "Shooting of Lee!"; *MMM-CLP* 2:854; "M. M. M.," *SLDH*, Mar. 25, 1877; "The Lee Execution," *NYH*, Mar. 25, 1877.

10. "Shooting of Lee!"; "The Lee Execution"; "The Last of Lee," *SLT*, Mar. 24, 1877; "Through the Heart"; "Retribution!," *SDRU*, Mar. 24, 1877.

11. "Shooting of Lee!"

12. "Shooting of Lee!"; "The Lee Execution"; Patterson, report, Mar. 26, 1877.

13. See "The Place of Execution," *DEN*, Mar. 24, 1877. One newspaper commented, "There is something needlessly dramatic and sensational in taking him to the Mountain Meadows as the scene of his execution. . . . The law should be above such demonstrations." "The Execution of John D. Lee," *Carson City Appeal*, Mar. 24, 1877. The following year the Utah state legislature passed a statute requiring that a death sentence "must be executed within the walls or yard of a jail or some convenient private place in the district." *Laws, Memorials, and Resolutions of the Territory of Utah, Passed at the Twenty-Third Session of the Legislative Assembly* (Salt Lake City: John W. Pike, 1878), 136.

14. "John D. Lee," *SLT*, Feb. 21, 1877. See also "John D. Lee," *SLT*, Feb. 14, 1877; "John D. Lee Sentenced," *SLT*, Mar. 9, 1877.

15. See "John D. Lee Sentenced"; "John D. Lee," *SLT*, Feb. 14, 1877; J. D. Lee to Joseph H. Lee, Oct. 26, 1876, HM 31216, JDLC; John D. Lee to Emma B. Lee, Oct. 26, 1876, HM 31213, JDLC; John D. Lee to Sarah C. W. Lee, Nov. 1, 1876, HM 31223, JDLC; John D. Lee to Sara Jane Lee Dalton, Nov. 16, 1876, HM 31227, JDLC; "Shooting of Lee!"

16. "The Lee Execution," *NYH*, Mar. 25, 1877.

17. "The Lee Execution"; "M. M. M.," *SLDH*, Mar. 25, 1877.

18. "Retribution!," *SDRU*, Mar. 24, 1877; "Shooting of Lee!"

19. "The Last of Lee," *SLT*, Mar. 24, 1877.

20. "Territorial Dispatches," *DEN*, Mar. 24, 1877; "Through the Heart."

21. "Territorial Dispatches," *DEN*, Mar. 24, 1877; "M. M. M.," *SLDH*, Mar. 25, 1877.

22. Patterson, report, Mar. 26, 1877; "Retribution!," *SDRU*, Mar. 24, 1877; "Shooting of Lee!," *SLT*, Mar. 30, 1877; "The Lee Execution," *NYH*, Mar. 25, 1877.

23. Collins R. Hakes, statement, Apr. 24, 1916, CM.

24. Anthony W. Ivins, interview by Edna Lee Brimhall and Anthon H. Lee, July 28, 1931, in Edna Lee Brimhall, Lee Family History Papers, CHL; A. W. Ivins to Mrs. G. T. Welch, Oct. 16, 1922, First Presidency Letterpress Copybook, vol. 64, CHL; "John D. Lee's Last Days of Life," *DNSJ*, Mar. 21, 1877.

25. JRS.

26. Hakes, statement, Apr. 24, 1916, CM; Patterson, report, Mar. 26, 1877, enclosed in Douglass to Townsend, Mar. 28, 1877, Correspondence Regarding JDL Trial and Execution, file 1013, AGO 1877, RG 94; Orson Welcome Huntsman, diary, Mar. 23, 1877, CHL. For a lower estimate, see "Execution of John D. Lee," *Provo (UT) Semi-Weekly Enquirer*, Mar. 24, 1877. References to Mormons at Mountain Meadows on the day of Lee's execution include A. W. Ivins to Mrs. G. T. Welch, Oct. 16, 1922, First Presidency Letterpress Copybook, vol. 64; Henry D. Holt, biographical questionnaire, Jan. 9, 1939, in "Utah Pioneer Biographies," 13:94, FHL; Sharon M. Bliss, comp., "Autobiographies/Biography of Tullis, Mangum, Pulsipher, Maughan, Davenport, Dahle, Griffin, etc.," typescript, 3, [1995], copy at FHL; Hamilton Wallace, autobiographical sketch, undated typescript, 2, Collection of Mormon Diaries, LOC, microfilm copy in CHL.

27. "M. M. M.," *SLDH*, Mar. 25, 1877; "Execution of John D. Lee," transcript, CM; "The Lee Execution," *NYH*, Mar. 25, 1877; Henry Inman and William F. Cody, *The Great Salt Lake Trail* (New York: MacMillan, 1898), 143.

28. "Shooting of Lee!" On Joseph Smith's words, see D&C 135:4.

29. "Shooting of Lee!"; "The Lee Execution," *NYH*, Mar. 25, 1877; JRS.

30. "The Lee Execution," *NYH*, Mar. 25, 1877. On identity of firing squad members, see *MMM-CLP*, 2:856. "I have requested my boys not to seek revenge for my killing, but to leave vengeance to God," Lee told a reporter at the Meadows before his death. "The Lee Execution," *NYH*, Mar. 25, 1877.

31. JRS; *MC* 2:206–7, 260n86.

32. JRS; "Through the Heart."

33. "The Lee Execution," *NYH*, Mar. 25, 1877.

34. JRS; "John D. Lee," *San Francisco Daily Bulletin*, Mar. 24, 1877.

35. JRS; "John D. Lee's Full Speech," *SDRU*, Apr. 7, 1877.

36. "The Last of Lee," *SLT*, Mar. 24, 1877.

37. "Vengeance," *NYH*, Mar. 24, 1877.

38. "The Lee Execution," *NYH*, Mar. 25, 1877; Josiah Rogerson to W. B. Dougall, telegram, Mar. 22, 1877, YOF.

39. "The Last of Lee," *SLT*, Mar. 24, 1877.

Chapter 46

1. "LLC"; "LC"; "Another Confession," *NYH*, Mar. 24, 1877; *MMM-CLP* 2:781–82.

2. "Lee's Confession," *NYH*, Mar. 22, 1877; "John D. Lee Makes a Confession of His Crimes," *San Francisco Chronicle*, Mar. 22, 1877; "Mountain Meadows," *San Francisco Daily Evening Post*, Mar. 22, 1877. On Lee's various statements, see *MMM-CLP* 2:781–809. When Bishop's version of the confession appeared in the *NYH*, Latter-day Saint newspaperman Charles W. Penrose observed that Lee's statements had "been touched up and interpolated by the writer, until they cover much broader ground and more sweeping charges than the convicted criminal intended." Penrose or another editor subtitled the article that contained Bishop's version, "A Little Lee and a Little Lawyer." "The Bishop Edition of Lee's 'Confession,'" *OJ*, Mar. 26, 1877; "Reported Confession of John D. Lee," *OJ*, Mar. 26, 1877.

3. "Lee's Confession," *NYH*, Mar. 22, 1877.

4. As one example, Bishop quoted Lee's journal in "Lee's Confession," though he placed it out of context. He took Lee's journal account for May 30, 1861, and placed it in 1859 with the visit of Judge John Cradlebaugh to southern Utah. Bishop's account falsely claimed Young accompanied Cradlebaugh to Mountain Meadows. "Lee's Confession," *NYH*, Mar. 22, 1877; *MC* 1:313–14.

5. "LLC"; "LC"; "Lee's Confession," *NYH*, Mar. 22, 1877.

6. "Gilman against Howard," *Pioche (NV) Weekly Record*, May 5, 1877.

7. "Howard's Defence," *NYH*, May 9, 1877; Charles Devens to Sumner Howard, Apr. 11, 1877, LSDOJ; "Miscellaneous," *SLT*, Apr. 13, 1877; "Brigham's Power," *SLT*, May 24, 1877.

8. "Brigham's Power."

9. *MMM-CLP* 2:781–86; Richard E. Turley Jr., "Problems with Mountain Meadows Massacre Sources," *Brigham Young University Studies* 47, no. 3 (2008): 147–51.

10. Presley Denny to S. B. Aden, Apr. 20, 1877, enclosed in Sumner Howard to Charles Devens, Nov. 12, 1877, MMML.

11. Jerome P. Cross to F. F. Aden, Jan. 23, 1878, SCF, box 545.

12. Sumner Howard to Charles Devens, Nov. 8, 1877.

13. "The Criminal Prosecutions," *SLT*, July 18, 1877.

14. Joel Hills Johnson to Nephi Johnson, Apr. 20, 1877, CHL.

15. Arrington, 398–400.

16. "Brigham Young as a Ruler," *SLT*, Aug. 30, 1877.

17. Sumner Howard to Charles Devens, Sept. 29, 1877, Jan. 2, 1878, LRS.

18. Jacob S. Boreman to Charles Devens, Jan. 7, 1879, draft, HM 16924, BC.

19. Jacob S. Boreman to Charles Devens, Jan. 7, 1879, draft, HM 16924, BC; Chas. Devens to Michael Shaughnessy, Dec. 15, 1879, LSDOJ; Jacob S. Boreman to Charles Devens, Nov. 20, 1879, LRS; Chas. Devens to Jacob S. Boreman, Dec. 15, 1879, BC.

20. John Gary Maxwell, *Robert Newton Baskin and the Making of Modern Utah* (Norman, OK: Arthur H. Clark Co., 2013), 179-90, 213-14; Barbara Jones Brown, "Manifestos, Mixed Messages, and Mexico: The Demise of 'Mainstream' Mormon Polygamy," in *The Persistence of Polygamy*, ed. Newell G. Bringhurst and Craig L. Foster (Independence, MO: John Whitmer Books, 2015), 27.

21. D&C, Official Declaration—1; Thomas G. Alexander, "The Odyssey of a Latter-day Prophet: Wilford Woodruff and the Manifesto of 1890," in *In the Whirlpool: The Pre-Manifesto Letters of President Wilford Woodruff to the William Atkin Family, 1885–1890*, ed. Reid L. Neilson (Norman, OK: Arthur H. Clark, 2011), 57–96.

22. "Judge R. N. Baskin Dies in Salt Lake," *SLT*, Aug. 27, 1918; Maxwell, *Robert Newton Baskin and the Making of Modern Utah*, 227–29.

23. "In Memory of Pioneer Leader," *DEN*, June 3, 1901.

24. "Judge Baskin," *DEN*, Aug. 27, 1918.

25. Gustive O. Larson, *The "Americanization" of Utah for Statehood* (San Marino, CA: Huntington Library, 1971), 283–304.

26. See, e.g., John M. Higbee, affidavit, June 15, 1896, CM; *AJ-DHM*, 220, 328; Joel W. White, affidavit, October 9, 1896, CM.

27. William Logan Hebner, *Southern Paiute: A Portrait* (Logan: Utah State University Press, 2010), 79; General Anderson quoted in Christopher Smith, "Forensic Study Aids Tribe's View of Mountain Meadows Massacre," *SLT*, Jan. 21, 2001.

28. Isabel T. Kelly, "Southern Paiute Bands," *American Anthropologist* 36 (1934): 552–53.

29. Hebner, *Southern Paiute*, 79.

30. Brooks1, 332; Lorraine Richardson Manderscheid, *Some Descendants of John Doyle Lee* (Bellevue, WA: Family Research and Development, 1996), 210–11, 214, 796–99.

31. George A. Hicks to B. Young, Feb. 18, 1877, Letters, MACF.

32. George A. Hicks to Parowan Stake High Council, Feb. 17, 1901, William R. Palmer Collection, Gerald R. Sherratt Library, Southern Utah University, Cedar City, UT.

33. George A. Hicks to Wilford Woodruff, Apr. 15, 1894, WWGC. On Woodruff's remarks, see Brian H. Stuy, *Collected Discourses Delivered by President Wilford Woodruff, His Two Counselors, the Twelve Apostles, and Others*, vol. 4 (Burbank, CA: B. H. S. Publishing, 1991), 72–73.

34. See the numerous endnote sources supporting *MAMM*, Appendix A, 243-49.

35. McGlashan.

36. LPCB 15:118–19; Reuben G. Miller, journal, Dec. 31, 1888, in Mormon Missionary Diaries, BYU, Digital Collections, http://contentdm.lib.byu.edu/cdm/compoundobject/collection/MMD/id/30894/rec/3; Albert Bacon, diary, May 19, 23, Aug. 11, 31, 1898, Mar. 22, 1899, CHL.

37. "A Nice Tramp," *SLT*, Jan. 11, 1877; "Arrivals," *MS* 39, no. 6 (Feb. 5, 1877): 91.

38. Arthur M. Richardson and Nicholas G. Morgan Sr., *The Life and Ministry of John Morgan* (Salt Lake City: Nicholas G. Morgan Sr., 1965), 134.

39. Patrick Q. Mason, *The Mormon Menace* (New York: Oxford University Press, 2011), 21–56, 110–11.

40. J. Golden Kimball, journal, Sept. 16, 1897, CHL.

41. Walter H. Durrant, journal, Feb. 13–14, 1900, CHL.

Chapter 47

1. *AJ-DHM*, 242–43.

2. George Spencer to E. Snow, Mar. 26, 1867, IC.

3. McGlashan.

4. J. H. Beadle, *Western Wilds, and the Men Who Redeem Them* (Cincinnati: Jones Brothers, 1878), 497, 502–3; Entry for George Spencer, May 10, 1871, in Missionary Department, Missionary registers, Book A, 19, CHL; *MatMM*, 262.

5. "Mountain Meadows Massacre: Joseph Clewes' Statement concerning It," *Salt Lake Daily Herald*, Apr. 5, 1877.

6. See *MU*, 293–301; Parowan Ward, Parowan Stake, General minutes, Nov. 18, 1874, CHL; "Our Beaver Letter," *SLT*, July 20, 1875; *MC* 2:383; "An Assassin Arrested," *SLT*, Aug. 29, 1876. On the indictments, see *MMM-CLP* 1:407–45.

7. KS; "Summons," *PDJ*, Jan. 29, 1876; "Mountain Meadow Massacre," *Visalia (CA) Weekly Delta*, Sept. 21, 1876; Priscilla K. Urie, biographical sketch of Philip Klingensmith, Dec. 28, 1919, Church History Department, Biographical sketches, CHL; *Pioneer Women of Faith and Fortitude* (Salt Lake City: International Society Daughters of Utah Pioneers, 1998), 2:1684; "Local Intelligence," *PDR*, Dec. 9, 15, 1875.

8. Juanita Brooks, ed., *Journal of the Southern Indian Mission* (Logan: Utah State University Press, 1972), 161.

9. KS.

10. Josiah Rogerson, untitled typescript pages, ca. 1911, 6–7, in CM; *MatMM*, 178–79.

11. *MMM-CLP* 1:493–503, 511–18, David O. McKay, diary, July 27, 1907, UofU; *AJ-DHM*, 141–62.

12. *MatMM*, 219, 259, 398n31; *MMM-CLP* 1:461–63.

13. Jacob S. Boreman to Charles Devens, Jan. 7, 1879, HM 16924, BC; Chas. Devens to Jacob S. Boreman, Dec. 15, 1879, BC; Chas. Devens to M[ichael] Shaughnessy, June 10, 1880, LSDOJ.

14. "Autobiography of James William Nixon the Second," ca. 1937, 5–6, MMMRF.

15. William C. Stewart to Brigham Young, Mar. 10, 1877, IC.

16. "The Story of the Mountain Meadows Massacre," *San Francisco Daily Morning Call*, Mar. 24, 1877; Charles Devens to Sumner Howard, Apr. 4, 1877, LSDOJ.

17. C. J. Arthur to John Taylor, Mar. 9, 1881, First Presidency, John Taylor Presidential Papers, 1877–87, copy in MMMRF; C. J. Arthur to John Taylor, Apr. 21, 1881, Taylor Presidential Papers, copy in MMMRF.

18. W. C. Stewart to Wilford Woodruff and Council, Nov. 1, 1890, WWGC.

19. [William C. Stewart to Erastus Snow,] Aug. 17, 1882, Taylor Presidential Papers. The clerical notation on the letter suggests it was addressed to Lorenzo Snow, but the context shows it was actually directed to Erastus Snow.

20. Stewart to Woodruff, Nov. 1, 1890, WWGC.

21. William C. Stewart to "Presidents Woodruff Canon & Smith," Jan. 4, 1891, WWGC; Stewart to Woodruff, Nov. 1, 1890, WWGC; L. John Nuttall to W. C. Stewart, Nov. 18, 1890.

22. John Ward Christian, dictation, [1886], H. H. Bancroft Manuscript Collection, BL.

23. George Teasdale to Wilford Woodruff, Jan. 24, 1895, Wilford Woodruff, Stake Correspondence Files, CHL.

24. *MatMM*, 199; "Another Judicial Movement," *DEN*, Feb. 24, 1875; "Local Intelligence," *PDR*, Aug. 21, 1875; Evelyn K. Jones and York F. Jones, *Mayors of Cedar City* (Cedar City, UT: Cedar City, Utah, Historical Preservation Commission and Southern Utah State College, 1986), 59; Wesley P. Larsen, *A History of Toquerville* (Cedar City, UT: by the author, 1985), 38; "Autobiography of James William Nixon the Second," 5–6; Cross to Aden, Jan. 23, 1878, House of Representatives, SCF, box 545; "History of John Mount Higbee," *Higbee Family Magazine* 3 (July 1957): 121; "History of Eunice Bladen, Wife of John Mount Higbee," *Higbee Family Magazine* 3 (July 1957): 129; "John Mo[u]nt Higbee," CM.

25. Bull Valley Snort, statement, Feb. 1894, photocopy of manuscript, Juanita Brooks Collection, UofU; "Eunice Higbee McRae Dies," 1953, typescript, in Florence S. Higbee, John M. Higbee and Mountain Meadows Massacre Papers, CHL; Regina [McRae] to Florence [S. Higbee], Oct. 30, 1950, typescript, in Higbee, John M. Higbee, and Mountain Meadows Massacre Papers.

26. *AJ-DHM*, 299–312; David H. Morris, journal, Feb. 1896, vol. 2, 45–46, typescript, CHL; John M. Higbee, affidavit, June 15, 1896, CM.

27. Rogerson, untitled typescript pages, ca. 1911, 7–8, in CM.

28. "Death of John M. Higbee," *DEN*, Dec. 19, 1904.

29. Hans P. Freece, *The Letters of an Apostate Mormon to His Son* (n.p.: by the author, 1908), 29.

30. Colorado, Conejos County, Manassa, 1880 U.S. Census, population schedule, 22, lists Haight under his alias Owen Owen.

31. [Haight] to "My Dear Wife," May 23, 1880, ICHC.

32. Franklin D. Richards, journal, Nov. 5, 1881, CHL; David Spilsbury, diary, Oct. 24, 1884, typescript, Janet Jenson papers regarding Isaac C. Haight, Haight biographical file, MMMRF; Woolley, 167–69; Burnham Ward, San Juan Stake, General Minutes, entry dated Mar. 2, 1884, vol. 9, 39, CHL; Slack, "A Biographical Study of Isaac Chauncey Haight," 94.

33. Penrose; "Mountain Meadows," *SLT*, Nov. 9, 1884.

34. O. Owen [Isaac C. Haight] to L. J. Nutt[all], ca. Nov. 1884, with postscript by Erastus Snow, Taylor Presidential Papers, photocopy received from Haight descendant Janet Jenson.

35. Woolley, 139–71. Original in ICHC.

36. Slack, "A Biographical Study of Isaac Chauncey Haight," 94–95, citing author's inter-
view with Caroline Keturah Parry, June 19, 1964; Woolley, 174–76; Fish, 283; Nathan
Ferris [Isaac Haight] to "My Dear Daughter and My Dear Ones," May 14, 1885, ICHC;
I. Horton [Isaac Haight] to "My Dear Daughter," June 15, 1885, ICHC; I. Horton [Isaac
Haight] to Roselia Haight Spilsbury, July 27, 1885, ICHC; I. Horton [Isaac Haight] to
Roselia Haight Spilsbury, Sept. 30, 1885, ICHC.

37. [Haight] to Spilsbury, July 27, 1885, ICHC.

38. Thomas H. Naylor, "The Mormons Colonize Sonora," *Arizona and the West* 20
(Winter 1978): 326–27, 340; George C. Williams to Jesse N. Smith, Jan. 28, 1895,
enclosed in Jesse N. Smith to Wilford Woodruff and counselors, Feb. 19, 1895, First
Presidency, Court Case Files, 1877–1916, CHL; George C. Williams, Reminiscence,
ca. 1915, typescript, CHL; JNSJ, July 18, 1885; Woolley, 179.

39. Hyrum Brinkerhoff to David Haight, Sept. 5, 1886, quoted in Woolley, 186; Hyrum
Brinkerhoff to Christopher Arthur, Sept. 8, 1886, telegram, quoted in Woolley, 187.

40. Raydene H. Cluff, "The High Price of Leadership: Isaac Chauncey Haight," in *Graham
County Historical Society 2004 Symposium Papers* (Safford, AZ: Graham County
Historical Society, ca. 2004), 16–17; Woolley, 96.

41. Wilford Woodruff, George Q. Cannon, and Jos. F. Smith to G. C. Williams, Mar. 8,
1895, typescript, CHL; George C. Williams to Jesse N. Smith, Jan. 28, 1895, enclosed
in Jesse N. Smith to Wilford Woodruff and counselors, Feb. 19, 1895, First Presidency,
Court Case Files; Naylor, "The Mormons Colonize Sonora," 325–42.

42. "Elias Morris Hurt," *SLH*, March 15, 1898; "Bishop Elias Morris," *SLH*, March
18, 1898.

43. *MatMM*, 180, 203–4; *AJ-DHM*, 329–30, 333; TM, 3548–661.

44. See, e.g., Lyman1, Sept. 21, 1895; *AJ-DHM*, 328–34; Nephi Johnson to Anthon
H. Lund, Mar. 1910, in CM; Nephi Johnson, conversation with Anthony W. Ivins,
Sept. 2, 1917, typescript, Anthony W. Ivins Collection, USHS.

45. Richard E. Turley Jr., *Juanita Brooks: "Ahead of Her Time"* (Salt Lake City: Alta Club, in
cooperation with the University of Utah J. Willard Marriott Library and the Division
of State History, 2017).

46. Juanita Brooks, *Quicksand and Cactus* (Salt Lake City: Howe Brothers, 1982), 215,
226–29; Brooks2.

Index

For the benefit of digital users, indexed terms that span two pages (e.g., 52–53) may, on occasion, appear on only one of those pages.

Abbreviations

LDS   Latter-day Saint(s)
MM   Mountain Meadows
MMM   Mountain Meadows Massacre

Figures are indicated by *f* following the page number

Utah Territory

Assaults on Emigrant Cattle Companies, 1857

1   City of Rocks: McKuen, Dunn, and Lincoln
    company attacked, ca. September 9

2   Warm Springs: McKuen, Dunn, and Lincoln
    company attacked, ca. September 9

3   Between Corn Creek and Beaver: Turner
    company attacked, September 8

4   Beaver: Combined Turner-Dukes-Collins
    company attacked, ca. September 9

5   Mountain Meadows: Arkansas company under
    attack and massacred, September 7–11

6   Big Wash: Turner-Dukes-Collins company
    attacked, ca. October 3